The first**writer**.com

Writers' Handbook
2022

The firstwriter.com

Writers' Handbook
2022

EDITOR
J. PAUL DYSON

Published in 2021 by JP&A Dyson
27 Old Gloucester Street, London WC1N 3AX, United Kingdom
Copyright JP&A Dyson

https://www.jpandadyson.com
https://www.firstwriter.com

ISBN 978-1-909935-37-2

Registered with the IP Rights Office
Copyright Registration Service
Ref: 3287952893

Foreword

The firstwriter.com Writers' Handbook returns for its 2022 edition with over 2,500 listings of literary agents, literary agencies, publishers, and magazines that have been updated in firstwriter.com's online databases between 2019 and 2021. This includes revised and updated listings from the previous edition and over 400 new entries.

Previous editions of this handbook have been bought by writers across the United States, Canada, and Europe; and ranked in the United Kingdom as the number one bestselling writing and publishing directory on Amazon. The 2022 edition continues this international outlook, giving writers all over the English-speaking world access to the global publishing markets.

Finding the information you need is made quick and easy with multiple tables, a detailed index, and unique paragraph numbers to help you get to the listings you're looking for.

The variety of tables helps you navigate the listings in different ways, and includes a Table of Authors, which lists over 3,000 authors and tells you who represents them, or who publishes them, or both.

The number of genres in the index has expanded to over 600. So, for example, while there was only one option for "Romance" in previous editions, you can now narrow this down to Historical Romance, Fantasy Romance, Supernatural / Paranormal Romance, Contemporary Romance, Diverse Romance, Erotic Romance, Feminist Romance, Christian Romance, or even Amish Romance.

The handbook also provides free online access to the entire current firstwriter.com databases, including over 2,300 magazines, over 2,300 literary agents and agencies, over 2,800 book publishers that don't charge fees, and constantly updated listings of current writing competitions, with typically more than 50 added each month.

For details on how to claim your free access please see the back of this book.

Included in the subscription

A subscription to the full website is not only free with this book, but comes packed with all the following features:

Advanced search features

- Save searches and save time – set up to 15 search parameters specific to your work, save them, and then access the search results with a single click whenever you log in. You can even save multiple different searches if you have different types of work you are looking to place.
- Add personal notes to listings, visible only to you and fully searchable – helping you to organise your actions.
- Set reminders on listings to notify you when to submit your work, when to follow up, when to expect a reply, or any other custom action.
- Track which listings you've viewed and when, to help you organise your search – any listings which have changed since you last viewed them will be highlighted for your attention.

Daily email updates

As a subscriber you will be able to take advantage of our email alert service, meaning you can specify your particular interests and we'll send you automatic email updates when we change or add a listing that matches them. So if you're interested in agents dealing in romantic fiction in the United States you can have us send you emails with the latest updates about them – keeping you up to date without even having to log in.

User feedback

Our agent, publisher, and magazine databases all include a user feedback feature that allows our subscribers to leave feedback on each listing – giving you not only the chance to have your say about the markets you contact, but giving a unique authors' perspective on the listings.

Save on copyright protection fees

If you're sending your work away to publishers, competitions, or literary agents, it's vital that you first protect your copyright. As a subscriber to firstwriter.com you can do this through our site and save 10% on the copyright registration fees normally payable for protecting your work internationally through the Intellectual Property Rights Office (https://www.CopyrightRegistrationService.com).

Monthly newsletter

When you subscribe to firstwriter.com you also receive our monthly email newsletter – described by one publishing company as "the best in the business" – including articles, news, and interviews for writers. And the best part is that you can continue to receive the newsletter even after you stop your paid subscription – at no cost!

For details on how to claim your free access please see the back of this book.

Contents

Index

Free Access

Glossary of Terms

This section explains common terms used in this handbook, and in the publishing industry more generally.

Academic

Listings in this book will be marked as targeting the academic market only if they publish material of an academic nature; e.g. academic theses, scientific papers, etc. The term is not used to indicate publications that publish general material aimed at people who happen to be in academia, or who are described as academic by virtue of being educated.

Adult

In publishing, "adult" simply refers to books that are aimed at adults, as opposed to books that are aimed at children, or young adults, etc. It is not a euphemism for pornographic or erotic content. Nor does it necessarily refer to content which is unsuitable for children; it is just not targeted at them. In this book, most ordinary mainstream publishers will be described as "adult", unless their books are specifically targeted at other groups (such as children, professionals, etc.).

Advance

Advances are up-front payments made by traditional publishers to authors, which are off-set against future royalties.

Agented

An *agented* submission is one which is submitted by a literary agent. If a publisher accepts only *agented* submissions then you will need a literary agent to submit the work on your behalf.

Author bio

A brief description of you and your life – normally in relation to your writing activity, but if intended for publication (particularly in magazines) may be broader in scope. May be similar to *Curriculum Vitae* (CV) or résumé, depending on context.

Bio

See *Author bio*.

Curriculum Vitae

A brief description of you, your qualifications, and accomplishments – normally in this context in relation to writing (any previous publications, or awards, etc.), but in the case of nonfiction proposals may also include relevant experience that qualifies you to write on the subject. Commonly abbreviated to "CV". May

also be referred to as a résumé. May be similar to *Author bio*, depending on context.

CV

See *Curriculum Vitae*.

International Reply Coupon

When submitting material overseas you may be required to enclose *International Reply Coupons*, which will enable the recipient to send a response and/or return your material at your cost. Not applicable/available in all countries, so check with your local Post Office for more information.

IRC

See *International Reply Coupon*.

Manuscript

Your complete piece of work – be it a novel, short story, or article, etc. – will be referred to as your manuscript. Commonly abbreviated to "ms" (singular) or "mss" (plural).

MS

See *Manuscript*.

MSS

See *Manuscript*.

Professional

Listings in this book will be marked as targeting the professional market if they publish material serving a particular profession: e.g. legal journals, medical journals, etc. The term is not used to indicate publications that publish general material aimed at a notional "professional class".

Proposal

A proposal is normally requested for nonfiction projects (where the book may not yet have been completed, or even begun). Proposals can consist of a number of components, such as an outline, table of contents, CV, marketing information, etc. but the exact requirements will vary from one publisher to another.

Query

Many agents and publishers will prefer to receive a query in the first instance, rather than your full *manuscript*. A query will typically

consist of a cover letter accompanied by a *synopsis* and/or sample chapter(s). Specific requirements will vary, however, so always check on a case by case basis.

Recommendation

If an agent is only accepting approaches by recommendation this means that they will only consider your work if it comes with a recommendation from an established professional in the industry, or an existing client.

RoW

Rest of world.

SAE

See *Stamped Addressed Envelope*. Can also be referred to as SASE.

SASE

Self-Addressed Stamped Envelope. Variation of SAE. See *Stamped Addressed Envelope*.

Simultaneous submission

A simultaneous submission is one which is sent to more than one market at the same time. Normally you will be sending your work to numerous different magazines, agents, and publishers at the same time, but some demand the right to consider it exclusively – i.e. they don't accept simultaneous submissions.

Stamped Addressed Envelope

Commonly abbreviated to "SAE". Can also be referred to as Self-Addressed Stamped Envelope, or SASE. When supplying an SAE, ensure that the envelope and postage is adequate for a reply or the return of your material, as required. If you are submitting overseas, remember that postage from your own country will not be accepted, and you may need to provide an *International Reply Coupon*.

Synopsis

A short outline of your story. This should cover all the main characters and events, including the ending. It is not the kind of "teaser" found on a book's back cover. The length of synopsis required can vary, but is generally between one and three pages.

TOC

Table of Contents. These are often requested as part of nonfiction proposals.

Unagented

An unagented submission is one which is not submitted through a literary agent. If a publisher accepts unagented submissions then you can approach them directly.

Unsolicited mss

A manuscript which has not been requested. Many agents and publishers will not accept unsolicited mss, but this does not necessarily mean they are closed to approaches – many will prefer to receive a short *query* in the first instance. If they like the idea, they will request the full work, which will then be a solicited manuscript.

The Writer's Roadmap

With most objectives in life, people recognise that there is a path to follow. Whether it is career progression, developing a relationship, or chasing your dreams, we normally understand that there are foundations to lay and baby steps to take before we'll be ready for the main event.

But for some reason, with writing (perhaps because so much of the journey of a writer happens in private, behind closed doors), people often overlook the process involved. They often have a plan of action which runs something like this:

1. Write novel.
2. Get novel published.

This is a bit like having a plan for success in tennis which runs:

3. Buy tennis racket.
4. Win Wimbledon.

It misses out all the practice that is going to be required; the competing in the minor competitions and the learning of the craft that will be needed in order to succeed in the major events; the time that will need to be spent gaining reputation and experience.

In this roadmap we'll be laying out what we think is the best path to follow to try and give yourself the best shot of success in the world of writing. You don't necessarily have to jump through all the hoops, and there will always be people who, like Pop Idol or reality TV contestants, get a lucky break that propels them to stardom without laying any of the foundations laid out below, but the aim here is to limit your reliance on luck and maximise your ability to shape your destiny yourself.

1: Write short material

Writers will very often start off by writing a novel. We would advise strongly against this. It's like leaving school one day and applying for a job as a CEO of an international corporation the next. Novels are the big league. They are expensive to produce, market, and distribute. They require significant investment and pose a significant financial risk to publishers. They are not a good place for new writers to try and cut their teeth. If you've already written your novel that's great – it's great experience and you'll have learned a lot – but we'd recommend shelving it for now (you can always come back to it later) and getting stuck into writing some short form material, such as poetry and short fiction.

This is what novelist George R. R. Martin, author of *A Game of Thrones*, has to say on the subject:

> "I would also suggest that any aspiring writer begin with short stories. These days, I meet far too many young writers who try to start off with a novel right off, or a trilogy, or even a nine-book series. That's like starting in at rock climbing by tackling Mt Everest. Short stories help you learn your craft."

You will find that writing short material will improve your writing no end. Writing short fiction allows you to play with lots of different stories and characters very quickly. Because you will probably only spend a few days on any given story you will quickly gain a lot of experience with plotting stories and will learn a lot about what works, what doesn't work, and what you personally are good at. When you write a novel, by contrast, you may spend years on a single story and one set of characters, making this learning process much slower.

Your writing will also be improved by the need to stick to a word limit. Writers who start their career by writing a novel often produce huge epics, the word counts of which they wear as a badge of honour, as if they demonstrate their commitment to and enthusiasm for writing. What they actually demonstrate is a naivety about the realities of getting published. The odds are already stacked against new writers getting a novel published, because of the cost and financial risk of publishing a novel. The bigger the novel, the more it will cost to print, warehouse, and distribute. Publishers will not look at a large word count and be impressed – they will be terrified. The longer the novel, the less chance it has of getting published.

A lengthy first novel also suggests that the writer has yet to learn one of the most critical skills a writer must possess to succeed: brevity. By writing short stories that fit the limits imposed by competitions and magazines you will learn this critical skill. You will learn to remove unnecessary words and passages, and you will find that your writing becomes leaner, more engaging, and more exciting as a result. Lengthy first novels are often rambling and sometimes boring – but once you've been forced to learn how to "trim the fat" by writing short stories, the good habits you've got into will transfer across when you start writing long form works, allowing you to write novels that are pacier and better to read. They will stand a better chance of publication not just because they are shorter and cheaper to produce, but they are also likely to be better written.

2: Get a professional critique

It's a good idea to get some professional feedback on your work at some point, and it's probably better to do this sooner, rather than later. There's no point spending a long time doing something that doesn't quite work if a little advice early on could have got you on the right track sooner. It's also a lot cheaper to get a short story critiqued than a whole novel, and if you can learn the necessary lessons now it will both minimise the cost and maximise the benefit of the advice.

Should you protect the copyright of short works before showing them to anyone?

This is a matter of personal preference. We'd suggest that it certainly isn't as important to register short works as full novels, as your short works are unlikely to be of much financial value to you. Having said that, films do sometimes get made which are based on short stories, in which case you'd want to have all your rights in order. If you do choose to register your short works this can be done for a relatively small amount online at https://www.copyrightregistrationservice.com/register.

3: Submit to competitions and magazines, and build a list of writing credits

Once you have got some short works that you are happy with you can start submitting them to competitions and small magazines. You can search for competitions at https://www.firstwriter.com/competitions and magazines at https://www.firstwriter.com/magazines. Prize money may not be huge, and you probably won't be paid for having your work appear in the kind of small literary magazines you will probably be approaching at first, but the objective here is to build up a list of writing credits to give you more credibility when approaching agents and publishers. You'll be much more likely to grab their attention if you can reel off a list of places where you have already been published, or prizes you have won.

4: Finish your novel and protect your copyright

Okay – so you've built up a list of writing credits, and you've decided it's time to either write a novel, or go back to the one you had already started (in which case you'll probably find yourself cutting out large chunks and making it a lot shorter!). Once you've got your novel to the point where you're happy to start submitting it for publication you should get it registered for copyright. Unlike the registration of short works, which we think is a matter of personal preference, we'd definitely recommend registering a novel, and doing so before you show it to anybody. That *includes* family and friends. Don't worry that you might want to change it – as long as you don't rewrite it to the point where it's not recognisable it will still be protected – the important thing is to get it registered without delay. You can protect it online at https://www.copyrightregistration service.com/register.

If you've already shown it to other people then just register it as soon as you can. Proving a claim to copyright is all about proving you had a copy of the work before anyone else, so time is of the essence.

5: Editing

These days, agents and publishers increasingly seem to expect manuscripts to have been professionally edited before being submitted to them – and no, getting your husband / wife / friend / relative to do it doesn't count. Ideally, you should have the whole manuscript professionally edited, but this can be expensive. Since most agents and publishers aren't going to want to see the whole manuscript in the first instance you can probably get away with just having the first three chapters edited. It may also be worth having your query letter and synopsis edited at the same time.

6: Submit to literary agents

There will be many publishers out there who will accept your submission directly, and on the face of it that might seem like a good idea, since you won't have to pay an agent 15% of your earnings.

However, all the biggest publishers are generally closed to direct submissions from authors, meaning that if you want the chance of getting a top publisher you're going to need a literary agent. You'll also probably find that their 15% fee is more than offset by the higher earnings you'll be likely to achieve.

To search for literary agents go to https://www.firstwriter.com/Agents. Start by being as specific in your search as possible. So if you've written a historical romance select "Fiction", "Romance", and "Historical". Once you've approached all the agents that specifically mention all three elements broaden your search to just "Fiction" and "Romance". As long as the new results don't specifically say they don't handle historical romance, these are still valid markets to approach. Finally, search for just "Fiction", as there are many agents who are willing to consider all kinds of fiction but don't specifically mention romance or historical.

Don't limit your approaches to just agents in your own country. With more and more agents accepting electronic queries it's now as easy to approach agents in other countries as in your own, and if you're ignoring either London or New York (the two main centres of English language publishing) you're cutting your chances of success in two.

7: Submit directly to publishers

Once you're certain that you've exhausted all potential agents for your work, you can start looking for publishers to submit your work directly to. You can search for publishers at https://www.firstwriter.com/publishers. Apply the same filtering as when you were searching for agents: start specific and gradually broaden, until you've exhausted all possibilities.

8: Self-publishing

In the past, once you got to the point where you'd submitted to all the publishers and agents who might be interested in your book, it would be time to pack away the manuscript in the attic, chalk it up to experience, and start writing another. However, these days writers have the option to take their book directly to market by publishing it themselves.

Before you decide to switch to self-publishing you must be sure that you've exhausted all traditional publishing possibilities – because once you've self-published your book you're unlikely to be able to submit it to agents and publishers. It will probably take a few years of exploring the world of traditional publishing to reach this point, but if you do then you've nothing to lose by giving self-publishing a shot. See our guide to self-publishing for details on how to proceed.

Why Choose Traditional Publishing

When **firstwriter.com** first started, back in 2001, there were only two games in town when it came to getting your book published: traditional publishing, and vanity publishing – and which you should pick was a no-brainer. Vanity publishing was little more than a scam that would leave you with an empty bank account and a house full of unsold books. If you were serious about being a writer, you had to follow the traditional publishing path.

Since then, there has been a self-publishing revolution, with new technologies and new printing methods giving writers a genuine opportunity to get their books into the market by themselves. So, is there still a reason for writers to choose traditional publishing?

The benefits of traditional publishing

Despite the allure and apparent ease of self-publishing, the traditional path still offers you the best chance of making a success of being a writer. There are rare cases where self-published writers make staggering fortunes and become internationally renowned on the back of their self-published books, but these cases are few and far between, and a tiny drop in the rapidly expanding ocean of self-published works. The vast majority of successful books – and the vast majority of successful writers – have their homes firmly in the established publishing houses. Even those self-published authors who find success usually end up moving to a traditional publisher in the end.

This is because the traditional publishers have the systems, the market presence, and the financial clout to *make* a book a bestseller. While successful self-published authors often owe their success in no small part to a decent dose of luck (a social media comment that goes viral; the right mention on the right media outlet at the right time), traditional publishers are in the business of engineering that success. They might not always succeed, but they have the marketing budgets and the distribution channels in place to give themselves, and the book they are promoting, the best possible chance.

And it's not just the marketing and the distribution. Getting signed with a traditional publisher brings a whole team of people with a wealth of expertise that will all work towards the success of the book. It will provide you with an editor who may have experience of working on previous bestsellers, who will not only help you get rid of mistakes in your work but may also help you refine it into a better book. They will help make sure that the quality of your content is good enough to make it in the marketplace.

The publishers will source a professional cover designer who will make your book look the part on the shelves and on the pages of the bookselling websites. They will have accountants who will handle the technicalities of tax regimes both home and abroad. They will have overseas contacts for establishing foreign publishing rights; translations; etc. They may even have contacts in the film industry, should there be a prospect of a movie adaptation. They will have experts working on every aspect of your book, right down to the printing and the warehousing and the shipping of the physical products. They will have people to manage the ebook conversion and the electronic distribution. As an author, you don't need to worry about any of this.

This means you get more time to simply be a writer. You may have to go on book tours, but even these will be organised for you by PR experts, who will also be handling all the press releases, etc.

And then there's the advances. Advances are up-front payments made by traditional publishers to authors, which are off-set against future royalties. So, an author might receive a $5,000 advance before their book is published. When the royalties start coming in, the publisher keeps the first $5,000 to off-set the advance. The good news for the author is that if the book flops and doesn't make $5,000 in royalties they still get to keep the full advance. In an uncertain profession, the security of an advance can be invaluable for an author – and of course it's not something available to self-published authors.

The drawbacks of traditional publishing

The main downside of traditional publishing is just that it's so hard to get into. If you choose to self-publish then – provided you have enough perseverance, the right help and advice, and perhaps a little bit of money – you are guaranteed to succeed and see your book in print and for sale. With traditional publishing, the cold hard fact is that most people who try will not succeed.

And for many of those people who fail it may not even be their fault. That aspect of traditional publishing which can bring so many benefits as compared to self-publishing – that of being part of a team – can also be part of its biggest drawback. It means that you have to get other people to buy into your book. It means that you have to rely on other people being competent enough to spot a bestseller. Many failed to spot the potential of the Harry Potter books. How many potential bestsellers never make it into print just because none of the professionals at the publishers' gates manage to recognise their potential?

So if you choose traditional publishing your destiny is not in your own hands – and for some writers the lack of exclusive control can also be a problem. Sometimes writers get defensive when editors try to tinker with their work, or annoyed when cover artists don't realise their vision the way they expect. But this is hardly a fair criticism of traditional publishing, as most writers (particularly when they are starting out) will benefit from advice from experienced professionals in the field, and will often only be shooting themselves in the foot if they insist on ignoring it.

The final main drawback with traditional publishing is that less of the sale price of each copy makes it to the writer. A typical royalty contract will give the writer 15%. With a self-published book, the author can expect to receive much more. So, all other things being equal, the self-published route can be more profitable – but, of course, all things are not equal. If self-publishing means lower sales (as is likely), then you will probably make less money overall. Remember, it's better to have 15% of something than 50% of nothing.

Conclusion

In conclusion, our advice to writers would be to aim for traditional publishing first. It might be a long shot, but if it works then you stand a much better chance of being successful. If you don't manage to get signed by an agent or a publisher then you still have the option of self-publishing, but make sure you don't get tempted to resort to self-publishing too soon – most agents and publishers won't consider self-published works, so this is a one-way street. Once you've self-published your work, you probably won't be able to change your mind and go back to the traditional publishers with your book unless it becomes a huge hit without them. It's therefore important that you exhaust all your traditional publishing options before making the leap to self-publishing. Be prepared for this to take perhaps a few years (lots of agents and publishers can take six months just to respond), and make sure you've submitted to everyone you can on *both* sides of the Atlantic (publishing is a global game these days, and you need to concentrate on the two main centres of English-language publishing (New York and London) equally) before you make the decision to self-publish instead.

Formatting Your Manuscript

Before submitting a manuscript to an agent, magazine, or publisher, it's important that you get the formatting right. There are industry norms covering everything from the size of your margins to the font you choose – get them wrong and you'll be marking yourself out as an amateur. Get them right, and agents and editors will be far more likely to take you seriously.

Fonts

Don't be tempted to "make your book stand out" by using fancy fonts. It *will* stand out, but not for any reason you'd want. Your entire manuscript should be in a monospaced font like Courier (not a proportional font, like Times Roman) at 12 points. (A monospaced font is one where each character takes up the same amount of space; a proportional font is where the letter "i" takes up less space than the letter "m".)

This goes for your text, your headings, your title, your name – everything. Your objective is to produce a manuscript that looks like it has been produced on a simple typewriter.

Italics / bold

Your job as the author is to indicate words that require emphasis, not to pick particular styles of font. This will be determined by the house style of the publisher in question. You indicate emphasis by underlining text; the publisher will decide whether they will use bold or italic to achieve this emphasis – you shouldn't use either in your text.

Margins

You should have a one inch (2.5 centimetre) margin around your entire page: top, bottom, left, and right.

Spacing

In terms of line spacing, your entire manuscript should be double spaced. Your word processor should provide an option for this, so you don't have to insert blank lines manually.

While line spacing should be double, spaces after punctuation should be single. If you're in the habit of putting two spaces after full stops this is the time to get out of that habit, and remove them from your manuscript. You're just creating extra work for the editor who will have to strip them all out.

Do not put blank lines between paragraphs. Start every paragraph (even those at the start of chapters) with an indent equivalent to five spaces. If you want a scene break then create a line with the "#" character centred in the middle. You don't need blank lines above or below this line.

Word count

You will need to provide an estimated word count on the front page of your manuscript. Tempting as it will be to simply use the word processor's word counting function to tell you exactly how many words there are in your manuscript, this is not what you should do. Instead, you should work out the maximum number of characters on a line, divide this number by six, and then multiply by the total number of lines in your manuscript.

Once you have got your estimated word count you need to round it to an approximate value. How you round will depend on the overall length of your manuscript:

- up to 1,500 words: round to the nearest 100;
- 1,500–10,000 words: round to the nearest 500;
- 10,000–25,000 words: round to the nearest 1,000;
- Over 25,000 words: round to the nearest 5,000.

The reason an agent or editor will need to know your word count is so that they can estimate how many pages it will make. Since actual pages include varying amounts of white space due to breaks in paragraphs, sections of speech, etc. the formula above will actually provide a better idea of how many pages will be required than an exact word count would.

And – perhaps more importantly – providing an exact word count will highlight you immediately as an amateur.

Layout of the front page

On the first page of the manuscript, place your name, address, and any other relevant contact details (such as phone number, email address, etc.) in the top left-hand corner. In the top right-hand corner write your approximate word count.

If you have registered your work for copyright protection, place the reference number two single lines (one double line) beneath your contact details. Since your manuscript will only be seen by agents or editors, not the public, this should be done as discreetly as possible, and you should refrain from using any official seal you may have been granted permissions to use. (For information on registering for copyright protection see "Protecting Your Copyright", below.)

Place your title halfway down the front page. Your title should be centred and would normally be in capital letters. You can make it bold or underlined if you want, but it should be the same size as the rest of the text.

From your title, go down two single lines (or one double line) and insert your byline. This should be centred and start with the word "By", followed by the name you are writing under. This can be your name or a pen name, but should be the name you want the work published under. However, make sure that the name in the top left-hand corner is your real, legal name.

From your byline, go down four single lines (or two double lines) and begin your manuscript.

Layout of the text

Print on only one side of the paper, even if your printer can print on both sides.

In the top right-hand corner of all pages except the first should be your running head. This should be comprised of the surname used in your byline; a keyword from your title, and the page number, e.g. "Myname / Mynovel Page 5".

Text should be left-aligned, *not* justified. This means that you should have a ragged right-hand edge to the text, with lines ending at different points. Make sure you don't have any sort of hyphenation function switched on in your word processor: if a word is too long to fit on a line it should be taken over to the next.

Start each new chapter a third of the way down the page with the centred chapter number / title, underlined. Drop down four single lines (two double lines) to the main text.

At the end of the manuscript you do not need to indicate the ending in any way: you don't need to write "The End", or "Ends", etc. The only exception to this is if your manuscript happens to end at the bottom of a page, in which case you can handwrite the word "End" at the bottom of the last page, after you have printed it out.

Protecting Your Copyright

Protecting your copyright is by no means a requirement before submitting your work, but you may feel that it is a prudent step that you would like to take before allowing strangers to see your material.

These days, you can register your work for copyright protection quickly and easily online. The Intellectual Property Rights Office operates a website called the "Copyright Registration Service" which allows you to do this:

- *https://www.CopyrightRegistrationService.com*

This website can be used for material created in any nation signed up to the Berne Convention. This includes the United States, United Kingdom, Canada, Australia, Ireland, New Zealand, and most other countries. There are around 180 countries in the world, and over 160 of them are part of the Berne Convention.

Provided you created your work in one of the Berne Convention nations, your work should be protected by copyright in all other Berne Convention nations. You can therefore protect your copyright around most of the world with a single registration, and because the process is entirely online you can have your work protected in a matter of minutes, without having to print and post a copy of your manuscript.

What is copyright?

Copyright is a form of intellectual property (often referred to as "IP"). Other forms of intellectual property include trade marks, designs, and patents. These categories refer to different kinds of ideas which may not exist in a physical form that can be owned as property in the traditional sense, but may nonetheless have value to the people who created them. These forms of intellectual property can be owned in the same way that physical property is owned, but – as with physical property – they can be subject to dispute and proper documentation is required to prove ownership.

The different types of intellectual property divide into these categories as follows:

- **Copyright:** copyright protects creative output such as books, poems, pictures, drawings, music, films, etc. Any work which can be recorded in some way can be protected by copyright, as long as it is original and of sufficient length. Copyright does not cover short phrases or names.

- **Trade marks:** trade marks cover words and/or images which distinguish the goods or services of one trader from another. Unlike copyright, trade marks can cover names and short phrases.

- **Designs:** designs cover the overall visual appearance of a product, such as its shape, etc.

- **Patents:** patents protect the technical or functional aspects of designs or inventions.

The specifics of the legal protection surrounding these various forms of intellectual property will vary from nation to nation, but there are also generally international conventions to which a lot if not most of the nations of the world subscribe. The information provided below outlines the common situation in many countries but you should be aware that this may not reflect the exact situation in every territory.

The two types of intellectual property most relevant to writers are copyright and trade marks. If a writer has written a novel, a short story, a poem, a script, or any other piece of writing then the contents themselves can be protected by copyright. The title, however, cannot be protected by copyright as it is a name. An author may therefore feel that they wish to consider protecting the title of their work by registering it as a trade mark, if they feel that it is particularly important and/or more valuable in itself than the cost of registering a trade mark.

If a writer wants to register the copyright for their work, or register the title of their work as a trade mark, there are generally registration fees to be paid. Despite the fact that copyright covers long works that could be hundreds of thousands of words long, while trade marks cover single words and short phrases, the cost for registering a trade mark is likely to be many times higher than that for registering a work for copyright protection. This is because trade marks must be unique and are checked against existing trade marks for potential conflicts. While works to be registered for copyright must also not infringe existing works, it is not practical to check the huge volume of new works to be registered for copyright against the even larger volume of all previously copyrighted works. Copyright registration therefore tends to simply archive the work in question as proof of the date at which the person registering the work was in possession of it.

In the case of both copyright and trade marks the law generally provides some protection even without any kind of registration, but registration provides the owner of the intellectual property with greater and more enforceable protection. In the case of copyright, the creator of a work usually automatically owns the copyright as soon as the work is recorded in some way (i.e. by writing it down or recording it electronically, etc.), however these rights can be difficult to prove if disputed, and therefore many countries (such as the United States) also offer an internal country-specific means of registering works. Some countries, like the United Kingdom, do not offer any such means of registration, however an international registration is available through the Intellectual Property Rights Office's Copyright Registration Service, and can be used regardless of any country-specific provisions. This can help protect copyright in all of the nations which are signatories of the Berne Convention.

In the case of trade marks, the symbol "™" can be applied to any mark which is being used as a trade mark, however greater protection is provided if this mark is registered, in which case the symbol "®" can be applied to the mark. It is often illegal to apply the "®" symbol to a trade mark which has not been registered. There are also options for international registrations of trade marks, which are administered by the World Intellectual Property Organization, however applications cannot be made to the WIPO directly – applications must be made through the relevant office of the applicant's country.

Copyright law and its history

The modern concept of copyright can be traced back to 1710 and the "Statute of Anne", which applied to England, Scotland, and Wales. Prior to this Act, governments had granted monopoly rights to publishers to produce works, but the 1710 Act was the first time that a right of ownership was acknowledged for the actual creator of a work.

From the outset, the attempt to protect the creator's rights was beset with problems due to the local nature of the laws, which applied in Britain only. This meant that lots of copyrighted works were reproduced without the permission of the author in Ireland, America, and in European countries. This not only hindered the ability of the London publishers to sell their legitimate copies of their books in these territories, but the unauthorised reproductions would also find their way into Britain, harming the home market as well.

A natural progression for copyright law was therefore its internationalisation, beginning in 1846 with a reciprocal agreement between Britain and Prussia, and culminating in a series of international treaties, the principal of which is the Berne Convention, which applies to over 160 countries.

Traditionally in the United Kingdom and the United States there has been a requirement to register a work with an official body in order to be able to claim copyright over it (Stationers Hall and the US Library of Congress respectively), however this has been changed by the Berne Convention, which requires signatory countries to grant copyright as an automatic right: i.e. the creator of a work immediately owns its copyright by virtue of creating it and recording it in some physical way (for instance by writing it down or making a recording of it, etc.). The United Kingdom and the United States have both been slow to fully adopt this approach. Though the United Kingdom signed the Berne Convention in 1887, it took 100 years for it to be fully implemented by the Copyright Designs and Patents Act 1988. The United States did not even sign the convention until 1989.

In the United States the US Library of Congress continues to provide archiving services for the purposes of copyright protection, but these are now optional. US citizens no longer need to register their work in order to be able to claim copyright over it. It is necessary, however, to be able to prove when the person who created it did so, and this is essentially the purpose of the registration today. In the United Kingdom, Stationers Hall has ceased to exist, and there is no longer any state-run means of registering the copyright to unpublished works, leaving the only available options as independent and/or international solutions such as the copyright registration service provided by the IP Rights Office.

Registering your work for copyright protection

Registering your work for copyright protection can help you protect your rights in relation to your work. Generally (particularly if you live in a Berne Convention country, as most people do) registration will not be compulsory in order to have rights over your work. Any time you create a unique original work you will in theory own the copyright over it, however you will need to be able to prove when you created it, which is the purpose of registering your work for copyright protection. There are other ways in which you might attempt to prove this, but registration provides better evidence than most other forms.

There are a range of different options for protecting your copyright that vary depending on where you live and the kind of coverage you want. Some countries, like the United States, provide internal means of registering the copyright of unpublished works, however the scope of these will tend to be restricted to the country in question. Other countries, like the United Kingdom, do not offer any specific government-sponsored system for registering the copyright of unpublished works. An international option is provided by the Intellectual Property Rights Office, which is not affiliated to any particular government or country. As long as you live in a Berne Convention country you should be able to benefit from using their Copyright Registration Service. You can register your work with the Intellectual Property Rights Office regardless of whether or not there are any specific arrangements in your home country (you may even choose to register with both to offer your work greater protection). Registration with the Intellectual Property Rights Office should provide you with protection throughout the area covered by the Berne Convention, which is most of the world.

Registering your work for copyright protection through the Intellectual Property Rights Office is an online process that can be completed in a few

minutes, provided you have your file in an accepted format and your file isn't too large (if your file is too large and cannot be reduced you may have to split it and take out two or more registrations covering it). There is a registration fee to pay ($45 / £25 / €40 at the time of writing) per file for registration, however if you are a subscriber to **firstwriter.com** you can benefit from a 10% discount when you start the registration process on our site.

When registering your work, you will need to give some consideration to what your work actually consists of. This is a straightforward question if your work is a novel, or a screenplay, but if it is a collection of poetry or short stories then the issue is more difficult. Should you register your collection as one file, or register each poem separately, which would be more expensive? Usually, you can answer this question by asking yourself what you propose to do with your collection. Do you intend to submit it to publishers as a collection only? Or do you intend to send the constituent parts separately to individual magazines? If the former is the case, then register the collection as a single work under the title of the collection. If the latter is the case then this could be unwise, as your copyright registration certificate will give the name of the collection only – which will not match the names of the individual poems or stories. If you can afford to, you should therefore register them separately. If you have so many poems and / or stories to register that you cannot afford to register them all separately, then registering them as a collection will be better than nothing.

Proper use of the copyright symbol

The first thing to note is that for copyright there is only one form of the symbol (©), unlike trade marks, where there is a symbol for registered trade marks (®) and a symbol for unregistered trade marks (™).

To qualify for use of the registered trade mark symbol (®) you must register your trade mark with the appropriate authority in your country, whereas the trade mark symbol (™) can be applied to any symbol you are using as a trade mark. Use of the copyright symbol is more similar to use of the trade mark symbol, as work does not need to be registered in order to use it.

You can place the copyright symbol on any original piece of work you have created. The normal format would be to include alongside the copyright symbol the year of first publication and the name of the copyright holder, however there are no particular legal requirements regarding this. While it has historically been a requirement in some jurisdictions to include a copyright notice on a work in order to be able to claim copyright over it, the Berne Convention does not allow such restrictions, and so any country signed up to the convention no longer has this requirement. However, in some jurisdictions failure to include such a notice can affect the damages you may be able to claim if anyone infringes your copyright.

A similar situation exists in relation to the phrase "All Rights Reserved". This phrase was a requirement in order to claim international copyright protection in countries signed up to the 1910 Buenos Aires Convention. However, since all countries signed up to the Buenos Aires Convention are now also signed up to the Berne Convention (which grants automatic copyright) this phrase has become superfluous. The phrase continues to be used frequently but is unlikely to have any legal consequences.

The Berne Convention

The Berne Convention covers 162 of the approximately 190 countries in the world, including most major nations. Countries which are signed up to the convention are compelled to offer the same protection to works created in other signatory nations as they would to works created in their own. Nations not signed up to the Berne Convention may have their own arrangements regarding copyright protection.

You can check if your country is signed up to the Berne Convention at the following website:

- *https://www.CopyrightRegistrationService.com*

The status of your country should be shown automatically on the right side of the screen. If not, you can select your country manually from the drop-down menu near the top right of the page.

Should You Self-Publish

Over recent years there has been an explosion in self-published books, as it has become easier and easier to publish your book yourself. This poses writers with a new quandary: continue to pursue publication through the traditional means, or jump into the world of self-publishing? As the rejections from traditional publishers pile up it can be tempting to reach for the control and certainty of self-publishing. Should you give into the temptation, or stick to your guns?

Isn't it just vanity publishing?

Modern self-publishing is quite different from the vanity publishing of times gone by. A vanity publisher would often pose or at least seek to appear to be a traditional publisher, inviting submissions and issuing congratulatory letters of acceptance to everyone who submitted – only slowly revealing the large fees the author would have to pay to cover the cost of printing the books.

Once the books were printed, the vanity publisher would deliver them to the author then cut and run. The author would be left with a big hole in their pocket and a mountain of boxes of books that they would be unlikely to ever sell a fraction of.

Modern self-publishing, on the other hand, is provided not by shady dealers but by some of the biggest companies involved in the publishing industry, including Penguin and Amazon. It doesn't have the large fees that vanity publishing did (depending on the path you choose and your own knowledge and technical ability it can cost almost nothing to get your book published); it *does* offer a viable means of selling your books (they can appear on the biggest bookselling websites around the world); and it *doesn't* leave you with a house full of unwanted books, because modern technology means that a copy of your book only gets printed when it's actually ordered.

That isn't to say that there aren't still shady characters out there trying to take advantage of authors' vanity by charging them enormous fees for publishing a book that stands very little chance of success, but it does mean that self-publishing – done right – can be a viable and cost effective way of an author taking their book to market.

The benefits of self-publishing

The main benefit of self-publishing, of course, is that the author gets control of whether their book is published or not. There is no need to spend years submitting to countless agents and publishers, building up countless heartbreaking rejection letters, and possibly accepting in the end that your dreams of publication will never come true – you can make them come true.

And this need not be pure vanity on the author's part. Almost every successful book – even such massive hits as *Harry Potter* – usually build up a string of rejections before someone finally accepts them. The professionals that authors rely on when going through the traditional publishing process – the literary agents and the editors – are often, it seems, just not that good at spotting what the public are going to buy. How many potential bestsellers might languish forever in the slush pile, just because agents and editors fail to spot them? What if your book is one of them? The traditional publishing process forces you to rely on the good judgment of others, but the self-publishing process enables you to sidestep that barrier and take your book directly to the public, so that readers can decide for themselves.

Self-publishing also allows you to keep control in other areas. You won't have an editor trying to change your text, and you'll have complete control over what kind of cover your book receives.

Finally, with no publisher or team of editors and accountants taking their slice, you'll probably get to keep a lot more of the retail price of every book you sell. So if you can sell the same amount of books as if you were traditionally published, you'll stand to make a lot more money.

The drawbacks of self-publishing

While self-publishing can guarantee that your book will be available for sale, it cannot guarantee that it will actually sell. Your self-published book will probably have a much lower chance of achieving significant sales than if it had been published traditionally, because it will lack the support that a mainstream publisher could bring. You will have no marketing support, no established position in the marketplace, and no PR – unless you do it yourself. You will have to arrange your own book tours; you will have to do your own sales pitches; you will have to set your own pricing structure; and you will have to manage your own accounts and tax affairs. If you're selling through Amazon or Smashwords or Apple (and if you're not, then why did you bother self-publishing in the first place?) you're going to need to fill in the relevant forms with the IRS (the US tax office) – whether you're a US citizen or not. If you're not a US citizen then you'll have to register with the IRS and complete the necessary tax forms, and potentially other forms for claiming treaty benefits so that you don't get taxed twice (in the US and your home country). And then of course you'll also have to register for tax purposes in your home nation and complete your own tax return there (though you would also have to do this as a traditionally published author).

It can all get very complicated, very confusing, and very lonely. Instead of being able to just be a writer you can find yourself writing less and less and becoming more and more embroiled in the business of publishing a book.

And while it's great to have control over your text and your cover, you'd be ill advised to ignore the value that professionals such as editors and cover designers can bring. It's tempting to think that you don't need an editor – that you've checked the book and had a friend or family member check it too, so it's probably fine – but a professional editor brings a totally different mindset to the process and will check things that won't have even occurred to you and your reader. Without a professional editor, you will almost certainly end up publishing a book which is full of embarrassing mistakes, and trust me – there is no feeling quite as deflating as opening up the first copy of your freshly printed book to see an obvious error jump out – or, even worse, to have it pointed out in an Amazon review, for all to see.

The cover is also incredibly important. Whether for sale on the shelf or on a website, the cover is normally the first point of contact your potential reader has with your book, and will cause them to form immediate opinions about it. A good cover can help a book sell well, but a bad one can kill its chances – and all too often self-published books have amateurish covers that will have readers flicking past them without a second glance.

Finally, the financial benefits of self-publishing can often be illusory. For starters, getting a higher proportion of the retail price is pretty irrelevant if you don't sell any copies. Fifty per cent of nothing is still nothing. Far better to have 15% of something. And then there's the advances. Advances are up-front payments made by traditional publishers to authors, which are off-set against future royalties. So, an author might receive a $5,000 advance before their book is published. When the royalties start coming in, the publisher keeps the first $5,000 to off-set the advance. The good news for the author is that if the book flops and doesn't make $5,000 in royalties they still get to keep the full advance. In an uncertain profession, the security of an advance can be invaluable for an author – and of course it's not something available to self-published authors.

Conclusion

Self-publishing can seem like a tempting shortcut to publication, but in reality it has its own challenges and difficulties. For the moment at least, traditional publishing still offers you the best shot of not only financial success, but also quality of life as a writer. With other people to handle all the other elements of publishing, you get to concentrate on doing what you love.

So we think that writers should always aim for traditional publishing first. It might be a long shot, but if it works then you stand a much better chance of being successful. If you don't manage to get signed by an agent or a publisher then you still have the option of self-publishing, but make sure you don't get tempted to resort to self-publishing too soon – most agents

and publishers won't consider self-published works, so this is a one-way street. Once you've self-published your work, you probably won't be able to change your mind and go back to the traditional publishers with your book unless it becomes a huge hit without them. It's therefore important that you exhaust all your traditional publishing options before making the leap to self-publishing. Be prepared for this to take perhaps a few years (lots of agents and publishers can take six months just to respond), and make sure you've submitted to everyone you can on *both* sides of the Atlantic (publishing is a global game these days, and you need to concentrate on the two main centres of English-language publishing (New York and London) equally) before you make the decision to self-publish instead.

However, once you have exhausted all options for traditional publishing, modern self-publishing does offer a genuine alternative path to success, and there are a growing number of self-published authors who have managed to sell millions of copies of their books. If you don't think traditional publishing is going to be an option, we definitely think you should give self-publishing a shot.

For directions on your path through the traditional publishing process see our Writers' Roadmap, above.

If you're sure you've already exhausted all your options for traditional publishing then see below for our quick guide to the self-publishing process.

The Self Publishing Process

Thinking about self-publishing your book? Make sure you go through all these steps first – and in the right order! Do them the wrong way round and you could find yourself wasting time and/or money.

1. Be sure you want to self-publish

You need to be 100% sure that you want to self-publish, because after you've done it there is no going back. Publishers and literary agents will not normally consider books that have been self-published, so if you wanted to get your book to print the old fashioned way you should stop now and rethink. Make absolutely sure that you've exhausted every possible opportunity for traditional publishing before you head down the self-publishing path.

For more information, see "Why choose traditional publishing?" and "Should you self-publish?", above.

2. Protect your copyright

Authors often wonder about what stage in the process they should protect their copyright – often thinking that it's best to leave it till the end so that there are no more changes to make to the book after it is registered.

However, this isn't the case. The key thing is to protect your work before you let other people see it – or, if you've already let other people see it, as soon as possible thereafter.

Don't worry about making small changes to your work after registering it – as long as the work is still recognisable as the same piece of work it will still be protected. Obviously, if you completely change everything you've written then you're going to need another registration, as it will effectively be a different book, but if you've just edited it and made minor alterations this won't affect your protection.

You can register you copyright online at https://www.copyrightregistrationservice.com.

3. Get your work edited

Editing is a vital step often overlooked by authors who self-publish. The result can often be an amateurish book littered with embarrassing mistakes. Any professionally published book will go through an editing process, and it's important that the same applies to your self-published book. It's also important to complete the editing process before beginning the layout, or you could find yourself having to start the layout again from scratch.

4. Choose your self-publishing path

Before you can go any further you are going to need to choose a size for your book, and in order to do that you are going to need to choose a self-publishing path.

There are various different ways of getting self-published, but in general these range from the expensive hands off approach, where you pay a company to do the hard work for you, to the cheap DIY approach, where you do as much as you can yourself.

At the top end, the hands off approach can cost you thousands. At the bottom end, the DIY approach allows you to publish your book for almost nothing.

5. Finalise your layout / typesetting

Before you can finalise your layout (often referred to in the industry as "typesetting") you need to be sure that you've finalised your content – which means having your full work professionally edited and all the necessary changes made. If you decide to make changes after this point it will be difficult and potentially costly, and will require you to go through many of the following steps all over again.

You also need to have selected your path to publication, so that you know what page sizes are available to you, and what page margins you are going to need to apply. If you create a layout that doesn't meet printing requirements (for instance, includes text too close to the edge of the page) then you will have to start the typesetting process all over again.

6. Organise your ISBN

Your book needs to have an ISBN. If you are using a self-publishing service then they may provide you with one of their own, but it is likely to come with restrictions, and the international record for your book will show your self-publishing service as the publisher.

You can acquire your own ISBNs directly from the ISBN issuer, but they do not sell them individually, so you will end up spending quite a lot of money buying more ISBNs than you need. You will, however, have control of the ISBN, and you will be shown as the publisher.

Alternatively, you can purchase a single ISBN at a lower price from an ISBN retailer. This should give you control over the ISBN, however the record for the book will show the ISBN retailer as the publisher, which you may not consider to be ideal.

Whatever you choose, you need to arrange your ISBN no later than this point, because it needs to appear in the preliminary pages (prelims) of your book.

7. Compile your prelims

Your prelims may include a variety of pages, but should always include a title page, a half title page, and an imprint/copyright page. You might then also include other elements, such as a foreword, table of contents, etc. You can only compile your table of contents at this stage, because you need to know your ISBN (this will be included on the copyright/imprint page) and the page numbers for your table of contents. You therefore need to make sure that you are happy with the typesetting and have no further changes to make before compiling your prelims.

8. Create your final press proof

Depending on the self-publishing path you have chosen, you may be able to use a Word file as your final document. However, you need to be careful. In order to print your book it will have to be converted into a press-ready PDF at some point. If a self-publishing service is doing this for you then you will probably find that they own the PDF file that is created, meaning you don't have control over your own press files. Some services will impose hefty charges (hundreds or even more than a thousand dollars) to release these press files.

It might also be the case that you won't get to see the final PDF, and therefore won't get chance to check it for any errors introduced by the conversion process. If it's an automated system, it may also be difficult to control the output you get from it.

We'd suggest that it's best to produce your own PDF files if possible. To do this you will need a copy of Adobe Acrobat Professional, and you will need to be familiar with the correct settings for creating print ready PDFs. Be careful to embed all fonts and make sure that all images are at 300 DPI.

9. Create your cover

Only once your press proof is finalised can you complete your cover design. That's because your cover includes not only the front cover and the back cover, but also (critically) the spine – and the width of the spine will vary according to the number of pages in your final press proof. In order to complete your cover design you therefore need to know your page size, your page count (including all prelims), and your ISBN, as this will appear on the back cover. You also need to get a barcode for your ISBN.

10. Produce your book

Once your cover and press proof are ready you can go through whichever self-publishing path you have chosen to create your book. With some

pathways the production of a print proof can be an optional extra that is only available at an extra cost – but we'd recommend standing that cost and getting a print version of your book to check. You never know exactly how it's going to come out until you have a physical copy in your hand.

If you're happy with the proof you can clear your book for release. You don't need to do anything to get it on online retailers like Amazon – they will automatically pick up the ISBN and add your book to their websites themselves.

11. Create an ebook version

In the modern day, having an ebook version of your book is imperative. Ebooks account for a significant proportion of all book sales and are a particularly effective vehicle for unknown and self-published authors.

There are various different file formats used by the different platforms, but .epub is emerging as a standard, and having your book in .epub format should enable you to access all the platforms with a single file.

12. Distribute your ebook

Unlike with print books, you will need to act yourself to get your ebooks into sales channels. At a minimum, you need to ensure that you get your ebook available for sale through Amazon, Apple, and Google Play.

Table of US Literary Agencies

Table of UK Literary Agencies

Table of US Literary Agents

Table of UK Literary Agents

Table of Canadian Literary Agents

Table of US Magazines

Table of UK Magazines

Table of Canadian Magazines

Table of Irish Magazines

Table of US Book Publishers

Table of UK Book Publishers

Table of Canadian Book Publishers

Table of Authors

Literary Agents and Agencies

For the most up-to-date listings of these and hundreds of other literary agents and agencies, visit https://www.firstwriter.com/Agents

To claim your free access to the site, please see the back of this book.

L0001 3 Seas Literary Agency
Literary Agency
PO Box 444, Sun Prairie, WI 53590
United States
Tel: +1 (608) 834-9317

threeseaslit@aol.com

https://www.threeseasagency.com
https://www.facebook.com/3-Seas-Literary-Agency-75205869856/
https://twitter.com/threeseaslit?lang=en

ADULT > **Fiction** > *Novels*
Fantasy; Romance; Science Fiction; Thrillers; Women's Fiction

CHILDREN'S > **Fiction** > *Middle Grade*

YOUNG ADULT > **Fiction** > *Novels*

How to send: Query Manager
How not to send: Email

Accepts queries through online submission system only. See website for full guidelines.

Literary Agents: Cori Deyoe (**L0263**); Stacey Graham (**L0409**); Michelle Grajkowski (**L0411**)

L0002 42 Management and Production
Literary Agency
Palladium House, 7th Floor, 1-4 Argyll Street, London, W1F 7TA
United Kingdom
Tel: +44 (0) 20 7292 0554

https://www.42mp.com

Professional Body: The Association of Authors' Agents (AAA)

A fully integrated management and production company, producing film, television and content, representing actors, writers, directors, producers, casting directors and media book rights; with offices in London and Los Angeles.

Literary Agents: Eugenie Furniss (**L0372**); Emily MacDonald (**L0653**); Marilia Savvides (**L0884**)

L0003 A.M. Heath & Company Limited, Author's Agents
Literary Agency
6 Warwick Court, Holborn, London, WC1R 5DJ
United Kingdom
Tel: +44 (0) 20 7242 2811

enquiries@amheath.com

https://amheath.com
https://twitter.com/AMHeathLtd
https://www.instagram.com/a.m.heath

Professional Body: The Association of Authors' Agents (AAA)

Fiction > *Novels*

Nonfiction > *Nonfiction Books*

Send: Query; Synopsis; Writing sample
How to send: Online submission system
How not to send: Post

Handles general commercial and literary fiction and nonfiction. Submit work with cover letter, synopsis, and writing sample up to 10,000 words, via online submission system only. No paper submissions. Aims to respond within six weeks.

Agency Assistant: Jessica Lee

Agency Assistant / Associate Agent: Florence Rees (**L0825**)

Literary Agents: Julia Churchill (**L0198**); Bill Hamilton (**L0438**); Victoria Hobbs (**L0472**); Zoe King; Oli Munson (**L0733**); Rebecca Ritchie (**L0838**); Euan Thorneycroft (**L0979**)

L0004 A3 Artists Agency
Literary Agency
The Empire State Building, 350 Fifth Ave. 38th Floor, New York, NY 10118, 750 North San Vicente Blvd., East Tower, 11th Floor, Los Angeles, CA 90069
United States
Tel: +1 (646) 486-4600

contactla@a3artistsagency.com
contactny@a3artistsagency.com

https://www.a3artistsagency.com/

Scripts
Film Scripts; *TV Scripts*

Closed to approaches.

L0005 Abner Stein
Literary Agency
Suite 137, China Works, 100 Black Prince Road, London, SE1 7SJ
United Kingdom

info@abnerstein.co.uk

http://www.abnerstein.co.uk

Professional Body: The Association of Authors' Agents (AAA)

Types: Fiction; Nonfiction
Markets: Adult; Children's

Agency based in London. Handles fiction, general nonfiction, and children's.

Literary Agents: Anna Carmichael (**L0160**); Rachel Clements (**L0203**); Caspian Dennis (**L0258**); Ben Fowler (**L0350**); Vanessa Kerr (**L0566**); Sandy Violette (**L1008**)

L0006 Stephanie Abou
Literary Agent
United States

Literary Agency: Massie & McQuilkin (**L0680**)

L0007 Above the Line Agency
Literary Agency
468 N. Camden Drive, #200, Beverly Hills, CA 90210
United States
Tel: +1 (310) 859-6115

abovethelineagency@gmail.com

http://www.abovethelineagency.com

Professional Body: Writers Guild of America (WGA)

Types: Scripts
Formats: Film Scripts; TV Scripts
Markets: Adult; Children's

Send: Query
Don't send: Full text

Costs: Offers services that writers have to pay for.

Send query via online web system only. Represents writers and directors; feature films, movies of the week, animation. Offers consultations at a rate of $200 per hour.

Literary Agents: Bruce Bartlett (*L0070*); Rima Greer (*L0422*)

L0008 Landa Acevedo-Scott
Literary Agent
United Kingdom

http://www.tiborjones.com/about/

Literary Agency: Tibor Jones & Associates (**L0982**)

L0009 Kwaku Acheampong
Literary Agent
United States

kwaku@carolynjenksagency.com

https://www.carolynjenksagency.com/agent/Kwaku-Acheampong

Literary Agency: Carolyn Jenks Agency (**L0164**)

ADULT
  Fiction > *Novels*
  Nonfiction > *Nonfiction Books*

NEW ADULT
  Fiction > *Novels*
  Nonfiction > *Nonfiction Books*

Send: Query; Writing sample
How to send: In the body of an email

Looking for fiction and nonfiction across most genres, though he has a special passion for new adult.

L0010 Adams Literary
Literary Agency
7845 Colony Road, C4 #215, Charlotte, NC 28226
United States
Tel: +1 (704) 542-1440
Fax: +1 (704) 542-1450

info@adamsliterary.com

http://www.adamsliterary.com

Types: Fiction
Markets: Children's; Young Adult

Closed to approaches.

Temporarily closed to submissions as at July 2019. Check website for current status. Handles books for children and young adults, from picture books to teen novels. No unsolicited MSS. Send query with complete ms via webform. See website for full submission guidelines.

Literary Agents: Josh Adams (*L0011*); Tracey Adams (*L0013*)

L0011 Josh Adams
Literary Agent
United States

Literary Agency: Adams Literary (**L0010**)

L0012 Seren Adams
Associate Agent
United Kingdom

SAdams@unitedagents.co.uk

https://www.unitedagents.co.uk/sadamsunitedagentscouk
https://twitter.com/serenadams

Literary Agency: United Agents (**L0992**)
Literary Agent: Anna Webber (**L1020**)

Fiction
  Novels: Literary
  Short Fiction: General

Nonfiction > *Nonfiction Books*: Narrative Nonfiction

Send: Query; Synopsis; Pitch; Market info
How to send: Email

Actively building her own list and loves reading excellent short fiction, unconventional literary novels, and compelling narrative non-fiction.

Authors: Kim Adrian; Jen Calleja; Sean Patrick Cooper; Al Crow; Lauren Aimee Curtis; Sam Diamond; Lucie Elven; Rakaya Fetuga; Ronan Fitzgerald; Amaryllis Gacioppo; Maria Giron; Lili Hamlyn; Catherine Humble; Blair James; Liza St. James; Ana Kinsella; Sonal Kohli; Aileen Maguire; Laura Maw; Sinéad Mooney; Caleb Azumah Nelson; Timothy Ogene; Joanna Pocock; Issa Quincy; Karina Lickorish Quinn; Gemma Reeves; Laura Robertson; Olivia Rosenthall; Alan Rossi; Taylor-Dior Rumble; Michael Salu; Lina Scheynius; Laura Southgate; Olivia Spring; Sean Stoker; Jordan Sullivan; Georgina Terry; Zakia Uddin; Kenechi Uzor; Lauren Wallach; Eva Warrick

L0013 Tracey Adams
Literary Agent
United States

Literary Agency: Adams Literary (**L0010**)

L0014 Phil Adie
Literary Agent
United Kingdom

http://nickturnermanagement.com/about-us/

Literary Agency: Nick Turner Management Ltd (**L0750**)

Represents writers and directors for film and television, and is currently building his client list.

L0015 Roxana Adle
Literary Agent
United Kingdom

Literary Agency: Independent Talent Group Ltd (**L0496**)

L0016 Aevitas
Literary Agency
19 West 21st Street, Suite 501, New York, NY 10010
United States
Tel: +1 (212) 765-6900

http://aevitascreative.com

Professional Body: Association of American Literary Agents (AALA)

Types: Fiction; Nonfiction
Subjects: Arts; Autobiography; Beauty; Business; Comedy / Humour; Commercial; Cookery; Culture; Design; Fashion; Health; History; Lifestyle; Literary; Nature; New Age; Personal Development; Politics; Psychology; Religion; Science; Technology
Markets: Adult; Children's; Young Adult

Send: Query
Don't send: Full text

See website for individual agent interests and query using online submission system.

Chief Executive Officers / Literary Agents:
David Kuhn (**L0584**); Todd Shuster (**L0911**)

Consulting Agents: Rob Arnold; Karen Brailsford

Literary Agencies: Aevitas Creative Management (ACM) UK (**L0017**); Sarah Lazin Books (**L0882**); Toby Mundy Associates Ltd (**L0984**)

Literary Agent / President: Esmond Harmsworth (**L0444**)

Literary Agent / Senior Partner: Jennifer Gates (**L0383**)

Literary Agents: Erica Bauman (**L0073**); Sarah Bowlin (**L0114**); Justin Brouckaert (**L0133**); Chris Bucci (**L0139**); Maggie Cooper (**L0220**); Jon Michael Darga (**L0241**); Lori Galvin (**L0378**); David Granger (**L0412**); Chelsey Heller; Georgia Frances King (**L0570**); Danya Kukafka (**L0585**); Sarah Lazin (**L0604**); Sarah Levitt (**L0612**); Will Lippincott (**L0620**); Jen Marshall (**L0676**); Penny Moore (**L0722**); Nate Muscato (**L0738**); Lauren Sharp (**L0903**); Michael Signorelli (**L0913**); Becky Sweren (**L0960**)

Literary Agents / Partners: Michelle Brower (**L0134**); Bridget Wagner Matzie (**L0685**); Jane von Mehren (**L0695**); Rick Richter (**L0834**)

Literary Agents / Senior Partners: Laura Nolan (**L0753**); Janet Silver (**L0917**)

L0017 Aevitas Creative Management (ACM) UK
Literary Agency
49 Greek Street, London, W1D 4EG
United Kingdom

ukenquiries@aevitascreative.com

https://aevitascreative.com/home/acm-uk/
https://twitter.com/AevitasCreative
https://www.facebook.com/AevitasCreative/

Literary Agency: Aevitas (**L0016**)

UK branch of a US agency, founded in 2019, representing writers and brands throughout the world.

Chief Executive Officer / Literary Agent: Toby Mundy (**L0731**)

Literary Agents: Trevor Dolby (**L0269**); Max Edwards (**L0291**); Natalie Jerome (**L0522**); Sara O' Keeffe (**L0563**); Simon Targett (**L0968**)

L0018 The Agency (London) Ltd
Literary Agency
24 Pottery Lane, Holland Park, London, W11 4LZ
United Kingdom

submissions@theagency.co.uk

http://www.theagency.co.uk

Professional Body: The Association of Authors' Agents (AAA)

ADULT > Scripts
 Film Scripts; *TV Scripts*; *Theatre Scripts*
CHILDREN'S > Fiction
 Middle Grade; *Novels*; *Picture Books*
TEEN > Fiction > Novels

YOUNG ADULT > Fiction > Novels

Send: Query; Synopsis; Writing sample
How to send: Email

Represents writers and authors for film, television, radio and the theatre. Also represents directors, producers, composers, and film and television rights in books, as well as authors of children's books from picture books to teen fiction. For script writers, only considers unsolicited material if it has been recommended by a producer, development executive or course tutor. If this is the case send CV, covering letter and details of your referee by email. Do not email more than one agent at a time. For directors, send CV, showreel and cover letter by email. For children's authors, send query by email with synopsis and first three chapters (middle grade, teen, or Young Adult) or complete ms (picture books) to address given on website.

Literary Agents: Ian Benson; Nicola Biltoo; Simon Blakey; Hannah Boulton; Hilary Delamere; Stephen Durbridge; Bethan Evans; Katie Haines; Jessica Hare (**L0443**); Emily Hickman; Jonathan Kinnersley; Julia Kreitman; Norman North; Nick Quinn; Leah Schmidt; Emily Smith; Tanya Tillett

L0019 AHA Talent Ltd
Literary Agency
2 Percy Street, London, W1T 1DD
United Kingdom
Tel: +44 (0) 20 7250 1760

mail@ahacreatives.co.uk

https://www.ahatalent.co.uk
https://twitter.com/AHAcreatives

Scripts
 Film Scripts; *Radio Scripts*; *TV Scripts*; *Theatre Scripts*

Send: Query; Author bio; Writing sample

Handles actors and creatives. Send query with CV/bio, and examples of your work.

Literary Agent: Amanda Fitzalan Howard (*L0485*)

L0020 The Ahearn Agency, Inc
Literary Agency
3436 Magazine St., #615, New Orleans, LA 70115
United States
Tel: +1 (504) 866-6434
Fax: +1 (504) 866-6434

pahearn@aol.com

http://www.ahearnagency.com

Fiction > Novels
 Suspense; Women's Fiction

Send: Query; Market info; Self-Addressed Stamped Envelope (SASE)
How to send: Email; Post
How not to send: Email attachment

Send one page query with SASE, description, length, market info, and any writing credits. Accepts email queries without attachments. Response in 2-3 months.

Specialises in women's fiction and suspense. No nonfiction, poetry, juvenile material or science fiction.

Authors: Michele Albert; Rexanne Becnel; Wendy Hilton; Sabrina Jeffries; Connie Koslow; Sandra Landry; Deb Marlowe; Meagan McKinney; Kate Moore; Gerri Russell; Susan Sipal

Literary Agent: Pamela G. Ahearn

L0021 Jamilah Ahmed
Associate Agent
United Kingdom

Literary Agency: Barbara Levy Literary Agency (**L0061**)

Fiction > Novels

Nonfiction > Nonfiction Books

Briefed with developing new writers in fiction and nonfiction.

L0022 Alan Brodie Representation Ltd
Literary Agency
Paddock Suite, The Courtyard, 55

Charterhouse Street, London, EC1M 6HA
United Kingdom
Tel: +44 (0) 20 7253 6226
Fax: +44 (0) 20 7183 7999

ABR@alanbrodie.com

http://www.alanbrodie.com

Types: Scripts
Formats: Film Scripts; Radio Scripts; TV Scripts; Theatre Scripts
Markets: Adult

Send: Query
Don't send: Full text
How to send: Email

Handles scripts only. No books. Approach with preliminary letter, recommendation from industry professional, and CV. Do not send a sample of work unless requested. No fiction, nonfiction, or poetry.

Literary Agents: Alan Brodie (*L0128*); Kara Fitzpatrick (*L0337*); Victoria Williams (*L1041*)

L0023 Michael Alcock
Literary Agent; Chair
United Kingdom

michael@johnsonandalcock.co.uk

http://www.johnsonandalcock.co.uk/michael-alcock

Literary Agency: Johnson & Alcock (**L0528**)

Nonfiction > Nonfiction Books
 Arts; Biography; Current Affairs; Food; Health; History; Lifestyle; Popular Science

Send: Query; Writing sample; Synopsis

L0024 Julian Alexander
Literary Agent; Company Director
United Kingdom

Literary Agency: The Soho Agency (**L0924**)

L0025 Alice Williams Literary
Literary Agency
United Kingdom
Tel: +44 (0) 20 7385 2118

submissions@alicewilliamsliterary.co.uk

https://www.alicewilliamsliterary.co.uk
https://twitter.com/alicelovesbooks
http://instagram.com/agentalicewilliams

Professional Body: The Association of Authors' Agents (AAA)

CHILDREN'S
 Fiction
  Middle Grade; *Novels*; *Picture Books*
 Nonfiction > Nonfiction Books

YOUNG ADULT
 Fiction > Novels
 Nonfiction > Nonfiction Books

Closed to approaches.

A specialist literary agency proudly representing writers and illustrators of picture books, young fiction, middle-grade, YA and non-fiction.

Literary Agent: Alice Williams (**L1036**)

L0026 Alive Literary Agency

Literary Agency
5001 Centennial Blvd #50742, Colorado Springs, CO 80908
United States

http://aliveliterary.com

Nonfiction > *Nonfiction Books*
 Lifestyle; Personal Development; Religion

How to send: By referral

Accepts queries from referred authors only. Works primarily with well-established, best-selling, and career authors.

Authors: Jamie Blaine; Michael Hyatt; Karen Kingsbury

Literary Agents: Andrea Heinecke; Lisa Jackson (*L0511*); Bryan Norman (*L0754*)

L0027 Allen O'Shea Literary Agency

Literary Agency
United States
Tel: +1 (203) 820-5967

marilyn@allenoshea.com

https://www.allenoshea.com

Professional Body: Association of American Literary Agents (AALA)

Types: Nonfiction
Subjects: Business; Cookery; Crafts; Culture; Finance; Health; History; Lifestyle; Politics; Science; Sport
Markets: Adult

Send: Query
Don't send: Full text
How to send: Email

Works mainly with nonfiction writers. Send query by email, describing why your work is unique, your experience, your platform, and any awards or honours received for your writing. See website for full guidelines.

L0028 Marilyn Allen

Literary Agent
United States

L0029 Elias Altman

Literary Agent
United States

Literary Agency: Massie & McQuilkin (**L0680**)

L0030 Ambassador Speakers Bureau & Literary Agency

Literary Agency
1107 Battlewood Street, Franklin, TN 37069
United States
Tel: +1 (615) 370-4700

info@ambassadorspeakers.com

https://www.ambassadorspeakers.com

Types: Fiction; Nonfiction
Subjects: Adventure; Autobiography; Commercial; Contemporary; Culture; Current Affairs; Finance; Health; History; How To; Legal; Lifestyle; Literary; Medicine; Personal Development; Politics; Religion; Women's Interests
Markets: Adult

Send: Query
Don't send: Full text
How to send: Email

Represents select authors and writers who are published by religious and general market publishers in the US and Europe. No short stories, children's books, screenplays, or poetry. Send query by email with short description. Submit work on invitation only.

L0031 The Ampersand Agency Ltd

Literary Agency
Ryman's Cottages, Little Tew, Chipping Norton, Oxfordshire, OX7 4JJ
United Kingdom
Tel: +44 (0) 1608 683677 / 683898
Fax: +44 (0) 1608 683449

submissions@theampersandagency.co.uk

http://www.theampersandagency.co.uk

Professional Body: The Association of Authors' Agents (AAA)

Fiction > *Novels*
 Contemporary; Crime; Fantasy; Historical Fiction; Literary; Science Fiction; Thrillers

Nonfiction > *Nonfiction Books*
 Biography; Current Affairs; History; Popular Science

Send: Query; Synopsis; Author bio; Writing sample
How to send: Email; Post

Costs: Author covers sundry admin costs.

We handle contemporary and historical novels, literary, crime, thrillers, fantasy, science fiction; non-fiction: current affairs, history, biography, popular science. Send query by post or email with brief bio, outline, and first three chapters. If emailing material, send as attachments rather than pasted into the body of the email. Also accepts science fiction, fantasy, horror, and Young Adult material to separate email address listed on website. No scripts except those by existing clients, no poetry, self-help or illustrated children's books. No

unpublished American writers, because in our experience British and European publishers aren't interested unless there is an American publisher on board. And we'd like to make it clear that American stamps are no use outside America!

Authors: Quentin Bates; Will Davis; Phillip Hunter; Vikas Swarup

Literary Agents: Peter Buckman; Jamie Cowen; Anne-Marie Doulton

L0032 Betsy Amster

Literary Agent
United States

Literary Agency: Betsy Amster Literary Enterprises (**L0094**)

L0033 Darley Anderson

Literary Agent
United Kingdom

https://www.darleyanderson.com/our-team

Literary Agency: The Darley Anderson Agency

ADULT > **Fiction** > *Novels*
 Noir; Romance; Thrillers

CHILDREN'S > **Fiction** > *Novels*: Animals

How to send: Email; Post

Looking specifically for thrillers and Scandi-Noir with a strong central character set in America or Ireland or other internationally appealing locations and tear-jerking love stories. He is looking specifically for children's books featuring an original series character and animal stories. Email submissions should be sent to the agent's assistant.

Agency Assistant: Rebeka Finch

Authors: Constance Briscoe; Chris Carter; Cathy Cassidy; Lee Child; Martina Cole; John Connolly; Liza Costello; Margaret Dickinson; Clare Dowling; Jack Ford; Tana French; Paul Hauck; Joan Jonker; Annie Murray; Abi Oliver; Adrian Plass; Hazel Prior; David Rhodes; Jacqui Rose; Stephen Spotswood; Erik Storey; Anna-Lou Weatherley; Lee Weeks

L0034 Andrew Lownie Literary Agency Ltd

Literary Agency
36 Great Smith Street, London, SW1P 3BU
United Kingdom
Tel: +44 (0) 20 7222 7574
Fax: +44 (0) 20 7222 7576

lownie@globalnet.co.uk

http://www.andrewlownie.co.uk
https://twitter.com/andrewlownie

Nonfiction > *Nonfiction Books*

Send: Query; Synopsis; Author bio; Market info; Writing sample
How to send: Email

This agency, founded in 1988, is now one of the UK's leading literary agencies with some two hundred nonfiction and fiction authors. It prides itself on its personal attention to its clients and specialises both in launching new writers and taking established writers to a new level of recognition.

Authors: Daniel Cowling; James Davies; Andy Donaldson; Angela Findlay; Katreen Hardt; Catherine Hewitt; Christian Jennings; David McClure; Danny Orbach; Linda Porter; Louise Ramsay; Dan Smith; Nicola Stow; Tim Tate; Ian Williams; Chris Woodford

Literary Agent: Andrew Lownie (*L0637*)

L0035 Andrew Nurnberg Associates, Ltd

Literary Agency
3-11 Eyre St Hill, London, EC1R 5ET
United Kingdom
Tel: +44 (0) 20 3327 0400

info@nurnberg.co.uk
submissions@nurnberg.co.uk

http://www.andrewnurnberg.com
https://twitter.com/nurnberg_agency
https://www.instagram.com/
andrewnurnbergassociates/?hl=en

Professional Body: The Association of Authors' Agents (AAA)

ADULT
  Fiction > *Novels*
  Nonfiction > *Nonfiction Books*

CHILDREN'S > **Fiction** > *Novels*

Does not want:

> **ADULT** > **Scripts**
>   *Film Scripts*; *Radio Scripts*; *TV Scripts*;
>   *Theatre Scripts*
> **CHILDREN'S** > **Fiction** > *Picture*
> *Books*

Send: Query; Synopsis; Writing sample
How to send: Email

Handles adult fiction and nonfiction, and children's fiction. No poetry, children's picture books, or scripts for film, TV, radio or theatre. Send query by email with one-page synopsis and first three chapters or 50 pages as attachments.

Literary Agency: The Wallace Literary Agency (**L1011**)

Literary Agents: Sarah Nundy (*L0758*); Andrew Nurnberg (*L0759*)

L0036 Nelle Andrew

Literary Agent
United Kingdom

nelle@rmliterary.co.uk

Literary Agency: Rachel Mills Literary (**L0819**)

Fiction > *Novels*
  Book Club Fiction; Commercial Women's Fiction; Crime; Feminism; Historical Fiction; Literary; Suspense; Thrillers

Nonfiction > *Nonfiction Books*: Narrative Nonfiction

Closed to approaches.

Looking for fiction and nonfiction. Loves historical, literary, commercial female fiction, reading group, suspense and thrillers and intelligent crime. Particularly interested in books that shine a light on new ideas or little known histories, diverse backgrounds, and emotionally moving narratives that resonate with modern complexities.

L0037 Andy Ross Agency

Literary Agency
767 Santa Ray Avenue, Oakland, CA 94610
United States
Tel: +1 (510) 238-8965

andyrossagency@hotmail.com

http://www.andyrossagency.com

Professional Body: Association of American Literary Agents (AALA)

Types: Fiction; Nonfiction
Subjects: Commercial; Contemporary; Culture; Current Affairs; History; Literary; Religion; Science
Markets: Adult; Young Adult

Send: Query
Don't send: Full text
How to send: Email

We encourage queries for material in our fields of interest. No poetry, short stories, adult romance, science fiction and fantasy, adult and teen paranormal, or film scripts. The agent has worked in the book business for 36 years, all of his working life. He was owner and general manager of Cody's Books in Berkeley, California from 1977-2006. Cody's has been recognised as one of America's great independent book stores. During this period, the agent was the primary trade book buyer. This experience has given him a unique understanding of the retail book market, of publishing trends and, most importantly and uniquely, the hand selling of books to book buyers. The agent is past president of the Northern California Booksellers Association, a board member and officer of the American Booksellers Association and a national spokesperson for issues concerning independent businesses. He has had significant profiles in the Wall Street Journal, Time Magazine, and the San Francisco Chronicle. Queries by email only. See website for full guidelines.

Literary Agent: Andy Ross (*L0861*)

L0038 Anne Clark Literary Agency

Literary Agency
United Kingdom

submissions@anneclarkliteraryagency.co.uk

https://www.anneclarkliteraryagency.co.uk

Professional Body: The Association of Authors' Agents (AAA)

CHILDREN'S
  Fiction
    Middle Grade; *Picture Books*
  Nonfiction > *Nonfiction Books*

YOUNG ADULT
  Fiction > *Novels*
  Nonfiction > *Nonfiction Books*

Send: Synopsis; Writing sample; Full text; Proposal
How to send: Email

Handles fiction and picture books for children and young adults. Send query by email only with the following pasted into the body of the email (not as an attachment): for fiction, include brief synopsis and first 3,000 words; for picture books, send complete ms; for nonfiction, send short proposal and the text of three sample pages. No submissions by post. See website for full guidelines.

Literary Agent: Anne Clark (*L0201*)

L0039 Anne Edelstein Literary Agency

Literary Agency
258 Riverside Drive #8D, New York, NY 10025
United States
Tel: +1 (212) 414-4923

information@aeliterary.com

https://aeliterary.com

Professional Body: Association of American Literary Agents (AALA)

Fiction > *Novels*
  Commercial; Literary

Nonfiction > *Nonfiction Books*
  Memoir; Narrative History; Psychology; Religion

Closed to approaches.

Send query letter with SASE and for fiction a summary of your novel plus the first 25 pages, or for nonfiction an outline of your book and one or two sample chapters. No queries by email.

Authors: Roderick Anscombe; Stephen Batchelor; Sophy Burnham; Mark Epstein; Kathleen Finneran; James Goodman; Patricia Hersch; His Holiness the Dalai Lama with Jeffrey Hopkins; Peter Levitt; Josip Novakovich; Natasha Rodijcic-Kane; James

Shapiro; Jody Shields; Russell Shorto; Rachel Simon; Sasha Troyan; Phyllis Vane

Literary Agent: Anne Edelstein

L0040 Annette Green Authors' Agency
Literary Agency
5 Henwoods Mount, Pembury, Kent, TN2 4BH
United Kingdom

annette@annettegreenagency.co.uk
david@annettegreenagency.co.uk

http://www.annettegreenagency.co.uk

Types: Fiction; Nonfiction
Formats: Film Scripts; TV Scripts
Subjects: Autobiography; Comedy / Humour; Commercial; Culture; Current Affairs; History; Horror; Literary; Music; Politics; Science; Sport; Thrillers
Markets: Adult; Children's; Young Adult

Send: Query
Don't send: Full text
How to send: Email

Costs: Offers services that writers have to pay for.

Send query by email with a brief synopsis (fiction) or overview (nonfiction), and the opening few chapters (up to about 10,000 words). No poetry, scripts, science fiction, or fantasy. Send Word documents rather than PDFs.

L0041 Jason Anthony
Literary Agent
United States

Literary Agency: Massie & McQuilkin (**L0680**)

Closed to approaches.

L0042 Antony Harwood Limited
Literary Agency
103 Walton Street, Oxford, OX2 6EB
United Kingdom
Tel: +44 (0) 1865 559615

mail@antonyharwood.com

http://www.antonyharwood.com

Fiction > *Novels*

Nonfiction > *Nonfiction Books*

Send: Query; Synopsis; Writing sample; Self-Addressed Stamped Envelope (SASE)
How to send: Email; Post

Handles fiction and nonfiction in every genre and category, except for screenwriting and poetry. Send brief outline and first 50 pages by email, or by post with SASE.

Authors: Christine Berry; Alastair Bonnett; Michael Bracewell; Peter Bunzl; Amanda Craig; Candida Crewe; David Dabydeen;

Tracy Darnton; Roy Dennis; Louise Doughty; Robert Edric; Anna Fleming; Sarah Gibson; Bob Gilbert; Caspar Henderson; Jill Hopper; Sally Huband; Gwyneth Lewis; Amy Liptrot; Fraser MacDonald; Stephen Rutt; Guy Shrubsole; Hugh Warwick

Literary Agents: Jonathan Gregory (**L0424**); Antony Harwood (*L0453*); James Macdonald Lockhart (**L0629**); Jo Williamson (**L1042**)

L0043 Zoe Apostolides
Literary Agent
United Kingdom

https://cmm.agency/about-us.php

Literary Agency: Coombs Moylett & Maclean Literary Agency (**L0217**)

ADULT
  Fiction > *Novels*
    Coming of Age; Crime; Historical Fiction; Horror; Mystery

  Nonfiction > *Nonfiction Books*

CHILDREN'S > **Fiction** > *Novels*

YOUNG ADULT > **Fiction** > *Novels*

Send: Synopsis; Writing sample
How to send: Online submission system

Manages a list of crime, historical, young adult and children's authors and is also looking to build a nonfiction list. She is especially interested in original horror novels, coming-of-age stories and any sort of whodunnit.

L0044 Apple Tree Literary Ltd
Literary Agency
86-90 Paul Street, London, EC2A 4NE
United Kingdom
Tel: +44 (0) 7515 876444

max@appletreeliterary.co.uk

http://appletreeliterary.co.uk

Types: Fiction; Nonfiction
Markets: Adult; Young Adult

Send: Query
Don't send: Full text
How to send: Email

Represents a range of authors, from journalism and academic non-fiction, to genre fiction and fiction for young adults. No poetry, self-help or lifestyle books, picture books, or romance novels. See website for full guidelines.

Literary Agent: Max Edwards (**L0291**)

L0045 Sophieclaire Armitage
Literary Agent
United Kingdom

Literary Agency: Noel Gay (**L0752**)

L0046 Victoria Wells Arms
Literary Agent
United States

submissions@wellsarms.com

https://www.hgliterary.com/victoria
https://twitter.com/VWArms

Literary Agencies: Wells Arms Literary; HG Literary (**L0467**)

CHILDREN'S > **Fiction**
  Middle Grade; Picture Books
YOUNG ADULT > **Fiction** > *Novels*

How to send: Email

L0047 Susan Armstrong
Literary Agent
United Kingdom

Literary Agency: C+W (Conville & Walsh) (**L0147**)

L0048 ASH Literary
Literary Agency
United Kingdom

info@ashliterary.com
submissions@ashliterary.com

https://www.ashliterary.com/
https://twitter.com/ashliterary
https://instagram.com/aliceisagent
https://querymanager.com/query/ASH_Literary

CHILDREN'S > **Fiction**
  Chapter Books: General
  Graphic Novels: Contemporary; Fantasy; Magical Realism; Surreal
  Middle Grade: Contemporary; Magical Realism
YOUNG ADULT > **Fiction**
  Graphic Novels: Contemporary; Fantasy; Magical Realism; Surreal
  Novels: General

Send: Synopsis; Writing sample
How to send: Query Manager

Looking for extraordinary stories for children that reflect and celebrate the diversity of our world. As of July 2021, our focus is on Middle Grade, particularly illustrated Middle Grade, and graphic novels across all ages.

Authors: Dina Al-Sabawi; Hannah Camacho; Ryan Crawford; Alex Falase-Koya; Niyla Farook; Kereen Getten; Gina Gonzales; Gavin Gray; Sarah Guillory; Ravena Guron; Radiya Hafiza; Anika Hussain; Jennifer Iacopelli; Nansubuga Isdahl; Samantha Joyce; Richard Mercado; Samuel Pollen; Ryan Robinson; Elizabeth Rounding; Kelly Sharpe; Cynthia So; Chitra Soundar; Claire Tomasi; Adelle Yeung

Literary Agent: Alice Sutherland-Hawes (**L0958**)

L0049 Isabel Atherton
Literary Agent
United Kingdom

Literary Agency: Creative Authors Ltd (**L0226**)

L0050 Charlotte Atyeo

Literary Agent
United Kingdom

charlotte@cclagents.com

https://cclagents.com/agent/charlotte-atyeo/
https://twitter.com/EverSoBookish

Literary Agency: Charlie Campbell Literary Agents (**L0188**)

Fiction > *Novels*: Literary

Nonfiction > *Nonfiction Books*
General, and in particular: Biography; Equality; Exercise; Feminism; Fitness; Gender; Memoir; Music; Nature; Sport

Send: Query; Synopsis; Writing sample; Outline
How to send: Email
How not to send: Post

Primarily looking for original and brilliantly written general non-fiction, biography and memoir, sport and exercise/fitness, music, nature writing, and feminism, gender and equality issues. On the fiction side, she is taking on a small number of literary novels.

Authors: Sofie Hagen; Ed Hawkins; Michael Holding; Jennifer Lane; Katy Massey; Susan Richardson; Sarah Shephard; Tatton Spiller; Jen Wight

L0051 AVAnti Productions & Management

Literary Agency
7 Parkside Mews, Hurst Road, Horsham, West Sussex, RH12 2SA
United Kingdom

avantiproductions@live.co.uk

https://www.avantiproductions.co.uk

Scripts > *Film Scripts*

Send: Full text
How to send: Email
How not to send: Post

Costs: Author covers sundry admin costs.

Talent and literary representation. Open to screenplay submissions for short films and feature films, but no theatre scripts.

Literary Agent: Veronica Lazar (**L0603**)

L0052 Ayesha Pande Literary

Literary Agency
128 West 132 Street, New York, NY 10027
United States
Tel: +1 (212) 283-5825

queries@pandeliterary.com

http://pandeliterary.com

A New York based boutique literary agency with a small and eclectic roster of clients. Submit queries via form on website. No poetry,

business books, cookbooks, screenplays or illustrated children's books.

Literary Agents: Jake Allgeier; Madison Smartt Bell (**L0085**); Stephany Evans (**L0314**); Serene Hakim (**L0436**); Annie Hwang (**L0492**); Kayla Lightner (**L0615**); Luba Ostashevsky (**L0772**); Ayesha Pande (**L0776**); Anjali Singh (**L0919**)

L0053 Matilda Ayris

Literary Agent
United Kingdom

Literary Agency: C+W (Conville & Walsh) (**L0147**)

L0054 Azantian Literary Agency

Literary Agency
United States

http://www.azantianlitagency.com
https://www.facebook.com/azantianlitagency/
https://twitter.com/jenazantian
https://www.instagram.com/azantianbooknerd/

Fiction > *Novels*

Nonfiction > *Nonfiction Books*

Committed to guiding the careers of both new and established voices in fiction and nonfiction, particularly those who have been historically underrepresented.

Associate Agents: Masha Gunic (**L0430**); Renae Moore (**L0723**); Amanda Rutter (**L0876**); Andrea Walker; Alexandra Weiss (**L1023**)

Literary Agents: Jennifer Azantian (**L0055**); Ben Baxter; T.S. Ferguson (**L0328**)

L0055 Jennifer Azantian

Literary Agent
United States

http://www.azantianlitagency.com/pages/team-ja.html

Literary Agency: Azantian Literary Agency (**L0054**)

ADULT > **Fiction** > *Novels*
General, and in particular: Fantasy; Psychological Horror; Science Fiction

CHILDREN'S > **Fiction**
Graphic Novels: Contemporary; Fantasy; Magical Realism
Middle Grade: General

YOUNG ADULT > **Fiction**
Graphic Novels: Contemporary; Fantasy; Magical Realism
Novels: General, and in particular: Mystery; Psychological Thrillers; Speculative

How to send: Query Manager

Focuses primarily on fiction across genres for mg, YA, and adult readers. Currently accepting submissions of graphic novels only.

L0056 Oliver Azis

Literary Agent
United Kingdom

Literary Agency: Independent Talent Group Ltd (**L0496**)

L0057 Becky Bagnell

Literary Agent
United Kingdom

Literary Agency: Lindsay Literary Agency (**L0619**)

L0058 Emma Bal

Literary Agent
United Kingdom

https://madeleinemilburn.co.uk/looking-for/emma-bal-what-im-looking-for/

Literary Agency: Madeleine Milburn Literary, TV & Film Agency (**L0664**)

Nonfiction > *Nonfiction Books*
Anthropology; Arts; Cookery; Culture; Economics; Food; Geography; History; Literature; Memoir; Narrative Nonfiction; Nature; Philosophy; Politics; Psychology; Science; Travel

Actively looking for: new perspectives in history, arts & culture, politics, economics, philosophy, psychology, and science; original approaches to travel and nature writing; unusual illustrated projects; thoughtful and dynamic cookery and food writing; and atypical narrative non-fiction and memoir. See agency listing for submission guidelines.

L0059 Natalie Ball

Literary Agent
United Kingdom

Literary Agency: Noel Gay (**L0752**)

L0060 Sarah Ballard

Literary Agent
United Kingdom

sballard@unitedagents.co.uk

https://www.unitedagents.co.uk/sballardunitedagentscouk

Literary Agency: United Agents (**L0992**)

Fiction > *Novels*

Nonfiction > *Nonfiction Books*
Feminism; History; Memoir

Does not want:

> **Fiction** > *Novels*
> Saga; Science Fiction

Closed to approaches.

I have extremely broad taste in fiction and non-fiction, but the underlying quality of the work that I'm interested in is a sense of urgency, and an attempt to make a change in the world, whether that is fiction with a compelling plot or structure overlaying a set of big ideas; memoir-ish non fiction flavoured with obsession and unfolding a hidden agenda; or meticulously researched history which changes our world view. I have a particular interest in feminism and feminist approaches – but exploring ideas or angles which are completely new to me is one of the great joys of my job. I prefer to work with writers who are more-or-less based in the UK, and are aiming to deliver a book every one or two years, and for whom I can add something to every area of their creative lives.

Associate Agent: Eli Keren (**L0564**)

L0061 Barbara Levy Literary Agency

Literary Agency
64 Greenhill, Hampstead High Street, London, NW3 5TZ
United Kingdom
Tel: +44 (0) 20 7435 9046

submissions@barbaralevyagency.com

http://barbaralevyagency.com
https://twitter.com/BLLA_NW3

Professional Body: The Association of Authors' Agents (AAA)

Types: Fiction; Nonfiction
Markets: Adult

Send: Query; Synopsis; Author bio; Writing sample
How to send: Email; Post

Send query with synopsis and first three chapters (approximately 50 pages) by email or by post with SAE. No poetry, plays, original screenplays, scripts or picture books for children.

Associate Agent: Jamilah Ahmed (**L0021**)

Literary Agents: Barbara Levy (*L0613*); Vicki Salter (*L0879*)

L0062 Stephen Barbara

Literary Agent
United States

Literary Agency: InkWell Management (**L0499**)

L0063 Bruce R. Barbour

Literary Agent
United States

Literary Agency: Literary Management Group, Inc. (**L0623**)

L0064 Julie Barer

Literary Agent
United States

Literary Agency: The Book Group (**L0109**)

L0065 Kate Barker

Literary Agent
United Kingdom

Literary Agency: Kate Barker Literary, TV, & Film Agency (**L0553**)

L0066 Barone Literary Agency

Literary Agency
United States

baronelit@outlook.com

http://www.baroneliteraryagency.com

Types: Fiction
Subjects: Erotic; History; Horror; Romance; Women's Interests
Markets: Adult; Young Adult

Closed to approaches.

Closed to submissions as at September 2019. Check website for current status.

Send query online form on website. Include synopsis and first three chapters. No plays, screenplays, picture books, middle grade, science fiction, paranormal, or nonfiction.

Literary Agent: Denise Barone (**L0067**)

L0067 Denise Barone

Literary Agent
United States

Literary Agency: Barone Literary Agency (**L0066**)

Authors: Laurie Albano; Michele Barrow-Belisle; Cathy Bennett; Sarah Biglow; KateMarie Collins; Jennifer Petersen Fraser; Yvette Geer; Suzanne Hay; Richard Moore; Rebekah Purdy; Curt Rude; Wyatt Shev; Anna Snow; Sharon Sullivan-Craver; Molly Zenk

L0068 Baror International, Inc.

Literary Agency
P.O. Box 868, Armonk, NY 10504-0868
United States

Heather@Barorint.com

http://www.barorint.com

ADULT
  Fiction > *Novels*
    Commercial; Fantasy; Literary; Science Fiction

  Nonfiction > *Nonfiction Books*

YOUNG ADULT > **Fiction** > *Novels*

Closed to approaches.

Specialises in the international and domestic representation of literary works in both fiction and nonfiction, including commercial fiction, literary, science fiction, fantasy, young adult and more.

Literary Agents: Danny Baror; Heather Baror-Shapiro

L0069 Nicola Barr

Literary Agent
United States

Literary Agency: The Bent Agency (**L0090**)

L0070 Bruce Bartlett

Literary Agent
United States

Literary Agency: Above the Line Agency (**L0007**)

L0071 Ethan Bassoff

Literary Agent
United States

Literary Agency: Massie & McQuilkin (**L0680**)
Professional Body: Association of American Literary Agents (AALA)

L0072 Bath Literary Agency

Literary Agency
5 Gloucester Road, Bath, BA1 7BH
United Kingdom

submissions@bathliteraryagency.com

https://www.bathliteraryagency.com
https://twitter.com/BathLitAgency
http://instagram.com/bathlitagency

Professional Body: The Association of Authors' Agents (AAA)

CHILDREN'S
  Fiction
    Middle Grade; Picture Books
  Poetry > *Picture Books*

YOUNG ADULT
  Fiction > *Novels*
  Nonfiction > *Nonfiction Books*

Send: Query; Synopsis; Writing sample; Full text; Self-Addressed Stamped Envelope (SASE)
How to send: Email; Post

Handles fiction and nonfiction for children, from picture books to Young Adult. Send query by email or by post with SAE for reply and return of materials if required, along with the first three chapters (fiction) or the full manuscript (picture books). See website for full details.

Literary Agent: Gill McLay

L0073 Erica Bauman

Literary Agent
United States

https://aevitascreative.com/agents/
https://querymanager.com/query/EricaBauman

Literary Agency: Aevitas (**L0016**)

ADULT > **Fiction**
  Graphic Novels: General

Novels: Commercial; Folklore, Myths, and Legends; Magic; Romantic Comedy; Speculative
CHILDREN'S > **Fiction** > *Graphic Novels*
YOUNG ADULT > **Fiction** > *Graphic Novels*
Closed to approaches.

Most interested in commercial novels that feature an exciting premise and lyrical, atmospheric writing; imaginative, genre-blending tales; speculative worlds filled with haunting, quietly wondrous magic; fresh retellings of mythology, ballet, opera, and classic literature; sharply funny rom-coms; graphic novels for all ages; fearless storytellers that tackle big ideas and contemporary issues; and working with and supporting marginalized authors and stories that represent the wide range of humanity.

L0074 Jan Baumer
Literary Agent
United States

jan@foliolitmanagement.com

https://www.foliolit.com/agents-1/jan-baumer

Literary Agency: Folio Literary Management, LLC (**L0343**)

Fiction > *Novels*
Allegory; Literary

Nonfiction > *Nonfiction Books*
Business; Comedy / Humour; Cookery; Health; Memoir; Narrative Nonfiction; Parenting; Prescriptive Nonfiction; Religion; Self Help; Spirituality; Wellbeing

Closed to approaches.

Interests as an agent are largely nonfiction, specifically spirituality, religion, self-help, health and wellness, parenting, memoir, and business with a spirituality or self-help angle. Also open to allegorical fiction, but it must have a literary voice and an author with the writing credentials to pull it off.

L0075 Veronique Baxter
Literary Agent; Company Director
United Kingdom

veroniquemanuscripts@davidhigham.co.uk

https://www.davidhigham.co.uk/agents-dh/veronique-baxter/

Literary Agency: David Higham Associates Ltd (**L0245**)

ADULT
Fiction > *Novels*
Historical Fiction; Literary; Speculative; Upmarket Crime; Upmarket Thrillers

Nonfiction > *Nonfiction Books*
Current Affairs; Feminism; History; Memoir; Narrative Nonfiction

CHILDREN'S > **Fiction** > *Middle Grade*: Adventure

YOUNG
ADULT > **Fiction** > *Novels*: Adventure

Agency Assistant: Sara Langham

Authors: Richard Adams; Naomi Alderman; Hannah Begbie; Carys Bray; Kevin Brockmeier; Glen Brown; Nick Butterworth; Nicola Davies; Jonathan Dimbleby; Berlie Doherty; Ellie Eaton; David Edmonds; Maz Evans; Jamila Gavin; Guinevere Glasfurd; Candy Guard; Saleem Haddad; Oliver Harris; Lisa Heathfield; Neil Hegarty; Emma Henderson; Edward Hogan; Phil Hogan; Ian Holding; Lucy Hounsom; Tristan Hughes; William Hussey; Will Iredale; Diana Wynne Jones; Claire King; Saci Lloyd; Kesia Lupo; Patrick Marnham; Geraldine McCaughrean; Jean McNeil; Sarah Mitchell

L0076 Maile Beal
Literary Agent
United States

maile@carolmannagency.com

https://www.carolmannagency.com/maile-beal
https://www.instagram.com/mailebeal/
https://twitter.com/MaileBeal

Literary Agency: Carol Mann Agency (**L0161**)

ADULT
Fiction > *Novels*: Commercial

Nonfiction
Illustrated Books: Comedy / Humour
Nonfiction Books: Cookery; Crime; Entertainment; Intersectional Feminism; Lifestyle; Narrative Nonfiction; Popular Culture; Social Issues
YOUNG ADULT > **Fiction** > *Novels*

Send: Query; Author bio; Writing sample
How to send: In the body of an email
How not to send: Post; Email attachment

L0077 Diana Beaumont
Literary Agent
United Kingdom

diana@marjacq.com

http://www.marjacq.com/diana-beaumont.html

Literary Agency: Marjacq Scripts Ltd (**L0672**)

Fiction > *Novels*
Book Club Fiction; Commercial; Contemporary; Crime; High Concept; Historical Fiction; Literary; Saga; Thrillers; Upmarket Women's Fiction

Nonfiction > *Nonfiction Books*
Cookery; Feminism; Lifestyle; Memoir; Social Justice

Closed to approaches.

Looking for upmarket women's commercial fiction with depth and heart, including reading group, historical, saga, uplit and contemporary stories that are irreverent and make her laugh; accessible literary fiction, high-concept crime

fiction and thrillers. On the non-fiction side: memoir, smart, funny feminists, lifestyle, cookery and social justice, and open to anything with a strong, original voice. She also encourages submissions from writers who have been traditionally under-represented.

Authors: Tanya Atapattu; Holly Baxter; Daisy Buchanan; Cecil Cameron; James Campbell; Angela Clarke; Mathew Clayton; Fiona Collins; Caroline Corcoran; Isabel Costello; Francesca Dorricott; Lilly Ebert; Dov Forman; Eve Harris; Louise Hulland; Catriona Innes; Amy Jones; Eve Makis; Andrea Mara; Francesca May; Claire McGowan; Adam Pearson; Alice Peterson; Das Petrou; Rachel Phipps; Carmen Reid; Samantha Renke; Lee Ridley; Diana Rosie; Frances Ryan; Jennifer Savin; Lucy Vine; James Wallman; Roz Watkins; Eva Woods

L0078 Rachel Beck
Literary Agent
United States

queryrachel@lizadawson.com

https://www.lizadawsonassociates.com/team/rachel-beck/

Literary Agency: Liza Dawson Associates (**L0625**)

ADULT
Fiction > *Novels*
Book Club Women's Fiction; Contemporary Romance; Domestic Suspense; Millennial Fiction; Upmarket Women's Fiction

Nonfiction > *Nonfiction Books*
Career Development; Feminism; Personal Development

YOUNG ADULT > **Fiction** > *Novels*
Contemporary; Cyberpunk; Post-Apocalyptic

Send: Query; Writing sample
How to send: In the body of an email

Believes that the right book can change or heal a life, and she wants to find those. But she's also interested in lighter fiction that helps you escape or simply makes you laugh after a tough day. Or nonfiction that teaches you something about an obscure topic, thus opening up a new world.

L0079 Emily Van Beek
Literary Agent; Partner
United States

emily@foliolitmanagement.com

https://www.publishersmarketplace.com/members/vanbeek/

Literary Agency: Folio Literary Management, LLC (**L0343**)

CHILDREN'S > **Fiction**
Middle Grade; *Picture Books*
YOUNG ADULT > **Fiction** > *Novels*

Adventure; Comedy / Humour; Dystopian Fiction; Fantasy; High Concept; Magical Realism; Supernatural / Paranormal

Send: Query; Writing sample
How to send: In the body of an email

L0080 Matt Belford

Literary Agent
United States

https://www.thetobiasagency.com/matt-belford
https://querymanager.com/query/MWBelford

Literary Agency: The Tobias Literary Agency
(**L0983**)

Fiction
Graphic Novels: General
Novels: Fantasy; Science Fiction
Nonfiction
Graphic Nonfiction: Memoir
Nonfiction Books: Popular

Send: Author bio; Query; Writing sample; Market info
How to send: Query Manager

Interested in receiving submissions for both graphic memoirs and graphic novels, as well as adult science fiction and fantasy, and some popular nonfiction. He is not interested in YA.

L0081 Bell Lomax Moreton Agency

Literary Agency
Suite C, 131 Queensway, Petts Wood, Kent, BR5 1DG
United Kingdom
Tel: +44 (0) 20 7930 4447
Fax: +44 (0) 1689 820061

agency@bell-lomax.co.uk

http://www.belllomaxmoreton.co.uk

Professional Body: The Association of Authors' Agents (AAA)

Types: Fiction; Nonfiction
Subjects: Biography; Business; Sport
Markets: Adult; Children's

How to send: Email

Considers most fiction, nonfiction, and children's book proposals. No poetry, short stories, novellas, textbooks, film scripts, stage plays, or science fiction. Send query by email with details of any previous work, short synopsis, and first three chapters (up to 50 pages). For children's picture books send complete ms. Also accepts postal submissions. See website for full guidelines.

Literary Agents: Eddie Bell (*L0082*); Jo Bell (*L0083*); June Bell (*L0084*); Lauren Gardner (*L0382*); Pat Lomax (*L0630*); Sarah McDonnell (*L0691*); Paul Moreton (*L0725*); Helen Mackenzie Smith (*L0922*)

L0082 Eddie Bell

Literary Agent
United Kingdom

Literary Agency: Bell Lomax Moreton Agency
(**L0081**)

L0083 Jo Bell

Literary Agent
United Kingdom

Literary Agency: Bell Lomax Moreton Agency
(**L0081**)

L0084 June Bell

Literary Agent
United Kingdom

Literary Agency: Bell Lomax Moreton Agency
(**L0081**)

L0085 Madison Smartt Bell

Literary Agent
United States

https://www.pandeliterary.com/about-pandeliterary

Literary Agency: Ayesha Pande Literary
(**L0052**)

Fiction > *Novels*
Literary; Noir; Police Procedural

L0086 Lorella Belli

Literary Agent
United Kingdom

Literary Agency: Lorella Belli Literary Agency
(LBLA) (**L0632**)

L0087 Faye Bender

Literary Agent
United States

Literary Agency: The Book Group (**L0109**)

L0088 Laura Bennett

Assistant Agent; Editor
United Kingdom

https://www.liverpool-literary.agency/about

Literary Agency: The Liverpool Literary Agency (**L0624**)

L0089 The Bent Agency (UK)

Literary Agency
17 Kelsall Mews, Richmond, TW9 4BP
United Kingdom

info@thebentagency.com

http://www.thebentagency.com

Professional Body: The Association of Authors' Agents (AAA)
Literary Agency: The Bent Agency (**L0090**)

ADULT
Fiction
Graphic Novels; Novels

Nonfiction > *Nonfiction Books*

CHILDREN'S > **Fiction**
Chapter Books; Graphic Novels; Middle Grade
YOUNG ADULT
Fiction
Graphic Novels; Novels
Nonfiction > *Nonfiction Books*

Send: Query
How to send: Email; Query Manager

UK office of established US agency. See website for individual agent interests and contact details and approach appropriate agent. Do not send submissions to general agency email address. See website for full submission guidelines.

Literary Agents: Molly Ker Hawn (**L0455**); Sarah Hornsley (**L0482**)

L0090 The Bent Agency

Literary Agency
529 W 42nd St, New York, NY 10036
United States

info@thebentagency.com

http://www.thebentagency.com

ADULT
Fiction
Graphic Novels; Novels
Nonfiction > *Nonfiction Books*

CHILDREN'S > **Fiction**
Chapter Books; Graphic Novels; Middle Grade
YOUNG ADULT
Fiction
Graphic Novels; Novels
Nonfiction > *Nonfiction Books*

Send: Query
How to send: Email; Query Manager

Accepts email or Query Manager queries only. See website for agent bios and specific interests and email addresses, then query one agent only. See website for full submission guidelines.

Literary Agency: The Bent Agency (UK)
(**L0089**)

Literary Agents: Nicola Barr (*L0069*); Jenny Bent (*L0091*); Victoria Cappello (*L0155*); Gemma Cooper (**L0219**); Claire Draper (*L0276*); Louise Fury (*L0373*); James Mustelier (**L0741**); Zoe Plant (**L0802**); John Silbersack (*L0915*); Laurel Symonds (**L0965**); Desiree Wilson (**L1045**)

L0091 Jenny Bent

Literary Agent
United States

Literary Agency: The Bent Agency (**L0090**)
Professional Body: Association of American Literary Agents (AALA)

L0092 **Berlin Associates**
Literary Agency
7 Tyers Gate, London, SE1 3HX
United Kingdom
Tel: +44 (0) 20 7836 1112
Fax: +44 (0) 20 7632 5296

submissions@berlinassociates.com

http://www.berlinassociates.com

Types: Scripts
Formats: Film Scripts; Radio Scripts; TV
Scripts; Theatre Scripts
Markets: Adult

Send: Query
Don't send: Full text
How to send: Email

Most clients through recommendation or
invitation, but accepts queries by email with
CV, experience, and outline of work you
would like to submit.

L0093 **John Berlyne**
Literary Agent
United Kingdom

http://zenoagency.com/about-us/

Literary Agency: Zeno Agency Ltd (**L1067**)

ADULT > **Fiction** > *Novels*
Crime; Fantasy; Historical Fiction; Horror;
Science Fiction; Space Opera; Thrillers;
Urban Fantasy

YOUNG ADULT > **Fiction** > *Novels*

Closed to approaches.

L0094 **Betsy Amster Literary
Enterprises**
Literary Agency
607 Foothill Blvd #1061, La Canada
Flintridge, CA 91012
United States

b.amster.assistant@gmail.com
b.amster.kidsbooks@gmail.com

http://amsterlit.com

Fiction > *Novels*
Literary; Mystery; Thrillers; Upmarket
Commercial Fiction; Upmarket Women's
Fiction

Nonfiction
Gift Books: General
Nonfiction Books: Biography; Career
Development; Cookery; Gardening; Health;
History; Lifestyle; Medicine; Narrative
Nonfiction; Nutrition; Parenting; Popular
Culture; Psychology; Self Help; Social
Issues; Travel; Women's Issues

How to send: Email
How not to send: Post

A full-service literary agency based in Los
Angeles, California. No romances,
screenplays, poetry, westerns, fantasy, horror,

science fiction, techno thrillers, spy capers,
apocalyptic scenarios, political or religious
arguments, or self-published books. See
website for full guidelines.

Authors: Amy Alkon; Dwight Allen; Will
Allen; Jess J. Araujo; Elaine N. Aron; Sandi
Ault; Lois Barr; Ariel Bernstein; Kim Boyce;
Helene Brenner; Karen Briner; Catheryn J.
Brockett; Karen Burns; Mónica Bustamante;
Joe P. Carr; Steven Carter; Lillian Castillo-
Speed; Robin Chotzinoff; Frank Clifford; Rob
Cohen; David Cundy; Leela Cyd; Margaret
Leslie Davis; Jan DeBlieu; David J. Diamond;
Martha O. Diamond; Phil Doran; Suzanne
Dunaway; Nick Dyer; J. Theron Elkins; Ruth
Andrew Ellenson; Loretta Ellsworth; James P.
Emswiler; Mary Ann Emswiler; Naomi Epel;
Alex Epstein; Karin Esterhammer; Jeannette
Faurot; Tom Fields-Meyer; Joline Godfrey;
Tanya Ward Goodman; Michael I. Goran;
Hindi Greenberg; Ellen Hawley; Marian
Henley; Charney Herst; Leigh Ann Hirschman;
Ariel Horn; Lisa Hunter; Jackie; Melissa
Jacobs; Janet Jaffe; Emily Katz; E. Barrie
Kavasch; Joy Keller; Eileen Kennedy-Moore;
Rachel Tawil Kenyon; Camille Landau; Carol
Lay; Anna Lefler; Margaret Lobenstine; Mark
Lowenthal; Paul Mandelbaum; Ivy Manning;
Melissa Martin; Domenico Minchilli;
Elizabeth Helman Minchilli; Wendy Mogel;
Sharon Montrose; Bonnie Frumkin Morales;
Yolanda Nava; Joy Nicholson; Judith Nies;
Susie Norris; Christopher Noxon; Lynette
Padwa; Neela Paniz; Kishani Perera; Cash
Peters; Barry Prizant; Winifred Reilly; Andrea
Richards; Eileen Roth; Adam Sappington;
Marjorie Barton Savage; Anthony Schmitz;
M.D. Edward Schneider; Kyle Schuneman;
George Shannon; Nancy Spiller; Allison Mia
Starcher; Louise Steinman; Bill Stern; Terry
Theise; Christina Baglivi Tinglof; Linda Venis;
MPH Emily Ventura; Marisel Vera; Elizabeth
Verdick; John Vorhaus; Hannah Voskuil;
Diana Wells; Tiare White; Chris Witt; Karen
Witynski; Steve D. Wolf; David Wollock;
Dawn Young

Literary Agent: Betsy Amster (*L0032*)

L0095 **Beverley Slopen
Literary Agency**
Literary Agency
131 Bloor St. W., Suite 711, Toronto, M5S
1S3
Canada
Tel: +1 (416) 964-9598
Fax: +1 (416) 921-7726

beverley@slopenagency.ca

http://www.slopenagency.com

Types: Fiction; Nonfiction
Subjects: Anthropology; Biography;
Commercial; Crime; History; Literary;
Personal Development
Markets: Adult; Children's

Send: Query
Don't send: Full text
How to send: Email

Send query by email with a few sample pages.
No hard copy submissions. Takes on few new
authors. Handles very few children's books,
and almost no romance, horror, or illustrated.
No poetry.

Literary Agent: Beverley Slopen (*L0921*)

L0096 **Elizabeth Bewley**
Literary Agent
United States

ebewley@sll.com

https://www.sll.com/our-team

Literary Agency: Sterling Lord Literistic, Inc.
(**L0940**)

ADULT
Fiction > *Novels*
High Concept; Romance; Upmarket
Commercial Fiction

Nonfiction > *Nonfiction Books:* Narrative
Nonfiction

CHILDREN'S > **Fiction**
Middle Grade; Picture Books
YOUNG ADULT > **Fiction** > *Novels*
High Concept; Romance

Send: Query; Synopsis; Writing sample
How to send: Online submission system; Email

On the children's side of her list, she represents
young adult and middle grade fiction, and the
occasional picture book. On the adult side, she
is eager to represent more upmarket
commercial fiction and narrative nonfiction.
Current submission wish list includes high-
concept young adult novels, especially from
underrepresented voices, accessible middle
grade novels that will foster a love of reading
(think: fun, funny, or both!), young adult
romance, high-concept adult love stories, and
any upmarket commercial fiction with a witty
voice and eye for detail.

L0097 **Bidnick & Company**
Literary Agency
United States

bidnick@comcast.net

Types: Nonfiction
Subjects: Commercial; Cookery
Markets: Adult

Send: Query
Don't send: Full text
How to send: Email

Handles cookbooks and commercial
nonfiction. Send query by email only.

Literary Agent: Carole Bidnick (*L0098*)

L0098 Carole Bidnick
Literary Agent
United States

Literary Agency: Bidnick & Company (**L0097**)

L0099 Victoria Birkett
Literary Agent
United Kingdom

https://milesstottagency.co.uk/representatives/
victoria-birkett/

Literary Agency: Miles Stott Children's
Literary Agency (**L0712**)

Author: Gill Lewis

L0100 The Blair Partnership
Literary Agency
PO Box, 7828, London, W1A 4GE
United Kingdom
Tel: +44 (0) 20 7504 2520

info@theblairpartnership.com

https://www.theblairpartnership.com

Professional Body: The Association of
Authors' Agents (AAA)

ADULT
 Fiction > *Novels*
  Book Club Fiction; Commercial; Crime;
  Detective Fiction; Dystopian Fiction; High
  Concept; Historical Fiction; Literary;
  Speculative; Thrillers; Upmarket;
  Women's Fiction

 Nonfiction > *Nonfiction Books*
  Crime; Lifestyle; Personal Development

CHILDREN'S
 Fiction
  Middle Grade: Adventure
  Novels: General, and in
  particular: Commercial
 Nonfiction > *Nonfiction Books*

TEEN > **Fiction** > *Novels*

YOUNG ADULT > **Fiction** > *Novels*

Send: Query; Synopsis; Proposal; Writing
sample
How to send: Word file email attachment; PDF
file email attachment

We welcome all submissions and consider
everything that is sent to the agency, though
we are not currently accepting submissions for
screenplays, short stories or poetry.

We welcome approaches from both debut
writers and established authors. We're very
happy to receive submissions from overseas, as
long as they're written in English.

Associate Agent: Jordan Lees (**L0608**)

Authors: Michael Byrne; Chris Hoy; Frank
Lampard; J.K. Rowling; Pete Townshend

Company Director / Literary Agent: Rory
Scarfe (**L0886**)

Literary Agents: Hattie Grunewald (**L0427**);
Josephine Hayes (**L0457**)

L0101 Blake Friedmann Literary Agency Ltd
Literary Agency
15 Highbury Place, London, N5 1QP
United Kingdom
Tel: +44 (0) 20 7387 0842

info@blakefriedmann.co.uk

http://www.blakefriedmann.co.uk

Professional Body: The Association of
Authors' Agents (AAA)

Types: Fiction; Nonfiction; Scripts
Formats: Film Scripts; Radio Scripts; TV
Scripts
Subjects: Autobiography; Commercial;
Contemporary; Cookery; Crime; Culture;
Current Affairs; Fantasy; Finance; History;
Literary; Mystery; Nature; Politics;
Psychology; Science; Science Fiction; Society;
Suspense; Technology; Thrillers; Travel;
Warfare; Women's Interests
Markets: Adult; Children's; Young Adult

Send: Query
Don't send: Full text
How to send: Email

Send query by email to a specific agent best
suited to your work. See website for full
submission guidelines, details of agents, and
individual agent contact details. Media
department currently only accepting
submissions from writers with produced
credits. Reply not guaranteed. If no response
within 8 weeks, assume rejection.

Authors: Gilbert Adair; Tatamkhulu Afrika;
Mary Akers; Ted Allbeury; Paul Ashton; MiMi
Aye

Literary Agents: Isobel Dixon (*L0267*); Samuel
Hodder (*L0474*); Juliet Pickering (*L0797*);
Tom Witcomb (*L1050*)

L0102 Caitlin Blasdell
Literary Agent
United States

Literary Agency: Liza Dawson Associates
(**L0625**)

L0103 Lyndsey Blessing
Literary Agent
United States

Literary Agency: InkWell Management
(**L0499**)

L0104 Brettne Bloom
Literary Agent
United States

Literary Agency: The Book Group (**L0109**)

L0105 Felicity Blunt
Literary Agent
United Kingdom

http://submissions.curtisbrown.co.uk/agents/

Literary Agency: Curtis Brown (**L0233**)

Fiction > *Novels*
 Domestic Suspense; Historical Fiction;
 Literary Thrillers; Psychological Suspense;
 Speculative

Nonfiction > *Nonfiction Books*
 Cookery; Food

Send: Full text; Synopsis; Author bio
How to send: Email

"Most simply put I am looking for good
stories, compellingly told. The books on my
list have one thing in common, the
combination of a distinctive voice and a great
narrative."

L0106 Camilla Bolton
Senior Agent
United Kingdom

camilla@darleyanderson.com

https://www.darleyanderson.com/our-team
https://twitter.com/CamillaJBolton

Literary Agency: The Darley Anderson Agency

Fiction > *Novels*
 Crime; Mystery; Suspense; Thrillers;
 Women's Fiction

How to send: Email attachment

Looking for accessible and commercial crime,
thrillers, mysteries, suspense and women's
fiction.

Authors: Haleh Agar; Emma Bamford; Vicki
Bradley; James Carol; Gloria Cook; A J Cross;
Jason Dean; Hayley Doyle; C. M. Ewan; G.R.
Halliday; Egan Hughes; Emma Kavanagh; T
M Logan; Imran Mahmood; L V Matthews;
Phoebe Morgan; B.A. Paris; Jo Platt; Meera
Shah; Rebecca Shaw; KL Slater; Kim Slater;
Sean Slater; Catherine Steadman; G X Todd;
Tim Weaver

L0107 Luigi Bonomi
Literary Agent
United Kingdom

http://www.lbabooks.com/agent/luigi-bonomi/

Literary Agency: LBA Books Ltd (**L0605**)

Fiction > *Novels*: Commercial

Nonfiction > *Nonfiction Books*: Commercial

Closed to approaches.

I love commercial fiction across all genres, as
well as intelligent non-fiction written for a
commercial audience, and am always on the
lookout for authors who aspire to hit the
bestseller list.

Authors: Will Adams; Lizzy Barber; James Becker; Jason Bray; Fern Britton; James Cheshire; Rosemary Conley; Gennaro Contaldo; Josephine Cox; Mason Cross; Louise Curtis; A.M. Dean; Dan Farnworth; Liz Fenwick; Judy Finnigan; Nick Foulkes; Mark Frary; Daniel Freeman; Susan Gee; David Gibbins; Jane Gordon; Tom Grass; Mark Griffin; Michael Gustafson; Rachel Hamilton; Richard Hammond; Duncan Harding; Matt Hilton; John Humphrys; Jessica Jarvli; Sarah Johnson; Annabel Kantaria; Catherine Kirwan; Guy Leschziner; Susan Lewis; Amy Lloyd; Richard Madeley; Tom Marcus; Ben Miller; Michael Morley; Anthony Mosawi; Karen Osman; S.A. Patrick; Andrew Pepper; Gervase Phinn; Richard Porter; Esther Rantzen; Madeleine Reiss; Alice Roberts; Simon Scarrow; Colin Shindler; Lucy Strange; Rachel de Thame; Alan Titchmarsh; Oliver Uberti; Phil Vickery; Tamsin Winter

L0108 The Book Bureau Literary Agency
Literary Agency
7 Duncairn Avenue, Bray, Co. Wicklow, Ireland
Tel: +353 (0) 1276 4996
Fax: +353 (0) 1276 4834

thebookbureau@oceanfree.net

Types: Fiction; Nonfiction
Subjects: Commercial; Crime; Literary; Thrillers; Women's Interests
Markets: Adult

Send: Query
Don't send: Full text
How to send: Email

Handles mainly general and literary fiction, plus some nonfiction. Particularly interested in women's, crime, Irish novels, and thrillers. Send query by email (preferred) or by post with SAE, synopsis, and first three chapters. Prefers single line spacing. No poetry, children's, horror, or science fiction. Strong editorial support provided before submission to publishers.

Literary Agent: Geraldine Nichol (*L0749*)

L0109 The Book Group
Literary Agency
20 West 20th Street, Suite 601, New York, NY 10011
United States
Tel: +1 (212) 803-3360

submissions@thebookgroup.com
info@thebookgroup.com

http://www.thebookgroup.com
https://www.facebook.com/thebookgrp
https://twitter.com/thebookgrp
https://www.instagram.com/thebookgrp/

Fiction > *Novels*

Nonfiction > *Nonfiction Books*

Send: Query; Writing sample
How to send: In the body of an email
How not to send: Email attachment; Post; Phone

Represents a broad range of fiction and nonfiction. No poetry or screenplays. Send query by email only with ten sample pages and the first and last name of the agent you are querying in the subject line (see website for individual agent interests). No attachments. Include all material in the body of the email. See website for full guidelines. Response only if interested.

Authors: Jenessa Abrams; Nishant Batsha; Rachel Broderick; Wendy Chin-Tanner; Tiana Clark; Tracy Clark-Flory; Chloe Cole; Ella Dawson; Kimberly Drew; Susie Dumond; Taylor Hahn; Alex Hoopes; Mike Lala; Melissa Larsen; Kristen Martin; Laura McKowen; Victoria Savanh; Sophia Shalmiyev; Rainesford Stauffer; Elissa Strauss; Sara Sutter; Noor Tagouri; Rachel Zarrow

Literary Agents: Julie Barer (*L0064*); Faye Bender (*L0087*); Brettne Bloom (*L0104*); Jamie Carr (**L0166**); Dana Murphy (*L0734*); Elisabeth Weed (*L1021*)

L0110 Bookseeker Agency
Literary Agency
PO Box 7535, Perth, PH2 1AF
United Kingdom
Tel: +44 (0) 1738 620688

bookseeker@blueyonder.co.uk

https://bookseekeragency.com
https://twitter.com/BookseekerAgent

Fiction > *Novels*

Poetry > *Any Poetic Form*

Send: Query; Synopsis; Writing sample
How to send: Email; Post

Handles fiction and (under some circumstances) poetry. No nonfiction. Send query by post or email outlining what you have written and your current projects, along with synopsis and sample chapter (novels).

Literary Agent: Paul Thompson (*L0977*)

L0111 BookStop Literary Agency, LLC
Literary Agency
67 Meadow View Road, Orinda, CA 94563
United States
Tel: +1 (925) 254-2664

info@bookstopliterary.com

http://www.bookstopliterary.com
https://www.facebook.com/bookstopliterary/
https://www.instagram.com/bookstopliterary/

CHILDREN'S
  Fiction
    Chapter Books; *Graphic Novels*; *Middle Grade*; *Novels*; *Picture Books*

  Nonfiction > *Nonfiction Books*

YOUNG ADULT > **Fiction** > *Novels*

Handles fiction and nonfiction for children and young adults.

Literary Agents: Minju Chang (**L0184**); Karyn Fischer (**L0336**); Kendra Marcus (**L0670**)

L0112 Stefanie Sanchez Von Borstel
Literary Agent
United States

https://www.fullcircleliterary.com/our-agents/stefanie-von-borstel/

Literary Agency: Full Circle Literary, LLC (**L0371**)
Professional Bodies: Society of Children's Book Writers and Illustrators (SCBWI); Association of American Literary Agents (AALA)

ADULT > **Nonfiction** > *Nonfiction Books*
  Creativity; Inspirational; Nature

CHILDREN'S
  Fiction
    Graphic Novels: General
    Middle Grade: Contemporary; Historical Fiction
  Nonfiction > *Middle Grade*

In adult nonfiction books, her focus is on creativity, inspiration, and nature. In middle grade fiction, she looks for memorable characters and voice. Open to submissions in the following categories only: illustrators, graphic novels, middle grade fiction/nonfiction by diverse creators.

L0113 Katie Shea Boutillier
Literary Agent
United States

Literary Agency: Donald Maass Literary Agency (**L0273**)

L0114 Sarah Bowlin
Literary Agent
Los Angeles
United States

https://aevitascreative.com/agents/

Literary Agency: Aevitas (**L0016**)

Fiction > *Novels*
  General, and in particular: Literary

Nonfiction > *Nonfiction Books*
  General, and in particular: Comedy / Humour; Dance; Food History; History; Narrative Nonfiction; Popular Culture; Wine

Closed to approaches.

Focused on bold, diverse voices in fiction and nonfiction. She's especially interested in stories of strong or difficult women and unexpected narratives of place, of identity, and of the shifting ways we see ourselves and each other. She's also interested in food history, wine, and dance.

L0115 Hannah Bowman
Literary Agent
United States

Literary Agency: Liza Dawson Associates (**L0625**)

L0116 Katherine Boyle
Literary Agent
United States

katherine@veritasliterary.com

http://www.veritasliterary.com

Literary Agency: Veritas Literary Agency (**L1002**)

ADULT
Fiction > *Novels*
Historical Fiction; Literary

Nonfiction > *Nonfiction Books*
Culture; History; Memoir; Narrative Nonfiction; Nature; Popular Culture; Women's Studies

CHILDREN'S > **Fiction**
Middle Grade; Picture Books
YOUNG ADULT > **Fiction** > *Novels*

L0117 Bradford Literary Agency
Literary Agency
5694 Mission Center Road # 347, San Diego, CA 92108
United States
Tel: +1 (619) 521-1201

hannah@bradfordlit.com

https://bradfordlit.com

ADULT
Fiction > *Novels*
Contemporary Romance; Erotic Romance; Historical Romance; Literary; Mystery; Romance; Romantic Suspense; Supernatural / Paranormal Romance; Thrillers; Upmarket Commercial Fiction; Urban Fantasy; Women's Fiction

Nonfiction > *Nonfiction Books*
Biography; Business; Comedy / Humour; Cookery; Food; History; Memoir; Parenting; Popular Culture; Relationships; Self Help; Social Issues

CHILDREN'S > **Fiction**
Novels; Picture Books

How to send: Query Manager; In the body of an email
How not to send: Email attachment

Represents a wide range of fiction and nonfiction. Send query by email with synopsis and first chapter (fiction), full ms (children's picture books), or proposal, including sample chapter (nonfiction). Select a particular agent

at the agency to submit to, and submit to only one agent at a time.

Literary Agents: Laura Bradford (**L0118**); Sarah LaPolla; Kari Sutherland (**L0957**); Jennifer Chen Tran (**L0986**); Katherine Wessbecher (**L1027**)

L0118 Laura Bradford
Literary Agent
United States

queries@bradfordlit.com

https://bradfordlit.com/about/laura-bradford/
http://www.twitter.com/bradfordlit

Literary Agency: Bradford Literary Agency (**L0117**)
Professional Bodies: Association of American Literary Agents (AALA); Romance Writers of America (RWA); Society of Children's Book Writers and Illustrators (SCBWI)

ADULT
Fiction
Graphic Novels: General
Novels: Contemporary Romance; Erotic Romance; Historical Fiction; Historical Romance; Mystery; Romance; Romantic Suspense; Speculative; Thrillers; Women's Fiction
Nonfiction > *Nonfiction Books*

CHILDREN'S > **Fiction** > *Middle Grade*

YOUNG ADULT > **Fiction** > *Novels*

Closed to approaches.

Interested in romance (historical, romantic suspense, category, contemporary, erotic), speculative fiction, women's fiction, mystery, thrillers, young adult, upper middle grade, illustration as well as some select non-fiction.

L0119 Brandt & Hochman Literary Agents, Inc.
Literary Agency
1501 Broadway, Suite 2605, New York, NY 10036
United States
Tel: +1 (212) 840-5760

http://brandthochman.com

See website for full submission guidelines and for details of individual agents' interests and direct contact details, then approach one agent specifically.

Literary Agents: Emily Forland (**L0345**); Gail Hochman (**L0473**); Jody Kahn (**L0544**); Marianne Merola (**L0699**); Emma Patterson (**L0782**); Henry Thayer (**L0973**); Mitchell Waters (**L1015**)

L0120 Hannah Brattesani
Literary Agent
United States

http://www.friedrichagency.com/about-alternate-2/

Literary Agency: The Friedrich Agency LLC (**L0367**)

Fiction > *Novels*: Literary

Nonfiction > *Nonfiction Books*
Culture; Lifestyle; Narrative Nonfiction; Popular Science

Send: Query
How to send: In the body of an email

L0121 The Brattle Agency LLC
Literary Agency
PO Box 380537, Cambridge, MA 02238
United States
Tel: +1 (617) 721-5375

submissions@thebrattleagency.com

https://thebrattleagency.com

Fiction
Graphic Novels: General
Novels: Literary

Nonfiction > *Nonfiction Books*
American History; Art History; Culture; European History; Music; Politics; Sport

Closed to approaches.

Accepts submissions only during one-month reading periods. See website for details.

L0122 The Bravo Blue Agency
Literary Agency
United Kingdom

charlotte@bravoblue.co.uk

https://www.bravoblue.co.uk

Literary Agency: Tibor Jones & Associates (**L0982**)

ADULT
Fiction > *Novels*
Commercial; Historical Fiction; Literary

Nonfiction > *Nonfiction Books*
Lifestyle; Narrative Nonfiction; Nature; Popular History; Science; Wellbeing

CHILDREN'S > **Fiction**
Early Readers; Middle Grade; Picture Books
YOUNG ADULT > **Fiction** > *Novels*

Send: Query; Author bio; Synopsis; Writing sample
How to send: Email

Literary Agent: Charlotte Colwill (**L0211**)

L0123 Helen Breitwieser
Literary Agent
United States

https://twitter.com/HelenBreit
http://aaronline.org/Sys/PublicProfile/2176619/417813

Professional Body: Association of American Literary Agents (AALA)
Literary Agency: Cornerstone Literary Agency (**L0221**)

Authors: Jackie Ashenden; Anne Barton; Anna Bennett; Bethany Blake; Marnee Blake; Maya Blake; Katherine Center; Zara Cox; Robert Evans; Beth Fantaskey; Jane Goodger; Sherilee Gray; C.S. Harris; Nicole Helm; Lisa Hendrix; Kate Hewitt; Rachael Johns; Diane Kelly; Rachel Lee; Fiona Lowe; Mary McKinley; Annabel Monaghan; Trish Morey; Kerry O'Connor; Mary-Anne O'Connor; Michael Paraskevas; Kayla Perrin; Candice Proctor; Kay Thomas; Christine Trent; Ursula Vernon; Tracy Anne Warren; Michelle Willingham; Maisey Yates

L0124 Bret Adams Ltd
Literary Agency
448 West 44th Street, New York, NY 10036
United States
Tel: +1 (212) 765-5630
Fax: +1 (212) 265-2212

http://www.bretadamsltd.net

Types: Scripts
Formats: Film Scripts; TV Scripts; Theatre Scripts
Markets: Adult

A full service agency representing writers, directors, designers, and actors.

Literary Agents: Mark Orsini (*L0771*); Bruce Ostler (*L0774*)

L0125 M. Courtney Briggs
Literary Agent
United States

Literary Agency: Derrick & Briggs, LLP (**L0259**)

L0126 The Bright Agency
Literary Agency
103-105 St John's Hill, London, SW11 1SY
United Kingdom
Tel: +44 (0) 20 7326 9140

mail@thebrightagency.com

https://thebrightagency.com
https://thebrightagency.com/uk/submissions/new

Media Company: The Bright Group International Limited

CHILDREN'S > **Fiction**
Chapter Books; *Middle Grade*; *Picture Books*

Send: Outline; Synopsis; Writing sample
How to send: Online contact form

Welcomes submissions from illustrators and authors who are looking for representation. Interested in children's picture book texts, chapter books and middle grade fiction. Provide an outline with a synopsis and the first three chapters.

Literary Agent: Vicki Willden-Lebrecht

L0127 Bright Group US Inc.
Literary Agency
50 West Street, C12, New York, NY 10006
United States
Tel: +1 (646) 578 6542

mail@thebrightagency.com

https://thebrightagency.com
https://thebrightagency.com/us/submissions/new

Media Company: The Bright Group International Limited

CHILDREN'S > **Fiction**
Chapter Books; *Middle Grade*; *Picture Books*

Send: Outline; Synopsis; Writing sample
How to send: Online contact form

Welcomes submissions from illustrators and authors who are looking for representation. Interested in children's picture book texts, chapter books and middle grade fiction. Provide an outline with a synopsis and the first three chapters.

L0128 Alan Brodie
Literary Agent
United Kingdom

Literary Agency: Alan Brodie Representation Ltd (**L0022**)

L0129 Alicia Brooks
Literary Agent
United States

Literary Agency: The Jean V. Naggar Literary Agency (**L0519**)

L0130 Philippa Brophy
Literary Agent; President
United States

https://www.sll.com/our-team
http://aaronline.org/Sys/PublicProfile/4090020/417813

Literary Agency: Sterling Lord Literistic, Inc. (**L0940**)
Professional Body: Association of American Literary Agents (AALA)

Fiction > **Novels**

Nonfiction > **Nonfiction Books**
General, and in particular: Journalism

Closed to approaches.

L0131 Brotherstone Creative Management
Literary Agency
Mortimer House, 37-41 Mortimer Street, London, W1T 3JH
United Kingdom
Tel: +44 (0) 7908 542886

submissions@bcm-agency.com
info@bcm-agency.com

http://bcm-agency.com

Professional Body: The Association of Authors' Agents (AAA)

Types: Fiction; Nonfiction
Subjects: Commercial; Literary
Markets: Adult

Send: Query; Writing sample; Synopsis
How to send: Email

Always on the search for talented new writers. Send query by email. For fiction, include the first three chapters or 50 pages and 2-page synopsis. For nonfiction, include detailed outline and sample chapter. No children's and young adult fiction, sci-fi and fantasy novels or unsolicited short story and poetry collections, or scripts.

Literary Agent: Charlie Brotherstone (*L0132*)

L0132 Charlie Brotherstone
Literary Agent
United Kingdom

Literary Agency: Brotherstone Creative Management (**L0131**)

L0133 Justin Brouckaert
Literary Agent
New York
United States

https://aevitascreative.com/agents/

Literary Agency: Aevitas (**L0016**)

Fiction
Novels: Literary
Short Fiction: Literary

Nonfiction > **Nonfiction Books**
Current Affairs; History; Journalism; Memoir; Narrative Nonfiction; Parenting; Politics; Sport; Travel

Send: Author bio; Outline; Market info; Writing sample
How to send: Online submission system

Actively seeking character-driven and formally inventive literary fiction and memoir, as well as narrative nonfiction in the areas of sports, internet culture, politics and current affairs, parenting, travel, and history. Regardless of genre, he is most passionate about projects that shine a light on underserved and overlooked communities and/or highlight unique relationships between people and places. He is especially interested in pairing with debut authors and helping them grow their careers.

L0134 Michelle Brower
Literary Agent; Partner
United States

https://aevitascreative.com/agents/

Literary Agency: Aevitas (**L0016**)

ADULT
Fiction > **Novels**

Book Club Fiction; Commercial; Literary; Suspense; Upmarket; Women's Fiction

Nonfiction > *Nonfiction Books*
Memoir; Narrative Nonfiction

CHILDREN'S > **Fiction** > *Middle Grade*

YOUNG ADULT > **Fiction** > *Novels*

Send: Pitch; Market info; Writing sample
How to send: Online submission system

Represents fiction and narrative nonfiction. Her interests include book club fiction (a commercial concept with a literary execution), literary fiction (including with an element of genre), and smart women's fiction. She also represents select young adult, middle grade, and memoir projects.

L0135 Andrea Brown
President; Literary Agent
United States

andrea@andreabrownlit.com

https://www.andreabrownlit.com/Team/Andrea-Brown

Literary Agency: Andrea Brown Literary Agency, Inc.
Professional Body: Association of American Literary Agents (AALA)

Closed to approaches.

L0136 Jenny Brown
Literary Agent
United Kingdom

Literary Agency: Jenny Brown Associates **(L0521)**

L0137 Browne & Miller Literary Associates
Literary Agency
52 Village Place, Hinsdale, IL 60521
United States
Tel: +1 (312) 922-3063

mail@browneandmiller.com

https://www.browneandmiller.com

Fiction > *Novels*: Commercial

Nonfiction > *Nonfiction Books*: Commercial

Send: Query
Don't send: Full text
How to send: Email

Handles books for the adult commercial book markets. No children's, young adult, science fiction, fantasy, horror, short stories, poetry, screenplays, or academic works. Send query only by email. No attachments.

Literary Agent: Danielle Egan-Miller

L0138 Vanessa Browne
Associate Agent
United Kingdom

https://madeleinemilburn.co.uk/team-member/vanessa-browne/

Literary Agency: Madeleine Milburn Literary, TV & Film Agency **(L0664)**
Literary Agent: Chloe Seager **(L0899)**

CHILDREN'S > **Fiction**
Middle Grade: Magic
Novels: Comedy / Humour; Commercial Fantasy; Contemporary; Drama; Family; High Concept; Social Commentary; Socio-Political
YOUNG ADULT > **Fiction** > *Novels*
Comedy / Humour; Commercial Fantasy; Contemporary; Drama; Family; High Concept; Social Commentary; Socio-Political

L0139 Chris Bucci
Literary Agent
New York
United States

https://aevitascreative.com/agents/

Literary Agency: Aevitas **(L0016)**

Fiction > *Novels*
Commercial; Historical Fiction; History; Literary; Mystery; Popular Culture; Popular Science; Thrillers

Nonfiction > *Nonfiction Books*
Narrative Nonfiction; Politics; Sport

Send: Author bio; Outline; Market info; Writing sample
How to send: Online submission system

Based in the New York Metropolitan area. Represents a broad range of fiction and nonfiction.

L0140 Danielle Bukowski
Foreign Rights Manager; Literary Agent
United States

https://www.sll.com/our-team

Literary Agency: Sterling Lord Literistic, Inc. **(L0940)**

Fiction > *Novels*
Commercial; Literary; Upmarket Women's Fiction

Nonfiction > *Nonfiction Books*

Send: Query; Synopsis; Writing sample
How to send: Online submission system

L0141 Megan Burkhart
Junior Agent
United States

megan@cyleyoung.com

https://cyleyoung.com/literary-agent/my-team/
https://meganlynneauthor.weebly.com/
https://www.facebook.com/meganlynne.13/
https://twitter.com/writemeganlynne
https://www.youtube.com/channel/UCv23mXzg-9PuXBnGDAuqmg

https://www.linkedin.com/in/megan-burkhart-93858814a/
https://www.instagram.com/authormeganlynne

Literary Agency: Cyle Young Literary Elite **(L0236)**

YOUNG ADULT > **Fiction** > *Novels*: Fantasy

Send: Query; Synopsis; Writing sample
How to send: Email

Costs: Offers services that writers have to pay for. Also offers editorial services.

Looks for YA fantasy and children's picture books, especially those with a strong narrative voice. Closed to picture book submissions as at June 2020.

L0142 Emelie Burl
Associate Agent
United States

emelie@schulmanagency.com

https://twitter.com/BigKidBookworm
https://www.facebook.com/emelie.s.samuelson
https://www.publishersmarketplace.com/members/Schulman/

Literary Agency: Susan Schulman Literary Agency **(L0955)**

ADULT > **Nonfiction** > *Nonfiction Books*: Popular Culture

CHILDREN'S > **Fiction** > *Middle Grade*
Comedy / Humour; Magic

YOUNG ADULT > **Fiction** > *Novels*
Comedy / Humour; Magic; Romantic Comedy

Focuses on children's, young adult, and pop culture nonfiction. Likes stories of hope and humor, rom-coms, strong female leads, and magic of all sorts. Also interested in LGBT+ and BIPOC. Not keen on murder.

L0143 Penelope Burns
Literary Agent
United States

Literary Agency: Gelfman Schneider / ICM Partners **(L0386)**

L0144 Juliet Burton
Literary Agent
United Kingdom

Literary Agency: Juliet Burton Literary Agency **(L0540)**

L0145 Kate Burton
Literary Agent
United Kingdom

Literary Agency: C+W (Conville & Walsh) **(L0147)**

L0146 Sheree Bykofsky
Literary Agent
United States

http://www.shereebee.com
http://aaronline.org/Sys/PublicProfile/2176625/417813

Literary Agency: Sheree Bykofsky Associates, Inc. (**L0908**)
Professional Body: Association of American Literary Agents (AALA)

L0147 C+W (Conville & Walsh)
Literary Agency
Haymarket House, 28-29 Haymarket, London, SW1Y 4SP
United Kingdom
Tel: +44 (0) 20 7393 4200

sue@cwagency.co.uk

http://cwagency.co.uk

Professional Body: The Association of Authors' Agents (AAA)

Types: Fiction; Nonfiction
Subjects: Autobiography; Comedy / Humour; Commercial; Crime; Current Affairs; Fantasy; History; Leisure; Lifestyle; Literary; Men's Interests; Mystery; Psychology; Science; Science Fiction; Sport; Suspense; Thrillers; Travel; Warfare; Women's Interests
Markets: Adult; Children's; Young Adult

Send: Query
Don't send: Full text

See website for agent profiles and submit to one particular agent only. Send submissions by email as Word .doc files only. No postal submissions. For fiction, please submit the first three sample chapters of the completed manuscript (or about 50 pages) with a one to two page synopsis. For nonfiction, send 30-page proposal. No poetry or scripts, or picture books. See website for full guidelines.

Author Estate: The Estate of Francis Bacon

Authors: Naoko Abe; Shahnaz Ahsan; Nigel Akehurst; Dolly Alderton; Keir Alexander; Piers Alexander; Robin Antalek; Ollie Aplin; Steven Appleby; Will Ashon; Stephen Baker; Damian Barr; Tony Barrell; Colin Barrett; Kevin Barry; Neil Bartlett; Brock Bastian; Sara Baume; Richard Beard; Francesca Beauman; Matt Beaumont; Patrick Benson; Mandy Berriman; Josie Bevan; Michael Bhaskar; Vanessa Black; Emma Blackery; Immodesty Blaize; David Bodanis; Lee Bofkin; Simon van Booy; Megan Bradbury; John Bradshaw; Kevin Breathnach; Michael Brooks; Iain Broome; The Wild Swimming Brothers; Dea Brovig; Bill Browder

Literary Agents: Susan Armstrong (*L0047*); Matilda Ayris (*L0053*); Kate Burton (*L0145*); Alexander Cochran (*L0206*); Clare Conville (*L0215*); Allison DeFrees (*L0255*); Emma Finn (*L0335*); Katie Greenstreet (*L0421*); Carrie

Kania (*L0546*); Sophie Lambert (*L0589*); Lucy Luck (*L0640*); Richard Pike (*L0799*); Jake Smith-Bosanquet (*L0923*)

L0148 CAA (Creative Artists Agency, LLC)
Literary Agency
2000 Avenue of the Stars, Los Angeles, CA 90067, 405 Lexington Avenue, 19th Floor, New York, NY 10174
United States
Tel: +1 (424) 288-2000
Fax: +1 (424) 288-2900

https://www.caa.com

Literary Agent: Cindy Uh (*L0990*)

L0149 Ellie Cahill-Nicholls
Literary Agent
United Kingdom

Literary Agency: Noel Gay (**L0752**)

L0150 William Callahan
Literary Agent
United States

Literary Agency: InkWell Management (**L0499**)

L0151 Linda Camacho
Literary Agent
United States

linda@galltzacker.com
QueryLinda@galltzacker.com

Literary Agency: Gallt & Zacker Literary Agency (**L0375**)

Fiction > *Novels*
 Romance; Women's Fiction

Send: Query; Writing sample
How to send: Email

L0152 Charlie Campbell
Literary Agent

charlie@cclagents.com

https://cclagents.com/agent/charlie-campbell/
https://twitter.com/ScapegoatCC

Literary Agency: Charlie Campbell Literary Agents (**L0188**)

ADULT
 Fiction > *Novels*
 Commercial; Crime; Historical Fiction; Literary; Thrillers

 Nonfiction > *Nonfiction Books*
 Business; Comedy / Humour; Commercial; History; Literary; Popular Science; Sport

CHILDREN'S > **Fiction** > *Novels*

Send: Query; Synopsis; Writing sample
How to send: Email

Primarily looking for crime and thrillers, as well as literary and historical fiction. In non-

fiction, his interests include sport, popular science, history, humour and business.

Authors: Guy Adams; SJ Bennett; Edward Brooke-Hitching; Theodore Brun; Andy Bull; Jen Campbell; Bonnie Chung; David Collins; Duncan Crowe; Iain Dey; Chris Dodd; Adam Fergusson; Jamie Fewery; Rebecca Front; Tom Gabbay; Julian Gough; David Higgins; Will Hill; Thomas W. Hodgkinson; Nicholas Hogg; Andrew Hosken; Simon Jones; Paul Levy; Bella Mackie; Shingi Mararike; Hugh Matheson; Anthony McGowan; Barry McKinley; Moin Mir; Anton Mosimann; Rebecca Myers; James Peak; Edvard Radzinsky; Amy Raphael; Andrea Stuart; Tom Tivnan; Hana Videen; Wendy Wason; Sioned Wiliam; Hywel Williams; Mike Woodhouse

L0153 Carrie Cantor
Literary Agent
United States

Literary Agency: Joelle Delbourgo Associates, Inc. (**L0527**)

L0154 Georgina Capel
Literary Agent
United Kingdom

Literary Agency: Georgina Capel Associates Ltd (**L0389**)

L0155 Victoria Cappello
Literary Agent
United States

Literary Agency: The Bent Agency (**L0090**)

L0156 Elise Capron
Literary Agent
United States

Literary Agency: Sandra Dijkstra Literary Agency

Closed to approaches.

L0157 Amber J. Caravéo
Literary Agent
United Kingdom

Literary Agency: Skylark Literary (**L0920**)

L0158 Michael V. Carlisle
Literary Agent
United States

Literary Agency: InkWell Management (**L0499**)

L0159 Agnes Carlowicz
Literary Agent
United States

agnes@carolmannagency.com

https://www.carolmannagency.com/agnes-carlowicz

https://twitter.com/AgnesCarlowicz
https://www.instagram.com/agnescarlowicz/

Literary Agency: Carol Mann Agency (**L0161**)

Fiction > *Novels*

Nonfiction > *Nonfiction Books*
Comedy / Humour; Crime; Intersectional
Feminism; Memoir; Popular Culture;
Wellbeing

Send: Query; Author bio; Writing sample;
Synopsis
How to send: In the body of an email

Her interests include both fiction and nonfiction, with a special passion for literature that
amplifies underrepresented voices and subverts
the status quo. Among others, she enjoys:
intersectional feminism, millennial self-care,
female-driven memoir, true-crime, and
humorous pop culture.

L0160 Anna Carmichael
Literary Agent
United Kingdom

anna@abnerstein.co.uk

Literary Agency: Abner Stein (**L0005**)

L0161 Carol Mann Agency
Literary Agency
55 Fifth Avenue, New York, NY 10003
United States
Tel: +1 (212) 206-5635

submissions@carolmannagency.com

https://www.carolmannagency.com

Send: Query; Author bio; Writing sample
How to send: In the body of an email
How not to send: Email attachment; Post;
Phone

Send query by email only, including synopsis,
brief bio, and first 25 pages, all pasted into the
body of your email. No attachments. No
submissions by post, or phone calls. Allow 3-4
weeks for response.

Authors: Jane Alexander; Clifton Hoodl Maria
Goodavage; Rachel Kelly

Literary Agents: Maile Beal (**L0076**); Agnes
Carlowicz (**L0159**); Gareth Esersky (**L0306**);
Iris Blasi (**L0506**); Carol Mann (**L0666**);
Myrsini Stephanides (**L0937**); Joanne Wyckoff
(**L1057**); Laura Yorke (**L1060**)

L0162 Caroline Davidson Literary Agency
Literary Agency
5 Queen Anne's Gardens, London, W4 1TU
United Kingdom
Tel: +44 (0) 20 8995 5768

enquiries@cdla.co.uk

https://www.cdla.co.uk

Professional Body: The Association of
Authors' Agents (AAA)

Types: Fiction; Nonfiction
Formats: Reference
Subjects: Archaeology; Architecture; Arts;
Biography; Cookery; Culture; Design;
Gardening; Health; History; Lifestyle;
Medicine; Nature; Politics; Psychology;
Science
Markets: Adult

Send: Query
Don't send: Full text
How not to send: Email

Send query by post only. See website for full
guidelines.

Authors: Emma Donoghue; John Phibbs

Literary Agent: Caroline Davidson (*L0247*)

L0163 Caroline Sheldon Literary Agency
Literary Agency
71 Hillgate Place, London, W8 7SS
United Kingdom
Tel: +44 (0) 20 7727 9102

info@carolinesheldon.co.uk

http://www.carolinesheldon.co.uk

Professional Body: The Association of
Authors' Agents (AAA)

ADULT > **Fiction** > *Novels*

CHILDREN'S > **Fiction**
Board Books; *Chapter Books*; *Early Readers*;
Middle Grade; *Novels*; *Picture Books*

Send: Query
How to send: Email

Interested in fiction and all types of children's
books. Send query by email only, addressed to
appropriate agent. Do not send submissions to
their individual email addresses.

Literary Agents: Caroline Sheldon; Felicity
Trew

L0164 Carolyn Jenks Agency
Literary Agency
30 Cambridge Park Drive, #3140, Cambridge,
MA 02140
United States

https://www.carolynjenksagency.com
https://www.facebook.com/
carolynjenksagency
https://twitter.com/TheJenksAgency

Company Director / Literary Agent: Carolyn
Jenks (**L0520**)

Literary Agents: Kwaku Acheampong
(**L0009**); Becca Crandall (**L0225**); Brenna
Girard (**L0395**); Molly McQuade

L0165 Heather Carr
Literary Agent
United States

Literary Agency: The Friedrich Agency LLC
(**L0367**)

L0166 Jamie Carr
Literary Agent
United States

http://www.thebookgroup.com/jamie-carr

Literary Agency: The Book Group (**L0109**)

Fiction > *Novels*
Literary; Upmarket Commercial Fiction

Nonfiction > *Nonfiction Books*
Culture; Food; Journalism; Narrative
Nonfiction

Send: Query; Writing sample
How to send: In the body of an email

Represents novelists, short story writers,
journalists, activists, and food and culture
writers. Most interested in adult literary and
upmarket commercial fiction and narrative
nonfiction, she is drawn to writing that is
voice-driven, highly transporting, from unique
perspectives and marginalized voices, and that
seeks to disrupt or reframe what appears to be
known.

Authors: Jenessa Abrams; Nishant Batsha;
Rachel Broderick; Wendy Chin-Tanner; Tiana
Clark; Tracy Clark-Flory; Chloe Cole; Ella
Dawson; Kimberly Drew; Susie Dumond;
Taylor Hahn; Alex Hoopes; Mike Lala;
Melissa Larsen; Kristen Martin; Laura
McKowen; Victoria Savanh; Sophia
Shalmiyev; Rainesford Stauffer; Elissa Strauss;
Sara Sutter; Noor Tagouri; Rachel Zarrow

L0167 Michael Carr
Literary Agent
United States

http://www.veritasliterary.com

Literary Agency: Veritas Literary Agency
(**L1002**)

Fiction > *Novels*
Fantasy; Historical Fiction; Science Fiction;
Women's Fiction

Nonfiction > *Nonfiction Books*

L0168 Lucy Carson
Literary Agent
United States

Literary Agency: The Friedrich Agency LLC
(**L0367**)

L0169 Rebecca Carter
Literary Agent
United Kingdom

http://www.janklowandnesbit.co.uk/node/404
https://rebeccacarterliteraryagent.

wordpress.com/
https://twitter.com/RebeccasBooks

Literary Agency: Janklow & Nesbit UK Ltd
(**L0516**)

ADULT
Fiction > *Novels*
Crime; Experimental

Nonfiction > *Nonfiction Books*
Biography; Creative Nonfiction; Cultural
Commentary; Design; Environment;
History; Memoir; Politics; Social
Commentary; Technology; Travel

CHILDREN'S
Fiction > *Novels*
Nonfiction > *Nonfiction Books*

Send: Query; Synopsis; Writing sample
How to send: Email

L0170 Claire Cartey
Literary Agent
United Kingdom

claire@holroydecartey.com

https://www.holroydecartey.com/about.html
https://www.holroydecartey.com/submissions.
html

Literary Agency: Holroyde Cartey (**L0478**)

CHILDREN'S > **Fiction**
Novels; *Picture Books*

Send: Synopsis; Full text
How to send: Email attachment

L0171 Casarotto Ramsay and Associates Ltd
Literary Agency
3rd Floor, 7 Savoy Court, Strand, London,
WC2R 0EX
United Kingdom
Tel: +44 (0) 20 7287 4450

info@casarotto.co.uk

https://www.casarotto.co.uk

Types: Scripts
Formats: Film Scripts; Radio Scripts; TV
Scripts; Theatre Scripts
Markets: Adult

Closed to approaches.

Handles scripts only – no books. Any
unsolicited scripts, treatments or other reading
materials will be deleted unread.

Authors: Alan Ayckbourn; Howard Brenton;
Caryl Churchill; Christopher Hampton; David
Hare; Nick Hornby; Amy Jephta; Sadie Jones;
Neil Jordan

Literary Agent: Jenne Casarotto (*L0172*)

L0172 Jenne Casarotto
Literary Agent
United Kingdom

Literary Agency: Casarotto Ramsay and
Associates Ltd (**L0171**)

L0173 Erin Casey
Literary Agent
United States

erin@galltzacker.com

Literary Agency: Gallt & Zacker Literary
Agency (**L0375**)

CHILDREN'S > **Fiction**
Middle Grade; *Picture Books*
YOUNG ADULT
Fiction
Graphic Novels; *Novels*
Nonfiction > *Nonfiction Books*

Closed to approaches.

L0174 Robert Caskie
Literary Agent
United Kingdom

robert@robertcaskie.com
submissions@robertcaskie.com

https://www.robertcaskie.com
https://twitter.com/rcaskie1

Literary Agency: Robert Caskie Ltd (**L0842**)

Fiction > *Novels*
Book Club Fiction; Commercial; Literary

Nonfiction > *Nonfiction Books*
Memoir; Narrative Nonfiction; Nature;
Politics; Social Issues

Send: Query; Writing sample; Proposal
How to send: Email

Keen to receive fiction and nonfiction writing
that stimulates debate, comments on the world
around us, and invokes an emotional response.

L0175 The Catchpole Agency
Literary Agency
53 Cranham Street, Oxford, OX2 6DD
United Kingdom
Tel: +44 (0) 7789 588070

submissions@thecatchpoleagency.co.uk

http://www.thecatchpoleagency.co.uk

Types: Fiction
Markets: Children's

Closed to approaches.

**Closed to submissions as at March 2019.
Check website for current status.** Works on
children's books with both artists and writers.
Send query by email with sample pasted
directly into the body of the email (the whole
text of a picture book or a couple of chapters of
a novel). No attachments. See website for full
guidelines.

Literary Agents: Celia Catchpole (*L0176*);
James Catchpole (*L0177*); Lucy Catchpole
(*L0178*)

L0176 Celia Catchpole
Literary Agent
United Kingdom

Literary Agency: The Catchpole Agency
(**L0175**)

L0177 James Catchpole
Literary Agent
United Kingdom

Literary Agency: The Catchpole Agency
(**L0175**)

L0178 Lucy Catchpole
Literary Agent
United Kingdom

Literary Agency: The Catchpole Agency
(**L0175**)

L0179 Cecily Ware Literary Agents
Literary Agency
30 Elsiedene Road, London, N21 2RP
United Kingdom
Tel: +44 (0) 20 7359 3787

info@cecilyware.com

http://www.cecilyware.com

Scripts
Radio Scripts; *TV Scripts*

Send: Full text; Author bio
How to send: Word file email attachment; PDF
file email attachment; Final Draft email
attachment

Handles television and radio writers and
producers. No books or theatre scripts.

Literary Agents: Carol Reyes; Gilly Schuster;
Warren Sherman

L0180 Jemiscoe Chambers-Black
Associate Agent
Los Angeles
United States

jemiscoe@andreabrownlit.com

https://www.andreabrownlit.com/agents.html
https://twitter.com/Jemiscoe
https://querymanager.com/query/Jemiscoe

Literary Agency: Andrea Brown Literary
Agency, Inc.

ADULT > **Fiction** > *Novels*
Comedy / Humour; Cozy Mysteries; Crime;
LGBTQIA; Literary; Low Fantasy;
Psychological Thrillers; Romance; Urban
Fantasy

CHILDREN'S > **Fiction**
Graphic Novels: General
Middle Grade: Adventure; Comedy /
Humour; Contemporary; Culture; Fantasy;
Folklore, Myths, and Legends; Ghost Stories;

Horror; LGBTQIA; Magical Realism;
Mystery; Supernatural / Paranormal
YOUNG ADULT > **Fiction** > *Novels*
Contemporary; Fantasy; Ghost Stories;
Horror; LGBTQIA; Mystery; Romance;
Romantic Comedy; Supernatural /
Paranormal

Send: Author bio; Query; Synopsis; Writing
sample; Pitch; Market info
How to send: Query Manager

Currently building her client list in the middle
grade, YA, and adult categories. She is also
interested in considering illustrators and
author-illustrators.

L0181 Jamie Chambliss
Literary Agent
United States

jamie@foliolitmanagement.com

https://www.foliolit.com/agents-1/jamie-
chambliss
https://twitter.com/JChambliss1

Literary Agency: Folio Literary Management,
LLC (**L0343**)

Fiction > *Novels*
Book Club Fiction; Literary; Upmarket

Nonfiction > *Nonfiction Books*
Food; History; Memoir; Narrative
Nonfiction; Popular Culture; Prescriptive
Nonfiction; Science; Sport

Closed to approaches.

L0182 Sonali Chanchani
Literary Agent
United States

sonali@foliolit.com

https://www.foliolit.com/agents-1/sonali-
chanchani

Literary Agency: Folio Literary Management,
LLC (**L0343**)

Fiction > *Novels*
Book Club Fiction; Crime; Folklore, Myths,
and Legends; Historical Fiction; Literary;
Magical Realism; Mystery; Psychological
Suspense; Thrillers; Upmarket Women's
Fiction

Nonfiction > *Nonfiction Books*
Culture; Narrative Nonfiction; Politics;
Social Justice; Society

Send: Query; Writing sample
How to send: In the body of an email

L0183 Anish Chandy
Literary Agent
India

Literary Agency: The Labyrinth Literary
Agency (**L0587**)

L0184 Minju Chang
Literary Agent
United States

Literary Agency: BookStop Literary Agency,
LLC (**L0111**)

CHILDREN'S
Fiction
Chapter Books; *Graphic Novels*; *Middle
Grade*; *Picture Books*
Nonfiction > *Nonfiction Books*

YOUNG ADULT > **Fiction** > *Novels*

How to send: By referral

Represents both fiction and nonfiction in all
children's book categories: picture books,
chapter books, middle-grade, graphic novels
and YA. She also represents illustrators and is
on the hunt for author-illustrators.

L0185 Nicola Chang
Literary Agent
United Kingdom

https://www.davidhigham.co.uk/agents-dh/
nicola-chang/

Literary Agency: David Higham Associates
Ltd (**L0245**)

Fiction > *Novels*
Contemporary; Historical Fiction;
International; Literary

Nonfiction > *Nonfiction Books*
Cookery; Cultural Criticism; Culture; Food;
Journalism; Mainstream; Memoir; Narrative
Nonfiction; Philosophy; Politics;
Psychology; Revisionist History; Society

Poetry > *Any Poetic Form*

Represents writers of fiction and nonfiction as
well as a small list of poets. Currently
accepting submissions and is primarily looking
for literary fiction and nonfiction of all kinds.

Authors: Rosanna Amaka; Iman Amrani;
Raymond Antrobus; Yemisí Aríbisálà; Amman
Brar; Symeon Brown; Judith Bryan; Stephen
Buoro; Jacqueline Crooks; Subhadra Das;
Olivia Dunnett; Orit Gat; Nikita Gill; Emma
Glass; Helen Goh; Will Harris; Alex Holder;
Jack Houston; Angela Hui; Sara Jafari; Keith
Jarrett; Bhanu Kapil; Lara Lee; Huw Lemmey;
Momtaza Mehri; Anna Metcalfe; Mark
Mukasa; Sri Owen; James Conor Patterson;
Riaz Phillips; Leone Ross; Saba Sams; Lisa
Smith; Varaidzo; Christian Weaver; Bryony
White

L0186 Chapman & Vincent
Literary Agency
21 Ellis Street, London, SW1X 9AL
United Kingdom

chapmanvincent@hotmail.co.uk

Professional Body: The Association of
Authors' Agents (AAA)

Types: Nonfiction
Subjects: Cookery; Gardening; History
Markets: Adult

Send: Query
Don't send: Full text
How to send: Email

Small agency handling illustrated nonfiction
only. Not actively seeking clients but will
consider queries by email. No attachments or
postal submissions.

Authors: George Carter; Leslie Geddes-Brown;
Lucinda Lambton; Eve Pollard

Literary Agents: Jennifer Chapman (*L0187*);
Gilly Vincent (*L1003*)

L0187 Jennifer Chapman
Literary Agent
United Kingdom

Literary Agency: Chapman & Vincent (**L0186**)

L0188 Charlie Campbell
Literary Agents
Literary Agency
United Kingdom

info@cclagents.com

http://cclagents.com

Professional Body: The Association of
Authors' Agents (AAA)

ADULT
Fiction > *Novels*
Commercial; Literary

Nonfiction > *Nonfiction Books*
General, and in particular: Biography;
Comedy / Humour; Cookery; History;
Lifestyle; Memoir; Music; Politics; Sport;
Wellbeing

CHILDREN'S
Fiction > *Novels*
Nonfiction > *Nonfiction Books*

Send: Query; Synopsis; Writing sample
How to send: Email

Author Estates: The Estate of Alan Rickman;
The Estate of Alfred H. Mendes

Authors: Guy Adams; Poppy Alexander;
Jennifer Lucy Allan; Jeremy Allen; SJ Bennett;
Leona Nichole Black; Owen Booth; Luce
Brett; Edward Brooke-Hitching; Theodore
Brun; Andy Bull; Jen Campbell; Bonnie
Chung; David Collins; Duncan Crowe; Iain
Dey; Chris Dodd; Lulah Ellender; Adam
Fergusson; Jamie Fewery; Liz Fraser; Rebecca
Front; Tom Gabbay; Julian Gough; Janet
Gover; Sarah Graham; Karen Gurney; Sofie
Hagen; Ed Hawkins; David Higgins; Maisie
Hill; Will Hill; Thomas W. Hodgkinson;
Nicholas Hogg; Michael Holding; Andrew
Hosken; Jo Iozzi; Heidi James; Simon Jones;
Jennifer Lane; Carlie Lee; Paul Levy; Fiona
Longmuir; Bella Mackie; Shingi Mararike;

Amanda Mason; Katy Massey; Hugh Matheson; Alison May; Hannah McCollum; Anthony McGowan; Barry McKinley; Moin Mir; Charlotte Mitchell; Anton Mosimann; Rebecca Myers; James Peak; Andrew Perry; Charlotte Philby; Edvard Radzinsky; Amy Ransom; Amy Raphael; Hamilton Richardson; Susan Richardson; Rebecca Schiller; Clare Seal; Matthew Shaw; Sarah Shephard; Michael Smith; Tatton Spiller; Andrea Stuart; Emma Svanberg; Harry Sword; James Thomas; Tom Tivnan; Luke Turner; Robin Turner; Hana Videen; Michael Volpe; Wendy Wason; Jen Wight; Sioned Wiliam; Hywel Williams; Mike Woodhouse; Liam Patrick Young

Chair: Patrick Janson-Smith

Literary Agents: Charlotte Atyeo (**L0050**); Charlie Campbell (**L0152**); Natalie Galustian (**L0377**); Julia Silk (**L0916**)

L0189 Mic Cheetham
Literary Agent
United Kingdom

mic@miccheetham.com

Literary Agency: Mic Cheetham Literary Agency (**L0701**)

L0190 The Cheney Agency
Literary Agency
39 West 14th Street, Suite 403, New York, NY 10011
United States
Tel: +1 (212) 277-8007
Fax: +1 (212) 614-0728

submissions@cheneyagency.com

http://cheneyassoc.com

Types: Fiction; Nonfiction
Subjects: Autobiography; Business; Commercial; Contemporary; Culture; Current Affairs; Finance; History; Horror; Literary; Literature; Politics; Romance; Science; Sport; Suspense; Thrillers; Women's Interests
Markets: Adult

Send: Query
Don't send: Full text
How to send: Email

Send query with up to three chapters of sample material by post with SASE, or by email. Response not guaranteed.

Literary Agents: Elyse Cheney (*L0191*); Allison Devereux (*L0262*); Adam Eaglin (*L0287*); Alice Whitwham (*L1034*)

L0191 Elyse Cheney
Literary Agent
United States

Literary Agency: The Cheney Agency (**L0190**)

L0192 Anwar Chentoufi
Literary Agent
United Kingdom

Literary Agency: Independent Talent Group Ltd (**L0496**)

L0193 Patrick Child
Literary Agent
United Kingdom

Literary Agency: Independent Talent Group Ltd (**L0496**)

L0194 Catherine Cho
Literary Agent
United Kingdom

https://twitter.com/catkcho

Literary Agency: Paper Literary (**L0777**)

Fiction > *Novels*
Family Saga; High Concept; Literary; Magical Realism; Psychological Suspense; Romance; Speculative; Thrillers; Upmarket

Nonfiction > *Nonfiction Books*
History; Lifestyle; Memoir; Narrative Nonfiction; Psychology; Science; Social Issues

L0195 Jennifer Christie
Literary Agent
United Kingdom

Literary Agency: Graham Maw Christie Literary Agency (**L0408**)

L0196 Christine Green Authors' Agent
Literary Agency
PO Box 70098, London, SE15 5AU
United Kingdom

info@christinegreen.co.uk

http://www.christinegreen.co.uk
http://twitter.com/#!/whitehorsemews

Professional Body: The Association of Authors' Agents (AAA)

Types: Fiction; Nonfiction
Subjects: Commercial; Literary
Markets: Adult; Young Adult

Send: Query
Don't send: Full text
How to send: Email

Focusses on fiction for adult and young adult, and also considers narrative nonfiction. No children's books, genre science-fiction/fantasy, poetry or scripts. Send query by email (preferred) or by post with SAE. No submissions by fax or CD. See website for full submission guidelines.

L0197 The Chudney Agency
Literary Agency
72 North State Road, Suite 501, Briarcliff

Manor, NY 10510
United States
Tel: +1 (201) 758-8739
Fax: +1 (201) 758-8739

steven@thechudneyagency.com

http://www.thechudneyagency.com

ADULT
Fiction > *Novels*
General, and in particular: Gender; Historical Fiction; LGBTQIA; Middle East; Mystery; Sexuality; Thrillers; Women's Fiction

Nonfiction
Gift Books: General
Illustrated Books: General
Nonfiction Books: Comedy / Humour

CHILDREN'S > **Fiction**
Chapter Books: General, and in particular: Comedy / Humour; Coming of Age; Contemporary; Culture; Gender; Historical Fiction; Literary; Mystery; Spirituality
Middle Grade: General, and in particular: Comedy / Humour; Coming of Age; Contemporary; Culture; Gender; Historical Fiction; Literary; Mystery; Spirituality
Picture Books: General

TEEN > **Fiction** > *Novels*
General, and in particular: Comedy / Humour; Coming of Age; Contemporary; Culture; Gender; Historical Fiction; Literary; Mystery; Spirituality

Send: Query
How to send: Email
How not to send: Post

Specialises in children's and teen books, but will also consider adult fiction. Send query only in first instance. Happy to accept queries by email. Submit material upon invitation only. No fantasy, science fiction, early readers, or scripts. See website for full guidelines.

Authors: Jessica Alexander; Mary Jane Beaufrand; Tess Hilmo; Kristen Landon

Literary Agent: Steven Chudney

L0198 Julia Churchill
Literary Agent
United Kingdom

https://amheath.com/agents/julia-churchill/
https://twitter.com/juliachurchill

Literary Agency: A.M. Heath & Company Limited, Author's Agents (**L0003**)

CHILDREN'S > **Fiction**
Novels; *Picture Books*
YOUNG ADULT > **Fiction** > *Novels*

L0199 Kayla Cichello
Literary Agent
United States

kayla.submission@gmail.com

http://www.upstartcrowliterary.com/agent/kayla-cichello/
https://twitter.com/SeriousKayla

Literary Agency: Upstart Crow Literary (**L0995**)

CHILDREN'S > Fiction
Middle Grade: General
Picture Books: Comedy / Humour

YOUNG ADULT > Fiction > *Novels*
Commercial; Dark Humour; Literary; Magical Realism; Mystery; Romance; Romantic Comedy; Suspense

How to send: Email

Seeking everything from heartfelt or humorous picture books (she has a soft spot for animal protagonists) to dynamic, unpredictable YA (she loves a good murder mystery or a clever rom-com).

L0200 Clare Hulton Literary Agency

Literary Agency
United Kingdom

info@clarehulton.co.uk

https://www.clarehulton.com

Professional Body: The Association of Authors' Agents (AAA)

Fiction > *Novels*

Nonfiction > *Nonfiction Books*
General, and in particular: Business; Cookery; Health; History; Lifestyle; Parenting; Philosophy; Pregnancy; Self Help

Send: Query
How to send: In the body of an email

Specialises in nonfiction, but also has a small commercial fiction list. Finds most authors through recommendation, but open to brief queries by email, explaining what your book is about. No attachments. If no response within two weeks, assume rejection.

Literary Agent: Clare Hulton (*L0487*)

L0201 Anne Clark
Literary Agent
United Kingdom

Literary Agency: Anne Clark Literary Agency (**L0038**)

L0202 Lucy Cleland
Literary Agent
United States

Literary Agency: Kneerim & Williams (**L0575**)

L0203 Rachel Clements
Literary Agent
United Kingdom

rachel@abnerstein.co.uk

Literary Agency: Abner Stein (**L0005**)

L0204 Mary Clemmey
Literary Agent
United Kingdom

Literary Agency: Mary Clemmey Literary Agency (**L0679**)

L0205 Jon Cobb
Associate Agent
United States

jon@hgliterary.com

https://www.hgliterary.com/jon
http://queryme.online/Cobb

Literary Agency: HG Literary (**L0467**)

ADULT > Fiction > *Novels*
African American; Fantasy; Literary; Mystery; Science Fiction; Thrillers

CHILDREN'S > Fiction > *Middle Grade*: Contemporary

YOUNG ADULT > Fiction > *Novels*

How to send: Query Manager

L0206 Alexander Cochran
Literary Agent
United Kingdom

Literary Agency: C+W (Conville & Walsh) (**L0147**)

L0207 Therese Coen
Literary Agent
United Kingdom

therese@hardmanswainson.com

https://www.hardmanswainson.com/agent/therese-coen/
https://twitter.com/theresecoen

Literary Agency: Hardman & Swainson (**L0441**)

ADULT > Fiction > *Novels*
Coming of Age; Crime; High Concept Romance; Historical Fiction

CHILDREN'S > Fiction > *Novels*
Adventure; Comedy / Humour; Fantasy; Space

Send: Query; Synopsis; Full text
How to send: Email

In terms of adult fiction, I have a soft spot for historical fiction, having read Early Modern History at university, but am also very much on the hunt for crime, coming-of-age stories and high-concept love stories. I love strong female characters, especially when they go through an evolution as the story progresses and gradually find that inner strength.

On the children's fiction front, I love all things fantasy and adventure – across lands, time and space, and involving strong friendships and strong lead characters. I want to be transported straight away when I start reading a manuscript. Right this moment, I would love to see something involving an Orient Express-style train, or maybe an Agatha Christie-type cruise boat (perhaps without the gruesome murder). I like very vivid, well-crafted and imaginative worlds, for example stories set in a toy factory or in an underwater world. I'd love some more adventures set in space, à la Star Trek and Wall-E. I want mysteries, quirky characters, explorers and imaginary friends.

L0208 Susan Lee Cohen
Literary Agent
United States

Literary Agency: Riverside Literary Agency (**L0839**)
Professional Body: Association of American Literary Agents (AALA)

L0209 Ann Collette
Literary Agent
United States

Literary Agency: Rees Literary Agency (**L0824**)

L0210 Frances Collin
Literary Agent
United States

Literary Agency: Frances Collin Literary Agent (**L0355**)

L0211 Charlotte Colwill
Literary Agent
United Kingdom

charlotte@bravoblue.co.uk

Literary Agencies: The Bravo Blue Agency (**L0122**); Tibor Jones & Associates (**L0982**)

L0212 Chris Combemale
Associate Agent
United States

https://www.sll.com/our-team

Literary Agency: Sterling Lord Literistic, Inc. (**L0940**)

Fiction > *Novels*
Commercial; Fantasy; Literary; Psychological Suspense; Speculative

Nonfiction
Essays: Economics; Food; Popular Science; Technology
Nonfiction Books: Economics; Food; Memoir; Popular Science; Technology

Send: Query; Synopsis; Proposal; Writing sample
How to send: Online submission system

Looking for a broad range of literary fiction and commercial fiction with an unexpected hook, from psychological suspense to speculative and fantasy. In non-fiction he is interested in memoir, essay, and expert-driven projects across subject areas with special attention to technology, food, pop-science, economics, and any book that asks big questions about forces of change.

L0213 **Concord Theatricals**
Literary Agency; Book Publisher
250 W. 57th Street, 6th Floor, New York, NY 10107-0102
United States
Tel: +1 (866) 979-0447

info@concordtheatricals.com

https://www.concordtheatricals.com/

Scripts > *Theatre Scripts*

Closed to approaches.

Publishes plays and represents writers of plays. Deals in well-known plays from Broadway and London's West End.

L0214 **Claire Paterson Conrad**
Literary Agent
United Kingdom

http://www.janklowandnesbit.co.uk/node/671

Literary Agency: Janklow & Nesbit UK Ltd (**L0516**)

Fiction > *Novels*

Nonfiction > *Nonfiction Books*
Biology; Creative Nonfiction; Environment; Nature; Popular Science

Send: Query; Synopsis; Writing sample; Outline
How to send: Email
How not to send: Post

Keen to represent more books about the natural world and our co-existence with it (whether that be popular science, biology, ecology or nature writing); books that celebrate women in science; books that help us understand the world and bring change; and creative nonfiction that blends genres. In fiction, gravitates towards atmospheric, character-driven novels that are rooted to a strong sense of place.

L0215 **Clare Conville**
Literary Agent
United Kingdom

Literary Agency: C+W (Conville & Walsh) (**L0147**)

L0216 **Clare Coombes**
Literary Agent
United Kingdom

https://www.liverpool-literary.agency/about

Literary Agency: The Liverpool Literary Agency (**L0624**)

Fiction > *Novels*
General, and in particular: Crime; Historical Fiction; Psychological Thrillers; Women's Fiction

Would love to see historical fiction, crime fiction, psychological thrillers and women's fiction, but as a new agent, she is open to all great writing with a strong hook in any area (excluding non-fiction, children's and YA).

L0217 **Coombs Moylett & Maclean Literary Agency**
Literary Agency
120 New Kings Road, London, SW6 4LZ
United Kingdom

info@cmm.agency

https://cmm.agency
https://www.instagram.com/cmmlitagency/
https://www.facebook.com/cmmlitagency/

ADULT
Fiction > *Novels*
Chick Lit; Commercial; Contemporary; Crime; Historical Fiction; Horror; Literary; Mystery; Suspense; Thrillers; Women's Fiction

Nonfiction > *Nonfiction Books*
General, and in particular: Biography; Crime; Current Affairs; Environment; Food; History; How To; Lifestyle; Narrative Nonfiction; Politics; Popular Science; Self Help

YOUNG ADULT > **Fiction** > *Novels*

Closed to approaches.

Send query with synopsis and first three chapters via online form. No submissions by email, fax or by post. No poetry, plays or scripts for film and TV. Whole books and postal submissions will not be read.

Editor / Literary Agent: Jamie Maclean (**L0659**)

Literary Agents: Zoe Apostolides (**L0043**); Elena Langtry (**L0596**); Lisa Moylett (**L0730**)

L0218 **Brandie Coonis**
Literary Agent
United States

Literary Agency: Rebecca Friedman Literary Agency (**L0821**)

L0219 **Gemma Cooper**
Literary Agent
United States

http://www.thebentagency.com/gemma-cooper

Literary Agency: The Bent Agency (**L0090**)

ADULT > **Fiction** > *Graphic Novels*: Comedy / Humour

CHILDREN'S
Fiction

Chapter Books; Graphic Novels; Illustrated Books; Middle Grade
Nonfiction > *Nonfiction Books*

YOUNG ADULT > **Fiction**
Graphic Novels; Illustrated Books

L0220 **Maggie Cooper**
Literary Agent
Boston, MA
United States

https://aevitascreative.com/agents/

Literary Agency: Aevitas (**L0016**)

Fiction > *Novels*
Feminist Romance; Historical Fiction; LGBTQIA; Literary

Nonfiction > *Nonfiction Books*
Cookery; Food

Represents imaginative, genre-bending literary fiction; capacious historical novels; beautifully told queer stories; and smart, feminist romance. Her other loves include unclassifiable book projects, food and cookbooks, and work by writers traditionally underrepresented in mainstream publishing.

L0221 **Cornerstone Literary Agency**
Literary Agency
United States

info@cornerstoneliterary.com

http://www.cornerstoneliterary.com

Fiction > *Novels*
Commercial; Literary

Nonfiction > *Nonfiction Books*: Narrative Nonfiction

Send: Query; Author bio; Writing sample; Self-Addressed Stamped Envelope (SASE)
How to send: Post; Email

Send query by post or by email. No business, how-to, photography books, poetry, screenplays, self-help or Westerns.

Literary Agent: Helen Breitwieser (**L0123**)

L0222 **The Cowles Agency**
Literary Agency
United States

katherine@cowlesagency.com

http://www.cowlesagency.com
https://twitter.com/cowlesagency
https://www.instagram.com/cowlesagency/

Nonfiction > *Nonfiction Books*
Business; Cookery; Design; Health; Memoir; Narrative Nonfiction; Photography

Authors: Bryant Austin; Catherine Bailey; Andy Baraghani; Nils Bernstein; Taylor Boetticher; Jon Bonne; Carrie Brown; Chris Burkhard; Courtney Burns; Gabriela Camara; Henry Carroll; Josef Centeno; Baylor

Chapman; Andrew Chau; Bin Chen; Mark Cushing; Sohla El-Waylly; Renee Erickson; Susan Fisher; Camille Fourmont; Andrea Gentl; Monica Khemsurov; Eric Kim; George King; Jessica Koslow; Lauri Krantz; Jeff Krasno; Chris Kronner; Travis Lett; Peter Liem; Kermit Lynch; Rick Martinez; Ignacio Mattos; Margarita Matzke; Emeran Mayer; Amy Merrick; Toponia Miller; Serena Mitnik-Miller; Sam Mogannam; Carla Lalli Music; Ivan Orkin; Rafael Pelayo; Mason St. Peter; Robin Petravic; Charles Phan; Natasha Pickowicz; Paulson Fontaine Press; Elisabeth Prueitt; Christian Puglisi; Chad Robertson; Sharon Robinson; Besha Rodell; Julia Sherman; Sheldon Simeon; Jill Singer; Garrett Snyder; David Tanis; Erica Tanov; Andrew Tarlow; Thaddeus Vogler; Eric Werner; Kris Yenbamroong; Chris Ying; Maria Zizka

Literary Agent: Katherine Cowles (**L0223**)

L0223 Katherine Cowles
Literary Agent
United States

katherine@cowlesagency.com

Literary Agency: The Cowles Agency (**L0222**)
Professional Bodies: Association of American Literary Agents (AALA); The Authors Guild

L0224 Peter Cox
Literary Agent
United Kingdom

Literary Agency: Redhammer (**L0823**)

L0225 Becca Crandall
Literary Agent
United States

becca@carolynjenksagency.com

https://www.carolynjenksagency.com/agent/BECCA-CRANDALL

Literary Agency: Carolyn Jenks Agency (**L0164**)

ADULT
  Fiction
    Graphic Novels; *Novels*
  Nonfiction > *Nonfiction Books*

CHILDREN'S > **Fiction**
  Middle Grade; *Picture Books*
YOUNG ADULT > **Fiction** > *Novels*

Send: Query; Writing sample
How to send: In the body of an email

L0226 Creative Authors Ltd
Literary Agency
United Kingdom

write@creativeauthors.co.uk

https://www.creativeauthors.co.uk

Types: Fiction; Nonfiction
Subjects: Arts; Autobiography; Business;

Comedy / Humour; Commercial; Cookery; Crafts; Crime; Culture; Health; History; Literary; Nature; Women's Interests
Markets: Adult; Children's

How to send: Email

As at April 2019, not accepting new fiction clients. See website for current situation. We are a dynamic literary agency – established to provide an attentive and unique platform for writers and scriptwriters and representing a growing list of clients. We're on the lookout for fresh talent and books with strong commercial potential. No unsolicited MSS, but considers queries by email. No paper submissions. Do not telephone regarding submissions.

Literary Agent: Isabel Atherton (*L0049*)

L0227 The Creative Rights Agency
Literary Agency
United Kingdom
Tel: +44 (0) 20 3371 7673

info@creativerightsagency.co.uk

http://www.creativerightsagency.co.uk

Fiction > *Novels*

Nonfiction > *Nonfiction Books*

Publishing, Licensing, Film/TV. Based in London.

Literary Agent: Richard Scrivener

L0228 Claudia Cross
Literary Agent; Partner
United States

https://www.foliolit.com/agents-1/claudia-cross
http://aaronline.org/Sys/PublicProfile/2176647/417813

Literary Agency: Folio Literary Management, LLC (**L0343**)
Professional Body: Association of American Literary Agents (AALA)

Closed to approaches.

L0229 Sara Crowe
Literary Agent
United States

Literary Agency: Pippin Properties, Inc (**L0801**)

L0230 Cull & Co. Ltd
Literary Agency
United Kingdom

tom@cullandco.com

https://cullandco.com
https://www.facebook.com/cullandco/
https://www.youtube.com/channel/UCp8AcbMXQ7UenhgFxX4XM6g

Professional Body: The Association of Authors' Agents (AAA)

Nonfiction > *Nonfiction Books*
  Biography; Crime; Memoir; Military; Narrative Nonfiction; Politics; Sport; Travel

Send: Synopsis; Writing sample; Author bio
How to send: Email

Handles full-length fiction and nonfiction for adults only. No children's picture books, poetry, plays or musical theatre. Primarily looking for authors from the UK and Ireland writing in English. Occasionally considers international writers but you must make it clear when submitting why you are looking for a literary agent in the UK.

L0231 Mary Cummings
Literary Agent
United States

Literary Agency: Great River Literary (**L0414**)
Professional Bodies: Association of American Literary Agents (AALA); Society of Children's Book Writers and Illustrators (SCBWI)

L0232 Michael Curry
Literary Agent
United States

Literary Agency: Donald Maass Literary Agency (**L0273**)

L0233 Curtis Brown
Literary Agency
Haymarket House, 28/29 Haymarket, London, SW1Y 4SP
United Kingdom
Tel: +44 (0) 20 7393 4400

info@curtisbrown.co.uk

http://www.curtisbrowncreative.co.uk

Professional Body: The Association of Authors' Agents (AAA)

Types: Fiction; Nonfiction; Scripts
Formats: Film Scripts; Radio Scripts; TV Scripts; Theatre Scripts
Subjects: Biography; Commercial; Crime; Fantasy; History; Literary; Science; Suspense; Thrillers
Markets: Adult; Children's; Young Adult

Send: Query
Don't send: Full text

Costs: Offers services that writers have to pay for.

Renowned and long established London agency. Handles general fiction and nonfiction, and scripts. Also represents directors, designers, and presenters. No longer accepts submissions by post or email – all submissions must be made using online submissions manager. Also offers services such as writing courses for which authors are charged.

Associate Agent: Viola Hayden (**L0456**)

Literary Agent / President: Jonathan Lloyd (**L0627**)

Literary Agents: Felicity Blunt (**L0105**); Sheila Crowley; Jonny Geller (**L0388**); Alice Lutyens (*L0646*); Lucy Morris (*L0727*); Cathryn Summerhayes (*L0954*); Gordon Wise (*L1048*)

L0234 Curtis Brown (Australia) Pty Ltd

Literary Agency
PO Box 19, Paddington, NSW, 2021
Australia

submission@curtisbrown.com.au

http://www.curtisbrown.com.au

Professional Body: Australian Literary Agents' Association (ALAA)

Fiction > *Novels*

Nonfiction > *Nonfiction Books*

How to send: Email

Accepts submission from within Australia and New Zealand only, during February, June, and October. No fantasy, sci-fi, stage/screenplays, poetry, self-help books, children's picture books, early reader books, young adult books, comic books, short stories, cookbooks, educational, corporate books or translations. Send query by email with synopsis up to two pages and first three chapters. See website for full guidelines.

Literary Agents: Clare Forster (*L0348*); Grace Heifetz (*L0462*); Fiona Inglis (*L0497*); Pippa Masson (*L0682*); Tara Wynne (*L1058*)

L0235 John Cusick

Literary Agent; Vice President
United States

https://www.publishersmarketplace.com/members/JohnC/
https://twitter.com/johnmcusick

Literary Agencies: Folio Literary Management, LLC (**L0343**); Folio Jr. (**L0342**)

ADULT > **Fiction** > *Novels*
Fantasy; Horror; Science Fiction; Suspense; Thrillers

CHILDREN'S > **Fiction** > *Middle Grade*
Comedy / Humour; Contemporary; Fantasy; Science Fiction; Speculative

YOUNG ADULT > **Fiction** > *Novels*
Comedy / Humour; Contemporary; Fantasy; Science Fiction; Speculative

Closed to approaches.

Authors: Courtney Alameda; Kayla Cagan; Josephine Cameron; Anna Carey; Marina Cohen; Paula Garner; Joan He; Christian McKay Heidicker; Sailor J; Jeramey Kraatz; Kristen Lippert-Martin; Julie Murphy; Abdi Nazemian; Jordan Reeves; Laura Sebastian;

Quinn Sosna-Spear; Sharon Biggs Waller; Don Zolidis

L0236 Cyle Young Literary Elite

Literary Agency
United States

submissions@cyleyoung.com

https://cyleyoung.com
https://www.facebook.com/cyle61?fref=ts
https://twitter.com/cyleyoung

Associate Agents: Hope Bolinger; Caroline George; Alyssa Roat

Author / Junior Agent: Del Duduit (**L0282**)

Author / Literary Agent: Cyle Young (**L1062**)

Junior Agents: Megan Burkhart (**L0141**); Jori Hanna; Chrysa Keenon; Kenzi Nevins

Literary Agent: Tessa Emily Hall (*L0437*)

L0237 Laura Dail

Literary Agent; President
United States

http://www.ldlainc.com/about
http://twitter.com/lcdail
http://aaronline.org/Sys/PublicProfile/2176649/417813

Literary Agency: Laura Dail Literary Agency (**L0599**)
Professional Body: Association of American Literary Agents (AALA)

Closed to approaches.

L0238 Judy Daish

Literary Agent
United Kingdom

Literary Agency: Judy Daish Associates Ltd (**L0536**)

L0239 Melissa Danaczko

Literary Agent
United States

Literary Agency: Stuart Krichevsky Literary Agency, Inc.

Closed to approaches.

L0240 Margaret Danko

Literary Agent
United States

submissions@paperoverboard.com

https://www.irenegoodman.com/margaret-danko

Literary Agency: Irene Goodman Literary Agency (IGLA) (**L0501**)

ADULT
  Fiction > *Novels*

Commercial; Contemporary; Historical Fiction; Literary; Magical Realism; Romantic Comedy; Suspense

  Nonfiction > *Nonfiction Books*
Comedy / Humour; Crime; Current Affairs; Health; Lifestyle; Politics; Popular Science; Wellbeing

YOUNG ADULT > **Fiction** > *Novels*: Fantasy

Send: Query
How to send: In the body of an email

Actively looking for attention-grabbing voices especially literary fiction with teeth, historical fiction with a dash of magical realism, fresh literary and commercial suspense, spooky contemporary and fantasy YA, narratives with a deep sense of place and history, quirky and heartwarming family stories, and rom-coms full of charm and whimsy. She is also interested in nonfiction in the areas of humor, lifestyle, popular science, health/wellness, true crime, politics, and current affairs. She does not represent Middle Grade or picture books.

L0241 Jon Michael Darga

Literary Agent
New York
United States

https://aevitascreative.com/agents/

Literary Agency: Aevitas (**L0016**)

ADULT
  Fiction > *Novels*
Fantasy; Literary; Science Fiction

  Nonfiction > *Nonfiction Books*
History; Memoir; Narrative Nonfiction; Popular Culture

YOUNG ADULT > **Fiction** > *Novels*

Send: Author bio; Outline; Pitch; Market info; Writing sample
How to send: Online submission system

Represents both nonfiction and fiction. He is most interested in voice-driven pop culture writing and histories that re-cast the narrative by emphasizing unexpected or unheard voices.

L0242 Darhansoff & Verrill Literary Agents

Literary Agency
529 11th Street, Third Floor, Brooklyn, NY 11215
United States
Tel: +1 (917) 305-1300

submissions@dvagency.com
info@dvagency.com

https://www.dvagency.com

ADULT
  Fiction > *Novels*
  Nonfiction > *Nonfiction Books*

YOUNG ADULT > **Fiction** > *Novels*

Send: Query; Writing sample
How to send: In the body of an email
How not to send: Post

Response only if interested. If no response within eight weeks, assume rejection.

Literary Agents: Liz Darhansoff; Charles Verrill

L0243 Darley Anderson Children's
Literary Agency
Unit 19, Matrix Studios, 91 Peterborough Road, London, SW6 3BU
United Kingdom
Tel: +44 (0) 20 7386 2674

childrens@darleyanderson.com

http://www.darleyandersonchildrens.com
http://twitter.com/DA_Childrens

Professional Body: The Association of Authors' Agents (AAA)

CHILDREN'S
  Fiction
    Chapter Books; *Middle Grade*; *Picture Books*
  Nonfiction > *Nonfiction Books*

YOUNG ADULT > *Fiction* > *Novels*

Send: Query; Synopsis; Writing sample; Author bio; Pitch
How to send: Word file email attachment; PDF file email attachment
How not to send: Post

Always on the look out for exciting, inspiring and original novels for both Young Adult and Middle-Grade readers, chapter books, picture books, and nonfiction.

Literary Agent: Clare Wallace (**L1012**)

L0244 David Godwin Associates
Literary Agency
2nd Floor, 40 Rosebery Avenue, Clerkenwell, London, EC1R 4RX
United Kingdom
Tel: +44 (0) 20 7240 9992

sebastiangodwin@
davidgodwinassociates.co.uk

http://www.davidgodwinassociates.com

Types: Fiction; Nonfiction
Subjects: Literary
Markets: Adult

Send: Query
Don't send: Full text
How to send: Email

Handles a range of nonfiction and fiction. Send query by email with synopsis and first 30 pages. No poetry. No picture books, except for existing clients.

Literary Agent: David Godwin (*L0401*)

L0245 David Higham Associates Ltd
Literary Agency
6th Floor, Waverley House, 7-12 Noel Street, London, W1F 8GQ
United Kingdom
Tel: +44 (0) 20 7434 5900
Fax: +44 (0) 20 7437 1072

dha@davidhigham.co.uk
submissions@davidhigham.co.uk
childrenssubmissions@davidhigham.co.uk

http://www.davidhigham.co.uk

Professional Body: The Association of Authors' Agents (AAA)

Agency Assistant: Sara Langham

Assistant Agent: David Evans (**L0313**)

Authors: Rachel Abbott; J. R. Ackerley; Richard Adams; Katie Agnew; Naomi Alderman; Tracy Alexander; Geraint Anderson; Michael Arditti; Hannah Begbie; Carys Bray; Kevin Brockmeier; Glen Brown; Rob Burnett; Nick Butterworth; Nicola Davies; Jonathan Dimbleby; Berlie Doherty; Ellie Eaton; David Edmonds; Maz Evans; Jamila Gavin; Guinevere Glasfurd; Candy Guard; Saleem Haddad; Oliver Harris; Lisa Heathfield; Neil Hegarty; Emma Henderson; Edward Hogan; Phil Hogan; Ian Holding; Lucy Hounsom; Jack Houston; Tristan Hughes; William Hussey; Will Iredale; Diana Wynne Jones; Claire King; Saci Lloyd; Kesia Lupo; Patrick Marnham; Geraldine McCaughrean; Jean McNeil; Anna Metcalfe; Sarah Mitchell; James Conor Patterson; Tasha Silva; Lisa Smith; Sureka Thanenthiran-Dharuman; Bryony White

Company Director / Literary Agent: Veronique Baxter (**L0075**)

Literary Agents: Olivia Barber; Nicola Chang (**L0185**); Elise Dillsworth (**L0266**); Jemima Forrester (**L0347**); Georgia Glover; Anthony Goff; Andrew Gordon; Lizzy Kremer; Harriet Moore; Caroline Walsh; Laura West; Jessica Woollard

L0246 David Luxton Associates
Literary Agency
United Kingdom

admin@davidluxtonassociates.co.uk

https://www.davidluxtonassociates.co.uk
https://twitter.com/DLuxAssociates
https://www.instagram.com/
davidluxtonassociates/

Professional Body: The Association of Authors' Agents (AAA)

Nonfiction > *Nonfiction Books*
  Food; Investigative Journalism; Lifestyle; Music; Nature; Photography; Sport

Send: Query; Synopsis; Writing sample; Author bio
How to send: Email
How not to send: Post

Specialises in nonfiction, including sport, celebrity biography, business & leadership, food-writing, nature-writing and lifestyle. No scripts or screenplays.

Literary Agents: David Luxton (**L0648**); Nick Walters (**L1014**); Rebecca Winfield (**L1047**)

L0247 Caroline Davidson
Literary Agent
United Kingdom

Literary Agency: Caroline Davidson Literary Agency (**L0162**)

L0248 Sarah Davies
Literary Agent
United States

https://www.greenhouseliterary.com/the-team/sarah-davies/
http://aaronline.org/Sys/PublicProfile/2715608/417813
https://querymanager.com/query/SarahDavies

Literary Agency: The Greenhouse Literary Agency (**L0420**)
Professional Body: Association of American Literary Agents (AALA)

ADULT > **Fiction** > *Novels*
  Suspense; Women's Fiction

CHILDREN'S
  Fiction
    Graphic Novels: General
    Middle Grade: Adventure; Magic; Magical Realism
  Nonfiction > *Nonfiction Books*

YOUNG ADULT > **Fiction** > *Novels*
  Contemporary Romance; Fantasy; France; Historical Fiction; Magical Realism; Middle East; Mystery; Romantic Comedy; Science; Thrillers; World War I; World War II

Does not want:

> **YOUNG ADULT** > **Fiction** > *Novels*
> American Civil War; American Revolution

Closed to approaches.

Seeking Fiction from Middle Grade through Young Adult and across all genres (note: she is currently closed to debut Picturebooks but does rep PBs by clients whom she's initially taken on for older fiction). She loves strong, hooky, layered plots, writing that is gorgeous but also conceptually strong, and stories that are really moving but make you think too. She is particularly seeking authors from under-represented backgrounds and stories with diverse settings and perspectives. She is also open, by referral, to women's fiction — especially in the suspense genre.

L0249 Chloe Davis
Assistant Agent
United Kingdom

http://www.darleyanderson.com/our-team

Literary Agent: Clare Wallace (**L1012**)
Literary Agency: The Darley Anderson Agency

CHILDREN'S > **Fiction** > *Middle Grade*: Adventure

YOUNG ADULT > **Fiction** > *Novels*: Contemporary Romance

Particularly enjoys reading submissions, especially middle grade adventures and contemporary YA love stories.

L0250 Meg Davis
Literary Agent
United Kingdom

meg@ki-agency.co.uk

https://ki-agency.co.uk/contact

Literary Agency: Ki Agency Ltd (**L0567**)

Fiction > *Novels*

Scripts
  Film Scripts; *TV Scripts*; *Theatre Scripts*

Happy to consider scripts in all genres, and books in some genres, especially genre fiction. Not a good bet for fiction that might be considered to be wearing a cardigan, or which is narrated by an animal.

L0251 Caroline Dawnay
Literary Agent
United Kingdom
Tel: +44 (0) 20 3214 0931

kaitken@unitedagents.co.uk

https://www.unitedagents.co.uk/
cdawnayunitedagentscouk

Literary Agency: United Agents (**L0992**)

Fiction > *Novels*: Literary

Nonfiction > *Nonfiction Books*

Send: Query; Author bio; Writing sample
How to send: Email

Interested in serious nonfiction and literary fiction. For submissions please email a short cover letter, biographical note and the first 10,000 words of your text.

Authors: Rennie Airth; Laura Beatty; Stephen Bernard; Alain de Botton; Susie Boyt; Christopher Brookmyre; James Buchan; Eleanor Catton; Charles Chadwick; Catherine Chidgey; Rupert Christiansen; Charles Clover; Peter Conrad; Jill Dawson; Guy Deutscher; Minoo Dinshaw; Gaston Dorren; Philip Eade; James Le Fanu; Tim Finch; Tom Fort; Richard

Francis; John Fuller; James Grant; Thomas Grant; Tessa Hadley; James Hall; Christopher de Hamel; Lynsey Hanley; Alexandra Harris; Jane Hasell-McCosh; David Hendy; Richard Holloway; Sheena Joughin; Adam Forrest Kay; Martin Kemp; Nick Lane; Richard Layard; Hermione Lee; Margaret MacMillan; Jan Morris; Chris Mullin; James Mylet; Jeremy Mynott; Virginia Nicholson; Constantine Phipps; Edward Platt; Jennifer Potter; Matthew Rice; Jane Ridley; Posy Simmonds; Helen Smith; Dan Snow; Donald Sturrock; Sasha Swire; Stephen Taylor; Tony Thompson; Francesca Wade; Nadia Wassef; Philip Ziegler; Sofka Zinovieff

L0252 Liza Dawson
Literary Agent
United States

Literary Agency: Liza Dawson Associates (**L0625**)

L0253 Liza DeBlock
Literary Agent
United Kingdom

ldbsubmissions@mushens-entertainment.com

https://www.mushens-entertainment.com/
submissions-guidelines

Literary Agency: Mushens Entertainment (**L0739**)

ADULT

  Fiction > *Novels*
    Commercial Fantasy; Historical Fiction; Romantic Comedy; Saga; Thrillers

  Nonfiction > *Nonfiction Books*
    Cookery; Current Affairs; Popular Science; Social History

YOUNG ADULT > **Fiction** > *Novels*
    Commercial Fantasy; Historical Fiction; Romantic Comedy; Saga; Thrillers

Closed to approaches.

Looking for both fiction and non fiction. For fiction, she is interested in adult and YA only. She is looking for historical fiction, commercial fantasy, romcom, saga, uplit, and thriller.

On the nonfiction side, she is looking for books that teach her something new or reframe a topic from an alternative point of view. This can include cookery, pop science, social history, and current events.

L0254 Stacia Decker
Literary Agent
United States

Literary Agency: Dunow, Carlson & Lerner Agency

Closed to approaches.

L0255 Allison DeFrees
Literary Agent
United Kingdom

Literary Agency: C+W (Conville & Walsh) (**L0147**)

L0256 Joelle Delbourgo
Literary Agent
United States

Literary Agency: Joelle Delbourgo Associates, Inc. (**L0527**)
Professional Body: Association of American Literary Agents (AALA)

L0257 The Dench Arnold Agency
Literary Agency
United Kingdom
Tel: +44 (0) 20 7437 4551
Fax: +44 (0) 20 7437 4551

fiona@denentharnold.com

https://www.dencharnold.com
https://www.instagram.com/
dencharnold_agency/
https://twitter.com/DenchArnold

Scripts
  Film Scripts; *TV Scripts*

Send: Query; Author bio; Synopsis
How to send: Email

Send query with CV and synopsis by email only. Represents writers, directors and heads of department (directors of photography, production designers, costume designers, editors and make-up designers).

Authors: Joe Ainsworth; Maurice Bessman; Giles Borg; William Borthwick; Peter Briggs; Karen Brown; Peter Chelsom; Rob Churchill; David Conolly; Hannah Davies; Jim Davies; Eric Deacon; Adrian Dunbar; Chris Fallon; Susanne Farrell; Matthew Faulk; Lucy Flannery; Ellis Freeman; Liam Gavin; Nicholas Gibbs; Steve Gough; Robert Hammond; James Handel; Michael Harvey; Jo Ho; David Lg Hughes; Julian Kemp; Malcolm Kohll; Anna Kythreotis; Sarah Lambert; Dominic Macdonald; Steve Mcateer; Alan Mcdonald; Kevin Molony; Courttia Newland; Matthew Newman; Omid Nooshin; Paul Parkes; Junior Rhone; Dave Simpson; Mark Skeet; Mark Stay; Francesca Tatini; Stewart Thomson; Alan Whiting; Terry Winsor; Kate Wood

Literary Agents: Michelle Arnold; Elizabeth Dench; Matthew Dench

L0258 Caspian Dennis
Literary Agent
United Kingdom

caspian@abnerstein.co.uk

Literary Agency: Abner Stein (**L0005**)

L0259 Derrick & Briggs, LLP
Literary Agency
BancFirst Tower, Suite 2700, 100 North
Broadway Avenue, Oklahoma City, OK 73102
United States
Tel: +1 (405) 235-1900
Fax: +1 (405) 235-1995

briggs@derrickandbriggs.com

http://derrickandbriggs.com

Types: Fiction; Nonfiction
Subjects: Autobiography; Commercial;
Contemporary; Health; Medicine; Nature;
Personal Development
Markets: Adult; Children's; Young Adult

Combines her primary work as a literary agent
with expertise in intellectual property,
entertainment law and estates and probate. Her
clients are published authors (exclusively),
theatres, and a variety of small businesses and
individuals.

Literary Agent: M. Courtney Briggs (*L0125*)

L0260 Dado Derviskadic
Literary Agent
United States
Tel: +1 (212) 400-1494

dado@foliolit.com

http://foliolit.com/dado-derviskadic

Literary Agency: Folio Literary Management,
LLC (**L0343**)

Fiction > *Novels*

Nonfiction > *Nonfiction Books*
  Biography; Cookery; Cultural History; Food;
  Health; Language; Memoir; Motivational
  Self-Help; Nutrition; Popular Culture;
  Popular Science

Send: Query; Writing sample; Proposal
How to send: In the body of an email

L0261 Francesca Devas
Literary Agent
United Kingdom

Literary Agency: Independent Talent Group
Ltd (**L0496**)

L0262 Allison Devereux
Literary Agent
United States

Literary Agency: The Cheney Agency (**L0190**)

L0263 Cori Deyoe
Literary Agent
United States

cori@threeseaslit.com

https://www.threeseasagency.com/cori-deyoe
https://querymanager.com/query/Cori3Seas

Literary Agency: 3 Seas Literary Agency
(**L0001**)

ADULT > **Fiction** > *Novels*
  Mystery; Romance; Thrillers; Women's
  Fiction

CHILDREN'S > **Fiction**
  Middle Grade; Picture Books
YOUNG ADULT > **Fiction** > *Novels*

Send: Query; Synopsis; Writing sample; Pitch;
Market info
How to send: Query Manager

Actively looking to expand her list of clients.
She represents all sub-genres of romance,
women's fiction, young adult, middle grade,
picture books, thrillers, mysteries and select
non-fiction.

L0264 DHH Literary Agency Ltd
Literary Agency
23-27 Cecil Court, London, WC2N 4EZ
United Kingdom
Tel: +44 (0) 20 3990 2452

enquiries@dhhliteraryagency.com

http://www.dhhliteraryagency.com

Professional Body: The Association of
Authors' Agents (AAA)

ADULT
  Fiction > *Novels*
  Nonfiction > *Nonfiction Books*

CHILDREN'S > **Fiction** > *Novels*

YOUNG ADULT > **Fiction** > *Novels*

Send: Query
Don't send: Full text

Accepts submissions by email only. No postal
submissions. See website for specific agent
interests and email addresses and approach one
agent only. Do not send submissions to generic
"enquiries" email address.

Associate Agents: Emily Glenister (**L0400**);
Tom Drake Lee (**L0607**)

Authors: Kishan Devani BEM; Graham
Bartlett; Louise Beech; R.C. Bridgestock;
Caraline Brown; Paul Burston; Paul Fraser
Collard; M.W. Craven; Heather Darwent;
Becca Day; Suzie Edge; Rachael Featherstone;
David Fennell; J.D. Fennell; Fishlove; Essie
Fox; Anita Frank; Erin Green; Lisa Hilton;
Dixie Innes; Valerie Jack; Ragnar Jonasson;
Carys Jones; Katrín Júlíusdóttir; Diana
Kessler; Caroline Lamond; Robin Laurance;
S.V. Leonard; Jean Levy; Sean Lusk; Jo
Lyons; Adrian Magson; Brian McGilloway;
Janie Millman; Noel O'Reilly; Vikki Patis;
Reagan Lee Ray; Ane Riel; Talia Samuels;
Robert Scragg; Victoria Selman; Andrew
Swanston; Eleanor Tattersfield; Jo Thomas;
Bar Tozino; Ronnie Turner; L.C. Tyler;
Stephen Walker; Jon Watts; A. J. West; Clare
Whitfield; Kathleen Whyman; Mic Wright;
Eva Björg Ægisdottir

Literary Agent / Managing Director: David H.
Headley (**L0458**)

Literary Agents: Broo Doherty (*L0268*); Harry
Illingworth (*L0495*); Hannah Sheppard
(*L0907*)

L0265 Diamond Kahn and Woods (DKW) Literary Agency Ltd
Literary Agency
United Kingdom
Tel: +44 (0) 20 3514 6544

info@dkwlitagency.co.uk

http://dkwlitagency.co.uk

Professional Body: The Association of
Authors' Agents (AAA)

Types: Fiction; Nonfiction
Subjects: Adventure; Archaeology; Biography;
Comedy / Humour; Commercial;
Contemporary; Crime; Culture; Fantasy;
Gothic; History; Literary; Politics; Science
Fiction; Society; Suspense; Thrillers
Markets: Adult; Children's; Young Adult

Closed to approaches.

**Closed to submissions as at September 2019.
Check website for current status.**

Send submissions by email. See website for
specific agent interests and contact details. Do
not send submissions to general agency email
address.

Literary Agents: Ella Diamond Kahn (**L0543**);
Bryony Woods (**L1055**)

L0266 Elise Dillsworth
Literary Agent
United Kingdom

elise@elisedillsworthagency.com

https://www.davidhigham.co.uk/agents-dh/
elise-dillsworth/

Literary Agencies: Elise Dillsworth Agency
(EDA) (**L0300**); David Higham Associates Ltd
(**L0245**)

Fiction > *Novels*
  Commercial; International; Literary

Nonfiction > *Nonfiction Books*
  Commercial; International; Literary

Represents literary and commercial fiction and
nonfiction, with a keen aim to reflect writing
that is international.

L0267 Isobel Dixon
Literary Agent
United Kingdom

Literary Agency: Blake Friedmann Literary
Agency Ltd (**L0101**)

L0268 **Broo Doherty**
Literary Agent
United Kingdom

Literary Agency: DHH Literary Agency Ltd
(**L0264**)

L0269 **Trevor Dolby**
Literary Agent
United Kingdom

https://aevitascreative.com/agents/#agent-7410

Literary Agency: Aevitas Creative
Management (ACM) UK (**L0017**)

Nonfiction > *Nonfiction Books*
Biography; Comedy / Humour; Memoir;
Military History; Narrative History; Nature;
Popular Culture; Popular Science

Send: Query; Writing sample
How to send: Online submission system

Looking for popular science with a clear
relevance to everyday life, narrative history,
military history, humour, biography, popular
culture, natural history and great memoirs by
passionate people whose lives have been well
lived.

L0270 **Adriana Dominguez**
Literary Agent
United States

https://www.fullcircleliterary.com/our-agents/
adriana-dominguez/

Literary Agency: Full Circle Literary, LLC
(**L0371**)

L0271 **Don Buchwald and
Associates**
Literary Agency
United States

info@buchwald.com

https://www.buchwald.com
https://twitter.com/buchwaldtalent
https://www.facebook.com/buchwaldtalent
https://www.instagram.com/buchwaldtalent

Professional Body: Writers Guild of America
(WGA)

Scripts
Film Scripts; *TV Scripts*; *Theatre Scripts*

Closed to approaches.

Does not accept unsolicited submissions of any
kind.

L0272 **Donaghy Literary Group**
Literary Agency
United States

stacey@donaghyliterary.com

http://www.donaghyliterary.com

ADULT > **Fiction** > *Novels*

Fantasy; Historical Fantasy; Historical
Fiction; Mystery; Romance; Science Fiction;
Suspense; Thrillers; Women's Fiction

YOUNG ADULT > **Fiction** > *Novels*
Fantasy; Historical Fantasy; Historical
Fiction; Mystery; Romance; Science Fiction;
Suspense; Thrillers; Women's Fiction

Send: Query
How to send: Online submission system

See website for individual agent interests, and
submit using online submission system.

Literary Agents: Amanda Ayers Barnett;
Stacey Donaghy; Liis McKinstry; Sue Miller;
Valerie Noble; Susan Spann

L0273 **Donald Maass Literary
Agency**
Literary Agency
1000 Dean Street, Suite 252, Brooklyn, NY
11238
United States
Tel: +1 (212) 727-8383
Fax: +1 (212) 727-3271

info@maassagency.com

http://www.maassagency.com

Professional Body: Association of American
Literary Agents (AALA)

Types: Fiction
Subjects: Comedy / Humour; Commercial;
Crime; Fantasy; History; Horror; Literary;
Mystery; Romance; Science Fiction; Suspense;
Thrillers; Westerns; Women's Interests
Markets: Adult; Young Adult

Send: Query
Don't send: Full text
How to send: Email

Welcomes all genres, in particular science
fiction, fantasy, mystery, suspense, horror,
romance, historical, literary and mainstream
novels. Send query to a specific agent, by
email, with "query" in the subject line. No
queries by post. See website for individual
agent interests and email addresses.

Authors: Saladin Ahmed; Sonya Bateman; Jim
Butcher

Literary Agents: Katie Shea Boutillier (*L0113*);
Michael Curry (*L0232*); Jennifer Goloboy
(*L0404*); Jennifer Jackson (*L0510*); Kat Kerr
(*L0565*); Donald Maass (*L0652*); Cameron
McClure (*L0688*); Caitlin McDonald (*L0690*);
Kiana Nguyen (*L0748*); Paul Stevens; Anne
Tibbets (**L0981**)

L0274 **Priya Doraswamy**
Literary Agent
United States

Literary Agency: Lotus Lane Literary (**L0633**)

L0275 **Dorie Simmonds
Agency**
Literary Agency
United Kingdom
Tel: +44 (0) 20 7736 0002

info@doriesimmonds.com

https://doriesimmonds.com/

Professional Body: The Association of
Authors' Agents (AAA)

ADULT
Fiction > *Novels*: Commercial

Nonfiction > *Nonfiction Books*

CHILDREN'S > **Fiction** > *Novels*

Send: Query; Writing sample; Author bio
How to send: PDF file email attachment; Word
file email attachment

Send query by email as Word or PDF
attachments. Include details on your
background and relevant writing experience,
and first three chapters or fifty pages. See
website for full details.

Literary Agents: Pearl Baxter; Dorie
Simmonds (**L0918**)

L0276 **Claire Draper**
Literary Agent
United States

Literary Agency: The Bent Agency (**L0090**)

L0277 **Catherine Drayton**
Literary Agent
United States

Literary Agency: InkWell Management
(**L0499**)

L0278 **The Drummond Agency**
Literary Agency
PO Box 572, Woodend, Vic, 3442
Australia
Tel: +61 (0) 3 5427 3644

sheila@drummondagency.com.au

http://www.drummondagency.com.au

Professional Body: Australian Literary Agents'
Association (ALAA)

Types: Fiction; Nonfiction
Formats: Film Scripts; Radio Scripts; TV
Scripts; Theatre Scripts
Subjects: Adventure; Anthropology; Antiques;
Archaeology; Architecture; Arts;
Autobiography; Business; Comedy / Humour;
Commercial; Cookery; Crime; Culture;
Current Affairs; Design; Drama;
Entertainment; Finance; Gardening; Health;
History; Horror; How To; Legal; Leisure;
Lifestyle; Literary Criticism; Media; Medicine;
Men's Interests; Music; Mystery; Nature;
Personal Development; Philosophy;
Photography; Politics; Psychology; Romance;

Satire; Science; Society; Spirituality; Suspense; Technology; Travel; Warfare; Women's Interests
Markets: Academic; Adult; Children's; Professional; Young Adult

Closed to approaches.

Costs: Author covers sundry admin costs.

Closed to submissions as at January 2019. Check website for current status. A small personalised agency with contacts with all major houses and a good network of sub agents in most territories.

Authors: Randa Abdel-Fattah; Alexandra Alt; Meredith Appleyard; Kate Belle; Deborah Burrows; Liz Byrski; Anne Connor; Janita Cunnington; Neil Curtis; Catherine DeVrye; Barbara Gaskell Denvil; Jill Dobson; Cath Ferla; Lee Fox; Ian Gow; Joan Grant; Carmen Gray; Susan Green; Des Guilfoyle; Sue Gunningham; Nicholas Hasluck; GS Johnston; Chantal Kayem; Stuart Kells; Elizabeth Kleinhenz; Veronicah Larkin; David Lawrence; Wenn Lawson; Kathryn Ledson; Casey Lever; Dianne Maguire; Jo McGahey; Tom McGill; Wilson McOrist; KB Mcgavin; Margaret Merrilees; Jane Messer; David Middleton; Phillip Middleton; Marianne Musgrove; Margareta Osborn; Ida Di Pastena; Kate Richards; A D Scott; Tom Skinner; Jennifer Smart; Jurgen Tampke; Glenna Thomson; Vikki Wakefield; Yvette Walker; Felicity Young; Claire Zorn

Literary Agent: Sheila Drummond (*L0279*)

L0279 Sheila Drummond
Literary Agent
Australia

Literary Agency: The Drummond Agency (**L0278**)

L0280 Alec Drysdale
Literary Agent
United Kingdom

Literary Agency: Independent Talent Group Ltd (**L0496**)

L0281 Robert Dudley
Literary Agent
United Kingdom

Literary Agency: Robert Dudley Agency (**L0843**)

L0282 Del Duduit
Junior Agent; Author
United States

https://cyleyoung.com/literary-agent/my-team/

Literary Agency: Cyle Young Literary Elite (**L0236**)
Literary Agent / Author: Cyle Young (**L1062**)

Nonfiction > *Nonfiction Books*

Christian Living; Cookery; Health; Inspirational; Leadership; Leisure; Lifestyle; Motivational Self-Help; Sport; Travel

L0283 Dunham Literary, Inc.
Literary Agency
United States

query@dunhamlit.com

https://www.dunhamlit.com

ADULT
  Fiction > *Novels*

  Nonfiction > *Nonfiction Books*: Narrative Nonfiction

CHILDREN'S > **Fiction**
  Novels; *Picture Books*

Send: Query; Writing sample
Don't send: Full text
How to send: In the body of an email
How not to send: Post; Fax; Phone; Email attachment

Handles quality fiction and nonfiction for adults and children. Send query by email only. See website for full guidelines. No approaches by post, phone or fax. No email attachments.

Literary Agents: Jennie Dunham (**L0284**); Bridget Smith; Leslie Zampetti (**L1066**)

L0284 Jennie Dunham
Literary Agent
United States

https://www.dunhamlit.com/jennie-dunham.html
http://aaronline.org/Sys/PublicProfile/2176658/417813

Literary Agency: Dunham Literary, Inc. (**L0283**)
Professional Bodies: Association of American Literary Agents (AALA); Society of Children's Book Writers and Illustrators (SCBWI)

ADULT
  Fiction
    Graphic Novels: General
    Novels: Comedy / Humour; Historical Fiction; LGBTQIA; Literary; Mystery; Thrillers; Women's Fiction
  Nonfiction > *Nonfiction Books*
    Biography; Current Affairs; Family; History; Memoir; Narrative Nonfiction; Parenting; Politics; Relationships; Science; Technology

CHILDREN'S > **Fiction**
  Middle Grade; *Picture Books*
NEW ADULT
  Fiction > *Novels*
  Nonfiction > *Nonfiction Books*

YOUNG ADULT > **Fiction** > *Novels*

Send: Query; Writing sample
Don't send: Full text
How to send: In the body of an email

How not to send: Post; Fax; Phone; Email attachment

Represents literary fiction and non-fiction for adults and children.

L0285 David Dunton
Literary Agent
United States

Literary Agency: Harvey Klinger, Inc (**L0452**)

L0286 E. J. McCarthy Agency
Literary Agency
United States

ejmagency@gmail.com

https://twitter.com/ejmccarthy

Nonfiction > *Nonfiction Books*
  Biography; History; Memoir; Military History; Sport

Send: Query
How to send: Email

Literary agency from former executive editor with experience at some of the world's largest publishing houses, specialising in military history, politics, history, biography, memoir, media, public policy, and sports.

Literary Agent: E. J. McCarthy

L0287 Adam Eaglin
Literary Agent
United States

Literary Agency: The Cheney Agency (**L0190**)

L0288 Chelsea Eberly
Literary Agent
United States

https://www.greenhouseliterary.com/the-team/chelsea-eberly/
https://twitter.com/chelseberly
https://www.publishersmarketplace.com/members/ChelseaEberly/
https://querymanager.com/query/ChelseaEberly

Literary Agency: The Greenhouse Literary Agency (**L0420**)

ADULT > **Fiction** > *Novels*
  Book Club Women's Fiction; Upmarket Women's Fiction
CHILDREN'S
  Fiction
    Graphic Novels: General
    Middle Grade: Adventure; Comedy / Humour; Fantasy; Mystery
    Picture Books: General

  Nonfiction
    Nonfiction Books; *Picture Books*
YOUNG ADULT
  Fiction

Graphic Novels: Comedy / Humour;
Contemporary; Fantasy; Magical Realism;
Romance
Novels: Commercial; Fantasy; Feminism;
Literary; Mystery; Romance; Social
Justice; Thrillers
Nonfiction > *Graphic Nonfiction*
General, and in particular: History

Does not want:

> **CHILDREN'S** > **Fiction** > *Middle
> Grade*: Horror
> **YOUNG
> ADULT** > **Fiction** > *Novels*: Horror

Closed to approaches.

Represents authors of middle grade, young
adult, graphic novels, and women's fiction, as
well as illustrators who write picture books.
She is actively building her list.

L0289 Eddison Pearson Ltd
Literary Agency
West Hill House, 6 Swains Lane, London, N6
6QS
United Kingdom
Tel: +44 (0) 20 7700 7763

enquiries@eddisonpearson.com

https://www.eddisonpearson.com
https://eddisonpearson.tumblr.com/
https://www.linkedin.com/in/clare-pearson-
epla
https://twitter.com/ClarePearson_EP

Professional Body: The Association of
Authors' Agents (AAA)

CHILDREN'S
  Fiction
    Novels: Contemporary; Historical Fiction
    Picture Books: General

  Poetry > *Any Poetic Form*

YOUNG ADULT > **Fiction** > *Novels*

Send: Query; Writing sample
How to send: Email
How not to send: Social Media; Post

A London-based literary agency providing a
personal service to a small stable of talented
authors, mainly of books for children and
young adults. Send query by email only for
auto-response containing up-to-date
submission guidelines and email address for
submissions. No submissions or enquiries by
post.

Authors: Valerie Bloom; Michael Catchpool;
Sue Heap; Caroline Lawrence; Robert
Muchamore; Mary Murphy; Megan Rix

Literary Agent: Clare Pearson (*L0783*)

L0290 Edwards Fuglewicz
Literary Agency
49 Great Ormond Street, London, WC1N 3HZ

United Kingdom
Tel: +44 (0) 20 7405 6725

jill@efla.co.uk

Professional Body: The Association of
Authors' Agents (AAA)

Types: Fiction; Nonfiction
Subjects: Biography; Commercial; History;
Literary
Markets: Adult

Handles literary and commercial fiction, and
nonfiction. No children's, science fiction,
horror, or email submissions.

Literary Agents: Ros Edwards (*L0292*);
Helenka Fuglewicz (*L0370*)

L0291 Max Edwards
Literary Agent
United Kingdom

max@appletreeliterary.co.uk

https://aevitascreative.com/agents/#agent-7412
http://appletreeliterary.co.uk/about/

Literary Agencies: Apple Tree Literary Ltd
(**L0044**); Aevitas Creative Management
(ACM) UK (**L0017**)

Fiction > *Novels*
  Commercial; Crime; Fantasy; High Concept;
  Science Fiction

Nonfiction > *Nonfiction Books*
  Arts; Football / Soccer; Journalism; Science;
  Sport

Send: Author bio; Query; Writing sample;
Synopsis
How to send: Email; Online submission system

Looking for commercial and genre novels, and
is a fan of novels that mix genres in a unique
way. Keen on high concepts, smart plots and
unique characters – twists and turns, good (and
bad) guys with depth and life. Also looking for
great stories that can be told through
nonfiction; either unique or surprising takes on
a subject, or something wildly original. Would
like to hear from academics mixing the arts
and science in a new way, journalists wanting
to take their writing beyond the article, sports
writers with a new way of exploring what we
play (particularly football/soccer), or writers
with an untold history to tell.

L0292 Ros Edwards
Literary Agent
United Kingdom

Literary Agency: Edwards Fuglewicz (**L0290**)

L0293 Silé Edwards
Literary Agent
United Kingdom

sesubmissions@mushens-entertainment.com

https://www.mushens-entertainment.com/
submissions
https://twitter.com/sileloquies

Literary Agency: Mushens Entertainment
(**L0739**)

Fiction > *Novels*
  Crime Thrilllers; Romantic Comedy;
  Upmarket

Nonfiction > *Nonfiction Books*
  Cookery; Food

Closed to approaches.

Looking for books that inform our
understanding of the world, society and the
ways we live. Interested in a range of Non-
Fiction from emotive life writing to topical
essay-like writing to projects on cookery and
food. She is particularly keen on finding
experts in their field who want to write about
what they know in a way that everyone can
understand, appreciate and enjoy.

Also accepts fiction submissions. She is open
to all genres, but especially interested in crime
thrillers, romantic comedies, poetry and
upmarket fiction.

L0294 Einstein Literary
Management
Literary Agency
United States
Tel: +1 (212) 221-8797

submissions@einsteinliterary.com

https://www.einsteinliterary.com
https://twitter.com/Einstein_Lit

ADULT
  Fiction > *Novels*
    Commercial; Literary

  Nonfiction > *Nonfiction Books*
    Cookery; Memoir; Narrative Nonfiction

CHILDREN'S > **Fiction** > *Novels*

YOUNG ADULT > **Fiction** > *Novels*

Closed to approaches.

Send query by email with first ten double-
spaced pages pasted into the body of the email.
No attachments. See website for details of
individual agents and their interests and
include the name of specific agent you are
submitting to in the subject line. No poetry,
textbooks, or screenplays. No queries by post
or by phone. Response only if interested.

Literary Agents: Susanna Einstein (**L0295**);
Susan Graham (**L0410**); Shana Kelly

L0295 Susanna Einstein
Literary Agent
United States

https://www.einsteinliterary.com/staff/
http://aaronline.org/Sys/PublicProfile/4557347/
417813

Literary Agency: Einstein Literary Management (**L0294**)
Professional Body: Association of American Literary Agents (AALA)

ADULT
Fiction > *Novels*
Commercial Women's Fiction; Crime; Upmarket Women's Fiction

Nonfiction > *Nonfiction Books*: Narrative Nonfiction

CHILDREN'S > **Fiction** > *Middle Grade*

YOUNG ADULT > **Fiction** > *Novels*

Has a particular fondness for crime fiction, upmarket commercial women's fiction, MG and YA fiction, and narrative non-fiction. She likes a good story well told.

L0296 Naomi Eisenbeiss

Literary Agent
United States

http://www.inkwellmanagement.com/staff/naomi-eisenbeiss

Literary Agency: InkWell Management (**L0499**)

Fiction > *Novels*: Literary

Nonfiction > *Nonfiction Books*
Memoir; Narrative Nonfiction

L0297 Caroline Eisenmann

Senior Agent
United States

ce@goldinlit.com

https://goldinlit.com/agents/

Literary Agency: Frances Goldin Literary Agency, Inc. (**L0356**)
Professional Body: Association of American Literary Agents (AALA)

Fiction > *Novels*
Literary; Social Issues; Upmarket

Nonfiction
Essays: General
Nonfiction Books: Biography; Cultural Criticism; History; Literary Memoir; Sub-Culture

How to send: Email

Particularly drawn to novels that engage with social issues, stories about obsession, and work that centers around intimacy and its discontents. Her nonfiction interests include deeply reported narratives (especially those that take the reader into the heart of a subculture), literary memoir, cultural criticism, essay collections, and history and biography with a surprising point of view.

Authors: Kyle Chayka; Ye Chun; Linda Rui Feng; Amanda Goldblatt; James Gregor; Peter Kispert; Theresa Levitt; Micah Nemerever;

Jenny Odell; Kate Wagner; Michelle Webster-Hein

L0298 Rachel Ekstrom

Literary Agent
United States
Tel: +1 (212) 400-1494

rekstrom@foliolitmanagement.com
rachel@foliolit.com

https://www.publishersmarketplace.com/members/ekstrach/
http://www.twitter.com/ekstromrachel

Literary Agency: Folio Literary Management, LLC (**L0343**)

ADULT
Fiction > *Novels*
General, and in particular: Dystopian Fiction; Health; Historical Fiction; Lifestyle; Literary; Mind, Body, Spirit; Mystery; Speculative; Suspense; Thrillers; Upmarket

Nonfiction > *Nonfiction Books*
Animals; Mental Health; Nature; Parenting; Psychology; Social Issues

CHILDREN'S
Fiction > *Middle Grade*
Nonfiction > *Nonfiction Books*

YOUNG ADULT
Fiction > *Novels*
Nonfiction > *Nonfiction Books*

Does not want:

> **ADULT**
> **Fiction** > *Novels*
> Cozy Mysteries; Hard Science Fiction; High / Epic Fantasy; Political Thrillers; Romance; Supernatural / Paranormal; Urban Fantasy
>
> **Nonfiction** > *Nonfiction Books*: Memoir
>
> **CHILDREN'S** > **Fiction** > *Picture Books*

Send: Query; Writing sample
How to send: In the body of an email

L0299 Elaine Markson Literary Agency

Literary Agency
116 West 23rd Street, 5th flr, New York, NY 10011
United States

https://www.marksonagency.com

Fiction > *Novels*

Nonfiction > *Nonfiction Books*

Literary Agent: Jeff Gerecke (**L0390**)

L0300 Elise Dillsworth Agency (EDA)

Literary Agency
United Kingdom

submissions@elisedillsworthagency.com

http://elisedillsworthagency.com

Types: Fiction; Nonfiction
Subjects: Autobiography; Commercial; Cookery; Literary; Travel
Markets: Adult

Send: Query
Don't send: Full text

Represents writers from around the world. Looking for literary and commercial fiction, and nonfiction (especially memoir, autobiography, biography, cookery and travel writing). No science fiction, fantasy, poetry, film scripts, or plays. No young adult, or children's, except for existing authors. Send query by email only (postal submissions no longer accepted). For fiction, include synopsis up to two pages and first three chapters, up to about 50 pages, as Word or PDF attachments. For nonfiction, send details of expertise / credentials, proposal, chapter outline, and writing sample of around 30 pages as a Word file attachment. See website for full guidelines. Allow eight weeks for response.

Literary Agent: Elise Dillsworth (**L0266**)

L0301 Ethan Ellenberg

Literary Agent; President
United States

agent@ethanellenberg.com

https://ethanellenberg.com
http://aaronline.org/Sys/PublicProfile/2176663/417813

Literary Agency: Ethan Ellenberg Literary Agency (**L0308**)
Professional Body: Association of American Literary Agents (AALA)

ADULT
Fiction > *Novels*
Commercial; Romance

Nonfiction > *Nonfiction Books*

CHILDREN'S > **Fiction**
Novels; *Picture Books*

L0302 Humphrey Elles-Hill

Literary Agent
United Kingdom

Literary Agency: Independent Talent Group Ltd (**L0496**)

L0303 Tracey Elliston

Literary Agent
United Kingdom

Literary Agency: Judy Daish Associates Ltd (**L0536**)

L0304 Zabé Ellor

Literary Agent
United States

https://www.jdlit.com/zabe-ellor
https://querymanager.com/query/ZabeEllor
https://twitter.com/ZREllor

Literary Agency: The Jennifer DeChiara
Literary Agency

ADULT
  Fiction
    Graphic Novels: General
    Novels: Commercial; Fantasy; Mystery;
    Science Fiction; Thrillers; Upmarket
    Contemporary Fiction
  Nonfiction > *Nonfiction Books*
    History; Science

CHILDREN'S > **Fiction**
  Graphic Novels: General
  Middle Grade: Adventure; Comedy /
  Humour; Speculative
YOUNG ADULT > **Fiction**
  Graphic Novels: General
  Novels: General, and in
  particular: Contemporary; Fantasy; Mystery;
  Romance; Science Fiction; Thrillers

Closed to approaches.

For fiction, send a query, a 1-2 page synopsis,
and the first 25 pages of your project. For
nonfiction, send a query and a sample chapter.
For graphic novels, send a query with a link to
your portfolio website. I strive to respond to all
queries in 12-14 weeks.

L0305 Jessica Errera

Literary Agent
United States

https://www.janerotrosen.com/agents
https://www.janerotrosen.com/contact-jessica-
errera

Literary Agency: Jane Rotrosen Agency

ADULT > **Fiction** > *Novels*
  Commercial Women's Fiction;
  Contemporary Romance; Historical Fiction;
  Suspense; Thrillers

YOUNG ADULT > **Fiction** > *Novels*

Looking for commercial women's fiction with
a fresh and fun hook, all genres of YA
(especially diverse stories), contemporary
romance, thrillers and suspense, the occasional
historical fiction, and anything that might be
read in a day on the beach.

L0306 Gareth Esersky

Literary Agent
United States

gesersky@verizon.net

https://www.carolmannagency.com/gareth-
esersky

Literary Agency: Carol Mann Agency (**L0161**)

Nonfiction > *Nonfiction Books*
  Health; Jewish Culture; Literary; Memoir;
  Narrative Nonfiction; Nutrition; Parenting;
  Psychology; Spirituality

Send: Query; Author bio; Writing sample
How to send: In the body of an email

Represents nonfiction authors whose work falls
into the following categories: health, nutrition,
psychology, parenting, spirituality, Judaica,
and literary and narrative nonfiction and
memoir.

L0307 Felicia Eth

Literary Agent
United States

Literary Agency: Felicia Eth Literary
Representation (**L0324**)

L0308 Ethan Ellenberg Literary Agency

Literary Agency
United States

agent@ethanellenberg.com

https://ethanellenberg.com

Professional Bodies: Science Fiction and
Fantasy Writers of America (SFWA); Society
of Children's Book Writers and Illustrators
(SCBWI); Romance Writers of America
(RWA); Mystery Writers of America (MWA)

ADULT
  Fiction > *Novels*
    General, and in particular: Commercial;
    Ethnic; Fantasy; Literary; Mystery;
    Romance; Science Fiction; Thrillers;
    Women's Fiction

  Nonfiction > *Nonfiction Books*
    General, and in particular: Adventure;
    Biography; Cookery; Crime; Current
    Affairs; Health; History; Memoir; New
    Age; Popular Culture; Psychology;
    Science; Spirituality

CHILDREN'S > **Fiction** > *Novels*

Send: Query; Synopsis; Writing sample;
Proposal
How to send: In the body of an email

Send query by email (no attachments; paste
material into the body of the email). For fiction
send synopsis and first 50 pages. For
nonfiction send proposal, author bio, and
sample chapters. For picture books send
complete MS. No poetry, short stories, or
scripts.

We have been in business for over 17 years.
We are a member of the AAR. We accept
unsolicited submissions and, of course, do not
charge reading fees.

Author Estates: The Estate of Bertrice Small;
The Estate of Johnny Quarles

Authors: G.A. Aiken; Jay Allan; Carac Allison;
Amanda Ashley; Claire Avery; Madeline
Baker; Sarah Banks; Jon Bergeron; Patty
Blount; Pat Bowne; Robin Bridges; Leah
Marie Brown; James Cambias; Elaine
Coffman; MaryJanice Davidson; Delilah
Devlin; John Domagalski; Ian Douglas; Bill
Ferris; Candace Fleming; Whitney Gaskell;
Susan Grant; James Hider; Ben Hillman;
Marthe Jocelyn; Aer-ki Jyr; William H. Keith;
Kay Kenyon; Marko Kloos; Travis Langley;
Shelly Laurenston; Georgie Lee; Michael
Livingston; Kevin Luthardt; Gail Z. Martin; Lt.
Col. Matt Martin; Thersa Matsuura; John
McCormack; Karen Miller; Lucy Monroe;
Helen Myers; J. Madison Newsome; Andre
Norton; Christopher Nuttall; Mel Odoam;
Melissa F. Olson; Tim Owens; Cindy Spencer
Pape; Thomas Philpott; Steven Popkes; Paladin
Press; Riptide Publishing; Clay Reynolds;
Matthew Rivett; Eric Rohmann; Peter Sasgen;
Charles Sasser; John Scalzi; Eric Schnabel;
Sharon Shinn; Susan Sizemore; Oz Spies;
Ferret Steinmetz; James Tabor; Dennis E.
Taylor; Kimberly Kaye Terry; Kate Tietje;
Judd Trichter; Margaret Vellez; Wendy
Wagner; Christine Warren; Jennifer Wilde;
Edward Willett; Robert Wolke; Rebecca York

Literary Agent / President: Ethan Ellenberg
(**L0301**)

Literary Agents: Evan Gregory (**L0423**); Bibi
Lewis (**L0614**)

L0309 Nicole Etherington

Assistant Agent
United Kingdom

nicole@hardmanswainson.com
submissions@hardmanswainson.com

https://www.hardmanswainson.com/agent/
nicole-etherington/
https://twitter.com/thewelshnicole

Literary Agency: Hardman & Swainson
(**L0441**)

Fiction > *Novels*
  Book Club Fiction; Contemporary; Literary

Nonfiction > *Nonfiction Books*

Send: Query; Synopsis; Full text
How to send: Email

Tastes lean towards literary and bookclub
fiction. In terms of nonfiction, drawn to books
that make readers think or explore familiar
topics in interesting ways. No submissions to
personal email address.

L0310 Eunice McMullen Children's Literary Agent Ltd

Literary Agency
Low Ibbotsholme Cottage, Off Bridge Lane,
Troutbeck Bridge, Windermere, Cumbria,
LA23 1HU
United Kingdom
Tel: +44 (0) 1539 448551

eunice@eunicemcmullen.co.uk

http://www.eunicemcmullen.co.uk

CHILDREN'S > Fiction
Middle Grade; *Novels*; *Picture Books*
TEEN > Fiction > Novels

Send: Query; Synopsis; Writing sample; Full text
How to send: Email

Enquire by email, including details about yourself, the opening chapters and synopsis, or two or three full texts for picture books. All types of material for children, particularly for those 9 and over. Strong list of authors and illustrators of picture books.

L0311 The Evan Marshall Agency

Literary Agency
1 Pacio Court, Roseland, NJ 07068-1121
United States
Tel: +1 (973) 287-6216

evan@evanmarshallagency.com

https://www.evanmarshallagency.com

Professional Body: Association of American Literary Agents (AALA)

Types: Fiction; Nonfiction
Markets: Adult; Young Adult

Send: Query
Don't send: Full text

Represents all genres of adult and young-adult full-length fiction. New clients by referral only.

Literary Agent: Evan Marshall (*L0675*)

L0312 Ann Evans

Literary Agent
United Kingdom

Literary Agency: Jonathan Clowes Ltd (**L0529**)

L0313 David Evans

Assistant Agent
United Kingdom

davidevans@davidhigham.co.uk

https://www.davidhigham.co.uk/agents-dh/david-evans/

Literary Agency: David Higham Associates Ltd (**L0245**)
Literary Agent: Andrew Gordon

ACADEMIC > Nonfiction > Nonfiction Books

ADULT
Fiction
Novels: Literary
Short Fiction: Literary

Nonfiction > Nonfiction Books
Culture; History; Journalism; Nature; Philosophy; Politics; Science

How to send: Email

Looking for literary fiction of style and ambition. He admires novelists who create memorable and unsettling voices, and short story writers with a keen sense of the poetic and absurd. In non-fiction, he enjoys projects of rigour, clarity and passion that can make small ideas radiate and big ideas graspable. He is particularly looking for works of academic research or journalistic investigation written for a wide readership, across areas such as culture, philosophy, politics, history, science, nature.

L0314 Stephany Evans

Literary Agent
United States

https://www.pandeliterary.com/about-pandeliterary
https://twitter.com/firerooster
http://aaronline.org/Sys/PublicProfile/2176670/417813

Literary Agency: Ayesha Pande Literary (**L0052**)
Professional Bodies: Association of American Literary Agents (AALA); Romance Writers of America (RWA); Mystery Writers of America (MWA); The Agents Round Table (ART)

Fiction > Novels
Commercial; Crime; Literary; Mystery; Romance; Thrillers; Upmarket Women's Fiction; Women's Fiction

Nonfiction > Nonfiction Books
Fitness; Food and Drink; Health; Lifestyle; Memoir; Narrative Nonfiction; Running; Spirituality; Sustainable Living; Wellbeing

Send: Pitch; Author bio; Synopsis; Writing sample
How to send: Online submission system

L0315 Lisa Eveleigh

Literary Agent
United Kingdom

Literary Agency: Richford Becklow Literary Agency (**L0833**)

L0316 Samantha Fabien

Literary Agent
United States

http://twitter.com/samanthashnh
http://aaronline.org/Sys/PublicProfile/48927898/417813
https://querymanager.com/query/samanthafabien

Professional Body: Association of American Literary Agents (AALA)

ADULT > Fiction
Graphic Novels: General
Novels: Book Club Fiction; Commercial; Fantasy; High Concept; Historical Fiction; Horror; Mystery; Psychological Thrillers;

Romantic Comedy; Speculative; Suspense; Thrillers; Upmarket Women's Fiction
CHILDREN'S > Fiction
Graphic Novels: General
Middle Grade: Contemporary; Grounded Fantasy; Horror; Mystery; Romance; Romantic Comedy; Speculative; Suspense; Thrillers
YOUNG ADULT > Fiction
Graphic Novels: General
Novels: Contemporary; Grounded Fantasy; Horror; Mystery; Romance; Romantic Comedy; Speculative; Suspense; Thrillers

Closed to approaches.

Across genres, I'm looking for high-concept, commercial fiction for adults and children that feature diverse, marginalized, and/or underrepresented voices with all-or-nothing stakes.

L0317 Fairbank Literary Representation

Literary Agency
P.O. Box 6, Hudson, NY 12534
United States
Tel: +1 (617) 576-0030

queries@fairbankliterary.com

https://fairbankliterary.com
https://www.publishersmarketplace.com/members/SorcheFairbank/
http://www.twitter.com/FairbankLit

ADULT
Fiction > Novels
International; Literary

Nonfiction
Gift Books: General
Nonfiction Books: Comedy / Humour; Crafts; Design; Food; Lifestyle; Memoir; Narrative Nonfiction; Popular Culture; Wine
CHILDREN'S > Fiction
Middle Grade; *Picture Books*

Send: Query; Writing sample
How to send: In the body of an email; Online contact form; Post
How not to send: Email attachment; Phone

Clients range from first-time authors to international best-sellers, prize winning-journalists to professionals at the top of their fields. Tastes tend toward literary and international fiction; voice-y novels with a strong sense of place; big memoir that goes beyond the me-moir; topical or narrative nonfiction with a strong interest in women's voices, global perspectives, and class and race issues; children's picture books & middle grade from illustrator/artists only; quality lifestyle books (food, wine, and design); pop culture; craft; and gift and humor books. Most likely to pick up works that are of social or cultural significance, newsworthy

Literary Agent: Sorche Elizabeth Fairbank

L0318 Delia Berrigan Fakis

Literary Agent
United States

Delia@MartinLit.com

http://www.martinliterarymanagement.com
https://twitter.com/PrimarilyProse

Literary Agency: Martin Literary Management

ADULT

Fiction > *Novels*
Commercial; Literary; Mystery

Nonfiction > *Nonfiction Books*
Business; Crime; Current Affairs; History;
Leadership; Memoir; Narrative Nonfiction;
Religion; Spirituality

CHILDREN'S > **Fiction** > *Picture Books*

Send: Query
How to send: Email

Most interested in representing adult
nonfiction, but will also consider select fiction
and children's picture books.

L0319 Holly Faulks

Literary Agent
United Kingdom

http://greeneheaton.co.uk/agents/holly-faulks/
https://twitter.com/hollycfaulks

Literary Agency: Greene & Heaton Ltd
(**L0419**)

Fiction > *Novels*
Literary; Upmarket Commercial Fiction

Nonfiction > *Nonfiction Books*
Current Affairs; Language; Lifestyle;
Memoir; Popular Science

Send: Synopsis; Writing sample
How to send: Email

Authors: Joseph Coward; Emma Garland; Lily
Hackett; Kit Heyam; Juliet Jacques; Iggy
LDN; Sara-Ella Ozbek; Jyoti Patel; Julie
Reverb; Ella Frances Sanders

L0320 Ariella Feiner

Literary Agent
United Kingdom

afeiner@unitedagents.co.uk

https://www.unitedagents.co.uk/
afeinerunitedagentscouk
https://twitter.com/ariellafeiner

Literary Agency: United Agents (**L0992**)

Fiction > *Novels*
Book Club Fiction; Crime; High Concept;
Historical Fiction; Thrillers

Nonfiction > *Nonfiction Books*
Cookery; Memoir

Send: Synopsis; Writing sample; Proposal
How to send: Email

Always open to submissions. In fiction, would
like to see crime and thrillers, issue-led books,
plot-driven stories, reading group books, high-
concept tales, a great elevator pitch, novels
with strong female characters, and historical
fiction with a twist. In nonfiction, is interested
in topics which feel untouched before now or
are inspiring, expert-led ideas, mouth-watering
cook books, narrative memoir, and
empowering female tales.

Authors: Francesca Armour-Chelu; Holly Bell;
Nargisse Benkabbou; Vicky Bennison; Mark
Bostridge; Robert Bryndza; Beth Cartwright;
Jane Casey; Alice Clark-Platts; John
Coldstream; Elle Croft; Laura Dockrill; Mike
Gayle; Paul Grzegorzek; Olia Hercules; Mina
Holland; Laura Jarratt; Lora Jones; Dean
Lomax; Emily Midorikawa; Robert Nicholls;
Selina Periampillai; Sarah Peverley; Natasha
Preston; Jane Riley; Nick Spalding; Danny
Wallace; Lucy Watson; Julie Welch; Kate
Williams; Louisa Young

L0321 The Feldstein Agency

*Literary Agency; Editorial Service;
Consultancy*
54 Abbey Street, Bangor, Northern Ireland,
BT20 4JB
United Kingdom
Tel: +44 (0) 2891 312485

submissions@thefeldsteinagency.co.uk

https://www.thefeldsteinagency.co.uk
https://twitter.com/feldsteinagency

Fiction > *Novels*

Nonfiction > *Nonfiction Books*

Does not want:

> **Fiction** > *Novels*
> Fantasy; Historical Fiction; Romance;
> Science Fiction

Send: Query; Synopsis; Author bio
How to send: Email

Costs: Offers services that writers have to pay
for. Offers editing, ghostwriting, and
consultancy services.

Handles adult fiction and nonfiction only. No
children's, young adult, romance, science
fiction, fantasy, poetry, scripts, or short stories.
Send query by email with 1-2 pages synopsis.
No reading fees or evaluation fees. The only
instance in which an author would be charged
a fee is for ghost-writing.

Consultant / Literary Agent: Paul Feldstein
(**L0322**)

Editor / Literary Agent: Susan Feldstein
(**L0323**)

L0322 Paul Feldstein

Literary Agent; Consultant
United Kingdom

paul@thefeldsteinagency.co.uk

*Literary Agency / Editorial Service /
Consultancy*: The Feldstein Agency (**L0321**)

L0323 Susan Feldstein

Literary Agent; Editor
United Kingdom

susan@thefeldsteinagency.co.uk

http://www.susanfeldstein.co.uk

*Literary Agency / Editorial Service /
Consultancy*: The Feldstein Agency (**L0321**)

L0324 Felicia Eth Literary Representation

Literary Agency
555 Bryant Street, Suite 350, Palo Alto, CA
94301
United States

feliciaeth.literary@gmail.com

https://ethliterary.com

Professional Body: Association of American
Literary Agents (AALA)

Types: Fiction; Nonfiction
Formats: Short Fiction
Subjects: Business; Cookery; Culture; History;
Lifestyle; Literary; Literature; Psychology;
Science; Sport; Suspense; Travel; Women's
Interests
Markets: Adult; Young Adult

Send: Query
Don't send: Full text
How to send: Email

Costs: Author covers sundry admin costs.

Send query by email or by post with SASE,
including details about yourself and your
project. Send sample pages upon invitation
only.

Literary Agent: Felicia Eth (*L0307*)

L0325 Felicity Bryan Associates

Literary Agency
2a North Parade Avenue, Banbury Road,
Oxford, OX2 6LX
United Kingdom
Tel: +44 (0) 1865 513816

submissions@felicitybryan.com

https://felicitybryan.com

Professional Body: The Association of
Authors' Agents (AAA)

Fiction > *Novels*
Book Club Fiction; Literary

Nonfiction > *Nonfiction Books*: Upmarket

Send: Query; Synopsis; Proposal; Writing
sample
How to send: Online submission system

Looking for accessible, upmarket non-fiction, written by an author with clear and demonstrable expertise (in practice, this means many years of professional work or PhD level study within the topic), and exciting, original 'bookclub' and literary debut fiction, particularly from underrepresented writers.

Author: Amy Key

Literary Agent: Angelique Tran Van Sang (**L0881**)

L0326 Felix de Wolfe

Literary Agency
20 Old Compton Street, London, W1D 4TW
United Kingdom
Tel: +44 (0) 20 7242 5066
Fax: +44 (0) 20 7242 8119

info@felixdewolfe.com

http://www.felixdewolfe.com

Types: Fiction; Scripts
Formats: Film Scripts; Radio Scripts; TV Scripts; Theatre Scripts
Markets: Adult

Send: Query
Don't send: Full text
How not to send: Email

Send query letter with SAE, short synopsis, and CV by post only, unless alternative arrangements have been made with the agency in advance. Quality fiction and scripts only. No nonfiction, children's books, or unsolicited MSS.

Authors: Kris Akabussi; Aileen Gonsalves; Bill MacIlwraith; Paul Todd

Literary Agents: Wendy Scozzaro (*L0898*); Caroline de Wolfe (*L1053*)

L0327 Hannah Ferguson

Literary Agent
United Kingdom

hannah@hardmanswainson.com
submissions@hardmanswainson.com

https://www.hardmanswainson.com/agent/hannah-ferguson/
https://twitter.com/AgentFergie

Literary Agency: Hardman & Swainson (**L0441**)

Fiction > *Novels*
  General, and in particular: Book Club Fiction; Commercial; Crime; Literary; Thrillers; Women's Fiction

Nonfiction > *Nonfiction Books*: Narrative Nonfiction

Send: Query; Synopsis; Full text
How to send: Email

Represents women's fiction, from the more literary to the very commercial. Likes book club reads that really capture a reader's attention or heart. Always on the lookout for

great crime and thrillers and interesting non-fiction.

L0328 T.S. Ferguson

Literary Agent
United States

http://www.azantianlitagency.com/pages/team-tf.html
https://querymanager.com/query/TSFerguson

Literary Agency: Azantian Literary Agency (**L0054**)

CHILDREN'S > **Fiction**
  Graphic Novels: General
  Middle Grade: General, and in particular: Adventure; Dark; Fairy Tales; Folklore, Myths, and Legends; High Concept; Horror; LGBTQIA
YOUNG ADULT > **Fiction**
  Graphic Novels: General
  Novels: General, and in particular: Adventure; Dark; Fairy Tales; Folklore, Myths, and Legends; High Concept; Horror; LGBTQIA

Does not want:

> **CHILDREN'S** > **Fiction** > *Middle Grade*
>   Hard Science Fiction; Sport
>
> **YOUNG ADULT** > **Fiction** > *Novels*
>   Hard Science Fiction; Sport

How to send: Query Manager

Looking for young adult and middle grade fiction across all genres that combines high-concept, hooky stories with writing and voice that feel standout. An addicting, page-turning quality is always a plus! He has a special place in his heart for dark and edgy stories (including but not limited to horror), fairy tales, mythology, action-adventure, LGBTQ stories, graphic novels, and stories by and about under-represented voices. He is not the best fit for sports-centric stories, high sci-fi, or non-fiction.

L0329 Julie Fergusson

Literary Agent
United Kingdom

http://thenorthlitagency.com/our-friends-in-the-north/
https://twitter.com/julie_fergusson

Literary Agency: The North Literary Agency (**L0755**)

Fiction > *Novels*
  Book Club Fiction; Domestic Suspense; Literary; Psychological Thrillers; Romantic Comedy; Speculative

Nonfiction > *Nonfiction Books*
  Popular Science; Social Justice

Closed to approaches.

Looking for fiction across a range of genres, particularly psychological thrillers, domestic suspense, near-future speculative, romcoms, reading group and literary fiction. She is interested in nonfiction that explores big ideas in the areas of popular science and social justice.

L0330 Fillingham Weston Associates

Literary Agency
20 Mortlake High Street, London, SW14 8JN
United Kingdom
Tel: +44 (0) 20 8748 5594

info@fillinghamweston.com
submissions@fillinghamweston.com

https://www.fillinghamweston.com
https://www.facebook.com/Fillingham-Weston-Associates-117304691662209
https://twitter.com/fwa_litagency
https://www.instagram.com/fillinghamwestonassociates/

ADULT > **Scripts**
  Film Scripts; *TV Scripts*; *Theatre Scripts*
CHILDREN'S > **Scripts**
  Film Scripts; *TV Scripts*; *Theatre Scripts*
YOUNG ADULT > **Scripts**
  Film Scripts; *TV Scripts*; *Theatre Scripts*

Send: Query; Author bio
How to send: Email

Represents writers and directors for stage, film and TV, as well as librettists, lyricists and composers in musical theatre. Does not represent books. See website for full submission guidelines.

Literary Agents: Janet Fillingham (*L0331*); Kate Weston (*L1028*)

L0331 Janet Fillingham

Literary Agent
United Kingdom

Literary Agency: Fillingham Weston Associates (**L0330**)

L0332 Film Rights Ltd in association with Laurence Fitch Ltd

Literary Agency
11 Pandora Road, London, NW6 1TS
United Kingdom
Tel: +44 (0) 20 8001 3040
Fax: +44 (0) 20 8711 3171

information@filmrights.ltd.uk

http://filmrights.ltd.uk

Types: Fiction; Scripts
Formats: Film Scripts; Radio Scripts; TV Scripts; Theatre Scripts
Subjects: Horror
Markets: Adult; Children's

Represents films, plays, and novels, for adults and children.

L0333 Alison Finch
Literary Agent
United Kingdom

Literary Agency: JFL Agency (**L0524**)

L0334 Stevie Finegan
Junior Agent
United Kingdom

finegan@zenoagency.com

http://zenoagency.com/news/stevie-finegan/
https://twitter.com/StevieFinegan

Literary Agency: Zeno Agency Ltd (**L1067**)

ADULT
Fiction
Graphic Novels: Feminism; LGBTQIA
Novels: High / Epic Fantasy; Soft Science Fiction
Nonfiction > *Nonfiction Books*
Feminism; Mental Health; Politics; Social Issues

CHILDREN'S > **Fiction**
Early Readers; *Middle Grade*; *Picture Books*

Closed to approaches.

Authors: Alice Bell; Mário Coelho; Craig Laurance Gidney; J.T. Greathouse; Anna McNuff; Adam Oyebanji; Farrah Riaz; Katherine Toran; R.R. Virdi; Angus Watson; Gary Wigglesworth; Jasmine Wigham; Yudhanjaya Wijeratne

L0335 Emma Finn
Literary Agent
United Kingdom

Literary Agency: C+W (Conville & Walsh) (**L0147**)

L0336 Karyn Fischer
Literary Agent
United States

http://www.bookstopliterary.com/submission.html
https://querymanager.com/query/KarynFischer

Literary Agency: BookStop Literary Agency, LLC (**L0111**)

CHILDREN'S > **Fiction** > *Middle Grade*
General, and in particular: Contemporary; Dark; Fantasy; Gothic; Historical Fiction; Literary Thrillers

YOUNG ADULT > **Fiction** > *Novels*
General, and in particular: Contemporary; Dark; Fantasy; Gothic; Historical Fiction; Literary Thrillers

Closed to approaches.

Particularly drawn to young adult and middle grade novels. Her favorite genres include gothic novels with twisty narratives and dark

secrets, historical fiction, literary thrillers, well-drawn fantasy, and heart-tugging contemporary stories. She's looking for anything with memorable characters, an engaging voice, and a tightrope-taut plot.

L0337 Kara Fitzpatrick
Literary Agent
United Kingdom

Literary Agency: Alan Brodie Representation Ltd (**L0022**)

L0338 Flannery Literary
Literary Agency
United States

jennifer@flanneryliterary.com

https://flanneryliterary.com

CHILDREN'S
Fiction
Novels; *Picture Books*
Nonfiction > *Nonfiction Books*

YOUNG ADULT
Fiction > *Novels*
Nonfiction > *Nonfiction Books*

Send: Query; Writing sample; Full text
How to send: Email
How not to send: Email attachment

Send query by email, with the word "Query" in the subject line. Include first 5-10 pages of your novel or full picture book text. Deals exclusively in children's and young adults' fiction and nonfiction, including picture books. See website for full guidelines.

Literary Agent: Jennifer Flannery

L0339 Caitie Flum
Literary Agent
United States

Literary Agency: Liza Dawson Associates (**L0625**)

L0340 Jacqueline Flynn
Literary Agent
United States

Literary Agency: Joelle Delbourgo Associates, Inc. (**L0527**)

L0341 Katherine Flynn
Literary Agent
United States

Literary Agency: Kneerim & Williams (**L0575**)

L0342 Folio Jr.
Literary Agency
United States

https://www.foliojr.com
https://twitter.com/FolioJr
https://www.instagram.com/foliojr/
https://www.facebook.com/FolioJr/

Literary Agency: Folio Literary Management, LLC (**L0343**)

Literary Agent / Vice President: John Cusick (**L0235**)

L0343 Folio Literary Management, LLC
Literary Agency
630 9th Avenue, Suite 1101, New York, NY 10036
United States
Tel: +1 (212) 400-1494
Fax: +1 (212) 967-0977

http://www.foliolit.com
https://www.facebook.com/folio.literary
https://twitter.com/FolioLiterary

Fiction > *Novels*
Commercial; Literary; Upmarket

Nonfiction > *Nonfiction Books*
Memoir; Narrative Nonfiction

Read agent bios on website and decide which agent to approach. Do not submit to multiple agents simultaneously. Each agent has different submission requirements: consult website for details. No unsolicited MSS or multiple submissions.

Affiliated Agents: Ruth Pomerance (**L0806**); Jeff Silberman (**L0914**)

Authors: Kareem Abdul-Jabbar; Dan Abrams; Gregg Allman; George Anastasia; Mario Andretti; Michael Baden; Joe Bonanno; Terry Bradshaw; Charles Brandt; Christi Clancy; John "Chick" Donohue; John Douglas; Lexie Elliott; Tamer Elnoury; Rickson Gracie; John Gray; Homer Hickam; Jacqueline Kelly; Harry Markopolos; Kevin Maurer; Mark Olshaker; Joe Pistone; Laura Prepon; Sheri Reynolds; Bill Russell; Christine Sneed

Literary Agencies: Folio Jr. (**L0342**); Harold Ober Associates, Inc. (**L0445**)

Literary Agents: Jan Baumer (**L0074**); Jamie Chambliss (**L0181**); Sonali Chanchani (**L0182**); Dado Derviskadic (**L0260**); Rachel Ekstrom (**L0298**); Michael Harriot (**L0446**); Melissa White (**L1031**)

Literary Agents / Partners: Emily Van Beek (**L0079**); Claudia Cross (**L0228**); Scott Hoffman (**L0476**); Jeff Kleinman (**L0573**); Steve Troha (**L0987**); Frank Weimann (**L1022**)

Literary Agents / Senior Vice Presidents: Erin Niumata (**L0751**); Marcy Posner (**L0809**)

Literary Agents / Vice Presidents: John Cusick (**L0235**); Erin Harris (**L0447**); Katherine Latshaw (**L0597**)

L0344 A for Authors
Literary Agency
73 Hurlingham Road, Bexleyheath, Kent, DA7 5PE

United Kingdom
Tel: +44 (0) 1322 463479

enquiries@aforauthors.co.uk

http://aforauthors.co.uk

Fiction > *Novels*
  Commercial; Literary

Closed to approaches.

Query by email only. Include synopsis and first three chapters (or up to 50 pages) and short author bio. All attachments must be Word format documents. No poetry, fantasy, SF, horror, erotica, or short stories. No submissions by post or by downloadable link.

Literary Agents: Annette Crossland; Bill Goodall

L0345 Emily Forland
Literary Agent
United States

eforland@bromasite.com

Literary Agency: Brandt & Hochman Literary Agents, Inc. (**L0119**)
Professional Body: Association of American Literary Agents (AALA)

ADULT
  Fiction
    Graphic Novels: General
    Novels: Comedy / Humour; Literary
  Nonfiction > *Nonfiction Books*
    General, and in particular: Biography; Cultural Criticism; Food; History; Memoir; Narrative Nonfiction

YOUNG ADULT > **Fiction** > *Novels*

Send: Query
How to send: Email

L0346 David Forrer
Literary Agent
United States

Literary Agency: InkWell Management (**L0499**)

L0347 Jemima Forrester
Literary Agent
United Kingdom

jemimaforrester@davidhigham.co.uk

https://www.davidhigham.co.uk/agents-dh/jemima-forrester/

Literary Agency: David Higham Associates Ltd (**L0245**)

Fiction > *Novels*
  Commercial; Crime; Feminism; High Concept; Historical Fiction; Literary; Psychological Suspense; Speculative; Thrillers; Upmarket; Women's Fiction

Nonfiction > *Nonfiction Books*
  Comedy / Humour; Cookery; Feminism; Lifestyle; Popular Culture

Send: Query; Synopsis; Writing sample
How to send: Email

Authors: Tessa Bickers; Lauren Bravo; Rob Burnett; Seerut K. Chawla; Lizzie Daykin; Sarah Daykin; Jessica George; Sarah J. Harris; Deborah Hewitt; Alex Hutchinson; Beth Lewis; Richard Lumsden; Deborah O'Donoghue; Alison Percival; Christina Pishiris; Tasha Silva; Michael Stewart; Rose Stokes; Sureka Thanenthiran-Dharuman; Adam Zmith

L0348 Clare Forster
Literary Agent
Australia

Literary Agency: Curtis Brown (Australia) Pty Ltd (**L0234**)

L0349 Roz Foster
Literary Agent
United States

Literary Agency: Frances Goldin Literary Agency, Inc. (**L0356**)

Fiction > *Novels*
  Commercial; Contemporary; Historical Fantasy; Historical Fiction; Literary; Multicultural; Science Fiction; Speculative; Upmarket

Nonfiction > *Nonfiction Books*
  Current Affairs; Design; History; Memoir; Politics; Science; Technology

L0350 Ben Fowler
Literary Agent
United Kingdom

ben@abnerstein.co.uk

Literary Agency: Abner Stein (**L0005**)

L0351 Fox & Howard Literary Agency
Literary Agency
39 Eland Road, London, SW11 5JX
United Kingdom
Tel: +44 (0) 20 7223 9452

enquiries@foxandhoward.co.uk

http://www.foxandhoward.co.uk

Professional Body: The Association of Authors' Agents (AAA)

Types: Nonfiction
Formats: Reference
Subjects: Biography; Business; Culture; Health; History; Lifestyle; Personal Development; Psychology; Spirituality
Markets: Adult

Closed to approaches.

Closed to submissions as at June 2019. Please check website for current status. Send query with synopsis and SAE for response. Small agency specialising in nonfiction that

works closely with its authors. No unsolicited MSS.

Literary Agents: Chelsey Fox (*L0352*); Charlotte Howard (*L0486*)

L0352 Chelsey Fox
Literary Agent
United Kingdom

Literary Agency: Fox & Howard Literary Agency (**L0351**)

L0353 Gráinne Fox
Literary Agent
United States

Literary Agency: Fletcher & Company

L0354 FRA (Futerman, Rose, & Associates)
Literary Agency
91 St Leonards Road, London, SW14 7BL
United Kingdom
Tel: +44 (0) 20 8255 7755

guy@futermanrose.co.uk

http://www.futermanrose.co.uk

Professional Body: The Association of Authors' Agents (AAA)

Nonfiction > *Nonfiction Books*
  General, and in particular: Entertainment; Media; Music; Politics; Sports Celebrity

Scripts
  Film Scripts; TV Scripts

Send: Query
Don't send: Full text
How to send: Email

Handles nonfiction on practically any subject, but particularly interested in politics, sport, show business and the music industry. Also handles scripts for film and television. No educational textbooks.

For nonfiction, send proposal including chapter breakdown, two or three sample chapters, and any relevant biographical detail.

For scripts, send sample episode or section of the script.

Accepts submissions by post (include SAE of return of work required) or by email with attachments.

See website for full guidelines.

Not currently accepting film and TV scripts.

Authors: Jill Anderson; Larry Barker; Nick Battle; Christian Piers Betley; Tracey Cheetham; Chengde Chen; Kevin Clarke; Lesley Crewe; Richard Digance; Peter Dobbie; Bobby Elliott; Paul Ferris; John French; Susan George; Keith Gillespie; Stephen Griffin; Paul Hendy; Terry Ilott; Sara Khan; Jerry Leider; Sue Lenier; Keith R. Lindsay; Stephen Lowe; Eric MacInnes; Paul Marsden; Paul Marx;

Tony McAndrew; Tony McMahon; Sir Vartan Melkonian; Michael Misick; Max Morgan-Witts; Sir Derek Morris; Peter Murphy; Judge Chris Nicholson; Antonia Owen; Tom Owen; Mary O'Hara; Ciarán O'Keeffe; Miriam O'Reilly; Zoe Paphitis; Liz Rettig; Kenneth G. Ross; Robin Callender Smith; Rt. Hon Iain Duncan Smith; Paul Stinchcombe; Felicity Fair Thompson; Bill Tidy; Mark White; Toyah Willcox; Simon Woodham; Tappy Wright; Allen Zeleski

Literary Agents: James Jacob; Guy Rose (*L0857*)

L0355 Frances Collin Literary Agent

Literary Agency
PO Box 33, Wayne, PA 19087-0033
United States
Tel: +1 (610) 254-0555
Fax: +1 (610) 254-5029

queries@francescollin.com

http://www.francescollin.com

Professional Body: Association of American Literary Agents (AALA)

Types: Fiction; Nonfiction
Subjects: Autobiography; Culture; Fantasy; History; Literary; Nature; Science Fiction; Travel; Women's Interests
Markets: Adult

Closed to approaches.

Send query by email (no attachments) or by post with SASE, or IRCs if outside the US. No queries by phone or fax.

Literary Agent: Frances Collin (*L0210*)

L0356 Frances Goldin Literary Agency, Inc.

Literary Agency
214 W 29th St., Suite 1006, New York, NY 10001
United States

agency@goldinlit.com

http://www.goldinlit.com

Professional Body: Association of American Literary Agents (AALA)

Types: Fiction; Nonfiction; Poetry; Translations
Formats: Film Scripts
Subjects: Arts; Autobiography; Commercial; Crime; Culture; Current Affairs; Entertainment; History; Legal; Literary; Nature; Philosophy; Politics; Science; Society; Sport; Technology; Thrillers; Travel
Markets: Adult; Children's; Young Adult

Send: Query
Don't send: Full text
How to send: Email

Submit to one agent only. See website for specific agent interests and preferred method of approach. No screenplays, romances (or most other genre fiction), and only rarely poetry. No work that is racist, sexist, ageist, homophobic, or pornographic.

Associate Agents: Sulamita Garbuz (**L0381**); Jade Wong-Baxter (**L1054**)

Authors: Susan Bordo; Monica Byrne; Mandy Catron; Pratap Chatterjee; David Cole; Cliff Conner; Dessa; Ray Douglas; Mark Edmundson; Shelley Fisher Fishkin; Bruce Grierson; Michael Hudson; Lynn Hunt; Margaret Jacob; Steven Jaffe; Barbara Kingsolver; Michelle Kuo; Anna Lappé; Daniel Medwed; Stephanie Mencimer; Rutu Modan; Alexandra Natapoff; Carla Peterson; Sam Polk; Janisse Ray; Gretchen Reynolds; Siva Vaidhyanathan; Mike Wallace; Helene Wecker

Literary Agents: Roz Foster (**L0349**); Frances Goldin; Ria Julien (**L0539**)

President / Senior Agent: Sam Stoloff (**L0946**)

Senior Agent: Caroline Eisenmann (**L0297**)

Senior Agents / Vice Presidents: Ellen Geiger (**L0384**); Matt McGowan (**L0693**)

L0357 Frances Kelly Agency

Literary Agency
111 Clifton Road, Kingston upon Thames, Surrey, KT2 6PL
United Kingdom
Tel: +44 (0) 20 8549 7830

Professional Body: The Association of Authors' Agents (AAA)

ACADEMIC > **Nonfiction**
 Nonfiction Books; *Reference*
ADULT > **Nonfiction**
 Nonfiction Books; *Reference*
PROFESSIONAL > **Nonfiction**
 Nonfiction Books; *Reference*

Send: Query; Synopsis; Author bio; Self-Addressed Stamped Envelope (SASE)
Don't send: Full text
How to send: Post

Send query with SAE, CV, and synopsis or brief description of work. Scripts handled for existing clients only. No unsolicited MSS.

Literary Agent: Frances Kelly

L0358 Will Francis

Literary Agent
United Kingdom

http://www.janklowandnesbit.co.uk/people/will-francis
https://twitter.com/zcosini

Literary Agency: Janklow & Nesbit UK Ltd (**L0516**)

Fiction > *Novels*: Literary

Nonfiction > *Nonfiction Books*
 History; Investigative Journalism; Popular Science

Send: Query; Synopsis; Writing sample
How to send: Email

L0359 Carol Franco

Literary Agent
United States

Literary Agency: Kneerim & Williams (**L0575**)

L0360 Fraser Ross Associates

Literary Agency
6/2 Wellington Place, Edinburgh, Scotland, EH6 7EQ
United Kingdom
Tel: +44 (0) 1315 532759

fraserrossassociates@gmail.com

http://www.fraserross.co.uk

Types: Fiction; Nonfiction
Subjects: Commercial; Literary
Markets: Adult; Children's

Send: Query
Don't send: Full text
How to send: Email

Send query by email or by post, including CV, the first three chapters and synopsis for fiction, or a one page proposal and the opening and a further two chapters for nonfiction. For picture books, send complete MS, without illustrations. No poetry, playscripts, screenplays, or individual short stories.

Authors: Jo Allan; Sorrel Anderson; Gill Arbuthnott; Tim Archbold; Alice Balfour; Barroux; Jason Beresford; Thomas Bloor; Ella Burfoot; Jill Calder; Simon Chapman; Judy Cumberbatch; Caroline Deacon; Emily Dodd; Lari Don; Christiane Dorion; Nicole Dryburgh; Jane Eagland; Teresa Flavin; Ciara Flood; Hannah Foley; Vivian French; Joe Friedman; Darren Gate; Roy Gill; Edward Hardy; Diana Hendry; Chris Higgins; Barry Hutchison; J D (Julie) Irwin; Cate James; Ann Kelley; Louise Kelly; Tanya Landman; Kate Leiper; Joan Lennon; Joan Lingard; Janis Mackay; L J Macwhirter; Kasia Matyjaszek; Eilidh Muldoon; Erica Mary Orchard; Judy Paterson; Helena Pielichaty; Sue Purkiss; Lynne Rickards; Jamie Rix; Karen Saunders; Dugald Steer; Chae Strathie; Kate Wakeling; Rosie Wallace

Literary Agents: Lindsey Fraser (*L0361*); Kathryn Ross (*L0862*)

L0361 Lindsey Fraser

Literary Agent
United Kingdom

Literary Agency: Fraser Ross Associates (**L0360**)

L0362 Robert Freedman
Literary Agent; President
United States

http://aaronline.org/Sys/PublicProfile/2176681/
417813

Literary Agency: Robert A. Freedman
Dramatic Agency, Inc. (**L0841**)
Professional Body: Association of American
Literary Agents (AALA)

Scripts > *Theatre Scripts*

L0363 Claire Friedman
Literary Agent
United States

http://www.inkwellmanagement.com/staff/
claire-friedman

Literary Agency: InkWell Management
(**L0499**)

ADULT
  Fiction > *Novels*: Commercial

  Nonfiction > *Nonfiction Books*: Narrative
  Nonfiction

CHILDREN'S > **Fiction** > *Novels*

YOUNG ADULT > **Fiction** > *Novels*

Send: Query; Writing sample
How to send: In the body of an email

L0364 Fredrica Friedman
Literary Agent

Professional Body: The Agents Round Table
(ART)
Literary Agency: Fredrica S. Friedman and Co.
Inc.

L0365 Jessica Friedman
Literary Agent
United States

https://www.sll.com/our-team

Literary Agency: Sterling Lord Literistic, Inc.
(**L0940**)

Fiction > *Novels*: Literary

Nonfiction > *Nonfiction Books*

Represents literary fiction and nonfiction.
Interested in distinctive voices and writing that
challenges the expected -- stylistically,
formally, or otherwise. Particularly drawn to
incisive, voice-driven writing and
underrepresented narratives.

L0366 Rebecca Friedman
Literary Agent
United States

Literary Agency: Rebecca Friedman Literary
Agency (**L0821**)

L0367 The Friedrich Agency LLC
Literary Agency
United States

mfriedrich@friedrichagency.com

http://www.friedrichagency.com

Types: Fiction; Nonfiction
Subjects: Commercial; Literary
Markets: Adult

Send: Query
Don't send: Full text
How to send: Email

See website for agent bios and individual
contact details, then submit to one by email
only. See website for full guidelines.

Literary Agents: Hannah Brattesani (**L0120**);
Heather Carr (*L0165*); Lucy Carson (*L0168*);
Molly Friedrich (*L0368*)

L0368 Molly Friedrich
Literary Agent
United States

Literary Agency: The Friedrich Agency LLC
(**L0367**)

L0369 Sarah Fuentes
Associate Agent
United States

Literary Agency: Fletcher & Company

L0370 Helenka Fuglewicz
Literary Agent
United Kingdom

Literary Agency: Edwards Fuglewicz (**L0290**)

L0371 Full Circle Literary, LLC
Literary Agency
3268 Governor Drive #323, San Diego, CA
92122
United States

info@fullcircleliterary.com

http://www.fullcircleliterary.com

Types: Fiction; Nonfiction
Subjects: Biography; Comedy / Humour;
Contemporary; Crafts; Culture; Current
Affairs; Design; Fantasy; History; How To;
Lifestyle; Literary; Nature; Science Fiction;
Women's Interests
Markets: Adult; Children's; Young Adult

Send: Query
Don't send: Full text

See website for individual agent interests and
submit using online submission system.

Literary Agents: Stefanie Sanchez Von Borstel
(**L0112**); Adriana Dominguez (**L0270**); Nicole
Geiger (**L0385**); Lilly Ghahremani (**L0392**);
Taylor Martindale Kean (**L0560**)

L0372 Eugenie Furniss
Literary Agent

eugeniefurniss@42mp.com

https://www.42mp.com/agents
https://twitter.com/Furniss

Literary Agency: 42 Management and
Production (**L0002**)

Fiction > *Novels*
  Comedy / Humour; Crime; Historical Fiction

Nonfiction > *Nonfiction Books*
  Biography; Finance; Memoir; Politics;
  Popular History

How to send: Email

Drawn to crime in all its guises and historical
fiction. On the nonfiction front seeks
biography and popular history, and politics.

L0373 Louise Fury
Literary Agent
United States

Literary Agency: The Bent Agency (**L0090**)

Closed to approaches.

L0374 The G Agency, LLC
Literary Agency
116 West 23rd Street, 5th floor, New York,
NY 10011
United States
Tel: +1 (718) 664-4505

Literary Agent: Jeff Gerecke (**L0390**)

L0375 Gallt & Zacker Literary Agency
Literary Agency
273 Charlton Avenue, South Orange, NJ 07079
United States
Tel: +1 (973) 761-6358

http://www.galltzacker.com

Handles fiction and nonfiction for children,
young adults, and adults. See website for
submission guidelines and specific agent
interests / contact details and approach relevant
agent by email.

Literary Agents: Linda Camacho (**L0151**); Erin
Casey (**L0173**); Nancy Gallt (**L0376**); Beth
Phelan (**L0795**); Marietta B. Zacker (**L1065**)

L0376 Nancy Gallt
Literary Agent
United States

nancy@galltzacker.com

Literary Agency: Gallt & Zacker Literary
Agency (**L0375**)

CHILDREN'S > **Fiction**
  Middle Grade; Picture Books
YOUNG ADULT
  Fiction > *Novels*
  Nonfiction > *Nonfiction Books*

Closed to approaches.

L0377 Natalie Galustian
Literary Agent
United Kingdom

natalie@cclagents.com

https://cclagents.com/agent/natalie-galustian/
https://twitter.com/natgalustian

Literary Agency: Charlie Campbell Literary Agents (**L0188**)

Fiction
 Novels: Literary
 Short Fiction: Literary

Nonfiction
 Essays: General
 Nonfiction Books: Arts; Biography; Comedy / Humour; Commercial; Cookery; Drama; History; Memoir; Music; Narrative Nonfiction

Send: Query; Synopsis; Writing sample; Outline
How to send: Email
How not to send: Post

Represents narrative and commercial non-fiction as well as literary fiction. She is primarily looking for strong new voices in non-fiction across musical, visual, dramatic and culinary arts, history, memoir, biography, essays and humour, along with some select fiction and short stories of literary quality.

Author Estates: The Estate of Alan Rickman; The Estate of Alfred H. Mendes

Authors: Jennifer Lucy Allan; Jeremy Allen; Lulah Ellender; Hannah McCollum; Charlotte Mitchell; Andrew Perry; Hamilton Richardson; Matthew Shaw; Michael Smith; Harry Sword; James Thomas; Luke Turner; Robin Turner; Michael Volpe; Liam Patrick Young

L0378 Lori Galvin
Literary Agent
Boston
United States

https://aevitascreative.com/agents/
https://querymanager.com/query/QueryLoriGalvin

Literary Agency: Aevitas (**L0016**)

Fiction > *Novels*
 General, and in particular: Crime; Women's Fiction

Nonfiction > *Nonfiction Books*
 Cookery; Food; Memoir

Send: Author bio; Query; Synopsis; Writing sample; Pitch; Market info
How to send: Query Manager

Represents both adult fiction (especially women's fiction and thrillers) and nonfiction (personal development and cookbooks).

L0379 Anna Gamble
Assistant Agent; Editor
United Kingdom

https://www.liverpool-literary.agency/about

Literary Agency: The Liverpool Literary Agency (**L0624**)

CHILDREN'S > **Fiction**
 Chapter Books: High Concept
 Middle Grade: Adventure

Would love to see high concept chapter books with a strong hook and middle grade fiction that really knows its audience and offers a sense of adventure.

L0380 Karen Gantz
Literary Agent
United States

Literary Agency: Karen Gantz Literary Management (**L0549**)

L0381 Sulamita Garbuz
Associate Agent
United States

sg@goldinlit.com

https://goldinlit.com/agents/

Literary Agency: Frances Goldin Literary Agency, Inc. (**L0356**)

Fiction > *Novels*
 Literary; Speculative

Nonfiction > *Nonfiction Books*
 Journalism; Memoir; Narrative Nonfiction; Psychology; Science; Social Justice

How to send: Email

Gravitates primarily towards nonfiction, with an emphasis on books with a social justice bent. Her areas of specialty include narrative nonfiction, memoir, psychology, science, and journalism. She is also looking for character driven literary fiction, and is especially excited by novels that use speculative or dreamlike elements to explore current social dynamics, stories of obsession and women misbehaving, and narratives about immigration and the 2nd generation experience.

L0382 Lauren Gardner
Literary Agent
United Kingdom

Literary Agency: Bell Lomax Moreton Agency (**L0081**)

L0383 Jennifer Gates
Senior Partner; Literary Agent
United States

https://aevitascreative.com/agents/

Literary Agency: Aevitas (**L0016**)

ADULT
 Fiction > *Novels*: Literary

Nonfiction > *Nonfiction Books*
 Current Affairs; Memoir; Narrative Nonfiction; Popular Culture

CHILDREN'S > **Fiction** > *Novels*

Send: Author bio; Pitch; Market info; Writing sample
How to send: Online submission system

Represents a range of nonfiction, including narrative and expert-driven works, memoir, current affairs, pop culture, as well as literary fiction and children's books.

L0384 Ellen Geiger
Senior Agent; Vice President
United States

https://goldinlit.com/agents/

Literary Agency: Frances Goldin Literary Agency, Inc. (**L0356**)

Fiction > *Novels*
 Culture; Historical Fiction; Literary Thrillers; Multicultural

Nonfiction > *Nonfiction Books*
 Biography; History; Investigative Journalism; Multicultural; Politics; Psychology; Religion; Social Issues; Women's Issues

Send: Query; Writing sample
How to send: Submittable

Represents a broad range of fiction and non-fiction. She has a lifelong interest in multicultural and social issues embracing change. History, biography, progressive politics, psychology, women's issues, religion and serious investigative journalism are special interests.

In fiction, she loves a good literary thriller, and novels in general that provoke and challenge the status quo, as well as historical and multicultural works. She is drawn to big themes which make a larger point about the culture and times we live in, such as Barbara Kingsolver's Poisonwood Bible. She is not the right agent for New Age, romance, how-to or right-wing politics.

L0385 Nicole Geiger
Literary Agent
United States

https://www.fullcircleliterary.com/submissions/
https://querymanager.com/query/NicoleFCL

Literary Agency: Full Circle Literary, LLC (**L0371**)

CHILDREN'S > **Fiction** > *Graphic Novels*
Closed to approaches.

Represents graphic novels for middle grade and younger only.

L0386 **Gelfman Schneider / ICM Partners**
Literary Agency
850 Seventh Avenue, Suite 903, New York, NY 10019
United States

mail@gelfmanschneider.com

http://www.gelfmanschneider.com

Professional Body: Association of American Literary Agents (AALA)

Types: Fiction; Nonfiction
Subjects: Autobiography; Commercial; Culture; Current Affairs; History; Literary; Mystery; Politics; Science; Suspense; Thrillers; Women's Interests
Markets: Adult; Young Adult

Send: Query
Don't send: Full text
How to send: Email

Costs: Author covers sundry admin costs.

Different agents within the agency have different submission guidelines. See website for full details. No screenplays, or poetry.

Literary Agents: Penelope Burns (*L0143*); Jane Gelfman (*L0387*); Heather Mitchell (*L0719*); Deborah Schneider (*L0890*)

L0387 **Jane Gelfman**
Literary Agent
United States

Literary Agency: Gelfman Schneider / ICM Partners (**L0386**)

L0388 **Jonny Geller**
Literary Agent
United Kingdom

http://submissions.curtisbrown.co.uk/agents/

Literary Agency: Curtis Brown (**L0233**)

Fiction > *Novels*
Commercial Women's Fiction; Literary; Thrillers

Nonfiction > *Nonfiction Books*: Journalism

Send: Query; Synopsis; Writing sample
How to send: Online submission system

"I am lucky enough to work with a fantastic range of writers – from authors of first class literary fiction to best selling thriller writers, from ground-breaking journalists to the very best writers in the field of women's commercial fiction – my focus is original fiction from writers who have a distinctive voice."

Associate Agent: Viola Hayden (**L0456**)

L0389 **Georgina Capel Associates Ltd**
Literary Agency
29 Wardour Street, London, W1D 6PS

United Kingdom
Tel: +44 (0) 20 7734 2414

georgina@georginacapel.com

http://www.georginacapel.com

Professional Body: The Association of Authors' Agents (AAA)

Types: Fiction; Nonfiction
Formats: Film Scripts; Radio Scripts; TV Scripts
Subjects: Biography; Commercial; History; Literary
Markets: Adult

Send: Query
Don't send: Full text
How to send: Email

Handles general fiction and nonfiction. Send query outlining writing history (for nonfiction, what qualifies you to write your book), with synopsis around 500 words and first three chapters, plus SAE or email address for reply. Submissions are not returned. Mark envelope for the attention of the Submissions Department. Accepts submissions by email, but prefers them by post. Response only if interested, normally within 6 weeks. Film and TV scripts handled for established clients only.

Authors: John Bew; Vince Cable; Daisy Dunn; Lauren Johnson

Literary Agent: Georgina Capel (*L0154*)

L0390 **Jeff Gerecke**
Literary Agent
United States

gagencyquery@gmail.com
jeff@gagencylit.com
jeff@marksonagency.com

https://www.publishersmarketplace.com/members/jeffg/
http://aaronline.org/Sys/PublicProfile/2176689/417813

Professional Body: Association of American Literary Agents (AALA)
Literary Agencies: The G Agency, LLC (**L0374**); Elaine Markson Literary Agency (**L0299**)

Fiction > *Novels*
General, and in particular: Commercial; Literary; Mystery

Nonfiction > *Nonfiction Books*
Biography; Business; Computers; Finance; History; Military History; Popular Culture; Sport; Technology

Send: Query; Writing sample
How to send: Email attachment

I am interested in commercial and literary fiction, as well as serious non-fiction and pop culture. My focus as an agent has always been on working with writers to shape their work for its greatest commercial potential. I provide lots

of editorial advice in sharpening manuscripts and proposals before submission.

L0391 **Josh Getzler**
Literary Agent; Partner
United States

josh@hgliterary.com

https://www.hgliterary.com/josh
https://twitter.com/jgetzler
http://www.publishersmarketplace.com/members/jgetzler/
http://aaronline.org/Sys/PublicProfile/2902758/417813
http://queryme.online/Getzler

Literary Agency: HG Literary (**L0467**)
Professional Body: Association of American Literary Agents (AALA)

ADULT
  Fiction > *Novels*
  Historical Fiction; Mystery; Thrillers; Women's Fiction

  Nonfiction > *Nonfiction Books*
  Business; History; Politics

CHILDREN'S > **Fiction** > *Middle Grade*
Comedy / Humour; Contemporary

Closed to approaches.

L0392 **Lilly Ghahremani**
Literary Agent
United States

https://www.fullcircleliterary.com/our-agents/lilly-ghahremani/
https://twitter.com/Wonderlilly

Literary Agency: Full Circle Literary, LLC (**L0371**)

Closed to approaches.

L0393 **Jim Gill**
Literary Agent
United Kingdom

jgill@unitedagents.co.uk

https://www.unitedagents.co.uk

Literary Agency: United Agents (**L0992**)

Fiction > *Novels*

Nonfiction > *Nonfiction Books*

Acts for a broad range of both fiction and non-fiction authors writing for the general-trade market, and is always on the look-out for the original and the excellent.

Authors: Ishbel Addyman; Dr Elizabeth Archibald; Joe Bennett; Mark Binelli; Jonathan Blyth; Lawrence Booth; Pete Brown; Christopher Bryant; Barnabas Calder; Justin Cartwright; Tom Chatfield; John Henry Clay; Sean Conway; Nicholas Crane; Emma Dibdin; Dominick Donald; Margaret Drabble; David Hart Dyke; Giles Foden; Tom Gregory; Sudhir Hazareesingh; Eleanor Henderson; Patrick

Hennessey; Mark Keating; Yasmin Khan; Jamie Kornegay; Robert Lautner; Thomas Leveritt; Joshua Levine; Matt Lewis; Rebecca Loncraine; Robert Low; Kevin Maher; Liam McIlvanney; Ciarán McMenamin; Steven Merritt Miner; Jonny Owen; Justin Pollard; Tony Pollard; Oliver Poole; James Rebanks; Jasper Rees; Harry Sidebottom; Ian Thomson; Joanna Trollope; Teddy Wayne; James Yorkston

L0394 Elena Giovinazzo
Literary Agent
United States

Literary Agency: Pippin Properties, Inc
(**L0801**)

L0395 Brenna Girard
Literary Agent
United States

brenna@carolynjenksagency.com

https://www.carolynjenksagency.com/agent/
BRENNA-GIRARD

Literary Agency: Carolyn Jenks Agency
(**L0164**)

Nonfiction > *Nonfiction Books*
General, and in particular: Business; Cookery

L0396 The Gislason Agency
Literary Agency
7362 University Avenue NE Ste 120, Fridley, MN 55432
United States
Tel: +1 (763) 220-2983
Fax: +1 (763) 571-1576

http://www.thegislasonagency.com

Fiction > *Novels*

Closed to approaches.

Costs: Offers services that writers have to pay for.

Represented fiction writers, including a mystery author who received critical acclaim in Publishers Weekly. Currently, she will only consider solicited authors. In some instances, she is willing to give people feedback on a writing project for a fee.

Authors: Linda Cook; Terence Faherty; Deborah Woodworth

Literary Agent: Barbara J. Gislason (*L0397*)

L0397 Barbara J. Gislason
Literary Agent
United States

Literary Agency: The Gislason Agency
(**L0396**)

L0398 Linda S. Glaz
Author; Literary Agent
United States

linda@hartlineliterary.com

http://hartlineagency.com/agentsandauthors/
https://www.facebook.com/linda.glaz
https://twitter.com/LindaGlaz

Literary Agency: Hartline Literary Agency
(**L0451**)
Professional Body: Advanced Writers and Speakers Association (AWSA)

Fiction > *Novels*
General, and in particular: Contemporary Romance; Historical Romance; Romance; Romantic Suspense

Nonfiction > *Nonfiction Books*

How to send: Email
How not to send: Post

Looking for nonfiction by experts in their field. In fiction, will consider anything well written, particularly romance, either contemporary, suspense, or historic. No children's or works that include graphic sexuality or profanity.

Authors: Karla Akins; Rick Barry; Kate Breslin; Lance Brown; Raquel Byrnes; J'nell Ciesielski; Ben Conlon; Angela Couch; Susan F. Craft; Rhonda Dragomir; Barbara Ellin Fox; Linda Gilden; Samantha Gomolka; Janet Grunst; Hilary Hamblin; Hilary Hamblin Voni Harris; Voni Harris; Julie Hatch; K Denise Holmberg; Dennis Lambert; A. D. Lawrence; Delores Liesner; Ashley Ludwig; Jessica Manfre; Merliyn Howton Marriott; Cheryl Linn Martin; Joy Massenburge; Dale McElhinney; Donna Mumma; Naomi Musch; Luke Negron; Jessica Nelson Tiffany Nicole; Candice Patterson; Carmen Peone; Karen Prough; DeBora Rachelle; Maria Reed; Cindy Regnier; Kathleen Rouser; Susan Browning Schulz; Colleen Scott; Laura Smith; Donnie Steven; Donnie Stevens; Patti Stockdale; Beth Summitt; Ken Swarner; Tiffany Tajiri; Donn Taylor; Donn Taylor Evelyn Taylor; Evelyn Taylor; Pegg Thomas; Tom Threadgill; Kari Trumbo; Susan L. Tuttle; Jennifer Uhlarik; Hannah Vanderpool; Denise Weimer; Karen Wingate; Maureen Wise; Frank Yates

L0399 Kerry Glencorse
Literary Agent
United Kingdom

https://www.susannalea.com/team-member/
kerry-glencorse/

Literary Agency: Susanna Lea Associates (UK)
(**L0956**)

Fiction > *Novels*
Crime; Historical Fiction; Literary; Thrillers; Upmarket Commercial Fiction; Women's Fiction

Nonfiction > *Nonfiction Books*
Cultural History; Memoir; Narrative Nonfiction; Nature; Popular Science; Social History

Send: Query; Synopsis; Writing sample
How to send: Email

Always on the lookout for new talent, especially in the areas of literary and upmarket commercial fiction; well-written genre fiction, including crime, thrillers, women's fiction, and historical. And on the non-fiction side: memoir, narrative non-fiction, popular science, natural science, social and cultural history.

L0400 Emily Glenister
Associate Agent
United Kingdom

eg.submission@dhhliteraryagency.com

http://www.dhhliteraryagency.com/emily-glenister.html
http://www.twitter.com/emily_glenister

Literary Agency: DHH Literary Agency Ltd
(**L0264**)

Fiction > *Novels*
Book Club Fiction; Commercial; Crime; Ghost Stories; Gothic; Historical Fiction; Romance; Thrillers; Upmarket Commercial Fiction; Upmarket Women's Fiction

Closed to approaches.

Looking for reading group and commercial novels, as well as diverse / own voices, with an emphasis on crime / thriller (not political or environmental), upmarket commercial women's fiction with a unique hook, epic love stories, post-eighteenth century history, and gothic novels / ghost stories.

Authors: Louise Beech; Heather Darwent; Becca Day; Suzie Edge; Carys Jones; Caroline Lamond; S.V. Leonard; Vikki Patis; Reagan Lee Ray; Reagan Lee Ray; Talia Samuels; Ronnie Turner; Kathleen Whyman

L0401 David Godwin
Literary Agent
United Kingdom

Literary Agency: David Godwin Associates
(**L0244**)

L0402 Ellen Goff
Associate Agent
United States

ellen@hgliterary.com

https://www.hgliterary.com/ellen

Literary Agency: HG Literary (**L0467**)

CHILDREN'S > **Fiction**
Middle Grade; Picture Books
YOUNG ADULT > **Fiction**
Graphic Novels: General
Novels: General, and in particular: Ghost Stories; Gothic; Historical Fiction

List consists of YA writers and illustrators, as well as middle grade and picture book writers. Interested in all genres and formats of YA, especially anything spooky, historical fiction, martial arts, graphic novels, and novels-in-verse. She has a soft spot for Shakespeare as well as southern gothic stories that remind her of her home state of Kentucky.

L0403 Veronica Goldstein
Associate Agent
United States

Literary Agency: Fletcher & Company

L0404 Jennifer Goloboy
Literary Agent
United States

Literary Agency: Donald Maass Literary Agency (**L0273**)

L0405 The Good Literary Agency
Literary Agency
United Kingdom

info@thegoodliteraryagency.org

https://www.thegoodliteraryagency.org
https://twitter.com/thegoodagencyuk

Professional Body: The Association of Authors' Agents (AAA)

ADULT
 Fiction
  Graphic Novels: General
  Novels: Crime; Family Saga; Fantasy; Historical Romance; Romance; Science Fiction; Thrillers
  Short Fiction: General

 Nonfiction
  Essays: General
  Nonfiction Books: Adventure; Biography; Economics; History; Lifestyle; Memoir; Nature; Poetry as a Subject; Politics; Popular Culture; Popular; Science; Self Help; Technology; Travel
CHILDREN'S
 Fiction > *Novels*
  Adventure; Comedy / Humour; Fantasy; Spy Thrilllers

 Nonfiction > *Nonfiction Books*
  Inspirational; Memoir; Self Help
YOUNG ADULT
 Fiction > *Novels*
  Adventure; Comedy / Humour; Fantasy; Spy Thrilllers

 Nonfiction > *Nonfiction Books*
  Inspirational; Memoir; Self Help

Send: Query
Don't send: Full text

Focused on discovering, developing and launching the careers of writers of colour, disability, working class, LGBTQ+ and anyone who feels their story is not being told in the mainstream. Writers must be born or resident in Britain. No poetry, plays, or screenplays.

Accepts submissions from the 1st to the 15th of each month only. See website for full guidelines and to submit via online form.

L0406 Howard Gooding
Literary Agent
United Kingdom

Literary Agency: Judy Daish Associates Ltd (**L0536**)

L0407 Irene Goodman
Literary Agent
United States

Literary Agency: Irene Goodman Literary Agency (IGLA) (**L0501**)

L0408 Graham Maw Christie Literary Agency
Literary Agency
37 Highbury Place, London, N5 1QP
United Kingdom
Tel: +44 (0) 7971 268342

submissions@grahammawchristie.com

http://www.grahammawchristie.com

Professional Body: The Association of Authors' Agents (AAA)

Types: Nonfiction
Formats: Reference
Subjects: Autobiography; Business; Comedy / Humour; Cookery; Crafts; Gardening; Health; History; Lifestyle; Personal Development; Philosophy; Science
Markets: Adult; Children's

Send: Query
Don't send: Full text
How to send: Email

No fiction, poetry, or scripts. Send query with one-page summary, a paragraph on the contents of each chapter, your qualifications for writing it, details of your online presence, market analysis, what you could do to help promote your book, and a sample chapter or two. Prefers approaches by email.

Literary Agents: Jennifer Christie (*L0195*); Jane Graham Maw (*L0687*)

L0409 Stacey Graham
Literary Agent
United States

stacey@threeseaslit.com

https://www.threeseasagency.com/copy-of-michelle-grajkowski
http://querymanager.com/Stacey3Seas

Literary Agency: 3 Seas Literary Agency (**L0001**)

ADULT
 Fiction > *Novels*: Romantic Comedy

 Nonfiction > *Nonfiction Books*

CHILDREN'S > **Fiction** > *Middle Grade*
  Comedy / Humour; Ghost Stories

How to send: Query Manager

Currently looking to expand her list with snappy Rom-Coms, hilarious/spooky middle grade, and weird nonfiction.

L0410 Susan Graham
Literary Agent
United States

https://www.einsteinliterary.com/staff/
http://aaronline.org/Sys/PublicProfile/
52451502/417813

Literary Agency: Einstein Literary Management (**L0294**)
Professional Body: Association of American Literary Agents (AALA)

ADULT > **Fiction** > *Novels*
  General, and in particular: Fantasy; LGBTQIA; Science Fiction

CHILDREN'S > **Fiction** > *Novels*
  General, and in particular: Fantasy; LGBTQIA; Science Fiction

YOUNG ADULT
 Fiction > *Novels*
  General, and in particular: Fantasy; LGBTQIA; Science Fiction

 Nonfiction > *Nonfiction Books*

Looking for children's and young adult fiction in all genres, but their favorite books are often science fiction and fantasy, especially written with a queer lens. They also enjoy picture books and represent graphic novels in all age categories and in all genres. They're particularly interested in friendships and sibling narratives, and monster protagonists are always a plus. They're looking for a good non-fiction or two for children or teens but don't know about what. For adult prose, they prefer genre fiction, and monster protagonists are still a plus. Works by and about marginalized voices are welcome and encouraged.

L0411 Michelle Grajkowski
Literary Agent
United States

michelle@threeseaslit.com

https://www.threeseasagency.com/michelle-grajkowski
http://querymanager.com/Michelle3Seas
http://aaronline.org/Sys/PublicProfile/2176701/417813

Literary Agency: 3 Seas Literary Agency (**L0001**)
Professional Body: Association of American Literary Agents (AALA)

ADULT
 Fiction > *Novels*
  Romance; Women's Fiction

 Nonfiction > *Nonfiction Books*

CHILDREN'S > **Fiction** > *Middle Grade*

How to send: Query Manager

Primarily represents romance, women's fiction, young adult and middle grade fiction along with select nonfiction projects with a terrific message. She is currently looking for fantastic writers with a voice of their own.

Authors: Katie MacAlister; Cathy McDavid; Kerrelyn Sparks; C.L. Wilson

L0412 David Granger
Literary Agent
New York
United States

https://aevitascreative.com/agents/

Literary Agency: Aevitas (**L0016**)

Nonfiction > *Nonfiction Books*
  Celebrity; Culture; Design; Food; Politics; Science; Technology

Closed to approaches.

Represents primarily non-fiction and is obsessed with topics across an extremely wide spectrum – politics; food culture; actual innovation in design, tech and science; fame. What binds these things is a yen for intensely original ideas and writing that pushes boundaries.

L0413 Olivia Gray
Literary Agent
United Kingdom

Literary Agency: Independent Talent Group Ltd (**L0496**)

L0414 Great River Literary
Literary Agency
United States

greatriverliterary@gmail.com

https://www.greatriverliterary.com

CHILDREN'S
  Fiction
    Board Books; *Chapter Books*; *Middle Grade*; *Picture Books*
  Nonfiction > *Nonfiction Books*: Literary

  Poetry > *Any Poetic Form*

YOUNG ADULT > **Fiction** > *Novels*

How to send: Email
How not to send: Email attachment; Phone; Post

An agency devoted exclusively to representing authors and author/illustrators of books for children and teens.

Literary Agent: Mary Cummings (*L0231*)

L0415 Donna Greaves
Literary Agent
United Kingdom

Literary Agency: Jo Unwin Literary Agency (**L0526**)

Closed to approaches.

L0416 Christine Green
Literary Agent
United Kingdom

L0417 Kathryn Green
Literary Agent
United States

Literary Agency: Kathryn Green Literary Agency, LLC (**L0557**)

L0418 Louise Greenberg
Literary Agent
United Kingdom

Literary Agency: Louise Greenberg Books Ltd (**L0634**)

L0419 Greene & Heaton Ltd
Literary Agency
37 Goldhawk Road, London, W12 8QQ
United Kingdom
Tel: +44 (0) 20 8749 0315

submissions@greeneheaton.co.uk
info@greeneheaton.co.uk

http://www.greeneheaton.co.uk
https://twitter.com/greeneandheaton

Professional Body: The Association of Authors' Agents (AAA)

Does not want:

CHILDREN'S > **Fiction** > *Picture Books*

Send: Query; Synopsis; Writing sample
Don't send: Full text
How to send: Email
How not to send: Post

Send query by email only, including synopsis and three chapters or approximately 50 pages. No submissions by post. No response unless interested. Handles all types of fiction and nonfiction, but no scripts or children's picture books.

Author Estates: The Estate of Julia Darling; The Estate of Sarah Gainham

Authors: Amen Alonge; Anthony Anaxagorou; Meg Arroll; Lucy Ashe; Louise Atkinson; Charlotte Bauer; Bridget; Lynne Bryan; Jason Byrne; Tom Campbell; Emma Chapman; Charles Cockell; Pam Corbin; Andrew Davidson; Russell Davies; Anna Davis; Patrick Drake; Nikki Duffy; Kim Duke; Lily Dunn; Suzannah Dunn; Jeremy Duns; Olaf Falafel; Hugh Fearnley-Whittingstall; Jane Fearnley-Whittingstall; Nick Fisher; Christopher Fitz-Simon; Christophe Galfard; Helen Giltrow; Francis Gimblett; Molly Greeley; Stuart

Heritage; Kit Heyam; Julian Hitch; Beatrice Hitchman; Wayne Holloway-Smith; Andrew Holmes; Alex Hourston; David Howard; Charles Jennings; Joan; D.B. John; Keith Kahn-Harris; Gabrielle Kimm; Esme King; Max Kinnings; David Kirk; Rikke Schmidt Kjærgaard; Joseph Knox; Sonya Kudei; William Leith; Dan Lepard; Robert Lewis; Eric Lindstrom; Kieran Long; Dorian Lynskey; Jolyon Maugham; James McGee; Gill Meller; Thomasina Miers; Lottie Moggach; Cathy Newman; Mary-Ann Ochota; Christopher Osborn; Iain Overton; John O'Connell; Pete Paphides; Jyoti Patel; Tom Phillips; Shivi Ramoutar; Richard Reed; Sam Rice; C. J. Sansom; Marcus du Sautoy; Indyana Schneider; Rebecca Seal; Paul Keers: Sediment; Laura Shepherd-Robinson; Mimi Spencer; Count Arthur Strong; Jacqueline Sutherland; Andrew Taylor; Ian Vince; John Vincent; Jennie Walker; Sarai Walker; Andrew Webb; Mark Wernham; Robyn Wilder; Will Wiles; Erin Young; Robyn Young; Andrew Ziminski

Literary Agents: Holly Faulks (**L0319**); Carol Heaton (**L0461**); Imogen Morrell (**L0726**); Judith Murray (**L0737**); Antony Topping (**L0985**); Laura Williams (**L1039**); Claudia Young (**L1061**)

L0420 The Greenhouse Literary Agency
Literary Agency

https://www.greenhouseliterary.com
https://www.facebook.com/The-Greenhouse-Literary-Agency-359292813053/?ref=nf

CHILDREN'S > **Fiction**
  Chapter Books; *Graphic Novels*; *Middle Grade*; *Picture Books*
YOUNG ADULT > **Fiction** > *Novels*

How to send: Query Manager

Transatlantic literary agency with agents in the US and UK. See individual agent details for more info.

Literary Agents: Sarah Davies (**L0248**); Chelsea Eberly (**L0288**); Polly Nolan; Kristin Ostby (**L0773**)

L0421 Katie Greenstreet
Literary Agent
United Kingdom

Literary Agency: C+W (Conville & Walsh) (**L0147**)

L0422 Rima Greer
Literary Agent
United States

Literary Agency: Above the Line Agency (**L0007**)

L0423 Evan Gregory
Literary Agent
United States

agent@ethanellenberg.com

https://ethanellenberg.com
https://twitter.com/#!/EvanJGregory
http://aaronline.org/Sys/PublicProfile/2309906/
417813

Literary Agency: Ethan Ellenberg Literary
Agency **(L0308)**
Professional Body: Association of American
Literary Agents (AALA)

ADULT
  Fiction > *Novels*
    Fantasy; Horror; Mystery; Science Fiction;
    Thrillers; Women's Fiction

  Nonfiction > *Nonfiction Books*
    Arts; Biography; Business; Cookery;
    Culture; Current Affairs; Entertainment;
    Family; Films; Food and Drink; Health;
    History; Memoir; Nature; Parenting;
    Photography; Politics; Popular Culture;
    Science; Sport; Technology; Travel

CHILDREN'S > **Fiction**
  Middle Grade; *Picture Books*
YOUNG ADULT > **Fiction** > *Novels*

Send: Query; Synopsis; Writing sample
How to send: Email
How not to send: Post

L0424 Jonathan Gregory
Literary Agent
United Kingdom

jonathan@antonyharwood.com

http://antonyharwood.com/jonathan-gregory/

Literary Agency: Antony Harwood Limited
(L0042)

Nonfiction > *Nonfiction Books*
  Biography; History; Medicine; Philosophy;
  Politics; Science

L0425 Alexandra Grese
Literary Agent
United States

Literary Agency: Freak Unleashed

L0426 Pam Gruber
Literary Agent
United States

pam.queries@irenegoodman.com

https://www.irenegoodman.com/pam-gruber
https://www.instagram.com/pjgruber/
https://twitter.com/Pamlet606

Literary Agency: Irene Goodman Literary
Agency (IGLA) **(L0501)**
ADULT
  Fiction > *Novels*

Coming of Age; Commercial; Fantasy;
Literary; Magical Realism; Romantic
Comedy; Speculative

  Nonfiction > *Nonfiction Books*

CHILDREN'S > **Fiction**
  Graphic Novels: General
  Middle Grade: Coming of Age; Commercial;
  Fantasy; Literary; Magical Realism;
  Romantic Comedy; Speculative
YOUNG ADULT > **Fiction**
  Graphic Novels: General
  Novels: Coming of Age; Commercial;
  Fantasy; Literary; Magical Realism;
  Romantic Comedy; Speculative

How to send: Email

Looking for adult, young adult, and middle
grade fiction with literary voices and
commercial hooks. She is particularly
interested in layered fantasy, speculative
fiction, fantastical realism, rom-coms, and
coming-of-age stories with a twist. She is also
open to middle grade and YA graphic novels,
as well as select narrative non-fiction on lesser-
known subjects. She would not be the best fit
for prescriptive non-fiction, anthologies, potty
humor, paranormal, or erotica.

L0427 Hattie Grunewald
Literary Agent
United Kingdom

https://www.theblairpartnership.com/
our_people/hattie-grunewald-literary-agent/

Literary Agency: The Blair Partnership
(L0100)

Fiction > *Novels*
  Book Club Fiction; Commercial; Crime;
  Historical Fiction; Thrillers; Upmarket;
  Women's Fiction

Nonfiction > *Nonfiction Books*
  Lifestyle; Personal Development

L0428 Robbie Guillory
Junior Agent; Editor; Proofreader
United Kingdom

https://katenashlit.co.uk/people/
https://twitter.com/RobbieGuillory

Literary Agency: Kate Nash Literary Agency
(L0555)

Fiction > *Novels*
  Commercial; Crime; Historical Fiction;
  Psychological Thrillers; Science Fiction

Nonfiction > *Nonfiction Books*: Nature

Send: Query; Synopsis; Writing sample
How to send: In the body of an email

Looking for outstanding writing across a
number of genres: stand-out commercial
fiction, science fiction that focuses on
communities and relationships whilst the
galaxy looks after itself, crime and
psychological thrillers with a difference,

gripping historical dramas, and beautiful
nonfiction with roots in the natural world.

L0429 Robert Guinsler
Senior Agent
United States

https://www.sll.com/our-team

Literary Agency: Sterling Lord Literistic, Inc.
(L0940)

Nonfiction > *Nonfiction Books*

Send: Query; Synopsis; Writing sample
How to send: Online submission system

L0430 Masha Gunic
Associate Agent
United States

http://www.azantianlitagency.com/pages/team-
mg.html
https://querymanager.com/query/MashaGunic

Literary Agency: Azantian Literary Agency
(L0054)

CHILDREN'S > **Fiction** > *Middle Grade*
  Adventure; Comedy / Humour;
  Contemporary; Fantasy; Historical Fiction;
  Horror

YOUNG ADULT > **Fiction** > *Novels*
  Commercial; Contemporary; Fantasy; High
  Concept; Historical Fiction; Literary;
  Magical Realism; Mystery; Science Fiction;
  Space Opera; Thrillers

How to send: Query Manager

Represents middle grade and young adult
novels.

L0431 Kanishka Gupta
Literary Agent
India

kanishka@writersside.com
kanishka500@gmail.com

https://www.facebook.com/kanishka.gupta.
754?frcf=ts
https://twitter.com/kan_writersside

L0432 Gurman Agency, LLC
Literary Agency
United States
Tel: +1 (212) 749-4618

assistant@gurmanagency.com

http://www.gurmanagency.com

Professional Body: Writers Guild of America
(WGA)

Scripts > *Theatre Scripts*

How to send: By referral

Represents playwrights, directors,
choreographers, composers and lyricists. New
clients by referral only, so prospective clients

should seek a referral rather than querying. No queries accepted.

Literary Agent: Susan Gurman (*L0433*)

L0433 Susan Gurman
Literary Agent
United States

Literary Agency: Gurman Agency, LLC (**L0432**)

L0434 Allan Guthrie
Literary Agent
United Kingdom

http://thenorthlitagency.com/our-friends-in-the-north/

Literary Agency: The North Literary Agency (**L0755**)

Fiction > *Novels*: Crime

Send: Query; Synopsis; Writing sample; Proposal
How to send: Email

Has worked in the book trade since 1996 and has been a literary agent since 2005. He is also an award-winning novelist, freelance editor and former publisher. His main area of interest is crime fiction.

L0435 Julie Gwinn
Literary Agent
United States

Literary Agency: The Seymour Agency (**L0902**)

L0436 Serene Hakim
Literary Agent
United States

https://www.pandeliterary.com/about-pandeliterary
https://twitter.com/serenemaria
http://aaronline.org/Sys/PublicProfile/52119398/417813

Literary Agency: Ayesha Pande Literary (**L0052**)
Professional Body: Association of American Literary Agents (AALA)

ADULT
  Fiction > *Novels*
    Feminism; International; LGBTQIA; Middle East

  Nonfiction > *Nonfiction Books*
    Feminism; International; LGBTQIA; Middle East
YOUNG ADULT
  Fiction > *Novels*
    Fantasy; Feminism; International; LGBTQIA; Middle East; Realistic; Science Fiction

  Nonfiction > *Nonfiction Books*

Feminism; International; LGBTQIA; Middle East

Send: Pitch; Author bio; Synopsis; Writing sample
How to send: Online submission system

L0437 Tessa Emily Hall
Literary Agent
United States

Literary Agency: Cyle Young Literary Elite (**L0236**)

L0438 Bill Hamilton
Literary Agent
United Kingdom

https://amheath.com/agents/bill-hamilton/

Literary Agency: A.M. Heath & Company Limited, Author's Agents (**L0003**)

Fiction > *Novels*

Nonfiction > *Nonfiction Books*

Agency Assistant / Associate Agent: Florence Rees (**L0825**)

L0439 The Hanbury Agency
Literary Agency
Suite 103, 88 Lower Marsh, London, SE1 7AB
United Kingdom

enquiries@hanburyagency.com

http://www.hanburyagency.com
https://www.facebook.com/HanburyAgency/
https://twitter.com/hanburyagency
https://www.instagram.com/the_hanbury_agency/

Professional Body: The Association of Authors' Agents (AAA)

Fiction > *Novels*

Nonfiction > *Nonfiction Books*
  Current Affairs; History; Popular Culture

Closed to approaches.

Closed to submissions as at August 2019. Check website for current status.

No film scripts, plays, poetry, books for children, self-help. Not accepting fantasy, science fiction, or misery memoirs. Send query by post with brief synopsis, first 30 pages (roughly), and your email address and phone number. No submissions by email. Do not include SAE, as no material is returned. Response not guaranteed, so assume rejection if no reply after 8 weeks.

Authors: George Alagiah; Simon Callow; Jane Glover; Bernard Hare; Imran Khan; Judith Lennox; Katie Price

Literary Agent: Margaret Hanbury

L0440 Carrie Hannigan
Literary Agent; Partner
United States

carrie@hgliterary.com

https://www.hgliterary.com/carrie
http://queryme.online/Hannigan

Literary Agency: HG Literary (**L0467**)
Professional Body: Association of American Literary Agents (AALA)

ADULT > **Nonfiction** > *Nonfiction Books*

CHILDREN'S
  Fiction
    Graphic Novels: General
    Novels: Comedy / Humour; Contemporary; Fantasy
  Nonfiction > *Nonfiction Books*

How to send: Query Manager

L0441 Hardman & Swainson
Literary Agency
S106, New Wing, Somerset House, Strand, London, WC2R 1LA
United Kingdom
Tel: +44 (0) 20 3701 7449

submissions@hardmanswainson.com

http://www.hardmanswainson.com
https://twitter.com/HardmanSwainson

Professional Body: The Association of Authors' Agents (AAA)

Send: Full text; Synopsis
How to send: Email
How not to send: Post

Agency launched June 2012 by former colleagues at an established agency. Welcomes submissions of fiction and nonfiction, but no submissions by post. See website for full submission guidelines.

Assistant Agent: Nicole Etherington (**L0309**)

Authors: Jennifer Barclay; Lilly Bartlett; Jackie Bateman; Alex Bell; Anna Bell; Jon Bounds; Oggy Boytchev; Paul Braddon; Cathy Bramley; Matt Brolly; Elizabeth Brooks; Isabelle Broom; Mark Broomfield; Tracy Buchanan; Meg Cabot; Elisabeth Carpenter; Simon Cheshire; Adrienne Chinn; Abby Clements; Helen Cox; Jeremy Craddock; Sara Crowe; Joshua Cunningham; Emma Darwin; Stuart David; Daniel M. Davis; Caroline Davison; Lisa Dickenson; Miranda Dickinson; Sarah Ditum; Carol Donaldson; Charlotte Duckworth; Simon David Eden; Rachel Edwards; Miranda Emmerson; Miguel Farias; Helen Fields; Rosie Fiore; Carrie Hope Fletcher; Giovanna Fletcher; Nicola Ford; Harry Freedman; Michele Gorman; James Gould-Bourn; Vanessa Greene; Kirsty Greenwood; Alastair Gunn; Tom Higham; Michael Jecks; Dinah Jefferies; Oskar Cox Jensen; Stuart Johnstone; Ishani Kar-Purkayastha; Elaine Kasket; Beth Kempton; Holly Kingston; Lucy Lawrie; Peter Laws; Christine Lehnen; Malinda Lo; Alice Loxton; Kevin Macneil; Katie Marsh; S R Masters; Cressida Mclaughlin; Ali Mcnamara; Susy

Mcphee; Siobhan Miller; Kr Moorhead; Martina Murphy; Julien Musolino; Helen Naylor; Nigel Packer; Lauren Price; Philip C Quaintrell; Martina Reilly; Caroline Roberts; Patrick Roberts; Nick Russell-Pavier; Nikola Scott; Catherine Simpson; Emma Slade; Danny Smith; Victoria Smith; Gareth Southwell; Elisabeth Spencer; Fiona Sussman; Eliska Tanzer; Sarah Tierney; Liz Trenow; Sarah Turner; Rebecca Wait; B P Walter; Louise Walters; Victoria Walters; Sue Watson; Alison White; Catherine Wikholm; Samantha Wilson; Laura Ziepe

Literary Agents: Therese Coen (**L0207**); Hannah Ferguson (**L0327**); Caroline Hardman (**L0442**); Joanna Swainson (**L0959**)

L0442 Caroline Hardman
Literary Agent
United Kingdom

submissions@hardmanswainson.com
caroline@hardmanswainson.com

http://www.hardmanswainson.com/agents/caroline-hardman/

Literary Agency: Hardman & Swainson (**L0441**)

Fiction > *Novels*
  Book Club Fiction; Crime; Historical Fiction; Literary; Thrillers; Upmarket Commercial Fiction

Nonfiction > *Nonfiction Books*
  Current Affairs; Feminism; Food; Health; Human Biology; Lifestyle; Medicine; Memoir; Narrative Nonfiction; Nutrition; Popular Science; Psychology; Wellbeing

Send: Synopsis; Full text
How to send: Email

Direct submissions to the agent, but send to the submissions email address, not her individual email address.

Authors: Katie Allen; Jennifer Barclay; Lilly Bartlett; Tracy Buchanan; Elisabeth Carpenter; HS Chandler; Emma Christie; Daniel M. Davis; Sarah Ditum; Andrew Doig; Charlotte Duckworth; Miranda Emmerson; Miguel Farias; Louise Fein; Helen Fields; Eliese Colette Goldbach; Michele Gorman; Paula Greenlees; Alastair Gunn; Dinah Jefferies; Helen Joyce; Ishani Kar-Purkayastha; Elaine Kasket; Beth Kempton; Alice Loxton; Martina Murphy; Helen Naylor; Jenni Nuttall; Julia Parry; Laura Pashby; Vanessa Potter; Martina Reilly; Nikola Scott; Joanne Sefton; Victoria Smith; Miss South; Elisabeth Spencer; Kathleen Stock; John Tregoning; Liz Trenow; Rebecca Wait; Alison White; Catherine Wikholm; Ryan Wilson; Eleanor Wood

L0443 Jessica Hare
Literary Agent
United Kingdom

jhare@theagency.co.uk

https://theagency.co.uk/the-agents/jessica-hare/
https://twitter.com/jcehare
https://instagram.com/jcehare

Literary Agency: The Agency (London) Ltd (**L0018**)

L0444 Esmond Harmsworth
Literary Agent; President
United States

https://aevitascreative.com/agents/

Literary Agency: Aevitas (**L0016**)

Fiction > *Novels*
  Crime; Historical Fiction; Horror; Literary; Mystery; Suspense; Thrillers

Nonfiction > *Nonfiction Books*
  Business; Culture; History; Politics; Psychology; Science

How to send: Online submission system

Represents serious nonfiction books on topics such as politics, psychology, culture, business, history and science. For fiction, he represents literary fiction, mystery and crime, thriller, suspense and horror, and historical novels.

L0445 Harold Ober Associates, Inc.
Literary Agency
United States

http://www.foliolit.com/harold-ober-associates

Literary Agency: Folio Literary Management, LLC (**L0343**)

Types: Fiction; Nonfiction
Markets: Adult; Children's

L0446 Michael Harriot
Literary Agent
United States

michael@foliolit.com

http://foliolit.com/michael-harriot

Literary Agency: Folio Literary Management, LLC (**L0343**)

Fiction > *Novels*
  Fantasy; Science Fiction

Nonfiction > *Nonfiction Books*
  Comic Books; Commercial; Films; Music; Narrative Nonfiction; Popular Culture; Prescriptive Nonfiction; Sport

Send: Proposal; Writing sample
How to send: Email attachment

L0447 Erin Harris
Literary Agent; Vice President
United States

eharris@foliolitmanagement.com

https://www.publishersmarketplace.com/members/eharris/
https://twitter.com/ErinHarrisFolio

Literary Agency: Folio Literary Management, LLC (**L0343**)
Professional Body: Association of American Literary Agents (AALA)

ADULT
Fiction
  Novels: Book Club Fiction; Family Saga; Folklore, Myths, and Legends; Historical Fiction; Literary Mystery; Suspense
  Short Fiction: General

Nonfiction
  Essays: General
  Nonfiction Books: High Concept; Memoir; Narrative Nonfiction; Social Issues
YOUNG ADULT > **Fiction** > *Novels*
  Contemporary; Fantasy; Speculative; Suspense

Send: Query; Writing sample
How to send: In the body of an email

L0448 Samara Harris
Literary Agent
United States

Literary Agency: Robert A. Freedman Dramatic Agency, Inc. (**L0841**)

L0449 Jim Hart
Literary Agent
United States

jim@hartlineliterary.com

https://www.hartlineagency.com/agents-and-authors

Literary Agency: Hartline Literary Agency (**L0451**)

Fiction > *Novels*
  Amish Romance; Contemporary Romance; Historical Romance; Romance; Romantic Suspense; Science Fiction; Speculative; Suspense; Thrillers; Women's Fiction

Nonfiction > *Nonfiction Books*
  Business; Christian Living; Leadership; Parenting; Self Help; Social Issues

Send: Query; Proposal
How to send: Email attachment

Serves both Christian and general markets. Currently most interested in non-fiction on the topics of Christian living, church growth, leadership, business, social issues, parenting, and some self-help. Non-fiction writers will need to show a strong platform in their area of expertise. He is not looking at memoirs or devotionals at this time.

Also looking at select fiction in these categories: suspense/thrillers, romance (contemporary, historical, suspense, Amish), women's fiction, and some speculative and sci-fi. Fiction writers should possess a strong and growing platform. He is not looking at children's or middle-grade fiction at this time.

Not looking at proposals for books that have been previously self-published. Please do not send proposals for books that include graphic language and sex.

Authors: David Awbrey; Diane Awbrey; Matt Aynes; Bethany Baker; Mark Baker; Sandra Barnes; Chaim Bentorah; Robin Bertram; Amy C. Blake; Laura C. Brandenberg; Suzanne Bratcher; Shanna Brickell; Kristi Burton Brown; Lainna Callentine; Terri Clark; Hope Toler Dougherty; F.R. D'Onofrio; Jacqueline Gillam Fairchild; Huey Freeman; Caroline Friday; Justin Gabriel; Anna Elizabeth Gant; Heidi Gaul; Chandler Gerber; PJ Gover; John Gray; Glenn Haggerty; Brandy Heineman; Chaka Heinz; Kim Taylor Henry; Bill Higgs; Dena Hobbs; Jason Hobbs; Erica Marie Hogan; Angela M. Hutchinson; Dalton Jantzen; Vicki Jantzen; Gary Keel; Ken Koopman; Anita Knight Kuhnley; R.J. Larson; Joseph Max Lewis; Marco Lupis; Kathi Macias; Paul Marshall; Vicki McCollum; Stephenia McGee; Kimberly M. Miller; Bonnie Mohr; Jairo de Oliveira; Kevin Ott; Ava Pennington; R.K. Pillai; Leigh Powers; Daniel Rhee; Penny Richards; Dominic Rivera; Katie Robles; Mary Selzer; James Shupp; Neil Silverberg; Greg Singleton; Martha Singleton; Adam Smith; Richard Spillman; Buck Storm; Robert C. Stroud; Jill Thomas; C Kevin Thompson; Mary Kay Tuberty; Hope Welborn; Beth E. Wescott; Karol Whaley; Jessica White; Beth Ann Ziarnik

L0450 Joyce A. Hart

Literary Agent; President
United States

joyce@hartlineliterary.com

http://hartlineliteraryagency.blogspot.com

Literary Agency: Hartline Literary Agency (**L0451**)

Fiction > *Novels*: Inspirational

Closed to approaches.

Over 35 years of experience marketing and promoting books. A pioneer of selling high quality fiction to the inspirational market.

Authors: Christy Barritt; Lorraine Beatty; Molly Noble Bull; Peggy Byers; Daniel Carl; Michael Carl; Dorothy Clark; Ace Collins; Dawn Crandall; Lena Nelson Dooley; Birdie Etchison; Suzanne Woods Fisher; Lisa Godfrees; Jeenie Gordon; Anne Greene; Pamela Griffin; Eleanor Gustafson; Ann Guyer; Lisa Harris; Sandra M. Hart; Rebecca Jepson; Melanie M. Jeschke; Mary Johnson; Jane Kirkpatrick; Zoe M. McCarthy; Rebekah Montgomery; Pola Marie Muzyka; Darrel Nelson; Melissa Ohden; Susan Titus Osborne; Carrie Fancett Pagels; Sam D. Pakan; Susan J. Reinhardt; Rita A. Schulte; Stacie Ruth

Stoelting; Ward Tanneberg; Diana Taylor; Margorie Vawter; Jacqueline Wheelock; Nancy Willich; Courtney Young

L0451 Hartline Literary Agency

Literary Agency
United States
Tel: +1 (412) 829-2483

http://www.hartlineliterary.com

Fiction > *Novels*

Nonfiction > *Nonfiction Books*

Costs: Offers services that writers have to pay for.

Specialises in Christian bookseller market, and particularly interested in adult fiction, nutritional, business, devotional, and self-help. No short fiction, screenplays, scripts, poetry, magazine articles, science fiction, fantasy, extraordinary violence, unnecessary profanity, gratuitous sexuality, or material that conflicts with the Christian worldview. Probably not the right agency for literary fiction, either. See website for detailed submission guidelines.

Note that this agency also offers literary services, which may be considered a conflict of interests.

Author / Literary Agent: Cyle Young (**L1062**)

Authors: Karla Akins; David Awbrey; Diane Awbrey; Matt Aynes; Bethany Baker; Mark Baker; Sandra Barnes; Rick Barry; Chaim Bentorah; Robin Bertram; Amy C. Blake; Laura C. Brandenberg; Suzanne Bratcher; Kate Breslin; Shanna Brickell; Kristi Burton Brown; Lance Brown; Raquel Byrnes; Lainna Callentine; J'nell Ciesielski; Terri Clark; David E. Clarke; Karen Condit; Ben Conlon; Angela Couch; Susan F. Craft; Hope Toler Dougherty; Rhonda Dragomir; F.R. D'Onofrio; Jacqueline Gillam Fairchild; Barbara Ellin Fox; Huey Freeman; Caroline Friday; Justin Gabriel; Anna Elizabeth Gant; Heidi Gaul; Chandler Gerber; Linda Gilden; Samantha Gomolka; PJ Gover; John Gray; Janet Grunst; Glenn Haggerty; Hilary Hamblin Voni Harris; Julie Hatch; Brandy Heineman; Chaka Heinz; Kim Taylor Henry; Bill Higgs; Dena Hobbs; Jason Hobbs; Erica Marie Hogan; K Denise Holmberg; Angela M. Hutchinson; Dalton Jantzen; Vicki Jantzen; Gary Keel; Ken Koopman; Anita Knight Kuhnley; Dennis Lambert; R.J. Larson; Julie Lavender; A. D. Lawrence; Joseph Max Lewis; Delores Liesner; Ashley Ludwig; Marco Lupis; Kathi Macias; Jessica Manfre; Merliyn Howton Marriott; Paul Marshall; Cheryl Linn Martin; Joy Massenburge; Vicki McCollum; Dale McElhinney; Stephenia McGee; Kimberly M. Miller; Bonnie Mohr; Donna Mumma; Naomi Musch; Luke Negron; Jessica Nelson Tiffany Nicole; Jairo de Oliveira; Kevin Ott; Candice Patterson; Ava Pennington; Carmen Peone; R.K. Pillai; Leigh Powers; Karen Prough; DeBora Rachelle; Maria Reed; Cindy Regnier;

Daniel Rhee; Penny Richards; Dominic Rivera; Katie Robles; Kathleen Rouser; Susan Browning Schulz; Colleen Scott; Mary Selzer; James Shupp; Neil Silverberg; Greg Singleton; Martha Singleton; Adam Smith; Laura Smith; Richard Spillman; Debbie Sprinkle; Donnie Steven; Donnie Stevens; Patti Stockdale; Buck Storm; Robert C. Stroud; Beth Summitt; Ken Swarner; Tiffany Tajiri; Donn Taylor Evelyn Taylor; Jill Thomas; Pegg Thomas; C Kevin Thompson; Tom Threadgill; Kari Trumbo; Mary Kay Tuberty; Susan L. Tuttle; Jennifer Uhlarik; Hannah Vanderpool; Denise Weimer; Beth E. Wescott; Karen Wingate; Maureen Wise; Frank Yates

Authors / Literary Agents: Linda S. Glaz (**L0398**); Patricia Riddle-Gaddis (**L0836**)

Literary Agent / President: Joyce A. Hart (**L0450**)

Literary Agents: Diana Flegal; Jim Hart (**L0449**)

L0452 Harvey Klinger, Inc

Literary Agency
300 West 55th Street, Suite 11V, New York, NY 10019
United States
Tel: +1 (212) 581-7068

queries@harveyklinger.com

http://www.harveyklinger.com

Professional Body: Association of American Literary Agents (AALA)

Types: Fiction; Nonfiction
Formats: Film Scripts; TV Scripts
Subjects: Adventure; Autobiography; Business; Comedy / Humour; Commercial; Contemporary; Cookery; Crafts; Crime; Culture; Current Affairs; Design; Fantasy; Health; History; Horror; How To; Lifestyle; Literary; Literature; Media; Medicine; Music; Mystery; Personal Development; Politics; Psychology; Romance; Science; Science Fiction; Spirituality; Sport; Suspense; Technology; Thrillers; Travel; Westerns; Women's Interests
Markets: Adult; Children's; Young Adult

Send: Query
Don't send: Full text
How to send: Email

Costs: Author covers sundry admin costs.

Send query by email. No submissions by post. Do not query more than one agent at the agency at a time. See website for individual agent interests and email addresses. No screenplays, or queries by phone or fax. See website for full submission guidelines.

Literary Agents: David Dunton (*L0285*); Harvey Klinger (*L0574*); Wendy Levinson (*L0611*); Rachel Ridout (*L0837*); Andrew Somberg (*L0928*)

L0453 **Antony Harwood**
Literary Agent
United Kingdom

Literary Agency: Antony Harwood Limited **(L0042)**

L0454 **Susan Hawk**
Literary Agent
United States

http://www.upstartcrowliterary.com/agent/susan-hawk/
https://twitter.com/@susanhawk

Literary Agency: Upstart Crow Literary **(L0995)**

CHILDREN'S
  Fiction
    Chapter Books; Middle Grade; Picture Books
  Nonfiction > *Nonfiction Books*

TEEN > **Fiction** > *Novels*

YOUNG ADULT > **Fiction** > *Novels*

Closed to approaches.

Represents work for children and teens only: picture books, chapter books, middle grade, and young adult, along with some non-fiction for young readers. She doesn't represent adult projects.

L0455 **Molly Ker Hawn**
Literary Agent
United Kingdom

hawnqueries@thebentagency.com

http://www.thebentagency.com/molly-ker-hawn
http://www.twitter.com/mollykh
https://www.publishersmarketplace.com/members/mkhawn

Literary Agency: The Bent Agency (UK) **(L0089)**

CHILDREN'S
  Fiction
    Graphic Novels; Middle Grade
  Nonfiction > *Nonfiction Books*

YOUNG ADULT > **Fiction**
  Graphic Novels; Novels

How to send: Email

I'm looking for middle grade and young adult fiction and graphic novels that are inventive, well-crafted, and rich with emotion. I'm also interested in non-fiction for readers ages 8–18. I like wit, but not snark; I prefer books that lean more toward literary than commercial, but of course, my perfect book neatly bridges the two. The fiction on my list all has a strong sense of authentic place, whether real or imaginary; I'm not the right agent for books with animal protagonists. Except maybe cats.

Assistant Agent: Martha Perotto-Wills **(L0788)**

L0456 **Viola Hayden**
Associate Agent
United Kingdom

http://submissions.curtisbrown.co.uk/agents/

Literary Agency: Curtis Brown **(L0233)**
Literary Agent: Jonny Geller **(L0388)**

Fiction > *Novels*

Nonfiction > *Nonfiction Books*

Send: Query; Synopsis; Writing sample
How to send: Online submission system

I am looking for confident writing that puts me at ease from the first page; a captivating voice or character, an exciting style, an unusual structure, an original premise or fresh take. A book that can't be replicated. If you have written a book like that – fiction or non-fiction – then it's on my wish list.

L0457 **Josephine Hayes**
Literary Agent
United Kingdom

josephinesubmissions@
theblairpartnership.com

https://www.theblairpartnership.com/our_people/josephine-hayes/
https://twitter.com/josephine_hayes

Literary Agency: The Blair Partnership **(L0100)**

CHILDREN'S > **Fiction**
  Board Books: Commercial; Contemporary
  Chapter Books: Commercial; Contemporary
  Early Readers: Commercial
  Middle Grade: Adventure; Comedy / Humour; Commercial; Contemporary; Low Fantasy; Mystery
  Picture Books: Commercial; Contemporary
TEEN > **Fiction** > *Novels*
  General, and in particular: Comedy / Humour

YOUNG ADULT > **Fiction** > *Novels*
  General, and in particular: Comedy / Humour; Romance

How to send: Email

Naturally gravitates towards quality middle-grade fiction, especially a good mystery or adventure with a dash of light fantasy (nothing high fantasy), or something whacky with a great sense of humour. In teen and YA fiction she loves an anti-hero, and is always keen to see strong young female characters taking centre stage. She's after a standout YA romance or something with strong relationships and characters who you fall in love with and think about even when you're not reading. Across 7+ to YA she's looking for humourous chapter books with series potential, particularly for readers at the younger end. She's also searching for children's author/illustrators for 2-7+ with a contemporary, quirky style and non-rhyming picture book texts.

L0458 **David H. Headley**
Literary Agent; Managing Director
United Kingdom

http://www.dhhliteraryagency.com/david-h-headley.html
https://twitter.com/davidhheadley

Literary Agency: DHH Literary Agency Ltd **(L0264)**

Fiction > *Novels*
  General, and in particular: Crime; High Concept; Suspense; Thrillers

Nonfiction > *Nonfiction Books*
  Biography; Food; History; Memoir; Politics; Popular Culture; Science

Closed to approaches.

Actively looking for: character-driven debuts and epic sweeping stories with big universal themes. Issue-driven crime and thrillers, high concepts and fear-inducing suspense. Thought-provoking stories, original narrative voices, uplifting fiction and emotional journeys – "stories that I don't want to end". Also accepts non-fiction submissions, from memoir, biography and history to politics, science, popular culture and food.

Authors: Kishan Devani BEM; Graham Bartlett; R.C. Bridgestock; Caraline Brown; Paul Burston; Paul Fraser Collard; M.W. Craven; Rachael Featherstone; David Fennell; J.D. Fennell; Fishlove; Essie Fox; Anita Frank; Erin Green; Lisa Hilton; Dixie Innes; Ragnar Jonasson; Katrín Júlíusdóttir; Jean Levy; Sean Lusk; Jo Lyons; Adrian Magson; Brian McGilloway; Janie Millman; Noel O'Reilly; Ane Riel; Robert Scragg; Victoria Selman; Andrew Swanston; Eleanor Tattersfield; Jo Thomas; Bar Tozino; L.C. Tyler; Stephen Walker; Jon Watts; A. J. West; Clare Whitfield; Mic Wright; Eva Björg Ægisdottir

L0459 **Duncan Heath**
Literary Agent
United Kingdom

Literary Agency: Independent Talent Group Ltd **(L0496)**

L0460 **Rupert Heath**
Literary Agent
United Kingdom

Literary Agency: Rupert Heath Literary Agency **(L0870)**

L0461 **Carol Heaton**
Literary Agent
United Kingdom

http://greeneheaton.co.uk/agents/carol-heaton/

Literary Agency: Greene & Heaton Ltd **(L0419)**

Fiction > *Novels*

Nonfiction > *Nonfiction Books*

Biography; Current Affairs; Gardening; Health; History; Travel

Closed to approaches.

Author Estate: The Estate of P.D. James

Authors: Stephen Anderton; Lewis Chester; Helen Craig; Charles Elliott; Michael Frayn; Richard Jenkyns

L0462 Grace Heifetz

Literary Agent
Australia

Literary Agency: Curtis Brown (Australia) Pty Ltd (**L0234**)

L0463 Jenny Heller

Literary Agent
United Kingdom

Literary Agency: Robertson Murray Literary Agency (**L0845**)

L0464 Saritza Hernandez

Literary Agent
United States

Literary Agency: Corvisiero Literary Agency

Closed to approaches.

L0465 Andrew Hewson

Literary Agent; Company Director
United Kingdom

http://www.johnsonandalcock.co.uk/andrew-hewson

Literary Agency: Johnson & Alcock (**L0528**)

Closed to approaches.

L0466 Lane Heymont

President; Literary Agent
United States

https://www.thetobiasagency.com/lane-heymont
https://querymanager.com/query/1291
http://aaronline.org/Sys/PublicProfile/27203936/417813

Literary Agency: The Tobias Literary Agency (**L0983**)
Professional Body: Association of American Literary Agents (AALA)

ADULT
 Fiction > *Novels*
  Commercial; Horror; Speculative; Women's Fiction

 Nonfiction > *Nonfiction Books*
  Celebrity; Culture; History; Popular Culture; Science

YOUNG ADULT > **Fiction** > *Novels*

Send: Author bio; Query; Market info; Writing sample
How to send: Query Manager

Represents a broad range of commercial fiction and serious nonfiction. In fiction, he is open to projects broadly defined as speculative fiction. He is most interested in horror defined however one defines it. This includes select young adult projects. He prefers contemporary settings and is always looking for own voices projects by BIPOC, LGBTQIA+, and other underrepresented cultures/identities in both fiction and nonfiction. In nonfiction, Lane acquires celebrity projects, science, cultural studies, history, and pop-culture.

L0467 HG Literary

Literary Agency
United States

https://www.hgliterary.com

Associate Agents: Jon Cobb (**L0205**); Ellen Goff (**L0402**)

Literary Agent / Vice President: Soumeya Bendimerad Roberts (**L0844**)

Literary Agents: Victoria Wells Arms (**L0046**); Julia Kardon (**L0548**); Rhea Lyons (**L0651**)

Literary Agents / Partners: Josh Getzler (**L0391**); Carrie Hannigan (**L0440**)

L0468 hhb agency ltd

Literary Agency
62 Grafton Way, London, W1T 5DW
United Kingdom
Tel: +44 (0) 20 7405 5525

http://www.hhbagency.com
https://twitter.com/hhbagencyltd

Professional Body: The Association of Authors' Agents (AAA)

Fiction > *Novels*

Nonfiction
 Illustrated Books: General
 Nonfiction Books: Biography; Comedy / Humour; Cookery; Crafts; Current Affairs; Entertainment; Food; History; Memoir; Politics; Popular Culture; Science; Sport

Closed to approaches.

Represents nonfiction writers, particularly in the areas of journalism, history and politics, travel and adventure, contemporary autobiography and biography, books about words and numbers, popular culture and quirky humour, entertainment and television, business, family memoir, food and cookery. Also handles commercial fiction. Not accepting unsolicited submissions as at September 2019.

Literary Agents: Heather Holden-Brown (**L0477**); Elly James (**L0513**)

L0469 Sophie Hicks

Literary Agent
United Kingdom

sophie@sophiehicksagency.com

http://www.sophiehicksagency.com/sophiehicks

Literary Agency: Sophie Hicks Agency (**L0931**)

ADULT
 Fiction > *Novels*
 Nonfiction > *Nonfiction Books*

CHILDREN'S > **Fiction** > *Middle Grade*

YOUNG ADULT > **Fiction** > *Novels*

Does not want:

Fiction > *Novels*: Women's Fiction

L0470 Hill Nadell Literary Agency

Literary Agency
6442 Santa Monica Blvd, Suite 201, Los Angeles, CA 90038
United States
Tel: +1 (310) 860-9605
Fax: +1 (323) 380-5206

queries@hillnadell.com

http://www.hillnadell.com

Types: Fiction; Nonfiction
Subjects: Autobiography; Commercial; Cookery; Culture; Current Affairs; Health; History; Legal; Literary; Nature; Politics; Science; Thrillers; Women's Interests
Markets: Adult; Young Adult

Send: Query
Don't send: Full text
How to send: Email

Costs: Author covers sundry admin costs.

Handles current affairs, food, memoirs and other narrative nonfiction, fiction, thrillers, upmarket women's fiction, literary fiction, genre fiction, graphic novels, and occasional young adult novels. No scripts or screenplays. Accepts queries both by post and by email. See website for full submission guidelines.

Literary Agent: Dara Hyde (*L0493*)

President: Bonnie Nadell

L0471 Sam Hiyate

Literary Agent; President; Chief Executive Officer
Canada

Literary Agency: The Rights Factory

Associate Agent / Author: Cecilia Lyra

Authors: Oscar Allueva; Ho Che Anderson; Michel Basilières; Margot Berwin; Charles Bongers; Alex Brueckmann; Varda Burstyn; Dave Butler; Timothy Christian; Elaine Dewar; Oonagh Duncan; Norine Dworkin-McDaniel; Benjamin Errett; Saad T. Farooqi; Bronwyn Fischer; Sara Flemington; Debbie Fox; Patricia Fulton; Rupinder Gill; Jesse Gilmour; Peter

Goddard; Lee Matthew Goldberg; Shinan Govani; Lee Gowan; Alexandra Grigorescu; Nadia Guo; Kamal Gupta; Nicole Hackett; Wes Hall; Denise Hearn; Alex Huntley; Cole Imperi; Chris Johns; Sam Juric; Andrew Kaufman; Michelle Kim; Sohan Koonar; Arkadi Kuhlmann; David Layton; David Leach; Barbra Leslie; Claire Letemendia; Emily Lipinski; Anneke Lucas; Natalie MacLean; Kiirsten May; Maureen Medved; Mark Milke; Elana Millman; Nathaniel G Moore; Sally Moore; Hal Niedzviecki; Rebecca Nison; Ell Orion; Brad Orsted; Kathryn Paulsen; Nick Pengelley; Katie Peyton; Bruce Philp; Barbara Radecki; Greg Rhyno; Alexandra Risen; John Semley; Leslie Shimotakahara; David Skuy; Michael Soussan; Robert Earl Stewart; Stephen Stohn; Jonathan Tepper; Diane Terrana; Chris Turner; Joanne Vannicola; Alex Varricchio; Maurice Vellekoop; Willow Verkerk; Cory Vitiello; Andy Walker; Kay Walker; Imogen Lloyd Webber; Emily Weedon; Jessica Westhead; Molly Roden Winter; Showey Yazdanian; E. Paul Zehr; Yvette d'Entremont

L0472 Victoria Hobbs

Literary Agent
United Kingdom

https://amheath.com/agents/victoria-hobbs/
http://twitter.com/victoriajhobbs

Literary Agency: A.M. Heath & Company Limited, Author's Agents (**L0003**)

Fiction > *Novels*
General, and in particular: Crime; Post-Apocalyptic; Thrillers

Nonfiction > *Nonfiction Books*
General, and in particular: Cookery; Food; Health; Narrative Nonfiction; Nature; Politics

Agency Assistant: Jessica Lee

L0473 Gail Hochman

Literary Agent
Brandt & Hochman Literary Agents, Inc., 1501 Broadway, Suite 2310, New York, NY 10036
United States

ghochman@bromasite.com

Literary Agency: Brandt & Hochman Literary Agents, Inc. (**L0119**)
Professional Body: Association of American Literary Agents (AALA)

ADULT
Fiction > *Novels*: Literary

Nonfiction > *Nonfiction Books*
General, and in particular: Literary Memoir

CHILDREN'S > **Fiction** > *Novels*

Send: Query
How to send: Email

L0474 Samuel Hodder

Literary Agent
United Kingdom

Literary Agency: Blake Friedmann Literary Agency Ltd (**L0101**)

L0475 Jodie Hodges

Literary Agent
United Kingdom
Tel: +44 (0) 20 3214 0891

jhodges@unitedagents.co.uk

https://www.unitedagents.co.uk/
jhodgesunitedagentscouk
http://twitter.com/jodiehodges31

Literary Agency: United Agents (**L0992**)

CHILDREN'S > **Fiction**
Middle Grade; *Picture Books*
TEEN > **Fiction** > *Novels*

YOUNG ADULT > **Fiction** > *Novels*

Send: Query; Synopsis; Writing sample; Full text
How to send: Email attachment
How not to send: Post

"I enjoy strong, original storytelling and a unique voice. I have a passion for funny writing for 7-12s and also a penchant for the realism of teenage life – be that gritty or hilarious – in writing for that age group. That said, I also love classic, epic adventure stories and a sprinkling of the fantastic."

"Additionally, I'm always searching for children's book illustrators or writer/illustrators with a contemporary, quirky style. A kind word of advice, though, please ensure your portfolio is ready for children's books. Make sure you're showing the best of yourself by showcasing the sort of illustration found in children's picture books in the UK."

Submit by email to the agent's assistant.

Agency Assistant: Molly Jamieson

Associate Agent: Emily Talbot (**L0966**)

L0476 Scott Hoffman

Literary Agent; Partner
United States

shoffman@foliolitmanagement.com

https://www.foliolit.com/agents-1/scott-hoffman

Literary Agency: Folio Literary Management, LLC (**L0343**)

Nonfiction > *Nonfiction Books*
Business; Fitness; Health; History; Psychology; Social Issues; Wellbeing

Send: Query; Writing sample
How to send: In the body of an email
How not to send: Email attachment

Send query by email with first ten pages. Assume rejection if no response within six weeks.

L0477 Heather Holden-Brown

Literary Agent
United Kingdom

heather@hhbagency.com

Literary Agency: hhb agency ltd (**L0468**)

L0478 Holroyde Cartey

Literary Agency
United Kingdom

http://www.holroydecartey.com

Professional Body: The Association of Authors' Agents (AAA)

Handles fiction and nonfiction for children of all ages, including picture books. Also represents illustrators. Welcomes submissions from debut and established authors and illustrators. Send query by email only, with cover letter, synopsis, and full ms as separate Word file attachments. See website for individual agent details and interests and approach one agent only. Aims to respond to every submission, within six weeks.

Literary Agents: Claire Cartey (**L0170**); Penny Holroyde (**L0479**)

L0479 Penny Holroyde

Literary Agent
United Kingdom

penny@holroydecartey.com

https://www.holroydecartey.com/about.html
https://www.holroydecartey.com/submissions.html

Literary Agency: Holroyde Cartey (**L0478**)

ADULT > **Fiction** > *Novels*

CHILDREN'S > **Fiction** > *Novels*

NEW ADULT > **Fiction** > *Novels*

YOUNG ADULT > **Fiction** > *Novels*

Send: Synopsis; Full text
How to send: Email attachment

L0480 Vanessa Holt

Literary Agent
United Kingdom

v.holt791@btinternet.com

Literary Agency: Vanessa Holt Ltd (**L0999**)

L0481 Kate Hordern

Literary Agent
United Kingdom

kate@khla.co.uk

https://twitter.com/katehordern

Literary Agency: Kate Hordern Literary Agency (**L0554**)

ADULT
Fiction > *Novels*
General, and in particular: Commercial;
Crime; Historical Fiction; Literary;
Psychological Suspense; Speculative;
Upmarket Women's Fiction

Nonfiction > *Nonfiction Books*
History; Memoir

CHILDREN'S > **Fiction** > *Middle Grade*

L0482 Sarah Hornsley
Literary Agent
United Kingdom

http://www.thebentagency.com/sarah-hornsley
https://twitter.com/SarahHornsley

Literary Agency: The Bent Agency (UK)
(**L0089**)

ADULT
Fiction > *Novels*
Commercial; Contemporary; Crime;
Historical Fiction; Horror; Literary;
Psychological Suspense; Speculative;
Thrillers

Nonfiction > *Nonfiction Books*
Cookery; Memoir; Popular Culture

YOUNG ADULT > **Fiction** > *Novels*

Closed to approaches.

My taste is varied and I'm looking for
commercial and accessible literary adult
fiction, YA and non-fiction. I am on the hunt
for adult contemporary fiction and in particular
I love novels which make me think about
society from a different angle or pose a moral
question. I'm also looking for a gorgeous love
story and I don't mind if this is high-concept
and hugely commercial or if it's more literary.
I also represent a range of crime and thrillers
full of twists and turns with interesting and
vivid settings. I'd also love to find an upmarket
historical novel which places women at the
forefront. In terms of non-fiction, I'm looking
for memoir and narrative non-fiction with
some social commentary. For YA, I'm
particularly interested in contemporary stories.

L0483 Millie Hoskins
Associate Agent
United Kingdom

https://www.unitedagents.co.uk/
mhoskinsunitedagentscouk

Literary Agency: United Agents (**L0992**)

Fiction > *Novels*
Commercial; Historical Fiction; Literary;
Thrillers; Upmarket; Women's Fiction

Nonfiction > *Nonfiction Books*
Memoir; Narrative Nonfiction

Send: Synopsis; Writing sample; Proposal
How to send: Email

On the lookout for exciting debut authors of
both commercial and literary upmarket fiction
of any genre (excluding SFF), with a particular
focus on women's fiction, thrillers and
historical fiction. Especially interested in
finding more great zeitgeist novels for our
generation and discovering new experiences
and places through people's writing. With
regards to non-fiction, largely drawn to
memoirs and narrative non-fiction with a
distinct writing style, an incredible story, or an
underrepresented voice or topic.

Authors: Amrou Al-Kadhi; Hina Belitz; LMK
Berry; Sophie Ellis Bextor; Quentin Blake;
Maggie Brookes; Emma Campbell; Brian
Catling; Jessie Cave; Leah Cowan; JP
Delaney; Rebecca Gibb; Susannah Hoffman;
Alison Irvine; Lenka Janiurek; Katie Kirby;
James McNicholas; Coco Mellors; Michelle
Morgan; Bobby Palmer; Philip Pullman;
Talulah Riley; LJ Ross; Kate Saunders; Mika
Simmons

L0484 Valerie Hoskins
Literary Agent
United Kingdom

Literary Agency: Valerie Hoskins Associates
(**L0998**)

L0485 Amanda Fitzalan Howard
Literary Agent
United Kingdom

Literary Agency: AHA Talent Ltd (**L0019**)

L0486 Charlotte Howard
Literary Agent
United Kingdom

Literary Agency: Fox & Howard Literary
Agency (**L0351**)

L0487 Clare Hulton
Literary Agent
United Kingdom

Literary Agency: Clare Hulton Literary Agency
(**L0200**)

L0488 Greg Hunt
Literary Agent
United Kingdom

Literary Agency: Independent Talent Group
Ltd (**L0496**)

L0489 Hunter Profiles
Literary Agency
London
United Kingdom

info@hunterprofiles.com

http://www.hunterprofiles.com

Fiction > *Novels*: Commercial

Nonfiction > *Nonfiction Books*: Commercial

Send: Query; Author bio; Synopsis; Writing
sample
How to send: Email
How not to send: Post

We specialise in commercial and narrative
fiction and nonfiction. We only accept
proposals by email. See website for submission
guidelines.

Author / Literary Agent / Publisher: Humfrey
Hunter (**L0490**)

L0490 Humfrey Hunter
Literary Agent; Publisher; Author
United Kingdom

https://www.silvertailbooks.com/author/
humfrey-hunter/

Literary Agency: Hunter Profiles (**L0489**)
Book Publisher: Silvertail Books (**P0763**)

A former journalist and public relations
consultant who is now a publisher and literary
agent.

L0491 Alexis Hurley
Literary Agent
United States

Literary Agency: InkWell Management
(**L0499**)

L0492 Annie Hwang
Literary Agent
United States

https://twitter.com/AnnieAHwang
https://www.publishersmarketplace.com/
members/hwangan/

Literary Agency: Ayesha Pande Literary
(**L0052**)

Fiction > *Novels*: Literary

Nonfiction > *Nonfiction Books*: Narrative
Nonfiction

Send: Pitch; Author bio; Synopsis; Writing
sample
How to send: Online submission system

Represents voice-driven literary fiction and
select nonfiction. In particular, she gravitates
toward subversive, genre-inflected literary
fiction and impactful mission-driven narrative
nonfiction that explores and grapples with the
complex, fundamental truths of our world.

L0493 Dara Hyde
Literary Agent
United States

Literary Agency: Hill Nadell Literary Agency
(**L0470**)

L0494 ILA (Intercontinental Literary Agency)
Literary Agency
5 New Concordia Wharf, Mill Street, London, SE1 2BB
United Kingdom
Tel: +44 (0) 20 7379 6611

ila@ila-agency.co.uk

http://www.ila-agency.co.uk

Professional Body: The Association of Authors' Agents (AAA)

ADULT
 Fiction in Translation > *Novels*
 Nonfiction in Translation > *Nonfiction Books*

CHILDREN'S > **Fiction in Translation** > *Novels*

Closed to approaches.

Handles translation rights only for, among others, the authors of LAW Ltd, London; Harold Matson Co. Inc., New York; PFD, London. Submissions accepted via client agencies and publishers only – no submissions from writers seeking agents.

Literary Agents: Sam Edenborough; Clementine Gaisman; Nicki Kennedy; Jenny Robson; Katherine West

L0495 Harry Illingworth
Literary Agent
United Kingdom

Literary Agency: DHH Literary Agency Ltd (**L0264**)

L0496 Independent Talent Group Ltd
Literary Agency
40 Whitfield Street, London, W1T 2RH
United Kingdom
Tel: +44 (0) 20 7636 6565

writersubmissions@independenttalent.com

http://www.independenttalent.com

Scripts
 Film Scripts; *Radio Scripts*; *TV Scripts*; *Theatre Scripts*

Closed to approaches.

Specialises in scripts and works in association with agencies in Los Angeles and New York. No submissions from North America.

Literary Agents: Roxana Adle (*L0015*); Oliver Azis (*L0056*); Anwar Chentoufi (*L0192*); Patrick Child (*L0193*); Francesca Devas (*L0261*); Alec Drysdale (*L0280*); Humphrey Elles-Hill (*L0302*); Olivia Gray (*L0413*); Duncan Heath (*L0459*); Greg Hunt (*L0488*); Jago Irwin (*L0507*); Georgia Kanner (*L0547*); Paul Lyon-Maris (*L0649*); Michael McCoy (*L0689*); Jennie Miller (*L0715*); Ikenna Obiekwe (*L0766*); Will Peterson (*L0794*);

Lyndsey Posner (*L0808*); Sue Rodgers (*L0852*); Laura Rourke (*L0867*); Alex Rusher (*L0873*); Paul Stevens (*L0942*); Jessica Stewart (*L0945*); Jessica Sykes (*L0963*); Jack Thomas (*L0974*); Sarah Williams (*L1040*); Hugo Young (*L1063*)

L0497 Fiona Inglis
Literary Agent
Australia

Literary Agency: Curtis Brown (Australia) Pty Ltd (**L0234**)

L0498 Ink and Colors Ltd
Literary Agency
Casella postale 10947, Cpd Milano Isola, 20110 Milano
Italy
Tel: +44 (0) 20 7558 8374

http://www.inkandcolors.com

ADULT
 Fiction > *Novels*
  General, and in particular: Commercial; Ethnic; Fantasy; Mystery; Romance; Science Fiction; Thrillers; Women's Fiction

 Nonfiction > *Nonfiction Books*
  General, and in particular: Adventure; Biography; Cookery; Crime; Current Affairs; Health; Memoir; New Age; Popular Culture; Psychology; Science; Spirituality

CHILDREN'S > **Fiction**
 Novels; *Picture Books*

Send: Query; Full text; Self-Addressed Stamped Envelope (SASE)
How to send: Post; Email
How not to send: Email attachment

Costs: Offers services that writers have to pay for.

International agency with offices in UK and Italy, representing Publishing Houses, Authors and Illustrators all over the world. On our website you'll find the submission guide and all information.

Accepts submissions by post with SASE or queries by email (no attachments).

firstwriter.com note: This agency submitted their details for inclusion in our database in January 2007. Upon receiving a negative feedback comment in June 2007 they have made demands that we remove the negative comment and have also made threats of legal action. We have offered to post their response to the negative comment, but this has only been met by further threats of legal action.

Literary Agent: Andrea Sabbadini

L0499 InkWell Management
Literary Agency
521 Fifth Avenue, 26th Floor, New York, NY

10175
United States
Tel: +1 (212) 922-3500
Fax: +1 (212) 922-0535

submissions@inkwellmanagement.com

http://www.inkwellmanagement.com

Types: Fiction; Nonfiction
Subjects: Business; Comedy / Humour; Commercial; Contemporary; Crime; Current Affairs; Finance; Health; History; Literary; Medicine; Mystery; Personal Development; Psychology; Thrillers
Markets: Adult

Send: Query
Don't send: Full text
How to send: Email

Accepts submissions in all genres, but no screenplays. Send query by email with up to two sample chapters. No large attachments. Response not guaranteed. Response within two months if interested. See website for full guidelines.

Literary Agents: Stephen Barbara (*L0062*); Lyndsey Blessing (*L0103*); William Callahan (*L0150*); Michael V. Carlisle (*L0158*); Sharon Chudnow; Catherine Drayton (*L0277*); Naomi Eisenbeiss (**L0296**); David Forrer (*L0346*); Claire Friedman (**L0363**); Emma Gougeon; Alexis Hurley (*L0491*); Nathaniel Jacks (*L0509*); Phoebe Low; George Lucas (*L0638*); Jessica Mileo (*L0711*); Christina Miller (**L0714**); Michael Mungiello (*L0732*); Jacqueline Murphy (*L0735*); Kristin van Ogtrop (*L0768*); Charlie Olsen (*L0769*); Richard Pine (*L0800*); Eliza Rothstein (**L0865**); Jessie Thorsted (*L0980*); Maria Whelan (**L1029**); Jenny Witherell (*L1051*); Kimberly Witherspoon (*L1052*)

L0500 InterSaga
Literary Agency
237 St Helier Avenue, Morden, Surrey, SM4 6JH
United Kingdom
Tel: +44 (0) 7534 013597

anna@intersaga.co.uk

http://www.intersaga.co.uk

Types: Fiction; Nonfiction; Poetry; Scripts
Formats: Reference
Subjects: Adventure; Autobiography; Commercial; Contemporary; Drama; Experimental; Fantasy; Literary; Literary Criticism; Romance; Satire; Science Fiction; Suspense; Thrillers; Traditional; Women's Interests
Markets: Adult; Children's; Young Adult

Send: Full text
How to send: Email

A literary agency that started in the heart of Chiswick. The managing director is a former bookseller and bookshop manager. You can read more on the website. All genres are welcome. We look forward to hearing from you!

Authors: Jane Clamp; Susan Lee Kerr; Kate Vick

L0501 Irene Goodman Literary Agency (IGLA)

Literary Agency
27 West 24th St., Suite 804, New York, NY 10010
United States

irene.queries@irenegoodman.com

http://www.irenegoodman.com

Professional Body: Association of American Literary Agents (AALA)

Types: Fiction; Nonfiction
Subjects: Autobiography; Beauty; Commercial; Contemporary; Cookery; Culture; Design; Fantasy; Fashion; History; Horror; Lifestyle; Literary; Mystery; Politics; Romance; Science; Science Fiction; Society; Suspense; Thrillers; Women's Interests
Markets: Adult; Children's; Young Adult

Send: Query
Don't send: Full text
How to send: Email

Select specific agent to approach based on details given on website (specific agent email addresses on website). Send query by email only with synopsis, bio, and first ten pages in the body of the email. No poetry, inspirational fiction, screenplays, or children's picture books. Response only if interested. See website for further details.

Literary Agents: Margaret Danko (**L0240**); Irene Goodman (*L0407*); Pam Gruber (**L0426**); Miriam Kriss (*L0582*); Natalie Lakosil (**L0588**); Victoria Marini (*L0671*); Lee O'Brien (**L0762**); Kim Perel (*L0786*); Barbara Poelle (*L0805*); Whitney Ross

L0502 Amy Ireson

Literary Agent
United Kingdom

Literary Agency: The Narrow Road Company (**L0743**)

L0503 Dan Ireson

Literary Agent
United Kingdom

Literary Agency: The Narrow Road Company (**L0743**)

L0504 James Ireson

Literary Agent
United Kingdom

Literary Agency: The Narrow Road Company (**L0743**)

L0505 Richard Ireson

Literary Agent
United Kingdom

richardireson@narrowroad.co.uk

Literary Agency: The Narrow Road Company (**L0743**)

Closed to approaches.

Do not approach directly. Approaches should be sent to the agency rather than individual agents.

L0506 Iris Blasi

Literary Agent
United States

iris@carolmannagency.com

https://www.carolmannagency.com/iris-blasi
https://twitter.com/IrisBlasi
https://www.instagram.com/irisblasi

Literary Agency: Carol Mann Agency (**L0161**)

Nonfiction > *Nonfiction Books*
Biography; Cultural Criticism; Current Affairs; Environment; Feminism; History; Intersectional Feminism; Memoir; Narrative Nonfiction; Nature; Politics; Popular Culture; Science; Social Justice; Sustainable Living

Send: Query; Author bio; Synopsis; Writing sample
How to send: In the body of an email
How not to send: Post

L0507 Jago Irwin

Literary Agent
United Kingdom

Literary Agency: Independent Talent Group Ltd (**L0496**)

L0508 J. de S. Associates, Inc.

Literary Agency
9 Shagbark Road, South Norwalk, CT 06854
United States
Tel: +1 (203) 838-7571
Fax: +1 (203) 866-2713

jdespoel@aol.com

http://www.jdesassociates.com

Types: Fiction; Nonfiction
Subjects: Commercial; Literary
Markets: Adult

Send: Query
Don't send: Full text
How to send: Email

Welcomes brief queries by post and by email, but no samples or other material unless requested.

Literary Agent: Jacques de Spoelberch (*L0933*)

L0509 Nathaniel Jacks

Literary Agent
United States

Literary Agency: InkWell Management (**L0499**)

L0510 Jennifer Jackson

Literary Agent
United States

Literary Agency: Donald Maass Literary Agency (**L0273**)

L0511 Lisa Jackson

Literary Agent
United States

Literary Agency: Alive Literary Agency (**L0026**)

L0512 The James Fitzgerald Agency

Literary Agency
PO Box 940, 70 Irish Road, Ranchos de Taos, NM 87557
United States
Tel: +1 (575) 758-2687

submissions@jfitzagency.com

https://jfitzagency.com

ADULT
Fiction > *Novels*
Crime; Popular Culture

Nonfiction
Illustrated Books: Popular Culture
Nonfiction Books: Adventure; Biography; Crime; Films; Food; History; Memoir; Music; Popular Culture; Religion; Socio-Political; Spirituality; Sport; TV
CHILDREN'S > **Fiction** > *Novels*

YOUNG ADULT > **Fiction** > *Novels*

Send: Full text; Synopsis; Author bio; Market info
How to send: Email attachment

Primarily represents books reflecting the popular culture of the day, in fiction, nonfiction, graphic and packaged books. No poetry or screenplays. All information must be submitted in English, even if the manuscript is in another language. See website for detailed submission guidelines.

Editorial Assistant: Anna Tatelman

Literary Agent: Dylan Lowy

Literary Agent / President: James Fitzgerald

L0513 Elly James

Literary Agent
United Kingdom

elly@hhbagency.com

Literary Agency: hhb agency ltd (**L0468**)

L0514 Jane Dowary Agency
Literary Agency
9B Little Street, Hawthorne, NJ 07506
United States

jane.dowary@gmail.com

http://www.janedowaryagency.mozello.com
https://accrispin.blogspot.com/2014/02/alert-jane-dowary-agency.html

Types: Fiction
Subjects: Adventure; Commercial;
Contemporary; Crime; Drama; Fantasy;
History; Horror; Literary; Mystery; Romance;
Satire; Science; Science Fiction; Suspense;
Thrillers
Markets: Adult; Children's; Young Adult

Send: Query
Don't send: Full text
How to send: Email

I only accept email queries. No queries by
regular mail, please. Please include a full
synopsis of the novel, first sample chapter, and
please let me know if the novel is complete and
if any other agent/Editor/Publisher/Movie
Producer has read the book (This will not stop
me from reading a project I am interested in).

Author: Gary B. Maier

Literary Agent: Julia Levin (**L0610**)

L0515 Jane Judd Literary Agency
Literary Agency
18 Belitha Villas, London, N1 1PD
United Kingdom
Tel: +44 (0) 20 7607 0273

https://www.janejudd.com
https://twitter.com/@Janelitagent

Professional Body: The Association of
Authors' Agents (AAA)

Fiction > *Novels*
   Commercial; Literary

Nonfiction > *Nonfiction Books*
   Cookery; Films; Sport

Closed to approaches.

**Closed to submissions as at December 2019.
Check website for current status.**

For fiction, send query with synopsis, first two
or three chapters, and SAE. For nonfiction
send first and/or other sample chapter,
synopsis, market info, chapter breakdown, and
any supporting evidence or articles. You may
telephone in advance to save time for both
parties. Also option of submitting online using
contact form on website. Particularly interested
in self-help, health, biography, popular history
and narrative nonfiction, general and historical
fiction and literary fiction.

Authors: Lynne Barrett-Lee; Michelle Birkby;
Andy Dougan; Quentin Falk; Cliff Goodwin;
Kathleen Griffin; Jill Mansell; David Winner

Literary Agent: Jane Judd (*L0535*)

L0516 Janklow & Nesbit UK Ltd
Literary Agency
13a Hillgate Street, London, W8 7SP
United Kingdom
Tel: +44 (0) 20 7243 2975

submissions@janklow.co.uk

http://www.janklowandnesbit.co.uk
https://twitter.com/JanklowUK

Professional Body: The Association of
Authors' Agents (AAA)

ADULT
   Fiction > *Novels*
      General, and in particular: Commercial;
      Literary

   Nonfiction > *Nonfiction Books*

CHILDREN'S > **Fiction** > *Novels*

YOUNG ADULT > **Fiction** > *Novels*

Send: Query; Synopsis; Writing sample
How to send: Email

Send query by email, including informative
covering letter providing background about
yourself and your writing; first three chapters /
approx. 50 pages; a brief synopsis for fiction,
or a full outline for nonfiction.

Literary Agents: Rebecca Carter (**L0169**);
Claire Paterson Conrad (**L0214**); Will Francis
(**L0358**); Hellie Ogden (**L0767**)

L0517 Oscar Janson-Smith
Literary Agent
United Kingdom

Literary Agency: Kruger Cowne (**L0583**)

L0518 Javelin
Literary Agency
203 South Union Street, Alexandria, VA
22314
United States
Tel: +1 (703) 490-8845

submissions@javelindc.com
hello@javelindc.com

http://javelindc.com

Nonfiction > *Nonfiction Books*
   History; Journalism; Politics; Science

Send: Proposal
How to send: Email

Represents presidential contenders, diplomats,
journalists, historians, scientists – and others
with a unique and compelling story to share.

L0519 The Jean V. Naggar Literary Agency
Literary Agency
216 East 75th Street, Suite 1E, New York, NY
10021

United States
Tel: +1 (212) 794-1082

jvnla@jvnla.com

http://www.jvnla.com

Professional Body: Association of American
Literary Agents (AALA)

Types: Fiction; Nonfiction
Subjects: Adventure; Autobiography; Comedy
/ Humour; Commercial; Cookery; Crime;
Culture; Current Affairs; Fantasy; Gothic;
Health; History; Lifestyle; Literary; Music;
Mystery; Personal Development; Psychology;
Romance; Science; Sport; Suspense; Thrillers;
Women's Interests
Markets: Adult; Children's; Young Adult

Send: Query
Don't send: Full text

Accepts queries via online submission system
only. See website for more details.

Literary Agents: Alicia Brooks (*L0129*); Jean
Naggar (*L0742*); Ariana Philips (**L0796**); Alice
Tasman (*L0969*); Jennifer Weltz (*L1025*)

L0520 Carolyn Jenks
Literary Agent; Company Director
United States

carolyn@carolynjenksagency.com

https://www.carolynjenksagency.com/agent/
CAROLYN-JENKS

Literary Agency: Carolyn Jenks Agency
(**L0164**)

Fiction > *Novels*

Nonfiction > *Nonfiction Books*

Send: Author bio; Writing sample; Pitch
How to send: In the body of an email

L0521 Jenny Brown Associates
Literary Agency
31 Marchmont Road, Edinburgh, Scotland,
EH9 1HU
United Kingdom
Tel: +44 (0) 1312 295334

submissions@jennybrownassociates.com

https://www.jennybrownassociates.com

Professional Body: The Association of
Authors' Agents (AAA)

Types: Fiction; Nonfiction
Subjects: Autobiography; Comedy / Humour;
Commercial; Crime; Culture; Finance; History;
Literary; Music; Romance; Science; Sport;
Thrillers; Women's Interests
Markets: Adult; Children's

Send: Query
Don't send: Full text

Submissions by email only. Accepts submissions only during specific reading periods. See website for details.

Literary Agents: Jenny Brown (*L0136*); Lucy Juckes (*L0534*)

L0522 Natalie Jerome
Literary Agent
United Kingdom

https://aevitascreative.com/agents/#agent-7411

Literary Agency: Aevitas Creative Management (ACM) UK (**L0017**)

ADULT > Nonfiction > *Nonfiction Books*
Commercial; Culture; Current Affairs; Entertainment; Food; Health; Music; Wellbeing

CHILDREN'S > **Fiction** > *Novels*

Send: Query; Writing sample
How to send: Online submission system

Has a specific interest in commercial nonfiction across areas of health and wellness, food, current events, culture, music and entertainment as well as looking for vibrant new authors in children's fiction.

L0523 JetReid Literary Agency
Literary Agency
151 1st Ave #257, New York, NY 10003
United States

http://www.jetreidliterary.com

Authors: Robin Becker; Bill Cameron; Gary Corby; Phillip DePoy; Stephanie Evans; Kennedy Foster; Lee Goodman; Dana Haynes; Patrick Lee; Thomas Lippman; Jeff Marks; Warren Richey; Terry Shames; Jeff Somers; Robert Stubblefield; Deb Vlock

Literary Agent: Janet Reid (**L0828**)

L0524 JFL Agency
Literary Agency
48 Charlotte Street, London, W1T 2NS
United Kingdom
Tel: +44 (0) 20 3137 8182

representation@jflagency.com
agents@jflagency.com

http://www.jflagency.com

Scripts
Film Scripts; *Radio Scripts*; *TV Scripts*; *Theatre Scripts*

Send: Query
How to send: Email

Handles scripts only (for television, film, theatre and radio). Considers approaches from established writers with broadcast experience, but only accepts submissions from new writers during specific periods – consult website for details.

Authors: Humphrey Barclay; Liam Beirne; Adam Bostock-Smith; Tim Brooke-Taylor; Ian Brown; Grant Cathro; Paul Charlton; Gabby Hutchinson Crouch; Bill Dare; Tim Dawson; Martin Day; Ed Dyson; Polly Eden; Jan Etherington; Sinéad Fagan; Anji Loman Field; Phil Ford; Patrick Gallagher; Ted Gannon; Lisa Gifford; Rob Gittins; Ben Harris; James Hendrie; Wayne Jackman; Tony Lee; Richard Leslie Lewis; Jane Marlow; Jonathan Morris; Cardy O'Donnell; Jim Pullin; Jackie Robb; Graeme Rooney; Gary Russell; David Semple; James Serafinowicz; Pete Sinclair; Paul Smith; Fraser Steele

Literary Agents: Alison Finch (*L0333*); Dominic Lord (*L0631*); Gary Wild (*L1035*)

L0525 Jim Donovan Literary
Literary Agency
5635 SMU Boulevard, Suite 201, Dallas, TX 75206
United States
Tel: +1 (214) 696-9411

jdliterary@sbcglobal.net

https://www.jimdonovanliterary.com

Fiction > *Novels*
Commercial; Literary; Mystery; Thrillers

Nonfiction > *Nonfiction Books*
American History; Biography; Military; Narrative Nonfiction; Popular Culture

Send: Query; Writing sample; Synopsis
How to send: Email; Post

Literary Agent: Melissa Shultz (*L0910*)

President: Jim Donovan

L0526 Jo Unwin Literary Agency
Literary Agency
West Wing, Somerset House, London, WC2R 1LA
United Kingdom
Tel: +44 (0) 20 7257 9599

submissions@jounwin.co.uk

http://www.jounwin.co.uk

Professional Body: The Association of Authors' Agents (AAA)

ADULT
Fiction > *Novels*
Nonfiction > *Nonfiction Books*

CHILDREN'S > Fiction > *Novels*

YOUNG ADULT > Fiction > *Novels*

Closed to approaches.

Handles literary fiction, commercial women's fiction, comic writing, narrative nonfiction, Young Adult fiction and fiction for children aged 9+. No poetry, picture books, or screenplays, except for existing clients. Accepts submissions by email. Mainly represents authors from the UK and Ireland, and sometimes Australia and New Zealand. Only represents US authors in very exceptional circumstances. See website for full guidelines.

Literary Agents: Donna Greaves (*L0415*); Rachel Mann (**L0667**); Milly Reilly (*L0829*); Jo Unwin (*L0994*)

L0527 Joelle Delbourgo Associates, Inc.
Literary Agency
101 Park St., Montclair, Montclair, NJ 07042
United States
Tel: +1 (973) 773-0836

joelle@delbourgo.com

http://www.delbourgo.com

Professional Body: Association of American Literary Agents (AALA)

ADULT
Fiction > *Novels*
Commercial; Fantasy; Literary; Mystery; Science Fiction; Thrillers

Nonfiction > *Nonfiction Books*
Biography; Business; Current Affairs; Health; History; Memoir; Mind, Body, Spirit; Narrative Nonfiction; Parenting; Popular Culture; Psychology; Science

CHILDREN'S
Fiction
Middle Grade; *Picture Books*
Nonfiction > *Nonfiction Books*

YOUNG ADULT
Fiction > *Novels*
Nonfiction > *Nonfiction Books*

Send: Query; Writing sample
How to send: Email
How not to send: Post

Costs: Author covers sundry admin costs.

A boutique literary agency based in the greater New York City area. We represent a wide range of authors writing for the adult trade market, from creative nonfiction to expert-driven nonfiction, commercial fiction to literary fiction, as well as new adult, young adult and middle grade fiction and nonfiction.

Authors: Tanya Acker; Jennifer Lynn Alvarez; Heather Anastasiu; Lisa Anselmo; Thomas Armstrong; Sara Au; Frances Bartkowski; Suzanne Bohan; Lynn Kiele Bonasia; Michele Borba; Robert Bornstein; Elizabeth Reid Boyd; Nora Bradbury-Haehl; Anne Greenwood Brown; Gay Browne; Ariel Burger; Craig Carlson; Debbie Cenziper; Rachael Cerrotti; Marj Charlier; John Christianson; Tara L. Clark; Gay Courter; Nancy Cowan; Karla Dougherty; Nancy Dreyfus; Charity Elder; Chris Farrell; Marilyn Fedewa; Laura Berman Fortgang; Susan Forward; Philip Freeman; Terry Gaspard; John Gaudet; Susan Gilbert-Collins; Ann E. Grant; Jonathon Grayson; Brenda Greene; Beth A. Grosshans; Julie L. Hall; Kate Harding; Laura Hartema; Kristi

Hedges; Holly Herrick; Helaina Hovitz; Erik Forrest Jackson; Theresa Kaminski; Rachelle Katz; Joseph Kelly; Stephen Kelly; Brynne S. Kennedy; Nancy Kennedy; Willem Kuyken; Mary Languirand; Missy Chase Lapine; Claire Lerner; Irene S. Levine; Alexandra Levitt; Geralyn Lucas; Lauren Mackler; Juliet Madison; Kerstin March; David J. Marsh; Chuck Martin; Lama Marut; Carol Masciola; Colleen O'Grady; Jim Obergefell; Elaine Neil Orr; Lindsey J. Palmer; Theresa Payton; Michelle Pearce; Julia Pimsleur; Gleb Raygorodetsky; Eliza Redgold; Michael Reichert; Ashley Rhodes-Courter; Paige Rien; Jillian Roberts; Tatsha Robertson; Lisa Romeo; Marilyn Simon Rothstein; Dale Russakoff; Michael Sadowski; Roberta Sandenbergh; Sue Scheff; Melissa Schorr; Ellen E. Schultz; Robert Sher; Heather Shumaker; Alexandra Silber; Pamela Slim; Laura Sobiech; Julie M. Stamm; Peter L. Stavinoha; Maryon Stewart; Nancy Rubin Stuart; Rachel Sulivan; Deborah J. Swiss; Jeff Sypeck; John Temple; Christopher Van Tilburg; Julie Valerie; Michael Volpatt; Caroline Welch; Kristin M. White; Barrie Wilson; Ben H. Winters; Jon Wuebben; Gabra Zackman; Peter Zheutlin; Gabe Zichermann

Literary Agents: Carrie Cantor (*L0153*); Joelle Delbourgo (*L0256*); Jacqueline Flynn (*L0340*)

L0528 Johnson & Alcock
Literary Agency
Bloomsbury House, 74-77 Great Russell Street, London, WC1B 3DA
United Kingdom
Tel: +44 (0) 20 7251 0125

http://www.johnsonandalcock.co.uk

Professional Body: The Association of Authors' Agents (AAA)

Send: Query; Synopsis; Writing sample
How to send: Email attachment
How not to send: Post

Send query by email to specific agent. Response only if interested. Include synopsis and first three chapters (approximately 50 pages).

Chair / Literary Agent: Michael Alcock (**L0023**)

Company Director / Literary Agent: Andrew Hewson (**L0465**)

Literary Agent / Managing Director: Anna Power (**L0811**)

Literary Agents: Liz Dennis; Becky Thomas; Ed Wilson (**L1046**)

L0529 Jonathan Clowes Ltd
Literary Agency
10 Iron Bridge House, Bridge Approach, London, NW1 8BD
United Kingdom

Tel: +44 (0) 20 7722 7674
Fax: +44 (0) 20 7722 7677

cara@jonathanclowes.co.uk

https://www.jonathanclowes.co.uk

Professional Body: The Association of Authors' Agents (AAA)

Types: Fiction; Nonfiction; Scripts
Formats: Film Scripts; Radio Scripts; TV Scripts; Theatre Scripts
Subjects: Commercial; Literary
Markets: Adult

Send: Query
Don't send: Full text
How to send: Email

Send query with synopsis and three chapters (or equivalent sample) by email. No science fiction, poetry, short stories, academic. Only considers film/TV clients with previous success in TV/film/theatre. If no response within six weeks, assume rejection.

Authors: Michael Baigent; David Bellamy; Oscar Brodkin; Angela Chadwick; Simon Critchley; Len Deighton; Maureen Duffy; Brian Freemantle; Miles Gibson; Victoria Glass; Rana Haddad; Francesca Hornak; Elizabeth Jane Howard; Ruqaya Izzidien; Richard Leigh; Doris Lessing; Mario Matassa; Clive McAlpin; Claire Miles; Teresa Forcades i Vila

Literary Agents: Ann Evans (*L0312*); Nemonie Craven Roderick (*L0851*); Cara Lee Simpson

L0530 Jonathan Pegg Literary Agency
Literary Agency
c/o Workshop, 47 Southgate Street, Winchester, SO23 7EH
United Kingdom
Tel: +44 (0) 1962 656101

submissions@jonathanpegg.com
info@jonathanpegg.com

https://jonathanpegg.com

Professional Body: The Association of Authors' Agents (AAA)

Fiction > *Novels*
   Historical Fiction; Literary; Suspense; Thrillers; Upmarket

Nonfiction
   Gift Books: Comedy / Humour
   Nonfiction Books: Biography; Business; Comedy / Humour; Current Affairs; History; Lifestyle; Memoir; Nature; Popular Psychology; Popular Science

Send: Query; Synopsis; Author bio; Market info; Writing sample
How to send: Email

Aims to read every submission and respond within a month, but cannot guarantee to do so in all cases.

Literary Agent: Jonathan Pegg

L0531 Jonathan Williams Literary Agency
Literary Agency
1 Urban Villas, Tivoli Terrace North, Dun Laoghaire, County Dublin, A96 YC95
Ireland
Tel: +353 (0) 1-280-3482
Fax: +353 (0) 1-280-3482

Types: Fiction; Nonfiction
Subjects: Literary
Markets: Adult

Costs: Offers services that writers have to pay for.

Agency also has agents in Holland, Italy, France, Spain, and Japan. Send SASE with IRCs if outside of Ireland. Charges a reading fee if a very fast decision is required.

Literary Agent: Rosney Mews

L0532 Robin Jones
Literary Agent
United Kingdom

https://twitter.com/AgentRobinJones

Literary Agency: Robin Jones Literary Agency (**L0847**)

L0533 Joy Harris Literary Agency, Inc.
Literary Agency
1501 Broadway, Suite 2605, New York, NY 10036
United States
Tel: +1 (212) 924-6269
Fax: +1 (212) 840-5776

submissions@joyharrisliterary.com

http://www.joyharrisliterary.com

Professional Body: Association of American Literary Agents (AALA)

Types: Fiction; Nonfiction; Translations
Formats: Short Fiction
Subjects: Autobiography; Comedy / Humour; Commercial; Culture; Experimental; History; Literary; Media; Mystery; Satire; Spirituality; Suspense; Women's Interests
Markets: Adult; Young Adult

Closed to approaches.

Costs: Author covers sundry admin costs.

Closed to submissions as at October 2019. Check website for current status.

Send query by email, including sample chapter or outline. No poetry, screenplays, genre fiction, self-help, or unsolicited mss. See website for full guidelines.

Literary Agents: Joy Harris; Adam Reed

L0534 Lucy Juckes
Literary Agent
United Kingdom

Literary Agency: Jenny Brown Associates
(**L0521**)

L0535 Jane Judd
Literary Agent
United Kingdom

Literary Agency: Jane Judd Literary Agency
(**L0515**)

L0536 Judy Daish Associates Ltd
Literary Agency
2 St Charles Place, London, W10 6EG
United Kingdom
Tel: +44 (0) 20 8964 8811
Fax: +44 (0) 20 8964 8966

judy@judydaish.com

http://www.judydaish.com

Types: Scripts
Formats: Film Scripts; Radio Scripts; TV Scripts; Theatre Scripts
Markets: Adult

Represents writers, directors, designers and choreographers for theatre, film, television, radio and opera. No books or unsolicited mss.

Literary Agents: Judy Daish (*L0238*); Tracey Elliston (*L0303*); Howard Gooding (*L0406*)

L0537 Julia Kingsford Ltd
Literary Agency
United Kingdom

query@juliakingsford.com

https://juliakingsford.com

Professional Body: The Association of Authors' Agents (AAA)

Closed to approaches.

Literary Agent: Julia Kingsford (**L0571**)

L0538 Julie Crisp Literary Agency
Literary Agency; Editorial Service
United Kingdom

julieacrisp@gmail.com

http://www.juliecrisp.co.uk
https://querymanager.com/query/2079

Professional Body: The Association of Authors' Agents (AAA)

Fiction > *Novels*
  Book Club Fiction; Crime; Fantasy; Historical Fiction; Science Fiction; Thrillers

How to send: Query Manager

Costs: Offers services that writers have to pay for.

Open to submissions and looking forward to considering any fantasy, science fiction, historical, bookclub, crime/thrillers. Would be particularly pleased to consider diverse and own voices novels.

Authors: E. J. Beaton; Heather Child; John Gwynne; Sam Hawke; Lucy Kissick; Devin Madson; Den Patrick; C. T. Rwizi; Nick Setchfield

L0539 Ria Julien
Literary Agent
United States

rj@goldinlit.com

https://francesgoldinliteraryagency.submittable.com/submit

Literary Agency: Frances Goldin Literary Agency, Inc. (**L0356**)

How to send: Submittable

L0540 Juliet Burton Literary Agency
Literary Agency
2 Clifton Avenue, London, W12 9DR
United Kingdom
Tel: +44 (0) 20 8762 0148

juliet.burton@julietburton.com

Professional Body: The Association of Authors' Agents (AAA)

Types: Fiction; Nonfiction
Subjects: Crime; Women's Interests
Markets: Adult

Send: Query
Don't send: Full text

Particularly interested in crime and women's fiction. Send query with SAE, synopsis, and two sample chapters. No poetry, plays, film scripts, children's, articles, academic material, science fiction, fantasy, or unsolicited MSS.

Literary Agent: Juliet Burton (*L0144*)

L0541 Juri Gabriel
Literary Agency
35 Camberwell Grove, London, SE5 8JA
United Kingdom
Tel: +44 (0) 20 7703 6186

juri@jurigabriel.com

Types: Fiction; Nonfiction
Markets: Adult

Send: Query
Don't send: Full text

Send query with 1-2 page synopsis and three sample chapters. Include SAE if submitting by post. No short stories, verse, articles, or books for children.

Authors: Nick Bradbury; Paul Genney; Robert Irwin; David Miller

L0542 K2 Literary
Literary Agency
Canada

https://k2literary.com
https://www.facebook.com/k2literary/
https://twitter.com/k2literary
https://instagram.com/k2literary

ADULT > **Fiction** > *Novels*

CHILDREN'S > **Fiction** > *Novels*

Closed to approaches.

Literary Agent: Kelvin Kong

L0543 Ella Diamond Kahn
Literary Agent
United Kingdom

http://dkwlitagency.co.uk/agents/
https://twitter.com/elladkahn

Literary Agency: Diamond Kahn and Woods (DKW) Literary Agency Ltd (**L0265**)

Closed to approaches.

L0544 Jody Kahn
Literary Agent
United States

jkahn@bromasite.com

http://brandthochman.com/agents
http://aaronline.org/Sys/PublicProfile/7225167/417813

Literary Agency: Brandt & Hochman Literary Agents, Inc. (**L0119**)
Professional Body: Association of American Literary Agents (AALA)

Fiction > *Novels*
  Comedy / Humour; Culture; Literary; Upmarket

Nonfiction > *Nonfiction Books*
  Culture; Food; History; Journalism; Literary Memoir; Narrative Nonfiction; Social Justice; Sport

Send: Query
How to send: Email

L0545 Kane Literary Agency
Literary Agency
United Kingdom

submissions@kaneliteraryagency.com
submissions@standenliteraryagency.com

https://www.kaneliteraryagency.com
https://www.facebook.com/kaneliteraryagency/
https://twitter.com/#!/YasminStanden

Professional Body: The Association of Authors' Agents (AAA)

Fiction > *Novels*

Nonfiction > *Nonfiction Books*
  Cookery; Lifestyle; Spirituality

Send: Query; Synopsis; Writing sample
How to send: Email

Send one-page synopsis and first three chapters by email only. No picture books. Responds if interested only. If no response in 6 weeks assume rejection.

Authors: Simon Arrowsmith; J Y Bee; Isabelle Brizee; Louise Cliffe-Minns; Sarah Harris; Vicki Howie; Zoe Marriott; Andrew Murray; Emily Nagle; Marisa Noelle

Literary Agent: Yasmin Standen

L0546 Carrie Kania
Literary Agent
United Kingdom

Literary Agency: C+W (Conville & Walsh) (**L0147**)

L0547 Georgia Kanner
Literary Agent
United Kingdom

Literary Agency: Independent Talent Group Ltd (**L0496**)

L0548 Julia Kardon
Literary Agent
United States

julia@hgliterary.com

https://www.hgliterary.com/julia
https://twitter.com/jlkardon
https://querymanager.com/query/JuliaKardon

Literary Agency: HG Literary (**L0467**)

Fiction > *Novels*
Literary; Upmarket

Nonfiction > *Nonfiction Books*
History; Journalism; Memoir; Narrative Nonfiction

How to send: Query Manager

L0549 Karen Gantz Literary Management
Literary Agency
United States

kgzahler@aol.com

https://karengantzliterarymanagement.com
https://www.facebook.com/
Karengantzliterarymanagement/
https://twitter.com/karengantz
https://www.instagram.com/karen_gantz/

Fiction > *Novels*

Nonfiction > *Nonfiction Books*
Cookery; Current Affairs; History; Lifestyle; Memoir; Narrative Nonfiction; Politics; Psychology; Religion

Send: Query; Synopsis
How to send: Email

Considers all genres but specialises in nonfiction. Send query and summary by email only.

Assistant Agent: Hester Malin (**L0665**)

Literary Agent: Karen Gantz (*L0380*)

L0550 Maryann Karinch
Literary Agent
United States

mak@rudyagency.com

http://rudyagency.com

Literary Agency: The Rudy Agency (**L0868**)

ADULT
Fiction > *Novels*
Adventure; Crime; Historical Fiction; Mystery; Suspense; Thrillers

Nonfiction > *Nonfiction Books*
Biography; Business; Career Development; Cookery; Culture; Current Affairs; Health; History; Lifestyle; Medicine; Memoir; Politics; Relationships; Science; Self Help; Society; Sport; Technology; Women's Issues

CHILDREN'S
Fiction > *Picture Books*
Nonfiction > *Nonfiction Books*

Send: Query
How to send: Email

Wants to see non-fiction projects from authors who are experts in their field. Will consider illustrated children's books and have a particular interest in non-fiction for children. Regarding fiction, likes action and suspense.

L0551 Michelle Kass
Literary Agent
United Kingdom

Literary Agency: Michelle Kass Associates (**L0706**)

L0552 Kiran Kataria
Literary Agent
United Kingdom

https://www.keanekataria.co.uk/agents/

Literary Agency: Keane Kataria Literary Agency (**L0561**)

L0553 Kate Barker Literary, TV, & Film Agency
Literary Agency
London,
United Kingdom
Tel: +44 (0) 20 7688 1638

kate@katebarker.net

https://www.katebarker.net

Professional Body: The Association of Authors' Agents (AAA)

Fiction > *Novels*
Book Club Fiction; Commercial; Contemporary; Crime; High Concept; Historical Fiction; Psychological Thrillers; Thrillers

Nonfiction > *Nonfiction Books*
History; Lifestyle; Memoir; Nature; Popular Psychology; Science; Wellbeing

Closed to approaches.

No science fiction (unless literary) and no fantasy or children's. Submit via website submission form.

Literary Agent: Kate Barker (*L0065*)

L0554 Kate Hordern Literary Agency
Literary Agency
18 Mortimer Road, Clifton, Bristol, BS8 4EY
United Kingdom
Tel: +44 (0) 1179 239368

kate@khla.co.uk
anne@khla.co.uk

https://khla.co.uk

Professional Body: The Association of Authors' Agents (AAA)

Send: Query; Writing sample; Synopsis
How to send: Email
How not to send: Post

Send query by email only with pitch, an outline or synopsis and the first three chapters. If no response within six weeks, assume rejection.

Authors: Garry Abson; Merryn Allingham; Lyn Andrews; Richard Bassett; Helen Carey; Sam Carrington; Jane Corry; Jeff Dawson; Rosemary Dun; Kylie Fitzpatrick; Leona Francombe; Mary Gibson; Catherine Hanley; Sven Hassel; David Helton; Duncan Hewitt; Julie Houston; Kathryn Hughes; Victoria Jenkins; Ewa Jozefkowicz; Julian Lees; Denzil Meyrick; P.J.Brackston; Will Randall; Dave Roberts; Abbie Ross; John Sadler; Alastair Sawday; Dominic Selwood; Genevieve Taylor; Sandy Taylor

Literary Agents: Kate Hordern (**L0481**); Anne Williams (*L1037*)

L0555 Kate Nash Literary Agency
Literary Agency
United Kingdom

submissions@katenashlit.co.uk

https://katenashlit.co.uk
https://www.facebook.com/
KateNashLiteraryAgency/
https://twitter.com/katenashagent
https://www.youtube.com/channel/
UCAugaYbUoZXD7wldntZ8DwQ

Professional Body: The Association of Authors' Agents (AAA)

ADULT
Fiction > *Novels*

Nonfiction > *Nonfiction Books*: Commercial

CHILDREN'S > **Fiction** > *Middle Grade*

YOUNG ADULT > **Fiction** > *Novels*

Send: Query; Synopsis; Writing sample; Pitch; Author bio
How to send: In the body of an email
How not to send: Email attachment

Open to approaches from both new and established authors. Represents general and genre fiction and popular nonfiction. No poetry, drama, or genre SFF. Send query by email with synopsis and first chapter (fiction) or up to three chapters (nonfiction) pasted into the body of the email (no attachments).

Editor / Junior Agent / Proofreader: Robbie Guillory (**L0428**)

Literary Agent: Kate Nash

L0556 Kathi J. Paton Literary Agency
Literary Agency
United States
Tel: +1 (212) 265-6586

kjplitbiz@optonline.net

http://www.PatonLiterary.com

Types: Fiction; Nonfiction
Subjects: Biography; Business; Comedy / Humour; Commercial; Culture; Current Affairs; Finance; Health; History; Lifestyle; Literary; Politics; Religion; Science; Sport; Technology
Markets: Adult

Send: Query
Don't send: Full text
How to send: Email

Costs: Offers services that writers have to pay for.

Send query with brief description by email only. No attachments or referrals to websites. Specialises in adult nonfiction. No science fiction, fantasy, horror, category romance, juvenile, young adult or self-published books. Response only if interested. Also offers editorial services.

Literary Agent: Kathi Paton (*L0781*)

L0557 Kathryn Green Literary Agency, LLC
Literary Agency
157 Columbus Avenue, Suite 510, New York, NY 10023
United States
Tel: +1 (212) 245-4225

query@kgreenagency.com
kathy@kgreenagency.com

https://www.kathryngreenliteraryagency.com
https://twitter.com/kathygreenlit

ADULT
Fiction > *Novels*
General, and in particular: Cozy Mysteries; Historical Fiction

Nonfiction > *Nonfiction Books*
General, and in particular: Comedy / Humour; History; Memoir; Parenting; Popular Culture

CHILDREN'S > **Fiction** > *Middle Grade*

YOUNG ADULT > **Fiction** > *Novels*

Does not want:

> **ADULT** > **Fiction** > *Novels*
> Fantasy; Science Fiction
>
> **CHILDREN'S** > **Fiction**
> *Middle Grade*: Fantasy; Science Fiction
> *Picture Books*: General
>
> **YOUNG ADULT** > **Fiction** > *Novels*
> Fantasy; Science Fiction

Send: Query
How to send: Email
How not to send: Post; Email attachment

Send query by email. Do not send samples unless requested. No science fiction, fantasy, children's picture books, screenplays, or poetry.

Literary Agent: Kathryn Green (*L0417*)

L0558 Simon Kavanagh
Literary Agent
United Kingdom

simon@miccheetham.com

Literary Agency: Mic Cheetham Literary Agency (**L0701**)

L0559 Kay Peddle Literary
Literary Agency
London
United Kingdom

https://kaypeddleliterary.co.uk/
https://www.instagram.com/kaypeddlebooks
http://twitter.com/kaypeddle

Professional Body: The Association of Authors' Agents (AAA)

Literary Agent: Kay Peddle (**L0784**)

L0560 Taylor Martindale Kean
Literary Agent
United States

https://www.fullcircleliterary.com/our-agents/taylor-martindale-kean/

Literary Agency: Full Circle Literary, LLC (**L0371**)

Closed to approaches.

L0561 Keane Kataria Literary Agency
Literary Agency
United Kingdom

info@keanekataria.co.uk

https://www.keanekataria.co.uk/submissions/

Fiction > *Novels*
Book Club Fiction; Commercial Women's Fiction; Contemporary; Cozy Mysteries; Historical Fiction; Romance; Saga

Send: Query; Synopsis; Writing sample
How to send: PDF file email attachment

Currently accepting submissions in the crime, domestic noir and commercial women's fiction genres. No thrillers, science fiction, fantasy or children's books. Send query by email only with synopsis and first three chapters. Attachments in PDF format only.

Literary Agents: Kiran Kataria (**L0552**); Sara Keane (**L0562**)

L0562 Sara Keane
Literary Agent
United Kingdom

https://www.keanekataria.co.uk/agents/

Literary Agency: Keane Kataria Literary Agency (**L0561**)

L0563 Sara O' Keeffe
Literary Agent
United Kingdom

sokeeffe@aevitascreative.com

https://www.saraokeeffe.co.uk
https://aevitascreative.com/agents/#agent-7942
https://www.instagram.com/sarabookcrazy/
https://twitter.com/okeeffe05

Literary Agency: Aevitas Creative Management (ACM) UK (**L0017**)

Fiction > *Novels*
Crime; Ireland; Science Fiction; Women's Fiction

Send: Writing sample; Query
How to send: Email

Has worked with major brand names in crime, science fiction and has a passion for Irish writing.

L0564 Eli Keren
Associate Agent
United Kingdom
Tel: +44 (0) 20 3214 0775

ekeren@unitedagents.co.uk

https://www.unitedagents.co.uk/ekerenunitedagentscouk
https://twitter.com/EliArieh

Literary Agency: United Agents (**L0992**)
Literary Agent: Sarah Ballard (**L0060**)

Fiction > *Novels*
Commercial; LGBTQIA; Literary; Magical
Realism; Speculative

Nonfiction > *Nonfiction Books*
General, and in particular: LGBTQIA;
Popular Science

Send: Query; Synopsis; Writing sample
How to send: Email

In non-fiction, I am particularly interested in
smart and engaging popular science. My own
background is in chemistry, but I'm fairly
omnivorous and happy to look at any nonfiction that grips me, be that science, history or
something else. I enjoy books by writers
completely obsessed with a niche subject who
are skilled enough communicators to make the
rest of the world fall in love with their passion
too, whatever that passion might be. I am
interested in any book that will change the
world for the better.

In fiction, I'm happy to look at commercial,
literary and anything in between across genres.
I don't tend to work with science-fiction or
high fantasy, but am open to grounded
speculative fiction and magical realism.

I do not represent authors for children's and
YA literature.

Authors: Marieke Bigg; Sarah Burton; Huho
Greenhalgh; Ioan Marc Jones; Johanna Lukate;
David Miles; Jem Poster; Claire Seeber; Sam
White

L0565 Kat Kerr
Literary Agent
United States

Literary Agency: Donald Maass Literary
Agency (**L0273**)

L0566 Vanessa Kerr
Literary Agent
United Kingdom

vanessa@abnerstein.co.uk

Literary Agency: Abner Stein (**L0005**)

L0567 Ki Agency Ltd
Literary Agency
Studio 105, Screenworks, 22 Highbury Grove,
London, N5 2ER
United Kingdom
Tel: +44 (0) 20 3214 8287

https://ki-agency.co.uk

Professional Bodies: The Association of
Authors' Agents (AAA); Personal Managers'
Association (PMA); Writers' Guild of Great
Britain (WGGB)

Fiction > *Novels*

Nonfiction > *Nonfiction Books*
Coaching; Leadership; Personal
Development

Scripts
Film Scripts; *TV Scripts*; *Theatre Scripts*

Send: Synopsis; Writing sample
How to send: Email attachment

Represents novelists and scriptwriters in all
media. No children's or poetry, or submissions
from writers in the US or Canada. Send
synopsis and first three chapters / first 50 pages
by email. See website for individual agent
interests.

Authors: John Allison; Fiona Barnett; Linda
Carey; Louise Carey; Mike Carey; Kate
Charlesworth; Helena Coggan; Daniel Depp;
Grant Dewar; Joanne Drayton; Diane Duane;
Matthew Feldman; Kitty Ferguson; Marianne
Gordon; Shaun Hutson; Annie Machon; Sarah
McManus; Robin Norwood; Anne Perry;
Adam Roberts; Kay Sexton; Angela Slatter;
Gillian Spraggs; Jesse Stuart; Nicole
Swengley; Catherine Webb

Literary Agents: Meg Davis (**L0250**); Roz
Kidd (**L0568**); Ruth Needham; Anne C. Perry
(**L0790**)

L0568 Roz Kidd
Literary Agent
United Kingdom

roz@ki-agency.co.uk

https://ki-agency.co.uk/contact

Literary Agency: Ki Agency Ltd (**L0567**)

Scripts
Film Scripts; *TV Scripts*; *Theatre Scripts*

Accepts submissions of scripts for film, TV or
theatre in any genre.

L0569 Natalie Kimber
Literary Agent
Canada

Literary Agency: The Rights Factory

ADULT
Fiction
Graphic Novels: General
Novels: Adventure; Commercial; Cookery;
Historical Fiction; Literary; Science Fiction
Nonfiction > *Nonfiction Books*
Creative Nonfiction; Memoir; Popular
Culture; Science; Spirituality; Sustainable
Living

YOUNG ADULT > **Fiction** > *Novels:* Boy
Books

Send: Query; Author bio; Writing sample
How to send: Email

L0570 Georgia Frances King
Literary Agent
United States

https://aevitascreative.com/agents/

Literary Agency: Aevitas (**L0016**)

Nonfiction > *Nonfiction Books*
Arts; Culture; Design; Futurism; Science;
Technology

Send: Query; Market info; Writing sample
How to send: Online submission system

Interested in nonfiction books about emerging
science and technology, futurism, design,
culture, and the arts, and supporting
underrepresented voices.

L0571 Julia Kingsford
Literary Agent

https://juliakingsford.com
https://twitter.com/juliakingsford

Literary Agency: Julia Kingsford Ltd (**L0537**)

Fiction > *Novels*

Nonfiction > *Nonfiction Books*

Closed to approaches.

L0572 Robert Kirby
Literary Agent
United Kingdom

https://www.unitedagents.co.uk/
rkirbyunitedagentscouk

Literary Agency: United Agents (**L0992**)

Fiction > *Novels*
Adventure; Commercial; Speculative

Nonfiction > *Nonfiction Books*
Cultural History; Environment; Psychology;
Science

Send: Synopsis; Writing sample
How to send: Email
How not to send: Post

I have an interest in science, psychology,
cultural history and environmental issues. I
enjoy gripping adventure fiction, speculative
fiction and emotionally driven commercial
fiction. Submissions should be sent to my
assistant by via email, with a synopsis and first
three chapters. Please do not send submissions
via the post.

Associate Agent: Kate Walsh (**L1013**)

L0573 Jeff Kleinman
Literary Agent; Partner
United States

jeff@foliolit.com

https://www.publishersmarketplace.com/
members/jkleinman/

Literary Agency: Folio Literary Management,
LLC (**L0343**)
Professional Body: Association of American
Literary Agents (AALA)

Fiction > *Novels*
Book Club Fiction; Literary; Suspense;
Thrillers; Upmarket

Nonfiction > *Nonfiction Books*

Animals; History; Memoir; Narrative Nonfiction

Send: Query; Writing sample; Synopsis
How to send: In the body of an email

L0574 Harvey Klinger

Literary Agent
United States

Literary Agency: Harvey Klinger, Inc (**L0452**)

L0575 Kneerim & Williams

Literary Agency
90 Canal Street, Boston, MA 02114
United States
Tel: +1 (617) 303-1650
Fax: +1 (617) 542-1660

submissions@kwlit.com

https://kwlit.com

Professional Body: Association of American Literary Agents (AALA)

Types: Fiction; Nonfiction
Subjects: Adventure; Anthropology; Archaeology; Autobiography; Business; Commercial; Crime; Culture; Current Affairs; Finance; Health; History; Legal; Lifestyle; Literary; Literature; Medicine; Nature; Politics; Psychology; Religion; Science; Society; Sport; Technology; Women's Interests
Markets: Adult

Send: Query
Don't send: Full text

Send query by email with synopsis, brief bio, and 10-20 pages of initial sample material in the body of the email. No attachments or queries by post or by phone. See website for full guidelines.

Literary Agents: Lucy Cleland (*L0202*); Katherine Flynn (*L0341*); Carol Franco (*L0359*); Jill Kneerim (*L0576*); Elaine Rogers (*L0855*); Carolyn Savarese (*L0883*); Matthew Valentinas (*L0997*); Ike Williams (*L1038*)

L0576 Jill Kneerim

Literary Agent
United States

Literary Agency: Kneerim & Williams (**L0575**)

L0577 Knight Features

Literary Agency
Trident Business Centre, 89 Bickersteth Road, London, SW17 9SH
United Kingdom
Tel: +44 (0) 20 7622 1467

http://www.knightfeatures.com

Nonfiction > *Nonfiction Books*
  Business; Military

Send: Proposal; Query; Self-Addressed Stamped Envelope (SASE)

How to send: Phone; Post; Online submission system

Make initial contact by phone or proposal through online submission system. If sending work by post, include SAE. Main areas of interest are: Motorsports, Graphic Novels, Business, History, Factual and Biographical/Autobiographical. Closed to fiction submissions as at February 2020.

Literary Agents: Samantha Ferris; Gaby Martin

L0578 Knight Hall Agency

Literary Agency
Lower Ground Floor, 7 Mallow Street, London, EC1Y 8RQ
United Kingdom
Tel: +44 (0) 20 3397 2901

office@knighthallagency.com

http://www.knighthallagency.com

Types: Scripts
Formats: Film Scripts; TV Scripts; Theatre Scripts
Subjects: Drama
Markets: Adult

Closed to approaches.

Note: Closed to submissions as at February 2020. Check website for current status.

Send query by post or email (no attachments). Only send sample if requested. Represents playwrights, screenwriters and writer-directors. Handles adaptation rights for novels, but does not handle books directly.

Authors: Simon Beaufoy; Jeremy Brock; Liz Lochhead; Martin McDonagh; Simon Nye

Literary Agent: Charlotte Knight

L0579 Kohner Agency

Literary Agency
9300 Wilshire Boulevard, Suite 555, Beverly Hills, CA 90212
United States
Tel: +1 (310) 550-1060

http://paulkohner.com

Closed to approaches.

The second oldest talent agency in Los Angeles, with a literary department boasting representation of 24 major publishing houses. No unsolicited submissions, ideas, or suggestions.

Literary Agents: Stephen Moore; Deborah Obad; Pearl Wexler

L0580 Stacey Kondla

Literary Agent
Canada

Literary Agency: The Rights Factory

L0581 Mary Krienke

Associate Agent
United States

https://www.sll.com/our-team

Literary Agency: Sterling Lord Literistic, Inc. (**L0940**)

Fiction > *Novels*
  Literary; Upmarket

Nonfiction > *Nonfiction Books*
  Culture; Health; Sexuality

Send: Query; Synopsis; Writing sample
How to send: Online submission system

Represents literary and upmarket fiction, voice-driven nonfiction, and memoir. She is particularly drawn to nonfiction that speaks to something essential and of-the-moment, especially work that engages with themes of culture, identity, sexuality, and health.

L0582 Miriam Kriss

Literary Agent
United States

Literary Agency: Irene Goodman Literary Agency (IGLA) (**L0501**)

L0583 Kruger Cowne

Literary Agency
Unit 7C, Chelsea Wharf, 15 Lots Road, London, SW10 0QJ
United Kingdom
Tel: +44 (0) 20 7352 2277

oscar@krugercowne.com

https://www.krugercowne.com
https://twitter.com/krugercowne
https://www.instagram.com/krugercowne/
https://www.facebook.com/krugercowne
https://www.linkedin.com/company/kruger-cowne
https://www.youtube.com/user/KrugerCowneTalent

Professional Body: The Association of Authors' Agents (AAA)

Types: Fiction; Nonfiction
Subjects: Adventure; Anthropology; Arts; Autobiography; Beauty; Business; Comedy / Humour; Commercial; Contemporary; Crime; Culture; Current Affairs; Erotic; Experimental; Fashion; Gothic; Health; History; Hobbies; How To; Lifestyle; Literary; Men's Interests; Music; Nature; New Age; Personal Development; Philosophy; Psychology; Satire; Science; Sport; Suspense; Thrillers; Warfare; Westerns; Women's Interests
Markets: Adult; Children's; Young Adult

Send: Full text
How to send: Email

A talent management agency, with an extremely strong literary arm.

The majority of the works handled by the agency fall into the category of celebrity nonfiction. However, also regularly work with journalists, entrepreneurs and influencers on projects, with a speciality in polemics, and speculative works on the future.

Occasionally take on exceptional fiction authors.

Authors: Akala; Bruce Dickinson; Bob Geldof; Kelly Holmes; Gail Porter

Literary Agent: Oscar Janson-Smith (*L0517*)

L0584 David Kuhn
Literary Agent; Chief Executive Officer
United States

https://aevitascreative.com/agents/

Literary Agency: Aevitas (**L0016**)

Nonfiction > *Nonfiction Books*
Culture; Current Affairs; Entertainment; Food; History; Memoir; Music; Politics

Closed to approaches.

Represents nonfiction books that will educate, entertain, and enlighten in the areas of memoir, current events, history, politics, culture, style, food, music, and entertainment.

L0585 Danya Kukafka
Literary Agent
United States

https://aevitascreative.com/agents/

Literary Agency: Aevitas (**L0016**)

Fiction > *Novels*
Experimental; Literary; Speculative; Suspense; Thrillers; Upmarket

Nonfiction > *Nonfiction Books*
Crime; Culture

Send: Query; Writing sample
How to send: Online submission system

She is interested literary fiction with particularly propulsive storylines. She is seeking literary suspense, sophisticated thrillers, speculative fiction, and experimental fiction—she also loves true crime that feels attuned to today's cultural conversations, as well as upmarket literary fiction you can read in one gulp.

L0586 The LA Literary Agency
Literary Agency
United States

ann@laliteraryagency.com

https://www.laliteraryagency.com

Fiction > *Novels*
Commercial; Literary

Nonfiction > *Nonfiction Books*
Biography; Business; Cookery; Health; History; Lifestyle; Memoir; Narrative

Nonfiction; Parenting; Psychology; Science; Sport

Send: Query; Proposal; Full text
How to send: Email attachment

Costs: Offers services that writers have to pay for. Sister company provides editorial services.

Send query with proposal (nonfiction) or full ms (fiction) by email. Response only if interested.

Literary Agents: Eric Lasher; Maureen Lasher

L0587 The Labyrinth Literary Agency
Literary Agency
India

ac@labyrinthagency.com

http://www.labyrinthagency.com
https://www.instagram.com/labyrinthagency/
https://twitter.com/LabyrinthAgency
https://twitter.com/LabyrinthAgency

Fiction > *Novels*

Nonfiction > *Nonfiction Books*

Send: Synopsis; Writing sample; Author bio
How to send: Email

Costs: Offers services that writers have to pay for. Offers editorial and advice services to authors with whom they do not have a business relationship.

Literary Agent: Anish Chandy (*L0183*)

L0588 Natalie Lakosil
Literary Agent
United States

https://www.adventuresinagentland.com
https://www.irenegoodman.com/natalie-lakosil
https://twitter.com/Natalie_Lakosil
http://www.manuscriptwishlist.com/mswl-post/natalie-lakosil/
https://querymanager.com/query/natlak

Literary Agency: Irene Goodman Literary Agency (IGLA) (**L0501**)

ADULT
Fiction > *Novels*
Cozy Mysteries; Crime; Thrillers; Upmarket Women's Fiction; Upmarket

Nonfiction > *Nonfiction Books*
Business; Parenting; Psychology; Science; Self Help

CHILDREN'S
Fiction
Chapter Books; *Middle Grade*; *Picture Books*
Nonfiction
Gift Books: General
Nonfiction Books: Biography; Comedy / Humour; Feminism; New Age; Social Issues
YOUNG ADULT > **Fiction** > *Novels*

How to send: Query Manager

Represents adult nonfiction, adult cozy mystery/crime, female-driven thrillers, upmarket women's/general fiction, illustrators, and all ages (picture book, chapter book, MG, YA) of children's literature, both fiction and nonfiction.

L0589 Sophie Lambert
Literary Agent
United Kingdom

Literary Agency: C+W (Conville & Walsh) (**L0147**)

L0590 Louise Lamont
Literary Agent
United Kingdom

louisesubmissions@lbabooks.com

http://www.lbabooks.com/agent/louise-lamont/

Literary Agency: LBA Books Ltd (**L0605**)

CHILDREN'S > **Fiction** > *Novels*
Adventure; Comedy / Humour

Does not want:

> **CHILDREN'S** > **Fiction** > *Picture Books*

How to send: Email

Authors: Lauren Ace; Nazneen Ahmed; Laura Archer; Chris Beardshaw; Lucy Beresford-Knox; Virginia Bergin; Katie Bonna; Anna Carey; Katie Clapham; Rebecca Cobb; Ping Coombes; Matt Edmondson; Clare Foges; Rosie French; Ellie Grace; Julia Gray; Helen Hancocks; Charlotte Haptie; Zinnie Harris; Eva Katzler; Lucy Mangan; Julie Mayhew; Anne Miller; Carol Morley; Eve Wersocki Morris; Jen Offord; Kavita Puri; Nicola Rayner; Fleur Sinclair; Jane Monckton Smith; Ria Voros; Laura Wood; Katherine Woodfine; Emma Yarlett

L0591 Andrew Lampack
Literary Agent
United States

Literary Agency: Peter Lampack Agency, Inc (**L0793**)

L0592 Sarah Landis
Literary Agent
United States

https://www.sll.com/our-team

Literary Agency: Sterling Lord Literistic, Inc. (**L0940**)

CHILDREN'S > **Fiction** > *Middle Grade*
Comedy / Humour; Contemporary; Fantasy

YOUNG ADULT > **Fiction** > *Novels*

Contemporary; Fantasy; High Concept; Historical Fiction; Mystery; Science Fiction; Thrillers

Send: Query; Synopsis; Writing sample
How to send: Online submission system

This agent is looking for middle grade and young adult books across all genres. She is particularly drawn to middle grade fantasy and contemporary with heart, humor, and magic. In the young adult space, she has an affinity for southern voices, high-concept plots, grounded sci-fi/fantasy, historical, mysteries and thrillers, and emotionally compelling contemporary.

L0593 Lina Langlee

Literary Agent
United Kingdom

http://thenorthlitagency.com/our-friends-in-the-north/
https://twitter.com/LinaLanglee

Literary Agency: The North Literary Agency (**L0755**)

ADULT
  Fiction > *Novels*
    Commercial; Crime; High Concept; Literary; Speculative; Thrillers

  Nonfiction > *Nonfiction Books*

CHILDREN'S > **Fiction** > *Middle Grade*

YOUNG ADULT > **Fiction** > *Novels*

Closed to approaches.

Looking for books across genres: commercial fiction with a great hook, literary fiction, speculative or high concept books that remain very readable, crime fiction that stands out, fun and moving Middle Grade, and any genre of Young Adult. In terms of nonfiction, interested either in 'the small made big' or 'the big made small': specialists that can make really niche subjects accessible and interesting to a wider market, or deeply personal accounts of the big issues we might all one day tackle.

L0594 Linda Langton

Literary Agent
United States

https://langtonsinternational.com/langtons-international/about-us/
https://www.linkedin.com/in/lindalangton

Literary Agency: Langtons International (**L0595**)

L0595 Langtons International

Literary Agency
United States

llangton@earthlink.net
langtonsinternational@gmail.com

https://langtonsinternational.com
https://www.facebook.com/LangtonsInternationalAgency

Fiction > *Novels*
  Literary; Mystery; Thrillers; Women's Fiction

Nonfiction > *Nonfiction Books*
  Business; Crime; Memoir; Self Help

Literary agency based in New York, specializing in business, self-help, memoir, and true crime, as well as mystery, thrillers, women's and literary fiction.

Literary Agent: Linda Langton (**L0594**)

L0596 Elena Langtry

Literary Agent
United Kingdom

https://cmm.agency/about-us.php

Literary Agency: Coombs Moylett & Maclean Literary Agency (**L0217**)

Fiction > *Novels*
  Commercial Women's Fiction; Psychological Thrillers

Nonfiction > *Nonfiction Books*
  Popular Science; Self Help

How to send: Online submission system

L0597 Katherine Latshaw

Literary Agent; Vice President
United States

klatshaw@foliolitmanagement.com

https://www.foliolit.com/agents-1/katherine-latshaw

Literary Agency: Folio Literary Management, LLC (**L0343**)

ADULT
  Fiction > *Novels*

  Nonfiction
    Essays: General
    Illustrated Books: General
    Nonfiction Books: Commercial; Cookery; Feminism; Health; Lifestyle; Memoir; Narrative Nonfiction; Popular Culture; Prescriptive Nonfiction; Wellbeing
CHILDREN'S > **Fiction** > *Middle Grade*

YOUNG ADULT > **Fiction** > *Novels*

How to send: Email

L0598 Jennifer Laughran

Senior Agent
United States

jennL@andreabrownlit.com

https://www.jenniferlaughran.com
https://www.andreabrownlit.com/Team/Jennifer-Laughran
http://twitter.com/literaticat
http://www.instagram.com/literaticat
https://querymanager.com/JenniferLaughran

https://www.publishersmarketplace.com/members/jennla/
https://www.manuscriptwishlist.com/mswl-post/jennifer-laughran/

Literary Agency: Andrea Brown Literary Agency, Inc.
Professional Body: Association of American Literary Agents (AALA)

CHILDREN'S > **Fiction** > *Middle Grade*

YOUNG ADULT > **Fiction** > *Novels*

Send: Query; Author bio; Writing sample
How to send: Query Manager

Always on the lookout for sparkling YA and middle grade fiction with unusual and unforgettable characters and vivid settings, she is drawn to nearly all kinds of books, whether realistic comedies or richly imagined magical adventures. However, the common thread in her favorite stories is an offbeat world-view.

L0599 Laura Dail Literary Agency

Literary Agency
121 West 27th Street, Suite 1201, New York, NY 10001
United States
Tel: +1 (212) 239-7477

queries@ldlainc.com

http://www.ldlainc.com
https://twitter.com/LDLiterary
https://www.instagram.com/lauradaillit/

How to send: Query Manager

Send query through online submission system only. Query one agent at a time with one project at a time.

Literary Agent / President: Laura Dail (**L0237**)

Literary Agents: Elana Roth Parker (**L0779**); Carrie Pestritto (**L0792**)

L0600 Sophie Laurimore

Literary Agent
United Kingdom

sohoagencysubmissions@gmail.com

https://thesohoagency.co.uk/agent/sophie-laurimore

Literary Agency: The Soho Agency (**L0924**)

Nonfiction > *Nonfiction Books*

Send: Writing sample; Synopsis; Query
How to send: Email attachment

L0601 Rowan Lawton

Company Director; Literary Agent
United Kingdom

https://twitter.com/Rowan_Lawton

Literary Agency: The Soho Agency (**L0924**)

Fiction > *Novels*

Book Club Fiction; Commercial Women's Fiction; Contemporary Romance; Crime; Domestic Suspense; Literary; Memoir; Romantic Comedy; Women's Fiction

L0602 Laxfield Literary Associates
Literary Agency
United Kingdom

submissions@laxfieldliterary.com

https://laxfieldliterary.com

Professional Body: The Association of Authors' Agents (AAA)

Fiction > *Novels*
Commercial; Literary

Nonfiction > *Nonfiction Books*
Creative Nonfiction; Memoir; Nature; Travel

Send: Query; Synopsis; Writing sample; Author bio; Outline
How to send: Word file email attachment

We are looking for fiction and non-fiction of the highest quality. We are keen to receive literary and commercial fiction. We are also looking for non-fiction, particularly creative non-fiction, travel writing, memoir and nature writing. We do not represent poetry, plays, children's books or YA.

L0603 Veronica Lazar
Literary Agent
United Kingdom

https://www.imdb.com/name/nm4400468/

Literary Agency: AVAnti Productions & Management (**L0051**)

L0604 Sarah Lazin
Literary Agent
United States

https://aevitascreative.com/agents/
http://lazinbooks.com/about-us/
http://aaronline.org/Sys/PublicProfile/1715266/417813

Literary Agencies: Sarah Lazin Books (**L0882**); Aevitas (**L0016**)
Professional Body: Association of American Literary Agents (AALA)

Nonfiction
Nonfiction Books: Biography; Current Affairs; Health; History; Journalism; Memoir; Parenting; Politics; Popular Culture; Social Issues
Reference: General

How to send: By referral

Represents a range of nonfiction writers working in fields such as popular culture, biography, history, politics, journalism, memoir, parenting, health, practical nonfiction, contemporary affairs, social issues, and general reference. She also handles fiction from

literary works and short stories to commercial novels, and represents some photographers and illustrators and several estates. She accepts submissions through referral only.

L0605 LBA Books Ltd
Literary Agency
91 Great Russell Street, London, WC1B 3PS
United Kingdom
Tel: +44 (0) 20 7637 1234

info@lbabooks.com

http://www.lbabooks.com

Professional Body: The Association of Authors' Agents (AAA)

Send query with synopsis and first three chapters to specific agent by email only. See website for specific agents' interests and email addresses. No scripts, short stories, or poetry.

Authors: Will Adams; Emily Adlam; Emad Ahmed; Sarah Alderson; Dominique Antiglio; Helen Arney; Lizzy Barber; James Becker; A.L. Bird; Darcie Boleyn; Christina Bradley; Jason Bray; Fern Britton; Amanda Brooke; Catherine Brookes; Julie Brunelle; Charlotte Butterfield; Anna Carey; Jo Carnegie; Lucie Cave; Rebecca Chance; James Cheshire; George Clarke; Rosemary Conley; Gennaro Contaldo; Emma Cooper; Josephine Cox; Mason Cross; Louise Curtis; A.M. Dean; Susie Donkin; Hannah Doyle; Elizabeth Drummond; Katherine Dyson; Kate Faithfull-Williams; Dan Farnworth; Liz Fenwick; Judy Finnigan; Bea Fitzgerald; Nick Foulkes; Mark Frary; Daniel Freeman; Susan Gee; David Gibbins; Lucy Goacher; Jane Gordon; Tom Grass; Mark Griffin; Michael Gustafson; Kate Hackworthy; Rachel Hamilton; Richard Hammond; Isabella Harcourt; Duncan Harding; Fiona Harper; Natalie Heaton; Matt Hilton; John Humphrys; Jessica Jarlvi; Sarah Johnson; Annabel Kantaria; Lesley Kara; Eva Katzler; Jenni Keer; Simon Kernick; Emily Kerr; Ella King; Margaret Kirk; Catherine Kirwan; Victoria Lamb; Amy Lavelle; Georgina Lees; Guy Leschziner; Susan Lewis; Lauren Libbert; Agnes Light; Freda Lightfoot; Jane Linfoot; Amy Lloyd; Rachael Lucas; Dee MacDonald; Richard Madeley; Lucy Mangan; Ian Marber; Tom Marcus; Sam Masters; James May; Julie Mayhew; Marina McCarron; Colin McDowell; Lisa Medved; David Meikle; Gavin Menzies; Ben Miller; Nicole Mones; Marcia Moody; Michael Morley; Anthony Mosawi; Elizabeth Moss; Steve Mould; Faya Nilsson; Jen Offord; Karen Osman; Sue Palmer; Angelique Panagos; S.A. Patrick; Seth Patrick; Andrew Pepper; Ivor Peters; Hannah Phillips; Melanie Phillips; Gervase Phinn; Catherine Piddington; Anna Pointer; Richard Porter; Suzy K Quinn; Esther Rantzen; Louisa Reid; Madeleine Reiss; Gillian Richmond; Alice Roberts; Bernadette Robinson; Amber Rose; Mike Rossiter; Simon Scarrow; Super Scrimpers; Heidi Shertok; Colin Shindler; Celia Silvani; Fleur Sinclair;

Jane Monckton Smith; Jack Steel; Zara Stoneley; Lucy Strange; Heidi Swain; Karen Swan; Joe Swift; Sophie Tanner; Rachel de Thame; Alan Titchmarsh; Andy Torbet; Jon Trace; Jonathan Trigell; Anna Turns; Oliver Uberti; Phil Vickery; Ria Voros; Claire Wade; Jennifer Wells; Kate Winter; Tamsin Winter; Terry Wogan; Peter Wood; Katherine Woodfine; Fiona Woodifield; Sally Worboyes; Emma Yarlett

Literary Agents: Luigi Bonomi (**L0107**); Louise Lamont (**L0590**); Amanda Preston (**L0815**); Hannah Schofield (**L0892**)

L0606 Ned Leavitt
Literary Agent
United States

Literary Agency: The Ned Leavitt Agency (**L0745**)

L0607 Tom Drake Lee
Associate Agent
United Kingdom

tdl.submission@dhhliteraryagency.com

http://www.dhhliteraryagency.com/tom-drake-lee.html
http://twitter.com/tomdrakelee

Literary Agency: DHH Literary Agency Ltd (**L0264**)

Fiction > *Novels*
Commercial; Literary

Nonfiction > *Nonfiction Books*
History; Memoir; Nature; Popular Science

Send: Synopsis; Writing sample
How to send: Email

Looking for commercial literary and genre fiction which tells stories and illuminates the human condition; fiction which has compelling plot, narrative and characters.

Also looking for non-fiction which tells us more about the world around us; nature writing, popular science, history and memoir.

No screenplays, short story / novellas, children's books / YA or Sci-Fi/Fantasy.

Authors: Valerie Jack; Diana Kessler; Robin Laurance

L0608 Jordan Lees
Associate Agent
United Kingdom

jordansubmissions@theblairpartnership.com

https://www.theblairpartnership.com/our_people/jordan-lees/

Literary Agency: The Blair Partnership (**L0100**)

Fiction > *Novels*
Book Club Fiction; Crime; Detective Fiction; Folklore, Myths, and Legends; High

Concept; Historical Fiction; Horror; Literary; Speculative; Thrillers

Nonfiction > *Nonfiction Books*
General, and in particular: Crime

Does not want:

Fiction > *Novels*: Spy Thrillers

Send: Synopsis; Proposal; Writing sample
How to send: Word file email attachment; PDF file email attachment
How not to send: WeTransfer; Dropbox; Google Docs email attachment; Google Docs shared document

Represents crime/thrillers of all stripes, book club fiction, historical fiction, literary fiction, true crime and smart non-fiction. Not currently looking for spy novels, sci-fi and fantasy, women's fiction, children's and YA.

L0609 Lindsay Leggett

Associate Agent
Canada

Literary Agency: The Rights Factory

ADULT > **Fiction**
Graphic Novels: General
Novels: Horror; LGBTQIA; Romance; Thrillers
CHILDREN'S > **Fiction** > *Middle Grade*

YOUNG ADULT > **Fiction** > *Novels*

Closed to approaches.

L0610 Julia Levin

Literary Agent
United States

https://accrispin.blogspot.com/2014/02/alert-jane-dowary-agency.html

Literary Agency: Jane Dowary Agency (**L0514**)

L0611 Wendy Levinson

Literary Agent
United States

Literary Agency: Harvey Klinger, Inc (**L0452**)

L0612 Sarah Levitt

Literary Agent
New York
United States

https://aevitascreative.com/agents/

Literary Agency: Aevitas (**L0016**)

Fiction > *Novels*: Literary

Nonfiction > *Nonfiction Books*
Comedy / Humour; History; Journalism; Memoir; Narrative Nonfiction; Popular Culture; Popular Science

Send: Author bio; Outline; Market info; Writing sample
How to send: Online submission system

Most interested in narrative nonfiction in the areas of popular science, big ideas, history, humor, pop culture, memoir, and reportage, in addition to voice-driven literary fiction with a bold plot and fresh, imaginative characters. She's excited by strong female and underrepresented voices, the strange and speculative, and projects that ignite cultural conversation.

L0613 Barbara Levy

Literary Agent
United Kingdom

Literary Agency: Barbara Levy Literary Agency (**L0061**)

L0614 Bibi Lewis

Literary Agent
United States

https://ethanellenberg.com/our-agents/

Literary Agency: Ethan Ellenberg Literary Agency (**L0308**)

ADULT > **Fiction** > *Novels*
Mystery; Romance; Thrillers; Women's Fiction

CHILDREN'S
Fiction > *Picture Books*
Nonfiction > *Picture Books*

YOUNG ADULT
Fiction > *Novels*
Nonfiction > *Nonfiction Books*

L0615 Kayla Lightner

Literary Agent
United States

https://www.pandeliterary.com/our-agents-pandeliterary
https://twitter.com/LightnerKayla

Literary Agency: Ayesha Pande Literary (**L0052**)
Professional Body: Association of American Literary Agents (AALA)

Fiction
Graphic Novels: General
Novels: Comedy / Humour; Contemporary; Crime; Domestic Suspense; Dystopian Fiction; Fantasy; Gothic; Historical Fiction; Horror; Literary; Magical Realism; Psychological Horror; Science Fiction; Thrillers; Upmarket
Nonfiction > *Nonfiction Books*
Comedy / Humour; Crime; Family Saga; Journalism; Memoir; Narrative Nonfiction; Sport

Send: Pitch; Synopsis; Author bio; Writing sample
How to send: Online submission system

I love discovering diverse and fresh new perspectives across commercial fiction, literary + upmarket fiction, non-fiction, and graphic novels. I'm particularly a fan of authors with singular voices that masterfully straddle the line between story-telling and teaching readers something new (about themselves, their communities, or the world we live in).

L0616 Limelight Management

Literary Agency
10 Filmer Mews, 75 Filmer Road, London, SW6 7JF
United Kingdom
Tel: +44 (0) 20 7384 9950

mail@limelightmanagement.com

https://www.limelightmanagement.com
https://www.facebook.com/pages/Limelight-Celebrity-Management-Ltd/399328580099859?fref=ts
https://twitter.com/Fionalimelight
https://www.youtube.com/channel/UCCmxquRk_blKqjR8jKRryFA
https://instagram.com/limelightcelebritymanagement/
https://www.linkedin.com/company-beta/11219861/

Professional Body: The Association of Authors' Agents (AAA)

Fiction > *Novels*
Commercial Women's Fiction; Crime; Historical Fiction; Mystery; Suspense; Thrillers

Nonfiction > *Nonfiction Books*
Arts; Autobiography; Biography; Business; Cookery; Crafts; Health; Nature; Popular Science; Sport; Travel

Send: Query; Synopsis; Writing sample; Author bio
How to send: Email

Always looking for exciting new authors. Send query by email with the word "Submission" in the subject line and synopsis and first three chapters as Word or Open Document attachments. Also include market info, and details of your professional life and writing ambitions. Film and TV scripts for existing clients only. See website for full guidelines.

Literary Agent: Fiona Lindsay

L0617 Linda Konner Literary Agency

Literary Agency
10 West 15 Street, Suite 1918, New York, NY 10011
United States

ldkonner@cs.com

http://www.lindakonnerliteraryagency.com

Types: Nonfiction
Formats: Reference
Subjects: Biography; Business; Cookery;

Culture; Entertainment; Finance; Health; How To; Lifestyle; Personal Development; Psychology; Science; Women's Interests
Markets: Adult

Send: Query
Don't send: Full text
How to send: Email

Costs: Author covers sundry admin costs.

Send one to two page query by email only. Attachments from unknown senders will be deleted unread. Nonfiction only. Books must be written by or with established experts in their field. No Fiction, Memoir, Religion, Spiritual/Christian, Children's/young adult, Games/puzzles, Humour, History, Politics, or unsolicited MSS. See website for full guidelines.

Literary Agent: Linda Konner

L0618 Linda Seifert Management
Literary Agency
United Kingdom
Tel: +44 (0) 20 3327 1180

contact@lindaseifert.com

http://www.lindaseifert.com

Professional Body: Personal Managers' Association (PMA)

ADULT > **Scripts**
  Film Scripts; *TV Scripts*
CHILDREN'S > **Scripts**
  Film Scripts; *TV Scripts*
Closed to approaches.

Costs: Author covers sundry admin costs.

A London-based management company representing screenwriters and directors for film and television. Our outstanding client list ranges from the highly established to the new and exciting emerging talent of tomorrow. Represents UK-based writers and directors only.

Literary Agent: Edward Hughes

L0619 Lindsay Literary Agency
Literary Agency
United Kingdom
Tel: +44 (0) 1420 831430

info@lindsayliteraryagency.co.uk

http://www.lindsayliteraryagency.co.uk
https://twitter.com/lindsaylit

Professional Body: The Association of Authors' Agents (AAA)

CHILDREN'S > **Fiction**
  Middle Grade; *Picture Books*
YOUNG ADULT > **Fiction** > *Novels*

Send: Query; Author bio; Pitch; Synopsis; Writing sample
How to send: Email

Send query by email only, including single-page synopsis and first three chapters. For picture books send complete ms. No submissions by post.

Authors: Helen Brandom; Pamela Butchart; Sital Gorasia Chapman; Christina Collins; Jim Daly; Donna David; Louise Finch; Sam Gayton; Ruth Hatfield; Larry Hayes; Peter Jones; Jay Joseph; Titania Krimpas; Mike Lancaster; Giles Paley-Phillips; Kate Peridot; Sharon Tregenza; Rachel Valentine; Sue Wallman; Jacqueline Whitehart; Joe Wilson

Literary Agent: Becky Bagnell (*L0057*)

L0620 Will Lippincott
Literary Agent
Los Angeles
United States

https://aevitascreative.com/agents/

Literary Agency: Aevitas (**L0016**)

Nonfiction > *Nonfiction Books*
  Current Affairs; Health; History; Journalism; Memoir; Narrative Nonfiction; Politics; Popular Culture; Science; Technology

Send: Query; Pitch; Market info; Writing sample
How to send: Online submission system

Agent based in Los Angeles. Interested in politics, journalistic narratives, history, health, technology, and memoir, with a special focus on multi-media storytelling.

L0621 The Lisa Ekus Group
Literary Agency
57 North Street, Hatfield, MA 01038
United States
Tel: +1 (413) 247-9325

info@tlegstaging.wpengine.com

https://lisaekus.com

Nonfiction > *Nonfiction Books*: Cookery

How to send: Online submission system

Handles cookery books only. Submit proposal through submission system on website.

Literary Agent: Lisa Ekus

L0622 Laurie Liss
Literary Agent; Executive Vice President
United States

https://www.sll.com/our-team
http://aaronline.org/Sys/PublicProfile/2176754/417813

Literary Agency: Sterling Lord Literistic, Inc. (**L0940**)
Professional Body: Association of American Literary Agents (AALA)

Fiction > *Novels*
  Commercial; Literary

Nonfiction > *Nonfiction Books*: Commercial

Send: Query; Synopsis; Writing sample
How to send: Online submission system

L0623 Literary Management Group, Inc.
Literary Agency
8530 Calistoga Way, Brentwood, TN 37027
United States
Tel: +1 (615) 812-4445

BruceBarbour@
LiteraryManagementGroup.com

https://literarymanagementgroup.com/

Nonfiction > *Nonfiction Books*
  Biography; Business; Lifestyle; Religion

Send: Query; Writing sample
How to send: Word file email attachment
How not to send: PDF file email attachment

Handles Christian books (defined as books which are consistent with the historical, orthodox teachings of the Christian fathers). Handles adult nonfiction only. No children's or illustrated books, poetry, memoirs, YA Fiction or text/academic books. Download proposal from website then complete and send with sample chapters.

Literary Agent: Bruce R. Barbour (*L0063*)

L0624 The Liverpool Literary Agency
Literary Agency
Liverpool
United Kingdom

submissions@liverpool-literary.agency

https://www.liverpool-literary.agency/
https://twitter.com/LiverpoolLit
https://www.instagram.com/
liverpool_literary_agency/

Professional Body: The Association of Authors' Agents (AAA)

ADULT > **Fiction** > *Novels*

CHILDREN'S > **Fiction**
  Chapter Books: High Concept
  Middle Grade: Adventure

Send: Query; Author bio; Market info; Synopsis; Writing sample
How to send: Email
How not to send: Post

Costs: Offers services that writers have to pay for. Also offers editorial services.

Literary agency based in Liverpool, focusing on helping writers from Northern England break into the publishing industry.

Assistant Agents / Editors: Laura Bennett (**L0088**); Anna Gamble (**L0379**)

Literary Agent: Clare Coombes (**L0216**)

L0625 Liza Dawson Associates
Literary Agency
121 West 27th Street, Suite 1201, New York, NY 10001
United States
Tel: +1 (973) 743-2535

queryliza@LizaDawsonAssociates.com

http://www.lizadawsonassociates.com

Professional Body: Association of American Literary Agents (AALA)

Types: Fiction; Nonfiction
Formats: Theatre Scripts
Subjects: Autobiography; Business; Comedy / Humour; Commercial; Culture; Current Affairs; Fantasy; History; Lifestyle; Literary; Medicine; Mystery; Personal Development; Politics; Psychology; Religion; Romance; Science; Science Fiction; Society; Suspense; Thrillers; Warfare; Women's Interests
Markets: Academic; Adult; Children's; Young Adult

See website for specific agent interests and query appropriate agent directly. Specific agent submission guidelines and contact details are available on website.

Authors: Marie Bostwick; Robyn Carr; Scott Hawkins; Marybeth Whalen

Literary Agents: Rachel Beck (**L0078**); Caitlin Blasdell (*L0102*); Hannah Bowman (*L0115*); Liza Dawson (*L0252*); Caitie Flum (*L0339*); Tom Miller (*L0716*)

L0626 The LKG Agency
Literary Agency
134 West 83rd Street, 3rd Floor, New York, NY 10024
United States

mgya@lkgagency.com
query@lkgagency.com

http://lkgagency.com

CHILDREN'S
Fiction > *Middle Grade*
General, and in particular: Contemporary; High / Epic Fantasy; Magical Realism; Science Fiction; Thrillers

Nonfiction > *Nonfiction Books*

YOUNG ADULT > **Fiction** > *Novels*

Does not want:

> CHILDREN'S > **Fiction** > *Middle Grade*: Horror

Send: Query; Synopsis; Writing sample
How to send: Email

Specializes in middle grade and young adult fiction. Within children's, is primarily drawn to contemporary and magical realism but is open to high fantasy, sci-fi, thriller, almost everything except maybe horror.

Literary Agents: Lauren Galit; Caitlen Rubino-Bradway

L0627 Jonathan Lloyd
Literary Agent; President
United Kingdom

Literary Agency: Curtis Brown (**L0233**)

Fiction > *Novels*

Nonfiction > *Nonfiction Books*

Send: Query; Synopsis; Writing sample
How to send: Online submission system

Represents a number of best-selling fiction authors who feature in the Guardian Top 100 annual list and he also has a wide range of non-fiction clients and well known autobiographers, from politicians to celebrities.

L0628 Rozzy Lloyd
Literary Agent
United Kingdom

Literary Agency: The Narrow Road Company (**L0743**)

L0629 James Macdonald Lockhart
Literary Agent
United Kingdom

james@antonyharwood.com

http://antonyharwood.com/james-macdonald-lockhart/

Literary Agency: Antony Harwood Limited (**L0042**)

Nonfiction > *Nonfiction Books*
History; Nature; Politics; Science; Travel

Authors: Christine Berry; Alastair Bonnett; Roy Dennis; Anna Fleming; Sarah Gibson; Bob Gilbert; Caspar Henderson; Jill Hopper; Sally Huband; Gwyneth Lewis; Amy Liptrot; Fraser MacDonald; Stephen Rutt; Guy Shrubsole; Hugh Warwick

L0630 Pat Lomax
Literary Agent
United Kingdom

Literary Agency: Bell Lomax Moreton Agency (**L0081**)

L0631 Dominic Lord
Literary Agent
United Kingdom

Literary Agency: JFL Agency (**L0524**)

L0632 Lorella Belli Literary Agency (LBLA)
Literary Agency
54 Hartford House, 35 Tavistock Crescent, Notting Hill, London, W11 1AY
United Kingdom
Tel: +44 (0) 20 7727 8547
Fax: +44 (0) 870 787 4194

info@lorellabelliagency.com

http://www.lorellabelliagency.com

Professional Body: The Association of Authors' Agents (AAA)

Types: Fiction; Nonfiction
Subjects: Literary
Markets: Adult

Send: Query
Don't send: Full text
How to send: Email

Send query by post or by email in first instance. No attachments. Particularly interested in multicultural / international writing, and books relating to Italy, or written in Italian; first novelists, and journalists; successful sel-published authors. Welcomes queries from new authors and will suggest revisions where appropriate. No poetry, children's, original scripts, academic, SF, or fantasy.

Authors: Shahena Ali; Zoe Bran; Emily Giffin; Nisha Minhas; Alanna Mitchell; Rick Mofina; Dave Singleton; Diana Winston; Carol Wright

Literary Agent: Lorella Belli (**L0086**)

L0633 Lotus Lane Literary
Literary Agency
United States

contact@lotuslit.com

https://lotuslit.com

Fiction > *Novels*

Nonfiction > *Nonfiction Books*

Closed to approaches.

Independent literary agency based in New Jersey, representing a diverse list of debut and seasoned authors. Handles adult fiction and nonfiction, and sells rights to the US, UK, Europe, and India.

Literary Agent: Priya Doraswamy (*L0274*)

L0634 Louise Greenberg Books Ltd
Literary Agency
The End House, Church Crescent, London, N3 1BG
United Kingdom
Tel: +44 (0) 20 8349 1179

louisegreenberg@btinternet.com

http://louisegreenbergbooks.co.uk

Professional Body: The Association of Authors' Agents (AAA)

Types: Fiction; Nonfiction
Subjects: Literary
Markets: Adult

Closed to approaches.

Not accepting new writers as at July 2019. Check website for current status. Handles full-length literary fiction and serious nonfiction only. Only considers new writers by recommendation.

Literary Agent: Louise Greenberg (*L0418*)

L0635 Lowenstein Associates, Inc.

Literary Agency
115 East 23rd Street, 4th Floor, New York, NY 10010
United States
Tel: +1 (212) 206-1630

assistant@bookhaven.com

http://www.lowensteinassociates.com

Professional Body: Association of American Literary Agents (AALA)

Types: Fiction; Nonfiction
Subjects: Autobiography; Business; Commercial; Contemporary; Crime; Culture; Health; Literary; Medicine; Mystery; Psychology; Science; Society; Thrillers; Women's Interests
Markets: Adult; Children's; Young Adult

Send: Query
Don't send: Full text
How to send: Email

Send query by email with one-page query letter and first ten pages pasted into the body of the email (fiction) or table of contents and (if available) proposal. See website for full guidelines. No Westerns, textbooks, children's picture books, or books in need of translation.

Literary Agents: Barbara Lowenstein (*L0636*); Mary South (*L0932*)

L0636 Barbara Lowenstein

Literary Agent
United States

Literary Agency: Lowenstein Associates, Inc. (**L0635**)

L0637 Andrew Lownie

Literary Agent
United Kingdom

Literary Agency: Andrew Lownie Literary Agency Ltd (**L0034**)

L0638 George Lucas

Literary Agent
United States

Literary Agency: InkWell Management (**L0499**)

L0639 Mark Lucas

Literary Agent; Chair
United Kingdom

Literary Agency: The Soho Agency (**L0924**)

L0640 Lucy Luck

Literary Agent
United Kingdom

Literary Agency: C+W (Conville & Walsh) (**L0147**)

L0641 Amanda Luedeke

Literary Agent; Vice President
United States

http://www.macgregorandluedeke.com/about/agents/amanda-luedeke/

Literary Agency: MacGregor & Luedeke (**L0655**)

L0642 Luithlen Agency

Literary Agency
United Kingdom

penny@luithlenagency.co.uk

http://www.luithlenagency.com

CHILDREN'S > **Fiction**
  Early Readers; Middle Grade; Novels
YOUNG ADULT > **Fiction** > *Novels*

Closed to approaches.

Closed to submissions as at March 2020. Check website for current status.

Authors: David Belbin; Jennifer Bell; Caroline Clough; Harry Edge; John Hickman; Stuart Hill; Pete Johnson; Maxine Linnell; Clive Mantle; Gary Morecombe; Alison Prince; Bali Rai; James Riordan; Jamie Scallion; Joe Standerline; Robert Swindells; Gareth Thompson; John Townsend; Dan Tunstall

Literary Agent: Jennifer Luithlen (*L0643*)

L0643 Jennifer Luithlen

Literary Agent
United Kingdom

Literary Agency: Luithlen Agency (**L0642**)

L0644 Eric Lupfer

Literary Agent
United States

Literary Agency: Fletcher & Company

L0645 Lutyens and Rubinstein

Literary Agency
21 Kensington Park Road, London, W11 2EU
United Kingdom
Tel: +44 (0) 20 7792 4855

submissions@lutyensrubinstein.co.uk

https://www.lutyensrubinstein.co.uk
https://twitter.com/LandRAgency
https://instagram.com/LandRAgency

Professional Body: The Association of Authors' Agents (AAA)

Fiction > *Novels*
  Commercial; Literary

Nonfiction > *Nonfiction Books*

Send: Query; Synopsis; Writing sample
How to send: Email
How not to send: Post

Send up to 5,000 words or first three chapters by email with covering letter and short synopsis. No film or TV scripts, or unsolicited submissions by hand or by post.

Literary Agent: Susannah Godman

L0646 Alice Lutyens

Literary Agent
United Kingdom

Literary Agency: Curtis Brown (**L0233**)

L0647 Reggie Lutz

Literary Agent
United States

Literary Agency: Prentis Literary (**L0814**)

L0648 David Luxton

Literary Agent
United Kingdom

https://www.davidluxtonassociates.co.uk/the-agency/

Literary Agency: David Luxton Associates (**L0246**)

Nonfiction > *Nonfiction Books*
  Food; Music; Politics; Sport

Principal interests are in the fields of sport, music, food-writing and politics and he represents a diverse range of authors including countless high-profile sports personalities.

L0649 Paul Lyon-Maris

Literary Agent
United Kingdom

Literary Agency: Independent Talent Group Ltd (**L0496**)

L0650 Jennifer Lyons

Literary Agent; President
United States

jenniferlyonsagency@gmail.com

https://www.jenniferlyonsliteraryagency.com/who-we-are/

Literary Agency: The Jennifer Lyons Literary Agency, LLC

ADULT
  Fiction > *Novels*

Commercial Women's Fiction; Literary; Upmarket

Nonfiction > *Nonfiction Books*: Narrative Nonfiction

CHILDREN'S > **Fiction** > *Middle Grade*

YOUNG ADULT > **Fiction** > *Novels*

Send: Query
How to send: Post; Email

Seeking: Literary fiction and upmarket, commercial women's fiction. Narrative nonfiction. Children's books, especially middle grade and young adult. Prefers hard copy queries, but can also be queried by email.

L0651 Rhea Lyons
Literary Agent
United States

rhea@hgliterary.com

https://www.hgliterary.com/rhea

Literary Agency: HG Literary (**L0467**)

ADULT
  Fiction
    Graphic Novels: General
    Novels: Commercial; Fantasy; Horror; Literary; Science Fiction
  Nonfiction > *Nonfiction Books*
    Journalism; Narrative Nonfiction

CHILDREN'S > **Nonfiction** > *Nonfiction Books*

Closed to approaches.

Looking to represent writers of fiction, nonfiction, and graphic novelists who want to confront and destroy the status quo. For fiction, she is looking for anything that could be deemed literary/commercial crossover with a speculative bend, as well as science fiction and fantasy -- both true to the genre as well as genre-busting -- told in an accessible, entertaining voice. She likes horror but more on the cerebral end, less on the gory end (slashers are a no). For nonfiction, she is looking for narrative nonfiction and journalistic deep-dives into a single subject, particular location, or that examines a moment in history from an underrepresented, international, or little-known point of view. For children's books, she is especially interested in nonfiction that inspires learning and creativity for all ages.

L0652 Donald Maass
Literary Agent
United States

Literary Agency: Donald Maass Literary Agency (**L0273**)

L0653 Emily MacDonald
Literary Agent
United Kingdom

emilymacdonald@42mp.com

https://www.42mp.com/agents
https://twitter.com/Ebh_mac

Literary Agency: 42 Management and Production (**L0002**)

Fiction > *Novels*: Literary

Nonfiction > *Nonfiction Books*
  History; Memoir; Narrative Nonfiction; Nature; Regional; Scotland

How to send: Email

Looking for literary fiction, narrative nonfiction with an investigative twist, and untold true stories, either personal or historical. Also interested in Scottish and regional voices with stories to tell.

L0654 Laura Macdougall
Literary Agent
United Kingdom

https://www.unitedagents.co.uk/lmacdougallunitedagentscouk

Literary Agency: United Agents (**L0992**)

Closed to approaches.

L0655 MacGregor & Luedeke
Literary Agency
PO Box 1316, Manzanita, OR 97130
United States
Tel: +1 (503) 389-4803

submissions@macgregorliterary.com

http://www.macgregorandluedeke.com
https://twitter.com/MacGregorLit

Types: Fiction; Nonfiction
Formats: Short Fiction
Subjects: Autobiography; Business; Comedy / Humour; Commercial; Contemporary; Crime; Culture; Current Affairs; Finance; History; How To; Lifestyle; Mystery; Personal Development; Religion; Romance; Sport; Suspense; Thrillers; Women's Interests
Markets: Academic; Adult

Send: Query
Don't send: Full text
How to send: Email

Costs: Author covers sundry admin costs.

Handles work in a variety of genres, but all from a Christian perspective. Currently closed to fiction submissions, but still accepting nonfiction. Send query with proposal / synopsis and first three chapters (approximately 50 pages). See website for full guidelines.

Authors: Don Brown; Davis Bunn; Rashawn Copeland; Sheila Gregoire; Rachel Hauck; James Byron Huggins; Steve Jackson; Jessica Kate; Rachel Linden; Holly Lorincz; Evelyn Lozada; Scott Parazynski; Jay Payleitner; Tom Satterly; Kimberly Stuart; David Thomas; Vincent Zandri

Literary Agent / President: Chip MacGregor (**L0656**)

Literary Agent / Vice President: Amanda Luedeke (**L0641**)

L0656 Chip MacGregor
Literary Agent; President
United States

http://www.macgregorandluedeke.com/about/agents/chip-macgregor/
http://aaronline.org/Sys/PublicProfile/2176764/417813

Literary Agency: MacGregor & Luedeke (**L0655**)
Professional Body: Association of American Literary Agents (AALA)

L0657 Joanna MacKenzie
Literary Agent
United States

https://nelsonagency.com/joanna-mackenzie/
https://www.publishersmarketplace.com/members/JoannaMacKenzie/
https://twitter.com/joannamackenzie
https://www.facebook.com/joanna.topor.mackenzie

Literary Agency: Nelson Literary Agency, LLC (**L0746**)

ADULT > **Fiction** > *Novels*
  High Concept; Magic; Mystery; Speculative; Thrillers; Witches; Women's Fiction

YOUNG ADULT > **Fiction** > *Novels*

Closed to approaches.

I'm looking for that epic adult or YA read that, at its center, beats with a universal heart. Anything set on a creepy island. Women's fiction featuring witches and touches of magic—especially as both pertain to women finding their voices and power. Mysteries/thrillers set in close-knit communities. (If those communities happen to be in the Midwest, all the better.) High-concept stories with a strong voice in the areas of women's fiction, mystery/thriller, and speculative. (Think Before I Go To Sleep by S.J Watson or Dark Matter by Blake Crouch.) Anything featuring fierce female heroines who will do whatever it takes to protect their brood. Smart and timely women's fiction where the personal intersects with the world at large. (Think This Is How It Always Is by Laurie Frankel or All We Ever Wanted by Emily Giffin.) Narratives about reinvention or the second and third acts of women's lives. Stories about the immigrant experience for both adult and YA (like The Namesake by Jhumpa Lahiri). Anything dealing with the relationships that make us who we are for both adult and YA. For all of the above, I am especially interested in diverse and marginalized voices.

Authors: Brooke Abrams; Kate Baer; Shana Galen; John Galligan; Jill Grunenwald; Alison Hammer; Robin Huber; Sarah Zachrich Jeng; Sierra Kincade; Karen Koh; Gillian Libby; Amanda Marbais; Jonathan Messinger; Meghan Scott Molin; Katrina Monroe; Kristen Simmons; Jennifer Springsteen; Stacy Stokes; Chrysler Szarlan; Ben Tanzer; Kathleen West.

L0658 Robert Mackwood

Literary Agent
Canada

Literary Agency: Seventh Avenue Literary Agency (**L0901**)

L0659 Jamie Maclean

Literary Agent; Editor
United Kingdom

https://cmm.agency/about-us.php

Literary Agency: Coombs Moylett & Maclean Literary Agency (**L0217**)
Magazine: Erotic Review (**M0192**)

Fiction > *Novels*
   Erotic; Historical Crime; Mystery; Thrillers

Nonfiction > *Nonfiction Books*
   Gender Politics; How To; Lifestyle; Relationships

Send: Synopsis; Writing sample
How to send: Online submission system

Specialises in both fiction and nonfiction and is particularly interested in sexual politics, relationship, lifestyle how-to's, erotica, thrillers, whodunit and historical crime.

L0660 Lauren MacLeod

Literary Agent
United States

https://www.strothmanagency.com/about
https://twitter.com/Lauren_MacLeod
http://aaronline.org/Sys/PublicProfile/12259463/417813

Literary Agency: The Strothman Agency (**L0951**)
Professional Body: Association of American Literary Agents (AALA)

ADULT
   Fiction > *Novels*: Literary

   Nonfiction > *Nonfiction Books*
      Crime; Feminism; Food; History; Narrative Nonfiction; Popular Culture; Science

CHILDREN'S > **Fiction** > *Middle Grade*

YOUNG ADULT
   Fiction > *Novels*
      General, and in particular: Environment; Politics; Social Issues

   Nonfiction > *Nonfiction Books*
      General, and in particular: Environment; Politics; Social Issues

Not accepting queries for adult novels, picture books, or chapter books for early readers at this time. She does not represent adult romance, adult SFF, or adult mysteries and thrillers.

L0661 Macnaughton Lord Representation

Literary Agency
United Kingdom
Tel: +44 (0) 20 7407 9201

info@mlrep.com

http://www.mlrep.com

Scripts
   Film Scripts; *TV Scripts*; *Theatre Scripts*

Closed to approaches.

Theatrical and literary agency representing established names and emerging talent in theatre, film, tv and the performing arts. No unsolicited mss.

Literary Agents: Rupert Lord; Helen Mumby; Davina Shah

L0662 Eve MacSweeney

Literary Agent
United States

Literary Agency: Fletcher & Company

L0663 Neeti Madan

Senior Agent
United States

https://www.sll.com/our-team

Literary Agency: Sterling Lord Literistic, Inc. (**L0940**)

Nonfiction > *Nonfiction Books*
   Journalism; Lifestyle; Memoir; Multicultural; Popular Culture; Women's Issues

Send: Query; Synopsis; Writing sample
How to send: Online submission system

L0664 Madeleine Milburn Literary, TV & Film Agency

Literary Agency
The Factory, 1 Park Hill, London, SW4 9NS
United Kingdom
Tel: +44 (0) 20 7499 7550

submissions@madeleinemilburn.com
childrens@madeleinemilburn.com
info@madeleinemilburn.com

https://madeleinemilburn.co.uk

Professional Body: The Association of Authors' Agents (AAA)

ADULT
   Fiction > *Novels*
   Nonfiction > *Nonfiction Books*

CHILDREN'S
   Fiction > *Novels*
   Nonfiction > *Nonfiction Books*

NEW ADULT
   Fiction > *Novels*
   Nonfiction > *Nonfiction Books*

TEEN
   Fiction > *Novels*
   Nonfiction > *Nonfiction Books*

YOUNG ADULT
   Fiction > *Novels*
   Nonfiction > *Nonfiction Books*

Send: Query; Synopsis; Pitch; Market info; Writing sample
How to send: Email attachment

Represents award-winning and bestselling authors of adult and children's fiction and non-fiction. Always looking for new writers. Address material to a specific agent. See website for full guidelines.

Associate Agent: Vanessa Browne (**L0138**)

Company Director / Literary Agent: Madeleine Milburn (**L0709**)

Literary Agent / Managing Director: Giles Milburn (**L0708**)

Literary Agents: Emma Bal (**L0058**); Chloe Seager (**L0899**); Hayley Steed (**L0935**)

L0665 Hester Malin

Assistant Agent
United States

https://karengantzliterarymanagement.com/about-1

Literary Agency: Karen Gantz Literary Management (**L0549**)

L0666 Carol Mann

Literary Agent
United States

https://www.carolmannagency.com/our-team

Literary Agency: Carol Mann Agency (**L0161**)
Professional Body: Association of American Literary Agents (AALA)

Fiction > *Novels*

Nonfiction > *Nonfiction Books*
   Current Affairs; Health; History; Medicine; Narrative Nonfiction; Parenting; Religion; Self Help; Spirituality

Send: Query; Author bio; Writing sample
How to send: In the body of an email

Specialises in nonfiction (health/medical, religion, spirituality, self-help, parenting, current affairs, history, narrative non-fiction) while also taking on the occasional fiction writer.

L0667 Rachel Mann

Literary Agent
United Kingdom

http://www.jounwin.co.uk/rachel-mann/

Literary Agency: Jo Unwin Literary Agency (**L0526**)

ADULT
Fiction > *Novels*

Nonfiction > *Nonfiction Books*
Comedy / Humour; Lifestyle

CHILDREN'S
Fiction > *Middle Grade*
Comedy / Humour; Commercial; High Concept

Nonfiction > *Nonfiction Books*
Comedy / Humour; Lifestyle

Does not want:

CHILDREN'S > **Fiction** > *Picture Books*

In all cases I want compelling voices, unpatronizing writing and vivid, complex characters. International settings and traditions, unconventional narratives, and progressive and/or radical social commentary will always get my attention. I'm particularly interested in writers from underrepresented backgrounds, especially if those stories are genre fiction, lifestyle or comic non-fiction, for both adults and children.

At the moment, I'm particularly on the look-out for funny, commercial and high-concept middle-grade series. I'd love to see strong hooks and rich worldbuilding, often with both humour and darkness.

I'm also looking for bold, voice-driven and emotionally engaging non-fiction across both adults' and children's.

L0668 Marcil O'Farrell Literary, LLC and Denise Marcil Literary Agency, LLC

Literary Agency
86 Dennis Street, Manhasset, NY 11030
United States
Tel: +1 (212) 337-3402

annemarie@marcilofarrellagency.com

https://www.marcilofarrellagency.com

Professional Body: Association of American Literary Agents (AALA)

Types: Nonfiction
Subjects: Business; Cookery; Health; Personal Development; Spirituality; Sport; Travel
Markets: Adult

Send: Query
Don't send: Full text
How to send: Email

Costs: Author covers sundry admin costs.

No fiction, memoirs, or screenplays. Send query up to 200 words by email.

Literary Agent: Denise Marcil (*L0669*)

L0669 Denise Marcil

Literary Agent
United States

Literary Agency: Marcil O'Farrell Literary, LLC and Denise Marcil Literary Agency, LLC (**L0668**)
Professional Body: The Agents Round Table (ART)

L0670 Kendra Marcus

Literary Agent
United States

http://www.bookstopliterary.com/submission.html

Literary Agency: BookStop Literary Agency, LLC (**L0111**)

CHILDREN'S
Fiction
Novels: General
Picture Books: Comedy / Humour

Nonfiction > *Nonfiction Books*
General, and in particular: History; Science

How to send: By referral

Gravitates toward quirky and funny picture books, fiction with unforgettable characters and stories that will bring her to tears. Unusual non-fiction, especially science presented in new ways and little gems of history are also her cup of tea. Stories with Hispanic or Latino characters are always welcome, and she is thrilled to find accomplished illustrators with a fresh style who can tell a strong story in pictures to accompany a text.

L0671 Victoria Marini

Literary Agent
United States

Literary Agency: Irene Goodman Literary Agency (IGLA) (**L0501**)
Professional Body: Association of American Literary Agents (AALA)

L0672 Marjacq Scripts Ltd

Literary Agency
The Space, 235 High Holborn, London, WC1V 7DN
United Kingdom
Tel: +44 (0) 20 7935 9499

enquiries@marjacq.com

http://www.marjacq.com
https://twitter.com/marjacqscripts

Professional Body: The Association of Authors' Agents (AAA)

ADULT
Fiction > *Novels*

Nonfiction > *Nonfiction Books*

Scripts
Film Scripts; *TV Scripts*
CHILDREN'S

Fiction > *Novels*
Nonfiction > *Nonfiction Books*

Send: Query
Don't send: Full text
How to send: Email
How not to send: Post

Accepts submissions by email only. For books, send query with synopsis and first 50 pages. For scripts, send short treatment and entire screenplay. Send only Word or PDF documents less than 2MB. Do not paste work into the body of the email. See website for full details. No children's picture books, poetry, plays or musical theatre.

Authors: Tanya Atapattu; Holly Baxter; Daisy Buchanan; Cecil Cameron; James Campbell; Angela Clarke; Mathew Clayton; Fiona Collins; Caroline Corcoran; Isabel Costello; Francesca Dorricott; Lilly Ebert; Dov Forman; Eve Harris; Louise Hulland; Catriona Innes; Amy Jones; Eve Makis; Andrea Mara; Francesca May; Claire McGowan; Adam Pearson; Alice Peterson; Das Petrou; Rachel Phipps; Carmen Reid; Samantha Renke; Lee Ridley; Diana Rosie; Frances Ryan; Jennifer Savin; Lucy Vine; James Wallman; Roz Watkins; Eva Woods

Literary Agents: Diana Beaumont (**L0077**); Leah Middleton (**L0707**); Philip Patterson; Imogen Pelham; Catherine Pellegrino; Sandra Sawicka

L0673 Mildred Marmur

Literary Agent
United States

Literary Agency: Mildred Marmur Associates, Ltd. (**L0710**)
Professional Body: Association of American Literary Agents (AALA)

L0674 Jill Marr

Literary Agent
United States

https://www.dijkstraagency.com/agent-page.php?agent_id=Marr
https://querymanager.com/query/JillMarr

Literary Agency: Sandra Dijkstra Literary Agency

Fiction > *Novels*
Book Club Fiction; Commercial; Historical Fiction; Horror; Mystery; Thrillers

Nonfiction > *Nonfiction Books*
Comedy / Humour; Current Affairs; Health; History; Memoir; Music; Narrative Nonfiction; Nutrition; Politics; Popular Culture; Science; Sport

How to send: Query Manager

Looking for fiction and non-fiction by BIPOC and Latinx writers, disabled persons, and people identifying as LGBTQ+, among others. She is interested in commercial fiction, with an emphasis on mysteries, thrillers, and horror, book club, and historical fiction. She is also looking for non-fiction by authors with a big, timely, smart message as well as historical projects that look at big picture issues. Jill is looking for non-fiction projects in the areas of current events, science, history, narrative non-fiction, sports, politics, health & nutrition, pop culture, humor, music, and very select memoir.

L0675 Evan Marshall

Literary Agent
United States

Literary Agency: The Evan Marshall Agency (**L0311**)

L0676 Jen Marshall

Literary Agent
New York
United States

https://aevitascreative.com/agents/

Literary Agency: Aevitas (**L0016**)

ADULT
Fiction
Graphic Novels: General
Novels: Adventure; Commercial; Crime; Drama; Horror; Literary; Popular Culture; Romance; Thrillers
Nonfiction > *Nonfiction Books*
Arts; Health; History; Mathematics; Narrative Nonfiction; Science

CHILDREN'S > *Fiction* > *Novels*

Send: Author bio; Outline; Pitch; Market info; Writing sample
How to send: Online submission system

Represents a range of fiction and nonfiction. She is most interested in: literary fiction, commercial fiction, crime, thrillers, style, pop culture, and compelling narrative nonfiction.

L0677 Joanna Marston

Literary Agent
United Kingdom

Literary Agency: Rosica Colin Ltd (**L0860**)

L0678 Sylvie Marston

Literary Agent
United Kingdom

Literary Agency: Rosica Colin Ltd (**L0860**)

L0679 Mary Clemmey Literary Agency

Literary Agency
6 Dunollie Road, London, NW5 2XP
United Kingdom
Tel: +44 (0) 20 7267 1290

mcwords@googlemail.com

Professional Body: The Association of Authors' Agents (AAA)

Types: Fiction; Nonfiction; Scripts
Formats: Film Scripts; Radio Scripts; TV Scripts; Theatre Scripts
Markets: Adult

Send: Query
Don't send: Full text
How not to send: Email

Send query with SAE and description of work only. Handles high-quality work with an international market. No children's books, science fiction, fantasy, or unsolicited MSS or submissions by email. Scripts handled for existing clients only. Do not submit a script or idea for a script unless you are already a client.

Literary Agent: Mary Clemmey (*L0204*)

L0680 Massie & McQuilkin

Literary Agency
27 West 20th Street, Suite 305, New York, NY 10011
United States
Tel: +1 (212) 352-2055
Fax: +1 (212) 352-2059

info@lmqlit.com

http://www.mmqlit.com

Types: Fiction; Nonfiction
Subjects: Autobiography; Comedy / Humour; Commercial; Crime; Culture; Current Affairs; Fantasy; Health; History; Literary; Politics; Psychology; Science; Society; Sport; Suspense; Thrillers; Women's Interests
Markets: Adult; Children's; Young Adult

Send: Query
Don't send: Full text
How to send: Email

Costs: Author covers sundry admin costs.

See website for specific agent interests and contact details. Query only one agent at a time.

Junior Agent: Max Moorhead (**L0724**)

Literary Agents: Stephanie Abou (*L0006*); Elias Altman (*L0029*); Jason Anthony (*L0041*); Ethan Bassoff (*L0071*); Laney Katz Becker; Maria Massie (*L0681*); Rob McQuilkin (*L0694*); Neil Olson (**L0770**); Sandra Pareja (**L0778**); Rayhane Sanders (**L0880**); Julie Stevenson (*L0943*); Lane Zachary (**L1064**); Renee Zuckerbrot (*L1069*)

L0681 Maria Massie

Literary Agent
United States

Literary Agency: Massie & McQuilkin (**L0680**)

L0682 Pippa Masson

Literary Agent
Australia

Literary Agency: Curtis Brown (Australia) Pty Ltd (**L0234**)

L0683 Peter Matson

Literary Agent; Chair
United States

https://www.sll.com/our-team

Literary Agency: Sterling Lord Literistic, Inc. (**L0940**)

Fiction > *Novels*

Nonfiction > *Nonfiction Books*
History; Science

Send: Query; Synopsis; Writing sample
How to send: Online submission system

L0684 Jennifer Mattson

Literary Agent
United States

Literary Agency: Andrea Brown Literary Agency, Inc.

Closed to approaches.

L0685 Bridget Wagner Matzie

Literary Agent; Partner
United States

https://aevitascreative.com/agents/

Literary Agency: Aevitas (**L0016**)

Fiction > *Novels*: Commercial

Nonfiction > *Nonfiction Books*

Closed to approaches.

Represents nonfiction and commercial fiction.

L0686 Shari Maurer

Literary Agent
United States

https://querymanager.com/query/1434

Literary Agency: The Stringer Literary Agency LLC (**L0949**)

ADULT
Fiction > *Novels*
Crime; Fantasy; Suspense; Thrillers; Upmarket Women's Fiction

Nonfiction > *Nonfiction Books*
Memoir; Narrative Nonfiction; Parenting; Popular Science

CHILDREN'S
Fiction
Middle Grade: Contemporary; Historical Fiction; Literary; Mystery
Picture Books: General

Nonfiction > *Middle Grade*

YOUNG ADULT
Fiction > *Novels*
Contemporary; Historical Fiction; Literary; Mystery

Nonfiction > *Nonfiction Books*

Does not want:

ADULT > Fiction > *Novels*: Erotic
Romance
CHILDREN'S > Fiction > *Middle
Grade*: Fantasy

Send: Query; Synopsis; Writing sample; Pitch
How to send: Query Manager

L0687 **Jane Graham Maw**
Literary Agent
United Kingdom

Literary Agency: Graham Maw Christie
Literary Agency (**L0408**)

L0688 **Cameron McClure**
Literary Agent
United States

Literary Agency: Donald Maass Literary
Agency (**L0273**)

L0689 **Michael McCoy**
Literary Agent
United Kingdom

Literary Agency: Independent Talent Group
Ltd (**L0496**)

L0690 **Caitlin McDonald**
Literary Agent
United States

Literary Agency: Donald Maass Literary
Agency (**L0273**)

L0691 **Sarah McDonnell**
Literary Agent
United Kingdom

Literary Agency: Bell Lomax Moreton Agency
(**L0081**)

L0692 **Holly McGhee**
Literary Agent
United States

Literary Agency: Pippin Properties, Inc
(**L0801**)

L0693 **Matt McGowan**
Senior Agent; Vice President
United States

mm@goldinlit.com

Literary Agency: Frances Goldin Literary
Agency, Inc. (**L0356**)

Fiction > *Novels*: Literary

Nonfiction
  Essays: General
  Nonfiction Books: Biography; Crime;
  Culture; Food; Football / Soccer; History;
  Journalism; Memoir; Narrative Nonfiction;
  Politics; Popular Culture; Popular Science;
  Sport; Sub-Culture; Travel

How to send: Email
Looking for emotionally, intellectually, and
formally adventurous work of all kinds and is
particularly interested in writers who believe
nonfiction can be as artful as fiction. Queries
for essays; literary fiction (strong but difficult
characters, examinations of place, sub-cultures,
and/or recent history or time periods);
researched narrative nonfiction; journalism;
politics; history; memoir; biography; cultural
studies; popular culture & science; sports
(particularly soccer); travel, crime, food,
literary graphic work (especially NF), are all
welcome.

L0694 **Rob McQuilkin**
Literary Agent
United States

Literary Agency: Massie & McQuilkin
(**L0680**)

L0695 **Jane von Mehren**
Literary Agent; Partner
United States

https://aevitascreative.com/agents/

Literary Agency: Aevitas (**L0016**)

Fiction > *Novels*
  Book Club Fiction; Historical Fiction;
  Literary

Nonfiction > *Nonfiction Books*
  Business; History; Memoir; Popular Culture;
  Science

Send: Query; Author bio; Market info; Writing
sample
How to send: Online submission system

Interested in narratives in the areas of business,
history, memoir, popular culture and science,
books that help us live our best lives, literary,
book club, and historical fiction.

L0696 **Mendel Media Group,
LLC**
Literary Agency
115 West 30th Street, Suite 209, New York,
NY 10001
United States
Tel: +1 (646) 239-9896

scott@mendelmedia.com

http://www.mendelmedia.com

Professional Body: Association of American
Literary Agents (AALA)

Types: Fiction; Nonfiction
Subjects: Autobiography; Comedy / Humour;
Commercial; Contemporary; Culture; Current
Affairs; Entertainment; Finance; History; How
To; Literary; Literature; Media; Mystery;
Personal Development; Politics; Religion;
Science; Thrillers; Women's Interests
Markets: Adult; Children's; Young Adult

Send: Query
Don't send: Full text
How to send: Email

Send query by email only. No longer accepts
submissions by post. For fiction, send synopsis
and first 20 pages. For nonfiction, send
proposal and sample chapters. See website for
full guidelines.

Literary Agent: Scott Mendel (*L0697*)

L0697 **Scott Mendel**
Literary Agent
United States

Literary Agency: Mendel Media Group, LLC
(**L0696**)

L0698 **Adam Mendlesohn**
Literary Agent
United Kingdom

Literary Agency: The Narrow Road Company
(**L0743**)

L0699 **Marianne Merola**
Literary Agent
United States

mmerola@bromasite.com

Literary Agency: Brandt & Hochman Literary
Agents, Inc. (**L0119**)
Professional Body: Association of American
Literary Agents (AALA)

ADULT
  Fiction > *Novels*
  Nonfiction > *Nonfiction Books*

CHILDREN'S > Fiction > *Novels*

Send: Query
How to send: Email

L0700 **Jackie Meyer**
Literary Agent
United States

Literary Agency: Whimsy Literary Agency,
LLC (**L1030**)

L0701 **Mic Cheetham Literary
Agency**
Literary Agency
62 Grafton Way, London, W1T 5DW
United Kingdom
Tel: +44 (0) 20 3976 7713

submissions@miccheetham.com

http://www.miccheetham.com

Fiction > *Novels*

Nonfiction > *Nonfiction Books*

Closed to approaches.

Agency with a deliberately small list. Only
takes on two or three new writers each year.
New writers are advised to acquaint
themselves with the work of the writers

currently represented by the agency before submitting their own work.

Authors: Carol Birch; Nm Browne; Pat Cadigan; Alan Campbell; Gregory Doran; Barbara Ewing; Ian Green; M John Harrison; Alice James; Ken MacLeod; Paul Mcauley; China Miéville; Sharon Penman; Antony Sher; Adrian Tchaikovsky

Literary Agents: Mic Cheetham (**L0189**); Simon Kavanagh (**L0558**)

L0702 The Michael Greer Literary Agency

Literary Agency
United Kingdom

melanie@michaelgreerliteraryagency.co.uk

http://www.michaelgreerliteraryagency.co.uk
https://twitter.com/SportLitAgent

ADULT
  Fiction > *Novels*: Urban

  Nonfiction > *Nonfiction Books*: Sport

YOUNG ADULT > **Fiction** > *Novels*

Send: Synopsis; Writing sample
How to send: Email

Costs: Author covers sundry admin costs.

Handles books in three areas: sport; City Fiction; and Young Adult. Send synopsis and three chapters by email.

Literary Agent: Melanie Michael-Greer (*L0704*)

L0703 Michael Snell Literary Agency

Literary Agency
PO Box 1206, Truro, MA 02666-1206
United States
Tel: +1 (508) 349-3718

query@michaelsnellagency.com

http://michaelsnellagency.com

Types: Fiction; Nonfiction
Subjects: Business; Health; How To; Lifestyle; Personal Development; Psychology; Science; Suspense; Thrillers; Travel; Women's Interests
Markets: Adult

Costs: Offers services that writers have to pay for.

Send query by post or by email. Specialises in business, how-to and self-help. No unsolicited MSS. Additional writing services available for a fee.

L0704 Melanie Michael-Greer

Literary Agent
United Kingdom

Literary Agency: The Michael Greer Literary Agency (**L0702**)

L0705 Micheline Steinberg Associates

Literary Agency
Suite 315, ScreenWorks, 22 Highbury Grove, London, N5 2ER
United Kingdom

info@steinplays.com

http://www.steinplays.com
https://twitter.com/steinbergassocs

Scripts
  Film Scripts; *Radio Scripts*; *TV Scripts*; *Theatre Scripts*

Send: Query
How to send: By referral

We're a mid-size agency in which all the agents have background in theatre and related media. We work closely with writers and the industry, developing writers work, managing their careers, and negotiating all rights. We also have affiliations with book agents and agents overseas including in the USA. Please note that we do not accept unsolicited submissions without a letter of recommendation from an industry professional. All unsolicited material will be deleted unread. Does not consider books.

Literary Agents: Jazz Adamson; Micheline Steinberg

L0706 Michelle Kass Associates

Literary Agency
85 Charing Cross Road, London, WC2H 0AA
United Kingdom
Tel: +44 (0) 20 7439 1624

office@michellekass.co.uk

http://www.michellekass.co.uk

Professional Body: The Association of Authors' Agents (AAA)

Fiction > *Novels*
  Commercial; Literary

Scripts
  Film Scripts; *TV Scripts*

How to send: Phone

Represents authors, dramatists/screenwriters, and screenwriters based in the UK and Ireland. Call before submitting.

Literary Agent: Michelle Kass (*L0551*)

L0707 Leah Middleton

Literary Agent
United Kingdom

leah@marjacq.com

http://www.marjacq.com/leah-middleton.html

Literary Agency: Marjacq Scripts Ltd (**L0672**)

Scripts

  Film Scripts: General, and in particular: Comedy / Humour
  TV Scripts: General, and in particular: Comedy / Humour

Send: Full text; Synopsis; Author bio
How to send: Email

Considers scripts across all formats and genres, but is particularly interested in comedy and returnable TV. No book submissions, or submissions from US screenwriters.

L0708 Giles Milburn

Literary Agent; Managing Director
United Kingdom

https://madeleinemilburn.co.uk/team-member/giles-milburn/

Literary Agency: Madeleine Milburn Literary, TV & Film Agency (**L0664**)

Fiction > *Novels*
  Book Club Fiction; Historical Crime; Historical Fiction; Thrillers

Nonfiction > *Nonfiction Books*
  Biography; Narrative Nonfiction

Send: Query; Pitch; Market info; Author bio; Synopsis; Writing sample
How to send: Email
How not to send: Post

Actively looking for: historical fiction for the book club market; marginalised voices in history; the next huge historical crime series; thrillers; familiar time periods from a new angle; old stories retold in new ways; gritty, real, transportive, warts-and-all historical fiction; characters caught in the build-up or aftermath of historical events; biographical / narrative non-fiction more incredible than any fiction.

L0709 Madeleine Milburn

Literary Agent; Company Director
United Kingdom

https://madeleinemilburn.co.uk/team-member/madeleine-milburn/

Literary Agency: Madeleine Milburn Literary, TV & Film Agency (**L0664**)

Fiction > *Novels*
  Book Club Fiction; Family Saga; Literary; Suspense; Thrillers

Send: Query; Pitch; Market info; Author bio; Synopsis; Writing sample
How to send: Email
How not to send: Post

Actively looking for character-led, voice-driven literary and book club fiction with a strong discussion point, moral dilemmas, family dramas with thought-provoking themes, quirky characters, original concepts, thrillers and suspense.

L0710 Mildred Marmur Associates, Ltd.
Literary Agency
2005 Palmer Avenue, Suite 127, Larchmont, NY 10538
United States

http://aaronline.org/Sys/PublicProfile/2176773/417813

Fiction > *Novels*

Nonfiction > *Nonfiction Books*

Literary agent based in Larchmont, New York.

Literary Agent: Mildred Marmur (*L0673*)

L0711 Jessica Mileo
Literary Agent
United States

Literary Agency: InkWell Management (**L0499**)

L0712 Miles Stott Children's Literary Agency
Literary Agency
East Hook Farm, Lower Quay Road, Hook, Haverfordwest, Pembrokeshire, SA62 4LR
United Kingdom
Tel: +44 (0) 7855 252043

fictionsubs@milesstottagency.co.uk
picturebooksubs@milesstottagency.co.uk

https://www.milesstottagency.co.uk
https://www.facebook.com/pages/Miles-Stott-Childrens-Literary-Agency/311096870669
https://twitter.com/MilesStott
https://www.instagram.com/milesstottagency/

Professional Body: The Association of Authors' Agents (AAA)

CHILDREN'S
  Fiction
    Middle Grade; *Novels*; *Picture Books*
  Nonfiction > *Nonfiction Books*

YOUNG ADULT > **Fiction** > *Novels*

Closed to approaches.

Handles Board books, Picture books, Novelty Books, Young fiction, Middle grade fiction, YA fiction, and Non-fiction. No poetry, musical works, or educational texts. For fiction send query with synopsis and first three chapters. For picture book submissions, send query by email only, with short covering letter, details about you and your background, and up to three stories. See website for full guidelines.

Authors: Kate Alizadeh; Kirsty Applebaum; Atinuke; Dominic Barker; Helen Baugh; Adam Beer; Rachel Bright; Mark Burgess; Ruth Doyle; Catherine Emmett; Jan Fearnley; Lu Fraser; Annelise Gray; Stacy Gregg; Frances Hardinge; Caryl Hart; Sophie Kirtley; Gill Lewis; Zoë Marriott; Julia Miranda; Tom Percival; Gareth Peter; Tom Pollock; Mark

Sperring; Amber Stewart; Leisa Stewart-Sharpe; Daniel Whelan

Literary Agents: Victoria Birkett (**L0099**); Caroline Hill-Trevor; Nancy Miles (**L0713**); Mandy Suhr (**L0953**)

L0713 Nancy Miles
Literary Agent
United Kingdom

nancy@milesstottagency.co.uk

https://www.milesstottagency.co.uk/about-nancy-miles.php

Literary Agency: Miles Stott Children's Literary Agency (**L0712**)

CHILDREN'S > **Fiction** > *Novels*
  Comedy / Humour; Contemporary; Fantasy; Historical Fiction; Science Fiction

YOUNG ADULT > **Fiction** > *Novels*
  Comedy / Humour; Contemporary; Fantasy; Historical Fiction; Science Fiction

"Whatever the book – funny, fantasy, sci-fi, contemporary, historical – and for whichever age, a strong voice, great characters and an engaging plot will be the first things to reel me in."

L0714 Christina Miller
Literary Agent
United States

http://www.inkwellmanagement.com/staff/christina-miller

Literary Agency: InkWell Management (**L0499**)

Fiction > *Novels*
  Historical Fiction; Mystery; Romance; Thrillers

L0715 Jennie Miller
Literary Agent
United Kingdom

Literary Agency: Independent Talent Group Ltd (**L0496**)

L0716 Tom Miller
Literary Agent
United States

Literary Agency: Liza Dawson Associates (**L0625**)

L0717 Rachel Mills
Literary Agent; Company Director
United Kingdom

rachel@rmliterary.co.uk

https://twitter.com/bookishyogini

Literary Agency: Rachel Mills Literary (**L0819**)

Nonfiction > *Nonfiction Books*

Biography; Current Affairs; Feminism; Food; Health; Memoir; Narrative Nonfiction; Nature; Popular Science; Psychology; Social Media; Sustainable Living; Wellbeing

Send: Query; Writing sample
How to send: Email

Looking for nonfiction on subjects including current affairs, feminism, psychology, popular science, well-being, narrative nonfiction, memoir, biography, food, nature, sustainability, health, social media and platform led projects.

Send email with as much detail about yourself and the project as possible, ideally with at least one sample chapter.

L0718 Philippa Milnes-Smith
Literary Agent; Managing Director
United Kingdom

https://www.facebook.com/philippa.milnessmith

Literary Agency: The Soho Agency (**L0924**)

L0719 Heather Mitchell
Literary Agent
United States

Literary Agency: Gelfman Schneider / ICM Partners (**L0386**)

L0720 MMB Creative
Literary Agency
The Old Truman Brewery, 91 Brick Lane, London, E1 6QL
United Kingdom
Tel: +44 (0) 20 3582 9370
Fax: +44 (0) 20 3582 9377

Nonfiction@mmbcreative.com
Childrenswriter@mmbcreative.com
Childrensillustrator@mmbcreative.com
irelandgenrefiction@mmbcreative.com
irelandliteraryfiction@mmbcreative.com
ukgenrefiction@mmbcreative.com
ukliteraryfiction@mmbcreative.com

https://mmbcreative.com

Professional Body: The Association of Authors' Agents (AAA)

ADULT
  Fiction > *Novels*
    Adventure; Commercial Women's Fiction; Crime; Horror; Ireland; Literary; Mystery; Thrillers

  Nonfiction > *Nonfiction Books*
    General, and in particular: Autobiography; Current Affairs; Food and Drink; History; Memoir; Popular Culture

YOUNG ADULT
  Fiction > *Novels*
  Nonfiction > *Nonfiction Books*

Send: Query; Synopsis; Author bio; Writing sample
How to send: Email

Send submissions as a single document including a synopsis, author biography, writing sample, and a brief statement on why you are interested in being represented by this agency. See website for full guidelines.

Literary Agents: Ivan Mulcahy; Sallyanne Sweeney

L0721 Caroline Montgomery
Literary Agent
United Kingdom

Literary Agency: Rupert Crew Ltd (**L0869**)

L0722 Penny Moore
Literary Agent
United States

https://aevitascreative.com/agents/
https://querymanager.com/query/LiteraryPenny

Literary Agency: Aevitas (**L0016**)

CHILDREN'S
 Fiction
  Middle Grade; Picture Books
 Nonfiction > *Nonfiction Books*

YOUNG ADULT
 Fiction > *Novels*
 Nonfiction > *Nonfiction Books*

Send: Author bio; Query; Writing sample; Market info
How to send: Query Manager

Mainly represents children's literature, including picture books, middle grade, and young adult. She also has an interest in select platform nonfiction projects that speak to younger audiences. Though she's interested in all genres, she's specifically seeking inventive works featuring breakout voices and compelling plot lines that will make young readers feel seen and heard for the first time.

L0723 Renae Moore
Associate Agent
United States

http://www.azantianlitagency.com/pages/team-rm.html
https://querymanager.com/query/renae

Literary Agency: Azantian Literary Agency (**L0054**)

ADULT > **Fiction** > *Novels*
 Literary Mystery; Literary; Speculative

YOUNG ADULT > **Fiction**
 Graphic Novels: Adventure; Coming of Age; Mystery; Speculative
 Novels: Adventure; Fantasy; Mystery; Romance; Science Fiction; Speculative

How to send: Query Manager

Gravitates to stories that have a balance of heart, mystery, magic, and adventure.

L0724 Max Moorhead
Junior Agent
United States

http://www.mmqlit.com/about/

Literary Agency: Massie & McQuilkin (**L0680**)

L0725 Paul Moreton
Literary Agent
United Kingdom

Literary Agency: Bell Lomax Moreton Agency (**L0081**)

L0726 Imogen Morrell
Literary Agent
United Kingdom

http://greeneheaton.co.uk/agents/imogen-morrell/
https://twitter.com/imogen_morrell

Literary Agency: Greene & Heaton Ltd (**L0419**)

Fiction > *Novels*
 Historical Fiction; LGBTQIA; Literary; Upmarket

Nonfiction
 Essays: General
 Nonfiction Books: Architecture; Fishing; Food; History; Language; Mental Health; Narrative Nonfiction; Nature; Politics

Send: Query; Synopsis; Writing sample
How to send: Email attachment

Looking for immersive, brilliantly plotted upmarket and literary fiction with a twist. In nonfiction, she's looking for proposals that find unexpected ways to talk about interesting things (architecture, food, nature, politics, history, identity) from academics, critics and journalists who are writing their specialist subject for trade publication. She also accepts submissions for narrative nonfiction, essay writing and food writing.

L0727 Lucy Morris
Literary Agent
United Kingdom

Literary Agency: Curtis Brown (**L0233**)

L0728 Natascha Morris
Senior Agent
United States

https://www.thetobiasagency.com/natascha-morris
https://querymanager.com/query/natascha

Literary Agency: The Tobias Literary Agency (**L0983**)

CHILDREN'S > **Fiction**

Middle Grade; Picture Books
YOUNG ADULT > **Fiction**
 Graphic Novels; Novels

How to send: Query Manager

Primarily looking for picture books, middle grade and young adult manuscripts across most genres, including graphic novels. She is also open to illustrator submissions.

L0729 Tasneem Motala
Assistant Agent
Canada

https://www.therightsfactory.com/submissions
https://querymanager.com/query/2005

Literary Agency: The Rights Factory

CHILDREN'S > **Fiction**
 Middle Grade; Picture Books
YOUNG ADULT > **Fiction** > *Novels*

Send: Query; Author bio; Writing sample; Pitch
How to send: Query Manager

Not currently accepting submissions from white people.

L0730 Lisa Moylett
Literary Agent
United Kingdom

https://cmm.agency/about-us.php
http://twitter.com/MoylettLisa

Literary Agency: Coombs Moylett & Maclean Literary Agency (**L0217**)

Fiction > *Novels*
 Commercial Women's Fiction; Crime; Ireland; Northern Ireland; Psychological Thrillers

Nonfiction > *Nonfiction Books*
 Politics; Popular Science

Send: Synopsis; Writing sample
How to send: Online submission system
How not to send: Email

Represents an eclectic list of authors and writers and is currently looking for well-written, commercial women's fiction.

L0731 Toby Mundy
Literary Agent; Chief Executive Officer
United Kingdom

https://aevitascreative.com/agents/#agent-7413

Literary Agencies: Toby Mundy Associates Ltd (**L0984**); Aevitas Creative Management (ACM) UK (**L0017**)

Fiction > *Novels*
 Literary; Thrillers

Nonfiction > *Nonfiction Books*
 Biography; Current Affairs; History; Memoir; Narrative Nonfiction; Popular Culture; Popular Science; Sport

Send: Query; Writing sample
How to send: Online submission system

Looking for gripping narrative nonfiction, and well written, mind-expanding works in the areas of history, biography, memoir, current affairs, sport, popular culture and popular science. Also represents a small number of thriller writers and literary novelists.

Authors: James Aldred; Michael Dine; Armand D'Angour; Jonathan Hillman; Graham Lawton; Mark Leonard; Isabel Losada; Kenan Malik; Peter Mead; Christopher Miller; Richard V. Reeves; Peter Ricketts; Donald Sassoon; Mark Sedgwick; Jeevan Vasagar; Owen Walker; Justin Webb; Christian Wolmar

L0732 Michael Mungiello
Literary Agent
United States

Literary Agency: InkWell Management (**L0499**)

L0733 Oli Munson
Literary Agent
United Kingdom

https://amheath.com/agents/oli-munson/
http://twitter.com/oliagent

Literary Agency: A.M. Heath & Company Limited, Author's Agents (**L0003**)

Fiction > *Novels*
Commercial; Crime; High Concept; Speculative; Suspense; Thrillers

Nonfiction > *Nonfiction Books*
Narrative Nonfiction; Social Issues; Sport

Agency Assistant / Associate Agent: Florence Rees (**L0825**)

L0734 Dana Murphy
Literary Agent
United States

Literary Agency: The Book Group (**L0109**)

L0735 Jacqueline Murphy
Literary Agent
United States

Literary Agency: InkWell Management (**L0499**)

L0736 Hilary Murray
Literary Agent
United Kingdom

Literary Agency: Robertson Murray Literary Agency (**L0845**)

L0737 Judith Murray
Literary Agent
United Kingdom

Literary Agency: Greene & Heaton Ltd (**L0419**)

Fiction > *Novels*
Crime; Historical Fiction; Literary; Thrillers; Women's Fiction

Nonfiction > *Nonfiction Books*
Biography; Cookery; History; Literary; Memoir; Travel

Authors: Poppy Adams; Mark Alder; Lucy Atkins; Laura Barnett; Mark Barrowcliffe; Charlotte Bauer; Darcey Bell; Caroline Bond; Lynne Bryan; Elizabeth Buchan; P. Kearney Byrne; Helen Callaghan; Lucy Clarke; Emma Cook; Kate Davies; Lydia Davis; Sabine Durrant; Samantha Ellis; Helen Fisher; Susanna Forrest; L. R. Fredericks; Andrea Gillies; Paula Gosling; Victoria Gosling; Stella Grey; Joanna Hall; Maeve Haran; Belinda Harley; Anjali Joseph; Esme King; M.D. Lachlan; Reif Larsen; Jardine Libaire; Rebecca Mackenzie; Ben Marcus; Ian McGuire; Laura McHugh; Ben McPherson; Kamin Mohammadi; Kate Morrison; Joanna Nadin; Jenny Offill; Temi Oh; Sean O'Connor; Helen Paris; Miranda Popkey; Jonathan Ray; Maria Realf; Karen Russell; Indyana Schneider; Jacqueline Sutherland; Clare Swatman; Susannah Walker; Jacqueline Ward; Patricia Wastvedt; Sarah Waters; Benjamin Wood; Anne Youngson

L0738 Nate Muscato
Literary Agent
New York
United States

https://aevitascreative.com/agents/

Literary Agency: Aevitas (**L0016**)

Fiction > *Novels*

Nonfiction > *Nonfiction Books*
Arts; Culture; Current Affairs; History

Send: Author bio; Outline; Pitch; Market info; Writing sample
How to send: Online submission system

Interested in fiction that plays with conventions of narrative and genre, and in nonfiction that contemplates and critiques the arts, culture, history, current events, and the future.

L0739 Mushens Entertainment
Literary Agency
London
United Kingdom

https://www.mushens-entertainment.com
https://twitter.com/MushensEnt

Professional Body: The Association of Authors' Agents (AAA)

London literary agency with a boutique feel. Represents a diverse range of Sunday Times and New York Times bestsellers, authors, actors, brands, and more.

Literary Agents: Liza DeBlock (**L0253**); Silé Edwards (**L0293**); Juliet Mushens (**L0740**)

L0740 Juliet Mushens
Literary Agent
United Kingdom

jmsubmissions@mushens-entertainment.com

Literary Agency: Mushens Entertainment (**L0739**)

ADULT > **Fiction** > *Novels*
Book Club Fiction; Crime; Fantasy; Ghost Stories; High Concept; Historical Fiction; Romantic Comedy; Science Fiction; Thrillers

YOUNG ADULT > **Fiction** > *Novels*

Closed to approaches.

Looking for adult fiction and YA only. She is looking for crime, thriller, YA, reading group fiction, ghost stories, historical fiction, SFF, romcoms, and high concept novels.

L0741 James Mustelier
Literary Agent
United States

http://www.thebentagency.com/james-mustelier
https://querymanager.com/query/1908

Literary Agency: The Bent Agency (**L0090**)

ADULT > **Fiction**
Novels: Comedy / Humour; Commercial; Crime; Horror; Literary; Mystery; Suspense; Thrillers
Short Fiction: General

YOUNG ADULT > **Fiction** > *Novels*

Closed to approaches.

L0742 Jean Naggar
Literary Agent
United States

Literary Agency: The Jean V. Naggar Literary Agency (**L0519**)

L0743 The Narrow Road Company
Literary Agency
1st Floor, 37 Great Queen Street, Covent Garden, London, WC2B 5AA
United Kingdom
Tel: +44 (0) 20 7831 4450

creatives@narrowroad.co.uk

https://narrowroad.co.uk/

Scripts
Film Scripts: General
Radio Scripts: General
TV Scripts: General
Theatre Scripts: Theatre

Send: Query
Don't send: Full text
How to send: Email
How not to send: Email attachment

Send query by email. Seeks writers with some experience and original ideas. Handles scripts only. No novels, poetry, unsolicited MSS, or email attachments.

Authors: Joe Graham; Richard Groves; Lincoln Hudson; Simon Macallum

Literary Agents: Amy Ireson (*L0502*); Dan Ireson (*L0503*); James Ireson (*L0504*); Richard Ireson (**L0505**); Rozzy Lloyd (*L0628*); Adam Mendlesohn (*L0698*); Sarah Veecock (*L1001*)

L0744 Natasha Kern Literary Agency

Literary Agency
United States

http://natashakernliterary.com

Fiction > *Novels*

Closed to approaches.

Closed to queries from unpublished writers. Focusses on developing the careers of established writers. Will continue to accept referrals through current clients or editors, and through conferences.

Authors: Tamera Alexander; Nikki Arana; Nina Bangs; Angela Benson; Cheryl Bolen; Maggie Brendan

Literary Agent: Natasha Kern

L0745 The Ned Leavitt Agency

Literary Agency
70 Wooster Street, Suite 4F, New York, NY 10012
United States
Tel: +1 (212) 334-0999

http://www.nedleavittagency.com

Professional Body: Association of American Literary Agents (AALA)

Types: Fiction; Nonfiction
Formats: Short Fiction
Subjects: Autobiography; Commercial; Health; Literary; Mystery; Science Fiction; Spirituality
Markets: Adult

Send: Query
Don't send: Full text

Accepts approaches by recommendation only.

Literary Agent: Ned Leavitt (*L0606*)

L0746 Nelson Literary Agency, LLC

Literary Agency
1732 Wazee Street, Suite 207, Denver, CO 80202
United States
Tel: +1 (303) 292-2805

info@nelsonagency.com

https://nelsonagency.com

Professional Body: Association of American Literary Agents (AALA)

ADULT > **Fiction** > *Novels*

CHILDREN'S > **Fiction**
Middle Grade; *Picture Books*
YOUNG ADULT > **Fiction** > *Novels*

Send: Query; Author bio; Writing sample
How to send: Query Manager

View individual agent interests and submit to one agent only.

Authors: Brooke Abrams; Kate Baer; L. Biehler; Jillian Boehme; Kristen Ciccarelli; Jessi Cole; Lisa Duffy; Doug Engstrom; Reese Eschmann; Shana Galen; John Galligan; Florence Gonsalves; Jill Grunenwald; Alison Hammer; Robin Huber; Sarah Zachrich Jeng; Becca Jones; Chloe Jory; Ausma Zehanat Khan; Sierra Kincade; Karen Koh; Gillian Libby; Maryann Jacob Macias; Amanda Marbais; Jonathan Messinger; Meghan Scott Molin; Katrina Monroe; Vanessa Montalban; Rosaria Munda; Jennifer Nissley; Lynette Noni; James Persichetti; Celesta Rimington; Laura Brooke Robson; Ehsaneh Sadr; Jeff Seymour; Kristen Simmons; Lisa Springer; Jennifer Springsteen; Stacy Stokes; Chrysler Szarlan; Ben Tanzer; Jordyn Taylor; Kathleen West

Literary Agents: Danielle Burby; Joanna MacKenzie (**L0657**); Kristin Nelson (**L0747**); Quressa Robinson (**L0849**)

L0747 Kristin Nelson

Literary Agent
United States

https://nelsonagency.com/kristin-nelson/
https://twitter.com/agentkristinNLA
https://querymanager.com/query/1350

Literary Agency: Nelson Literary Agency, LLC (**L0746**)
Professional Body: Association of American Literary Agents (AALA)

ADULT > **Fiction** > *Novels*
Commercial; Fantasy; High Concept; Historical Fiction; Literary; Science Fiction; Speculative; Thrillers

YOUNG ADULT > **Fiction** > *Novels*

Send: Author bio; Query; Writing sample
How to send: Query Manager

My goal as an agent is simple: I want every client of mine to make a living solely from writing and 90% of my authors do without help from any other source of income.

L0748 Kiana Nguyen

Literary Agent
United States

Literary Agency: Donald Maass Literary Agency (**L0273**)

L0749 Geraldine Nichol

Literary Agent
Ireland

Literary Agency: The Book Bureau Literary Agency (**L0108**)

L0750 Nick Turner Management Ltd

Literary Agency
27 Meadow Place, London, SW8 1XZ
United Kingdom
Tel: +44 (0) 20 3723 8833

http://nickturnermanagement.com
https://uk.linkedin.com/in/nicolas-turner-2a84a1103
https://twitter.com/NickTurnerMgmt

ADULT > **Scripts**
Film Scripts; *Radio Scripts*; *TV Scripts*
CHILDREN'S > **Scripts** > *TV Scripts*

How to send: By referral

Creative talent agency representing a broad mix of writers, directors and producers working across feature-film, television drama, comedy, children's, continuing-drama and radio. No unsolicited submissions. New clients come through producer or personal recommendations only.

Literary Agents: Phil Adie (**L0014**); Nick Turner (*L0988*)

L0751 Erin Niumata

Literary Agent; Senior Vice President
United States
Tel: +1 (212) 400-1494

erin@foliolit.com

https://www.foliolit.com/agents-1/erin-niumata
https://www.instagram.com/ecniumata/?hl=en
https://twitter.com/ecniumata?ref_src=twsrc%5Egoogle%7Ctwcamp%5Eserp%7Ctwgr%5Eauthor

Literary Agency: Folio Literary Management, LLC (**L0343**)

Fiction > *Novels*
Book Club Fiction; Commercial Women's Fiction; Commercial; Historical Fiction; Mystery; Romance; Romantic Comedy; Thrillers; Women's Fiction

Nonfiction > *Nonfiction Books*
Commercial; Cookery; Memoir; Narrative Nonfiction; Prescriptive Nonfiction

Closed to approaches.

Looking for commercial nonfiction, from prescriptive and practical to narrative and memoir, as well as a select list of fiction including mysteries, rom-coms, and commercial women's fiction.

L0752 Noel Gay

Literary Agency
1st Floor, 2 Stephen Street, Fitzrovia, London, W1T 1AN
United Kingdom
Tel: +44 (0) 20 7836 3941

info@noelgay.com

https://www.noelgay.com
https://twitter.com/NoelGay19

Scripts
Film Scripts; *Radio Scripts*; *TV Scripts*;
Theatre Scripts

Agency representing writers, directors,
performers, presenters, comedians, etc.

Literary Agents: Sophieclaire Armitage
(*L0045*); Natalie Ball (*L0059*); Philip Bell;
Ellie Cahill-Nicholls (*L0149*)

L0753 Laura Nolan
Literary Agent; Senior Partner
United States

https://aevitascreative.com/agents/

Literary Agency: Aevitas (**L0016**)
Professional Body: Association of American
Literary Agents (AALA)

Fiction > *Novels*: Upmarket Commercial
Fiction

Nonfiction > *Nonfiction Books*
Alternative Health; Celebrity; Cookery;
Food; Investigative Journalism; Lifestyle;
Music; Politics; Science; Women's Issues

Send: Query; Writing sample
How to send: Online submission system

Represents platform-driven narrative
nonfiction in the areas of celebrity, music,
investigative journalism, women's issues,
alternative health, and lifestyle. She is
passionate about cookbooks and food narrative
informed by politics or science. She is seeking
challenging ideas, incisive writing that asks
"big" questions, and artists who are successful
in one medium but whose talents and passion
translate into narrative.

L0754 Bryan Norman
Literary Agent
United States

Literary Agency: Alive Literary Agency
(**L0026**)

L0755 The North Literary Agency
Literary Agency
The Chapel, Market Place, Corbridge,
Northumberland, NE45 5AW
United Kingdom

hello@thenorthlitagency.com

http://thenorthlitagency.com

Fiction > *Novels*

Nonfiction > *Nonfiction Books*: Narrative
Nonfiction

Send: Query; Synopsis; Proposal; Writing
sample
How to send: Email

Looking for all types of fiction and narrative
nonfiction. No academic writing, poetry, self-
help, picture books or screenplays. No
submissions by post.

Literary Agents: Julie Fergusson (**L0329**);
Allan Guthrie (**L0434**); Lina Langlee (**L0593**);
Kevin Pocklington (**L0803**); Mark "Stan"
Stanton (**L0934**)

L0756 Northbank Talent Management
Literary Agency
United Kingdom
Tel: +44 (0) 20 3973 0835

info@northbanktalent.com
fiction@northbanktalent.com
nonfiction@northbanktalent.com
childrens@northbanktalent.com

https://www.northbanktalent.com
https://twitter.com/NorthbankTalent
https://www.facebook.com/northbanktalent/
https://www.instagram.com/northbanktalent
https://www.linkedin.com/company/
northbank-talent-management/
https://www.youtube.com/channel/
UCKEAHOg6Y2G3NOy146k9y4A?view_as=
subscriber

Professional Body: The Association of
Authors' Agents (AAA)

ADULT
  Fiction > *Novels*
  Nonfiction > *Nonfiction Books*

CHILDREN'S
  Fiction > *Middle Grade*: Commercial

  Nonfiction > *Nonfiction Books*

YOUNG ADULT > **Fiction** > *Novels*

Send: Query; Synopsis; Writing sample
How to send: Email

Literary and talent agency based in central
London. Actively seeking new clients. Send
query by email with synopsis and first three
chapters as Word or Open Document
attachments to appropriate email address.

Literary Agents: Martin Redfern (*L0822*);
Hannah Weatherill (*L1019*)

L0757 Trodayne Northern
Literary Agent; President
United States

Literary Agency: Prentis Literary (**L0814**)

L0758 Sarah Nundy
Literary Agent
United Kingdom

Literary Agency: Andrew Nurnberg
Associates, Ltd (**L0035**)

L0759 Andrew Nurnberg
Literary Agent
United Kingdom

Literary Agency: Andrew Nurnberg
Associates, Ltd (**L0035**)

L0760 Haskell Nussbaum
Associate Agent
Canada

Literary Agency: The Rights Factory

L0761 NY Creative Management
Literary Agency
United States

http://www.nycreative.com

Types: Fiction; Nonfiction
Markets: Children's

Send: Synopsis

Send one-page synopsis by email, giving a
brief, informative paragraph about your novel,
non-fiction book, screenplay or magazine-
length article, giving the main idea and basic
structure of your project.

Literary Agent: Jeff Schmidt (**L0889**)

L0762 Lee O'Brien
Literary Agent
United States

Lee.queries@irenegoodman.com

https://www.irenegoodman.com/lee-obrien

Literary Agency: Irene Goodman Literary
Agency (IGLA) (**L0501**)

Fiction > *Novels*
  LGBTQIA; Magic; Romance

How to send: Email

Across all age categories, they're looking for
books with clear stakes and an immersive
world, as well as anything with lots of
atmosphere, magic, monsters, intrigue, or a
plot full of twists and turns. They're actively
seeking underrepresented voices, and they
have a particular soft spot for queer romance
(whether it's an epic love story or a first
crush), ace rep, and trans kids with swords.

L0763 Faith O'Grady
Literary Agent
108 Upper Leeson Street, Dublin 4
Ireland
Tel: + 353 1 637 5000
Fax: + 353 1 667 1256

info@lisarichards.ie

http://lisarichards.ie/writers#.YAgtljlxdaS

Literary Agency: The Lisa Richards Agency

ADULT
  Fiction > *Novels*

Nonfiction > *Nonfiction Books*
Biography; Comedy / Humour; History;
Lifestyle; Memoir; Motorsports; Narrative
Nonfiction; Popular Culture; Self Help

CHILDREN'S > **Fiction**
Chapter Books; *Middle Grade*

Does not want:

ADULT
Fiction > *Novels*
Horror; Science Fiction
Scripts
Film Scripts; *TV Scripts*
CHILDREN'S > **Fiction** > *Picture Books*

Send: Query; Writing sample; Self-Addressed
Stamped Envelope (SASE); Proposal
How to send: Email; Post

If sending fiction, please limit your submission
to the first three or four chapters, and include a
covering letter and an SAE if required. If
sending non-fiction, please send a detailed
proposal about your book, a sample chapter
and a cover letter. Every effort will be made to
respond to submissions within 3 months of
receipt.

L0764 Niamh O'Grady
Associate Agent
United Kingdom

https://www.thesohoagency.co.uk/agent/
niamh-ogrady

Literary Agency: The Soho Agency (**L0924**)

Fiction > *Novels*
Book Club Fiction; Comedy / Humour;
Family; Literary; Relationships

Nonfiction > *Nonfiction Books*
Comedy / Humour; Narrative Nonfiction

Send: Query; Synopsis; Writing sample
How to send: Email attachment

Actively looking for accessible literary and
reading-group fiction, and narrative nonfiction. She is drawn to books with heart and
humour, thought-provoking writing and
distinctive, compelling voices. She particularly
loves novels that explore family and
relationships and wants to read stories that
leave an emotional impact, with characters that
stay with her long after the final page. She is
keen to find new Irish and Northern writing
talent.

L0765 Coleen O'Shea
Literary Agent
United States

Professional Body: Association of American
Literary Agents (AALA)

L0766 Ikenna Obiekwe
Literary Agent
United Kingdom

Literary Agency: Independent Talent Group
Ltd (**L0496**)

L0767 Hellie Ogden
Literary Agent
United Kingdom

submissions@janklow.co.uk

http://www.janklowandnesbit.co.uk/node/483
https://twitter.com/HellieOgden

Literary Agency: Janklow & Nesbit UK Ltd
(**L0516**)

ADULT
Fiction > *Novels*
Book Club Fiction; Commercial; Crime;
High Concept Thrillers; Historical Fiction;
Literary; Psychological Thrillers;
Romance; Upmarket

Nonfiction > *Nonfiction Books*
Cookery; Lifestyle; Memoir; Narrative
Nonfiction; Nature

CHILDREN'S > **Fiction** > *Middle Grade*
General, and in particular: Adventure; Magic

YOUNG ADULT > **Fiction** > *Novels*

How to send: Email

Represents fiction, children's books and nonfiction and enjoys novels with bold
storytelling, moving prose and vivid, thought-
provoking characters. In non-fiction she is
looking for unique personal stories,
campaigners, memoir and nature writing,
cookery, lifestyle, and work that has a social
following with cross-media potential. As an
editorially focused agent, she has a keen
interest in helping to develop and nurture debut
writers.

L0768 Kristin van Ogtrop
Literary Agent
United States

Literary Agency: InkWell Management
(**L0499**)

L0769 Charlie Olsen
Literary Agent
United States

Literary Agency: InkWell Management
(**L0499**)

L0770 Neil Olson
Literary Agent
United States

neil@mmqlit.com

Literary Agency: Massie & McQuilkin
(**L0680**)

Fiction > *Novels*

Nonfiction > *Nonfiction Books*
Biography; Environment; History; Travel

How to send: Email

L0771 Mark Orsini
Literary Agent
United States

Literary Agency: Bret Adams Ltd (**L0124**)

L0772 Luba Ostashevsky
Literary Agent
United States

https://www.pandeliterary.com/about-
pandeliterary

Literary Agency: Ayesha Pande Literary
(**L0052**)

Nonfiction > *Nonfiction Books*
Health; History; Popular Science

Send: Pitch; Author bio; Synopsis; Writing
sample
How to send: Online submission system

Interested in nonfiction popular science
projects, written by either research scientists,
medical or mental health professionals, or
journalists. Not comfortable representing
fiction, cookbooks, YA, self help, nor business
or politics (unless directly about science).

L0773 Kristin Ostby
Literary Agent
United States

https://www.greenhouseliterary.com/the-team/
kristin-ostby/
https://querymanager.com/query/kristinostby

Literary Agency: The Greenhouse Literary
Agency (**L0420**)

ADULT > **Fiction** > *Novels*
Literary; Upmarket

CHILDREN'S > **Fiction**
Graphic Novels: General
Middle Grade: Comedy / Humour;
Commercial; Fantasy; Feminism; Historical
Fiction; LGBTQIA; Literary; Mystery;
Science Fiction; Social Issues
Picture Books: General

YOUNG ADULT > **Fiction** > *Novels*
Adventure; Comedy / Humour; Fantasy;
Feminism; Historical Fiction; LGBTQIA;
Literary; Mystery; Romance; Science Fiction

How to send: Query Manager

Represents authors of middle grade and young
adult fiction, as well as picture book
author/illustrators and select adult fiction. She
is primarily seeking tightly written, tightly
plotted, fast-paced commercial middle-grade
and young adult fiction—adventure, mystery,
and contemporary humor—as well as young
adult romance.

L0774 Bruce Ostler
Literary Agent
United States

Literary Agency: Bret Adams Ltd (**L0124**)

L0775 Anne Marie O'Farrell
Literary Agent

Professional Body: The Agents Round Table (ART)

L0776 Ayesha Pande
Literary Agent
United States

https://www.pandeliterary.com/about-pandeliterary
https://twitter.com/agent_ayesha
http://aaronline.org/Sys/PublicProfile/2455085/417813

Literary Agency: Ayesha Pande Literary (**L0052**)
Professional Bodies: Association of American Literary Agents (AALA); The Agents Round Table (ART)

ADULT
  Fiction > *Novels*: Literary

  Nonfiction > *Nonfiction Books*
    Biography; Cultural Commentary; History; Memoir; Narrative Nonfiction

YOUNG ADULT > **Fiction** > *Novels*

Send: Pitch; Author bio; Synopsis; Writing sample
How to send: Online submission system

While her interests are wide-ranging and eclectic, she works mostly with literary fiction, narrative nonfiction across a broad range of topics including history and cultural commentary, memoir and biography, and the occasional work of young adult fiction. She is drawn to distinctive voices with a compelling point of view and memorable characters.

L0777 Paper Literary
Literary Agency
United Kingdom

submissions@paperliterary.com

https://www.paperliterary.com

Professional Body: The Association of Authors' Agents (AAA)

Literary Agent: Catherine Cho (**L0194**)

L0778 Sandra Pareja
Literary Agent
United States

sandra@mmqlit.com

http://www.mmqlit.com/about/

Literary Agency: Massie & McQuilkin (**L0680**)

Fiction > *Novels*: Literary

Nonfiction > *Nonfiction Books*: Narrative Nonfiction

Poetry > *Poetry Collections*

How to send: Email

Looking for authentic, unconventional literary voices in fiction, nonfiction and sometimes poetry. Query by email.

L0779 Elana Roth Parker
Literary Agent
United States

http://www.ldlainc.com/submissions/
http://www.manuscriptwishlist.com/mswl-post/elana-roth-parker/
https://querymanager.com/query/queryelana
http://aaronline.org/Sys/PublicProfile/43775067/417813

Literary Agency: Laura Dail Literary Agency (**L0599**)
Professional Body: Association of American Literary Agents (AALA)

CHILDREN'S
  Fiction
    Graphic Novels: Commercial
    Middle Grade: Adventure; Comedy / Humour; High Concept; Romance
  Nonfiction > *Nonfiction Books*: Narrative Nonfiction

TEEN > **Nonfiction** > *Nonfiction Books*: Narrative Nonfiction

YOUNG ADULT > **Fiction**
    Graphic Novels: Commercial
    Novels: Adventure; Comedy / Humour; High Concept; Romance

Closed to approaches.

Commercial and high-concept middle-grade and young adult fiction (all genres, but maybe avoid Christmas, talking animal books, or anything nightmare-inducing); commercial or fanciful graphic novels for middle-grade and young adult audiences (author/illustrators preferred); narrative non-fiction for children and teens; picture books by referral only.

L0780 Marina De Pass
Associate Agent
United Kingdom

https://www.thesohoagency.co.uk/agent/marina-de-pass
https://twitter.com/marinadepass

Literary Agency: The Soho Agency (**L0924**)

Fiction > *Novels*
    Book Club Fiction; Crime; Folklore, Myths, and Legends; Historical Fiction; Literary; Romance; Romantic Comedy; Thrillers; Upmarket Commercial Fiction

Send: Query; Synopsis; Writing sample
How to send: Email attachment

Loves upmarket commercial, book club and accessible literary fiction in all its forms – from twisty crime and thrillers to smart rom-coms and epic, sweeping love stories to historical fiction – and is actively looking to take on clients in this area.

L0781 Kathi Paton
Literary Agent
United States

Literary Agency: Kathi J. Paton Literary Agency (**L0556**)

L0782 Emma Patterson
Literary Agent
United States

epatterson@bromasite.com

Literary Agency: Brandt & Hochman Literary Agents, Inc. (**L0119**)
Professional Body: Association of American Literary Agents (AALA)

ADULT
  Fiction > *Novels*
    Historical Fiction; Literary; Upmarket

  Nonfiction > *Nonfiction Books*
    Investigative Journalism; Memoir; Narrative Nonfiction; Popular History

YOUNG ADULT > **Fiction** > *Novels*
    Historical Fiction; Literary; Upmarket

Send: Query
How to send: Email

L0783 Clare Pearson
Literary Agent
United Kingdom

Literary Agency: Eddison Pearson Ltd (**L0289**)

L0784 Kay Peddle
Literary Agent
United Kingdom

kay@kaypeddleliterary.co.uk

https://kaypeddleliterary.co.uk/about-us
http://instagram.com/kaypeddlebooks
http://twitter.com/kaypeddle

Literary Agency: Kay Peddle Literary (**L0559**)

Nonfiction > *Nonfiction Books*
    Cookery; Current Affairs; Food; History; Journalism; Literary Memoir; Narrative Nonfiction; Nature; Politics; Popular Science; Social Justice; Travel

Send: Query; Pitch; Proposal; Author bio; Market info; Writing sample; Outline
How to send: Word file email attachment

Looking for books that spark discussion, that have the potential to change opinions and reveal hidden aspects of a familiar story. Interested in narrative nonfiction; literary memoir; cookery and food writing; travel writing; nature writing; journalism with a social justice angle; politics; current affairs; history and popular science.

L0785 Peregrine Whittlesey Agency
Literary Agency
United States

https://www.linkedin.com/in/peregrine-whittlesey-33423830

Types: Scripts
Formats: Film Scripts; TV Scripts; Theatre Scripts
Markets: Adult

Handles mainly theatre scripts, plus a small number of film/TV scripts by playwrights who also write for screen.

Literary Agent: Peregrine Whittlesey (*L1033*)

L0786 Kim Perel
Literary Agent
United States

Literary Agency: Irene Goodman Literary Agency (IGLA) (**L0501**)

L0787 Kristina Perez
Associate Agent
United Kingdom

perez@zenoagency.com

http://zenoagency.com/agents/kristina-perez/
https://twitter.com/kperezagent

Literary Agency: Zeno Agency Ltd (**L1067**)

ADULT
 Fiction > *Novels*
  Dystopian Fiction; Fantasy; Feminism; Historical Fantasy; Historical Romance; Magical Realism; Retellings; Romance; Science Fiction; Space Opera; Supernatural / Paranormal Romance; Witches

 Nonfiction > *Nonfiction Books*

CHILDREN'S
 Fiction > *Middle Grade*
  Fantasy; Historical Fiction

 Poetry > *Novels in Verse*

YOUNG ADULT
 Fiction > *Novels*
  Coming of Age; Contemporary; Fantasy; Folklore, Myths, and Legends; Ghost Stories; Historical Fiction; LGBTQIA; Retellings; Romantic Comedy; Soft Science Fiction; Theatre; Vampires

 Nonfiction > *Nonfiction Books*

 Poetry > *Novels in Verse*

Does not want:

 Fiction > *Novels*
  Contemporary Romance; Hard Science Fiction

Closed to approaches.

Accepts submissions only from BAME and other marginalised creators.

Authors: Alexia Casale; Sharon Emmerichs; Jennifer Wolf Kam; Erin Rose Kim; Troy Tassier; Vincent Tirado; Khadija L. VanBrakle; Stephen Vines; Cristin Williams; Josh Winning; Yuchi Zhang

L0788 Martha Perotto-Wills
Assistant Agent
United Kingdom

http://www.thebentagency.com/martha-perotto-wills

Literary Agent: Molly Ker Hawn (**L0455**)

Fiction > *Novels*

Closed to approaches.

Particularly enjoys self-aware spookiness, joyful radicalism, eccentric glamour, and anything that could be described as 'an intelligent romp'.

L0789 Perry Literary, Inc.
Literary Agency
211 South Ridge Street, Suite 2, Rye Brook, NY 10573
United States

jperry@perryliterary.com

https://www.perryliterary.com

Types: Fiction; Nonfiction
Formats: Film Scripts; TV Scripts
Subjects: Biography; Business; Cookery; Crime; Culture; Current Affairs; Finance; History; Legal; Lifestyle; Literary; Medicine; Music; Personal Development; Philosophy; Politics; Psychology; Science; Society; Sport; Technology; Travel
Markets: Adult; Children's

How to send: Email

Send query by email with first ten pages in the body of the email (or full manuscript for picture books). No attachments. See website for full guidelines.

Literary Agent: Joseph Perry (*L0791*)

L0790 Anne C. Perry
Literary Agent
United Kingdom

anne@ki-agency.co.uk

https://ki-agency.co.uk/contact

Literary Agency: Ki Agency Ltd (**L0567**)

ADULT
 Fiction > *Novels*

 Nonfiction > *Nonfiction Books*
  Adventure; Dinosaurs; Dorset; Memoir; Nature; Popular History; Popular Science; Robots; Romance

YOUNG ADULT > **Fiction** > *Novels*

Closed to approaches.

Happy to accept fiction submissions in all genres. In non-fiction, she is looking for popular science, natural history, popular history and memoirs. She loves dinosaurs, robots, the Dorset coast, and Oxford commas.

L0791 Joseph Perry
Literary Agent
United States

Literary Agency: Perry Literary, Inc. (**L0789**)

L0792 Carrie Pestritto
Literary Agent
United States

http://www.ldlainc.com/about
http://aaronline.org/Sys/PublicProfile/53765008/417813
http://twitter.com/literarycarrie
https://literarycarrie.wixsite.com/blog
http://www.manuscriptwishlist.com/mswl-post/carrie-pestritto/

Literary Agency: Laura Dail Literary Agency (**L0599**)
Professional Body: Association of American Literary Agents (AALA)

ADULT
 Fiction > *Novels*
  Comedy / Humour; Commercial; Cozy Mysteries; Historical Fiction; LGBTQIA; Relationships; Romance; Romantic Comedy; Suspense; Thrillers; Upmarket Women's Fiction

 Nonfiction > *Nonfiction Books*
  Biography; Commercial; History; LGBTQIA; Memoir; Narrative Nonfiction; Popular Science; Prescriptive Nonfiction

CHILDREN'S > **Fiction**
 Chapter Books: Adventure; Fantasy; High Concept; Mystery; Science Fiction; Thrillers
 Middle Grade: Adventure; Commercial; Contemporary; Fantasy; High Concept; Historical Fiction; Horror; Mystery; Science Fiction; Thrillers
YOUNG ADULT > **Fiction** > *Novels*
 Adventure; Commercial; Contemporary; Fantasy; High Concept; Historical Fiction; Horror; Mystery; Science Fiction; Thrillers

How to send: Query Manager

Loves the thrill of finding new authors with strong, unique voices and working closely with her clients. Always strives to help create books that will introduce readers to new worlds and is drawn in by relatable characters, meticulous world-building, and unusual, compelling premises.

L0793 Peter Lampack Agency, Inc
Literary Agency
The Empire State Building, 350 Fifth Avenue, Suite 5300, New York, NY 10118
United States
Tel: +1 (212) 687-9106
Fax: +1 (212) 687-9109

andrew@peterlampackagency.com

https://www.peterlampackagency.com

Types: Fiction; Nonfiction
Subjects: Commercial; Literary
Markets: Adult

Send: Query
Don't send: Full text
How to send: Email

Specialises in commercial and literary fiction as well as nonfiction by recognised experts in a given field. Send query by email only, with cover letter, author bio, sample chapter, and 1-2 page synopsis. No children's books, horror, romance, westerns, science fiction or screenplays.

Authors: Russell Blake; Sandra Burton; Thomas Caplan; Linda Cirino; J.M. Coetzee; Clive Cussler; Stephen Horn; Judith Kelman; Paul Kemprecos; Brian Lysaght; Gerry Spence; Fred Mustard Stewart

Literary Agent: Andrew Lampack (*L0591*)

L0794 Will Peterson
Literary Agent
United Kingdom

Literary Agency: Independent Talent Group Ltd (**L0496**)

L0795 Beth Phelan
Literary Agent
United States

QueryBeth@galltzacker.com
beth@galltzacker.com

https://www.galltzacker.com/submissions.html
https://querymanager.com/query/querybeth

Literary Agency: Gallt & Zacker Literary Agency (**L0375**)

CHILDREN'S
Fiction > *Middle Grade*
Contemporary; Fantasy

Nonfiction > *Middle Grade*

YOUNG ADULT
Fiction > *Novels*
Contemporary; Fantasy

Nonfiction > *Nonfiction Books*

How to send: Email; Query Manager

Gravitates toward stories and characters that inspire, and anything with a touch of humor and the bittersweet. She is very interested in powerful and unique storytelling, offbeat

contemporary fiction, immersive fantasy, and profoundly resonant voices.

L0796 Ariana Philips
Literary Agent
United States

https://www.jvnla.com/our-team.php
https://twitter.com/ArianaPhilips

Literary Agency: The Jean V. Naggar Literary Agency (**L0519**)

ADULT
Fiction > *Novels*
Commercial; Family Saga; Historical Fiction; Literary; Romantic Comedy; Upmarket Women's Fiction

Nonfiction
Gift Books: General
Illustrated Books: General
Nonfiction Books: Comedy / Humour; Cookery; Crime; Food; Lifestyle; Literary Memoir; Narrative Nonfiction; Popular Culture; Popular History; Prescriptive Nonfiction; Science; Social Issues; Sport; Travel

CHILDREN'S > **Fiction** > *Middle Grade*
Adventure; Magic; Mystery

YOUNG ADULT > **Fiction** > *Novels*
Contemporary; Romantic Comedy

Send: Query; Author bio
How to send: Online submission system

Loves to find new talent and work with her clients to develop strong proposals and manuscripts. She enjoys being the author's advocate, often being their first editor, business manager, and trusted confidante. Her personal agenting philosophy is to take on an author for the duration of their career and help guide them through the ever-changing publishing landscape. She is actively building her client list while also handling audio, permissions, and electronic rights for the agency.

L0797 Juliet Pickering
Literary Agent
United Kingdom

Literary Agency: Blake Friedmann Literary Agency Ltd (**L0101**)

L0798 Nell Pierce
Associate Agent
United States

https://www.sll.com/our-team

Literary Agency: Sterling Lord Literistic, Inc. (**L0940**)

Fiction > *Novels*
Commercial; Literary

Nonfiction > *Nonfiction Books*
Language; Narrative Nonfiction

Send: Query; Synopsis; Writing sample
How to send: Online submission system

Looking for literary and commercial fiction, narrative nonfiction, character-driven young adult novels, and books about language and linguistics.

L0799 Richard Pike
Literary Agent
United Kingdom

Literary Agency: C+W (Conville & Walsh) (**L0147**)

L0800 Richard Pine
Literary Agent
United States

Literary Agency: InkWell Management (**L0499**)

L0801 Pippin Properties, Inc
Literary Agency
110 West 40th Street, Suite 1704, New York, NY 10016
United States
Tel: +1 (212) 338-9310
Fax: +1 (212) 338-9579

info@pippinproperties.com

http://www.pippinproperties.com

Professional Body: Association of American Literary Agents (AALA)

Types: Fiction
Markets: Adult; Children's; Young Adult

Send: Query
Don't send: Full text
How to send: Email

Costs: Author covers sundry admin costs.

Devoted primarily to picture books, middle-grade, and young adult novels, but also represents adult projects on occasion. Send query by email with synopsis, first chapter, or entire picture book manuscript in the body of your email. No attachments. See website for full guidelines.

Literary Agents: Sara Crowe (*L0229*); Elena Giovinazzo (*L0394*); Holly McGhee (*L0692*)

L0802 Zoe Plant
Literary Agent
United States

plantqueries@thebentagency.com

http://www.thebentagency.com/zoe-plant
https://www.twitter.com/zoeplant89

Literary Agency: The Bent Agency (**L0090**)

ADULT > **Fiction** > *Novels*
Fantasy; Horror; Science Fiction; Speculative

CHILDREN'S > **Fiction** > *Middle Grade*

YOUNG ADULT > **Fiction** > *Novels*

How to send: Email

I am looking for middle grade and young adult fiction across all genres, as well as adult science-fiction, fantasy, horror and speculative fiction. My tastes lean towards the commercial, and I am particularly interested in seeing submissions from writers from traditionally underrepresented backgrounds.

L0803 Kevin Pocklington
Literary Agent
United Kingdom

http://thenorthlitagency.com/our-friends-in-the-north/

Literary Agency: The North Literary Agency (**L0755**)

Fiction > *Novels*
 Crime; Literary

Nonfiction > *Nonfiction Books*

Send: Query; Synopsis; Writing sample; Proposal
How to send: Email

Looking for a wide range of nonfiction submissions and would like to develop a fiction list with new authors, including accessible literary fiction and crime titles.

L0804 Rebecca Podos
Literary Agent
United States

Literary Agency: Rees Literary Agency (**L0824**)

L0805 Barbara Poelle
Literary Agent
United States

Literary Agency: Irene Goodman Literary Agency (IGLA) (**L0501**)

L0806 Ruth Pomerance
Affiliated Agent
United States

http://foliolit.com/ruth-pomerance

Literary Agency: Folio Literary Management, LLC (**L0343**)

Fiction > *Novels*: Commercial

Nonfiction > *Nonfiction Books*: Narrative Nonfiction

Does not want:

> **Nonfiction** > *Nonfiction Books*: Prescriptive Nonfiction

Closed to approaches.

L0807 Pontas Copyright Agency, S.L.
Literary Agency
P.O. Box / Apartat postal # 11, E-08183

Castellterçol (Barcelona)
Spain
Tel: (+34) 93 218 22 12

info@pontas-agency.com

http://www.pontas-agency.com

Fiction > *Novels*

Send: Author bio; Writing sample
How to send: Email

International literary and film agency accepting submissions of adult fiction in English and French by email only. Include at least the first five chapters and the author's biography.

L0808 Lyndsey Posner
Literary Agent
United Kingdom

Literary Agency: Independent Talent Group Ltd (**L0496**)

L0809 Marcy Posner
Literary Agent; Senior Vice President
United States

marcy@foliolit.com

https://www.foliolit.com/agents-1/marcy-posner

Literary Agency: Folio Literary Management, LLC (**L0343**)
ADULT
 Fiction > *Novels*
  Historical Fiction; Psychological Suspense; Thrillers; Women's Fiction

 Nonfiction > *Nonfiction Books*
  History; Narrative Nonfiction; Popular Science

CHILDREN'S
 Fiction > *Middle Grade*
 Nonfiction > *Middle Grade*

YOUNG ADULT
 Fiction > *Novels*
 Nonfiction > *Nonfiction Books*

Does not want:

> **ADULT** > **Fiction** > *Novels*
> Fantasy; Science Fiction
>
> **CHILDREN'S** > **Fiction**
> *Middle Grade*: Fantasy; Science Fiction
> *Picture Books*: General
>
> **YOUNG ADULT** > **Fiction** > *Novels*
> Fantasy; Science Fiction

Closed to approaches.

Looking for women's fiction, thrillers, historical fiction, history, psychology, narrative non-fiction. YA and middle grade, fiction and non-fiction. No genre fiction for any age especially sci-fi and fantasy.

Authors: Christi Clancy; Lexie Elliott; Jacqueline Kelly; Sheri Reynolds; Christine Sneed

L0810 Elizabeth Poteet
Literary Agent
United States

Literary Agency: The Seymour Agency (**L0902**)

L0811 Anna Power
Literary Agent; Managing Director
Bloomsbury House, 74-77 Great Russell Street, London, WC1B 3DA
United Kingdom

anna@johnsonandalcock.co.uk

http://www.johnsonandalcock.co.uk/anna-power
https://twitter.com/APowerAgent

Literary Agency: Johnson & Alcock (**L0528**)

Fiction > *Novels*
 Book Club Fiction; Commercial; Crime; Literary; Psychological Suspense; Upmarket Women's Fiction

Nonfiction > *Nonfiction Books*
 Cultural Criticism; Current Affairs; Food; History; Memoir; Popular Science

Send: Query; Synopsis; Writing sample
How to send: Email attachment
How not to send: Post

L0812 Marta Praeger
Literary Agent
United States

http://aaronline.org/Sys/PublicProfile/1715282/417813

Literary Agency: Robert A. Freedman Dramatic Agency, Inc. (**L0841**)
Professional Body: Association of American Literary Agents (AALA)

Scripts > *Theatre Scripts*

L0813 Tanusri Prasanna
Literary Agent
United States

tpsubmissions@defliterary.com

https://www.defliterary.com/agent/tanusri-prasanna/

Literary Agency: DeFiore and Company
ADULT
 Fiction > *Novels*: Diversity

 Nonfiction > *Nonfiction Books*
  Comedy / Humour; Memoir; Narrative Nonfiction; Social Justice

CHILDREN'S
 Fiction

Middle Grade: Coming of Age; Contemporary; High / Epic Fantasy; Romance; School; Suspense
Picture Books: General, and in particular: Comedy / Humour
Nonfiction > *Nonfiction Books*

YOUNG ADULT > **Fiction** > *Novels*
Coming of Age; Contemporary; High / Epic Fantasy; Romance; School; Suspense

Send: Pitch; Author bio; Writing sample
How to send: Email

Looks for accessible and wide-reaching, narrative nonfiction set against themes in social justice and representation; memoirs that speak to these issues with authenticity, humor, and heart; and select fiction featuring diverse perspectives, experiences, and even storytelling styles. For YA and middle-grade, she gravitates towards contemporary coming-of-age stories, and ambitious, world-building fantasies. She's drawn to charming and relatable romances, well-plotted and voice-driven suspense, and stories set in schools or interesting neighborhoods. In the picture book space, she loves wry humor and twisty endings, as well as meaningful, concept-driven texts. She also represents children's nonfiction that excites the imagination and curiosity of young readers.

L0814 Prentis Literary

Literary Agency
PMB 496, 6830 NE Bothell Way, Suite C, Kenmore, WA 98028
United States

info@prentisliterary.com

https://www.prentisliterary.com

ADULT
Fiction > *Novels*
Fantasy; Horror; LGBTQIA; Literary; Mystery; Romance; Science Fiction; Suspense; Thrillers; Women's Fiction

Nonfiction > *Nonfiction Books*: Memoir

CHILDREN'S > **Fiction**
Chapter Books; *Early Readers*; *Middle Grade*; *Picture Books*
YOUNG ADULT > **Fiction** > *Novels*

Closed to approaches.

Agency with a historic focus on science fiction and fantasy, but now working with well crafted stories in a variety of genres.

Literary Agents: Autumn Frisse; Reggie Lutz (*L0647*)

Literary Agents / Presidents: Trodayne Northern (*L0757*); Leslie Varney (*L1000*)

L0815 Amanda Preston

Literary Agent
United Kingdom

amandasubmissions@lbabooks.com

http://www.lbabooks.com/agent/amanda-preston/

Literary Agency: LBA Books Ltd (**L0605**)

Fiction > *Novels*
Book Club Fiction; Commercial; Crime Thrilllers; Psychological Suspense; Women's Fiction

Nonfiction > *Nonfiction Books*

Closed to approaches.

Authors: Emily Adlam; Sarah Alderson; Dominique Antiglio; A.L. Bird; Darcie Boleyn; Christina Bradley; Catherine Brookes; Jo Carnegie; Lucie Cave; Rebecca Chance; Emma Cooper; Susie Donkin; Hannah Doyle; Katherine Dyson; Kate Faithfull-Williams; Kate Hackworthy; Fiona Harper; Natalie Heaton; Lesley Kara; Simon Kernick; Emily Kerr; Ella King; Amy Lavelle; Georgina Lees; Freda Lightfoot; Jane Linfoot; Rachael Lucas; Dee MacDonald; Ian Marber; Colin McDowell; Lisa Medved; Marcia Moody; Angelique Panagos; Hannah Phillips; Catherine Piddington; Anna Pointer; Suzy K Quinn; Gillian Richmond; Zara Stoneley; Heidi Swain; Karen Swan; Sophie Tanner; Jonathan Trigell; Anna Turns; Claire Wade; Kate Winter; Fiona Woodifield

L0816 Rufus Purdy

Literary Agent
United Kingdom

Literary Agency: The Two Piers Literary Agency (**L0989**)

L0817 Queen Literary Agency, Inc.

Literary Agency
30 East 60th Street, Suite 1004, New York, NY 10024
United States
Tel: +1 (212) 974-8333
Fax: +1 (212) 974-8347

submissions@queenliterary.com

http://www.queenliterary.com

Types: Fiction; Nonfiction
Subjects: Business; Commercial; Cookery; History; Literary; Mystery; Psychology; Science; Sport; Thrillers
Markets: Adult

Send: Query
Don't send: Full text
How to send: Email

Founded by a former publishing executive, most recently head of IMG WORLDWIDE'S literary division. Handles a wide range of nonfiction titles, with a particular interest in business books, food writing, science and popular psychology, as well as books by well-known chefs, radio and television personalities and sports figures. Also handles commercial and literary fiction, including historical fiction, mysteries, and thrillers.

Literary Agent: Lisa Queen (*L0818*)

L0818 Lisa Queen

Literary Agent
United States

Literary Agency: Queen Literary Agency, Inc. (**L0817**)

L0819 Rachel Mills Literary

Literary Agency
M27, South Wing, Somerset House, Strand, London, WC2R 1LA
United Kingdom

submissions@rmliterary.co.uk

https://www.rachelmillsliterary.co.uk
https://twitter.com/bookishyogini
https://www.instagram.com/rachelmillsliterary/

Professional Body: The Association of Authors' Agents (AAA)

How to send: Email

As an agency we are particularly interested in female voices, and in showcasing talent which deserves to be heard, regardless of age or background. We seek to work with authors whose careers we can help build over the long term, across multiple projects.

Company Director / Literary Agent: Rachel Mills (**L0717**)

Literary Agent: Nelle Andrew (**L0036**)

L0820 Kiele Raymond

Literary Agent
United States

Literary Agency: Thompson Literary Agency (**L0975**)

L0821 Rebecca Friedman Literary Agency

Literary Agency
United States

queries@rfliterary.com

https://rfliterary.com

Types: Fiction; Nonfiction
Subjects: Autobiography; Commercial; Contemporary; Cookery; Lifestyle; Literary; Romance; Suspense; Women's Interests
Markets: Adult; Young Adult

Send: Query
Don't send: Full text
How to send: Email

See website for full submission guidelines and specific agent interests and contact details. Aims to respond in 6-8 weeks, but may take longer.

Literary Agents: Brandie Coonis (*L0218*); Rebecca Friedman (*L0366*); Abby Schulman (**L0893**)

L0822 Martin Redfern
Literary Agent
United Kingdom

Literary Agency: Northbank Talent Management (**L0756**)

L0823 Redhammer
Literary Agency
United Kingdom

https://redhammer.info
https://www.facebook.com/RealLitopia
https://twitter.com/Litopia
https://www.linkedin.com/in/petecox/
https://studio.youtube.com/channel/
UCmbrM2ciaxb4hHQFfnSeOpg

Fiction > *Novels*

Nonfiction > *Nonfiction Books*

Send: Pitch; Writing sample
How to send: Online submission system

Runs weekly pop-up submission sessions where you can watch your submission being discussed.

Literary Agent: Peter Cox (*L0224*)

L0824 Rees Literary Agency
Literary Agency
One Westinghouse Plaza, Suite A203, Boston, MA 02136-2075
United States
Tel: +1 (617) 227-9014

lorin@reesagency.com

http://www.reesagency.com

Professional Body: Association of American Literary Agents (AALA)

Types: Fiction; Nonfiction
Formats: Film Scripts
Subjects: Autobiography; Business; Comedy / Humour; Commercial; Contemporary; Culture; Fantasy; History; Horror; Literary; Mystery; Personal Development; Psychology; Romance; Science; Science Fiction; Suspense; Thrillers; Warfare; Westerns; Women's Interests
Markets: Adult; Children's; Young Adult

Send: Query
Don't send: Full text
How to send: Email

See website for specific agents' interests and submission requirements.

Authors: Tom Cooper; Siobhan Fallon; S.M. Hulse; Nicco Mele

Literary Agents: Ann Collette (*L0209*); Rebecca Podos (*L0804*); Lorin Rees (*L0826*)

L0825 Florence Rees
Agency Assistant; Associate Agent
United Kingdom

florence.rees@amheath.com

https://amheath.com/agents/florence-rees/
https://twitter.com/florencerees93

Literary Agency: A.M. Heath & Company Limited, Author's Agents (**L0003**)
Literary Agents: Bill Hamilton (**L0438**); Oli Munson (**L0733**)

Fiction > *Novels*
Fantasy; Science Fiction

Nonfiction > *Nonfiction Books*
Environment; Memoir; Sustainable Living

L0826 Lorin Rees
Literary Agent
United States

Literary Agency: Rees Literary Agency (**L0824**)

L0827 Regina Ryan Publishing Enterprises
Literary Agency
251 Central Park West, #7D, New York, NY 10024
United States
Tel: +1 (212) 787-5589

queries@reginaryanbooks.com

http://www.reginaryanbooks.com

Professional Body: Association of American Literary Agents (AALA)

Types: Nonfiction
Formats: Reference
Subjects: Adventure; Architecture; Autobiography; Business; Cookery; Gardening; Health; History; Legal; Leisure; Lifestyle; Nature; Politics; Psychology; Science; Spirituality; Sport; Travel; Women's Interests
Markets: Adult

Send: Full text
How to send: Email

Costs: Author covers sundry admin costs.

Send submissions through email. See website for full guidelines.

Authors: Ben Austro; Randi Minetor; Doug Whynott

Literary Agent: Regina Ryan (*L0877*)

L0828 Janet Reid
Literary Agent
United States

Janet@JetReidLiterary.com

http://www.jetreidliterary.com
http://jetreidliterary.blogspot.com/
https://queryshark.blogspot.com/
http://aaronline.org/Sys/PublicProfile/2176820/

417813
https://www.publishersmarketplace.com/members/JanetReid/

Literary Agency: JetReid Literary Agency (**L0523**)
Professional Bodies: Association of American Literary Agents (AALA); Mystery Writers of America (MWA); Society of Children's Book Writers and Illustrators (SCBWI)

ADULT
  Fiction > *Novels*
  Commercial; Crime; Domestic Suspense; Literary; Mystery; Thrillers

  Nonfiction > *Nonfiction Books*
  Biography; History; Memoir; Narrative Nonfiction; Science

CHILDREN'S > **Nonfiction**
  Middle Grade: Biography; History
  Picture Books: Biography; History

Send: Query; Writing sample; Author bio; Proposal
How to send: In the body of an email
How not to send: Email attachment

New York literary agent with a list consisting mainly of crime novels and thrillers, and narrative nonfiction in history and biography.

Authors: Robin Becker; Bill Cameron; Gary Corby; Phillip DePoy; Stephanie Evans; Kennedy Foster; Lee Goodman; Dana Haynes; Patrick Lee; Thomas Lippman; Jeff Marks; Warren Richey; Terry Shames; Jeff Somers; Robert Stubblefield; Deb Vlock

L0829 Milly Reilly
Literary Agent
United Kingdom

Literary Agency: Jo Unwin Literary Agency (**L0526**)

L0830 Laura Rennert
Executive Agent
United States

ljrennert@mac.com

http://www.litagentlaurarennert.com
https://www.andreabrownlit.com/Team/Laura-Rennert
https://www.publishersmarketplace.com/members/LauraRennert/
https://www.manuscriptwishlist.com/mswl-post/laura-rennert/
https://querymanager.com/query/LauraRennert

Literary Agency: Andrea Brown Literary Agency, Inc.

ADULT > **Fiction**
  Graphic Novels: General
  Novels: Commercial; Fantasy; Folklore, Myths, and Legends; Gothic; Historical Fiction; Horror; Literary; Police Procedural; Science Fiction; Social Issues; Speculative; Thrillers
CHILDREN'S > **Fiction**

Chapter Books; Middle Grade; Picture Books
YOUNG ADULT > **Fiction** > *Novels*

Send: Query; Author bio; Writing sample
How to send: Email

Specializes in all categories of children's books, from picture books to young adult. On the adult side, she represents literary-commercial fiction, thrillers, horror, sci-fi/fantasy, speculative fiction, and select historical fiction. Her sweet spot in the market is literary voice and commercial conception.

L0831 Nicole Resciniti
Literary Agent
United States

Literary Agency: The Seymour Agency **(L0902)**

L0832 Nicki Richesin
Literary Agent
United States

https://www.dclagency.com

Literary Agency: Dunow, Carlson & Lerner Agency

ADULT > **Fiction** > *Novels*
Literary; Upmarket

YOUNG ADULT
Fiction > *Novels*

Nonfiction > *Nonfiction Books*
Biography; Cookery; Diversity; Feminism; Films; Investigative Journalism; Memoir; Music; Popular Culture; TV

Represents literary and upmarket fiction, and young adult fiction. She also focuses on nonfiction including investigative journalism, pop culture (especially film/TV and music), biography, cooking, and memoir that makes an impact and becomes part of a larger cultural conversation. She is particularly interested in discovering underrepresented voices from around the world exploring identity, feminism, and social diversity.

L0833 Richford Becklow Literary Agency
Literary Agency
United Kingdom
Tel: +44 (0) 1728 660879 / + 44 (0) 7510 023823

lisa.eveleigh@richfordbecklow.co.uk

https://www.richfordbecklow.com
https://www.facebook.com/RichfordBecklowLiteraryAgency/
https://twitter.com/richfordbecklow

Fiction > *Novels*
Crime; Fantasy; Historical Fiction; Literary; Romance; Saga

Nonfiction > *Nonfiction Books*
Biography; Memoir

Closed to approaches.

Company founded in 2012 by an experienced agent, previously at the longest established literary agency in the world. Interested in fiction and nonfiction. See website for full submission guidelines.

Author Estate: The Estate of Leila Berg

Authors: Caroline Ashton; Amanda Austen; Hugo Barnacle; Stephen Buck; Anne Corlett; Iestyn Edwards; Gray Freeman; Sam Giles; Jane Gordon-Cumming; R P Marshall; Carol McGrath; Madalyn Morgan; Sophie Parkin; Robert Ross; Lakshmi Raj Sharma; Tony Slattery; Jonathan Socrates; Adrienne Vaughan; Grace Wynne-Jones

Literary Agent: Lisa Eveleigh (*L0315*)

L0834 Rick Richter
Literary Agent; Partner
United States

https://aevitascreative.com/agents/

Literary Agency: Aevitas **(L0016)**

ADULT
Fiction > *Novels*: Thrillers

Nonfiction > *Nonfiction Books*
Celebrity Memoir; Crime; Food; History; Memoir; Music; Narrative Nonfiction; Politics; Popular Culture; Religion; Self Help; Social Issues; Sports Celebrity

CHILDREN'S > **Fiction**
Middle Grade; Picture Books
YOUNG ADULT > **Fiction** > *Novels*

Send: Author bio; Market info; Writing sample
How to send: Online submission system

Areas of interest include self-help, pop culture, memoir, history, thriller, true crime, political and social issues, narrative food writing, and faith. He has deep experience and interest in children's books.

L0835 Rick Broadhead & Associates Literary Agency
Literary Agency
47 St. Clair Avenue West, Suite 501, Toronto, Ontario, M4V 3A5
Canada
Tel: +1 (416) 929-0516

submissions@rbaliterary.com

http://www.rbaliterary.com

Professional Body: The Authors Guild

Nonfiction > *Nonfiction Books*
Biography; Business; Comedy / Humour; Crime; Current Affairs; Environment; Health; History; Investigative Journalism; Medicine; National Security; Nature; Politics; Popular Culture; Science; Secret Intelligence; Self Help

Send: Query
How to send: Email

Welcomes queries by email. Send brief query outlining your project and your credentials. Responds only if interested. No screenplays, poetry, children's books, or fiction.

Literary Agent: Rick Broadhead

L0836 Patricia Riddle-Gaddis
Author; Literary Agent
United States

patricia@hartlineliterary.com

http://hartlineagency.com/agentsandauthors/

Literary Agency: Hartline Literary Agency **(L0451)**

ADULT
Fiction > *Novels*
Cozy Mysteries; Romance

Nonfiction > *Nonfiction Books*

YOUNG ADULT > **Fiction** > *Novels*

Interested in obtaining sweet romance, cozy mysteries, and young adult categories. (think Princess Diaries and a modern Nancy Drew.) She will also consider a range of nonfiction.

Authors: Marlys Johnson; Karl A. Schultz; Norma F. Swanson

L0837 Rachel Ridout
Literary Agent
United States

Literary Agency: Harvey Klinger, Inc **(L0452)**

L0838 Rebecca Ritchie
Literary Agent
United Kingdom

https://amheath.com/agents/rebecca-ritchie/
https://twitter.com/Becky_Ritchie1

Literary Agency: A.M. Heath & Company Limited, Author's Agents **(L0003)**

Fiction > *Novels*
Book Club Fiction; Comedy / Humour; Commercial; Contemporary Women's Fiction; Crime; High Concept; Historical Fiction; Police Procedural; Psychological Suspense; Romance; Saga; Thrillers

Nonfiction > *Nonfiction Books*
Cookery; Health; Travel; Wellbeing

L0839 Riverside Literary Agency
Literary Agency
41 Simon Keets Road, Leyden, MA 01337
United States
Tel: +1 (413) 772-0067
Fax: +1 (413) 772-0969

rivlit@sover.net

http://www.riversideliteraryagency.com

Types: Fiction; Nonfiction
Markets: Adult

Costs: Author covers sundry admin costs.

Agency based in Leyden, Massachusetts.

Literary Agent: Susan Lee Cohen (*L0208*)

L0840 Carina Rizvi
Literary Agent
United Kingdom

Literary Agency: The Soho Agency (**L0924**)

L0841 Robert A. Freedman Dramatic Agency, Inc.
Literary Agency
1501 Broadway, Suite 2310, New York, NY 10036
United States
Tel: +1 (212) 840-5760

info@robertfreedmanagency.com
mprfda@gmail.com
mp@bromasite.com

https://www.robertfreedmanagency.com
https://www.facebook.com/RAFagency/
https://twitter.com/RFreedmanAgency
https://www.linkedin.com/company/robert-a-freedman-dramatic-agency-inc/

Professional Body: Writers Guild of America (WGA)

Scripts
  Film Scripts; TV Scripts; Theatre Scripts

Dramatic literary agency based in New York City representing playwrights and film and television writers.

Literary Agent / President: Robert Freedman (**L0362**)

Literary Agents: Samara Harris (*L0448*); Marta Praeger (**L0812**)

L0842 Robert Caskie Ltd
Literary Agency
United Kingdom

submissions@robertcaskie.com

https://www.robertcaskie.com/
https://twitter.com/rcaskie1

Literary Agent: Robert Caskie (**L0174**)

L0843 Robert Dudley Agency
Literary Agency
135A Bridge Street, Ashford, Kent, TN25 5DP
United Kingdom

info@robertdudleyagency.co.uk

http://www.robertdudleyagency.co.uk

Types: Nonfiction
Subjects: Adventure; Biography; Business; Current Affairs; History; Medicine; Personal Development; Sport; Technology; Travel; Warfare
Markets: Adult

Send: Full text
How to send: Email

Specialises in nonfiction. No fiction submissions. Send submissions by email, preferably in Word format, as opposed to PDF.

Literary Agent: Robert Dudley (*L0281*)

L0844 Soumeya Bendimerad Roberts
Literary Agent; Vice President
United States

soumeya@hgliterary.com

https://www.hgliterary.com/soumeya
https://querymanager.com/query/SBR
https://www.publishersmarketplace.com/members/SoumeyaRoberts/

Literary Agency: HG Literary (**L0467**)
Professional Body: Association of American Literary Agents (AALA)

ADULT
  Fiction
    Novels: Literary; Postcolonialism; Upmarket
    Short Fiction Collections: Literary

  Nonfiction
    Essays: Personal Essays
    Nonfiction Books: Crafts; Design; How To; Lifestyle; Memoir; Narrative Nonfiction; Prescriptive Nonfiction
CHILDREN'S > **Fiction** > *Middle Grade:* Realistic

YOUNG ADULT > **Fiction** > *Novels:* Realistic

Send: Query; Synopsis; Writing sample
How to send: Query Manager

Represents literary novels and collections, upmarket fiction, and non-fiction, both narrative and prescriptive. Though she is primarily seeking Adult genres, she also represents select, realistic middle-grade and YA. She is particularly, but not exclusively, interested in fiction that reflects on the post-colonial world, marginalized and liminal spaces, and narratives by people of color. In non-fiction, she is primarily looking for idea-driven or voice-forward memoirs, personal essay collections, and narrative non-fiction of all stripes. She also represents a curated list of practical and how-to books by makers across creative fields including design, craft, and lifestyle.

L0845 Robertson Murray Literary Agency
Literary Agency
3rd Floor, 37 Great Portland Street, London, W1W 8QH
United Kingdom
Tel: +44 (0) 20 7580 0702

info@robertsonmurray.com

https://robertsonmurray.com

Types: Fiction; Nonfiction
Subjects: Autobiography; Comedy / Humour; Commercial; Cookery; Current Affairs; History; Lifestyle; Literary; Science; Society; Sport
Markets: Adult; Children's; Young Adult

Send: Query
Don't send: Full text

No science fiction, academic books, scripts, or poetry. Submit online through form on website. No postal submissions. Currently closed to submissions of children's books as at April 2019. See website current status and for full guidelines.

Literary Agents: Jenny Heller (*L0463*); Hilary Murray (*L0736*); Charlotte Robertson (*L0846*)

L0846 Charlotte Robertson
Literary Agent
United Kingdom

Literary Agency: Robertson Murray Literary Agency (**L0845**)

L0847 Robin Jones Literary Agency
Literary Agency
66 High Street, Dorchester on Thames, OX10 7HN
United Kingdom
Tel: +44 (0) 1865 341486

robijones@gmail.com

https://twitter.com/AgentRobinJones

Fiction > *Novels*
  Commercial; Literary; Russia

Nonfiction > *Nonfiction Books*
  Commercial; Russia

Send: Query; Synopsis; Writing sample

Costs: Offers services that writers have to pay for.

Literary agency founded in 2007 by an agent who has previously worked at four other agencies, and was the UK scout for international publishers in 11 countries. Handles commercial and literary fiction and nonfiction for adults. Welcomes Russian language fiction and nonfiction. No children's, poetry, young adult, or original scripts. Send query with synopsis and 50-page sample. Also editorial services.

Literary Agent: Robin Jones (**L0532**)

L0848 Lloyd Robinson
Literary Agent
United States

Literary Agency: Suite A Management

L0849 Quressa Robinson
Literary Agent
United States

https://nelsonagency.com/submission-guidelines/
https://querymanager.com/query/1066

Literary Agency: Nelson Literary Agency, LLC (**L0746**)

ADULT
Fiction > *Novels*
Fantasy; Science Fiction; Westerns

Nonfiction > *Nonfiction Books*
Literary Memoir; Narrative Nonfiction; Popular Science

CHILDREN'S > **Fiction** > *Middle Grade*
Contemporary; Fantasy; Literary; Science Fiction

YOUNG ADULT > **Fiction** > *Novels*
Contemporary; Fantasy; Romantic Comedy; Science Fiction

Closed to approaches.

L0850 Rochelle Stevens & Co.
Literary Agency
2 Terretts Place, Upper Street, London, N1 1QZ
United Kingdom
Tel: +44 (0) 20 7359 3900

info@rochellestevens.com

http://www.rochellestevens.com
http://twitter.com/TerrettsPlace
http://www.rochellestevens.com/submissions/#

Scripts
Film Scripts; *Radio Scripts*; *TV Scripts*; *Theatre Scripts*

Send: Query; Author bio; Synopsis; Writing sample
How to send: Email

Handles script writers for film, television, theatre, and radio. No longer handles writers of fiction, nonfiction, or children's books. See website for full submission guidelines.

Literary Agents: Frances Arnold; Rochelle Stevens

L0851 Nemonie Craven Roderick
Literary Agent
United Kingdom

Literary Agency: Jonathan Clowes Ltd (**L0529**)

L0852 Sue Rodgers
Literary Agent
United Kingdom

Literary Agency: Independent Talent Group Ltd (**L0496**)

L0853 Jennifer Rofe
Senior Agent
United States

jennifer@andreabrownlit.com

https://www.andreabrownlit.com/Team/Jennifer-Rof%C3%A9
http://twitter.com/jenrofe
http://instagram.com/jenrofe
https://www.publishersmarketplace.com/members/jenrofe/
https://www.manuscriptwishlist.com/mswl-post/jennifer-rofe/
http://queryme.online/jenrofe

Literary Agency: Andrea Brown Literary Agency, Inc.

CHILDREN'S > **Fiction**
Middle Grade: General, and in particular: Commercial; Contemporary; Fantasy; Historical Fiction; Literary; Magic
Picture Books: General

Send: Query; Author bio; Writing sample
How to send: Query Manager

Always seeking distinct voices and richly developed characters. Middle grade has long been her soft spot and she's open to all genres in this category—literary, commercial, contemporary, magical, fantastical, historical, and everything in between. She especially appreciates stories that make her both laugh and cry, and that offer an unexpected view into the pre-teen experience. In picture books, she likes funny, character-driven projects; beautifully imagined and written stories; and milestone moments with a twist.

L0854 Roger Hancock Ltd
Literary Agency
4th Floor, 7-10 Chandos Street, Cavendish Square, London, W1G 9DQ
United Kingdom
Tel: +44 (0) 20 8341 7243

enquiries@rogerhancock.com

http://www.rogerhancock.com

Types: Scripts
Subjects: Comedy / Humour; Drama; Entertainment
Markets: Adult

Handles scripts only. Interested in comedy dramas and light entertainment. No books or unsolicited MSS.

L0855 Elaine Rogers
Literary Agent
United States

Literary Agency: Kneerim & Williams (**L0575**)

L0856 Maria Rogers
Associate Agent
United States

https://www.thetobiasagency.com/maria-rogers
https://querymanager.com/query/MRogers

Literary Agency: The Tobias Literary Agency (**L0983**)

ADULT > **Nonfiction** > *Nonfiction Books*
Cultural Criticism; Journalism; Science

CHILDREN'S > **Nonfiction** > *Nonfiction Books*
Classics / Ancient World; Contemporary

Send: Query; Synopsis; Writing sample; Pitch; Market info
How to send: Query Manager

Currently looking for non-fiction that explores big events from new angles, whip-smart cultural criticism, as well as original and urgent journalism and science writing. She's also on the lookout for books to engage kids in non-fiction topics, from ancient history to contemporary issues. She is not currently considering poetry, picture books, romance, science fiction, or fantasy at this time.

L0857 Guy Rose
Literary Agent
United Kingdom

Literary Agency: FRA (Futerman, Rose, & Associates) (**L0354**)

L0858 The Rosenberg Group
Literary Agency
United States

http://www.rosenberggroup.com
https://querymanager.com/query/QueryManagerRosenbergGroup

Professional Body: Association of American Literary Agents (AALA)

ACADEMIC > **Nonfiction** > *Nonfiction Books*

ADULT
Fiction > *Novels*
Romance; Women's Fiction

Nonfiction > *Nonfiction Books*
General, and in particular: Apiculture (Beekeeping); History; Psychology; Wine

How to send: Query Manager

Represents romance and women's fiction for an adult audience, nonfiction, and college textbooks.

Literary Agent: Barbara Collins Rosenberg (*L0859*)

L0859 Barbara Collins Rosenberg
Literary Agent
United States

Literary Agency: The Rosenberg Group (**L0858**)

L0860 Rosica Colin Ltd
Literary Agency
1 Clareville Grove Mews, London, SW7 5AH
United Kingdom
Tel: +44 (0) 20 7370 1080

Types: Fiction; Nonfiction; Scripts
Formats: Film Scripts; Radio Scripts; TV
Scripts; Theatre Scripts
Subjects: Autobiography; Beauty; Comedy /
Humour; Cookery; Crime; Current Affairs;
Erotic; Fantasy; Fashion; Gardening; Health;
History; Horror; Leisure; Lifestyle; Literary;
Men's Interests; Mystery; Nature; Psychology;
Religion; Romance; Science; Sport; Suspense;
Thrillers; Travel; Warfare; Women's Interests
Markets: Academic; Adult; Children's

Send: Query
Don't send: Full text

Send query with SAE, CV, synopsis, and list of
other agents and publishers where MS has
already been sent. Considers any full-length
mss (except science fiction and poetry), but
send synopsis only in initial query.

Literary Agents: Joanna Marston (*L0677*);
Sylvie Marston (*L0678*)

L0861 Andy Ross
Literary Agent
United States

Literary Agency: Andy Ross Agency (**L0037**)

L0862 Kathryn Ross
Literary Agent
United Kingdom

Literary Agency: Fraser Ross Associates
(**L0360**)

L0863 Zoe Ross
Literary Agent
United Kingdom

zross@unitedagents.co.uk

https://www.unitedagents.co.uk/
zrossunitedagentscouk

Literary Agency: United Agents (**L0992**)

Fiction > *Novels*: Literary

Nonfiction > *Nonfiction Books*
Food; Narrative Nonfiction

Works with a list of writers ranging from
exciting new voices in literary fiction and
narrative non-fiction, to award-winning food
writers and academics. With a background in
modern languages and psychoanalysis, she has
a particular taste for stylish prose, sly humour
and complex characterisation in fiction, and for
challenging ideas and questions of identity
across all genres.

L0864 Stefanie Rossitto
Literary Agent
United States

https://www.thetobiasagency.com/stefanie-
rossitto
https://querymanager.com/query/1927

Literary Agency: The Tobias Literary Agency
(**L0983**)

Fiction > *Novels*
Historical Fiction; Historical Romance;
Medieval; Romance

How to send: Query Manager

Currently looking for historical fiction, and
funny, witty, modern romances. She also
enjoys anything and everything medieval as
well as exciting historical romances and/or
fiction based on real characters.

L0865 Eliza Rothstein
Literary Agent
United States

http://www.inkwellmanagement.com/staff/
eliza-rothstein
https://twitter.com/elizaloren

Literary Agency: InkWell Management
(**L0499**)

Fiction > *Novels*
Commercial; Literary

Nonfiction > *Nonfiction Books*
Business; Comedy / Humour; Food;
Journalism; Medicine; Memoir; Narrative
Nonfiction; Popular Culture; Psychology;
Science; Technology

Send: Query; Writing sample
How to send: In the body of an email

Represents memoir, literary and commercial
fiction, and a wide range of journalists and
nonfiction authors who seek to generate deep
conversations, inspire social and systemic
change, or advance our understanding of our
minds and bodies. In addition to finding
publishers for their books, she helps writers
expand their reach by placing essays and
journalism in publications ranging from The
New York Times and The Atlantic to National
Geographic and Sports Illustrated. She is
particularly interested in the intersection of
narrative writing with topics of psychology,
medicine, science, food, technology, business,
humor and pop culture. She is also drawn to
literary fiction that explores diverse
communities or intergenerational stories,
commercial fiction that crosses genre borders,
and fiction from Latinx and Spanish-speaking
writers.

L0866 Steph Roundsmith
Literary Agent; Editor
United Kingdom

Literary Agency / Editorial Service: Steph
Roundsmith Agent and Editor (**L0936**)

L0867 Laura Rourke
Literary Agent
United Kingdom

Literary Agency: Independent Talent Group
Ltd (**L0496**)

L0868 The Rudy Agency
Literary Agency
Estes Park, CO
United States
Tel: +1 (970) 577-8500

http://www.rudyagency.com

Agency representing both fiction and
nonfiction.

Literary Agents: Hilary Claggett; Maryann
Karinch (**L0550**); Lauren Manoy; Geoffrey
Stone

L0869 Rupert Crew Ltd
Literary Agency
Southgate, 7 Linden Avenue, Dorchester,
Dorset, DT1 1EJ
United Kingdom
Tel: +44 (0) 1305 260335

info@rupertcrew.co.uk

http://www.rupertcrew.co.uk

Professional Body: The Association of
Authors' Agents (AAA)

Types: Fiction; Nonfiction
Markets: Adult

Closed to approaches.

**Closed to submissions as at August2019.
Check website for current status.**

Send query with SAE, synopsis, and first two
or three consecutive chapters. International
representation, handling volume and subsidiary
rights in fiction and nonfiction properties. No
Short Stories, Science Fiction, Fantasy, Horror,
Poetry or original scripts for Theatre,
Television and Film. Email address for
correspondence only. No response by post and
no return of material with insufficient return
postage.

Literary Agent: Caroline Montgomery (*L0721*)

L0870 Rupert Heath Literary Agency
Literary Agency
United Kingdom

emailagency@rupertheath.com

http://www.rupertheath.com
https://twitter.com/RupertHeathLit
https://www.facebook.com/RupertHeathLit/
https://www.pinterest.com/rupertheathlit/
https://www.youtube.com/user/RupertHeathLit
http://www.linkedin.com/company/rupert-
heath-literary-agency

Professional Body: The Association of Authors' Agents (AAA)

Fiction > *Novels*
Commercial; Crime; Historical Fiction; Literary; Science Fiction; Thrillers

Nonfiction > *Nonfiction Books*
Arts; Autobiography; Biography; Comedy / Humour; Current Affairs; History; Nature; Politics; Popular Culture; Popular Science

Send: Query; Author bio; Outline
How to send: Email

Send query giving some information about yourself and the work you would like to submit by email. Response only if interested.

Authors: Michael Arnold; Mark Blake; Paddy Docherty; Peter Doggett; Nina Lyon; Lorna Martin; Christopher Moore

Literary Agent: Rupert Heath (*L0460*)

L0871 The Ruppin Agency
Literary Agency
London,
United Kingdom

submissions@ruppinagency.com

https://www.ruppinagency.com/
https://twitter.com/ruppinagency

Fiction > *Novels*
Commercial; Crime; Historical Fiction; Literary; Mystery; Thrillers

Nonfiction > *Nonfiction Books*
Memoir; Narrative Nonfiction; Nature; Science; Social Issues

Send: Synopsis; Writing sample
How to send: Email

Literary agency set up by a former bookseller, offering writers a new perspective on finding the right publisher for their work. Keen to find writers with something to say about society today and particularly looking for storylines that showcase voices and communities that have tended to be overlooked by the publishing world, although that should deter no-one from sending their writing. No poetry, children's, young adult, graphic novels, plays and film scripts, self-help or lifestyle (including cookery, gardening, or interiors), religious or other esoteric titles, illustrated, academic, business or professional titles.

Literary Agent: Jonathan Ruppin (*L0872*)

L0872 Jonathan Ruppin
Literary Agent
United Kingdom

Literary Agency: The Ruppin Agency (**L0871**)

L0873 Alex Rusher
Literary Agent
United Kingdom

Literary Agency: Independent Talent Group Ltd (**L0496**)

L0874 Laetitia Rutherford
Literary Agent
United Kingdom

https://www.watsonlittle.com/agent/laetitia-rutherford/
http://www.twitter.com/laetitialit

Literary Agency: Watson, Little Ltd

Fiction > *Novels*
Crime; Literary; Upmarket

Nonfiction > *Nonfiction Books*
Contemporary; Culture; Environment; Gender; Nature; Parenting; Sexuality

Send: Query; Synopsis; Writing sample
How to send: Email

I represent a broad and diverse list of authors, ranging across Fiction and contemporary Non Fiction, and including literary prizewinners and commercial bestsellers. In Fiction, my special areas are Literary, Upmarket Fiction and Crime.

Author Estate: The Estate of Christine Evans

Authors: R.G. Adams; Lucy Ayrton; Petrina Banfield; Jenny Blackhurst; Andrew Brown; Clare Brown; Ursula Brunetti; Emile Chabal; Ajay Chowdhury; Cynthia Clark; Vivianne Crowley; Jeremy Daldry; Rebecca Elliott; Robin Harvie; JM Hewitt; Samson Kambalu; Rosie Lewis; Holan Liang; Chrissie Manby; Lindiwe Maqhubela; Alex Marwood; Thabi Moeketsi; Tamsin Omond; Matt Rendell; Richard Owain Roberts; Amos Ruiz; Anika Scott; Zoe Somerville; Shane Spall; Akemi Tanaka; Geeta Vara; Vincent Vincent; Jeremy Williams

L0875 Jim Rutman
Senior Agent
United States

https://www.sll.com/our-team
http://aaronline.org/Sys/PublicProfile/4090054/417813

Literary Agency: Sterling Lord Literistic, Inc. (**L0940**)
Professional Body: Association of American Literary Agents (AALA)

Fiction > *Novels*

Nonfiction > *Nonfiction Books*
Culture; History

Send: Query; Synopsis; Writing sample
How to send: Online submission system

Represents formally adventurous and stylistically diverse authors of fiction as well as a variety of journalists and critics whose non-fiction work examines an array of cultural and historical subjects.

L0876 Amanda Rutter
Associate Agent
United States

http://www.azantianlitagency.com/pages/team-ar.html

Literary Agency: Azantian Literary Agency (**L0054**)

ADULT > **Fiction** > *Novels*
Fantasy; Science Fiction

CHILDREN'S > **Fiction** > *Middle Grade*
Fantasy; Science Fiction

YOUNG ADULT > **Fiction** > *Novels*
Fantasy; Science Fiction

Send: Query; Synopsis; Writing sample
How to send: Query Manager

Looking for adult, YA and MG fantasy and science fiction. She is particularly keen to find hopeful science fiction, political fantasy and fresh takes on familiar tropes. Stories that definitely agree with her include: enemy to friend dynamics, women in STEM environments, antagonists with realistic motivations, and characters that overcome challenges in surprising ways. Stories that don't appeal include steampunk and zombie fiction! She would like to see witty dialogue, strong world building, and tales about characters from diverse backgrounds that don't concentrate on issues, but explore all facets of life.

L0877 Regina Ryan
Literary Agent
United States

Literary Agency: Regina Ryan Publishing Enterprises (**L0827**)
Professional Body: The Agents Round Table (ART)

L0878 Lesley Sabga
Literary Agent
United States

Literary Agency: The Seymour Agency (**L0902**)

L0879 Vicki Salter
Literary Agent
United Kingdom

Literary Agency: Barbara Levy Literary Agency (**L0061**)

L0880 Rayhane Sanders
Literary Agent
United States

http://www.mmqlit.com/about/

Literary Agency: Massie & McQuilkin (**L0680**)
Professional Body: Association of American Literary Agents (AALA)

ADULT
Fiction
Graphic Novels: General
Novels: Book Club Fiction; Historical
Fiction; Literary; Upmarket
Nonfiction
Essays: General
Nonfiction Books: Memoir; Narrative
Nonfiction
YOUNG ADULT > *Fiction* > *Novels*

Does not want:

> **YOUNG**
> **ADULT** > **Fiction** > *Novels*: Speculative

Represents and is on the lookout for literary
and historical fiction, upmarket book-club
fiction and comic novels, select YA (no
speculative elements, please), propulsive
narrative nonfiction, linked essay collections,
and select memoir. She likes projects that are
voice-centered and site-specific, whether that
be a place, profession, or subculture. Though
quality of writing is the most important factor,
she is particularly interested in fresh voices
telling fresh stories we haven't heard before
(including for YA audiences), and is fond of
immigrant stories and stories concerned with
race, sexuality, specific cultural settings, cross-
cultural themes, and notions of identity.

L0881 Angelique Tran Van Sang
Literary Agent
United Kingdom

Literary Agency: Felicity Bryan Associates
(**L0325**)

Fiction > *Novels*: Literary

Nonfiction > *Nonfiction Books*
Arts; History; Literature; Memoir; Narrative
Nonfiction; Philosophy; Politics

Send: Query; Synopsis; Writing sample
How to send: Online submission system

Actively building a list of authors of literary
fiction and narrative non-fiction. Interested in
essays and longform narratives that have a
distinctive voice. Also partial to an exquisitely
written memoir, ideally one that weaves in art,
literature, history, politics or philosophy.

Author: Amy Key

L0882 Sarah Lazin Books
Literary Agency
19 West 21st Street, Suite 501, New York, NY
10001
United States
Tel: +1 (212) 765-6900

http://lazinbooks.com

Literary Agency: Aevitas (**L0016**)

A full-service boutique agency founded in
1983. The agency is active in licensing first
serial, audio, and e-book rights.

As of June 1st, 2018, Sarah Lazin Books has
joined Aevitas Creative Management.

Authors: Marcus Baram; Patricia Romanowski
Bashe; Michael Benson; Jenny Blake; Ianthe
Brautigan; Richard Brautigan; Bill Brewster;
Frank Broughton; Kate Brown; E. Jean Carroll;
Ted Chapin; Robert Christgau; Julie Clow;
Broughton Coburn; Charles R. Cross; Stephen
DeAngelo; Anthony DeCurtis; Jim Dickinson;
Banning Eyre; Jim Farber; Ben Fong-Torres;
Georgia Freedman; Elysa Gardner; Richard
Gehr; Nelson George; Holly George-Warren;
Richard Goldstein; Jane Gottesman; Shirley
Halperin; John Harris; Elizabeth Hess; Janet
Hopson; Bill Ivey; Laura Joplin; Jason King;
Michael Lang; Bernie Lierow; Diane Lierow;
Alan Light; Kurt Loder; Kim MacQuarrie;
Hans J. Massaquoi; Ed McCormack; Evelyn
McDonnell; Kembrew McLeod; Dennis
McNally; Paula Mejia; Joan Morgan; Robert
K. Oermann; Robert Palmer; Sheri Parks;
Patricia Pearson; Bruce Porter; Ann Powers;
Parke Puterbaugh; Amy Rigby; Suze Rotolo;
Chris Salewicz; Ben Sandmel; Sylvie
Simmons; Ed Stafford; Robin Stone; Dominic
Streatfeild; Ned Sublette; John Swenson; John
Szwed; Paul Trynka; Jessica Vitkus; Elijah
Wald; David Wild; Frank Wildman; Sue
Williamson; Chris Willman; Douglas Wolk;
Emily Zemler

Literary Agent: Sarah Lazin (**L0604**)

L0883 Carolyn Savarese
Literary Agent
United States

Literary Agency: Kneerim & Williams (**L0575**)

L0884 Marilia Savvides
Literary Agent
United Kingdom

mariliasavvides@42mp.com

https://www.42mp.com/agents
https://twitter.com/MariliaSavvides

Literary Agency: 42 Management and
Production (**L0002**)

Fiction > *Novels*
Book Club Fiction; Crime; Dark; High
Concept Thrillers; Horror; Legal Thrillers;
Psychological Suspense; Speculative

Nonfiction > *Nonfiction Books*
Crime; Investigative Journalism; Memoir;
Narrative History; Popular Psychology;
Popular Science

How to send: Email

On the hunt for high-concept thrillers, crime,
psychological suspense, horror and
speculative, genre-bending fiction, reading
group fiction in the vein of Jodi Picoult or

Liane Moriarty; pop science / psychology,
narrative history, true crime and investigative
journalism.

L0885 Sophie Scard
Literary Agent
United Kingdom

SScard@unitedagents.co.uk

https://www.unitedagents.co.uk/
sscardunitedagentscouk

Literary Agency: United Agents (**L0992**)

Fiction > *Novels*

Nonfiction > *Nonfiction Books*

Send: Query; Author bio; Writing sample
How to send: Email

Actively building her client list, and is looking
for excellent writing of all types, fiction or
nonfiction. For submissions please email a
brief cover letter along with a biographical
note and the first 10,000 words of your text.

Authors: Oana Aristide; Joan Bakewell;
Stephen Bernard; Christopher Brookmyre;
Robin Bunce; Alex Alvina Chamberland; Clare
Chambers; Tom Chivers; Jill Dawson;
Susannah Dickey; Minoo Dinshaw; Tim Finch;
Ysenda Maxtone Graham; Charlotte
Grimshaw; Camilla Grudova; Tessa Hadley;
Lynsey Hanley; Jack Hartnell; Richard
Holloway; Annaleese Jochems; Tobias Kelly;
Clement Knox; Laura Kounine; Nakul
Krishna; Samara Linton; Jan Morris; Anna
Neima; Ambrose Parry; Ruth Pavey; Juno
Roche; Saumya Roy; Tracey Slaughter; Emily
Thomas; Ryan Turner; James Vincent;
Francesca Wade; Stephen Walsh

L0886 Rory Scarfe
Literary Agent; Company Director
United Kingdom

https://www.theblairpartnership.com/
our_people/rory-scarfe/

Literary Agency: The Blair Partnership
(**L0100**)

Fiction > *Novels*: Commercial

Nonfiction > *Nonfiction Books*: Commercial

Scripts
Film Scripts; *TV Scripts*

L0887 Christopher Schelling
Literary Agent
United States

Literary Agency: Selectric Artists (**L0900**)

L0888 Wendy Schmalz
Literary Agent
United States

Literary Agency: Wendy Schmalz Agency
(**L1026**)

L0889 Jeff Schmidt
Literary Agent

jschmidt@nycreative.com

http://www.nycreative.com/contact.html

Literary Agency: NY Creative Management
(**L0761**)

L0890 Deborah Schneider
Literary Agent
United States

Literary Agency: Gelfman Schneider / ICM
Partners (**L0386**)
Professional Body: Association of American
Literary Agents (AALA)

L0891 Kathy Schneider
Literary Agent
United States

Literary Agency: Jane Rotrosen Agency

Fiction > *Novels*
Literary; Upmarket

Nonfiction > *Nonfiction Books*
Business; Current Affairs; Health; Narrative
Nonfiction; Personal Development; Popular
Culture; Women's Interests

L0892 Hannah Schofield
Literary Agent
United Kingdom

hannahsubmissions@lbabooks.com

http://www.lbabooks.com/agent/hannah-
schofield/

Literary Agency: LBA Books Ltd (**L0605**)

ADULT > **Fiction** > *Novels*
Book Club Fiction; Commercial; High
Concept Romance; Historical Fiction;
Romantic Comedy; Suspense; Thrillers;
Women's Fiction

YOUNG ADULT > **Fiction** > *Novels*

How to send: Email

Currently building a list of commercial and
reading-group fiction.

Authors: Emad Ahmed; Amanda Brooke;
Charlotte Butterfield; Elizabeth Drummond;
Bea Fitzgerald; Lucy Goacher; Isabella
Harcourt; Jenni Keer; Amy Lavelle; Marina
McCarron; Heidi Shertok; Celia Silvani

L0893 Abby Schulman
Literary Agent
United States

Abby@rfliterary.com

Literary Agency: Rebecca Friedman Literary
Agency (**L0821**)

YOUNG ADULT > **Fiction** > *Novels*: Fantasy

Closed to approaches.

L0894 Susan Schulman
Literary Agent
United States

Literary Agency: Susan Schulman Literary
Agency (**L0955**)

L0895 The Science Factory
Literary Agency
Scheideweg 34C, Hamburg, 20253
Germany
Tel: + 49 40 4327 4959; +44 (0) 20 7193 7296
(Skype)

info@sciencefactory.co.uk

https://www.sciencefactory.co.uk

Types: Fiction; Nonfiction
Subjects: Autobiography; Current Affairs;
History; Medicine; Music; Politics; Science;
Technology; Travel
Markets: Adult

Send: Query; Writing sample
Don't send: Full text
How to send: Email

Specialises in science, technology, medicine,
and natural history, but will also consider other
areas of nonfiction. Novelists handled only
occasionally, and if there is some special
relevance to the agency (e.g. a thriller about
scientists, or a novel of ideas). See website for
full submission guidelines.

Literary Agents: Jeff Shreve (**L0909**); Tisse
Takagi; Peter Tallack

L0896 Kevin Conroy Scott
Literary Agent
United Kingdom

http://www.tiborjones.com/about/

Literary Agency: Tibor Jones & Associates
(**L0982**)

L0897 Rosemary Scoular
Literary Agent
United Kingdom

https://www.unitedagents.co.uk/
rscoularunitedagentscouk

Literary Agency: United Agents (**L0992**)

Nonfiction > *Nonfiction Books*
Adventure; Arts; Food; History; Investigative
Journalism; Memoir; Politics; Popular
Science; Travel

Focuses on nonfiction, from food writing to
history, popular science, travel and adventure,
politics and investigative journalism, the arts
and memoir of all kinds.

L0898 Wendy Scozzaro
Literary Agent
United Kingdom

Literary Agency: Felix de Wolfe (**L0326**)

L0899 Chloe Seager
Literary Agent
United Kingdom

https://madeleinemilburn.co.uk/team-member/
19023/

Literary Agency: Madeleine Milburn Literary,
TV & Film Agency (**L0664**)

CHILDREN'S
Fiction > *Middle Grade*
Nonfiction > *Middle Grade*

TEEN > **Fiction** > *Novels*

YOUNG ADULT
Fiction > *Novels*
Nonfiction > *Nonfiction Books*

Send: Query; Pitch; Market info; Author bio;
Synopsis; Writing sample
How to send: Email
How not to send: Post

Actively looking for: Middle Grade age 7 and
up; clean teen; young adult; non-fiction MG
and YA.

Associate Agent: Vanessa Browne (**L0138**)

L0900 Selectric Artists
Literary Agency
9 Union Square #123, Southbury, CT 06488
United States
Tel: +1 (347) 668-5426

query@selectricartists.com

https://www.selectricartists.com

ADULT
Fiction
Graphic Novels: General
Novels: Commercial; Science Fiction;
Thrillers
Nonfiction
Graphic Nonfiction: General
Nonfiction Books: Memoir; Narrative
Nonfiction
YOUNG ADULT > **Fiction** > *Novels*
Fantasy; Science Fiction

Send: Query; Full text
How to send: Email

Send query by email with your manuscript
attached as a .doc, .pdf, or .pages file. Put the
word "query" in the subject line. No queries by
phone. Response only if interested.

Literary Agent: Christopher Schelling (*L0887*)

L0901 Seventh Avenue
Literary Agency
Literary Agency
Canada

info@seventhavenuelit.com

http://www.seventhavenuelit.com

Types: Nonfiction
Markets: Adult

Describes itself as one of Canada's largest nonfiction and personal management agencies.

Literary Agent: Robert Mackwood (*L0658*)

L0902 The Seymour Agency
Literary Agency
475 Miner Street Road, Canton, NY 13617
United States

nicole@theseymouragency.com

https://www.theseymouragency.com

Professional Body: Association of American Literary Agents (AALA)

Types: Fiction; Nonfiction
Subjects: Adventure; Autobiography; Comedy / Humour; Contemporary; Cookery; Fantasy; History; Horror; Mystery; Personal Development; Religion; Romance; Science Fiction; Suspense; Thrillers; Warfare; Women's Interests
Markets: Adult; Children's; Young Adult

Send: Query
Don't send: Full text
How to send: Email

Brief email queries accepted (no attachments), including first five pages pasted into the bottom of your email. All agents prefer queries by email. See website for full submission guidelines and specific interests of each agent.

Literary Agents: Julie Gwinn (*L0435*); Elizabeth Poteet (*L0810*); Nicole Resciniti (*L0831*); Lesley Sabga (*L0878*); Tina Wainscott (*L1009*); Jennifer Wills (*L1044*)

L0903 Lauren Sharp
Literary Agent
United States

https://aevitascreative.com/agents/

Literary Agency: Aevitas (*L0016*)

Nonfiction > *Nonfiction Books*
Current Affairs; History; Narrative Nonfiction; Politics; Science

Represents nonfiction in the areas of politics, history, current affairs, narrative nonfiction, and science.

L0904 The Shaw Agency
Literary Agency
United Kingdom

https://www.theshawagency.co.uk

ADULT
Fiction > *Novels*
Commercial; Literary

Nonfiction > *Nonfiction Books*
Lifestyle; Narrative Nonfiction; Wellbeing

CHILDREN'S > **Fiction** > *Novels*

TEEN > **Fiction** > *Novels*

Send: Query; Pitch; Synopsis; Writing sample
Don't send: Full text
How to send: Online contact form

Handles literary and commercial fiction, crime fiction, powerful and quirky nonfiction, teen and children's books. Send query through online form with one-page synopsis, first 10 pages, and email address for response. See website for full guidelines.

Literary Agent: Kate Shaw (*L0905*)

L0905 Kate Shaw
Literary Agent
United Kingdom

Literary Agency: The Shaw Agency (*L0904*)

L0906 Sheil Land Associates Ltd
Literary Agency
52 Doughty Street, London, WC1N 2LS
United Kingdom
Tel: +44 (0) 20 7405 9351
Fax: +44 (0) 20 7831 2127

info@sheilland.co.uk

http://www.sheilland.co.uk

ADULT
Fiction > *Novels*
Book Club Fiction; Commercial Women's Fiction; Contemporary; Crime; Family Saga; Fantasy; Ghost Stories; Historical Fiction; Horror; Literary; Mystery; Romance; Science Fiction; Thrillers

Nonfiction
Gift Books: Comedy / Humour
Nonfiction Books: Biography; Cookery; Gardening; Lifestyle; Memoir; Mind, Body, Spirit; Personal Development; Politics; Popular Science; Psychology; Travel
Scripts
Film Scripts; *TV Scripts*; *Theatre Scripts*
CHILDREN'S
Fiction > *Novels*

Scripts
Animation Scripts; *TV Scripts*
YOUNG ADULT > **Fiction** > *Novels*

Send: Query
Don't send: Full text
How to send: Email

Send query with synopsis, CV, and first three chapters (or around 50 pages), by post addressed to "The Submissions Dept", or by email. If posting mss, do not send only copy as submissions are recycled and responses sent by email. If you require response by post, include SAE.

Authors: Peter Ackroyd; Melvyn Bragg; Susan Hill; David Lister; Catherine Robertson; Jonathan Steele

Literary Agents: Piers Blofeld; Ian Drury; Lucy Fawcett; Vivien Green; Sonia Land; Donna McCafferty; David Taylor (*L0970*)

L0907 Hannah Sheppard
Literary Agent
United Kingdom

Literary Agency: DHH Literary Agency Ltd (*L0264*)

L0908 Sheree Bykofsky Associates, Inc.
Literary Agency
4326 Harbor Beach Boulevard, PO Box 706, Brigantine, NJ 08203
United States

submitbee@aol.com
shereebee@aol.com

http://www.shereebee.com

Fiction > *Novels*
Commercial; Literary; Mystery

Nonfiction > *Nonfiction Books*
Biography; Business; Comedy / Humour; Cookery; Current Affairs; Films; Games; Health; Multicultural; Music; Parenting; Personal Development; Psychology; Spirituality; Women's Interests

Send: Query; Synopsis; Writing sample
Don't send: Full text
How to send: Email
How not to send: Fax; Post

Send query by email only. Include one page query, and for fiction a one page synopsis, and first page of manuscript, all in the body of the email. No attachments. Always looking for a bestseller in any category, but generally not interested in horror, westerns, occult, picture books, or fantasy.

Authors: Jeffrey Fox; Sue Hitzmann; Jason Kelly

Literary Agent: Sheree Bykofsky (*L0146*)

L0909 Jeff Shreve
Literary Agent
United States

https://www.sciencefactory.co.uk/agents

Literary Agency: The Science Factory (*L0895*)

Nonfiction > *Nonfiction Books*
Astronomy; Biology; Business; Genetics; Health; Neuroscience; Personal Development; Physics; Technology

L0910 Melissa Shultz
Literary Agent
United States

Literary Agency: Jim Donovan Literary (*L0525*)

L0911 Todd Shuster
Literary Agent; Chief Executive Officer
United States

Literary Agency: Aevitas (**L0016**)

Fiction > *Novels*
Commercial; Literary; Mystery; Thrillers

Nonfiction > *Nonfiction Books*
Business; Current Affairs; Health; History;
Memoir; Politics; Wellbeing

Closed to approaches.

Represents both fiction and nonfiction. His
nonfiction list primarily focuses on current
affairs, politics and civil rights, health and
wellness, memoir, business, and history. His
fiction list includes both literary and
commercial novels, including mysteries and
thrillers.

L0912 Signature Literary Agency
Literary Agency
4200 Wisconsin Ave, NW #106-233,
Washington, DC 20016
United States

gary@signaturelit.com

http://www.signaturelit.com

ADULT
  Fiction
    Graphic Novels: General
    Novels: Commercial; Historical Fiction;
    Literary; Mystery; Thrillers
  Nonfiction > *Nonfiction Books*
    Biography; Comedy / Humour; Current
    Affairs; Entertainment; History; How To;
    Memoir; Narrative Nonfiction; Popular
    Culture; Science

YOUNG ADULT > **Fiction** > *Novels*

Send: Query
How to send: Email

Costs: Author covers sundry admin costs.

Agency with agents based in Washington DC
and North Carolina. Send all queries by email
only.

Literary Agents: Gary Heidt; Ellen Pepus;
Amy Tipton

L0913 Michael Signorelli
Literary Agent
United States

https://aevitascreative.com/agents/

Literary Agency: Aevitas (**L0016**)

Fiction > *Novels*
Commercial; Literary; Thrillers

Nonfiction > *Nonfiction Books*
Adventure; Culture; Current Affairs; History;
Narrative Nonfiction; Nature; Science; Sport

Send: Pitch; Market info; Writing sample
How to send: Online submission system

Oversees a list of literary and commercial
fiction as well as nonfiction spanning nature,
science, adventure, current affairs, sports, and
cultural history.

L0914 Jeff Silberman
Affiliated Agent
United States

jsilberman@foliolitmanagement.com

https://www.publishersmarketplace.com/
members/silberjeff/

Literary Agency: Folio Literary Management,
LLC (**L0343**)
Professional Body: Association of American
Literary Agents (AALA)

Fiction > *Novels*
Book Club Fiction; Literary

Nonfiction > *Nonfiction Books*
Biography; Comedy / Humour; Cookery;
Current Affairs; Food; Health; History;
Lifestyle; Memoir; Politics; Popular Culture;
Science; Sport; Technology

Send: Query; Writing sample
How to send: In the body of an email

L0915 John Silbersack
Literary Agent
United States

Literary Agency: The Bent Agency (**L0090**)

L0916 Julia Silk
Literary Agent
United Kingdom

julia@cclagents.com

https://cclagents.com/agent/julia-silk/
https://twitter.com/juliasreading
https://www.instagram.com/juliasreading/
https://www.pinterest.co.uk/juliasreadingbo/
my-favourite-books/

Literary Agency: Charlie Campbell Literary
Agents (**L0188**)

Fiction > *Novels*
Commercial; Crime; Historical Fiction;
Literary; Upmarket Thrillers

Nonfiction > *Nonfiction Books*
Health; Journalism; Wellbeing

Send: Query; Writing sample
How to send: Email

Particularly looking for crime with a series
character, upmarket thrillers, and a compelling
historical novel with a strong voice. In nonfiction she is also keen to hear from journalists
and experts illuminating new stories and
previously unexplored subjects, and on the
practical side she represents a number of
writers in health and wellbeing and is
interested in original evidence-based proposals

in this area from experts with a strong
platform.

Authors: Poppy Alexander; Leona Nichole
Black; Owen Booth; Luce Brett; Liz Fraser;
Janet Gover; Sarah Graham; Karen Gurney;
Maisie Hill; Jo Iozzi; Heidi James; Carlie Lee;
Fiona Longmuir; Amanda Mason; Alison May;
Charlotte Philby; Amy Ransom; Rebecca
Schiller; Clare Seal; Emma Svanberg

L0917 Janet Silver
Literary Agent; Senior Partner
United States

https://aevitascreative.com/agents/

Literary Agency: Aevitas (**L0016**)

Fiction > *Novels*: Literary

Nonfiction > *Nonfiction Books*
Biography; Creative Nonfiction; History;
Memoir; Narrative Nonfiction; Philosophy;
Women's Studies

Send: Query; Writing sample
How to send: Online submission system

Represents literary fiction, memoir, and
creative/narrative nonfiction with a compelling
storyline. In both fiction and nonfiction, she
seeks diverse, singular voices, and unique
perspectives.

L0918 Dorie Simmonds
Literary Agent
United Kingdom

https://doriesimmonds.com/about-us
https://twitter.com/Dorie_Simmonds

Literary Agency: Dorie Simmonds Agency
(**L0275**)

Will consider material from any genre except
reference books and children's picture books.

L0919 Anjali Singh
Literary Agent
United States

https://www.pandeliterary.com/about-
pandeliterary
https://twitter.com/agent_anjali
http://aaronline.org/Sys/PublicProfile/
52119428/417813

Literary Agency: Ayesha Pande Literary
(**L0052**)
Professional Body: Association of American
Literary Agents (AALA)

ADULT
  Fiction
    Graphic Novels: General
    Novels: Literary

  Nonfiction > *Nonfiction Books*: Narrative
  Nonfiction

CHILDREN'S > **Fiction** > *Graphic Novels*

YOUNG ADULT > **Fiction** > *Graphic Novels*

Closed to approaches.

Looking for new voices, character-driven fiction or nonfiction works that reflect an engagement with the world around us, literary thrillers, memoirs, YA literature and graphic novels.

L0920 Skylark Literary

Literary Agency
19 Parkway, Weybridge, Surrey, KT13 9HD
United Kingdom
Tel: +44 (0) 20 8144 7440

submissions@skylark-literary.com
info@skylark-literary.com

http://www.skylark-literary.com
https://twitter.com/SkylarkLit
http://www.facebook.com/skylarkliteraryltd

Professional Body: The Association of Authors' Agents (AAA)

CHILDREN'S > **Fiction**
Chapter Books; *Early Readers*; *Middle Grade*
YOUNG ADULT > **Fiction** > *Novels*

Send: Full text; Synopsis
How to send: Word file email attachment

Handles fiction for children, from chapter books for emerging readers up to young adult / crossover titles. No picture books. Send query by email with one-page synopsis and full ms. No postal submissions.

Literary Agents: Amber J. Caravéo (*L0157*); Joanna Moult

L0921 Beverley Slopen

Literary Agent
Canada

Literary Agency: Beverley Slopen Literary Agency (**L0095**)

L0922 Helen Mackenzie Smith

Literary Agent
United Kingdom

Literary Agency: Bell Lomax Moreton Agency (**L0081**)

L0923 Jake Smith-Bosanquet

Literary Agent
United Kingdom

Literary Agency: C+W (Conville & Walsh) (**L0147**)

L0924 The Soho Agency

Literary Agency
16–17 Wardour Mews, London, W1F 8AT
United Kingdom
Tel: +44 (0) 20 7471 7900

sohoagencysubmissions@gmail.com
sohoagencychildrenssubmissions@gmail.com

http://www.thesohoagency.co.uk
https://twitter.com/TheSohoAgencyUK
https://www.instagram.com/thesohoagencyuk/

Professional Bodies: The Association of Authors' Agents (AAA); Personal Managers' Association (PMA); Association of Illustrators (AOI)

Fiction > *Novels*

Nonfiction > *Nonfiction Books*

Send: Query; Synopsis; Writing sample
How to send: Email attachment

Send query by email only. Include short synopsis and the first three chapters or up to 30 pages. For children's books under 1,000 words, submit complete ms. See website for separate email address for children's submissions. No plays, poetry, or textbooks. Film and TV scripts handled for existing clients only.

Associate Agents: Niamh O'Grady (**L0764**); Marina De Pass (**L0780**)

Chair / Literary Agent: Mark Lucas (*L0639*)

Company Director / Literary Agent: Rowan Lawton (**L0601**)

Company Directors / Literary Agents: Julian Alexander (*L0024*); Araminta Whitley (*L1032*)

Literary Agent / Managing Director: Philippa Milnes-Smith (**L0718**)

Literary Agents: Ben Clark; Sophie Laurimore (**L0600**); Jamie Mitchell; Carina Rizvi (*L0840*); Alice Saunders

L0925 Solow Literary Enterprises, Inc.

Literary Agency
United States

info@solowliterary.com

http://www.solowliterary.com
https://www.facebook.com/SolowLiterary
https://twitter.com/SolowLiterary

Nonfiction > *Nonfiction Books*
Business; Culture; Education; Health; Memoir; Narrative Nonfiction; Nature; Psychology; Science; Wellbeing

Send: Query
Don't send: Full text
How to send: Email

Handles nonfiction in the stated areas only. Send single-page query by email, providing information on what your book is about; why you think it has to be written; and why you are the best person to write it. Response only if interested.

Foreign Rights Manager: Taryn Fagerness

Literary Agent: Bonnie Solow (*L0926*)

L0926 Bonnie Solow

Literary Agent
United States

Literary Agency: Solow Literary Enterprises, Inc. (**L0925**)
Professional Bodies: Association of American Literary Agents (AALA); The Authors Guild

L0927 Jennifer March Soloway

Literary Agent
United States

soloway@andreabrownlit.com

https://querymanager.com/query/JenniferMarchSoloway
https://twitter.com/marchsoloway

Literary Agency: Andrea Brown Literary Agency, Inc.

ADULT > **Fiction** > *Novels*
Commercial; Crime; Literary; Psychological Suspense

CHILDREN'S > **Fiction**
Middle Grade: Adventure; Comedy / Humour; Contemporary; Fantasy; Ghost Stories; Mystery; Realistic
Picture Books: General, and in particular: Comedy / Humour
YOUNG ADULT > **Fiction** > *Novels*
Family; Literary; Mental Health; Psychological Horror; Relationships; Romance; Sexuality; Suspense; Thrillers

Send: Query; Pitch; Writing sample
How to send: Query Manager

Represents authors and illustrators of picture book, middle grade, and YA stories, and is actively building her list. Although she specializes in children's literature, she also represents adult fiction, both literary and commercial, particularly crime and psychological suspense projects.

L0928 Andrew Somberg

Literary Agent
United States

Literary Agency: Harvey Klinger, Inc (**L0452**)

L0929 Kelly Sonnack

Senior Agent
United States

https://www.andreabrownlit.com/agents.html
https://twitter.com/KSonnack

Literary Agency: Andrea Brown Literary Agency, Inc.

CHILDREN'S > **Fiction** > *Picture Books*

YOUNG ADULT > **Fiction**
Graphic Novels; *Novels*

How to send: By referral

L0930 Kaitlin Sooklal

Assistant Agent
Canada

https://www.therightsfactory.com/Agents/kaitlin-sooklal/

L0931 Sophie Hicks Agency

Literary Agency
60 Gray's Inn Road, London, WC1X 8LU
United Kingdom
Tel: +44 (0) 20 3735 8870

info@sophiehicksagency.com

http://www.sophiehicksagency.com
https://twitter.com/SophieHicksAg
https://www.instagram.com/
sophiehicksagency/

Professional Body: The Association of
Authors' Agents (AAA)

ADULT
  Fiction > *Novels*
  Nonfiction > *Nonfiction Books*

CHILDREN'S > **Fiction** > *Novels*

Send: Query; Writing sample; Synopsis
How to send: Email

Welcomes submissions. Send query by email
with sample pages attached as Word or PDF
documents. See website for full guidelines and
specific submissions email addresses. No
poetry or scripts for theatre, film or television,
and not currently accepting illustrated books
for children.

Literary Agents: Sophie Hicks (**L0469**); Sarah
Williams

L0932 Mary South

Literary Agent
United States

Literary Agency: Lowenstein Associates, Inc.
(**L0635**)

L0933 Jacques de Spoelberch

Literary Agent
United States

Literary Agency: J. de S. Associates, Inc.
(**L0508**)

L0934 Mark "Stan" Stanton

Literary Agent
United Kingdom

http://thenorthlitagency.com/our-friends-in-
the-north/
https://twitter.com/litagent007

Literary Agency: The North Literary Agency
(**L0755**)

Fiction > *Novels*
  Book Club Fiction; Crime; High Concept;
  Historical Fiction; Politics; Romantic
  Comedy; Satire; Thrillers

Nonfiction > *Nonfiction Books*
  Biography; Politics; Popular Culture; Popular
  Science; Sport

Send: Query; Synopsis; Writing sample;
Proposal
How to send: Email

Actively searching for new novelists and
nonfiction projects, particularly in the areas of
sport, culture and politics.

L0935 Hayley Steed

Literary Agent
United Kingdom

https://madeleinemilburn.co.uk/looking-for/
hayley-steed-im-looking/

Literary Agency: Madeleine Milburn Literary,
TV & Film Agency (**L0664**)

Fiction > *Novels*
  Book Club Fiction; Commercial; Crime;
  High Concept; Magical Realism; Mystery;
  Romance; Suspense; Thrillers; Upmarket

Send: Query; Pitch; Market info; Author bio;
Synopsis; Writing sample
How to send: Email
How not to send: Post

Actively looking for: commercial and bookclub fiction across all genres including
women's fiction; uplifting love stories;
suspense and mystery; upmarket general
fiction; high concept novels; original crime;
character-driven thrillers; emotional epics;
complex characters; magical realism and cross-
genre books.

L0936 Steph Roundsmith
Agent and Editor

Literary Agency; Editorial Service
United Kingdom

agent@stephroundsmith.co.uk

http://www.stephroundsmith.co.uk
https://twitter.com/StephRoundsmith

CHILDREN'S
  Fiction > *Novels*
  Nonfiction > *Nonfiction Books*

Closed to approaches.

Costs: Offers services that writers have to pay
for.

Interested in any genre for children under 12.
Also offers proofreading and editorial services.

Authors: Paul Adshead; Greg Dobbins; Jen
Dodds; Sara Fellows; Julian Green; Diana
Shaw

Editor / Literary Agent: Steph Roundsmith
(*L0866*)

L0937 Myrsini Stephanides

Literary Agent
United States

myrsini@carolmannagency.com

https://www.carolmannagency.com/myrsini-
stephanides
https://twitter.com/myrrr
https://www.instagram.com/myrsini_s/
https://www.goodreads.com/author/show/
2512266.Myrsini_Stephanides

Literary Agency: Carol Mann Agency (**L0161**)

ADULT > **Nonfiction** > *Nonfiction Books*
  General, and in particular: Activism;
  Business; Comedy / Humour; Inspirational;
  Memoir; Mind, Body, Spirit; Music;
  Narrative Nonfiction; Politics; Popular
  Culture; Popular Science; Science
  Journalism; Self Help; Social Justice

CHILDREN'S > **Nonfiction** > *Nonfiction
Books*

Send: Query
How to send: Email
How not to send: Post

Handles adult and children's nonfiction
(illustrated or narrative) in the following areas:
pop culture and music; humor of all kinds,
popular science and science journalism,
narrative nonfiction, memoir, business, self-
help and self-care; inspiration; mind, body,
spirit; politics; social justice and activism.

Authors: Huda Al-Marashi; Claire Belton;
Kelsey Crowe; John Doerr; Cyndy Etler; Laura
Garnett; Matthew Inman; Jarrett Lerner; Emily
McDowell; Martine Rothblatt; Hannah Shaw;
Jen Waite

L0938 Stephanie Tade Literary
Agency

Literary Agency
United States

https://www.stephanietadeagency.com

Nonfiction > *Nonfiction Books*: Mind, Body,
Spirit

Send: Query
How to send: Online contact form

A full service literary agency with a focus on
nonfiction, particularly in the categories of
physical, psychological, and spiritual wellbeing.

Literary Agent: Stephanie Tade

L0939 Jenny Stephens

Literary Agent
United States

https://www.sll.com/our-team

Literary Agency: Sterling Lord Literistic, Inc.
(**L0940**)

Nonfiction > *Nonfiction Books*
  Cookery; Cultural Criticism; Economics;
  Environment; Food; History; Lifestyle;
  Nature; Science; Social Justice

Send: Query; Synopsis; Writing sample
How to send: Online submission system

L0940 Sterling Lord Literistic,
Inc.

Literary Agency
115 Broadway, New York, NY 10006
United States

Tel: +1 (212) 780-6050
Fax: +1 (212) 780-6095

info@sll.com

https://www.sll.com

Send: Query; Synopsis; Writing sample
How to send: Online submission system

Select one agent to query and approach via online form on website.

Associate Agents: Chris Combemale (**L0212**); Mary Krienke (**L0581**); Nell Pierce (**L0798**)

Chair / Literary Agent: Peter Matson (**L0683**)

Executive Vice President / Literary Agent: Laurie Liss (**L0622**)

Foreign Rights Director: Szilvia Molnar

Foreign Rights Manager / Literary Agent: Danielle Bukowski (**L0140**)

Literary Agent / President: Philippa Brophy (**L0130**)

Literary Agent / Vice President: Douglas Stewart (**L0944**)

Literary Agents: Elizabeth Bewley (**L0096**); Brian Egan; Celeste Fine; Jessica Friedman (**L0365**); Sarah Landis (**L0592**); Sterling Lord; John Maas; Alison MacKeen; Martha Millard; George Nicholson; Sarah Passick; Jenny Stephens (**L0939**)

Senior Agents: Robert Guinsler (**L0429**); Neeti Madan (**L0663**); Jim Rutman (**L0875**)

L0941 Sternig & Byrne Literary Agency
Literary Agency
2370 S. 107th Street, Apt 4, Milwaukee, Wisconsin 53227-2036
United States
Tel: +1 (414) 328-8034

jackbyrne@hotmail.com

https://sternig-byrne-agency.com

Professional Bodies: Science Fiction and Fantasy Writers of America (SFWA); Mystery Writers of America (MWA)

Fiction > *Novels*
  Fantasy; Mystery; Science Fiction

Send: Query; Self-Addressed Stamped Envelope (SASE)
How to send: Email; Post
How not to send: Email attachment; Links to material online

Send brief query by post or email in first instance (if sending by email send in the body of the mail, do not send attachments). Will request further materials if interested. Currently only considering science fiction, fantasy, and mysteries. Preference given to writers with a publishing history.

Authors: Katherine Addison; John Haefele; Lael Littke; Kelly McCullough; Sarah

Monette; Moira Moore; Jo Walton; David Michael Williams; John C. Wright

Literary Agent: Jack Byrne

L0942 Paul Stevens
Literary Agent
United Kingdom

Literary Agency: Independent Talent Group Ltd (**L0496**)

L0943 Julie Stevenson
Literary Agent
United States

Literary Agency: Massie & McQuilkin (**L0680**)

L0944 Douglas Stewart
Literary Agent; Vice President
United States

https://www.sll.com/our-team

Literary Agency: Sterling Lord Literistic, Inc. (**L0940**)

ADULT > **Fiction** > *Novels*
  Commercial; Literary

CHILDREN'S > **Fiction** > *Novels*

YOUNG ADULT > **Fiction** > *Novels*

Send: Query; Synopsis; Writing sample
How to send: Online submission system

L0945 Jessica Stewart
Literary Agent
United Kingdom

Literary Agency: Independent Talent Group Ltd (**L0496**)

L0946 Sam Stoloff
President; Senior Agent
United States

https://goldinlit.com/agents/

Literary Agency: Frances Goldin Literary Agency, Inc. (**L0356**)

Fiction
  Graphic Novels: Literary
  Novels: Literary; Speculative
Nonfiction
  Graphic Nonfiction: General
  Nonfiction Books: Culture; Current Affairs; Environment; Food; History; Journalism; Legal; Memoir; Narrative Nonfiction; Philosophy; Politics; Science; Sociology; Sustainable Living; Technology

Send: Query; Writing sample
How to send: Submittable

Interested in books that advance the public conversation on crucial issues and groundbreaking work of all kinds, including literary fiction, memoir, history, accessible sociology and philosophy, cultural studies,

serious journalism on contemporary and international affairs, and narrative and topical nonfiction with a progressive orientation. Among his particular interests are literary graphic fiction and nonfiction, works on environmental sustainability, books on legal affairs and the justice system, works that dissect the right wing and American imperialism, the history of race in America, the history of science and technology, and books on food culture and history. His taste in fiction ranges from the psychologically realistic, to first-rate speculative literature.

Authors: Susan Bordo; Monica Byrne; Mandy Catron; Pratap Chatterjee; David Cole; Cliff Conner; Dessa; Ray Douglas; Mark Edmundson; Shelley Fisher Fishkin; Bruce Grierson; Michael Hudson; Lynn Hunt; Margaret Jacob; Steven Jaffe; Barbara Kingsolver; Michelle Kuo; Anna Lappé; Daniel Medwed; Stephanie Mencimer; Rutu Modan; Alexandra Natapoff; Carla Peterson; Sam Polk; Janisse Ray; Gretchen Reynolds; Siva Vaidhyanathan; Mike Wallace; Helene Wecker

L0947 Strachan Literary Agency
Literary Agency
P.O. Box 2091, Annapolis, MD 21404
United States

Query@StrachanLit.com

http://www.strachanlit.com

Types: Fiction; Nonfiction
Subjects: Autobiography; Comedy / Humour; Commercial; Cookery; Crime; Gardening; Health; Lifestyle; Literary; Mystery; Personal Development; Religion; Suspense; Thrillers; Travel; Women's Interests
Markets: Adult; Children's; Young Adult

Send: Query
Don't send: Full text

Send query through online form on website, providing a brief description of your book as well as your biographical information and writing credits or professional experience. No samples or mss unless requested. No picture books, genre fiction, poetry, or screenplays.

Literary Agents: Laura Strachan (*L0948*); Marisa Zeppieri (*L1068*)

L0948 Laura Strachan
Literary Agent
United States

Literary Agency: Strachan Literary Agency (**L0947**)

L0949 The Stringer Literary Agency LLC

Literary Agency
PO Box 111255, Naples, FL 34108
United States

https://www.stringerlit.com
https://www.instagram.com/stringerlit/
https://www.pinterest.com/stringerlit/
https://www.facebook.com/StringerLit
https://twitter.com/MarleneStringer

Professional Bodies: Association of American Literary Agents (AALA); Mystery Writers of America (MWA); Society of Children's Book Writers and Illustrators (SCBWI); The Authors Guild; Women's Fiction Writers Association (WFWA)

ADULT > **Fiction** > *Novels*

CHILDREN'S > **Fiction**
  Middle Grade; *Picture Books*
YOUNG ADULT > **Fiction** > *Novels*

A full-service literary agency specializing in commercial fiction since 2008.

Authors: Melissa Amateis; Caroline L. Bayley; Emily Bleeker; Marta Bliese; Anna Bradley; Emily Cavanagh; Don Dixon; Charlie Donlea; Pat Esden; Alyxandra Harvey; Erica Hayes; Charlie N Holmberg; Suzanne Johnson; Kristin Kisska; Kallie Lane; Caitlin McFarland; Liane Merciel; Sophie Munday; Melanie Novak; Liz Perrine; Molly Pierce; Emily Rittel-King; Alexandra Rushe; Luanne G. Smith; Kate Pawson Studer; Andrea Thalasinos; Tessa Wegert; Bethany Wiggins; Clare Zeschky

Literary Agents: Shari Maurer (**L0686**); Marlene Stringer (**L0950**)

L0950 Marlene Stringer

Literary Agent
United States

http://aaronline.org/Sys/PublicProfile/5108942/417813
https://querymanager.com/query/StringerLit

Literary Agency: The Stringer Literary Agency LLC (**L0949**)

ADULT
  Fiction > *Novels*
    Book Club Fiction; Commercial; Contemporary Crime; Contemporary Fantasy; Contemporary Women's Fiction; Crime; Fantasy; Historical Crime; Historical Fiction; Literary; Magical Realism; Mystery; Romance; Suspense; Thrillers; Upmarket Women's Fiction; Women's Fiction

  Nonfiction > *Nonfiction Books*: Narrative Nonfiction

CHILDREN'S > **Fiction** > *Middle Grade*

YOUNG ADULT > **Fiction** > *Novels*
  Contemporary; Fantasy

Send: Author bio; Query; Synopsis; Writing sample; Pitch; Market info
How to send: By referral; Conferences

L0951 The Strothman Agency

Literary Agency
63 East 9th Street, 10X, New York, NY 10003
United States

strothmanagency@gmail.com
info@strothmanagency.com

https://www.strothmanagency.com/
https://twitter.com/StrothmanAgency
https://www.facebook.com/StrothmanAgency/

Closed to approaches.

Only accepts electronic submissions. Physical query letters will be recycled unopened. Do not send entire manuscripts or attachments unless requested. All unrequested attachments will be deleted unread. Does not accept or respond to queries via fax or telephone.

Literary Agents: Lauren MacLeod (**L0660**); Wendy Strothman (**L0952**)

L0952 Wendy Strothman

Literary Agent
United States

https://www.strothmanagency.com/about
http://aaronline.org/Sys/PublicProfile/2176866/417813

Literary Agency: The Strothman Agency (**L0951**)
Professional Body: Association of American Literary Agents (AALA)

Nonfiction > *Nonfiction Books*
  Current Affairs; History; Narrative Journalism; Narrative Nonfiction; Nature; Science

Send: Query
Don't send: Full text
How to send: Email
How not to send: Email attachment; Fax; Phone

Looking for books that matter, books that change the way we think about things we take for granted, that tell stories that readers can't forget, and advance scholarship and knowledge. History, narrative nonfiction, narrative journalism, science and nature, and current affairs.

L0953 Mandy Suhr

Literary Agent
United Kingdom

https://milesstottagency.co.uk/representatives/mandy-suhr/

Literary Agency: Miles Stott Children's Literary Agency (**L0712**)

CHILDREN'S > **Fiction** > *Picture Books*

"I offer an experienced guiding hand to authors and illustrators, new and established, keen to work within this exciting genre. As well as editorial development of a style or story, I'll also help navigate through the business of publishing and that all important contract, ensuring each of my clients gets the best possible deal."

Authors: Rachel Bright; Lu Fraser

L0954 Cathryn Summerhayes

Literary Agent
United Kingdom

Literary Agency: Curtis Brown (**L0233**)

L0955 Susan Schulman Literary Agency

Literary Agency
454 West 44th Street, New York, NY 10036
United States
Tel: +1 (212) 713-1633

Susan@Schulmanagency.com

https://twitter.com/SusanSchulman

Professional Body: Association of American Literary Agents (AALA)

Fiction > *Novels*
  General, and in particular: Commercial; Literary; Women's Fiction

Nonfiction > *Nonfiction Books*
  Creativity; Economics; Finance; Health; History; Legal; Memoir; Mind, Body, Spirit; Politics; Psychology; Social Issues; Writing

Send: Query; Synopsis; Writing sample; Author bio
How to send: Email

Handles commercial and literary fiction and non-fiction, specifically narrative memoir, politics, economics, social issues, history, urban planning, finance, law, health, psychology, body/mind/sprit, and creativity and writing.

Associate Agent: Emelie Burl (**L0142**)

Literary Agent: Susan Schulman (*L0894*)

L0956 Susanna Lea Associates (UK)

Literary Agency
South Wing, Somerset House, Strand, London, WC2R 1LA
United Kingdom
Tel: +44 (0) 20 7287 7757

london@susannalea.com

https://www.susannalea.com

Professional Body: The Association of Authors' Agents (AAA)

Fiction > *Novels*

Nonfiction > *Nonfiction Books*

Send: Query; Synopsis; Writing sample
How to send: Email

Literary agency with offices in Paris, London, and New York. Always on the lookout for exciting new talent. No poetry, plays, screen plays, science fiction, educational text books, short stories or illustrated works. No queries by fax or post. Accepts queries by email only. Include cover letter, synopsis, and first three chapters or proposal. Response not guaranteed.

Literary Agent: Kerry Glencorse (**L0399**)

L0957 Kari Sutherland
Literary Agent
United States

https://bradfordlit.com/about/kari-sutherland/
https://querymanager.com/query/
Kari_Sutherland_Query_Form
https://twitter.com/KariSutherland

Literary Agency: Bradford Literary Agency (**L0117**)

ADULT > **Fiction** > *Novels*
  Gothic; International; Magic; Psychology; Saga; Suspense; Upmarket Women's Fiction
CHILDREN'S
  Fiction
    Chapter Books: General
    Graphic Novels: General
    Middle Grade: Adventure; Contemporary Romance; Drama; Environment; Fantasy; Social Justice; Social Media; Suspense; Technology
    Picture Books: General
  Nonfiction > *Nonfiction Books*
    Beauty; Environment; Health; History; Information Science; Science

YOUNG ADULT > **Fiction**
  Graphic Novels: General
  Novels: Adventure; Contemporary Romance; Drama; Environment; Fantasy; Social Justice; Social Media; Suspense; Technology

Closed to approaches.

Open to genres from picture books through adult. Most interested in finding stories full of heart; ones that carry readers to faraway places or deep into a character's mind; action-packed page-turners that surprise her; dark dramas with touches of humor; and, above all, a voice that leaps off the page. She is actively seeking diverse voices across all genres.

L0958 Alice Sutherland-Hawes
Literary Agent
United Kingdom

https://www.ashliterary.com/#about

Literary Agency: ASH Literary (**L0048**)

Authors: Dina Al-Sabawi; Hannah Camacho; Ryan Crawford; Alex Falase-Koya; Niyla Farook; Kereen Getten; Gina Gonzales; Gavin Gray; Sarah Guillory; Ravena Guron; Radiya

Hafiza; Anika Hussain; Jennifer Iacopelli; Nansubuga Isdahl; Samantha Joyce; Richard Mercado; Samuel Pollen; Ryan Robinson; Elizabeth Rounding; Cynthia So; Chitra Soundar; Claire Tomasi; Adelle Yeung

L0959 Joanna Swainson
Literary Agent
United Kingdom

submissions@hardmanswainson.com

http://www.hardmanswainson.com/agents/
joanna-swainson/
https://twitter.com/JoannaSwainson

Literary Agency: Hardman & Swainson (**L0441**)

Fiction > *Novels*
  Comedy / Humour; Commercial; Contemporary; Crime; Folk Horror; Ghost Stories; Historical Fiction; Horror; Literary; Speculative; Thrillers

Nonfiction > *Nonfiction Books*
  Memoir; Narrative Nonfiction; Nature; Popular History; Science

Send: Synopsis; Full text
How to send: Email
How not to send: Post

Authors: Jon Bounds; Oggy Boytchev; Paul Braddon; Matt Brolly; Elizabeth Brooks; Mark Broomfield; Adrienne Chinn; Helen Cox; Jeremy Craddock; Sara Crowe; Emma Darwin; Stuart David; Caroline Davison; Carol Donaldson; Simon David Eden; Rachel Edwards; Nicola Ford; Harry Freedman; James Gould-Bourn; Tom Higham; Michael Jecks; Oskar Cox Jensen; Stuart Johnstone; Lucy Lawrie; Peter Laws; Kevin Macneil; S R Masters; Lauren Price; Philip C Quaintrell; Patrick Roberts; Nick Russell-Pavier; Catherine Simpson; Danny Smith; Eliska Tanzer; Sarah Tierney; B P Walter; Samantha Wilson

L0960 Becky Sweren
Literary Agent
United States

https://aevitascreative.com/agents/#agent-7413

Literary Agency: Aevitas (**L0016**)

Nonfiction > *Nonfiction Books*
  Culture; History; Investigative Journalism; Memoir

Closed to approaches.

Authors: Jesse Ball; Mark Braude; Adin Dobkin; Beck Dorey-Stein; Renee Dudley; Penina Eilberg-Schwartz; Valerie Fridland; Nicholas Griffin; Lawrence Jackson; Mohamad Jebara; Faith Jones; Jillian Keenan; Jake Keiser; Sulaiman Khatib; Ali Kriegsman; Daniel Levin; Eric M. O'Neill; Matteson Perry; Pen Rhodeen; Mohammed Al Samawi; Laurie Segall; Shabtai Shavit; Gabourey

Sidibe; Judith E. Stein; Noa Tishby; Steven Ujifusa; Jack Viertel; Lijia Zhang

L0961 Swetky Literary Agency
Literary Agency
929 W. Sunset Blvd #21-285, St. George, UT 84770
United States
Tel: +1 (719) 859-2211
Fax: +1 (435) 579-5000

swetkyagency@amsaw.org

http://www.swetkyagency.com

Types: Fiction; Nonfiction
Markets: Adult

Send: Query
Don't send: Full text

Submit query using submission form on website.

Literary Agent: Faye Swetky (*L0962*)

L0962 Faye Swetky
Literary Agent
United States

Literary Agency: Swetky Literary Agency (**L0961**)

L0963 Jessica Sykes
Literary Agent
United Kingdom

Literary Agency: Independent Talent Group Ltd (**L0496**)

L0964 SYLA – Susan Yearwood Literary Agency
Literary Agency
2 Knebworth House, Londesborough Road, Stoke Newington, London, N16 8RL
United Kingdom
Tel: +44 (0) 20 7503 0954

submissions@susanyearwoodagency.com

https://susanyearwoodagency.com

Professional Body: The Association of Authors' Agents (AAA)

ADULT
  Fiction > *Novels*
  Nonfiction > *Nonfiction Books*

CHILDREN'S > **Fiction** > *Novels*

YOUNG ADULT > **Fiction** > *Novels*

Send: Query; Author bio; Writing sample; Synopsis
How to send: Email attachment

Send query by email, including synopsis and first thirty pages as Word or PDF attachment.

Authors: Catherine Balavage; Lucy Basey; Angela Cairns; Fran Clark; Sarah Dobbs; Selina Flavius; Kimberley Glover; Liz Kolbeck; Prajwal Parajuly; Susan Quirke;

Sarupa Shah; Jacqueline Shaw; Suzanne Snow; Sarah Stephenson; Kerry Young

Literary Agent: Susan Yearwood (**L1059**)

L0965 Laurel Symonds
Literary Agent
United States

http://www.thebentagency.com/laurel-symonds

Literary Agency: The Bent Agency (**L0090**)

CHILDREN'S
Fiction
Chapter Books; *Graphic Novels*; *Illustrated Books*; *Middle Grade*; *Picture Books*
Nonfiction > *Nonfiction Books*

YOUNG ADULT > **Fiction**
Graphic Novels; *Novels*

Closed to approaches.

I am seeking young adult and middle grade fiction with a special interest in contemporary and fantasy-with-a-twist. I look for engaging voices, commercial hooks, and immersive worlds. My YA tastes are pretty commercial whereas my middle grade tastes can skew more literary and I'm especially interested in middle grade that might lend itself to illustration.

For picture books, graphic novels, and other illustrated work, my tastes are diverse, ranging from sophisticated to quirky to gently humorous. I am interested in art in all mediums, but especially appreciate a smart use of color and perspective.

I also represent select nonfiction for children and young adults, especially projects about STEM or history with age-appropriate hooks and series potential.

L0966 Emily Talbot
Associate Agent
United Kingdom

etalbot@unitedagents.co.uk

https://www.unitedagents.co.uk/etalbotunitedagentscouk

Literary Agency: United Agents (**L0992**)
Literary Agent: Jodie Hodges (**L0475**)

CHILDREN'S > **Fiction**
Middle Grade; *Picture Books*
TEEN > **Fiction** > *Novels*

YOUNG ADULT > **Fiction** > *Novels*

Send: Query; Synopsis; Writing sample

Represents children's illustrators and authors of picture books, middle grade, teenage and YA.

Authors: Aysha Awwad; Susanna Bailey; Abigail Balfe; Alex Barrow; Becky Baur; Gabby Dawnay; Sophie Deen; Chloe Douglass; Ed Eaves; Alison Guile; James Harris; Sam Hearn; Benjamin Hughes; James Lent; Rebecca Lewis-Oakes; Maggie Li; Roger

McGough; Becka Moor; Polly Owen; Keith Robinson; Andy Sagar; Jion Sheibani; Qian Shi; Georgina Stevens; Barry Timms; Jacqueline Tucker; Kael Tudor; Lucy Unwin; Maddy Vian; Lucia Vinti

L0967 Amy Tannenbaum
Literary Agent
United States

atannenbaum@janerotrosen.com

https://www.janerotrosen.com/agents
https://www.janerotrosen.com/contact-amy-tannenbaum

Literary Agency: Jane Rotrosen Agency

Fiction > *Novels*
Commercial; Contemporary Romance; Literary; Psychological Suspense; Thrillers; Women's Fiction

Nonfiction > *Nonfiction Books*: Narrative Nonfiction

Send: Query
How to send: In the body of an email
How not to send: Email attachment

Represents clients who write across a variety of genres including women's fiction, contemporary romance, thriller and psychological suspense. She is particularly interested in those categories, as well as fiction that falls into the sweet spot between literary and commercial, and works by diverse voices.

L0968 Simon Targett
Literary Agent
United Kingdom

https://aevitascreative.com/agents/#agent-7409

Literary Agency: Aevitas Creative Management (ACM) UK (**L0017**)

Fiction > *Novels*: Historical Fiction

Nonfiction > *Nonfiction Books*
Biography; Business; Current Affairs; Genealogy; History; Journalism; Leadership; Music; Nature; Popular Science; Sport; Travel

Send: Market info; Writing sample
How to send: Online submission system

Interested in a wide range of nonfiction, including business and leadership, history, journalism, current affairs, biography, sport, music, popular science, nature, travel, genealogy. Will also consider historical fiction. The common factor is an emphasis on big ideas, great stories, and fine writing.

L0969 Alice Tasman
Literary Agent
United States

Literary Agency: The Jean V. Naggar Literary Agency (**L0519**)

L0970 David Taylor
Literary Agent
United Kingdom

Literary Agency: Sheil Land Associates Ltd (**L0906**)

Scripts
Film Scripts; *TV Scripts*; *Theatre Scripts*

L0971 Teresa Chris Literary Agency Ltd
Literary Agency
43 Musard Road, London, W6 8NR
United Kingdom
Tel: +44 (0) 20 7386 0633

teresachris@litagency.co.uk

http://www.teresachrisliteraryagency.co.uk

Professional Body: The Association of Authors' Agents (AAA)

Fiction > *Novels*
Commercial Women's Fiction; Commercial; Crime; Literary

Does not want:

Fiction > *Novels*
Fantasy; Horror; Science Fiction

Send: Query; Synopsis; Writing sample; Self-Addressed Stamped Envelope (SASE)
How to send: Domestic Post; Email if overseas

Welcomes submissions. Overseas authors must approach by email, otherwise submit by post. Send query with SAE, first three chapters, and one-page synopsis. Specialises in crime fiction and commercial women's fiction. No poetry, short stories, fantasy, science fiction, horror, or children's fiction.

Authors: Stephanie Austin; Lily Baxter; Ginny Bell; M A Bennett; Victoria Blake; Stephen Booth; Benita Brown; Rory Clements; Julie Cohen; Dilly Court; Martin Davies; Ellie Dean; Linda Finlay; Marina Fiorato; Emily Freud; Kate Furnivall; Annie Groves; Clare Harvey; Debby Holt; Hunter; Corrie Jackson; Jim Kelly; Danuta Kot; Linscott; Tamara McKinley; Jane McMorland; Charlotte Parsons; Stuart Pawson; Caro Peacock/Gillian; Nicola Pryce; Eileen Ramsay; Kate Rhodes; Mary-Jane Riley; Caroline Scott; Marsali Taylor; Jane Wenham-Jones

L0972 Paige Terlip
Associate Agent
United States

paige@andreabrownlit.com

https://www.andreabrownlit.com/agents.html
https://twitter.com/pterlip
https://www.instagram.com/pterlip/

Literary Agency: Andrea Brown Literary Agency, Inc.

ADULT

Fiction > *Novels*
Cozy Mysteries; Fantasy; High Concept; Magic; Psychological Suspense; Science Fiction; Thrillers; Upmarket

Nonfiction > *Nonfiction Books*
Mind, Body, Spirit; Narrative Nonfiction; Self Help

CHILDREN'S > **Fiction**
Chapter Books; *Middle Grade*; *Picture Books*

YOUNG ADULT > **Fiction** > *Novels*
High Concept; Magic

Send: Author bio; Query; Writing sample; Pitch; Market info
How to send: Query Manager

Represents all categories of children's books from picture books to young adult, as well as select adult fiction and nonfiction. She is also actively building her list of illustrators and is especially looking for author-illustrators and graphic novel illustrators.

L0973 Henry Thayer
Literary Agent
United States

hthayer@bromasite.com

Literary Agency: Brandt & Hochman Literary Agents, Inc. (**L0119**)
Professional Body: Association of American Literary Agents (AALA)

Fiction > *Novels*
General, and in particular: Literary

Nonfiction > *Nonfiction Books*
General, and in particular: American History; Popular Music; Sport

Send: Query
How to send: Email

L0974 Jack Thomas
Literary Agent
United Kingdom

Literary Agency: Independent Talent Group Ltd (**L0496**)

L0975 Thompson Literary Agency
Literary Agency
115 West 29th St, Third Floor, New York, NY 10001
United States
Tel: +1 (347) 281-7685

submissions@thompsonliterary.com

https://thompsonliterary.com

Professional Body: Association of American Literary Agents (AALA)

Types: Fiction; Nonfiction
Subjects: Arts; Autobiography; Beauty; Commercial; Cookery; Culture; Fashion;

Health; History; Literary; Music; Politics; Science; Spirituality; Sport
Markets: Adult; Children's; Young Adult

Send: Query
Don't send: Full text
How to send: Email

Accepts commercial and literary fiction, but specialises in nonfiction. See website for list of agent interests and address submission by email to specific agent.

Literary Agents: Kiele Raymond (*L0820*); Meg Thompson (*L0976*); John Thorn (*L0978*)

L0976 Meg Thompson
Literary Agent
United States

Literary Agency: Thompson Literary Agency (**L0975**)

L0977 Paul Thompson
Literary Agent
United Kingdom

Literary Agency: Bookseeker Agency (**L0110**)

L0978 John Thorn
Literary Agent
United States

Literary Agency: Thompson Literary Agency (**L0975**)

L0979 Euan Thorneycroft
Literary Agent
United Kingdom

https://amheath.com/agents/euan-thorneycroft/
http://twitter.com/EuanThorneycrof

Literary Agency: A.M. Heath & Company Limited, Author's Agents (**L0003**)

Fiction > *Novels*
Crime; Historical Fiction; Literary; Thrillers

Nonfiction > *Nonfiction Books*
History; Memoir; Nature; Politics; Science; Technology

Agency Assistant: Jessica Lee

L0980 Jessie Thorsted
Literary Agent
United States

Literary Agency: InkWell Management (**L0499**)

L0981 Anne Tibbets
Literary Agent
United States

http://maassagency.com/anne-tibbets/
https://querymanager.com/query/AnneTibbets

Literary Agency: Donald Maass Literary Agency (**L0273**)

ADULT > **Fiction** > *Novels*

Amateur Investigator; Cozy Mysteries; Diversity; Domestic Thriller; Fantasy; Feminism; High Concept; Historical Fiction; Horror; LGBTQIA; Mystery; Police Procedural; Psychological Horror; Romance; Romantic Comedy; Romantic Suspense; Science Fiction; Thrillers; Women's Fiction

YOUNG ADULT > **Fiction** > *Novels*
Diversity; Feminism; Historical Fiction; LGBTQIA; Thrillers

Send: Author bio; Query; Synopsis; Writing sample
How to send: Query Manager

Represents adult and young adult commercial genre, primarily thrillers, mysteries, science fiction, fantasy, horror, and historical women's fiction.

L0982 Tibor Jones & Associates
Literary Agency
PO Box 74604, London, SW2 9NH
United Kingdom

enquiries@tiborjones.com

http://www.tiborjones.com
https://twitter.com/TiborJones

Fiction > *Novels*

Nonfiction > *Nonfiction Books*

Send: Query; Synopsis; Author bio; Writing sample
How to send: Email

Welcomes fiction and nonfiction proposals from writers who are looking to publish something different. Send query by email giving details about you and your writing background, with one-page synopsis and first five pages of the novel/proposal.

Literary Agency: The Bravo Blue Agency (**L0122**)

Literary Agents: Landa Acevedo-Scott (**L0008**); Charlotte Colwill (**L0211**); Kevin Conroy Scott (**L0896**)

L0983 The Tobias Literary Agency
Literary Agency
United States

https://www.thetobiasagency.com
https://twitter.com/TheTobiasAgency
https://www.facebook.com/TobiasLiteraryAgency
https://www.instagram.com/thetobiasliteraryagency/

Specializes in all Intellectual Property matters in the publishing industry, from the seed of an idea to the day a book hits the shelves. A full-service literary agency headquartered in New York City with satellite offices in Boston, Nashville, and soon-to-be Los Angeles. Represents established and debut authors.

Associate Agent: Maria Rogers (**L0856**)

Literary Agent / President: Lane Heymont (**L0466**)

Literary Agents: Matt Belford (**L0080**); Stefanie Rossitto (**L0864**)

Senior Agent: Natascha Morris (**L0728**)

L0984 Toby Mundy Associates Ltd

Literary Agency
38 Berkeley Square, London, W1J 5AE
United Kingdom
Tel: +44 (0) 20 3713 0067

submissions@tma-agency.com

http://tma-agency.com
https://twitter.com/tma_agency
https://facebook.com/tobymundyassociates
https://flipboard.com/@tobymundy/publishing-futures-rkd4uodqy

Literary Agency: Aevitas (**L0016**)

Fiction > *Novels*

Nonfiction > *Nonfiction Books*

Send: Query; Synopsis; Writing sample
How to send: Email; By referral

Accepts submissions upon recommendation only. Send query by email with brief synopsis, first chapter, and a note about yourself, all pasted into the body of the email.

Chief Executive Officer / Literary Agent: Toby Mundy (**L0731**)

L0985 Antony Topping

Literary Agent
United Kingdom

http://greeneheaton.co.uk/agents/antony-topping/

Literary Agency: Greene & Heaton Ltd (**L0419**)

Fiction > *Novels*
Contemporary; Historical Literary; Historical Thrillers

Nonfiction > *Nonfiction Books*
Comedy / Humour; Food; Science

Authors: Amen Alonge; Meg Arroll; Lucy Ashe; Louise Atkinson; Helena Attlee; James Bridle; Jason Byrne; Tom Campbell; Emma Chapman; Charles Cockell; Pam Corbin; Andrew Davidson; Russell Davies; Anna Davis; Patrick Drake; Nikki Duffy; Suzannah Dunn; Jeremy Duns; Olaf Falafel; Hugh Fearnley-Whittingstall; Jane Fearnley-Whittingstall; Nick Fisher; Christopher Fitz-Simon; Christophe Galfard; Stuart Heritage; Julian Hitch; Andrew Holmes; Alex Hourston; D.B. John; Keith Kahn-Harris; Max Kinnings; David Kirk; Rikke Schmidt Kjærgaard; Joseph Knox; William Leith; Dan Lepard; Robert Lewis; Kieran Long; Dorian Lynskey; Jolyon Maugham; James McGee; Gill Meller;

Thomasina Miers; Lottie Moggach; Cathy Newman; Mary-Ann Ochota; Christopher Osborn; Iain Overton; John O'Connell; Pete Paphides; Tom Phillips; Shivi Ramoutar; Richard Reed; Sam Rice; C. J. Sansom; Marcus du Sautoy; Rebecca Seal; Laura Shepherd-Robinson; Mimi Spencer; Count Arthur Strong; Andrew Taylor; Ian Vince; John Vincent; Jennie Walker; Andrew Webb; Mark Wernham; Robyn Wilder; Will Wiles; Erin Young; Robyn Young; Andrew Ziminski

L0986 Jennifer Chen Tran

Literary Agent
United States

http://bradfordlit.com/about/jennifer-chen-tran-agent/
https://twitter.com/jenchentran
https://querymanager.com/query/jenchentran

Literary Agency: Bradford Literary Agency (**L0117**)

ADULT
Fiction > *Novels*
Contemporary Women's Fiction; Literary; Upmarket Women's Fiction; Women's Fiction

Nonfiction > *Nonfiction Books*
Beauty; Biography; Business; Cookery; Current Affairs; Design; Fashion; Health; History; How To; Investigative Journalism; Lifestyle; Medicine; Memoir; Mind, Body, Spirit; Music; Narrative Nonfiction; Parenting; Popular Culture; Psychology; Relationships; Travel

CHILDREN'S
Fiction > *Graphic Novels*

Nonfiction > *Nonfiction Books*
Cookery; Creativity; History; Popular Science

YOUNG ADULT > **Fiction**
Graphic Novels; Novels

How to send: Query Manager

Very interested in diverse writers and #ownvoices from underrepresented/ marginalized communities, strong and conflicted characters who are not afraid to take emotional risks, stories about multi-generational conflict, war and post-war fiction, and writing with a developed sense of place. In non-fiction, she loves books that broaden her world view or shed new light on 'big ideas.'

L0987 Steve Troha

Literary Agent; Partner
United States

https://www.publishersmarketplace.com/members/stroha/
http://aaronline.org/Sys/PublicProfile/5633367/417813

Literary Agency: Folio Literary Management, LLC (**L0343**)

Professional Body: Association of American Literary Agents (AALA)

L0988 Nick Turner

Literary Agent
United Kingdom

Literary Agency: Nick Turner Management Ltd (**L0750**)

L0989 The Two Piers Literary Agency

Literary Agency
Brighton
United Kingdom

hello@twopiersagency.com

https://twopiersagency.com
https://twitter.com/TwoPiersAgency
https://www.facebook.com/TwoPiersAgency
https://www.instagram.com/twopiersagency/

ADULT
Fiction > *Novels*
Nonfiction > *Nonfiction Books*

CHILDREN'S > **Fiction** > *Middle Grade*

YOUNG ADULT > **Fiction** > *Novels*

Send: Query; Synopsis; Writing sample; Author bio
How to send: Online submission system

Costs: Offers services that writers have to pay for. Sister company provides online novel-writing course.

Literary agency based in Brighton, which represents writers from all over the world and sells their work into the UK, US and international territories. An editorially focused agency that works closely with authors to produce manuscripts that are as strong as they can possibly be before submitting them to publishers.

Literary Agent: Rufus Purdy (*L0816*)

L0990 Cindy Uh

Literary Agent
United States

Literary Agency: CAA (Creative Artists Agency, LLC) (**L0148**)

L0991 Union Literary

Literary Agency
30 Vandam Street, Suite 5A, New York, NY 10013
United States
Tel: +1 (212) 255-2112

queries@threeseaslit.com

https://www.unionliterary.com

Professional Body: Association of American Literary Agents (AALA)

Types: Fiction; Nonfiction
Subjects: Autobiography; Business; Cookery;

History; Literary; Science; Society
Markets: Adult

Send: Query
Don't send: Full text
How to send: Email

Prefers queries by email. Include a proposal and sample chapter for nonfiction, or a synopsis and sample pages for fiction. See website for specific agent interests and contact details, and approach one agent only. Response only if interested.

Literary Agents: Christina Clifford; Taylor Curtin; Trena Keating

L0992 United Agents

Literary Agency
12-26 Lexington Street, London, W1F 0LE
United Kingdom
Tel: +44 (0) 20 3214 0800
Fax: +44 (0) 20 3214 0802

info@unitedagents.co.uk

https://www.unitedagents.co.uk
https://twitter.com/UnitedAgents
https://www.instagram.com/unitedagents/

Professional Body: The Association of Authors' Agents (AAA)

Fiction > *Novels*

Nonfiction > *Nonfiction Books*

Send: Query; Pitch; Market info; Synopsis; Writing sample
How to send: Email
How not to send: Post

Do not approach the book department generally. Consult website and view details of each agent before selecting a specific agent to approach personally. Accepts submissions by email only. Submissions by post will not be returned or responded to.

Agency Assistants: Molly Jamieson; Olivia Martin

Associate Agents: Seren Adams (**L0012**); Millie Hoskins (**L0483**); Eli Keren (**L0564**); Emily Talbot (**L0966**); Kate Walsh (**L1013**)

Authors: Kim Adrian; Amrou Al-Kadhi; Laura Albert; Rosie Alison; Nina Allan; Karin Altenberg; Jessica Anthony; Oana Aristide; Aysha Awwad; Susanna Bailey; Adam Baker; Joan Bakewell; Abigail Balfe; Alex Barrow; Becky Baur; Deborah Bee; Hina Belitz; Alan Bennett; Stephen Bernard; LMK Berry; Sophie Ellis Bextor; Marieke Bigg; Mark Blacklock; Quentin Blake; Stefan Merrill Block; Ezekiel Boone; Melitta Breznik; Molly Brodak; Maggie Brookes; Christopher Brookmyre; Sylvia Brownrigg; Robin Bunce; John Burnside; Sarah Burton; Jen Calleja; Emma Campbell; Robin Carhart-Harris; Brian Catling; Carl Cattermole; Jessie Cave; Alex Alvina Chamberland; Clare Chambers; Roland Chambers; Tom Chivers; Emma Cline;

Amanda Coe; Sean Patrick Cooper; Wendy Cope; Marion Coutts; Leah Cowan; Al Crow; Dan Cruickshank; Lauren Aimee Curtis; Rosie Dastgir; Carys Davies; Gabby Dawnay; Jill Dawson; Tim Dee; Sophie Deen; JP Delaney; Sam Diamond; Susannah Dickey; Minoo Dinshaw; Paddy Docherty; Chloe Douglass; Miranda Doyle; Dennis Duncan; Douglas Dunn; Elanor Dymott; Ben Eastham; Ed Eaves; Christy Edwall; Lucie Elven; Chris England; Hermione Eyre; James Fenton; Toby Ferris; Rakaya Fetuga; Tim Finch; Ronan Fitzgerald; William Fowler; Amaryllis Gacioppo; Rivka Galchen; William Ghosh; Rebecca Gibb; Maria Giron; Sue Glover; Rebecca Gowers; Ysenda Maxtone Graham; Huho Greenhalgh; Charlotte Grimshaw; Camilla Grudova; Alison Guile; Tessa Hadley; Lili Hamlyn; Lynsey Hanley; Robert Hardman; James Harris; David Harsent; Jack Hartnell; Samantha Harvey; Will Hayward; Sam Hearn; Colin Heber-Percy; Sheila Heti; Ben Hinshaw; Susannah Hoffman; Michael Hofmann; Richard Holloway; Joseph Hone; Benjamin Hughes; Caoilinn Hughes; Catherine Humble; Mark Hussey; Nicholas Hytner; Alison Irvine; William Irvine; Mick Jackson; Blair James; Liza St. James; Lenka Janiurek; Annaleese Jochems; Ioan Marc Jones; Peter Stephan Jungk; Francesca Kay; I. J. Kay; Tobias Kelly; Katharine Kilalea; Ana Kinsella; Katie Kirby; Clement Knox; Sonal Kohli; Laura Kounine; Nakul Krishna; Richard Lambert; James Lasdun; David Lawrence; Paul Lay; Mike Leigh; James Lent; Louise Levene; Rebecca Lewis-Oakes; Nell Leyshon; Maggie Li; Samara Linton; Victor Lodato; Tom Lubbock; Johanna Lukate; Anna Mackmin; Caroline Maclean; Deirdre Madden; Aileen Maguire; Emily St. John Mandel; Adam Mars-Jones; Philip Marsden; Andrew Martin; Anita Mason; Laura Maw; Simon Mawer; Patrick McGinley; Roger McGough; Daisy McNally; James McNicholas; Coco Mellors; Livi Michael; David Miles; Peter Moffat; Sinéad Mooney; Becka Moor; Michelle Morgan; Jan Morris; Ottessa Moshfegh; Sarah Moss; John Mullan; Nicholas Murray; Malik Al Nasir; Anna Neima; Caleb Azumah Nelson; Anthea Nicholson; Trevor Norton; Alissa Nutting; Redmond O'Hanlon; Timothy Ogene; Nat Ogle; David Olusoga; Alice Oswald; Polly Owen; Bobby Palmer; William Palmer; Tim Parks; Ambrose Parry; Ian Pattison; Ruth Pavey; Helen Pike; Joanna Pocock; Jem Poster; Miranda Pountney; Philip Pullman; Issa Quincy; Karina Lickorish Quinn; Julya Rabinowich; Natasha Randall; Victoria Redel; Gemma Reeves; Ruth Rendell; Talulah Riley; Sam Riviere; Michael Symmons Roberts; Michèle Roberts; Laura Robertson; Keith Robinson; Juno Roche; Jane Rogers; Michael Rosen; Olivia Rosenthall; LJ Ross; Alan Rossi; Saumya Roy; Taylor-Dior Rumble; Andy Sagar; Michael Salu; Kate Saunders; Lina Scheynius; Claire Seeber; Jenn Shapland; Jion

Sheibani; Qian Shi; Mika Simmons; Tracey Slaughter; Laura Southgate; Olivia Spring; Alexander Starritt; Wendell Steavenson; Georgina Stevens; Sean Stoker; Alexander Stuart; Jordan Sullivan; Alain Claude Sulzer; David Szalay; George Szirtes; Georgina Terry; Emily Thomas; Barry Timms; Jacqueline Tucker; Kael Tudor; Peter Turnbull; Ryan Turner; Zakia Uddin; Lucy Unwin; Kenechi Uzor; Maddy Vian; James Vincent; Lucia Vinti; Francesca Wade; Lauren Wallach; Stephen Walsh; Natasha Walter; James Walvin; Eva Warrick; Gavin Weightman; Sam White; Derek Wilson; Gaby Wood; Rohullah Yakobi; An Yu; Zinovy Zinik; Tirdad Zolghadr

Literary Agents: Sarah Ballard (**L0060**); Caroline Dawnay (**L0251**); Ariella Feiner (**L0320**); Jim Gill (**L0393**); Jodie Hodges (**L0475**); Robert Kirby (**L0572**); Laura Macdougall (**L0654**); Zoe Ross (**L0863**); Sophie Scard (**L0885**); Rosemary Scoular (**L0897**); Charles Walker (**L1010**); Anna Webber (**L1020**)

L0993 United Talent Agency (UTA)

Literary Agency
888 Seventh Avenue, Seventh Floor, New York, NY 10106
United States
Tel: +1 (212) 659-2600

https://www.unitedtalent.com

Types: Fiction; Nonfiction
Subjects: Business; History; Literary; Science; Science Fiction
Markets: Adult

Send: Query
Don't send: Full text

Multimedia agency representing recording artists, celebrities, and with a literary agency operating out of the New York and London offices. Accepts queries by referral only.

L0994 Jo Unwin

Literary Agent
United Kingdom

Literary Agency: Jo Unwin Literary Agency (**L0526**)

L0995 Upstart Crow Literary

Literary Agency
594 Dean Street, Office 47, Brooklyn, NY 11238
United States

http://www.upstartcrowliterary.com

ADULT
  Fiction > *Novels*
  Nonfiction > *Nonfiction Books*

CHILDREN'S > **Fiction**
  Middle Grade; Novels; Picture Books

YOUNG ADULT > **Fiction** > *Novels*

Send: Query
How to send: Email

Send query by email with 20 pages of your ms, in the body of an email. No attachments or hard copy submissions. See website for more details, and specific agent interests and contact details.

Literary Agents: Danielle Chiotti; Kayla Cichello (**L0199**); Susan Hawk (**L0454**)

L0996 Laura Usselman
Literary Agent
United States

http://skagency.com/agents/laura-usselman/

Literary Agency: Stuart Krichevsky Literary Agency, Inc.

Fiction > *Novels*

Nonfiction > *Nonfiction Books*
General, and in particular: Memoir

Represents adult fiction and nonfiction. Her fiction interests include character-centered fiction of all stripes, from the formally strange to the family saga. For nonfiction, she is interested in thoughtful narrative nonfiction for younger readers, restlessly curious idea books, and voice-driven memoir.

Authors: Katherine Blunt; Victoria Facelli; Sarah Jaffe; Rachel McCarthy James; Madeline Ostrander; Robin Page; Soraya Palmer; David Shih; Sofi Thanhauser; Kaitlyn Tiffany

L0997 Matthew Valentinas
Literary Agent
United States

Literary Agency: Kneerim & Williams (**L0575**)

L0998 Valerie Hoskins Associates
Literary Agency
20 Charlotte Street, London, W1T 2NA
United Kingdom
Tel: +44 (0) 20 7637 4490

info@vhassociates.co.uk

http://www.vhassociates.co.uk

Scripts
Film Scripts; *Radio Scripts*; *TV Scripts*

Send: Query; Self-Addressed Stamped Envelope (SASE)
Don't send: Full text

Small agency extremely limited as to the number of new clients that can be taken on. Allow up to eight weeks for response to submissions.

Literary Agents: Valerie Hoskins (*L0484*); Rebecca Watson (*L1017*)

L0999 Vanessa Holt Ltd
Literary Agency
1422/4 London Road, Leigh On Sea, Essex, SS9 2UL
United Kingdom

v.holt791@btinternet.com

https://find-and-update.company-information. service.gov.uk/company/02391626

Professional Body: The Association of Authors' Agents (AAA)

Fiction > *Novels*

Nonfiction > *Nonfiction Books*

Literary Agent: Vanessa Holt (**L0480**)

L1000 Leslie Varney
Literary Agent; President
United States

Literary Agency: Prentis Literary (**L0814**)

L1001 Sarah Veecock
Literary Agent
United Kingdom

Literary Agency: The Narrow Road Company (**L0743**)

L1002 Veritas Literary Agency
Literary Agency
601 Van Ness Avenue, Opera Plaza Suite E, San Francisco, CA 94102
United States

submissions@veritasliterary.com

http://www.veritasliterary.com
https://www.twitter.com/verlit

Professional Body: Association of American Literary Agents (AALA)

ADULT
Fiction > *Novels*
Commercial; Fantasy; Historical Fiction; Speculative; Women's Fiction

Nonfiction > *Nonfiction Books*
Biography; Cultural History; History; Memoir; Narrative Nonfiction; Nature; Popular Culture; Popular Science; Women's Studies

CHILDREN'S > **Fiction** > *Middle Grade*

YOUNG ADULT > **Fiction** > *Novels*

Send: Query; Writing sample
How to send: In the body of an email
How not to send: Post

Send query or proposal by email only. Submit further information on request only. For fiction, include cover letter listing previously published work, one-page summary and first five pages. For nonfiction, include author bio, overview, chapter-by-chapter summary, sample chapters or text, and analysis of competing titles.

Literary Agents: Katherine Boyle (**L0116**); Michael Carr (**L0167**)

Literary Scout: Chiara Rosati

L1003 Gilly Vincent
Literary Agent
United Kingdom

Literary Agency: Chapman & Vincent (**L0186**)

L1004 The Vines Agency, Inc.
Literary Agency
320 7th Avenue, Suite 178, Brooklyn, NY 11215
United States
Tel: +1 (212) 777-5522
Fax: +1 (718) 228-4536

http://www.vinesagency.com

Professional Bodies: The Authors Guild; Writers Guild of America (WGA)

Fiction > *Novels*
Commercial; Historical Fiction; Literary; Mystery; Science Fiction

Nonfiction > *Nonfiction Books*: Commercial
Closed to approaches.

This agency is closed to new clients and is no longer accepting query letters or submissions.

Authors: Laura Doyle; Shawne Johnson; Bernice McFadden; Christine Moriarty; Don Winslow; Moon Unit Zappa

Literary Agent: James C. Vines (*L1005*)

L1005 James C. Vines
Literary Agent
United States

Literary Agency: The Vines Agency, Inc. (**L1004**)

L1006 The Viney Agency
Literary Agency
21, Dartmouth Park Ave, London, NW5 IJL
United Kingdom

charlie@thevineyagency.com

http://thevineyagency.com

Professional Body: The Association of Authors' Agents (AAA)

ADULT
Fiction > *Novels*

Nonfiction > *Nonfiction Books*
Biography; History; Journalism

CHILDREN'S > **Fiction** > *Novels*

Send: Query
Don't send: Full text
How not to send: Email

Handles high quality nonfiction, and adult and children's fiction. See website for examples of the kinds of books represented. Send query by first or second class post.

Literary Agent: Charlie Viney (*L1007*)

L1007 Charlie Viney
Literary Agent
United Kingdom

Literary Agency: The Viney Agency (**L1006**)

L1008 Sandy Violette
Literary Agent
United Kingdom

sandy@abnerstein.co.uk

Literary Agency: Abner Stein (**L0005**)

L1009 Tina Wainscott
Literary Agent
United States

Literary Agency: The Seymour Agency
(**L0902**)

L1010 Charles Walker
Literary Agent
United Kingdom
Tel: +44 (0) 20 3214 0874

cwalker@unitedagents.co.uk

https://www.unitedagents.co.uk/
cwalkerunitedagentscouk

Literary Agency: United Agents (**L0992**)

Fiction > *Novels*
  Crime; Historical Fiction; Literary; Science
  Fiction

Nonfiction > *Nonfiction Books*
  History; Memoir

Send: Query; Synopsis; Writing sample
How to send: Email

In nonfiction deals mainly in history and
memoir. In fiction, leans toward literary
fiction, although it can contain historical and
crime and very occasionally sci-fi. Send query
by email to assistant.

Agency Assistant: Olivia Martin

Authors: Adam Baker; Alan Bennett; Wendy
Cope; Dan Cruickshank; Paddy Docherty;
Douglas Dunn; Chris England; Sue Glover;
Robert Hardman; David Harsent; Colin Heber-
Percy; Mark Hussey; Richard Lambert; David
Lawrence; Paul Lay; Mike Leigh; Anita
Mason; Simon Mawer; Patrick McGinley;
Roger McGough; Livi Michael; Peter Moffat;
Nicholas Murray; Malik Al Nasir; Redmond
O'Hanlon; David Olusoga; William Palmer;
Ruth Rendell; Michèle Roberts; Jane Rogers;
Michael Rosen; Alexander Stuart; Peter
Turnbull; James Walvin; Gavin Weightman;
Derek Wilson

L1011 The Wallace Literary Agency
Literary Agency
United States

contact@wallaceliteraryagency.com

http://www.wallaceliteraryagency.com

Literary Agencies: Robin Straus Agency, Inc.;
Andrew Nurnberg Associates, Ltd (**L0035**)

L1012 Clare Wallace
Literary Agent
United Kingdom

https://www.darleyandersonchildrens.com/
about-us
https://twitter.com/LitAgentClare

Literary Agencies: The Darley Anderson
Agency; Darley Anderson Children's (**L0243**)

ADULT > **Fiction** > *Novels*: Commercial
Women's Fiction

CHILDREN'S > **Fiction**
  Middle Grade; *Picture Books*
TEEN > **Fiction** > *Novels*

YOUNG ADULT > **Fiction** > *Novels*

Scouting for new authors of picture books,
middle grade, teenage, YA and illustrators.
Also represents a boutique list of commercial
and accessible literary women's fiction but is
closed to new submissions.

Assistant Agent: Chloe Davis (**L0249**)

Authors: Honor Cargill-Martin; Sophie
Cousens; Tom Ellen; Kerry Fisher; Martyn
Ford; Polly Ho-Yen; Phaedra Patrick; Beth
Reekles; Pat Sowa; Deirdre Sullivan;
Samantha Tonge

L1013 Kate Walsh
Associate Agent
United Kingdom
Tel: +44 (0) 20 3214 0884

kwalsh@unitedagents.co.uk

https://www.unitedagents.co.uk/
kwalshunitedagentscouk

Literary Agency: United Agents (**L0992**)
Literary Agent: Robert Kirby (**L0572**)

Fiction > *Novels*

Nonfiction > *Nonfiction Books*
  Commercial; Current Affairs; Politics

Send: Query; Synopsis; Writing sample
How to send: Email

Actively building her list. She's on the lookout
mainly for commercial non-fiction, particularly
with a political or current affairs slant, and
anything that feels like a fresh and original
way of looking at the world. She is especially
drawn to 20th and 21st century affairs, and
anyone willing to speculate on what comes
next. Whilst working mainly with non-fiction,
she is always excited to read anything, fiction
or non-, with a strong and transporting sense of
place and time.

Authors: Will Hayward; Rohullah Yakobi

L1014 Nick Walters
Literary Agent
United Kingdom

nick@davidluxtonassociates.co.uk

https://www.davidluxtonassociates.co.uk/the-
agency/

Literary Agency: David Luxton Associates
(**L0246**)

Nonfiction > *Nonfiction Books*
  Commercial; Leadership; Lifestyle; Self
  Help; Sport

Send: Synopsis; Writing sample; Author bio
How to send: Email

Agent and Rights Manager. Principle interests
are in the fields of sport, true crime, current
affairs, lifestyle and self-help.

L1015 Mitchell Waters
Literary Agent
United States

mwaters@bromasite.com

https://brandthochman.com/agents
http://aaronline.org/Sys/PublicProfile/1681270/
417813

Literary Agency: Brandt & Hochman Literary
Agents, Inc. (**L0119**)
Professional Body: Association of American
Literary Agents (AALA)

ADULT
  Fiction > *Novels*
    Comedy / Humour; Commercial; Historical
    Fiction; Literary; Mystery

  Nonfiction > *Nonfiction Books*
    Biography; History; Memoir

YOUNG
ADULT > **Fiction** > *Novels*: Realistic

How to send: Email

L1016 Mackenzie Brady Watson
Literary Agent
United States

mbwquery@skagency.com

http://skagency.com/agents/mackenzie-brady-
watson/

Literary Agency: Stuart Krichevsky Literary
Agency, Inc.

ADULT > **Nonfiction** > *Nonfiction Books*
  Business; Food; Investigative Journalism;
  Memoir; Narrative Nonfiction; Science;
  Sociology

YOUNG ADULT > **Fiction** > *Novels*

Focuses on narrative non-fiction for all ages
and select Young Adult fiction. As a former
genetics lab technician, she has a great passion
for science books, especially if they are
historically driven or revolutionize current

theory, as well as sociology, investigative journalism, food writing, memoir, and business books. She particularly appreciates work that sheds light on marginalized experiences and helps contribute to the cultural conversation.

Authors: Roxanna Asgarian; Ahmed Badr; Lyndsie Bourgon; Hannah Brencher; Caren Cooper; Hope Ewing; Kathryn Finney; Kit Fox; Katie Fricas; Olivia Gatwood; Jessica Goudeau; Rose Hackman; Anita Hannig; Sarah Jaffe; R. Dean Johnson; Sophie Lucido Johnson; Megan Kimble; Audrea Lim; Catherine Lo; Michael Loynd; Jennifer Lunden; P.E. Moskowitz; José Olivarez; Karen Pinchin; Shelley Puhak; Lydia Reeder; Victoria Reihana; Margot Lee Shetterly; Brie Spangler; Rachel Swaby; Sarah Vogel; Kimberley Welman; Christina Wilcox; Nina Willner; Bernice Yeung; Sara Zin

L1017 Rebecca Watson

Literary Agent
United Kingdom

Literary Agency: Valerie Hoskins Associates (**L0998**)

L1018 Jessica Watterson

Literary Agent
United States

https://www.dijkstraagency.com/agent-page.php?agent_id=Watterson
https://querymanager.com/query/jessicawatterson

Literary Agency: Sandra Dijkstra Literary Agency

ADULT > Fiction > *Novels*
Cozy Mysteries; Romance; Women's Fiction

CHILDREN'S
Fiction > *Picture Books*

Nonfiction > *Nonfiction Books*: Popular Culture

YOUNG ADULT > Fiction > *Novels*
Contemporary; Romance

Closed to approaches.

Most interested in all genres of romance. Also loves women's fiction and is open to select Cozy Mysteries. In Young Adult, will consider just about anything in the contemporary sphere, particularly with some romance. Will also consider author-illustrated books and nonfiction on Pop Culture by authors who have established platforms.

L1019 Hannah Weatherill

Literary Agent
United Kingdom

Literary Agency: Northbank Talent Management (**L0756**)

L1020 Anna Webber

Literary Agent
United Kingdom
Tel: +44 (0) 20 3214 0876

awebber@unitedagents.co.uk

https://www.unitedagents.co.uk/awebberunitedagentscouk
https://twitter.com/aeewebber

Literary Agency: United Agents (**L0992**)

Fiction > *Novels*

Nonfiction > *Nonfiction Books*: Literary

Poetry > *Any Poetic Form*

Send: Synopsis; Writing sample; Proposal

Represents both fiction and non-fiction, with a special focus on literary fiction and voice-driven non-fiction. She is open for submissions, but can only take on a small number of new clients per year.

Associate Agent: Seren Adams (**L0012**)

Authors: Laura Albert; Rosie Alison; Nina Allan; Karin Altenberg; Jessica Anthony; Deborah Bee; Mark Blacklock; Stefan Merrill Block; Ezekiel Boone; Melitta Breznik; Molly Brodak; Sylvia Brownrigg; John Burnside; Robin Carhart-Harris; Carl Cattermole; Roland Chambers; Emma Cline; Amanda Coe; Marion Coutts; Rosie Dastgir; Carys Davies; Tim Dee; Miranda Doyle; Dennis Duncan; Elanor Dymott; Ben Eastham; Christy Edwall; Hermione Eyre; James Fenton; Toby Ferris; William Fowler; Rivka Galchen; William Ghosh; Rebecca Gowers; Samantha Harvey; Sheila Heti; Ben Hinshaw; Michael Hofmann; Joseph Hone; Caoilinn Hughes; Nicholas Hytner; William Irvine; Mick Jackson; Peter Stephan Jungk; Francesca Kay; I. J. Kay; Katharine Kilalea; James Lasdun; Louise Levene; Nell Leyshon; Victor Lodato; Tom Lubbock; Anna Mackmin; Caroline Maclean; Deirdre Madden; Emily St. John Mandel; Adam Mars-Jones; Philip Marsden; Andrew Martin; Daisy McNally; Ottessa Moshfegh; Sarah Moss; John Mullan; Anthea Nicholson; Trevor Norton; Alissa Nutting; Nat Ogle; Alice Oswald; Tim Parks; Ian Pattison; Helen Pike; Miranda Pountney; Julya Rabinowich; Natasha Randall; Victoria Redel; Sam Riviere; Michael Symmons Roberts; Jenn Shapland; Alexander Starritt; Wendell Steavenson; Alain Claude Sulzer; David Szalay; George Szirtes; Natasha Walter; Gaby Wood; An Yu; Zinovy Zinik; Tirdad Zolghadr

L1021 Elisabeth Weed

Literary Agent
United States

Literary Agency: The Book Group (**L0109**)

L1022 Frank Weimann

Literary Agent; Partner
United States
Tel: +1 (212) 400-1494

fweimann@foliolit.com

https://www.publishersmarketplace.com/members/weimann/

Literary Agency: Folio Literary Management, LLC (**L0343**)

Nonfiction > *Nonfiction Books*
General, and in particular: African American; Biography; Business; CIA; Celebrity; Comedy / Humour; Finance; Health; History; Mafia; Memoir; Military; Narrative Nonfiction; Pets; Prescriptive Nonfiction; Religion; Science; Special Forces; Sport

Send: Query; Writing sample
How to send: In the body of an email

Authors: Kareem Abdul-Jabbar; Dan Abrams; Gregg Allman; George Anastasia; Mario Andretti; Michael Baden; Joe Bonanno; Terry Bradshaw; Charles Brandt; John "Chick" Donohue; John Douglas; Tamer Elnoury; Rickson Gracie; John Gray; Homer Hickam; Harry Markopolos; Kevin Maurer; Maria Menounos; Mark Olshaker; Joe Pistone; Laura Prepon; Bill Russell

L1023 Alexandra Weiss

Associate Agent
United States

http://www.azantianlitagency.com/pages/team-awe.html
https://querymanager.com/query/AlexandraWeiss

Literary Agency: Azantian Literary Agency (**L0054**)

ADULT > Nonfiction
Gift Books: General
Nonfiction Books: Environment; Mental Health; Science; Space
CHILDREN'S
Fiction
Graphic Novels; *Picture Books*
Nonfiction
Chapter Books: General
Middle Grade: Adventure; Contemporary; Magic; Science Fiction; Time Travel
Picture Books: General

YOUNG ADULT > Fiction
Graphic Novels: General
Novels: Coming of Age; Contemporary; Folklore, Myths, and Legends; Low Fantasy; Magical Realism; Romantic Comedy; Soft Science Fiction

Closed to approaches.

Represents fiction and nonfiction picture books, middle grade, young adult, graphic novels, and select adult nonfiction.

L1024 Karmen Wells

Associate Agent
Canada

karmen@therightsfactory.com

https://www.therightsfactory.com/Agents/
Karmen-Wells
https://twitter.com/KarmenEdits

Literary Agency: The Rights Factory

Fiction > *Novels*
  Comedy / Humour; Coming of Age;
  Commercial; Drama; Dystopian Fiction;
  High Concept; Horror; LGBTQIA; Literary;
  Popular Culture; Science Fiction

Nonfiction > *Nonfiction Books*: Narrative
Nonfiction

Send: Query; Pitch; Author bio; Writing
sample
How to send: Email

Looking for published or to-be-published
books to represent to producers for film or TV
adaptation.

Authors: Daniel Barnett; Kelly Florence;
Rhonda J. Garcia; Jessica Guess; Meg Hafdahl;
Tim Meyer; Hailey Piper

L1025 Jennifer Weltz

Literary Agent
United States

Literary Agency: The Jean V. Naggar Literary
Agency (**L0519**)

L1026 Wendy Schmalz Agency

Literary Agency
402 Union St. #831, Hudson, NY 12534
United States

wendy@schmalzagency.com

http://www.schmalzagency.com

CHILDREN'S
  Fiction > *Middle Grade*
  Nonfiction > *Middle Grade*

YOUNG ADULT
  Fiction > *Novels*
  Nonfiction > *Nonfiction Books*

Send: Query; Synopsis
Don't send: Full text; Writing sample
How to send: Email

Handles books for middle grade and young
adults. No science fiction, fantasy, or picture
books. Send query by email. No unsolicited
mss or sample chapters. If no response after
two weeks, assume no interest.

Literary Agent: Wendy Schmalz (*L0888*)

L1027 Katherine Wessbecher

Literary Agent
United States

https://bradfordlit.com/about/katherine-
wessbecher/
https://twitter.com/KatWessbecher

Literary Agency: Bradford Literary Agency
(**L0117**)

ADULT
  Fiction > *Novels*
    Commercial; Literary; Upmarket

  Nonfiction
    Graphic Nonfiction: General
    Nonfiction Books: Narrative Nonfiction

CHILDREN'S
  Fiction
    Middle Grade: Epistolary; Fantasy;
    Historical Fiction
    Picture Books: General

  Nonfiction
    Graphic Nonfiction: General
    Nonfiction Books: Narrative Nonfiction

YOUNG ADULT
  Fiction > *Novels*
    Epistolary; Fantasy; Historical Fiction

  Nonfiction
    Graphic Nonfiction: General
    Nonfiction Books: Narrative Nonfiction

Does not want:

Fiction > *Novels*
  High / Epic Fantasy; Romance;
  Science Fiction; Thrillers

Nonfiction > *Nonfiction Books*
  Business; Memoir

Poetry > *Any Poetic Form*

Scripts
  Film Scripts; *TV Scripts*

Closed to approaches.

Looking for children's books (picture books
through YA), upmarket adult fiction, and
narrative nonfiction for all ages.

L1028 Kate Weston

Literary Agent
United Kingdom

Literary Agency: Fillingham Weston
Associates (**L0330**)

L1029 Maria Whelan

Literary Agent
United States

http://www.inkwellmanagement.com/staff/
maria-whelan

Literary Agency: InkWell Management
(**L0499**)

Fiction > *Novels*
  Comedy / Humour; Literary; Magical
  Realism; Upmarket Women's Fiction

Nonfiction > *Nonfiction Books*

  General, and in particular: Society

Send: Query; Writing sample
How to send: In the body of an email

Enjoys literary fiction, magical realism,
upmarket women's fiction and humor, as well
as non-fiction, revolving around peculiar topics
especially overlooked facets of society.

L1030 Whimsy Literary Agency, LLC

Literary Agency
49 North 8th Street, 6G, Brooklyn, NY 11249
United States
Tel: +1 (212) 674-7162

whimsynyc@aol.com

http://whimsyliteraryagency.com

Types: Nonfiction
Subjects: Arts; Autobiography; Business;
Comedy / Humour; Cookery; Current Affairs;
Design; Finance; Health; History; How To;
Lifestyle; Literature; New Age; Personal
Development; Photography; Psychology;
Technology; Women's Interests
Markets: Adult

Send: Query
Don't send: Full text

No unsolicited mss. Send query in first
instance. Response only if interested.

Literary Agent: Jackie Meyer (*L0700*)

L1031 Melissa White

Literary Agent
United States

melissa@foliolit.com

https://www.publishersmarketplace.com/
members/sarverm/

Literary Agency: Folio Literary Management,
LLC (**L0343**)

ADULT
  Fiction > *Novels*

  Nonfiction > *Nonfiction Books*
    Business; Cookery; Health; Memoir;
    Narrative Nonfiction; Parenting; Wellbeing

CHILDREN'S > **Fiction**
  Chapter Books: Contemporary
  Middle Grade: Contemporary

YOUNG ADULT > **Fiction** > *Novels*
  Contemporary; Fantasy; Historical Fiction;
  Magical Realism; Science Fiction; Thrillers

Does not want:

CHILDREN'S > **Fiction** > *Middle
Grade*: Adventure

Closed to approaches.

L1032 Araminta Whitley
Literary Agent; Company Director
United Kingdom

Literary Agency: The Soho Agency (**L0924**)

L1033 Peregrine Whittlesey
Literary Agent
United States

Literary Agency: Peregrine Whittlesey Agency (**L0785**)

L1034 Alice Whitwham
Literary Agent
United States

Literary Agency: The Cheney Agency (**L0190**)

L1035 Gary Wild
Literary Agent
United Kingdom

Literary Agency: JFL Agency (**L0524**)

L1036 Alice Williams
Literary Agent
United Kingdom

alice@alicewilliamsliterary.co.uk

https://twitter.com/alicelovesbooks

Literary Agency: Alice Williams Literary (**L0025**)

L1037 Anne Williams
Literary Agent
United Kingdom

Literary Agency: Kate Hordern Literary Agency (**L0554**)

L1038 Ike Williams
Literary Agent
United States

Literary Agency: Kneerim & Williams (**L0575**)

Closed to approaches.

L1039 Laura Williams
Literary Agent
United Kingdom

lwilliams@greeneheaton.co.uk

http://greeneheaton.co.uk/agents/laura-williams/
https://twitter.com/laurabirdland

Literary Agency: Greene & Heaton Ltd (**L0419**)

ADULT > **Fiction** > *Novels*
Commercial; Ghost Stories; Gothic; Horror; Literary; Psychological Thrillers

YOUNG ADULT
Fiction > *Novels*
Contemporary; High Concept

Nonfiction > *Nonfiction Books*: Narrative Nonfiction

Authors: Eve Ainsworth; Catherine Barter; Anna Day; Sue Divin; Helen Dring; Maggy Van Eijk; Zoe Feeney; Gabrielle Fernie; Louise Finnigan; Sarah Goodwin; Oliver Grant; Molly Greeley; Maria Hummer; Jem Lester; Claire McGlasson; Gemma Milne; Barney Norris; Nina De Pass; Richard Roper; Zuzana Ruzickova; Nancy Springer; John Sutherland; Alyssa Warren; Gill Wyness; Bella Younger

L1040 Sarah Williams
Literary Agent
United Kingdom

Literary Agency: Independent Talent Group Ltd (**L0496**)

L1041 Victoria Williams
Literary Agent
United Kingdom

Literary Agency: Alan Brodie Representation Ltd (**L0022**)

L1042 Jo Williamson
Literary Agent
United Kingdom

jo@antonyharwood.com

http://antonyharwood.com/jo-williamson/

Literary Agency: Antony Harwood Limited (**L0042**)

CHILDREN'S > **Fiction**
Middle Grade: Adventure
Picture Books: General

YOUNG ADULT > **Fiction** > *Novels*

L1043 Kathryn Willms
Associate Agent
Canada

kathryn@therightsfactory.com

https://www.therightsfactory.com/Agents/Kathryn-Willms
https://querymanager.com/query/2039

Literary Agency: The Rights Factory

Nonfiction > *Nonfiction Books*
Environment; Food and Drink; Nature; Social Justice; Sport

Closed to approaches.

Currently focused on building her non-fiction list in sports, social justice, nature/environmental topics, and food and drink. However, as a generalist who simply likes "good books," she's open to a variety of genres. She is passionate about bringing ambitious, unconventional, and joyous books into the world, would rather laugh than cry, and is ultimately a sucker for a good story compellingly told.

Authors: Lynda Calvert; Meghan Chayka; Alyssa Huizing; Lisa Brahin Weinblatt

L1044 Jennifer Wills
Literary Agent
United States

Literary Agency: The Seymour Agency (**L0902**)
Professional Body: Association of American Literary Agents (AALA)

L1045 Desiree Wilson
Literary Agent
United States

http://www.thebentagency.com/desiree-wilson
https://twitter.com/swindlesoiree

Literary Agency: The Bent Agency (**L0090**)

Fiction
Graphic Novels: General
Novels: Contemporary; Fantasy; Horror; Science Fiction; Speculative
Short Fiction: General

Nonfiction > *Nonfiction Books*: Narrative Nonfiction

Closed to approaches.

I am currently looking for middle-grade, young adult, and adult horror novels; narrative memoirs, especially from BIPOC communities; lush, dark, speculative science fiction and fantasy for young adult and adult readers; YA fantasy, especially adaptations of non-Western folklore and mythos, or interpretations of Western folklore/mythos centering nontraditional protagonists; and short story collections of LGBTQ+ fiction. I am also accepting graphic novel pitches that fall within the above genres, as well as graphic narratives meant to teach complex skills and/or practical information.

L1046 Ed Wilson
Literary Agent
United Kingdom
Tel: +44 (0) 20 7251 0125

ed@johnsonandalcock.co.uk

http://www.johnsonandalcock.co.uk/ed-wilson
https://twitter.com/literarywhore

Literary Agency: Johnson & Alcock (**L0528**)

ADULT
Fiction
Graphic Novels: General
Novels: Commercial; Crime; Experimental; Fantasy; High Concept; Literary; Science Fiction; Speculative; Thrillers
Nonfiction > *Nonfiction Books*
History; Nature; Politics; Popular Culture; Sport

YOUNG ADULT > **Fiction** > *Novels*

Send: Query; Synopsis; Writing sample
How to send: Email attachment

With a background studying postmodern American literature he doesn't fear the experimental, speculative, and downright weird. He is actively building a SFF list and is always on the lookout for books that transcend genre. He's open to all forms of high concept writing, intelligent crime and thrillers. He represents some YA, but only books at the older end, and with crossover potential to an adult market.

His non-fiction tastes cover a wide range: from politics and serious history, to sport, natural history and popular culture. He loves intelligent and original graphic novels and infographics, and anything quirky. He is not currently taking on any children's authors and does not represent poetry or scripts.

L1047 Rebecca Winfield
Literary Agent
United Kingdom

https://www.davidluxtonassociates.co.uk/the-agency/

Literary Agency: David Luxton Associates (**L0246**)

Nonfiction
  Nonfiction Books: History; Memoir; Travel
  Reference: Popular Reference

Send: Synopsis; Writing sample; Author bio
How to send: Email
How not to send: Post

L1048 Gordon Wise
Literary Agent
United Kingdom

Literary Agency: Curtis Brown (**L0233**)

L1049 Caryn Wiseman
Executive Agent
United States

https://www.andreabrownlit.com/agents.html
https://querymanager.com/query/CarynWiseman
https://www.facebook.com/caryn.wiseman
https://twitter.com/CarynWiseman

Literary Agency: Andrea Brown Literary Agency, Inc.

CHILDREN'S
  Fiction
    Chapter Books: General, and in particular: Diversity; Social Justice
    Graphic Novels: General, and in particular: Diversity; Social Justice
    Middle Grade: General, and in particular: Diversity; Social Justice
    Picture Books: General, and in particular: Diversity; Social Justice
  Nonfiction
    Nonfiction Books: General, and in particular: Diversity; Social Justice

Picture Books: General, and in particular: Biography; Diversity; Social Justice
YOUNG ADULT
  Fiction > *Novels*
    General, and in particular: Diversity; Romance; Social Justice

  Nonfiction > *Nonfiction Books*
    General, and in particular: Diversity; Social Justice

Send: Author bio; Query; Writing sample; Pitch; Market info
How to send: Query Manager

Drawn to contemporary YA and middle grade with a strong voice, multifaceted characters, complex relationships, beautiful writing, and a well-developed hook. Great world-building is essential, whether it's a real time and place that becomes almost a character in a book, or a light fantasy element in a unique story that's grounded in reality. Zombies, horror, and high fantasy will, most likely, never appeal. She is particularly interested in books for children and teens that explore themes of diversity and social justice. She would be thrilled to see more books by underrepresented authors that deeply explore their culture, as well as books in which the ethnicity of the character is not the issue. She adores a swoon-worthy, layered romance; a funny or poignant middle grade novel with a hook that makes it stand out from the crowd would hold great appeal; and she's partial to lyrical, non-institutional picture book biographies and character-driven, not-too-sweet picture book fiction, particularly by author-illustrators.

L1050 Tom Witcomb
Literary Agent
United Kingdom

Literary Agency: Blake Friedmann Literary Agency Ltd (**L0101**)

L1051 Jenny Witherell
Literary Agent
United States

Literary Agency: InkWell Management (**L0499**)

L1052 Kimberly Witherspoon
Literary Agent
United States

Literary Agency: InkWell Management (**L0499**)

L1053 Caroline de Wolfe
Literary Agent
United Kingdom

Literary Agency: Felix de Wolfe (**L0326**)

L1054 Jade Wong-Baxter
Associate Agent
United States

jwb@goldinlit.com

https://goldinlit.com/contact/

Literary Agency: Frances Goldin Literary Agency, Inc. (**L0356**)

Fiction > *Novels*
  Literary; Magical Realism; Upmarket

Nonfiction > *Nonfiction Books*
  Cultural Criticism; History; Memoir; Narrative Nonfiction; Popular Culture

Send: Query; Writing sample
How to send: Email

L1055 Bryony Woods
Literary Agent
United Kingdom

http://dkwlitagency.co.uk/agents/
https://twitter.com/BryonyWoods

Literary Agency: Diamond Kahn and Woods (DKW) Literary Agency Ltd (**L0265**)

Closed to approaches.

L1056 Writers' Representatives, LLC
Literary Agency
116 W. 14th St., 11th Fl., New York, NY 10011-7305
United States
Tel: +1 (212) 620-0023
Fax: +1 (212) 620-0023

transom@writersreps.com

http://www.writersreps.com

Types: Fiction; Nonfiction; Poetry
Formats: Reference
Subjects: Autobiography; Business; Comedy / Humour; Cookery; Current Affairs; Finance; History; Legal; Literary; Literary Criticism; Mystery; Personal Development; Philosophy; Politics; Science; Thrillers
Markets: Adult

Send: Full text
How to send: Email

Costs: Author covers sundry admin costs.

Send email describing your project and yourself, or send proposal, outline, CV, and sample chapters, or complete unsolicited MS, with SASE. See website for submission requirements in FAQ section. Specialises in serious and literary fiction and nonfiction. No screenplays. No science fiction or children's or young adult fiction unless it aspires to serious literature.

L1057 Joanne Wyckoff
Literary Agent
United States

joanne@carolmannagency.com

https://www.carolmannagency.com/joanne-wyckoff

Literary Agency: Carol Mann Agency (**L0161**)

Nonfiction > *Nonfiction Books*
General, and in particular: African American Issues; Animals; Comedy / Humour; Culture; Education; Food; Health; History; Memoir; Narrative Journalism; Narrative Nonfiction; Nature; Psychology; Religion; Science; Spirituality; Sport; Wellbeing; Women's Issues

Send: Query
How to send: Email

Represents a wide array of nonfiction. Has vast experience working with academics and experts in diverse fields, helping them develop and write books for a broad market. She also has a particular love of the memoir, narrative nonfiction, the personal narrative, and narrative journalism. She is always looking for writers with strong, original voices who explore a subject in new and surprising ways. Her list includes books in psychology, women's issues, history, education, science, health and wellness, sports, humour, food and culture, natural history and anything about animals, religion and spirituality, and African American issues.

L1058 Tara Wynne
Literary Agent
Australia

Literary Agency: Curtis Brown (Australia) Pty Ltd (**L0234**)

L1059 Susan Yearwood
Literary Agent
United Kingdom

submissions@susanyearwoodagency.com

https://susanyearwoodagency.com

Literary Agency: SYLA – Susan Yearwood Literary Agency (**L0964**)

ADULT
 Fiction > *Novels*
 Book Club Fiction; Commercial; Crime; Romance; Saga; Thrillers

 Nonfiction > *Nonfiction Books*
 General, and in particular: Business; Cookery; Finance; Lifestyle; Self Help; Wellbeing

CHILDREN'S > **Fiction** > *Middle Grade*

TEEN > **Fiction** > *Novels*

YOUNG ADULT > **Fiction** > *Novels*

Send: Query; Author bio; Writing sample; Synopsis
How to send: Email attachment

Looks for book club fiction, commercial fiction including romance and saga, genre fiction i.e. crime/thriller, children's aged 9+ and teen/young adult novels as well as non-fiction, particularly business and finance, self-help and well-being, and lifestyle, including cookery.

Authors: Catherine Balavage; Lucy Basey; Angela Cairns; Fran Clark; Sarah Dobbs; Selina Flavius; Kimberley Glover; Liz Kolbeck; Prajwal Parajuly; Susan Quirke; Sarupa Shah; Jacqueline Shaw; Suzanne Snow; Sarah Stephenson; Kerry Young

L1060 Laura Yorke
Literary Agent
United States

https://www.carolmannagency.com/laura-yorke

Literary Agency: Carol Mann Agency (**L0161**)

L1061 Claudia Young
Literary Agent
United Kingdom

http://greeneheaton.co.uk/agents/claudia-young/
https://twitter.com/ClaudiaL_Young

Literary Agency: Greene & Heaton Ltd (**L0419**)

Fiction > *Novels*
 Contemporary; Crime; Historical Fiction; Literary; Thrillers

Nonfiction > *Nonfiction Books*
 Comedy / Humour; Cookery; Food Journalism; Travel

Closed to approaches.

Currently on maternity leave as at May 2020.

Authors: Sam Akbar; Anthony Anaxagorou; Ros Atkinson; Jordan Bourke; Aine Carlin; Matt Chapple; Martha Collison; Jack Cooke; Kevan Davis; Kim Duke; Ella Frears; Francis Gimblett; Lewis Goodall; Peter Harper; Alice Hart; Wayne Holloway-Smith; Lizzie King; Vanessa King; Jenny Lee; Eleanor Maidment; Janina Matthewson; Val Payne; Alice Procter; Rejina Pyo; James Ramsden; Rosie Ramsden; Charlie Ryrie; Kat Sadler; Viviane Schwarz; Tim Sebastian; Dale Shaw; Rachel de Thample; Regina Wong

L1062 Cyle Young
Literary Agent; Author
United States

cyle@hartlineliterary.com
submissions@cyleyoung.com

https://cyleyoung.com
http://hartlineagency.com/agentsandauthors/
https://www.facebook.com/cyleyoung

Literary Agencies: Hartline Literary Agency (**L0451**); Cyle Young Literary Elite (**L0236**)

ADULT

Fiction > *Novels*
 Amish Romance; Christianity; Fantasy; Romance; Science Fiction; Speculative

Nonfiction > *Nonfiction Books*
 Christianity; Leadership; Parenting; Self Help

Scripts
 Film Scripts; *TV Scripts*

CHILDREN'S > **Fiction**
 Chapter Books; *Early Readers*; *Middle Grade*; *Picture Books*

YOUNG ADULT > **Fiction** > *Novels*

How to send: Conferences; Online pitch events
How not to send: Email

Represents work in both the General and Christian markets.

Author / Junior Agent: Del Duduit (**L0282**)

Authors: Dreama Archibald; Starr Ayers; Deborah Bailey; Marie E. Bast; Del Bates; Don Best; Lisa E. Betz; Cherrilynn Bisbano; Adam Blumer; Catherine Brakefield; Clare Campbell; George Cargill; Andy Clapp; Ray Comfort; Karen Condit; Elaine Marie Cooper; Jacy Corral; Shelley Cummings; Robin Currie; Callie Daruk; Bryan Davis; Melody Delgado; Rene Dick; Joyce K. Ellis; Diana Estell; Ryan Farr; C. Hope Flinchbaugh; Jennifer Froelich; Mary Gardner; Carla Gasser; Darlo Gemeinhardt; Annette Griffin; P.K. Hallinan; Jennifer Hallmark; Ruth Hartman; Cindy Huff; Carlton Hughes; Nancy L. Hull; Pauline Hylton; Kathy Ide; Ashley Kirby Jones; Jeff Jones; Stephanie Kehr; Marcie Keithley; Lisa Kibler; Victoria Kimble; Cary Knox; D.L. Koontz; Julie Lavender; Sarah Limardo; Beckie Lindsey; Jan Lis; Robin Luftig; Jayme Mansfield; Lori Marett; Jann Martin; Jake McCandless; Britt Mooney; Kay Mortimer; Susan Neal; Shelley Pierce; Dana Romanin; Andrew Roth; Patty Schell; Nicole Schrader; Olivia Schwab; Tim Shoemaker; Susan Holt Simpson; Donna L. H. Smith; John Snyder; Debbie Sprinkle; Kendra Stanton-Lee; Bruce A. Stewart; Cecil Stokes; Melissa Stroh; Janet Surette; Rachel Swanson; Elaine Tomski; John Turney; Bill Watkins; Molly White; Y.K. Willemse; Jean Wilund; Jean Wise

L1063 Hugo Young
Literary Agent
United Kingdom

Literary Agency: Independent Talent Group Ltd (**L0496**)

L1064 Lane Zachary
Literary Agent
United States

lane@mmqlit.com

http://www.mmqlit.com/about/
http://www.mmqlit.com/contact/

Literary Agency: Massie & McQuilkin (**L0680**)

Fiction > *Novels*

Nonfiction > *Nonfiction Books*

Send: Query
How to send: Email

Looking for books of nonfiction and fiction that are beautifully crafted and have the capacity to change the way in which we see and live in the world. Response only if interested. If no response within 6 weeks, assume rejection.

L1065 Marietta B. Zacker
Literary Agent
United States

marietta@galltzacker.com
querymarietta@galltzacker.com

https://www.galltzacker.com/submissions.html
https://querymanager.com/query/querymarietta

Literary Agency: Gallt & Zacker Literary Agency (**L0375**)

CHILDREN'S > **Fiction**
  Middle Grade; *Picture Books*
YOUNG ADULT
  Fiction
    Graphic Novels; *Novels*
  Nonfiction > *Nonfiction Books*

How to send: Query Manager; Email

Currently only accepting queries from illustrators and author/illustrators.

L1066 Leslie Zampetti
Literary Agent
United States

https://www.dunhamlit.com/leslie-zampetti.html
http://aaronline.org/Sys/PublicProfile/46970641/417813
https://twitter.com/leslie_zampetti
https://www.facebook.com/AgentLeslieZampetti/
https://www.instagram.com/literarylesliez/

Literary Agency: Dunham Literary, Inc. (**L0283**)
Professional Bodies: Association of American Literary Agents (AALA); Society of Children's Book Writers and Illustrators (SCBWI)

ADULT
  Fiction > *Novels*
    Historical Fiction; Literary Mystery; Upmarket Romance

  Nonfiction > *Nonfiction Books*
    Crime; Literature; Memoir
CHILDREN'S
  Fiction > *Middle Grade*
    Baseball; Contemporary; Florida; Historical Fiction; Mystery; Romance

  Nonfiction > *Picture Books*
    Comedy / Humour; Diversity; Florida

  Poetry > *Novels in Verse*

YOUNG ADULT > **Fiction** > *Novels*
    Baseball; Contemporary; Florida; Historical Fiction; Mystery; Romance

Send: Query
Don't send: Full text
How to send: Email
How not to send: Phone; Fax; Email attachment; Post

Seeks middle grade and young adult novels, especially mysteries and contemporary fiction. Historical fiction with a specific hook to the time and place, novels in verse, and off-the-beaten-path romances are on her wish list. For picture books, she prefers nonfiction that tells a story almost too good to be true, stories that show everyday diversity to mirror under-represented readers and open windows to others (per Dr. Rudine Sims Bishop), witty wordplay, and dry, sly humor. Drawn to books about Florida, odd homes, and kids with book smarts and big hearts.

For adult fiction, she is interested in literary mysteries, upmarket romance with interfaith or marginalized couples, and historical fiction set in regions other than Europe and North America. For nonfiction, she finds narrative nonfiction that straddles the boundaries between crime, memoir, and literature especially appealing. An armchair adventurer, she enjoys experiencing wild places and extreme challenges from the comfort of her chair. Though she reads widely, she's not a fit for political thrillers, inspirational Christian fiction, memoirs about violence against women, or hard sci-fi.

L1067 Zeno Agency Ltd
Literary Agency
Primrose Hill Business Centre, 110 Gloucester Avenue, London, NW1 8HX
United Kingdom
Tel: +44 (0) 20 7096 0927

louisebuckleyagent@gmail.com

http://zenoagency.com

Professional Body: The Association of Authors' Agents (AAA)

Types: Fiction; Nonfiction
Subjects: Autobiography; Commercial; Cookery; Crime; Fantasy; Health; History; Horror; Lifestyle; Literary; Nature; Science Fiction; Society; Suspense; Thrillers; Women's Interests
Markets: Adult; Children's; Young Adult

London-based literary agency specialising in Science Fiction, Fantasy, and Horror, but expanding into other areas such as crime, thrillers, women's fiction, and young adult fiction. Adult fiction must be at least 75,000 words and children's fiction should be at least 50,000 words. Send query by email with synopsis up to two pages, and first three chapters (or approximately 50 double-spaced pages) as attachments in .docx or .pdf format. No submissions by post.

Associate Agent: Kristina Perez (**L0787**)

Authors: Alice Bell; Mário Coelho; Craig Laurance Gidney; J.T. Greathouse; Jennifer Wolf Kam; Anna McNuff; Adam Oyebanji; Farrah Riaz; Troy Tassier; Katherine Toran; R.R. Virdi; Angus Watson; Gary Wigglesworth; Jasmine Wigham; Yudhanjaya Wijeratne

Junior Agent: Stevie Finegan (**L0334**)

Literary Agents: John Berlyne (**L0093**); Louise Buckley

L1068 Marisa Zeppieri
Literary Agent
United States

Literary Agency: Strachan Literary Agency (**L0947**)

L1069 Renee Zuckerbrot
Literary Agent
United States

Literary Agency: Massie & McQuilkin (**L0680**)

Magazines

For the most up-to-date listings of these and hundreds of other magazines, visit https://www.firstwriter.com/magazines

To claim your free access to the site, please see the back of this book.

M0001 110% Gaming
Magazine
United Kingdom

Newspaper Publisher / Magazine Publisher:
DC Thomson Media

M0002 The 2River View
Online Magazine
Santa Rosa, CA 95404
United States

Be1ong@2river.org

https://www.2river.org
https://2river.submittable.com/submit

Poetry > *Any Poetic Form*

Send: Full text
How to send: Submittable

Considers unpublished poems only. Submit via online submission system. See website for more details.

Editor: Richard Long

M0003 30 North
Magazine
United States

https://30northliterarymagazine.com

Fiction > *Short Fiction*: Literary

Nonfiction > *Short Nonfiction*: Creative Nonfiction

Poetry > *Any Poetic Form*

Send: Full text
How to send: Submittable

Publishes previously unpublished poetry, fiction, creative non-fiction, and art by undergraduate writers and artists. Submit via online submission system.

M0004 32 Poems
Magazine
Washington & Jefferson College, Department of English, 60 S. Lincoln Street, Washington, PA 15301
United States

submissions@32poems.com

http://32poems.com

Nonfiction > *Reviews*: Poetry as a Subject

Poetry > *Any Poetic Form*

Send: Full text
How to send: Submittable; Duosuma

Costs: A fee is charged for online submissions. $3 fee for online submissions.

Publishes poems and reviews of recent poetry collections. Submit via online submission systems. Will re-open to postal submissions in January 2022.

Editor: George David Clark

Managing Editor: Elisabeth Clark

M0005 34th Parallel
Magazine
United States

https://34thparallel.net

Fiction > *Short Fiction*: Literary

Nonfiction
   Articles: Journalism
   Essays: Creative Nonfiction

Poetry > *Any Poetic Form*

Send: Full text

Costs: A fee is charged upon submission. $14.50 fee includes download of latest digital edition.

Publishes fiction, creative nonfiction, essays, scripts, poetry, and artwork. Submit via online submission system.

M0006 365 Tomorrows
Magazine
United States

submissions@365tomorrows.com

https://365tomorrows.com

Types: Fiction
Formats: Short Fiction
Subjects: Science Fiction
Markets: Adult

Send: Full text

Website publishing daily flash fiction up to 600 words. Accepts all kinds of science fiction. Submit via form on website.

M0007 aaduna
Magazine
144 Genesee Street Suite 102-259, Auburn, New York 13021
United States

submissionsmanager@aaduna.org

http://www.aaduna.org

Types: Fiction; Nonfiction; Poetry
Subjects: Literary
Markets: Adult

Send: Full text
How to send: Email

Publishes fiction, poetry, and nonfiction. Submissions must be sent both by post and by email. See website for full guidelines.

M0008 AARP The Magazine
Magazine
c/o Editorial Submissions, 601 E St. NW, Washington, DC 20049
United States

AARPMagazine@aarp.org

https://www.aarp.org/magazine/

Types: Nonfiction
Formats: Articles; Essays
Subjects: Cookery; Finance; Health; Lifestyle; Travel
Markets: Adult

Send: Query
Don't send: Full text
How to send: Email

Magazine for those over 50. Rarely uses unsolicited ideas but will review those submitted in accordance with the guidelines on the website.

M0009 About Place Journal
Magazine
PO Box 24, Black Earth, WI 53515-0424
United States

blackearthinstitute@gmail.com

https://aboutplacejournal.org

Fiction > *Short Fiction*: Literary

Nonfiction
   Essays: General
   Short Nonfiction: Creative Nonfiction

Poetry > *Any Poetic Form*
Closed to approaches.

Publishes poetry, fiction, and essays / creative nonfiction. Accepts submissions during specific submission windows. See website for details and for themes.

M0010 The Account
Magazine
United States

poetryprosethought@gmail.com

http://theaccountmagazine.com

Types: Fiction; Nonfiction; Poetry
Formats: Essays; Short Fiction
Subjects: Literary
Markets: Adult

Send: Full text

Accepts poetry, fiction, and creative nonfiction, between May 1 and September 1, annually, and between November 15 and March 1. Send 3-5 poems, essays up to 6,000 words, or fiction between 1,000 and 6,000 words, through online submission system. Each piece of work must be accompanied by an account between 150 and 500 words, giving voice to the artist's approach.

Editors: Brianna Noll, Poetry Editor; Jennifer Hawe, Nonfiction Editor; M. Milks, Fiction Editor; Tyler Mills, Editor-in-Chief; Christina Stoddard, Managing Editor/ Publicist

M0011 Accountancy Age
Magazine
United Kingdom

michael.mccaw@contentive.com

https://www.accountancyage.com

PROFESSIONAL > **Nonfiction** > *Articles*
Accounting; Business; Finance

Weekly magazine publishing articles on accountancy, business, and the financial world.

Editors: Michael McCaw; Beth McLoughlin

M0012 ACR Journal
Magazine
United Kingdom

Magazine Publisher: Warners Group Publications

M0013 Acumen
Magazine
6 The Mount, Higher Furzeham, Brixham, South Devon, TQ5 8QY
United Kingdom
Tel: +44 (0) 1803 851098

patriciaoxley6@gmail.com

http://www.acumen-poetry.co.uk

Types: Nonfiction; Poetry
Formats: Articles

Subjects: Literary; Literary Criticism
Markets: Adult

Send: Full text
How to send: Email

Magazine publishing poetry, articles, and features connected to poetry. Send submissions with SAE and author details on each page, or submit by email as Word attachment. See website for full submission guidelines.

Editor: Patricia Oxley

M0014 Ad Astra
Magazine
United States

adastra@nss.org

https://space.nss.org/ad-astra-the-magazine-of-the-national-space-society/

Nonfiction
Articles: Space
News: Space

Send: Query; Author bio; Writing sample; Full text
How to send: Email

Non-technical magazine, reporting on a broad range of space-related topics, including domestic and international space policy and programs, transportation, commercialisation, planetary science, extraterrestrial resources, colonisation, education, and space advocacy. No science fiction or UFO stories. Accepts unsolicited mss, but prefers queries from writers seeking assignments, including details of author expertise, credits, and writing samples.

Editor: Frank Sietzen Jr

M0015 Agenda
Magazine
Harts Cottage, Stonehurst Lane, Five Ashes, Mayfield, East Sussex, TN20 6LL
United Kingdom
Tel: +44 (0) 1825 831994

submissions@agendapoetry.co.uk

http://www.agendapoetry.co.uk

Types: Poetry
Formats: Essays; Reviews
Subjects: Literary; Literary Criticism
Markets: Adult

Send: Full text
How to send: Email

Publishes poems, critical essays, and reviews. Send up to five poems or up to two essays / reviews with email address, age, and short bio. No previously published material. Submit by email only, with each piece in a separate Word attachment. Accepts work only during specific submission windows – see website for current status.

Editor: Patricia McCarthy

M0016 Agony Opera
Online Magazine
188 A/23 Maniktala Main Road, Parvati Residency, flat-304, Opposite Kankurgachhi post office
India
Tel: +919831778983

hiyamukherjeephysics@gmail.com

https://www.agonyopera.com

Fiction in Translation > *Short Fiction*
Contemporary; Culture; Erotic; Experimental; Fantasy; Literary; New Age; Philosophy; Politics; Social Commentary; Speculative; Surreal

Fiction > *Short Fiction*
Contemporary; Culture; Erotic; Experimental; Fantasy; Literary; New Age; Philosophy; Politics; Social Commentary; Speculative; Surreal

Poetry in Translation > *Any Poetic Form*
Experimental; Literary; Surreal

Poetry > *Any Poetic Form*
Experimental; Literary; Surreal

How to send: Email

We like things edgy, experimental (be it in language or form), surreal, magic-real, speculative, avant-garde. In short anything out of the box.

We have a soft spot for literature which makes a staunch stand on politics. And by politics, we mean the politics regarding the rights of the 99%, not the other way round. Though, we must admit socialist realism doesn't excite us that much.

M0017 Agricultural History
Magazine
Kennesaw State University, Dept. of History and Philosophy, 402 Bartow Ave., Kennesaw, GA 30144
United States

aghistory@kennesaw.edu

http://www.aghistorysociety.org/journal/

Types: Nonfiction
Formats: Articles
Subjects: History; Nature
Markets: Academic

Send: Full text

Publishes articles on all aspects of the history of agriculture and rural life with no geographical or temporal limits. Submit via online submission system. See website for full guidelines.

Editor: Albert Way

M0018 Air & Space Magazine
Magazine
Smithsonian Institution, PO Box 37012, MRC

513, Washington, DC 20013-7012
United States

editors@si.edu

https://www.airspacemag.com
https://www.facebook.com/AirSpaceMag
https://twitter.com/airspacemag
http://instagram.com/airspacemag

Magazine Publisher / Book Publisher:
Smithsonian Institution (**P0775**)

Nonfiction > *Articles*
Aviation; Military Aviation; Space

Send: Query
How to send: Email; Online submission system

General interest magazine about flight. Submit proposal by email or through online submission system.

Editor: George Larson

M0019 Aleph
Magazine
The Sidney M. Edelstein Center, The Hebrew University of Jerusalem, Givat Ram, 91904
Jerusalem
Israel
Tel: +972.2.658.56
Fax: +972.2.658.67.09

edelstein.aleph@mail.huji.ac.il

https://iupress.org/journals/aleph/

ACADEMIC > **Nonfiction** > *Essays*
History; Judaism; Science

Send: Full text

Magazine devoted to the exploration of the interface between Judaism and science in history.

Editors: Resianne Fontaine; Reimund Leicht

M0020 Alternatives Journal
Magazine
PO Box 26016 College PO, Kitchener ON
N2G 0A4
Canada
Tel: +1 (519) 578-2327

https://www.alternativesjournal.ca
http://twitter.com/AlternativesJ
https://www.youtube.com/user/
alternativesjournal
https://www.facebook.com/AlternativesJ

Nonfiction > *Articles*
Environment; Sustainable Living

Publishes features, articles, and news on environmental action and ideas.

Editor: Nicola Ross

M0021 Ambit
Magazine
Staithe House, Main Road, Brancaster Staithe,
Norfolk, PE31 8BP

United Kingdom
Tel: +44 (0) 7715 233221

contact@ambitmagazine.co.uk

http://ambitmagazine.co.uk

Types: Fiction; Poetry
Formats: Short Fiction
Subjects: Arts; Literary
Markets: Adult

Send: Full text

An international magazine. Potential contributors are advised to read a copy before submitting work. Send up to 5 poems, a story up to 5,000 words, or flash fiction up to 1,000 words. Submit via online portal, or by post if unable to use online portal. No submissions by email. Accepts submission only during specific submission windows – see website for details.

M0022 America's Civil War
Magazine
United States

acw@historynet.com

http://americascivilwarmag.com
https://www.historynet.com/magazines/mag-acw

Magazine Publisher: HistoryNet LLC

Nonfiction > *Articles*: American Civil War

Publishes material on the American Civil War, including features and articles for columns on the subjects of weapons, units, eye-witness accounts, and profiles of figures involved.

M0023 American Book Review
Magazine
School of Arts & Sciences, University of Houston-Victoria, 3007 N. Ben Wilson,
Victoria, TX 77901
United States
Tel: +1 (361) 570-4848

americanbookreview@uhv.edu

http://americanbookreview.org

Nonfiction > *Reviews*
Cultural Criticism; Fiction as a Subject;
Literary Criticism; Poetry as a Subject

Closed to approaches.

Specializes in reviews of frequently neglected works of fiction, poetry, and literary and cultural criticism from small, regional, university, ethnic, avant-garde, and women's presses. In nonfiction, reviews important books of criticism, biographies, and cultural studies. No reviews of "how-to" or "self-help" books. Would consider a review of innovative children's literature, but not usually part of the preferred content. Prefers books that have been published in the past six months, but will review books that have been published in the past year. No unsolicited reviews.

Editor: Lisa Savage

M0024 American Heritage
Online Magazine
United States

https://www.americanheritage.com
https://www.facebook.com/ameriheritage/
https://twitter.com/AmeriHeritage

Nonfiction > *Articles*
American History; Culture; Travel; United States

Magazine of American history, travel, food and culture. Originally a print magazine, now an online magazine as of 2017.

Editor: Richard Snow

M0025 The American Poetry Journal (APJ)
Magazine
United States

apjpoetry@gmail.com

https://www.apjpoetry.org

Types: Poetry
Markets: Adult

Send: Full text

Publishes three issues per year in print and online editions, an annual anthology, and a chapbook series. Publishes poetry from diverse backgrounds and orientations, from new and established voices. We publish work that is committed, distinct and moving.

Editor: Jessica Fischoff

M0026 Amethyst Review
Online Magazine
United Kingdom

amethystreview@gmail.com
Sarah.Poet@gmail.com

https://amethystmagazine.org
https://www.facebook.com/AmethystReview/

Fiction > *Short Fiction*: Spirituality

Nonfiction > *Short Nonfiction*: Spirituality

Poetry > *Any Poetic Form*: Spirituality

Send: Full text; Author bio
How to send: Word file email attachment; In the body of an email

Publishes work that engages in some way with spirituality or the sacred. Submit up to five poems (of any length) and / or prose pieces of up to 2,000 words. Simultaneous submissions if notification of acceptance elsewhere is provided. No previously published work. Send submissions by email with author bio of around 50 words. See website for full guidelines.

Editor: Sarah Law

M0027 Anaverde Magazine

Magazine
38713 Tierra Subida Avenue #128, Palmdale, CA 93551
United States
Tel: +1 (661) 200-9156

hello@anaverde-magazine.com

http://www.anaverde-magazine.com
http://www.facebook.com/anaverdemagazine
http://www.twitter.com/anaverdemagazine
https://www.instagram.com/anaverdemagazine

Fiction > *Short Fiction*

Nonfiction
Articles: Arts; Beauty; Crafts; Culture;
Design; Entertainment; Fashion; Finance;
Gardening; Health; Hobbies; Leisure;
Lifestyle; Nature; Spirituality; Women's
Interests
Interviews: General

Send: Full text
How to send: Email

First issue in June 2020. The publication is mailed directly to the residents in the Anaverde community, which is located in the Antelope Valley.

Editors: Malena Jackson; Samantha Jennings

M0028 And Magazine

Magazine
India

https://andmagazine824063762.wordpress.com

Fiction > *Short Fiction*: Literary

Nonfiction > *Articles*

Poetry > *Any Poetic Form*

Send your best work poems, article, essay, paper, artwork in MS word file and images in jpeg format by email.

All the accepted accepted works will be published with ISBN No. and will available in major bookstores worldwide.

M0029 The Antigonish Review

Magazine
PO Box 5000, Antigonish, Nova Scotia, B2G 2W5
Canada
Tel: +1 (902) 867-3962
Fax: +1 (902) 867-5563

tar@stfx.ca

https://antigonishreview.com
https://twitter.com/antigonishrevie
https://www.facebook.com/The-Antigonish-Review-332083480162513/
https://www.linkedin.com/in/the-antigonish-review-7602052a

Fiction in Translation > *Short Fiction*: Literary

Fiction > *Short Fiction*: Literary

Nonfiction > *Essays*
Creative Nonfiction; Culture; History;
Memoir; Sport; Travel

Poetry in Translation > *Any Poetic Form*

Poetry > *Any Poetic Form*

Send: Full text
How to send: Submittable
How not to send: Post; Email

Costs: A fee is charged upon submission. $5 for prose; $2 for poetry.

Submit via online portal only. Submit no more than 6-8 poems (preferably 3-4) and submit no more till a response is received. Considers poetry on any subject written from any point of view and in any form. For fiction, send only one story at a time. Also publishes poetry and prose translated into English from other languages (be sure to indicate source language). Also considers critical articles and essays that are fresh, vigorous, and free from jargon. Welcomes creative nonfiction. No email submissions, postal submissions, or simultaneous submissions.

M0030 The Antioch Review

Magazine
One Morgan Place, Yellow Springs, OH 45387
United States
Tel: +1 (937) 769-1365

review@antiochcollege.edu

http://review.antiochcollege.org

Fiction > *Short Fiction*: Literary

Nonfiction
Essays: General
Reviews: Literature

Poetry > *Any Poetic Form*

Closed to approaches.

Send MS with SASE for return. Strongly encourages potential contributors to buy a sample copy and peruse the magazine before submitting. Considers fiction from September 1 to May 31 only, and accepts poetry from September 1 to April 30 only. Do not mix poetry and prose submissions in the same envelope. No email submissions or unsolicited book reviews.

Editor: Robert S. Fogarty

M0031 Aquila

Magazine
United Kingdom
Tel: +44 (0) 1323 431313

submissions@aquila.co.uk

https://www.aquila.co.uk
https://www.facebook.com/AquilaChildrensMagazine
https://twitter.com/aquilamag

CHILDREN'S
Fiction > *Short Fiction*

Nonfiction > *Articles*
General, and in particular: History; Science

How to send: Email

Describes itself as the ultimate intelligent read for inquisitive kids. Full of exuberant articles and challenging puzzles that will get the whole family involved, every issue covers science, history and general knowledge.

M0032 The Architectural Review

Magazine
69-77 Paul Street, London, EC2A 4NW
United Kingdom
Tel: +44 (0) 20 3953 2000

https://www.architectural-review.com

Magazine Publisher: EMAP Publishing

PROFESSIONAL > **Nonfiction** > *Articles*
Architecture; Design

Magazine of architecture and design aimed at professionals.

Editor: Paul Finch

M0033 Arena Fantasy

Magazine
11 East Street, Bicester, Oxfordshire, OX26 2EY
United Kingdom
Tel: +44 (0) 7528 924361

submissions@arenafantasymagazine.co.uk

https://arenafantasymagazine.co.uk

Fiction > *Short Fiction*: Fantasy

Nonfiction > *Articles*
Creative Writing; Fantasy

Send: Query; Outline; Author bio
How to send: Email

Fantasy ezine that publishes every quarter. We specialise in fantasy stories as well as articles that help authors old and new. There are also competitions and a myriad of tools that will help you grow as an author.

Submissions – Prose and Artwork

Query via email initially. Your query should contain your Name, Pseudonym email address and contact details. Please give us a brief overview of your piece and a brief bio of anything you have published before if we like your work we will let you know and invite you to submit your piece.

Editor: Andy Hesford

M0034 Areopagus Magazine

Magazine
United Kingdom

editor@areopagus.org.uk

https://www.areopagus.org.uk

Fiction > *Short Fiction*

Christianity; Evangelism

Nonfiction > *Articles*
Christianity; Evangelism

Poetry > *Any Poetic Form*
Christianity; Evangelism

Send: Full text
How to send: Email; Domestic Post

Costs: A subscription is required in order to submit. £5 for electronic subscription / £15 for print.

A Christian-based arena for creative writers. A forum for debate on contemporary issues relating to Christianity and wider issues. A chance for new writers to have their work published for the first time. We can only consider MSS which are submitted by subscribers to the magazine. Subscribers may submit by email, or by post if within the UK.

Editor: Julian Barritt

M0035 Arkansas Review

Magazine
Department of English and Philosophy, PO Box 1890, State University, AR 72467
United States
Tel: +1 (870) 972-3043
Fax: +1 (870) 972-3045

arkansasreview@astate.edu

http://arkreview.org

Types: Fiction; Nonfiction; Poetry
Formats: Articles; Essays; Short Fiction
Subjects: Anthropology; Arts; Culture; History; Literature; Music; Politics; Sociology
Markets: Academic; Adult

Send: Full text
How to send: Email

Publishes articles in various disciplines focusing on the seven-state Mississippi River Delta, aimed at a general academic audience. Also publishes creative work including poetry, essays, fiction, and artwork that evoke or respond to the culture or nature of the delta. Academic articles should be submitted by post or by email. Creative material should be submitted through online system. Allow 3-12 months for response.

Editor: Marcus Tribbett

M0036 The Armourer

Magazine
United Kingdom

Magazine Publisher: Warners Group Publications

M0037 Art Monthly

Magazine
12 Carlton House Terrace, London, SW1Y 5AH
United Kingdom
Tel: +44 (0) 20 7240 0389

info@artmonthly.co.uk

http://www.artmonthly.co.uk
https://www.twitter.com/artmonthly
https://www.facebook.com/artmonthly
https://instagram.com/art_monthly_uk

Nonfiction
Articles: Arts
Interviews: Arts
Reviews: Arts

Magazine of contemporary visual art. Publishes in-depth features, interviews with artists, profiles on emerging artists and coverage of major trends and developments by independent critics.

Editor: Patricia Bickers

M0038 Art Quarterly

Magazine
Art Fund, 2 Granary Square, King's Cross, London, N1C 4BH
United Kingdom
Tel: +44 (0) 20 7225 4856

artquarterly@artfund.org

https://www.artfund.org/about-us/art-quarterly

Types: Nonfiction
Formats: Articles
Subjects: Arts
Markets: Adult

Arts magazine publishing features on artists, galleries and museums.

M0039 Art Times Journal

Online Magazine
PO Box 730, Mount Marion, NY 12456
United States
Tel: +1 (914) 246-6944
Fax: +1 (914) 246-6944

info@arttimesjournal.com

https://www.arttimesjournal.com
http://www.youtube.com/user/arttimes
https://facebook.com/ArtTimesJournal
https://twitter.com/ARTTIMESjournal
https://www.instagram.com/arttimesjournal/

Fiction > *Short Fiction*: Literary

Nonfiction > *Articles*
Arts; Culture

Poetry > *Any Poetic Form*

Send: Full text; Self-Addressed Stamped Envelope (SASE)
How to send: Email; Post

Formerly a print journal, online-only since 2016. Publishes articles on arts and culture, literary fiction, poetry, and opinion pieces relating to creativity and the arts. Prefers submissions by email but will accept submissions by post with SASE. See website for full guidelines.

Editor: Raymond J. Steiner

M0040 ARTEMISpoetry

Magazine
3 Springfield Close, East Preston, West Sussex, BN16 2SZ
United Kingdom

editor@poetrypf.co.uk

http://www.secondlightlive.co.uk/artemis.shtml

Types: Poetry
Subjects: Literary
Markets: Adult

Send: Full text
How to send: Email

For poems by women. Submit up to four poems, up to 200 lines total, by post only. Poems must be unpublished and not out for submission elsewhere. See website for full guidelines.

Editors: Kathy Miles; Lyn Moir; Dilys Wood

M0041 The Artist

Magazine
The Maltings, West Street, Bourne, Lincolnshire, PE10 9PH
United Kingdom
Tel: +44 (0) 1580 763673

https://www.painters-online.co.uk
https://www.facebook.com/paintersonline
https://twitter.com/artpublishing
https://www.instagram.com/paintersonline/
https://www.pinterest.co.uk/paintersonline/

Magazine Publisher: Warners Group Publications

Nonfiction > *Articles*: Arts

Written by artists for artists, since 1931, this magazine has inspired generations of passionate, practising artists from experienced amateur up to professionals, with practical painting and drawing articles and projects, designed to improve painting technique.

Editor: Sally Bulgin

M0042 ARTmosterrific

Online Magazine
19 Ila-Orangun Street, Ketu
Nigeria
Tel: 08164187014

dhadarms@gmail.com
Prose@artmosterrific.com
Editor@artmosterrific.com
Poetry@artmosterrific.com

https://artmosterrific.com
https://facebook.com/artmosterrific
https://twitter.com/artmosterrific
https://instagram.com/_artmosterrific
https://duotrope.com/listing/31866/artmosterrific-magazine

Fiction > *Short Fiction*

Nonfiction > *Essays*

Contemporary; Personal Essays

Poetry > *Any Poetic Form*

Closed to approaches.

An online platform and community by and for African undergraduates. It runs on five sections, all different and independent from one another: Virtual residence where 3 college writers are mentored to complete a book of art; the African Prize for Undergraduates awarded every year to an African undergraduate; the Biannual Chapbook that works as an anthology, exploring thematic issues in society, the Online Issue/Mag (Prose, Poetry, Essay, Photography), and the Community (with webinars, Book Chat, Bookstore, Physical Conference, etc). Check our submission page for detailed information on each section, and feel free to subscribe to our newsletter.

Editorial Calendar

Issue Submission (January — February)

Virtual Residence (March — April)

Chapbook Submission (May — June)

Funso Oris Prize / African Prize For Undergraduates (June — July)

ISSUE SUBMISSION (August — September)

CHAPBOOK SUBMISSION (October — November)

Dates and time for community programmes, such as the book chat, webinar, undergraduate-led auditorium conference, are subject to factors.

A literary publication that features fiction, poetry, creative nonfiction, and photography for everything that makes you sleep, keeps you awake, breaks your heart and repairs it. Everything that rusts and unrusts you. Send us your flaws and strengths, awesome and bizarre, brilliant and outrageous. However, please note that while we accept all submissions, we are especially on the lookout for works by African undergraduates. Send us your terrific work anyways!

M0043 Arts & Letters

Magazine
United States
Tel: +1 (478) 445-1289

https://artsandletters.gcsu.edu
https://artsandletters.submittable.com/submit
https://www.facebook.com/artslettersgc
https://twitter.com/ArtsLettersGC
https://artsandlettersjournal.tumblr.com/

Fiction > *Short Fiction*: Literary

Nonfiction > *Short Nonfiction*: Creative Nonfiction

Poetry > *Any Poetic Form*

Send: Full text
How to send: Submittable

Costs: A fee is charged upon submission. $3 submission fee.

Send between four and six poems, or up to 25 pages (typed, double-spaced) of fiction or creative nonfiction. Accepts submissions between August 1 and January 31.

Editor: Martin Lammon

M0044 Asimov's Science Fiction

Magazine
United States

asimovs@dellmagazines.com

https://www.asimovs.com
http://asimovs.magazinesubmissions.com/

Magazine Publisher: Dell Magazines

Fiction > *Short Fiction*
Fantasy; Science Fiction; Slipstream; Surreal

Poetry > *Any Poetic Form*
Fantasy; Science Fiction; Slipstream; Surreal

Does not want:

Fiction > *Short Fiction*: Sword and Sorcery

How to send: Online submission system; Post

Seeks serious, character-orientated science fiction and (borderline) fantasy, slipstream, and surreal. The characters should always be the main focus, rather than the science. Humour will be considered. No simultaneous submissions, sword-and-sorcery, horror, explicit sex, or violence.

Editor: Gardner Dozois

M0045 Ask

Magazine
United States

Magazine Publisher: Cricket Media, Inc.

M0046 Atlanta Review

Magazine
Suite 333, 686 Cherry St. NW, Atlanta, GA 30332-0161
United States

atlantareview@gatech.edu

http://atlantareview.com
https://atlantareview.submittable.com/submit
https://twitter.com/ATLReview
https://www.facebook.com/atlantareview
https://www.instagram.com/atlantareviewpojo/

Poetry > *Any Poetic Form*

Closed to approaches.

Costs: A fee is charged for online submissions. $3.

Accepts submissions of poetry between January 1 and June 1, and between September

15 and December 1. Submit online ($3 submission fee) or by post with SASE.

M0047 The Atlantic

Magazine
United States

politics@theatlantic.com
culture@theatlantic.com
science@theatlantic.com
family@theatlantic.com
education@theatlantic.com
global@theatlantic.com
ideas@theatlantic.com
fiction@theatlantic.com
poetry@theatlantic.com

https://www.theatlantic.com
https://support.theatlantic.com/hc/en-us/articles/360011374734-Submit-a-piece-for-editorial-consideration-at-The-Atlantic
https://www.facebook.com/TheAtlantic
https://www.instagram.com/theatlantic
https://www.youtube.com/user/TheAtlantic
https://twitter.com/TheAtlantic
https://www.linkedin.com/company/the-atlantic
https://flipboard.com/@theatlantic

Fiction > *Short Fiction*

Nonfiction > *Articles*
Business; Culture; Education; Family; Health; International; Literature; Politics; Science; Technology

Poetry > *Any Poetic Form*

Send: Pitch; Full text
How to send: Word file email attachment; PDF file email attachment; In the body of an email

Always interested in great nonfiction, fiction, and poetry. A general familiarity with what we have published in the past is the best guide to what we're looking for. All manuscripts should be submitted as a Word document or PDF. Succinct pitches may be submitted in the body of an email.

Editor: Cullen Murphy

M0048 Auroras & Blossoms Poetry Journal

Online Magazine
United Kingdom

info@abpoetryjournal.com

https://www.abpoetryjournal.com

ADULT > **Poetry** > *Any Poetic Form*

YOUNG ADULT > **Poetry** > *Any Poetic Form*

Closed to approaches.

Costs: A fee is charged upon submission. $4 minimum for priority listing.

Electronic poetry journal co-founded by two authors. They are family friendly, publishing "positive poetry/content. Positive as in stimulating, optimistic, confident, uplifting, inspirational." They accept work from adult writers/poets and teen poets (13-16).

We are a family-friendly magazine, so we expect clean language. No dirty words at all. We also don't want anything related to erotica or politics.

Apart from that, we are open to everything, as long as the message is good and uplifting.

When poets send us their pieces, we ask them to tell us why they think they would make a good fit for the journal. We want to ensure that they understand that the message is just as important as the language itself. There must be an energy behind the pieces that really make us think hard and ultimately inspires the reader, not just the poet themselves.

Editors / Poets: David Ellis; Cendrine Marrouat

M0049 Aviation News

Magazine
United Kingdom

https://www.key.aero/aviationnews

Magazine Publisher: Key Publishing

Nonfiction
   Articles: Aviation
   News: Aviation

Publishes news and features related to aviation, including military, civil, business, historical, contemporary, aircraft, airports, and equipment.

Editors: David Baker; Jamie Ewan

M0050 Awen

Magazine
Atlantean Publishing, 4 Pierrot Steps, 71 Kursaal Way, Southend-on-Sea, Essex, SS1 2UY
United Kingdom

atlanteanpublishing@hotmail.com

http://atlanteanpublishing.wikia.com/wiki/Awen

Book Publisher / Magazine Publisher: Atlantean Publishing (**P0057**)

Fiction > *Short Fiction*

Poetry > *Any Poetic Form*

Closed to approaches.

Now normally eight A4 sides in length, it contains poetry and short prose fiction and has appeared four times a year since 2013. Submit by post or by email.

Editor: David-John Tyrer

M0051 Backcountry Magazine

Magazine
60 Main Street, PO Box 190, Jeffersonville, VT 05464

United States
Tel: +1 (802) 644-6606

https://backcountrymagazine.com

Nonfiction > *Articles*
   Skiing; Snowboarding

Send: Query
How to send: Email

Magazine of skiing and snowboarding. Send query by email.

Editor: Lucy Higgins

Managing Editor: Betsy Manero

M0052 Bacopa Literary Review

Magazine
United States

https://writersalliance.org/bacopa-literary-review/

Fiction > *Short Fiction*: Literary

Nonfiction > *Short Nonfiction*: Creative Nonfiction

Poetry > *Any Poetic Form*

Closed to approaches.

Annual print journal publishing short stories, creative nonfiction, poetry, and prose poetry. Accepts submissions only through annual contest that runs from March 18 to May 17 annually.

M0053 Bad Nudes

Magazine
Canada

submit.badnudes@gmail.com

http://www.badnudes.com

Types: Fiction; Poetry
Formats: Short Fiction
Subjects: Experimental; Literary
Markets: Adult

Send: Full text
How to send: Email

Strives to pair bold, experimental poetry and fiction with innovative design to create a magazine that is both relevant and thought-provoking. Submit one story up to 3,000 words, or up to five poems up to ten pages total.

M0054 The Baffler

Magazine
19 West 21st Street #1001, New York, NY 10010
United States
Tel: +1 (212) 390-1569

https://thebaffler.com

Types: Fiction; Nonfiction; Poetry
Formats: Articles; Essays; Short Fiction
Subjects: Comedy / Humour; Culture; Politics; Satire
Markets: Adult

Send: Query
Don't send: Full text

Describes itself as "America's leading voice of interesting and unexpected left-wing political criticism, cultural analysis, short stories, poems and art". Submit pitch using online form on website.

Editor: Jonathon Sturgeon

M0055 Banipal

Magazine
1 Gough Square, London, EC4A 3DE
United Kingdom

editor@banipal.co.uk

http://www.banipal.co.uk

Types: Fiction; Poetry; Translations
Formats: Articles; Reviews; Short Fiction
Markets: Adult

Send: Query
Don't send: Full text
How to send: Email

Contemporary Arab authors in English translations. Publishes new and established writers, and diverse material including translations, poetry, short stories, novel excerpts, profiles, interviews, appreciations, book reviews, reports of literary festivals, conferences, and prizes. Welcomes submissions by post, but queries only by email. Unsolicited email submissions with attachments will be automatically deleted. Response in 3-6 months.

Editor: Margaret Obank

M0056 Bard

Magazine
Atlantean Publishing, 4 Pierrot Steps, 71 Kursaal Way, Southend-on-Sea, Essex, SS1 2UY
United Kingdom

atlanteanpublishing@hotmail.com

http://atlanteanpublishing.wikia.com/wiki/Bard
https://atlanteanpublishing.wordpress.com
https://www.facebook.com/groups/169974286448031/

Book Publisher / Magazine Publisher: Atlantean Publishing (**P0057**)

Poetry > *Any Poetic Form*

Closed to approaches.

Flyer-style broadsheet of poetry released roughly monthly and available for free to subscribers of the publisher's magazines. Occasionally runs themed issues but generally open to any and all poetry. See website for full submission guidelines.

M0057 Bare Fiction Magazine
Magazine
177 Copthorne Road, Shrewsbury, Shropshire, SY3 8NA
United Kingdom

info@barefiction.co.uk

https://www.barefictionmagazine.co.uk

Types: Fiction; Nonfiction; Poetry; Scripts
Formats: Essays; Interviews; Reviews; Short Fiction; Theatre Scripts
Subjects: Drama; Literary; Literature
Markets: Adult

Closed to approaches.

Closed to submissions as at March 2019. Check website for current status. Publishes poetry, fiction and plays, literary review, interviews and commentary. Does not accept submissions at all times – check website for current status and sign up to newsletter to be notified when submissions next open.

M0058 Barren Magazine
Magazine
United States

info@barrenmagazine.com

https://barrenmagazine.com

Types: Fiction; Nonfiction; Poetry
Formats: Short Fiction
Subjects: Literary; Photography
Markets: Adult

Send: Full text
How to send: Email

An Alt.Lit Introspective. A literary publication that features fiction, poetry, creative nonfiction, and photography for hard truths, long stares, and gritty lenses. We revel in the shadow-spaces that make up the human condition, and aim to find antitheses to that which defines us: light in darkness; beauty in ugliness; peace in disarray. We invite you to explore it with us.

Editor: Jason D. Ramsey

M0059 BBC Countryfile Magazine
Magazine
Eagle House, Bristol, BS1 4ST
United Kingdom
Tel: +44 (0) 1173 147399

editor@countryfile.com

http://www.countryfile.com

Nonfiction > *Articles*
Countryside; Nature

Send: Query
Don't send: Full text

Magazine on British countryside and rural life. Send queries with ideas by email. No unsolicited mss.

Editor: Fergus Collins

M0060 BBC Gardeners' World Magazine
Magazine
Immediate Media, 2nd Floor, Vineyard House, 44 Brook Green, Hammersmith, London, W6 7BT
United Kingdom
Tel: +44 (0) 20 7150 5770

magazine@gardenersworld.com

https://www.gardenersworld.com
https://www.facebook.com/GWmagazine
http://uk.pinterest.com/gwmag
https://twitter.com/gwmag
https://www.youtube.com/channel/UC8kRP4T6HbZnsheHCuIB_FQ
https://www.instagram.com/gardenersworldmag/

Magazine Publisher: Immediate Media Co.

Nonfiction > *Articles:* Gardening

Publishes advice and ideas about gardening.

Editor: Adam Pasco

M0061 BBC Music Magazine
Magazine
Eagle House, Colston Avenue, Bristol, BS1 4ST
United Kingdom

music@classical-music.com

https://www.classical-music.com
https://www.facebook.com/classicalmagazine
https://twitter.com/MusicMagazine
https://www.youtube.com/channel/UC0TNxfRDOfvSlieR6Zq51eg
https://www.instagram.com/musicmagazinepics/

Nonfiction > *Articles:* Classical Music

Monthly magazine covering all areas of classical music.

Editor: Oliver Condy

M0062 Beano
Magazine
United Kingdom

Newspaper Publisher / Magazine Publisher: DC Thomson Media

M0063 The Beano
Magazine
185 Fleet Street, London, EC4A 2HS
United Kingdom

https://www.beano.com

CHILDREN'S > **Fiction** > *Cartoons:* Comedy / Humour

Publishes comic strips for children aged 6-12.

M0064 Beat Scene
Magazine
United Kingdom

kevbeatscene@gmail.com

https://www.beatscene.net

Nonfiction > *Articles:* Beat Generation

A magazine about the Beat Generation, Jack Kerouac, William Burroughs, Allen Ginsberg, Lawrence Ferlinghetti, Gary Snyder, Michael McClure, Philip Whalen, Anne Waldman, Joanne Kyger, Charles Bukowski and others.

Editor: Kevin Ring

M0065 Beir Bua Journal
Online Magazine
Ireland

BeirBuaJournal@gmail.com

https://beirbuajournal.wordpress.com
https://twitter.com/beirbuajournal
https://instagram.com/beirbuajournal
https://www.youtube.com/channel/UCdlyd1MKVthfnqJ__fW99Aw
https://www.facebook.com/BeirBuaJournal/

Poetry
Any Poetic Form: Avant-Garde; Experimental; Ireland; Motherhood; Postmodernism; Religion; Women's Issues
Experimental Poetry: General
Visual Poetry: General

Closed to approaches.

Costs: Offers services that writers have to pay for. Offers expedited submissions and feedback for a fee.

Interested in conceptual poetics of new language, women's issues, motherhood, slanted unreality, polarity and plurality of time, religion, Ireland's history. Would love more Irish women experimental poets.

M0066 Bella
Magazine
Academic House, 24-28 Oval Road, London, NW1 7DT
United Kingdom

Bella.Hotline@bauermedia.co.uk

https://www.bellamagazine.co.uk
https://twitter.com/#!/bellamagazineUK
http://facebook.com/bellamagazineUK
https://www.instagram.com/bellamagazineuk/

Magazine Publisher: Bauer Media Group

Nonfiction > *Articles*
Celebrity; Diet; Fashion; Real Life Stories; Travel

Send: Query
How to send: Email

Human interest magazine for women, publishing articles on celebs, diet, style, travel, and real-life stories. Send query by email.

Editor: Jayne Marsden

M0067 Bellingham Review

Magazine
MS-9053, Western Washington University,
Bellingham, WA 98225
United States
Tel: +1 (360) 650-4863

bellingham.review@wwu.edu

http://bhreview.org

Types: Fiction; Nonfiction; Poetry
Formats: Essays; Short Fiction
Subjects: Literary
Markets: Adult

Send submissions of prose up to 6,000 words, or up to three poems, via online submission system only. Submit material between September 15 and December 1 only. Simultaneous submissions accepted provided immediate notification is given of acceptance elsewhere.

Editor: Bailey Cunningham

M0068 Belmont Story Review

Magazine
United States

belmontstoryreview@gmail.com

https://belmontstoryreview.wixsite.com/
website
https://belmontstoryreview.submittable.com/
submit

Fiction > *Short Fiction*

Nonfiction > *Short Nonfiction*: Creative
Nonfiction

Poetry > *Any Poetic Form*

Closed to approaches.

Established in 2016, the magazine aims to surprise and delight readers through an eclectic mix of storytelling which includes fiction, personal essay, poetry, songwriting, drama, graphic narrative, and photography; as well as creative reportage, including coverage of music, film, creativity and collaboration, and the intersection of faith and culture.

We seek to publish new and established writers passionate about their craft, fearlessly encountering difficult ideas, seeking to explore human experience in all its broken blessedness.

M0069 Beloit Fiction Journal

Magazine
Box 11, Beloit College, 700 College Street,
Beloit, WI 53511
United States

https://www.beloit.edu/fiction-journal/
https://beloitfictionjournal.submittable.com/
submit

Fiction > *Short Fiction*: Literary

How to send: Submittable

Costs: A fee is charged upon submission. $3
per submission.

Open to literary fiction on any subject or theme, up to 13,000 words. Also accepts flash fiction. Showcases new writers as well as established writers. Simultaneous submissions are accepted.

Editor: Heather Skyler

M0070 Best

Magazine
United Kingdom

best@hearst.co.uk

https://www.hearst.co.uk/brands/best
https://www.facebook.com/bestmagazine/
https://twitter.com/BestMagOfficial

Magazine Publisher: Hearst Magazines UK

Nonfiction > *Articles*
  Beauty; Celebrity; Diet; Fashion; Finance;
  Real Life Stories; Recipes; TV

Jam packed with amazing real-life stories, showbiz news, diet, recipes, fashion, beauty advice and so much more.

Editor: for fiction Pat Richardson.

M0071 Better Than Starbucks

Magazine
PO Box 673, Mayo, FL 32066
United States
Tel: +1 (561) 719-8627

betterthanstarbucks2@gmail.com

https://www.betterthanstarbucks.org

ADULT
  Fiction > *Short Fiction*

  Nonfiction > *Short Nonfiction*: Creative
  Nonfiction

  Poetry in Translation > *Any Poetic Form*

  Poetry
    Any Poetic Form: Africa; Comedy /
    Humour; International
    Experimental Poetry: General
    Formal Poetry: General
    Free Verse: General
    Haiku: General
    Prose Poetry: General

CHILDREN'S > **Poetry** > *Any Poetic Form*

Send: Full text; Author bio
How to send: Email

Publishes African Poetry, International Poetry, Prose Poetry, Forms as well as Formal Poetry, Poetry Translations, Experimental Poetry and poetry for children. Encourages sentiment in poetry. Also publishes Fiction, Flash Fiction, Micro Fiction and Creative Nonfiction. Submitted opinion pieces will be considered.

Editor: Vera Ignatowitsch

M0072 Big Fiction

Online Magazine
Seattle University, English Dept, c/o Juan
Carlos Reyes, P.O. Box 222000, Seattle, WA
98122-1090
United States

editors@bigfiction.com

https://www.bigfictionmagazine.org

Fiction > *Novelette*

Nonfiction
  Essays: General
  Reviews: Fiction as a Subject
  Short Nonfiction: Creative Nonfiction

Closed to approaches.

Costs: A fee is charged upon submission. $5
for novelettes; $3 for essays.

Literary magazine devoted to longer short fiction, between 7,500 and 20,000 words.

M0073 The Big Ugly Review

Online Magazine
2703 Seventh Street, Box 345, Berkeley, CA
94710
United States

elizabethstix@gmail.com

http://www.biguglyreview.com

Types: Fiction; Nonfiction; Poetry
Formats: Essays
Subjects: Commercial; Experimental; Literary
Markets: Adult

Send full MS as Word or Word-compatible attachment by email. Publishes poetry, fiction, flash fiction, creative nonfiction and personal essays in themed issues online. All material submitted must be related to theme for upcoming issue, which is available on website along with individual email addresses for different editors.

Editor: Elizabeth Bernstein

M0074 BIGnews

Magazine
United States

http://www.mainchance.org

Fiction > *Short Fiction*

Nonfiction
  Articles: Arts; Literature
  Essays: Arts; Literature
  Interviews: Arts; Literature

Publishes features, interviews, personal essays, short stories, and serialised novels from the outsider's perspective. Interested in presenting the art and literature of the outsider, rather than simply drumming up sympathy for the homeless.

Editor: Ron Grunberg

M0075 Bike Magazine

Magazine
United Kingdom

https://www.bikemagazine.co.uk
https://www.facebook.com/bikemagazineUK
https://twitter.com/BikeMagazine

Magazine Publisher: Bauer Media Group

Nonfiction > *Articles*: Motorbikes

Your definitive guide to the world of motorcycling. Every issue features incredible motorcycling travel stories from our team and readers with amazing adventures and epic photography. Plus there's expert opinion on all the new motorcycles available in the UK, giving you all the details you need to choose your next bike.

Editors: John Westlake; Hugo Wilson

M0076 Bikers Club

Online Magazine
7B Tejal Bhuvan, N.P.Thakkar Road, Vile Parle, Mumbai 400057
India
Tel: +91 9820189969

rm@bikersclub.in

https://www.bikersclub.in
https://www.facebook.com/bikersclubapp/
https://www.instagram.com/bikersclubapp/
https://twitter.com/Bikersclubapp

Nonfiction
 Articles: Biker Lifestyle; Motorbikes; Motorcycling; Motorsports; Travel
 Interviews: Motorbikes; Motorcycling; Motorsports
 Reviews: Motorbikes

Send: Full text
How to send: Email

Monthly digitally issued magazine dedicated to the bikers and the traveller worldwide. It includes interview, reviews of bikes and destinations, lifestyles, shout out, current affairs and travel stories.

Editor: Rahul Mehta

M0077 Black Beauty & Hair

Magazine
United Kingdom

info@blackbeautyandhair.com

http://www.blackbeautyandhair.com
https://www.facebook.com/BlackBeautyandHair
https://twitter.com/BlackBeautyMag
https://www.youtube.com/user/blackbeautymag
http://instagram.com/BlackBeautyMag
https://www.pinterest.com/blackbeautyhair/

Nonfiction > *Articles*
 Beauty; Fashion; Hairstyles; Weddings

Publishes articles and features on black hair, beauty, fashion, and lifestyle. Also publishes bridal features.

Editor: Irene Shelley

M0078 Black Moon Magazine

Online Magazine
United States

blackmoonmageditors@gmail.com

http://box5887.temp.domains/~blackmy8/
https://www.facebook.com/BlackMoonMagazine
https://www.instagram.com/black.moon.mag/
https://twitter.com/Black_Moon_Mag

Fiction > *Short Fiction*

Nonfiction
 Interviews: Literature
 Reviews: Books

Poetry > *Any Poetic Form*

Send: Full text; Query; Author bio
How to send: Email attachment

Submit up to three short stories between 1,000 and 8,000 words, or up to five poems of up to five pages each. Also accepts book reviews and interviews with professionals in the writing community for online publication.

M0079 Black Static

Magazine
United Kingdom

http://ttapress.com/blackstatic/

Magazine Publisher / Book Publisher: TTA Press (**P0839**)

Fiction > *Short Fiction*
 Dark; Horror

Send: Full text
How to send: Submittable

Always open to unsolicited submissions of new dark/horror stories up to a maximum of 10,000 words.

Editor: Andy Cox

M0080 Blithe Spirit

Magazine
United Kingdom

ed.blithespirit@gmail.com

http://britishhaikusociety.org.uk

Poetry > *Haiku*

Send: Full text
How to send: Email

Only accepts submissions from members, however members do not enjoy an automatic right to publication – quality is key. Non-members may appear as featured writers. All work must be original. Submissions should be sent by email with a covering note.

Editor: Caroline Skanne

M0081 Blue Collar Review

Magazine
PO 11417, Norfolk, VA 23517
United States

red-ink@earthlink.net

https://www.partisanpress.org

Book Publisher: Partisan Press (**P0615**)

Fiction > *Short Fiction*: Working Class

Nonfiction
 Essays: Culture; Working Class
 Reviews: General

Poetry > *Any Poetic Form*: Working Class

Send: Full text; Self-Addressed Stamped Envelope (SASE)

Magazine that aims to "expand and promote a progressive working class vision of culture that inspires us and that moves us forward as a class". Submit up to five poems or short stories, essays, or reviews up to 1,000 words by post with SASE for response.

M0082 Blue Earth Review

Magazine
230 Armstrong Hall, Minnesota State University, Mankato, Mankato, MN 56001
United States

blueearthreview@gmail.com

https://blueearthreview.mnsu.edu
https://www.facebook.com/theblueearthreview/
https://twitter.com/BlueEarthReview

Fiction > *Short Fiction*

Nonfiction
 Essays: Personal Essays
 Short Nonfiction: Creative Nonfiction; Memoir
Poetry > *Any Poetic Form*

Send: Full text
How to send: Submittable

Publishes fiction, creative nonfiction and poetry. Fiction can be of any length, but hopefully under 15 manuscript pages. Interested in creative nonfiction (memoir and personal essay) with contemporary themes. No literary criticism. Submit up to five poems at a time.

Managing Editor: Christina Olson

M0083 Booklaunch

Magazine
12 Wellfield Avenue, London, N10 2EA, United Kingdom

book@booklaunch.london

https://www.booklaunch.london
https://www.facebook.com/booklaunch.london/
https://twitter.com/booklaunch_ldn
https://www.youtube.com/channel/

UCNQfRhWa8DdObMJ9xxxvveA/videos
https://www.instagram.com/
booklaunchlondon/

Fiction > *Novel Excerpts*

Nonfiction > *Book Extracts*

Poetry > *Book Extracts*

Does not want:

> **Fiction** > *Novel Excerpts*
> Erotic; Fantasy; Gothic; Romance;
> Suspense; Westerns
>
> **Nonfiction** > *Nonfiction Books*
> Hobbies; How To; Leisure; New Age;
> Self Help; Spirituality

Send: Full text
How to send: PDF file email attachment

Costs: A fee is charged for publication.

Carries extracts from new and newish books.
Its editorial balance is largely towards nonfiction but also accepts novels and poetry. (See
past issues on website.) Tabloid format with
space for approx 1,600 words per page. Does
not run extracts at less than a page. Charges for
inclusion. Has the largest print run of any
books magazine in the UK. Page rate a fifth of
that of rival publications. Uploads and archives
every print edition. Helps its authors to record
audio tracks to its YouTube channel. Contact
by email for ratecard.

M0084 Brain, Child

Magazine
PO Box 714, Lexington, VA 24450
United States
Tel: +1 (540) 463-4817

editor@brainchildmag.com

http://www.brainchildmag.com

Types: Fiction
Formats: Articles; Essays; News; Reviews;
Short Fiction
Subjects: Comedy / Humour

Closed to approaches.

Magazine on modern motherhood. Send MSS
with cover letter and SASE, or pasted into the
body of an email with "Submission" in the
subject heading. For features, news items, and
debate essays query first with clips.
Simultaneous submissions are accepted,
provided immediate notification is given of
acceptance elsewhere.

Core focus is on insightful personal essays,
using illustrative anecdotes, a personal voice,
and a down-to-earth tone. Humour is
appreciated. Sentimentality isn't.

Also publishes more traditional features based
on reporting rather than introspection. Also
publishes short fiction, parody, and book
reviews. See website for full details.

Editor: Jennifer Niesslein and Stephanie
Wilkinson

M0085 Brick

Magazine
P.O. Box 609, STN P, Toronto, ON, M5S 2Y4
Canada

info@brickmag.com

https://brickmag.com/
https://twitter.com/brickMAG
https://facebook.com/brickmagazine
https://instagram.com/brickliterary

Nonfiction
Essays: Arts; City and Town Planning;
Dance; Food; History; Literature; Music;
Photography; Science; Sport; Travel; Writing
Interviews: Arts; Literature; Performing Arts
Reviews: Arts; Literature; Performing Arts
Short Nonfiction: Literary; Memoir

Send entire submission in first instance. Please
read magazine before submitting. Accepts
unsolicited nonfiction submissions on a variety
of subjects between March 1 and April 30 and
between September 1 and October 31 each
year. No unsolicited fiction or poetry.

Editor: Vivien Leong

M0086 British Medical Journal (BMJ)

Magazine
BMA House, Tavistock Square, London,
WC1H 9JP
United Kingdom
Tel: +44 (0) 20 7387 4410
Fax: +44 (0) 20 7383 6418

papersadmin@bmj.com

https://www.bmj.com

Types: Nonfiction
Formats: Articles; News
Subjects: Medicine
Markets: Professional

Leading medical journal for healthcare
professionals. Papers can be submitted using
online submission system available via
website.

Editor: Fiona Godlee

M0087 British Railway Modelling

Magazine
United Kingdom

Magazine Publisher: Warners Group
Publications

M0088 Brittle Star

Magazine
Diversity House, 72 Nottingham Road, Arnold,
Nottingham, NG5 6LF
United Kingdom

brittlestar.subs@gmail.com

http://www.brittlestar.org.uk
http://www.twitter.com/brittlestarmag

Fiction > *Short Fiction*: Literary

Poetry > *Any Poetic Form*

Send: Full text; Self-Addressed Stamped
Envelope (SASE)
How to send: Post

Publishes original and unpublished poetry and
short stories. Send 1-4 poems or 1-2 stories of
up to 2,000 words each. Include short bio of up
to 40 words. No simultaneous submissions.
Also reviews of first, full poetry collections
and single-author short fiction collections.

M0089 The Broons

Magazine
United Kingdom

Newspaper Publisher / Magazine Publisher:
DC Thomson Media

M0090 Brush Talks

Magazine
United States

editor@brushtalks.com

http://www.brushtalks.com
https://twitter.com/BrushTalks

Nonfiction > *Essays*
Arts; China; Culture; History; Memoir;
Narrative Nonfiction; Science; Technology;
Travel

Poetry in Translation > *Any Poetic
Form*: China

Poetry > *Any Poetic Form*: China

Send: Full text
How to send: Email attachment

A journal of creative nonfiction, photography,
and poetry related to China. Articles can take
many forms: general essays, travel essays,
profiles, memoir, and narrative nonfiction. We
seek submissions about places, people, history,
culture, the arts, science and technology —
anything related to China that is well written,
creative, and true (we do not publish fiction).
Rolling submissions, no fee. Please visit our
website for more information and read the
guidelines before submitting.

M0091 The Burlington Magazine

Magazine
14-16 Duke's Road, London, WC1H 9SZ
United Kingdom
Tel: +44 (0) 20 7388 1228

mhall@burlington.org.uk

http://www.burlington.org.uk

Types: Nonfiction
Formats: Articles; Reviews

Subjects: Arts; History
Markets: Adult

Monthly magazine devoted to the fine and decorative arts. Publishes concise articles based on original research, presenting new works, art-historical discoveries and fresh interpretations.

Editor: Michael Hall

M0092 Business London
Magazine
210 Dundas St., Suite 201, London, ON N6A 5J3
Canada

https://lfpress.com/category/business-london/

Media Company: The London Free Press

PROFESSIONAL > **Nonfiction** > *Articles:* Business

Business magazine for southwestern Ontario.

Editor: Sarah Jones

Managing Editor: Madisyn Latham

M0093 Buttered Toast
Magazine
United States

https://www.toadhalleditions.ink/buttered-toast

Book Publisher / Self Publishing Service: Toad Hall Editions (**P0828**)

CHILDREN'S
Fiction > *Short Fiction*

Nonfiction
Essays: General
Short Nonfiction: Creative Nonfiction

Poetry > *Any Poetic Form*

Costs: A fee is charged upon submission. $7 per submission. Fee is waived for those who require assistance.

Annual journal publishing work by and for young people up to 18 years old.

M0094 Button
Magazine
PO Box 77, Westminster, MA 01473
United States

sally@moonsigns.net

http://www.moonsigns.net/Button-frame.htm

Fiction > *Short Fiction*

Poetry > *Any Poetic Form*

Send: Full text
How to send: Post; Email if overseas
How not to send: Email if not overseas

Send SASE for writers guidelines, and / or purchase a copy of the magazine for guidance on style. Magazine of poetry, fiction, and gracious living.

Editor: Sally Cragin

Fiction Editor: W.M. Davies

M0095 Cabildo Quarterly
Magazine
United States

cabildoquarterly@gmail.com

https://cabildoquarterly.tumblr.com

Types: Fiction; Poetry
Formats: Short Fiction
Subjects: Literary
Markets: Adult

Send: Full text
How to send: Email

Punk-influenced broadsheet journal based in Cape Cod and Bangor ME. Publishes material both in print and online. Send one or two unpublished stories or up to five unpublished poems, by email. See website for full guidelines and separate email address for poetry submissions.

M0096 Caesura
Magazine

United States

caesura@pcsj.org

http://www.pcsj.org/caesura.html

Types: Fiction; Nonfiction; Poetry
Formats: Interviews; Reviews; Short Fiction
Subjects: Literary; Literary Criticism
Markets: Adult

Literary journal publishing poems, short fiction, nonfiction, critical work, book reviews, and interviews.

M0097 The Cafe Irreal
Magazine
United States

editors@cafeirreal.com

http://cafeirreal.alicewhittenburg.com

Types: Fiction
Formats: Short Fiction
Subjects: Literary
Markets: Adult

Send: Full text
How to send: Email

Quarterly webzine publishing fantastic fiction resembling the work of writers such as Franz Kafka and Jorge Luis Borges. Send stories up to 2,000 in the body of an email. No simultaneous submissions.

M0098 Cahoodaloodaling
Magazine
United States

cahoodaloodaling@gmail.com

https://cahoodaloodaling.com
https://cahoodaloodaling.submittable.com/submit

Fiction > *Short Fiction*

Nonfiction
Articles: Publishing; Writing
Essays: Publishing; Writing
Interviews: General
Reviews: Books

Poetry > *Any Poetic Form*

Send: Full text
How to send: Submittable

Themed triannual journal, publishing poetry, fiction, and articles and essays that are either about writing and publishing, or match the current submission call. See website for upcoming themes, and to submit via online submission system. If you would like your book reviewing, query by email with a brief sample.

Editor: Raquel Thorne

M0099 Cake Craft
Magazine
United Kingdom

Magazine Publisher: Warners Group Publications

M0100 Cake Craft Guides
Magazine
United Kingdom

Magazine Publisher: Warners Group Publications

M0101 Campervan
Magazine
United Kingdom

Magazine Publisher: Warners Group Publications

M0102 Camping Magazine
Magazine
United Kingdom

Magazine Publisher: Warners Group Publications

M0103 Candis
Magazine
Newhall Publications Ltd, Newhall Lane, Hoylake, Wirral, CH47 4BQ
United Kingdom
Tel: +44 (0) 1516 323232

info@newhallpublishing.com

https://www.candis.co.uk

Types: Nonfiction
Formats: Articles
Subjects: Cookery; Health; Lifestyle; Travel
Markets: Adult

Publishes features on food, health, travel, and charity.

M0104 Caravan
Magazine
United Kingdom

Magazine Publisher: Warners Group Publications

M0105 The Casket of Fictional Delights
Online Magazine
United Kingdom

https://thecasket.co.uk
https://www.facebook.com/casketfiction/
https://twitter.com/casketfiction
https://uk.pinterest.com/thecasket/

Fiction > *Short Fiction*

Send: Full text
How to send: By referral

Online magazine publishing flash fiction and short stories. Submissions by invitation and recommendation only.

Editor: Joanna Sterling

M0106 Cat World
Magazine
PO Box 2258, Pulborough, West Sussex, RH20 9BA
United Kingdom
Tel: +44 (0) 1903 884988

support@ashdown.co.uk

http://www.catworld.co.uk

Types: Nonfiction
Formats: Articles; News
Subjects: Comedy / Humour; Nature
Markets: Adult

Publishes articles about cats and cat ownership.

M0107 Cemetery Dance
Magazine
132-B Industry Lane, Unit 7, Forest Hill, MD 21050
United States
Tel: +1 (410) 588-5901
Fax: +1 (410) 588-5904

info@cemeterydance.com

https://www.cemeterydance.com/
https://www.cemeterydance.com/cemetery-dance-magazine.html

Fiction > *Short Fiction*
Dark; Horror; Mystery; Suspense

Nonfiction
Articles: Dark; Horror; Mystery; Suspense
Interviews: Dark; Horror; Mystery; Suspense
News: Dark; Horror; Mystery; Suspense
Reviews: Dark; Horror; Mystery; Suspense

Closed to approaches.

Publishes horror, dark mystery, crime, and suspense stories which are powerful, emotional, pacy, and original.

Editor: Richard Chizmar

M0108 Chapman
Magazine
4 Broughton Place, Edinburgh, EH1 3RX
United Kingdom
Tel: +44 (0) 131 557 2207

chapman-pub@blueyonder.co.uk

http://www.chapman-pub.co.uk

Fiction > *Short Fiction*: Literary

Nonfiction > *Articles*: Literary Criticism

Poetry > *Any Poetic Form*

Send: Full text; Self-Addressed Stamped Envelope (SASE)
How to send: Post
How not to send: Email

Describes itself as Scotland's leading literary magazine, publishing new creative writing: poetry, fiction, discussion of cultural affairs, theatre, reviews and the arts in general, plus critical essays. It publishes international as well as Scottish writers and is a dynamic force for artistic and cultural change and development. Always open to new writers and ideas.

Fiction may be of any length, but average is around 3,000 words. Send one piece at a time. Poetry submissions should contain between four and ten poems. Single poems are not usually published.

Articles and reviews are usually commissioned and ideas should be discussed with the editor in advance.

All submissions must include an SAE or IRCs or email address for response. No submissions by email.

Editor: Joy Hendry

M0109 Charleston Style and Design Magazine
Magazine
United States

https://www.charlestonstyleanddesign.com
https://www.facebook.com/Charleston-Style-Design-Magazine-108903839161607/
https://www.instagram.com/chasstyleanddesign/
https://twitter.com/CharlestonSDMa1
https://www.pinterest.com/charlestonsdmag/

Nonfiction > *Articles*
Architecture; Arts; Design; Fashion; Food; Lifestyle; Travel; Wine

Design and lifestyle magazine for the Lowcountry, covering architects, designers and builders, home projects, lifestyle trends,

restaurants, wines, fashions, art galleries, and travel destinations.

Editor: Mary Love

M0110 Chat
Magazine
TI Media, 161 Marsh Wall, London, London, E14 9AP
United Kingdom
Tel: +44 (0) 20 3148 5000

chat_magazine@ti-media.com

https://www.ti-media.com

Types: Nonfiction
Formats: Articles
Subjects: Comedy / Humour; Lifestyle; Women's Interests
Markets: Adult

Send: Full text

General interest women's magazine. Approach in writing with ideas only after becoming familiar with the magazine and the kind of material it publishes. No fiction.

M0111 Cholla Needles
Magazine
United States

editor@chollaneedles.com

https://www.chollaneedles.com

Poetry > *Any Poetic Form*: Literary

Send: Full text
How to send: Email

We look for poetry that reaches readers, with a special emphasis on poetry that readers desire to return to. Each issue contains 10 distinctly different poets, and we are very happy to introduce new writers to our audience in each issue. We have no restriction as to writing style or format, but do expect that the work submitted is ready for an audience. Payment in US is by contributor's copy, and outside the US is by pdf copy.

M0112 Christianity & Literature
Magazine
Department of English, Azusa Pacific University, 901 E. Alosta Avenue, Azusa, CA 91702-7000
United States

cal@apu.edu

https://www.christianityandliterature.com/journal

Types: Nonfiction; Poetry
Formats: Articles; Essays; Reviews
Subjects: Literature; Religion
Markets: Academic; Adult

Send: Full text

Journal devoted to the scholarly exploration of how literature engages Christian thought, experience, and practice. Submit articles and essays via online submission system. Send poems by post only. Book reviews by invitation only. See website for full details.

Editor: Mark Eaton

M0113 Church Music Quarterly
Magazine
RSCM, 19 The Close, Salisbury, Wiltshire, SP1 2EB
United Kingdom
Tel: +44 (0) 1722 424848

cmq@rscm.com

https://www.rscm.org.uk/our-resources/magazines/church-music-quarterly/

Nonfiction > *Articles*: Church Music

Send: Full text
How to send: Email; Post

Publishes reports, press releases and letters on or related to church music.

Editor: Esther Jones

M0114 The Cincinnati Review
Magazine
PO Box 210069, Cincinnati, Ohio 45221-0069
United States

editors@cincinnatireview.com

https://www.cincinnatireview.com/
https://facebook.com/CincinnatiReview
https://twitter.com/CincinnReview
https://www.youtube.com/channel/UCbDPomwAnBAddHtuKKh4HqA

Fiction > *Short Fiction*: Literary

Nonfiction > *Short Nonfiction*
Creative Nonfiction; Literary

Poetry in Translation > *Any Poetic Form*

Poetry > *Any Poetic Form*

How to send: Online submission system

Submit up to ten pages of poetry, up to forty pages of double-spaced fiction, or up to twenty pages of double-spaced literary nonfiction between September 1 and January 1. Accepts micro submissions year-round, except when accepting contest submissions.

Editors: Michael Griffith; Kristen Iversen; Rebecca Lindenberg

Fiction Editor: Brock Clarke

Managing Editor: Nicola Mason

Poetry Editor: Jim Cummins

M0115 Cirque
Magazine
United States

cirquejournal@gmail.com

https://cirquejournal.com

Fiction > *Short Fiction*: North Pacific Rim

Nonfiction
Reviews: North Pacific Rim
Short Nonfiction: North Pacific Rim

Poetry > *Any Poetic Form*: North Pacific Rim

Scripts > *Theatre Scripts*: North Pacific Rim

Send: Full text
How to send: Submittable

Publishes short stories, poems, creative nonfiction, translations, and plays by writers born in, or resident for at least five years in, the North Pacific Rim (Alaska, Washington, Oregon, Idaho, Montana, Hawaii, Yukon Territory, Alberta, and British Columbia). Submit via online submission system.

Editor: Sandra Kleven

M0116 Civil War Times
Magazine
United States

Magazine Publisher: HistoryNet LLC

M0117 Classic & Sports Car
Magazine
United Kingdom

https://www.classicandsportscar.com
https://www.facebook.com/candscmagazine
https://twitter.com/candscmagazine?lang=en
https://www.youtube.com/user/candscmagazine
https://www.instagram.com/classicandsportscar

Magazine Publisher: Haymarket Media Group

Nonfiction > *Articles*
Classic Cars; Sports Cars

Describes itself as "the world's best-selling classic car magazine, and the undisputed authority for anyone buying, owning, selling, maintaining or even just dreaming about classic cars".

Editor: James Elliott

Editor-in-Chief: Alastair Clements

M0118 Click
Magazine
United States

Magazine Publisher: Cricket Media, Inc.

M0119 Climbing
Magazine
United States

https://www.climbing.com
https://www.facebook.com/climbingmagazine
https://twitter.com/climbingmag
https://www.youtube.com/user/ClimbingMagazine
https://www.instagram.com/climbingmagazine

Magazine Publisher: Outside Interactive Inc.

Nonfiction > *Articles*: Climbing

Climbing photography and writing magazine.

Editor: Jeff Achey

M0120 Clubhouse Magazine
Magazine
Focus on the Family, 8605 Explorer Drive, Colorado Springs, CO 80920
United States
Tel: +1 (800) 232-6459

https://www.clubhousemagazine.com

Types: Fiction; Nonfiction
Formats: Essays; Interviews; Short Fiction
Subjects: Comedy / Humour; Fantasy; History; Religion; Science Fiction
Markets: Children's

Send: Full text

Magazine for boys and girls aged 8-12 providing wholesome, educational material with Scriptural or moral insight. Avoid bible stories, poems, and strictly informational pieces. See website for full guidelines.

Assistant Editor: Rachel Pfeiffer

M0121 Coin Collector
Magazine
United Kingdom

Magazine Publisher: Warners Group Publications

M0122 Coin News
Magazine
No 40, Southernhay East, Exeter, Devon, EX1 1PE
United Kingdom
Tel: +44 (0) 1404 46972

info@tokenpublishing.com

https://www.tokenpublishing.com

Types: Nonfiction
Formats: Articles; News
Subjects: Hobbies
Markets: Adult

Magazine covering coin collecting.

M0123 Collectors Magazine
Magazine
United Kingdom

Magazine Publisher: Warners Group Publications

M0124 The Comics Journal
Magazine
7563 Lake City Way NE, Seattle, WA 98115
United States

editorial@tcj.com

http://tcj.com

Book Publisher: Fantagraphics

Nonfiction > *Articles*: Comic Books

Send: Pitch
How to send: Email

Journal covering comics as an art form. Send pitch by email with subject line "Submission Inquiry".

Managing Editor: Dirk Deppey

News Editor: Michael Dean

M0125 Commando
Magazine
185 Fleet Street, London, EC4A 2HS
United Kingdom

generalenquiries@commandomag.com

https://www.commandocomics.com
https://www.facebook.com/Commando-Comics-168688426504994

Newspaper Publisher / Magazine Publisher: DC Thomson Media

ADULT > **Fiction** > *Cartoons*
Adventure; Warfare

CHILDREN'S > **Fiction** > *Cartoons*
Adventure; Warfare

YOUNG ADULT > **Fiction** > *Cartoons*
Adventure; Warfare

Publishes stories of action and adventure set in times of war, told in graphic novel format. May be wars of the modern age or ancient wars, or even occasionally wars of the future.

M0126 The Common Tongue Magazine
Online Magazine
United States

submissions@commontonguezine.com

https://www.commontonguezine.com
https://twitter.com/commontonguemag
https://www.facebook.com/commontonguezine/

Fiction > *Short Fiction*
Dark Fantasy; High / Epic Fantasy

Nonfiction > *Articles*
Fantasy; Writing

Poetry > *Any Poetic Form*: Dark Fantasy

Send: Full text
How to send: Online submission system

Writer's submissions must adhere to our guidelines to be considered for publication in our magazine. While we allow our writers a vast amount of room for creativity and writer's interpretation, we want to be sure that they support us in our quest for retaining that dark, dangerous tone that invokes our brand image.

We currently pay 3 cents USD per word for prose; $20 for a poem.

We invite all writers, regardless of level, to submit their short story submissions. We appreciate everyone's interest in the magazine and seek to honor that interest. While we are proud of being a leader in fantasy publications, we are also foremost writers and artists, and so we have extreme pride in supporting our contributors and those that make this all possible.

If you are interested in submitting short stories to be published in our bimonthly magazine, please review the writer guidelines to be considered on our website.

Online Magazine: The Undercommons (**M0533**)

M0127 Commonweal
Magazine
475 Riverside Drive, Room 405, New York, NY 10115
United States
Tel: +1 (212) 662-4200

editors@commonwealmagazine.org

https://www.commonwealmagazine.org
https://www.facebook.com/commonwealmagazine
https://twitter.com/commonwealmag

Nonfiction > *Articles*
Culture; Politics; Religion

Poetry > *Any Poetic Form*

How to send: Submittable

Journal of opinion edited by Catholic lay people. Publishes articles on religion, literature, and the arts. More interested in articles which examine the links between "worldly" concerns and religious beliefs than churchy or devotional pieces. Also publishes poetry.

Editor: Paul Baumann

M0128 Condé Nast Traveller
Magazine
United Kingdom

https://www.cntraveller.com
https://www.facebook.com/CNTraveller/
https://twitter.com/cntraveller
https://www.instagram.com/condenasttraveller/
https://www.youtube.com/user/condenasttraveller
https://www.pinterest.co.uk/cntraveller/

Magazine Publisher: Condé Nast Britain

Nonfiction > *Articles*: Travel

A luxury travel magazine aimed at the upmarket, independent traveller.

Editor: Abigail Chisman

M0129 Conjunctions
Magazine
21 East 10th St., #3E, New York, NY 10003
United States

conjunctions@bard.edu

http://www.conjunctions.com
https://conjunctions.submittable.com/submit
http://www.facebook.com/pages/Conjunctions/133404885505
https://www.instagram.com/_conjunctions/
https://twitter.com/_conjunctions

Fiction > *Short Fiction*: Literary

Nonfiction > *Short Nonfiction*: Creative Nonfiction

Poetry > *Any Poetic Form*

Send: Full text; Self-Addressed Stamped Envelope (SASE)
How to send: Post; Submittable

Publishes short and long form fiction, poetry, and creative nonfiction. No academic essays or book reviews. Do not query or send samples – submit complete ms through by post with SASE or using online submission system. See website for full guidelines.

Editor: Bradford Morrow

Online Magazine: Conjunctions Online (**M0130**)

M0130 Conjunctions Online
Online Magazine
21 E 10th Street, #3E, New York, NY 10003
United States

http://www.conjunctions.com/online/
https://conjunctions.submittable.com/submit
http://www.facebook.com/pages/Conjunctions/133404885505
https://www.instagram.com/_conjunctions/
https://twitter.com/_conjunctions

Magazine: Conjunctions (**M0129**)

Fiction > *Short Fiction*

Nonfiction > *Short Nonfiction*: Creative Nonfiction

Poetry > *Any Poetic Form*

How to send: Post; Submittable

Weekly online magazine. No thematic restrictions. Postal submissions are accepted year-round, but online submissions are open only during specific windows.

M0131 Conscience
Magazine
1436 U St. NW, Suite 301, Washington, DC 20009-3997
United States

conscience@catholicsforchoice.org

https://consciencemag.org
https://twitter.com/Catholic4Choice
https://www.facebook.com/CatholicsforChoice

Nonfiction > *Articles*
  Christianity; Feminism; Gender; Politics;
  Sexuality; Social Issues

How to send: Email

Magazine offers in-depth, cutting-edge
coverage of vital contemporary issues,
including reproductive rights, sexuality and
gender, feminism, the religious right, church
and state issues and US politics. Send
submissions by email.

M0132 Copper Nickel

Magazine
United States

wayne.miller@ucdenver.edu

http://copper-nickel.org

Types: Fiction; Nonfiction; Poetry;
Translations
Formats: Essays; Short Fiction
Subjects: Literary
Markets: Adult

Send: Full text

Submit four to six poems, or one story or one
essay at a time. Wait at least six months
between submissions. Submit via online
submission system.

Fiction Editor: Teague Bohlen

Fiction Editor / Nonfiction Editor: Joanna
Luloff

Managing Editor: Wayne Miller

Poetry Editors: Brian Barker; Nicky Beer

M0133 The Corridor of Uncertainty

Magazine
United Kingdom

clarky@corridorofuncertainty.com

https://www.corridorofuncertainty.com
https://twitter.com/clarkyfanzine

Types: Nonfiction
Formats: Articles
Subjects: Sport
Markets: Adult

How to send: Email

A Yorkshire cricket fansite which encourages
discussion on Yorkshire cricket and cricket in
general.

Editor: James Buttler

M0134 Cosmopolitan

Magazine
House of Hearst, 30 Panton Street, London,
SW1Y 4AJ
United Kingdom
Tel: +44 (0) 1858 438423

cosmopolitan-UK@hearst.co.uk

https://www.cosmopolitan.com/uk
https://facebook.com/cosmopolitanuk
https://twitter.com/CosmopolitanUK
https://www.pinterest.com/cosmopolitanuk/
https://instagram.com/cosmopolitanuk
https://www.youtube.com/user/cosmopolitanuk

Magazine Publisher: Hearst Magazines UK

Nonfiction > *Articles*
  Beauty; Current Affairs; Entertainment;
  Fashion; Health; Politics; Relationships; Sex

Magazine aimed at modern-minded women in
their mid-twenties, including a range of
articles, particularly on careers, relationships,
and news.

Editor: Sam Baker

Features Editor: Catherine Gray

M0135 Country Life

Magazine
Pinehurst 2, Pinehurst Road, Farnborough
Business Park, Farnborough, Hants, GU14
7BF
United Kingdom
Tel: +44 (0) 1252 555062

mark.hedges@ti-media.com

https://www.countrylife.co.uk

Types: Nonfiction
Formats: Articles; News
Subjects: Architecture; Arts; Current Affairs;
Lifestyle; Nature; Sport
Markets: Adult

Magazine covering all aspects of country
living. Looks for strong, well informed
material rather than material by amateur
enthusiasts.

Editor: Mark Hedges

M0136 Country Living

Magazine
House of Hearst, 30 Panton Street, London,
SW1Y 4AJ
United Kingdom

https://www.countryliving.com
https://www.facebook.com/countrylivinguk
https://twitter.com/countrylivinguk
https://www.pinterest.com/UKcountryliving/
https://www.instagram.com/countrylivinguk/

Magazine Publisher: Hearst Magazines UK

Nonfiction > *Articles*
  Country Lifestyle; Countryside; Crafts;
  Gardening; Houses; Nature; Recipes; Travel;
  Wellbeing

Magazine for people who love the country,
whether they live in it or not. Includes articles
on the countryside, wildlife, conservation,
gardens, houses, rural life, etc.

Editor: Susy Smith

M0137 Country Smallholding

Magazine
Archant SW, Unit 3, Old Station Road,
Barnstaple, EX32 8PB
United Kingdom
Tel: +44 (0) 1271 341652

editorial.csh@archant.co.uk

https://www.countrysmallholding.com/
https://www.facebook.com/
countrysmallholding
https://twitter.com/ctysmallholding

Nonfiction > *Articles*
  Country Lifestyle; Countryside; Gardening;
  Self-Sufficiency; Smallholdings

Magazine for smallholders, small farmers and
landowners, and those interested in both rural
and urban self-sufficiency.

Editor: Diane Cowgill

M0138 Cowboys & Indians

Magazine
Three Forest Plaza, 12221 Merit Drive, Suite
1610, Dallas, Texas 75251
United States
Tel: +1 (386) 246-0179

queries@cowboysindians.com

https://www.cowboysindians.com
https://www.facebook.com/cowboysindians/
http://pinterest.com/cowboysindians/
http://www.twitter.com/CI_Magazine
http://instagram.com/
cowboysindiansmagazine#

Nonfiction > *Articles*
  American West; Arts; Culture;
  Entertainment; Fashion; Food and Drink;
  Houses; Ranch Lifestyle; Ranches; Travel

Magazine focusing on the past and present of
the American West, including both historical
and lifestyle material.

M0139 Crab Orchard Review

Magazine
Southern Illinois University, Department of
English, 1000 Faner Drive, Mail Code 4503,
Southern Illinois University Carbondale,
Carbondale, IL 62901
United States
Tel: +1 (618) 453-6833
Fax: +1 (618) 453-8224

https://craborchardreview.siu.edu

Fiction > *Short Fiction*

Nonfiction > *Essays*

Poetry > *Any Poetic Form*

Closed to approaches.

Closed to submissions for the foreseeable
future following the death of the editor in
December 2019. Check website for current
status.

Editors: Allison Joseph; Jon Tribble

Prose Editor: Carolyn Alessio

M0140 Crannog Magazine
Magazine
Ireland

submissions@crannogmagazine.com

http://www.crannogmagazine.com

Fiction > *Short Fiction*: Literary

Poetry > *Any Poetic Form*

Send: Full text

A literary magazine publishing fiction and poetry only. No reviews or nonfiction. Published twice yearly in March and September. Accepts submissions in June and November. Authors who have been previously published in the magazine are recommended to purchase a copy of the current issue (or take out a subscription); for authors who have not been previously published in the magazine this is a requirement. Send up to one story or up to three poems by email only. No postal submissions.

Editor: Sandra Bunting, Tony O'Dwyer, Ger Burke, Jarlath Fahy

M0141 Cream City Review
Magazine
Department of English, University of Wisconsin-Milwaukee, P.O. Box 413, Milwaukee, WI 53201
United States

poetry@creamcityreview.org
fiction@creamcityreview.org
nonfiction@creamcityreview.org
art@creamcityreview.org
io@creamcityreview.org

https://uwm.edu/creamcityreview/
https://www.facebook.com/creamcityreview/
https://twitter.com/creamcityreview
https://www.instagram.com/cream_city_review/

Fiction > *Short Fiction*

Nonfiction > *Short Nonfiction*: Creative Nonfiction

Poetry > *Any Poetic Form*

Send: Full text
How to send: Submittable

Send prose up to 20 pages, or up to five poems of any length. Open to submissions January 1 to April 1 and August 1 to November 1.

M0142 Creative Nonfiction
Magazine
607 College Avenue, Pittsburgh, PA 15232
United States
Tel: +1 (412) 404-2975
Fax: +1 412-345-3767

information@creativenonfiction.org

https://creativenonfiction.org
https://creativenonfiction.submittable.com/submit/
https://www.facebook.com/creativenonfiction
https://twitter.com/cnfonline
https://instagram.com/creativenonfiction/

Nonfiction > *Essays*
   Creative Nonfiction; Memoir; Personal Essays

How to send: Submittable

Publishes all types of creative nonfiction, from immersion reportage to lyric essay to memoir and personal essays. See website for specific submission calls and their topics, or submit a pitch for a column year-round.

Editor: Lee Gutkind

M0143 Crimewave
Magazine
United Kingdom

http://www.ttapress.com/crimewave/

Magazine Publisher / Book Publisher: TTA Press (**P0839**)

Fiction > *Short Fiction*
   Crime; Mystery

Send: Full text
How to send: Submittable

Publishes crime and mystery short stories. See website for complete guidelines.

Editor: Andy Cox

M0144 Critical Quarterly
Magazine
Newbury, Crediton, Devon, EX17 5HA
United Kingdom

CQpoetry@gmail.com

http://onlinelibrary.wiley.com/journal/10.1111/(ISSN)1467-8705

Types: Fiction; Nonfiction; Poetry
Formats: Essays; Short Fiction
Subjects: Culture; Literary; Literary Criticism
Markets: Adult

Send: Full text
How to send: Email

Publishes literary criticism, cultural studies, poetry and fiction. Send submissions by email. See website for separate email address for submissions of criticism.

Editors: Clare Bucknell; Colin MacCabe

M0145 CrossStitcher
Magazine
United Kingdom

Magazine Publisher: Warners Group Publications

M0146 Cruising World
Magazine
480 N. Orlando Ave. Suite 236, Winter Park, FL 32789
United States
Tel: +1 (407) 628-4802

https://www.cruisingworld.com
https://www.facebook.com/cruisingworld/
https://twitter.com/cruisingworld/
https://www.instagram.com/cruisingworldmag/
https://www.youtube.com/c/cruisingworld

Media Company: Bonnier Corporation

Nonfiction > *Articles*
   Boats; Sailing

Send: Full text
How to send: Email

Magazine for owners of sailboats between 20 and 50 feet in length. Authors should familiarise themselves with the magazine before approaching.

Editor: Mark Pillsbury

M0147 Crystal Magazine
Magazine
3 Bowness Avenue, Prenton, Birkenhead, CH43 0SD
United Kingdom
Tel: +44 (0) 7769 790676

christinecrystal@hotmail.com

http://www.christinecrystal.blogspot.com

Fiction > *Short Fiction*
   Adventure; Comedy / Humour; Fantasy; Horror; Mystery; Romance; Science Fiction; Suspense; Thrillers; Westerns

Nonfiction > *Articles*
   Comedy / Humour; Literature; Nature; Travel

Poetry > *Any Poetic Form*

Send: Full text
How to send: Email

Costs: A subscription is required in order to submit. £21 UK / £25 RoW.

MAGAZINE: A4, 40-page, spiral-bound bi-monthly

FOR: subscribers only

CONTENTS: poems, stories (true and fiction) and articles

COLOUR IMAGES: carefully selected to enhance work

WORDSMITHING: a very popular regular feature written just for the magazine

LETTERS: usually pages

NEWS: an opportunity to share writing achievements

EXTRA: occasionally free booklets, bumper issues, gifts

SURPRISE COMPETITIONS: open to all writers.

TWENTY YEARS OLD!

FREE GIFT!

Editor: Christine Carr

M0148 Cumbria

Magazine
Country Publications Limited, The Gatehouse, Skipton Castle, Skipton, BD23 1AL
United Kingdom
Tel: +44 (0) 1756 701381
Fax: +44 (0) 1756 701326

johnm@dalesman.co.uk

http://www.cumbriamagazine.co.uk

Types: Nonfiction
Formats: Articles
Subjects: Nature; Travel
Markets: Adult

Regional magazine focusing on the nature of and walks in the Lake District.

Editor: John Manning

M0149 CutBank

Magazine
University of Montana, English Dept, LA 133, Missoula, MT 59812
United States

editor.cutbank@gmail.com

http://www.cutbankonline.org
https://cutbank.submittable.com/submit
https://twitter.com/cutbankonline
http://instagram.com/cutbankmag
https://www.facebook.com/cutbanklitmag/

Fiction > *Short Fiction*

Nonfiction > *Short Nonfiction*: Creative Nonfiction

Poetry > *Any Poetic Form*

Closed to approaches.

Costs: A fee is charged upon submission. $5 reading fee.

Accepts poetry, fiction, creative nonfiction, and visual art submissions. Please only submit online; paper submissions will be recycled.

M0150 Cyphers

Magazine
3 Selskar Terrace, Ranelagh, Dublin 6
Ireland

letters@cyphers.ie

http://www.cyphers.ie

Types: Fiction; Poetry; Translations
Formats: Short Fiction
Subjects: Literary
Markets: Adult

Send: Full text
How not to send: Email

Publishes poetry and fiction in English and Irish, from Ireland and around the world. Translations are welcome. No unsolicited critical articles. Submissions by post only. Attachments sent by email will be deleted. See website for full guidelines.

M0151 Daily Science Fiction

Magazine
United States

https://dailysciencefiction.com

Types: Fiction
Formats: Short Fiction
Subjects: Fantasy; Science Fiction
Markets: Adult

Send: Full text

Publishes speculative fiction stories from 100 to 1,500 words, including science fiction, fantasy, slipstream, etc. Send submissions through online submissions system

M0152 Dalesman

Magazine
The Gatehouse, Skipton Castle, Skipton, North Yorkshire, BD23 1AL
United Kingdom
Tel: +44 (0) 1756 701033

jon@dalesman.co.uk

http://www.dalesman.co.uk

Book Publisher / Magazine Publisher:
Dalesman Publishing Co. Ltd (**P0209**)

Nonfiction > *Articles*: Yorkshire

Magazine publishing material of Yorkshire interest.

Editor: Paul Jackson

M0153 The Dalhousie Review

Magazine
Dalhousie University, Halifax, Nova Scotia, B3H 4R2
Canada

dalhousie.review@dal.ca

https://ojs.library.dal.ca/dalhousiereview

Types: Fiction; Nonfiction; Poetry
Formats: Essays; Reviews; Short Fiction
Subjects: Literary
Markets: Adult

Send: Full text
How to send: Email

Publishes fiction, poetry, essays, and book reviews. Submit up to five poems at a time. Query before submitting reviews. See website for full submission guidelines.

M0154 Dame

Magazine
United States

editorial@damemagazine.com

https://www.damemagazine.com

Types: Nonfiction
Formats: Articles; Essays; News
Subjects: Arts; Business; Culture; Finance; Health; Nature; Politics; Science; Technology; Women's Interests
Markets: Adult

Magazine of news and opinion from a female perspective.

Editor: Kera Bolonik

M0155 Dancing Times

Magazine
United Kingdom
Tel: +44 (0) 20 7250 3006

https://www.facebook.com/1dancingtimes/
https://twitter.com/dancingtimes

Nonfiction
  Articles: Dance
  News: Dance
  Reviews: Dance

Monthly magazine of dance, publishing features, news, and review.

M0156 DargonZine

Magazine
United States

editor@dargonzine.org

http://dargonzine.org

Types: Fiction
Formats: Short Fiction
Subjects: Fantasy
Markets: Adult

Send: Full text

Electronic magazine publishing fantasy fiction based in a shared world, where authors write in a common milieu, sharing settings, mythos, and characters. To submit, writers need to join (free until a year after first publication) and work with a mentor to produce a piece of work that will fit the shared world.

M0157 The Dark Horse

Magazine
PO Box 8342, Kilwinning, KA13 9AL
United Kingdom

https://www.thedarkhorsemagazine.com
https://www.facebook.com/The-Dark-Horse-Magazine-184043168311270/
https://twitter.com/thedarkhorsemag

Poetry > *Any Poetic Form*

Send: Full text; Self-Addressed Stamped Envelope (SASE)
How to send: Post
How not to send: Email

International literary magazine committed to British, Irish and American poetry. Send submissions by post only, to UK or US editorial addresses. No simultaneous submissions. See website for full guidelines.

Editor: Gerry Cambridge

M0158 Dark Tales
Magazine
7 Offley Street, Worcester, WR3 8BH
United Kingdom

stories@darktales.co.uk

http://www.darktales.co.uk

Fiction > *Short Fiction*
Horror; Speculative

Send: Full text
How to send: Email; Post

Costs: A fee is charged upon submission; Offers services that writers have to pay for.

Created as an outlet primarily for unpublished writers of sci-fi, dark fantasy and horror short stories. Published stories are the winners and shortlisted entries from the monthly competition (£4 entry fee). Also offers optional critiques.

Editor: Sean Jeffery

M0159 Darts World
Magazine
United Kingdom

info@dartsworld.com

https://www.dartsworld.com
https://www.facebook.com/
dartsworldmagazine
https://twitter.com/darts_world

Nonfiction
Articles: Darts
News: Darts

Publishes articles and news on the subject of darts only.

Editor: Tony Wood

M0160 The Dawntreader
Magazine
24 Forest Houses, Halwill, Beaworthy, Devon, EX21 5UU
United Kingdom

dawnidp@gmail.com

https://www.indigodreams.co.uk/the-dawntreader

Types: Fiction; Nonfiction; Poetry
Formats: Articles; Short Fiction
Subjects: Literary; Nature; Spirituality
Markets: Adult

Send: Full text

A quarterly publication specialising in myth, legend; in the landscape, nature; spirituality and love; the mystic, the environment. Welcomes poetry up to 40 lines, and prose, articles, and local legends up to 1,000 words.

Editor: Ronnie Goodyer

M0161 Decision
Magazine
United States

https://decisionmagazine.com
https://www.facebook.com/Decisionmagazine/
https://twitter.com/DecisionNews

Nonfiction
Articles: Christianity; Evangelism; Politics
News: Christianity; Evangelism; Politics

Magazine publishing news and articles of relevance to Christians and evangelism.

Editor: Bob Paulson

M0162 Deep Overstock Magazine
Magazine
United States

submissions@deepoverstock.com

https://deepoverstock.com/issues/
https://deepoverstock.com/submission-guidelines/

Book Publisher / Magazine Publisher: Deep Overstock Publishing (**P0222**)

Fiction > *Short Fiction*

Nonfiction > *Essays*

Poetry > *Any Poetic Form*

Send: Full text; Author bio
How to send: In the body of an email

Accepts fiction, poetry, and essays. Issues are themed. Check website for current theme. Prefers essays and fiction to be under 3,000 words. Accepts up to seven poems per theme.

M0163 Deracine
Magazine
United States

deracinemagazine@gmail.com

http://deracinemagazine.wordpress.com

Types: Fiction; Poetry
Subjects: Contemporary; Experimental; Gothic; Literary; Literature
Markets: Adult; Professional; Young Adult

Send: Full text
How to send: Email

A literary magazine featuring dark, psychological fiction, poetry, and art. Started in 2017, we are a nonprofit publication. Our goal is to share literature that raises awareness of and expresses psychological issues and feelings of displacement through the literary gothic. We're open to a variety of styles, including writing that is minimalistic or that has elements of fantasy or horror, so long as it fits within our theme.

Editor: Victoria Elghasen and Michelle Baleka

M0164 Descant
Magazine
c/o TCU Department of English, Box 297270, 2850 S. University Dr., Fort Worth, TX 76129
United States

descant@tcu.edu

https://descant.tcu.edu

Types: Fiction; Poetry
Formats: Short Fiction
Subjects: Literary
Markets: Adult

Send: Full text

Submit one story up to 5,000 words, or up to five poems via online submission system, or by post with SASE. Closed to submissions in April, May, June, July, and August. See website for full guidelines.

M0165 Diecast Collection
Magazine
United Kingdom

Magazine Publisher: Warners Group Publications

M0166 Diver Magazine
Magazine
Suite B, 74 Oldfield Road, Hampton, Middlesex, TW12 2HR
United Kingdom
Tel: +44 (0) 20 8941 8152

nigel@divermag.co.uk

https://divernet.com/contact/

Formats: Articles; News
Subjects: Hobbies; Sport; Technology; Travel
Markets: Adult

Magazine covering every aspect of recreational scuba diving, especially in the realms of gear testing and surveys, diving holiday destinations, and advances in technology and techniques.

M0167 Dogs Monthly
Magazine
The Old Print House, 62 The High Street, Chobham, Surrey, GU24 8AA
United Kingdom
Tel: +44 (0) 1276 858880

https://dogsmonthly.co.uk
https://www.facebook.com/DogsMonthly
https://www.instagram.com/
dogsmonthlymagazine/
https://twitter.com/dogsmonthly

Nonfiction > *Articles*: Dogs

Send: Query
How to send: Online contact form; Phone; Post

Magazine for dog enthusiasts publishing articles on breeds, topical news, and features. Contact through form on website, or by phone or post in first instance.

Editor: Caroline Davis

M0168 Dolls House and Miniature Scene
Magazine
United Kingdom

Magazine Publisher: Warners Group
Publications

M0169 Dorset Life
Magazine
7, The Leanne, Sandford Lane, Wareham,
Dorset, BH20 4DY
United Kingdom
Tel: +44 (0) 1929 551264

editor@dorsetlife.co.uk

https://www.dorsetlife.co.uk

Types: Nonfiction
Formats: Articles
Markets: Adult

County magazine for Dorset.

Editor:

M0170 Downstate Story
Magazine
1825 Maple Ridge, Peoria, IL 61614
United States
Tel: +1 (309) 688-1409

ehopkins7@prodigy.net

https://www.downstatestory.com

Types: Fiction
Formats: Short Fiction
Subjects: Literary
Markets: Adult

A regional magazine featuring mostly writers
from Illinois and the Midwest. As of 2012,
online only.

Editor: Elaine Hopkins

M0171 The Drake Magazine
Magazine
PO Box 11546, Denver, CO 80211
United States
Tel: +1 (303) 917-9006

info@drakemag.com

https://drakemag.com/
https://www.instagram.com/thedrakemagazine/
https://twitter.com/Drakemagazine
https://www.facebook.com/
TheDrakeMagazine/
http://feeds.feedburner.com/Drakemag

Nonfiction > *Articles*: Fishing

Send: Query
Don't send: Full text
How to send: Post; Email

Fishing magazine publishing educational and
entertaining fishing stories. Does not publish
how-to and where-to stories, but rather pieces

which tell stories in a literary way. See website
for details.

Editor: Tom Bie

M0172 Dream Catcher
Magazine
109 Wensley Drive, Leeds, LS7 2LU
United Kingdom

http://www.dreamcatchermagazine.co.uk

Fiction > *Short Fiction*

Nonfiction > *Interviews*

Poetry > *Any Poetic Form*

Send: Full text
How to send: Post

Send submissions by post, following
guidelines on website. No electronic
submissions.

Editor: Wendy Pratt

M0173 The Dublin Review
Magazine
PO Box 7948, Dublin 1
Ireland

enquiry@thedublinreview.com

https://thedublinreview.com

Types: Fiction; Nonfiction
Formats: Essays; Short Fiction
Subjects: Literary; Literary Criticism
Markets: Adult

Send: Full text

Publishes essays, criticism, reportage, and
fiction for a general, intelligent readership. No
poetry. Accepts submissions by post with
email address for response, but prefers
submissions by via form on website. Physical
material is not returned, so do not include
return postage. No response without email
address.

M0174 E/The Environmental Magazine
Online Magazine
United States

http://www.emagazine.com
https://www.facebook.com/askearthtalk/
https://twitter.com/EEnviroMag

Nonfiction
  Articles: Environment; Nature; Sustainable
  Living
  News: Environment

Send: Query
How to send: Online contact form

Former print magazine (now online only)
focusing on environmental issues, dispensing
news and information and advising people on
how they can make a difference. Potential
contributors should query in the first instance
via contact form on website.

Editor: Jim Motavalli

M0175 EAP: The Magazine
Magazine
United States

tod@exterminatingangel.com

http://exterminatingangel.com/eap-the-
magazine/

Types: Fiction; Poetry
Formats: Short Fiction
Subjects: Literary
Markets: Adult

Online publication established in 2012. See
website for latest issue and next deadline for
submissions.

Editor: Tod Davies

M0176 Early American Life
Magazine
Firelands Media Group LLC, 16759 West Park
Circle Drive, Chagrin Falls, Ohio 44023
United States
Tel: +1 (440) 543-8566

queries@firelandsmedia.com

https://www.ealonline.com

Types: Nonfiction
Formats: Articles
Subjects: Antiques; Architecture; Crafts;
History
Markets: Adult

Send: Full text
How to send: Email

Magazine aimed at people with an interest in
the style of the period 1600-1840 in America,
and its use in their modern homes and lives.
Covers architecture, antiques, etc. Will
consider unsolicited mss but prefers initial
queries by email.

M0177 Eclipse Lit
Magazine
United States

hello@eclipselit.org

https://www.eclipselit.org
https://twitter.com/eclipse_lit
http://www.instagram.com/jlfaccend

Fiction > *Short Fiction*: Literary

Nonfiction > *Essays*

Poetry > *Any Poetic Form*

How to send: Email

We are a nonprofit literary magazine that
focuses on sharing the work of writers and
artists while benefiting a different organization
through each issue. Our mission is to give an
outlet for writers to heal through art while
benefiting organizations dedicated to helping
people with trauma.

M0178 Economica

Magazine
United Kingdom

economica@lse.ac.uk

https://onlinelibrary.wiley.com/journal/
14680335

Types: Nonfiction
Formats: Articles
Subjects: Business; Finance
Markets: Academic

Send: Full text
How to send: Email

Academic journal or economics. See website
for submission guidelines.

Editors: Nava Ashraf; Oriana Bandiera; Tim
Besley; Francesco Caselli; Maitreesh Ghatak;
Stephen Machin; Ian Martin; Gianmarco
Ottaviano

M0179 The Economist

Magazine
The Adelphi, 1-11 John Adam Street, London,
WC2N 6HT
United Kingdom
Tel: +44 (0) 20 7830 7000

https://www.economist.com
https://www.facebook.com/theeconomist
https://www.instagram.com/theeconomist
https://www.twitter.com/theeconomist
https://www.linkedin.com/company/the-
economist
https://www.youtube.com/user/
economistmagazine

Nonfiction
  Articles: Business; Current Affairs; Finance;
  Politics
  News: Business; Current Affairs; Finance;
  Politics

Magazine covering economics, business,
finance, politics, and current affairs.

M0180 Ecotone

Magazine
Department of Creative Writing, University of
North Carolina Wilmington, 601 South
College Road, Wilmington, NC 28403-5938
United States

info@ecotonejournal.com

https://ecotonemagazine.org

Types: Fiction; Nonfiction; Poetry
Subjects: Literary
Markets: Adult

Send: Full text

Publishes work from a wide range of voices.
Particularly interested in hearing from writers
historically underrepresented in literary
publishing and in place-based contexts: people
of colour, Indigenous people, people with
disabilities, gender-nonconforming people,

LGBTQIA+, women, and others. Check
website for specific reading periods and submit
prose up to 30 double-spaced pages or 3-5
poems by post with SAE or using online
system ($3 charge). No hard copy submissions
from outside the US.

Editor: David Gessner

M0181 Edinburgh Review

Magazine
United Kingdom

https://edinburgh-review.com
https://www.facebook.com/Edinburgh-
Review-202034306209/
https://twitter.com/EdinburghReview

Fiction > *Short Fiction*: Literary

Nonfiction > *Essays*
  Arts; Culture; Literary Criticism; Literature;
  Philosophy; Politics

Poetry > *Any Poetic Form*

Closed to approaches.

Publishes Scottish and international fiction and
accessible essays on the relationship of
philosophy to the visual and literary arts.

Editor: Brian McCabe

M0182 Edison Literary Review

Magazine
13 Waverly Drive East, Edison, NJ 08817
United States

http://edisonliteraryreview.org

Types: Poetry
Subjects: Literary
Markets: Adult

Submit 3-5 poems. Poems under 40 lines stand
a better chance of acceptance. Will accept
submissions by post with SASE, but prefers
submissions via form on website.

M0183 The Ekphrastic Review

Online Magazine
Canada

theekphrasticreview@gmail.com

https://www.ekphrastic.net

Fiction > *Short Fiction*

Nonfiction
  Articles: Arts
  Interviews: Literature
  Reviews: Literature
  Short Nonfiction: General

Poetry in Translation > *Any Poetic
Form*: Arts

Poetry > *Any Poetic Form*: Arts

Send: Full text
How to send: Email

Publishes poetry that responds to, explores, or
is inspired by a piece of art, and fiction and

nonfiction of any kind, including book
interviews or profiles, and articles about
ekphrastic writing. Accepts submissions during
specific windows only (see website for details).

Editor: Lorette C. Luzajic

M0184 El Portal

Magazine
United States

el.portal@enmu.edu

https://elportaljournal.com

Types: Fiction; Nonfiction; Poetry
Formats: Essays; Short Fiction
Subjects: Literary
Markets: Adult

Send: Full text
How to send: Email

Accepts submissions of flash fiction up to 500
words, short stories and creative nonfiction up
to 4,000 words, or up to five poems, by email.
See website for full guidelines.

Editor: Jennifer Baros

M0185 The Elks Magazine

Magazine
425 West Diversey Parkway, Chicago, IL
60614
United States

magnews@elks.org

https://www.elks.org/elksmag/

Nonfiction > *Articles*
  Americana; Finance; Health; History;
  Leisure; Nature; Retirement; Science; Sport;
  Technology

Send: Full text; Self-Addressed Stamped
Envelope (SASE)
How to send: Post; Email

Publishes features of general interest. Seeks
articles that are fresh, thought provoking, well
researched, and well documented. Typical
readership consists of individuals over 40, with
some college, an above-average income, from
towns of half a million or less. Send
submissions by email or by post with SASE.
No religious, political, or first-person articles,
or poetry.

Editor: Anna L. Idol

M0186 Elle

Magazine
30 Panton Street, Leicester Square, London,
SW1Y 4AJ
United Kingdom
Tel: +44 (0) 1858 438796

ellefeatures@elleuk.com

https://www.elle.com/uk/
https://www.facebook.com/ELLEuk
https://twitter.com/ELLEUK
https://www.pinterest.com/ellemag/

https://www.instagram.com/elleuk/
https://www.youtube.com/user/ELLEUKTV

Magazine Publisher: Hearst Magazines UK

Nonfiction
  Articles: Beauty; Culture; Fashion;
  Horoscopes; Lifestyle
  News: Celebrity

Send: Query; Author bio
How to send: Email

For features, send query with CV by email.

Editor: Lorraine Candy

Features Editor: Anna Pursglove

M0187 Empire

Magazine
United Kingdom

https://www.empireonline.com
http://facebook.com/empiremagazine
http://twitter.com/empiremagazine

Magazine Publisher: Bauer Media Group

Nonfiction
  Articles: Cinemas / Movie Theaters; Film
  Industry; Films; Technology
  News: Cinemas / Movie Theaters; Film
  Industry; Films; Technology
  Reviews: Films; Technology

Magazine of films and film-makers, as well as
some attention to supporting technologies.
Publishes behind-the-scenes articles, news, and
reviews.

Editor: Colin Kennedy

M0188 Emrys Journal

Magazine
Emrys Foundation, P.O. Box 8813, Greenville,
SC 29604
United States
Tel: +1 (864) 202-4906

info@emrys.org

https://www.emrys.org
https://www.facebook.com/EmrysFoundation
https://twitter.com/EmrysFoundation
https://www.instagram.com/emrysfoundation/
https://www.youtube.com/playlist?list=
PL36cHhWtnzVMd45OyB6TspqM9xwBZfc
My

Fiction > *Short Fiction*

Nonfiction > *Short Nonfiction*: Creative
Nonfiction

Poetry > *Any Poetic Form*

Closed to approaches.

Literary journal publishing fiction, poetry, and
creative nonfiction. Submit via online
submission system during specific submission
windows.

Editor: Katherine Burgess

M0189 Enchanted Living

Magazine
United States

submissions@faeriemag.com

https://enchantedlivingmag.com

Types: Fiction; Nonfiction; Poetry
Formats: Articles
Subjects: Arts; Beauty; Crafts; Design;
Fantasy; Fashion; Nature; Travel
Markets: Adult

Send: Full text
How to send: Email

A quarterly print magazine that celebrates all
things enchanted. Publishes photography,
recipes, original fiction and poetry, travel
pieces, artist profiles, home decor,
otherworldly beauty tips, craft tutorials, and
more. Send submissions by email. See website
for specific email address for poetry.

M0190 Entrepreneur

Magazine
18061 Fitch, Irvine CA, 92614
United States

https://www.entrepreneur.com/
https://www.facebook.com/EntMagazine
https://twitter.com/entrepreneur
https://www.linkedin.com/company/
entrepreneur-media
https://www.pinterest.com/entrepreneurmedia
https://www.instagram.com/entrepreneur/
https://www.youtube.com/user/
EntrepreneurOnline

Nonfiction > *Articles*
  Business; Entrepreneurship; Finance; How
  To

Magazine for people who have started and are
running their own business, providing news o
current trends, practical how-to articles,
features on combining work and life, etc. Runs
features and several regular columns, as well
as an inner magazine on start-ups.

Editor: Karen Axelton

M0191 EQy Magazine (Scottish Equestrian Year)

Magazine
Wyvex Media, Fettes Park, 496 Ferry Road,
Edinburgh, EH5 2DL
United Kingdom
Tel: +44 (0) 1315 511000

heddy@eqymagazine.co.uk

https://www.eqymagazine.co.uk

Types: Nonfiction
Subjects: Nature
Markets: Adult

Luxury magazine published once a year,
covering Scottish equestrianism.

M0192 Erotic Review

Magazine
United Kingdom

editorial@ermagazine.org

http://eroticreviewmagazine.com

Types: Fiction; Nonfiction
Formats: Articles; Reviews; Short Fiction
Subjects: Erotic; Lifestyle
Markets: Adult

Send: Full text
How to send: Email

Literary lifestyle publication about sex and
sexuality aimed at sophisticated, intelligent and
mature readers. Print version has been retired
and is now online only. Publishes features,
articles, short stories, and reviews. See website
for full submission guidelines.

Editor / Literary Agent: Jamie Maclean
(L0659)

M0193 Event

Magazine
PO Box 2503, New Westminster, BC, V3L
5B2
Canada
Tel: +1 (604) 527-5293

event@douglascollege.ca

https://www.eventmagazine.ca
https://twitter.com/EVENTmags
https://www.facebook.com/eventmagazine
http://www.youtube.com/channel/
UCKuYlH5b3uRaitKO4lCk8zA?feature=
watch

Fiction > *Short Fiction*

Nonfiction
  Reviews: Books
  Short Nonfiction: Creative Nonfiction

Poetry > *Any Poetic Form*

Closed to approaches.

One of Western Canada's longest-running
literary magazines. Welcomes submissions in
English from around the world during specific
submission windows.

M0194 Fabula Argentea

Magazine
United States

fabargmagazine@gmail.com

https://www.fabulaargentea.com

Types: Fiction
Formats: Short Fiction
Markets: Adult

Send: Full text

Online magazine publishing fiction up to 8,000
words. Submit via online submission system.

M0195 Faces

Magazine
1751 Pinnacle Drive, Suite 600, McLean, VA
22102
United States

faces@cricketmedia.com

http://cricketmedia.com/Faces-travel-
magazine-for-kids

Magazine Publisher: Cricket Media, Inc.

CHILDREN'S
Fiction > *Short Fiction*: Folklore, Myths, and
Legends
Nonfiction
Articles: Culture; Lifestyle; Travel
Interviews: Culture; Lifestyle; Travel

Send: Query
Don't send: Full text
How to send: Email

Magazine for children aged 9-14 covering the
ways in which people living in other countries
and cultures live. All issues are themed so
essential to check upcoming themes before
querying. Send query with one-page outline of
proposed article and detailed bibliography of
materials. See website for full details.

Editor: Elizabeth Crooker Carpentiere

M0196 Fangoria

Magazine
United States

editorial@fangoria.com

https://fangoria.com
https://www.facebook.com/FANGORIA/
https://twitter.com/fangoria
https://www.instagram.com/fangoria
https://www.youtube.com/user/
fangoriamagazine

Nonfiction
Articles: Films; Horror
Reviews: Films; Horror

Send: Pitch; Writing sample
How to send: Email

Horror entertainment magazine founded in
1979. Send pitch with writing sample by email.

Editor: Anthony Timpone

M0197 Farm & Ranch Living

Magazine
1610 North 2nd Street, Suite 102, Milwaukee,
WI 53212
United States

feedback@farmandranchliving.com

http://www.farmandranchliving.com

PROFESSIONAL > **Nonfiction** > *Articles*: F
arming

Send: Full text
How to send: Online submission system

Reader-written magazine about farming and
life on a ranch, publishing personal stories and
photographs. Submit via online submission
system.

M0198 Farming Magazine

Magazine
United States
Tel: +1 (330) 674-1892

editor@farmingmagazine.net

https://www.farmingmagazine.net

Types: Nonfiction
Formats: Articles
Subjects: Lifestyle; Nature
Markets: Adult; Professional

Send: Full text
How to send: Email

Magazine that celebrates the joys of farming
well and living well on a small, ecologically-
conscious scale.

M0199 Fashion x Film

Magazine
United States

info@fashionxfilm.com

https://fashionxfilm.com

Types: Nonfiction
Formats: Articles; Film Scripts
Subjects: Beauty; Culture; Fashion
Markets: Academic; Adult

Send: Full text
How to send: Email

Online publication dedicated to unravelling the
hidden meaning of fashion in film, be it
through a single work, a director's oeuvre, or
some common theme. Aims for an academic,
cerebral tone. Send queries or complete
submissions by email. See website for full
guidelines.

M0200 Fate

Magazine
PO Box 774, Hendersonville, NC 28793
United States
Tel: +1 (828) 702-3032

Phyllis@fatemag.com

https://www.fatemag.com
https://www.youtube.com/channel/UCAjXG-
tsjV5VJM-i-afsvqA
https://twitter.com/Fate_Magazine
https://instagram.com/fatemagazine

Nonfiction > *Articles*
Mystery; Science; Supernatural / Paranormal

How to send: Post; Email

Magazine of mysterious and unexplained
phenomena.

Editor-in-Chief: Phyllis Galde

M0201 Faultline

Magazine
UCI Department of English, 435 Humanities
Instructional Building, Irvine, CA 92697-2650
United States
Tel: +1 (949) 824-1573

faultline@uci.edu
ucifaultline@gmail.com

https://faultline.sites.uci.edu/
https://www.facebook.com/uci.faultline
https://twitter.com/faultline_journ

Fiction in Translation > *Short Fiction*

Fiction > *Short Fiction*

Nonfiction in Translation > *Short
Nonfiction*: Creative Nonfiction

Nonfiction > *Short Nonfiction*: Creative
Nonfiction

Poetry in Translation > *Any Poetic Form*

Poetry > *Any Poetic Form*

Closed to approaches.

Send up to five poems or up to 20 pages of
fiction or creative nonfiction, between October
15 and December 15 only.

Fiction Editor: Sara Joyce Robinson

Poetry Editor: Lisa P. Sutton

M0202 FellowScript

Magazine
c/o Box 463, Glendon, Alberta
Canada
Tel: +1 (780) 646-3068

fellowscripteditor2@gmail.com

https://inscribe.org/fellowscript/

Types: Nonfiction; Poetry
Formats: Articles; Reviews
Subjects: Hobbies; Religion
Markets: Adult

Magazine for Christian writers. Includes
articles and book and market reviews of
interest to writers, and also poetry. See website
for full guidelines.

Editor: Nina Morey

M0203 Feminist Review

Magazine
c/o Centre for Gender Studies, SOAS
University of London, Thornhaugh Street,
LONDON, WC1H 0XG
United Kingdom

feministreview@soas.ac.uk

https://journals.sagepub.com/home/fer
https://twitter.com/FeministReview_

Book Publisher / Magazine Publisher: Sage
Publications (**P0725**)

ACADEMIC > **Nonfiction** > *Articles*: Femini
sm

Send: Full text
How to send: Online submission system

A peer reviewed, interdisciplinary journal contributing to new agendas for feminism. The journal invites critical reflection on the relationship between materiality and representation, theory and practice, subjectivity and communities, contemporary and historical formations.

Editor: Joanna Hoare, Assistant Editor

M0204 Feminist Studies

Magazine
4137 Susquehannna Hall, 4200 Lehigh Road, University of Maryland, College Park, MD 20742
United States
Tel: +1 (301) 405-7415
Fax: +1 (301) 405-8395

info@feministstudies.org
submit@feministstudies.org
creative@feministstudies.org
art@feministstudies.org
review@feministstudies.org

http://www.feministstudies.org

ACADEMIC > **Nonfiction** > *Essays*
   Cultural Criticism; Literary Criticism
ADULT
   Fiction > *Short Fiction*: Feminism

   Nonfiction > *Articles*
      Arts; Culture; Feminism

   Poetry > *Any Poetic Form*: Feminism

Send: Full text; Proposal; Writing sample; Author bio
How to send: Email

Feminist journal publishing research and criticism, creative writing, art, essays, and other forms of writing and visual expression. See website for submission guidelines and specific submission email addresses.

M0205 Fenland Poetry Journal

Magazine
PO Box 234, Wisbech, PE14 4EZ
United Kingdom

fenlandpoetryjournal@gmail.com

https://fenlandpoetryjournal.co.uk

Poetry > *Any Poetic Form*
   Contemporary; Literary

Send: Full text
How not to send: Email

Contemporary poetry journal accepting submissions from anywhere in the world, though particularly encouraged from Fenland. No line limits. Send up to six poems by post only with SASE. No email submissions.

M0206 FHM

Online Magazine
United Kingdom

editor@fhm.com

http://www.fhm.com

Nonfiction
   Articles: Cars; Entertainment; Fashion; Lifestyle; Sex; Sport
   Interviews: General

Formerly the world's best-selling print male lifestyle magazine, now an online magazine.

Editor: Ross Brown

M0207 Fiction

Magazine
c/o Department of English, City College of New York, Convent Ave. at 138th Street, New York, NY 10031
United States

fictionmageditors@gmail.com

http://www.fictioninc.com
http://submissions.fictioninc.com/
http://instagram.com/fiction.magazine
https://twitter.com/fictionmag
https://www.facebook.com/fiction.mag/

Fiction > *Short Fiction*: Literary

Closed to approaches.

Accepts short stories, novelettes, and novellas of any length (though staying under 5,000 words is encouraged). Submit by post or using online submission system between October 15 and April 15 only.

Editor: Mark J. Mirsky

M0208 The Fiddlehead

Magazine
Campus House, 11 Garland Court, University of New Brunswick, PO Box 4400, Fredericton NB, E3B 5A3
Canada
Tel: +1 (506) 453-3501

fiddlehd@unb.ca

https://thefiddlehead.ca
https://twitter.com/TheFiddlehd
http://www.facebook.com/pages/The-Fiddlehead-Atlantic-Canadas-International-Literary-Journal/174825212565312

Fiction
   Novel Excerpts; *Short Fiction*
Nonfiction > *Short Nonfiction*: Creative Nonfiction

Poetry > *Any Poetic Form*

Send: Query; Author bio; Full text
How to send: Submittable; Post

Publishes poetry, fiction, and creative nonfiction in a variety of styles, including experimental genres. Also publishes excerpts from longer works, and reviews. Submit up to six poems (up to 12 pages total), or a piece of fiction up to 6,000 words. All submissions must be original and unpublished. Prefers submissions through online submission system (Feb 15 to April 30 and Sep 15 to November 30 only), but will accept submissions by post. See website for full details.

M0209 Film Review

Online Magazine
United States

https://filmreviewonline.com
https://www.facebook.com/Film-Review-Online-139186982814321

Nonfiction
   Interviews: Celebrity; Entertainment; Films; TV
   News: Cinemas / Movie Theaters; Film Industry; Films; TV
   Reviews: Films; TV

Film and TV website publishing reviews, profiles, interviews, and news. Includes editors based in New York, Los Angeles, and London.

Editor: Neil Corry

M0210 Firmament

Magazine
United States

support@sublunaryeditions.com

https://sublunaryeditions.com/firmament
https://oleada.io/publication/sublunary-editions

Book Publisher / Magazine Publisher: Sublunary Editions (**P0802**)

Fiction > *Short Fiction*

Nonfiction > *Interviews*

Features new writing from around the world, along with in-depth interviews, excerpts from upcoming titles, regular columns, and more.

M0211 The First Line

Magazine
PO Box 250382, Plano, Texas 75025-0382
United States

submission@thefirstline.com

http://www.thefirstline.com

Fiction > *Short Fiction*

Nonfiction > *Essays*: Literary Criticism

Poetry > *Any Poetic Form*

Send: Full text; Self-Addressed Stamped Envelope (SASE)
How to send: Word file email attachment; Post
How not to send: PDF file email attachment; Google Docs shared document

Prefers submissions by email, but will also accept submissions by post with SASE. Prefers attachments as a Word or Word Perfect file. Stories must begin with the appropriate first line for that issue, as provided on the website.

Occasionally accepts poems starting with the specified first line. Also accepts essays on your favourite first line from a book.

M0212 Five Points

Magazine
Georgia State University, P.O. Box 3999,
Atlanta, GA 30302-3999
United States

http://fivepoints.gsu.edu

Fiction in Translation
   Novel Excerpts: Literary
   Short Fiction: Literary

Fiction > *Short Fiction*: Literary

Nonfiction in Translation > *Essays*

Nonfiction > *Short Nonfiction*
   General, and in particular: Literary

Poetry in Translation > *Any Poetic Form*

Poetry > *Any Poetic Form*

Send: Full text
How to send: Submittable
How not to send: Post

Costs: A fee is charged upon submission.

Welcomes unsolicited submissions of fiction, poetry, flash fiction and nonfiction, and literary nonfiction. Submit through online submission system.

Editor: Megan Sexton

M0213 Flaneur

Online Magazine
United Kingdom

editor@flaneur.me.uk

http://www.flaneur.me.uk

Nonfiction > *Articles*
   Arts; Films; Food and Drink; Literature;
   Music; Politics; Sport; TV; Theatre; Travel

Send: Full text
How to send: In the body of an email

Online magazine of arts, culture, politics, and sport.

Editor: J Powell

M0214 Flash: The International Short-Short Story Magazine

Magazine
Department of English, University of Chester,
Parkgate Road, Chester, CH1 4BJ
United Kingdom

flash.magazine@chester.ac.uk

http://www.chester.ac.uk/flash.magazine

Types: Fiction
Formats: Short Fiction
Subjects: Literary
Markets: Adult

Send: Full text
How to send: Email

Publishes flash fiction up to 360 words, including the title. Send up to four pieces per issue. Attach submissions to a single email. See website for full submission guidelines.

Editors: Dr Peter Blair; Dr Ashley Chantler

M0215 Florida Living

Magazine
999 Douglas Avenue, Suite 3301, Altamonte
Springs, FL 32714
United States

Publisher@FloridaMagazine.com

https://www.floridamagazine.com

Nonfiction > *Articles*
   Florida; Food; History; Lifestyle; Outdoor
   Activities; Travel

General interest magazine covering Florida lifestyle and travel. Focuses on the state's history and heritage, outdoor activities, travel and vacations, food, dining, scenic beauty, greenways and trails, state parks, homes and gardens, and every other aspect of life and travel in Florida.

M0216 Focus

Magazine
United Kingdom

devhotmail@yahoo.co.uk

https://bsfa.co.uk/focus

Professional Body: BSFA (British Science Fiction Association)

Nonfiction > *Articles*
   Creative Writing; Science Fiction

Send: Query
How to send: Email

Writing magazine, devoted to the craft and practice of writing genre fiction. Publishes articles on writing science fiction. Query by email.

Editor: Dev Agarwal

M0217 Folio

Magazine
United States

folio.editors@gmail.com

https://www.american.edu/cas/literature/folio/
https://www.facebook.com/FolioLitJournal/
https://twitter.com/FolioLitJournal
https://www.linkedin.com/in/folio-literary-journal-a235a8b4
http://folio-lit-journal.tumblr.com/

Fiction > *Short Fiction*: Literary

Nonfiction > *Essays*: Creative Nonfiction

Poetry > *Any Poetic Form*

Closed to approaches.

Accepts submissions of fiction, nonfiction, and poetry on specific themes during specific submission windows. See website for details.

M0218 Fortean Times: The Journal of Strange Phenomena

Magazine
Dennis Publishing, 31-32 Alfred Place,
London, WC1E 7DP
United Kingdom

drsutton@forteantimes.com

http://subscribe.forteantimes.com

Types: Nonfiction
Formats: Articles; News; Reviews
Markets: Adult

Publishes accounts of strange phenomena, experiences, curiosities, mysteries, prodigies, and portents. No fiction or poetry.

Editor: David Sutton

M0219 Foundation: The International Review of Science Fiction

Magazine
19 Beech Green, Dunstable, Bedfordshire,
LU6 1EB
United Kingdom

sff@beccon.org

https://www.sf-foundation.org/about-the-sff-journal

Nonfiction
   Articles: Science Fiction
   Reviews: Books; Science Fiction

Describes itself as the essential critical review of science fiction, publishing articles up to 6,000 words and reviews up to 1,500 words.

Editor: Dr Farah Mendlesohn

M0220 The Fourth River

Magazine
United States

4thriver@gmail.com

https://www.thefourthriver.com
https://twitter.com/thefourthriver
https://www.instagram.com/thefourthriver/
https://www.facebook.com/TheFourthRiver

Fiction > *Short Fiction*: Literary

Nonfiction > *Short Nonfiction*: Creative
Nonfiction

Poetry > *Any Poetic Form*

Send: Full text
How to send: Submittable

Costs: A fee is charged upon submission. $3 submission fee.

Print and digital literary magazine publishing creative writing that explores the relationship between humans and their environments, whether natural or man-made. Submit 3-5 poems or prose up to 4,000 words between July 1 and September 1 for print, or December 1 and February 1 for online, via online submission system. No submissions by email.

M0221 **The Frogmore Papers**
Magazine
21 Mildmay Road, Lewes, East Sussex, BN7 1PJ
United Kingdom

frogmorepress@gmail.com

http://www.frogmorepress.co.uk

Fiction
   Novel Excerpts; Short Fiction
Poetry > *Any Poetic Form*

Send: Full text; Self-Addressed Stamped Envelope (SASE)
How to send: Domestic Post; Email if overseas

Poetry and prose by new and established authors. There is no house style but the extremes of tradition and experiment are equally unlikely to find favour.

Send between four and six poems, or up to two prose pieces.

Editor: Jeremy Page

M0222 **Fugue**
Magazine
United States

fugue@uidaho.edu

https://fuguejournal.com
https://twitter.com/FugueJournal
https://www.instagram.com/fugue_journal/
https://www.facebook.com/fuguejournal/

Fiction > *Short Fiction*

Nonfiction
   Essays: General
   Reviews: Books

Poetry > *Any Poetic Form*

Send: Full text
How to send: Submittable

Costs: A fee is charged upon submission. $3.

Submit 3 to 5 poems, up to two short shorts, one story, or one essay per submission. Accepts submissions online only, between September 1 and May 1. Submission service charges $3 per submission.

Editors: Scott Dorsch; Ryan Downum; Emmy Newman; Steven Pfau; Clare Shearer; Keene Short

M0223 **Funny Times**
Magazine
PO Box 18530, Cleveland Heights, OH 44118
United States
Tel: +1 (888) 386-6984

info@funnytimes.com

https://funnytimes.com
https://www.facebook.com/TheFunnyTimes

Fiction
   Cartoons: Business; Comedy / Humour; Current Affairs; Food; Pets; Politics; Relationships; Religion; Technology
   Short Fiction: Business; Comedy / Humour; Current Affairs; Food; Pets; Politics; Relationships; Religion; Technology

Send: Full text; Self-Addressed Stamped Envelope (SASE)
How to send: Post

Send query with SASE and details of previous publishing history (where applicable). Publishes funny stories and cartoons only. No fax or email submissions.

Editor: Raymond Lesser, Susan Wolpert

M0224 **The Furrow**
Magazine
St Patrick's College, Maynooth, Co. Kildare
Ireland
Tel: 01-7083741
Fax: 01-7083908

editor.furrow@spcm.ie

https://thefurrow.ie

Formats: Articles
Subjects: Religion
Markets: Adult

A monthly journal for the contemporary Church, providing a forum for discussion of challenges facing the Church today and of the resources available to meet them.

Editor: Pádraig Corkery

M0225 **The Future Fire**
Online Magazine
United Kingdom

fiction@futurefire.net
nonfiction@futurefire.net

http://futurefire.net

Fiction > *Short Fiction*
   Crime; Environment; Feminism; LGBTQIA; Mystery; Noir; Postcolonialism; Speculative

Nonfiction > *Reviews*
   Arts; Books; Films; Magazines

Poetry > *Any Poetic Form*
   Environment; Feminism; LGBTQIA; Postcolonialism; Speculative

Send: Full text
How to send: Email attachment

Magazine of social political and speculative cyber fiction. Publishes short stories generally up to 10,000 words, however may consider stories up to 17,500. Also publishes nonfiction reviews. Accepts email submissions for fiction; for reviews send query by email before submitting material. See website for full submission guidelines.

Editors: Djibril Alayad; Bruce Stenning

M0226 **Garden & Gun**
Magazine
701 E. Bay Street, #115, Charleston, SC 29403
United States

editorial@gardenandgun.com

https://gardenandgun.com

Types: Nonfiction
Formats: Articles
Subjects: Arts; Cookery; Culture; Gardening; Lifestyle; Music; Sport; Travel
Markets: Adult

Lifestyle magazine devoted to to the New South and the Caribbean.

M0227 **Garden Rail**
Magazine
United Kingdom

Magazine Publisher: Warners Group Publications

M0228 **The Garden**
Magazine
The Royal Horticultural Society, 80 Vincent Square, London, SW1P 2PE
United Kingdom
Tel: +44 (0) 20 3176 5800

thegarden@rhs.org.uk

https://www.rhs.org.uk/about-the-rhs/publications/the-garden

Magazine Publisher: The Royal Horticultural Society (RHS)

Nonfiction > *Articles:* Gardening

Gardening magazine publishing practical garden design ideas, plant profiles and outstanding gardens large and small. Also carries news of flower shows, special garden openings, books, etc.

Editor: Ian Hodgson

M0229 **Gateway**
Magazine
Missouri Historical Society, PO Box 775460, St. Louis, MO 63177
United States

https://mohistory.org/publications/gateway/

Nonfiction > *Articles*
   African American; Civil Rights; Culture; History; Missouri; Music; Society; Theatre

Magazine covering St. Louis's and Missouri's historical and contemporary cultural, social, and political issues. Particularly interested in articles and essays on preservation and architecture; folk culture and oral history; music and theatre traditions; civil rights and African American history, as well as original poetry, photography, and literature.

Editor: Victoria W. Monks

M0230 Geochemistry: Exploration, Environment, Analysis
Magazine
United Kingdom

Book Publisher / Magazine Publisher: The
Geological Society Publishing House (**P0322**)

M0231 German Life
Magazine
PO Box 3000, Denville, NJ 07834-9723
United States
Tel: +1 (866) 867-0251

comments@germanlife.com

https://germanlife.com
http://www.facebook.com/https://www.
facebook.com/germanlifemag/

Magazine Publisher: Zeitgeist Publishing

Nonfiction > *Articles*
  Austria; Culture; Germany; Politics; Social
  Commentary; Switzerland

Magazine on German history, culture, and
travel, and the way in which Germany and
German immigrants have helped shape
America.

Editor: Mark Slider

M0232 Gertrude
Online Magazine
United States

EditorGertrudePress@gmail.com

https://www.gertrudepress.org

Fiction > *Short Fiction*
  General, and in particular: LGBTQIA

Nonfiction
  Essays: Creative Nonfiction; LGBTQIA
  Short Nonfiction: Creative Nonfiction;
  LGBTQIA; Memoir
  Poetry > *Any Poetic Form*
  General, and in particular: LGBTQIA

Send: Full text
How to send: Submittable

Costs: A fee is charged upon submission. £3
submission fee.

Online LGBTQA journal publishing fiction,
poetry, and creative nonfiction. Subject matter
need not be LGBTQA-specific, and writers
from all backgrounds are welcomed. Submit
fiction or creative nonfiction up to 3,000
words, or up to five poems (no line limit, but
under 40 lines preferred), via online
submission system. For book reviews and
interviews, email editor with proposal. See
website for full guidelines.

Editor: Tammy

M0233 Get Creative With...
Magazine
United Kingdom

Magazine Publisher: Warners Group
Publications

M0234 Gibbons Stamp Monthly
Magazine
399 Strand, London, WC2R 0LX
United Kingdom
Tel: +44 (0) 1425 472363

http://www.gibbonsstampmonthly.com

Types: Nonfiction
Formats: Articles; News
Subjects: Hobbies
Markets: Adult

Magazine publishing features and news
relating to stamps.

M0235 The Gin Kin
Online Magazine
United Kingdom

https://www.theginkin.com

Newspaper Publisher / Magazine Publisher:
DC Thomson Media

M0236 Golf Tips
Magazine
iGolf Sports Network LLC, 13800 Panama
City Beach PKWY, Suite 106D, #138, Panama
City Beach, FL 32407
United States
Tel: +1 (850) 588-1550

ted@igolfsportsnetwork.com

https://www.golftipsmag.com

Nonfiction > *Articles*
  Golf; How To; Travel

Publishes tips, guides, and features on golf.

M0237 Good Homes
Magazine
United Kingdom

https://www.goodhomesmagazine.com
https://www.facebook.com/GoodHomes
https://uk.pinterest.com/goodhomes/
https://twitter.com/GoodHomesMag
https://www.instagram.com/goodhomesmag/

Magazine Publisher: Media 10

Nonfiction > *Articles*
  Decorating; Interior Design

Magazine of decorating and interior design.

Editor: Lisa Allen

M0238 The Good Ski Guide
Magazine
1 Esher Place Avenue, KT10 8PU

United Kingdom
Tel: +44 (0) 1372 469874

johnh@goodholidayideas.com

https://www.goodskiguide.com/
https://www.facebook.com/goodskiguide.
official
https://twitter.com/officialGSG
https://www.youtube.com/goodskiguideoffical

Nonfiction > *Articles*
  Skiing; Travel

Magazine of skiing and ski resorts.

Editors: Nick Dalton; John Hill

M0239 Graffiti Magazine
Magazine
United Kingdom

writersinthebrewery@yahoo.co.uk

https://www.facebook.com/pages/Graffiti-
Magazine/63653000411

Fiction > *Short Fiction*

Poetry > *Any Poetic Form*

Publishes poetry and prose. Each edition has a
short story competition.

Editor: Rona Laycock

M0240 Granta
Magazine
12 Addison Avenue, Holland Park, London,
W11 4QR
United Kingdom
Tel: +44 (0) 20 7605 1360
Fax: +44 (0) 20 7605 1361

editorial@granta.com

https://granta.com

Fiction > *Short Fiction*

Nonfiction > *Short Nonfiction*

Poetry > *Any Poetic Form*

Send: Full text
How to send: Submittable

Costs: A fee is charged upon submission. £3
for prose; £2 for poems.

Submit one story or essay, or up to four poems,
via online submission system. £3 charge for
prose submissions; £2 for poems. No specific
length limits for prose, but most pieces are
between 3,000 and 6,000 words. Unlikely to
read anything over 10,000 words.

Editor: Sigrid Rausing

M0241 Grazia
Magazine
Media House, Peterborough Business Park,
Lynch Wood, Peterborough, PE2 6EA
United Kingdom
Tel: +44 (0) 1858 438884

graziadaily@graziamagazine.co.uk

https://graziadaily.co.uk

Types: Nonfiction
Formats: Articles; News
Subjects: Beauty; Fashion; Lifestyle; Women's Interests
Markets: Adult

Weekly glossy women's magazine published for more than 50 years in Italy, now brought to the UK market. Publishes articles and news aimed at women aged between 25 and 45.

M0242 The Great Outdoors (TGO)
Magazine
Kelsey Media Ltd, The Granary, Downs Court, Yalding Hil, Yalding, Kent, ME18 6AL
United Kingdom

carey.davies@kelsey.co.uk

https://www.tgomagazine.co.uk

Magazine Publisher: Kelsey Media

Nonfiction > *Articles*: Walking

Magazine publishing articles on walking and back-packing.

Editor: Carey Davies

M0243 Grit
Magazine
1503 S.W. 42nd St., Topeka, KS 66609
United States
Tel: +1 (785) 274-4300
Fax: +1 (785) 274-4305

Letters@grit.com

https://www.grit.com
https://www.facebook.com/GritMagazine/
https://www.pinterest.com/gritmagazine
https://www.instagram.com/grit1882/
https://www.youtube.com/user/
MotherEarthNewsMag
https://twitter.com/GritMagazine

Nonfiction > *Articles*
Farming; Gardening; Rural Living; Urban Farming

Send: Query
Don't send: Full text
How to send: Word file email attachment

Family magazine distributed across America, with a positive approach to life, providing a voice for rural lifestyle farmers. Potential contributors must be knowledgeable on rural life. Send query in first instance, preferably by email (with the word "Query" in the subject line).

Editor: K.C. Compton

Editorial Director: Oscar H. Will

M0244 GUD Magazine
Magazine
United States

mike@ktf-design.com

http://www.gudmagazine.com

Types: Fiction; Nonfiction; Poetry
Formats: Articles; Essays; Interviews; Short Fiction
Subjects: Arts; Comedy / Humour; Fantasy; History; Horror; Literary; Mystery; Romance; Science Fiction; Suspense
Markets: Adult

Closed to approaches.

Note: Closed to submissions as at November 2016. See website for current status. What you've been looking for in a magazine. Published two times a year, we provoke with words and art. We bring you stories that engage. Essays and interviews that make you think harder. Poetry that bares reality, more subtly interprets what it means to be human. We're aiming to make each issue roughly two hundred pages of content, 450 words (or a single poem or piece of art) per page. Information for how to subscribe will be available shortly. Subscribe and discover a new magazine that looks good, feels good in the hand, and delivers content that will make you hungry for more.

Editor: Kaolin Fire, Mike Coombes, Sue Miller, Sal Coraccio

M0245 Gutter Magazine
Magazine
United Kingdom

contactguttermagazine@gmail.com

https://www.guttermag.co.uk/

Fiction > *Short Fiction*
International; Literary; Scotland

Nonfiction > *Essays*
Creative Nonfiction; International; Literary; Scotland

Poetry > *Any Poetic Form*
International; Scotland

Scripts > *Theatre Scripts*
International; Literary; Scotland

Closed to approaches.

Publishes poetry, short stories, and drama. Publishes work by writers born or living in Scotland alongside international writing. Send up to five poems up to 120 lines total, or prose up to 3,000 words. Submit through online submission system. See website for full guidelines.

Editors: Colin Begg; Kate MacLeary; Laura Waddell

M0246 Haiku Journal
Magazine
Prolific Press Inc., ICO HJ Editor, PO Box 5315, Johnstown, PA 15904
United States

Editor@HaikuJournal.org

https://haikujournal.org

Types: Poetry
Subjects: Literary
Markets: Adult

Send: Full text

Magazine publishing Haiku. Submit via online submission system available on website.

Editor: Glenn Lyvers

M0247 Haikuniverse
Magazine
United States

info@haikuniverse.com

http://www.haikuniverse.com

Types: Poetry
Subjects: Literary
Markets: Adult

Send: Full text

Daily online publication of haiku and micro-poems. Submit online using website submission form.

M0248 Hair
Magazine
United Kingdom

http://hairmagazine.co.uk

Magazine Publisher: Haversham Publications Ltd

Nonfiction > *Articles*: Hairstyles

Magazine on hair and beauty, publishing articles and features on trends in fashion and hair styling.

M0249 Harper's Magazine
Magazine
666 Broadway, 11th Floor, New York, NY 10012
United States
Tel: +1 (212) 420-5720

harpers@harpers.org

https://harpers.org
https://twitter.com/Harpers
https://www.facebook.com/HarpersMagazine/
https://www.instagram.com/harpersmagazine/

Fiction > *Short Fiction*

Nonfiction
Articles: Culture; Current Affairs; Environment; Journalism; Politics; Society
Essays: Culture; Current Affairs; Environment; Politics; Society

Send: Query; Full text; Self-Addressed Stamped Envelope (SASE)
How to send: Post
How not to send: Email

Current affairs magazine publishing topical essays, and fiction. Considers unsolicited fiction MSS, however no unsolicited nonfiction (query in first instance). All queries and submissions must be sent by post.

Editor: Roger D. Hodge

M0250 Harpur Palate
Magazine
Binghamton University, English Department, P.O. Box 6000, Binghamton, NY 13902-6000
United States

harpur.palate@gmail.com

https://harpurpalate.binghamton.edu
https://twitter.com/harpurpalate
https://www.instagram.com/harpurpalate
https://www.facebook.com/harpurpalate
https://harpurpalate.submittable.com/submit

Fiction > *Short Fiction*

Nonfiction > *Short Nonfiction*: Creative Nonfiction

Poetry > *Any Poetic Form*

Closed to approaches.

Submit up to five poems, up to 15 pages total; prose up to 5,500 words; or three pieces of short prose up to 1,000 words each. Submit through online submission system.

M0251 Harvard Magazine
Magazine
7 Ware Street, Cambridge, Mass. 02138-4037
United States
Tel: +1 (617) 495-5746
Fax: +1 (617) 495-0324

https://www.harvardmagazine.com
https://www.facebook.com/HarvardMagazine
https://twitter.com/harvardmagazine
https://www.linkedin.com/company/harvard-magazine
https://www.youtube.com/user/HarvardMagazine
https://www.instagram.com/harvardmagazine/

Nonfiction > *Articles*: Harvard

Send: Query
How to send: Email

Magazine for faculty, alumni, and students of the university. Aims to keep alumni connected to the university community, covering the work and thinking being done at the university, and raising contemporary social and political issues and reflecting upon them. Also includes alumni news. Send query to the editor by email.

Editor: John S. Rosenberg

M0252 Heat Pumps Today
Magazine
United Kingdom

Magazine Publisher: Warners Group Publications

M0253 The Helix
Magazine
United States

helixmagazine@gmail.com

https://helixmagazine.org

Fiction > *Short Fiction*

Nonfiction > *Short Nonfiction*

Poetry > *Any Poetic Form*

Closed to approaches.

Publishes fiction, creative nonfiction, poetry, plays, and art. Submit prose up to 3,000 words each, or up to four poems.

Editor: Victoria-Lynn Bell

M0254 Hello!
Magazine
Wellington House, 69-71 Upper Ground, London, SE1 9PQ
United Kingdom
Tel: +44 (0) 20 7667 8721

holly.nesbitt-larking@hellomagazine.com

https://www.hellomagazine.com

Types: Nonfiction
Formats: Articles; Interviews; News
Subjects: Beauty; Culture; Fashion; Lifestyle; Women's Interests
Markets: Adult

Magazine of celebrity and lifestyle.

Editor: Holly Nesbitt-Larking

M0255 Here Comes Everyone
Magazine
United Kingdom

http://herecomeseveryone.me

Types: Fiction; Nonfiction; Poetry
Formats: Articles
Subjects: Literary
Markets: Adult

Send: Full text

Biannual literature and arts magazine publishing poetry, fiction, articles, and artwork. Each issue is themed. See website for upcoming themes and to submit.

Editors: Matthew Barton; Raef Boylan

M0256 Hi-Fi News
Magazine
United Kingdom

https://www.hifinews.com
https://www.facebook.com/pages/Hi-Fi-News-Record-Review/299204350193416
https://twitter.com/hifinewsmag

Magazine Publisher: AV Tech Media Ltd

Nonfiction
 News: Audio Technology
 Reviews: Audio Technology

Reviews audiophile-oriented sound-reproduction and recording equipment, and includes information on new products and developments in audio.

Editor: Paul Miller

M0257 Highway News
Magazine
1525 River Road, Marietta, PA 17547
United States
Tel: +1 (717) 426-9977

info@tfcglobal.org

https://tfcglobal.org/highway-news/current-issue/

Nonfiction > *Articles*
 Hauliers; Religion

Religious magazine aimed at truck drivers and their families. Publishes testimonials, teachings, and human interest stories that have a foundation in Biblical/Christian values.

Editor: Jennifer Landis

M0258 History Scotland
Magazine
United Kingdom

Magazine Publisher: Warners Group Publications

M0259 Homes & Antiques
Magazine
United Kingdom

https://www.homesandantiques.com
https://www.facebook.com/homesantiques
http://uk.pinterest.com/homesantiques
https://twitter.com/@homes_antiques
https://www.youtube.com/channel/UChlvNbVVoLcWle1xHnuAZlQ
https://www.instagram.com/homes_antiques

Magazine Publisher: Immediate Media Co.

Nonfiction > *Articles*
 Antiques; Decorating; Interior Design

Magazine of home interest, antiques, and collectibles.

Editor: Angela Linforth

M0260 Horse & Rider
Magazine
5720 Flatiron Parkway, Boulder, CO, 80301
United States
Tel: +1 (303) 253-6405

HorseandRider@equinenetwork.com

https://my.horseandrider.com
https://www.facebook.com/HorseandRider
https://www.pinterest.com/hrsrdrmag/
https://www.instagram.com/horseandridermag/
https://twitter.com/Horse_and_Rider

Magazine Publisher: Equine Network

Nonfiction > *Articles*

American West; Horses; Travel

Provides all you need for today's Western horse life. Learn from top professional trainers, clinicians, and horse-keeping experts. Experience Western life. Travel to Western destinations and scenic trails. Your resource to live today's Western horse life.

Editor: Debbie Moors, Associate Editor

M0261 Horse and Rider
Magazine
DJ Murphy Publishers Ltd, Olive Studio, Grange Road, Tilford, Farnham, Surrey, GU10 2DQ
United Kingdom
Tel: +44 (0) 1428 601020

editor@djmurphy.co.uk

https://www.horseandrideruk.com

Magazine Publisher: DJ Murphy Publishers Ltd

Nonfiction > *Articles*
  Equestrian; Horses

Magazine on horses, including news, instructional features, etc. Aimed mainly at horse-owners.

Editor: Louise Kittle

M0262 Hotel Amerika
Magazine
C/O The Department of Creative Writing, Columbia College Chicago, 600 South Michigan Avenue, Chicago, IL 60605
United States
Tel: +1 (312) 369-8175

http://www.hotelamerika.net

Fiction > *Short Fiction*: Literary

Nonfiction > *Essays*

Poetry > *Any Poetic Form*

Closed to approaches.

Costs: A fee is charged upon submission. $3.00.

Submissions will be considered between September 1 and April 1. Materials received after April 1 and before September 1 will not be considered.

Editor: David Lazar

M0263 Hoxie Gorge Review
Magazine
United States

editor@hoxiegorgereview.com

http://hoxiegorgereview.com

Types: Fiction; Nonfiction; Poetry
Subjects: Literary
Markets: Adult

Send: Full text

Online literary journal publishing poetry, fiction, and creative nonfiction. Submit via website through online submission system.

Editor: Heather Bartlett

M0264 Hunger Mountain
Magazine
36 College Street, Montpelier, VT 05602
United States
Tel: +1 (802) 828-8844

hungermtn@vcfa.edu

https://hungermtn.org

Fiction in Translation > *Short Fiction*: Literary

Fiction > *Short Fiction*: Literary

Nonfiction in Translation > *Short Nonfiction*: Creative Nonfiction

Nonfiction > *Short Nonfiction*: Creative Nonfiction

Poetry in Translation > *Any Poetic Form*

Poetry > *Any Poetic Form*

Closed to approaches.

Submit prose up to 8,000 words, or up to three flash pieces, or up to five poems, via online submission system. Accepts general submissions between May 1 and October 15, and contest submissions between November 1 and March 1.

Editor: Caroline Mercurio

M0265 I-70 Review
Magazine
913 Joseph Drive, Lawrence, KS 66044
United States

i70review@gmail.com

http://i70review.fieldinfoserv.com

Fiction > *Short Fiction*

Poetry > *Any Poetic Form*

Send: Full text; Author bio
How to send: Word file email attachment

Accepts submissions of fiction and flash fiction or 3-5 poems, by email, during the reading period that runs from July 1 to December 31. Accepts simultaneous submissions. See website for full details.

M0266 Ibbetson Street
Magazine
25 School Street, Somerville, MA 02143
United States
Tel: +1 (617) 628-2313

tapestryofvoices@yahoo.com

http://ibbetsonpress.com

Types: Poetry
Subjects: Literary
Markets: Adult

Publishes poetry that is not too abstract. Looks for simplicity and economy of words. Send 3-5 poems with author bio in the body of an email with "Poetry Submission" in the subject line. No attachments.

Editors: Harris Gardner; Lawrence Kessenich; Emily Pineau

M0267 Ibsen Studies
Magazine
Norway

https://www.tandfonline.com/toc/sibs20/current

Types: Nonfiction
Formats: Articles; Essays
Subjects: Literature
Markets: Academic

Publishes scholarly articles on the life and works of Henrik Ibsen. See website for submission guidelines.

Editor: Ellen Rees

M0268 Iconoclast
Magazine
1675 Amazon Road, Mohegan Lake, NY 10547-1804
United States

http://www.iconoclastliterarymagazine.com

Fiction > *Short Fiction*: Literary

Poetry > *Any Poetic Form*

Send: Full text
How to send: Post

Publishes poetry and prose from authors interested in the creation, sharing, and transmission of ideas, imaginings, and experiences. Send prose up to 3,500 words or poetry up to two pages with SASE. See website for full guidelines.

Editor: Phil Wagner

M0269 Idaho Review
Magazine
Boise State University, 1910 University Drive, Boise, Idaho 83725
United States

mwieland@boisestate.edu

https://www.idahoreview.org
https://theidahoreview.submittable.com/submit
http://www.facebook.com/10213528569031037
http://twitter.com/idahoreview
http://www.instagram.com/theidahoreview

Fiction > *Short Fiction*: Literary

Nonfiction
  Essays: General
  Short Nonfiction: Creative Nonfiction

Poetry > *Any Poetic Form*

Closed to approaches.

Costs: A fee is charged for online submissions. $3 to submit online.

Annual literary journal publishing poetry and fiction. No specific limit for fiction, but most of the stories accepted are under 25 double-spaced pages. For poetry, submit up to five poems. Reading period runs from September to March (see website for specific dates for this year). Accepts submissions by post with SASE, but prefers submissions through online submission system ($3 fee).

M0270 Ideal Home

Magazine
161 Marsh Wall, London, E14 9AP
United Kingdom

ideal_home@futurenet.com

https://www.idealhome.co.uk
https://www.facebook.com/idealhome.co.uk
https://twitter.com/idealhome
https://www.pinterest.co.uk/idealhomemag/
https://www.instagram.com/idealhomeuk/

Magazine Publisher: Future

Nonfiction > *Articles*
    Gardening; Interior Design

Monthly magazine on the home, covering interior design, decoration, furnishing, home improvements, gardening, etc.

Editor: Susan Rose

M0271 Identity Theory

Magazine
United States

editor@identitytheory.com

http://www.identitytheory.com

Types: Fiction; Nonfiction; Poetry
Formats: Essays; Interviews; Short Fiction
Subjects: Literary
Markets: Adult

Send: Full text

Online literary magazine. Send fiction or essays up to 4,000 words through Submittable or through specific email address, or 3-5 unpublished poems in the body of an email. See website for different email addresses for different types of submissions.

Editor: Matt Borondy

M0272 Iman Collective

Online Magazine
Nigeria

imancollectivemag@gmail.com

https://imancollective.wordpress.com

Fiction > *Short Fiction*
    Islam; Literary

Nonfiction > *Short Nonfiction*
    Islam; Literary

Poetry > *Any Poetic Form*

Islam; Literary

Send: Query
How to send: Email

This is a quarterly magazine publishing Muslim literature in the genres of poetry, fiction, and nonfiction.

M0273 The Independent Publishing Magazine

Magazine
United Kingdom

mickrooney@
theindependentpublishingmagazine.com

http://www.
theindependentpublishingmagazine.com

Types: Nonfiction
Formats: Articles; News
Subjects: Media
Markets: Adult

Magazine covering the self-publishing industry specifically and the wider publishing industry generally.

Editor: Mick Rooney

M0274 Indiana Review

Magazine
Indiana University, Indiana Review Journal, Department of English, Lindley 215, 150 S Woodlawn Ave, Bloomington, IN 47405-7104
United States

inreview@indiana.edu

https://indianareview.org
https://twitter.com/indianareview
https://www.facebook.com/IndianaReview

Fiction in Translation > *Short Fiction*: Literary

Fiction > *Short Fiction*: Literary

Nonfiction in Translation > *Essays*

Nonfiction > *Essays*

Poetry in Translation > *Any Poetic Form*

Poetry > *Any Poetic Form*

Closed to approaches.

Costs: A fee is charged upon submission. $3 per submission.

Send fiction or nonfiction up 6,000 words or 3-6 poems per submission, during specific submission windows only (see website for details). No submissions by post or by email – all submissions must be made through online submission manager ($3 fee). See website for full guidelines, and to submit.

Editor: Tessa Yang

Editor-in-Chief: Mariah Gese

M0275 InfoWorld

Online Magazine
140 Kendrick Street, Building B, Needham, MA 02494
United States

https://www.infoworld.com
https://www.linkedin.com/company/164364
https://twitter.com/infoworld
https://www.facebook.com/InfoWorld

Magazine Publisher: IDG Communications, Inc.

PROFESSIONAL > **Nonfiction** > *Articles*
    Computers; Technology

Closed to approaches.

The leading voice in emerging enterprise technology, is the go-to resource for developers, architects, and business leaders launching next-generation initiatives on scalable cloud platforms, where such future-focused tech as AI/machine learning, big data analytics, and NoSQL databases evolve continuously. Does not publish contributed articles.

Editor: Steve Fox, Editor in Chief

M0276 Ink Sweat and Tears

Online Magazine
United Kingdom

inksweatandtearssubmissions@gmail.com

http://www.inksweatandtears.co.uk

Nonfiction > *Reviews*
    Literature; Poetry as a Subject

Poetry
    Any Poetic Form; Haibun; Haiga; Haiku; Prose Poetry

Send: Full text
How to send: Email

UK-based webzine publishing poetry, prose, prose-poetry, word and image pieces, and poetry reviews. Send 4-6 pieces by email only. Accepts unsolicited reviews of poetry and short story collections. See website for full guidelines.

Editor: Helen Ivory

M0277 Inspiralist

Online Magazine
United Kingdom

Newspaper Publisher / Magazine Publisher: DC Thomson Media

M0278 InStyle

Magazine
United States
Tel: +1 (800) 274-6200

letters@instylemag.com

https://www.instyle.com
https://www.facebook.com/InStyle

https://twitter.com/InStyle
https://www.pinterest.com/instyle/
https://www.instagram.com/instylemagazine/

Magazine Publisher: Meredith Corporation

Nonfiction
Articles: Beauty; Celebrity; Fashion; Hairstyles; How To; Lifestyle; Politics; Popular Culture; Social Issues
News: General

Magazine providing readers with a mix of fashion and beauty advice and celebrity news and lifestyle.

Editor: Louise Chunn

M0279 Insurance Age
Magazine
Infopro Digital, 133 Houndsditch, London, EC3A 7BX
United Kingdom
Tel: +44 (0) 20 7316 9000
Fax: +44 (0) 20 7681 3401

sian.barton@infopro-digital.com

https://www.insuranceage.co.uk

Types: Nonfiction
Formats: Articles; News
Subjects: Business; Finance
Markets: Professional

Publishes news and features on the insurance industry.

Editor: Sian Barton

M0280 International Piano
Magazine
St Jude's Church, Dulwich Road, London, SE24 0PB
United Kingdom

international.piano@rhinegold.co.uk

http://www.rhinegold.co.uk
https://www.rhinegold.co.uk/rhinegold-publishing/magazines/international-piano/
https://twitter.com/IP_mag
https://www.facebook.com/internationalpiano/
https://www.instagram.com/internationalpianomagazine
https://www.youtube.com/channel/UCOKPU5skkhcvQRjXVkou10Q

Magazine Publisher: Rhinegold Publishing

ACADEMIC > **Nonfiction** > *Articles*: Piano

ADULT > **Nonfiction** > *Articles*: Piano

PROFESSIONAL > **Nonfiction** > *Articles*: Piano

Offers a rich mix of inspiration and guidance to pianists and piano fans around the world, from dedicated amateurs and students to professional pianists, teachers and aficionados.

Editor: Jeremy Siepmann

M0281 The Interpreter's House
Online Magazine
United Kingdom

interpretershousesubmissions@gmail.com

https://theinterpretershouse.org

Fiction > *Short Fiction*

Nonfiction
Essays; *Interviews*; *Reviews*
Poetry > *Any Poetic Form*

Send up to five poems or up to two short stories by email during specific submission windows (see website for details).

Editor: Georgi Gill

M0282 Interzone
Magazine
United Kingdom

https://ttapress.com/interzone/
https://tta.submittable.com/submit

Magazine Publisher / Book Publisher: TTA Press (**P0839**)

Fiction > *Short Fiction*
Fantasy; Science Fiction

Send: Full text
How to send: Submittable

Publishes science fiction and fantasy short stories up to about 10,000 words. See website for full guidelines and online submission system.

Editor: Andy Cox

M0283 Investors Chronicle
Magazine
United Kingdom

john.hughman@ft.com

https://www.investorschronicle.co.uk

Types: Nonfiction
Formats: Articles; News
Subjects: Business; Finance
Markets: Professional

Magazine for investors.

Editor: John Hughman

M0284 The Iowa Review
Magazine
The University of Iowa, 308 English-Philosophy Building, Iowa City, IA 52242
United States
Tel: +1 (319) 335-0462
Fax: +1 (319) 335-2535

iowa-review@uiowa.edu

http://www.iowareview.org

Types: Fiction; Poetry; Translations
Formats: Essays; Reviews; Short Fiction
Subjects: Literary
Markets: Adult

Send: Full text

Publishes poetry, fiction, and nonfiction. Submit in September, October, and November only, via online submission system ($4 charge for non-subscribers) or by post with SASE. Accepts prose up to 25 pages and poetry up to 8 pages (query by email if your poem is longer). Do not mix genres in a single envelope. Work must be unpublished. Simultaneous submissions accepted if immediate notification of acceptance elsewhere is given.

Editor: Lynne Nugent

M0285 Ireland's Own
Magazine
Channing House, Rowe Street, Wexford
Ireland

info@irelandsown.ie

https://irelandsown.ie

Types: Fiction; Nonfiction
Formats: Articles; Short Fiction
Subjects: Literary; Traditional
Markets: Adult; Children's; Young Adult

Magazine publishing stories and articles of Irish interest for the whole family, plus puzzles and games.

Editor: Sean Nolan

M0286 Irish Pages
Magazine
129 Ormeau Road, Belfast, BT7 1SH
United Kingdom
Tel: +44 (0) 2890 434800

editor@irishpages.org

https://irishpages.org

Types: Fiction; Nonfiction; Poetry; Translations
Formats: Essays; Reviews; Short Fiction
Subjects: Autobiography; History; Literary; Nature; Science
Markets: Adult

Send: Full text
How not to send: Email

Non-partisan and non-sectarian literary journal publishing writing from the island of Ireland and elsewhere in equal measure. Publishes work in English, and in the Irish Language or Ulster Scots with English translations or glosses. Accepts submissions throughout the year by post only with stamps, coupons or cash for return postage (no self-addressed envelope is needed). See website for more details.

M0287 Iron Cross
Magazine
United Kingdom

Magazine Publisher: Warners Group Publications

M0288 Island

Magazine
PO Box 4703, Hobart TAS 7000
Australia
Tel: +61 (0) 3 6234 1462

admin@islandmag.com

https://islandmag.com
https://island.submittable.com/submit

Fiction > *Short Fiction*

Nonfiction
  Articles; *Essays*
Poetry > *Any Poetic Form*

How to send: Submittable

Welcomes submissions of nonfiction, fiction and poetry from Australia, New Zealand and the Pacific, as well as from Australians living abroad. See website for details and to submit using online submission system.

Online Magazine: Island Online (**M0289**)

M0289 Island Online

Online Magazine
Australia

admin@islandmag.com
ben@islandmag.com

https://islandmag.com/online
https://island.submittable.com/submit
http://www.facebook.com/islandmagtas
http://instagram.com/islandmagtas
https://twitter.com/IslandMagTas

Magazine: Island (**M0288**)

Fiction > *Short Fiction*
  Arts; Culture; Environment; Experimental; Literary; Nature; Society

Nonfiction > *Essays*
  Arts; Culture; Environment; Nature; Society

How to send: Submittable

Digital publishing platform operated in conjunction with longstanding print magazine.

M0290 J Journal

Magazine
Department of English, John Jay College of Criminal Justice, 524 West 59th Street, 7th Floor, New York, NY 10019
United States

submissionsjjournal@gmail.com

http://jjournal2.jjay.cuny.edu/jjournal/

Types: Fiction; Nonfiction; Poetry
Formats: Essays; Short Fiction
Subjects: Crime; Legal; Literary
Markets: Adult

Send: Full text
How to send: Email

Publishes fiction, creative nonfiction (1st person narrative, personal essay, memoir) and poetry that examines questions of justice,

either obliquely or directly addressing crime and the criminal justice system. Unlikely to publish genre fiction. Send up to three poems or prose up to 6,000 words.

M0291 J.J. Outre Review

Magazine
United States

thejjoutrereview@gmail.com

https://darkpassagespublishing.com

Types: Fiction
Formats: Short Fiction
Subjects: Adventure; Crime; Experimental; Fantasy; Horror; Literary; Mystery; Science Fiction; Suspense; Thrillers
Markets: Adult

Send: Full text

Semi-annual online journal with an annual print issue. Publishes genre fiction with strong literary elements. Welcomes the bizarre and experimental. Not interested in zombies, vampires, werewolves, fairies, shapeshifters or fan-fic. Submit up to three stories at a time via online submission system.

M0292 Jaggery

Magazine
United States

editor@jaggerylit.com

http://jaggerylit.com

Types: Fiction; Nonfiction; Poetry
Formats: Essays; Interviews; Reviews; Short Fiction
Markets: Adult

Send: Full text

Publishes fiction, poetry, essays, interviews and reviews from or about South Asia and its diasporas. Submit online via online submission system.

Editor: Anu Mahadev

M0293 Jewish Chronicle

Magazine
United Kingdom

editorial@thejc.com

https://www.thejc.com
https://www.instagram.com/thejewishchronicle/
https://twitter.com/jewishchron
https://www.facebook.com/pages/The-Jewish-Chronicle/99875692725
https://www.pinterest.co.uk/thejewishchroni/

Nonfiction
  Articles: Jewish Culture; Judaism; Lifestyle
  News: Jewish Culture; Judaism; Sport

Weekly paper publishing material of Jewish interest. No fiction.

M0294 Journal of Apicultural Research

Magazine
United Kingdom

https://www.tandfonline.com/toc/tjar20/current

ACADEMIC > **Nonfiction** > *Articles*: Apiculture (Beekeeping)

Send: Full text
How to send: Online submission system

Publishes research articles, theoretical papers, notes, comments and authoritative reviews on scientific aspects of the biology, ecology, natural history and culture of all types of bee.

M0295 Journal of the Geological Society

Magazine
United Kingdom

Book Publisher / Magazine Publisher: The Geological Society Publishing House (**P0322**)

M0296 Juniper

Magazine
United Kingdom

Newspaper Publisher / Magazine Publisher: DC Thomson Media

M0297 Kairos

Magazine
United States

submissions.kairos@gmail.com

http://kairoslit.com

Types: Fiction; Nonfiction; Poetry
Formats: Articles; Short Fiction
Subjects: Literary
Markets: Adult

Send: Full text
How to send: Email

Publishes poetry, fiction, creative nonfiction, and opinion / editorial pieces. Submit up to five poems or prose up to 10,000 words.

M0298 Kaleidoscope

Magazine
701 South Main Street, Akron, OH 44311-1019
United States
Tel: +1 (330) 762-9755

kaleidoscope@udsakron.org

http://www.udsakron.org/kaleidoscope.aspx

Types: Fiction; Poetry
Formats: Articles; Reviews; Short Fiction
Subjects: Arts; Autobiography; Culture; Health; Literary; Sociology
Markets: Adult

Send: Full text
How to send: Email

Publishes material examining experiences of disability through literature and the fine arts. Seeking material that challenges and overcomes stereotypical, patronising, and sentimental attitudes about disability. Writers with and without disabilities are welcome to submit their work. Writers should avoid using offensive language and always put the person before the disability. All MSS should be submitted by email or through the website. Poetry submissions should consist of up to five poems and use strong imagery and evocative language. Short stories should demonstrate effective technique, thought-provoking subject matter, and a mature grasp of the art of story-telling.

Editor: Gail Willmott

M0299 The Kenyon Review
Magazine
Finn House, 102 W. Wiggin Street, Kenyon College, Gambier, OH 43022-9623
United States
Tel: +1 (740) 427-5208
Fax: +1 (740) 427-5417

kenyonreview@kenyon.edu

https://kenyonreview.org

Types: Fiction; Nonfiction; Poetry; Scripts; Translations
Formats: Essays; Reviews; Short Fiction
Subjects: Arts; Literary
Markets: Adult

Submit through online submission system. Send short fiction up to 7,500 words, poetry up to six poems, or plays or excerpts up to 30 pages, with SASE. Translations are also accepted, but author is responsible for permissions. No unsolicited interviews or submissions by email or post.

Editor: David H. Lynn

Managing Editor: Abigail Wadsworth Serfass

M0300 Kerning
Magazine
United States

https://www.toadhalleditions.ink/kerning-a-space-for-words

Book Publisher / Self Publishing Service: Toad Hall Editions (**P0828**)

Fiction > *Short Fiction*

Nonfiction
    Essays: General
    Short Nonfiction: Creative Nonfiction

Poetry > *Any Poetic Form*

Closed to approaches.

Costs: A fee is charged upon submission. $7.

Publishes work by women and gender diverse people only.

M0301 Kids Alive!
Magazine
The Salvation Army, 101 Newington Causeway, London, SE1 6BN
United Kingdom
Tel: +44 (0) 20 7367 4910

kidsalive@salvationarmy.org.uk

https://www.salvationarmy.org.uk/publications/kids-alive

CHILDREN'S
    Fiction > *Cartoons*: Christianity

    Nonfiction > *Articles*: Christianity

Christian children's magazine publishing puzzles, comic strips, etc.

Editor: Justin Reeves

M0302 La Presa
Magazine
United States

leegould@embajadoraspress.com

https://embajadoraspress.com/index.php/la-presa/

Types: Fiction; Nonfiction; Poetry
Formats: Essays; Short Fiction
Subjects: Autobiography; Literary
Markets: Adult

Send: Full text
How to send: Email

Publishes poetry and prose, in English and Spanish, by writers from Canada, the US, and Mexico. Publishes poems and poem sequences, creative nonfiction, fiction, memoir, flash fiction, essays and vignettes. Also eager to publish longer work. Send submissions by email.

M0303 LabLit.com
Magazine
United States

editorial@lablit.com

http://www.lablit.com

Types: Fiction; Nonfiction; Poetry
Formats: Essays; Interviews; Short Fiction
Subjects: Comedy / Humour; Science
Markets: Adult

Send: Full text
How to send: Email

Magazine for scientists and non-scientists, publishing profiles, interviews, essays, humour, cartoons, reviews, poetry, and fiction related to science (but no science fiction). Send submissions by email.

Editor: Dr Jennifer Rohn

M0304 Land Rover Monthly
Magazine
United Kingdom

Magazine Publisher: Warners Group Publications

M0305 Leisure Painter
Magazine
The Maltings, West Street, Bourne, Lincolnshire, PE10 9PH
United Kingdom

https://www.painters-online.co.uk

Magazine Publisher: Warners Group Publications

Nonfiction > *Articles*: Painting

Magazine offering artistic inspiration, guidance, tuition and encouragement for beginners and amateur artists. Includes features and step-by-step painting and drawing demonstrations.

Editor: Ingrid Lyon

M0306 Life and Work
Magazine
121 George Street, Edinburgh, EH2 4YN
United Kingdom
Tel: +44 (0) 1312 255722

magazine@lifeandwork.org

https://www.lifeandwork.org

Types: Nonfiction
Formats: Articles; News
Subjects: Religion
Markets: Adult

Magazine of the Church of Scotland.

M0307 Light & Life
Magazine
United States

https://lightandlife.fm
https://twitter.com/lightandlifemag
https://www.facebook.com/lightandlifemagazine
https://www.youtube.com/channel/UCr8nd1V-UnRFTBeCTSPB68A
https://vimeo.com/llcomm
https://www.linkedin.com/company/559925
https://www.flickr.com/photos/llcomm/

Nonfiction > *Articles*: Methodism

Bimonthly magazine that exists to promote thoughtful Christian discipleship from a Wesleyan-Arminian perspective.

Editor: Doug Newton

Executive Editor: Jeff Finley

M0308 Lighthouse
Magazine
United Kingdom

submissions@lighthouse.gatehousepress.com

http://www.gatehousepress.com/lighthouse/

Types: Fiction; Poetry
Formats: Short Fiction

Subjects: Contemporary; Literary
Markets: Adult

Send: Full text
How to send: Email

Magazine of contemporary fiction and poetry, aimed at a UK audience. Submit up to four poems, one piece of fiction or up to two flash fictions by email as attachments. No previously published material or simultaneous submissions. See website for full guidelines.

M0309 Lincolnshire Life

Magazine
County House, 9 Checkpoint Court, Sadler Road, Lincoln, LN6 3PW
United Kingdom
Tel: +44 (0) 1522 689671

studio@lincolnshirelife.co.uk

https://www.lincolnshirelife.co.uk
http://www.facebook.com/lincolnshirelife
https://twitter.com/lincslife

Nonfiction > *Articles*
Business; Contemporary; Culture; Food; History; Leisure; Lifestyle; Lincolnshire

A monthly magazine devoted to the history, culture and contemporary life of Lincolnshire, England.

Editor: Judy Theobald

M0310 The Linguist

Magazine
Chartered Institute of Linguists (CIOL), 7th Floor, 167 Fleet Street, London, EC4A 2EA
United Kingdom
Tel: +44 (0) 20 7940 3100

https://www.ciol.org.uk/the-linguist

Types: Nonfiction
Formats: Articles; News
Subjects: Science
Markets: Professional

Magazine for language professionals.

M0311 Literal Latté

Online Magazine
200 East 10th Street, Suite 240, New York, NY 10003
United States
Tel: +1 (212) 260-5532

http://www.literal-latte.com
https://twitter.com/LiteralLatte
http://www.facebook.com/pages/Literal-Latte/108582045833559

Fiction > *Short Fiction*

Nonfiction > *Essays*: Personal Essays

Poetry > *Any Poetic Form*

Scripts > *Theatre Scripts*

Closed to approaches.

Costs: A fee is charged for online submissions.

Submit unpublished stories or personal essays, up to 10,000 words, or short plays or poems, up to 4,000 words, with bio, by post with SASE or via online submission system ($3 fee).

Editor: Jeff Bockman

M0312 Literary Mama

Online Magazine
United States

LMinfo@literarymama.com
LMreviews@literarymama.com
LMnonfiction@literarymama.com
LMfiction@literarymama.com
LMpoetry@literarymama.com

https://literarymama.com
http://www.facebook.com/litmama
http://twitter.com/literarymama
https://www.instagram.com/literary_mama/

Fiction > *Short Fiction*: Motherhood

Nonfiction
Reviews: Books; Motherhood
Short Nonfiction: Creative Nonfiction; Motherhood
Poetry > *Any Poetic Form*: Motherhood

Send: Full text; Query
How to send: In the body of an email

Online magazine publishing fiction, poetry, creative nonfiction, and book reviews focusing on mother writers, and the complexities and many faces of motherhood. Accepts submissions in the text of emails only – no snail mail submissions. See website for full submission guidelines.

Editor: Amy Hudock

M0313 Litro Magazine

Magazine
90 York Way, London, N1 9AG
United Kingdom
Tel: +44 (0) 20 3371 9971

info@litro.co.uk
editorial@litro.co.uk

https://www.litro.co.uk
https://www.facebook.com/Litromedia/
https://open.spotify.com/show/78fpfD5ejecJXXdsVHGJqb
https://www.instagram.com/litromedia/
https://twitter.com/litromagazine

Fiction > *Short Fiction*

Nonfiction > *Short Nonfiction*
Literary Journalism; Memoir; Travel

Accepts short fiction, flash/micro fiction, nonfiction (memoir, literary journalism, travel narratives, etc), and original artwork (photographs, illustrations, paintings, etc) based on the designated monthly theme. Works translated into English are also welcome. See website for upcoming themes.

M0314 Living

Magazine
United Kingdom

Newspaper Publisher / Magazine Publisher: DC Thomson Media

M0315 Loaded

Online Magazine
United Kingdom

https://loaded.co.uk
https://www.facebook.com/LoadedMagazine
https://twitter.com/loadedonline
https://www.pinterest.com/loadedonline/

Nonfiction
Articles: Entertainment; Lifestyle; Sport; Women
News: General

Online men's lifestyle magazine. Originally a print publication, now online only.

Editors: Scott Manson; Andrew Woods

M0316 The London Magazine

Magazine
Flat 5, 11 Queen's Gate, London, SW7 5EL
United Kingdom
Tel: +44 (0) 20 7584 5977

info@thelondonmagazine.org

http://thelondonmagazine.org

Types: Fiction; Nonfiction; Poetry
Formats: Articles; Essays; Reviews; Short Fiction
Subjects: Arts; Autobiography; Literary; Literary Criticism
Markets: Adult

Send: Full text

Send submissions through online submission system or by email. Does not normally publish science fiction or fantasy writing, or erotica. Will consider postal submissions, but prefers submissions electronically. See website for full guidelines and to access online submission system.

M0317 London Review of Books

Magazine
28 Little Russell Street, London, WC1A 2HN
United Kingdom
Tel: +44 (0) 20 7209 1101
Fax: +44 (0) 20 7209 1151

edit@lrb.co.uk

https://www.lrb.co.uk

Types: Nonfiction; Poetry
Formats: Articles; Essays; Film Scripts; Reviews
Subjects: Arts; Culture; Literary; Literature; Politics; Science
Markets: Adult

Publishes poems, reviews, reportage, memoir, articles, and blogposts. Send submissions by email or by post (with SAE).

M0318 Long Poem Magazine

Magazine
20 Spencer Rise, London, NW5 1AP
United Kingdom

longpoemmagazine@gmail.com

http://longpoemmagazine.org.uk

Types: Nonfiction; Poetry
Formats: Essays; Reviews
Subjects: Literary; Literature
Markets: Adult

Closed to approaches.

Magazine dedicated to publishing long poems and sequences. Publishes unpublished poems of at least 75 lines (but no book length poems). Also publishes essays on aspects of the long poem and reviews of books featuring long poems or sequences. Send submissions by email as Word file attachments. Does not accept poems submitted in the body of emails. See website for full guidelines and submission months. Poems submitted outside submission months will be discarded.

M0319 Louisiana Literature

Magazine
United States

lalit@selu.edu

http://www.louisianaliterature.org
https://twitter.com/LaLiterature
https://louisianaliterature.submittable.com/submit

Fiction > *Short Fiction*: Literary

Nonfiction > *Essays*: Creative Nonfiction

Poetry > *Any Poetic Form*

Send: Full text
How to send: Submittable

Literary journal publishing fiction, poetry, and creative nonfiction. Submit via online system available at the website.

Editor: Dr Jack Bedell

M0320 The MacGuffin

Magazine
Schoolcraft College, 18600 Haggerty Road, Livonia, MI 48152
United States
Tel: +1 (734) 462-5327

macguffin@schoolcraft.edu

https://schoolcraft.edu/macguffin

Types: Fiction; Nonfiction; Poetry
Formats: Short Fiction
Subjects: Experimental; Literary; Traditional
Markets: Adult

Send: Full text
How to send: Email

Publishes fiction, creative nonfiction, and poetry. Send complete MS by post with return postage, or by email as a Word document attachment. Submissions in the body of the email will not be accepted. Submit up to five poems or up to two stories.

M0321 Machine Knitting Monthly

Magazine
PO Box 1479, Maidenhead, Berkshire, SL6 8YX
United Kingdom
Tel: +44 (0) 1628 783080

mail@machineknittingmonthly.net

https://machineknittingmonthly.net

Nonfiction > *Articles*: Knitting

Editor: Anne Smith

M0322 MacroMicroCosm

Magazine
Canada

literary@vraeydamedia.ca

https://www.vraeydamedia.ca/macromicrocosm

Types: Fiction; Nonfiction; Poetry
Formats: Interviews; Reviews
Subjects: Fantasy; Literary; Literary Criticism; Philosophy; Science; Science Fiction
Markets: Adult

Send: Full text
How to send: Email

A quarterly digital literary and art journal dedicated to speculative fiction, art and literary criticism. Send submissions by email.

M0323 Mad

Magazine
United States

Customer_Service@Mad-Magazine.us

https://www.madmagazine.com

Formats: Articles
Subjects: Comedy / Humour; Current Affairs; Politics; Satire; Sport
Markets: Adult; Young Adult

Send: Query
Don't send: Full text

Humour magazine welcoming pitches of up to three article ideas via the form on the website.

M0324 Magma

Magazine
23 Pine Walk, Carshalton, SM5 4ES
United Kingdom

info@magmapoetry.com

https://magmapoetry.com

Types: Nonfiction; Poetry
Formats: Reviews
Subjects: Literary; Literature
Markets: Adult

Send: Full text

Prefers submissions through online submission system. Postal submissions accepted from the UK only, and must include SAE. No submissions by email. Accepts poems and artwork. Poems are considered for one issue only – they are not held over from one issue to the next. Seeks poems that give a direct sense of what it is to live today – honest about feelings, alert about world, sometimes funny, always well crafted. Also publishes reviews of books and pamphlets of poetry. See website for details.

Editor: Laurie Smith

M0325 Making Cards

Magazine
United Kingdom

Magazine Publisher: Warners Group Publications

M0326 Management Today

Magazine
Bridge House, 69 London Road, Twickenham, TW1 3SP
United Kingdom
Tel: +44 (0) 20 8267 4967

adam.gale@haymarket.com

https://www.managementtoday.co.uk

Types: Nonfiction
Formats: Articles
Subjects: Business
Markets: Professional

Send: Query
Don't send: Full text
How to send: Email

Publishes features and articles on general business and management topics. Send query with brief synopsis by email only.

Editors: Adam Gale; Kate Magee

M0327 Manoa

Magazine
University of Hawai'i at Mānoa, Department of English, 1733 Donaghho Road, Honolulu, HI 96822
United States
Tel: +1 (808) 956-3070
Fax: +1 (808) 956-3083

mjournal-l@lists.hawaii.edu

https://manoa.hawaii.edu/manoajournal/

ACADEMIC > **Nonfiction** > *Essays*
 Asia; Culture; Literature; Pacific

ADULT

Fiction in Translation > *Short Fiction*
Asia; Pacific

Fiction > *Short Fiction*
Asia; Pacific

Poetry in Translation > *Any Poetic Form*
Asia; Pacific

Poetry > *Any Poetic Form*
Asia; Pacific

Closed to approaches.

A Pacific journal, however material does not need to be related to the Pacific, or by authors from the region.

Editor: Frank Stewart

M0328 marie claire

Magazine
300 West 57th Street, New York, NY 10019
United States

https://www.marieclaire.com
https://www.facebook.com/MarieClaire
https://twitter.com/marieclaire
https://www.pinterest.com/MarieClaire
https://instagram.com/marieclairemag
https://www.youtube.com/c/MarieClaire

Nonfiction > *Articles*
Beauty; Career Development; Celebrity; Culture; Fashion; Finance; Fitness; Food and Drink; Health; Horoscopes; Politics; Relationships; Sex; Travel; Women's Interests

Lifestyle magazine aimed at the younger working woman.

M0329 Marlin

Magazine
World Publications, 460 North Orlando Ave, Suite 200, Winter Park, FL 32789
United States

editor@marlinmag.com

https://www.marlinmag.com
https://www.facebook.com/marlinmag/
https://twitter.com/MarlinMagazine/
http://instagram.com/marlinmag/
http://www.youtube.com/MarlinMagazine/

Nonfiction > *Articles*
Boats; How To; Offshore Gamefishing; Travel

Publishes articles, features, and news items relating to offshore fishing, destinations, personalities, fishery regulations, the boating industry and related topics, including how-to and technical information.

Editor: Dave Ferrel

M0330 The Massachusetts Review

Magazine
Photo Lab 309, University of Massachusetts, Amherst, MA 01003

United States
Tel: +1 (413) 545-2689
Fax: +1 (413) 577-0740

massrev@external.umass.edu

http://www.massreview.org
https://www.facebook.com/pages/The-Massachusetts-Review/40580092594
https://twitter.com/MassReview
http://instagram.com/themassachusettsreview?ref=badge
http://themassreview.tumblr.com/

Fiction in Translation > *Short Fiction*: Literary

Fiction > *Short Fiction*: Literary

Nonfiction in Translation > *Essays*
Arts; Current Affairs; Drama; Literature; Music; Philosophy; Science

Nonfiction
Articles: Arts; Current Affairs; Drama; Literature; Music; Philosophy; Science
Essays: Arts; Current Affairs; Drama; Literature; Music; Philosophy; Science

Poetry in Translation > *Any Poetic Form*

Poetry > *Any Poetic Form*

Closed to approaches.

Costs: A fee is charged for online submissions. $3.

Send one story of up to 25–30 pages or up to six poems of any length (though rarely publishes poems of more than 100 lines). White people may not submit between May 1 and September 30. Others may submit year-round, and may use email if the online submission system is closed. White people are not permitted to submit by email. Articles and essays of breadth and depth are considered, as well as discussions of leading writers; of art, music, and drama; analyses of trends in literature, science, philosophy, and public affairs. No plays, reviews of single books, or submissions by fax or email.

Editor: David Lenson

M0331 Maxim

Magazine
United States

Editor@maxim.com

https://www.maxim.com
https://www.facebook.com/maximmagazine
https://twitter.com/MaximMag
https://www.youtube.com/user/videosbyMaxim
https://www.instagram.com/maximmag
https://pinterest.com/maximmag

Nonfiction > *Articles*
Cars; Entertainment; Fashion; Food and Drink; Luxury Lifestyle; Sport; Technology; Travel; Women

Glossy magazine for men publishing articles and features on entertainment, fashion, sex,

sport, travel, motoring, and tech. No poetry or fiction.

Editor: Tom Loxley

M0332 Mayfair Times

Magazine
United Kingdom

https://mayfairtimes.co.uk
https://www.facebook.com/mayfairtimes/
https://twitter.com/MayfairTimes
https://instagram.com/Mayfair.Times

Nonfiction
Articles: Arts; Business; Culture; Fashion; Finance; Food and Drink; Houses; Lifestyle; Local; Travel
News: Local

A monthly luxury lifestyle magazine, which has been serving the people of Mayfair, Marylebone and St James's for 35 years.

M0333 Medal News

Magazine
No 40, Southernhay East, Exeter, Devon, EX1 1PE
United Kingdom
Tel: +44 (0) 1404 46972

info@tokenpublishing.com

http://www.tokenpublishing.com

Types: Nonfiction
Formats: Articles; News
Subjects: History; Warfare
Markets: Adult

Send: Full text

Magazine covering medals and the history surrounding them. Welcomes unsolicited MSS, but prior approach by phone or in writing preferred.

M0334 Meetinghouse

Magazine
United States

submissions@meetinghousemag.org

https://www.meetinghousemag.org
https://twitter.com/meethousemag

Fiction > *Short Fiction*

Poetry > *Any Poetic Form*

Closed to approaches.

A literary magazine that provides a space for diverse voices to speak with one another. Submit up to two pieces of prose and up to five poems per submission.

M0335 Men's Health

Magazine
Hearst UK, 30 Panton Street, Leicester Square, London, SW1Y 4AJ
United Kingdom

https://www.menshealth.com/uk

Types: Nonfiction
Formats: Articles
Subjects: Health; Lifestyle; Medicine; Men's Interests
Markets: Adult

Publishes articles related to the health of men, including such topics as fitness, stress, sex, nutrition, and health in general.

M0336 Metropolis Magazine
Magazine
101 Park Ave, 4th Floor, New York, NY 10178
United States
Tel: +1 (212) 934-2800

info@metropolismag.com

https://www.metropolismag.com/
https://www.facebook.com/MetropolisMag
https://twitter.com/MetropolisMag
https://www.linkedin.com/company/metropolis-magazine
https://www.instagram.com/metropolismag/

Magazine Publisher: Sandow

Nonfiction > *Articles*
Architecture; Arts; City and Town Planning; Culture; Design; Interior Design; Sustainable Living; Technology

Magazine examining contemporary life through design: architecture, interior design, product design, graphic design, crafts, planning, and preservation.

M0337 MHQ
Magazine
United States

Magazine Publisher: HistoryNet LLC

M0338 Michigan Quarterly Review
Magazine
3277 Angell Hall, 435 S. State Street, Ann Arbor, MI 48109-1003
United States
Tel: +1 (734) 764-9265

mqr@umich.edu

https://sites.lsa.umich.edu/mqr/
https://mqr.submittable.com/submit

Fiction in Translation > *Short Fiction*

Fiction > *Short Fiction*

Nonfiction
Articles; *Essays*
Poetry in Translation > *Any Poetic Form*

Poetry > *Any Poetic Form*

How to send: Submittable

An interdisciplinary and international literary journal, combining distinctive voices in poetry, fiction, and nonfiction, as well as works in translation.

Editor: Laurence Goldstein

M0339 Mid-American Review
Magazine
Department of English, Bowling Green State University, Bowling Green, OH 43403
United States
Tel: +1 (419) 372-2725

mar@bgsu.edu

https://casit.bgsu.edu/midamericanreview/

Fiction in Translation > *Short Fiction*: Literary

Fiction > *Short Fiction*: Literary

Nonfiction
Essays: General
Reviews: Books

Poetry in Translation > *Any Poetic Form*

Poetry > *Any Poetic Form*

How to send: Online submission system; Post

Accepts fiction, poetry, translations, and nonfiction (including personal essays, essays on writing, and short reviews). Submit by post with SASE or through online submission system.

Editor: Michael Czyzniejewski

M0340 Midway Journal
Magazine
United States

editors@midwayjournal.com

http://midwayjournal.com

Types: Fiction; Nonfiction; Poetry
Subjects: Literary
Markets: Adult

Send: Full text

Accepts submissions of fiction, poetry, and creative nonfiction via online submission system between January 1 and May 1 each year. Seeks aesthetically ambitious work that invokes the colliding and converging energies of the fairgrounds. See website for full guidelines.

Fiction Editor: Ralph Pennel

Nonfiction Editor: Allie Mariano

Poetry Editors: Mariela Lemus; Paige Riehl

M0341 Military History
Magazine
1919 Gallows Road, Ste 400, Vienna, VA 22182
United States

militaryhistory@historynet.com

https://www.historynet.com/magazines/mag-mh

Magazine Publisher: HistoryNet LLC

Nonfiction > *Articles*: Military History

Send: Query
Don't send: Full text
How to send: Email

Magazine of military history. No unsolicited MSS. Send one-page query with details of any previous writing experience. Potential contributors advised to familiarise themselves with the magazine before approaching.

Editor: Michael Robbins

M0342 Miniature Wargames
Magazine
United Kingdom

Magazine Publisher: Warners Group Publications

M0343 MiniWorld Magazine
Magazine
The Granary, Downs Court, Yalding Hill, Yalding, Kent, ME18 6AL
United Kingdom
Tel: +44 (0) 1959 541444

mw.ed@kelsey.co.uk

https://miniworld.co.uk
http://www.facebook.com/miniworldmagazine
https://twitter.com/MagMiniWorld

Magazine Publisher: Kelsey Media

Nonfiction > *Articles*: Mini Cars

Magazine devoted to the mini, including technical advice, tuning, restoration, social history, maintenance, etc.

Editor: Monty Watkins

M0344 Mississippi Review
Magazine
118 College Drive #5144, Hattiesburg, Mississippi 39406-0001
United States
Tel: +1 (601) 266-4321

msreview@usm.edu

http://sites.usm.edu/mississippi-review/

Fiction > *Short Fiction*

Nonfiction > *Essays*

Poetry > *Any Poetic Form*

Costs: A fee is charged upon submission. $16 competition entry fee.

Publishes work submitted to competition only. No unsolicited MSS. See website for competition details.

Editor: Frederick Barthelme

Managing Editor: Rie Fortenberry

M0345 The Missouri Review
Magazine
357 McReynolds Hall, University of Missouri, Columbia, MO 65211
United States

question@moreview.com

https://www.missourireview.com
https://www.facebook.com/themissourireview
https://twitter.com/missouri_review
https://www.instagram.com/themissourireview/

Fiction > *Short Fiction*

Nonfiction > *Essays*

Poetry > *Any Poetic Form*

Does not want:

Nonfiction > *Essays*: Literary Criticism

Send: Query; Self-Addressed Stamped Envelope (SASE); Full text
How to send: Post; Online submission system

Costs: A fee is charged for online submissions. $4 submission fee for online submissions.

Publishes poetry, fiction, and essays of general interest. No literary criticism. Submit by post with SASE, or via online system. There is a $4 charge for online submissions.

Editor: Speer Morgan

M0346 Modern Poetry in Translation

Magazine
United Kingdom

http://modernpoetryintranslation.com
https://twitter.com/MPTmagazine
https://www.instagram.com/modernpoetryintranslation/

Poetry in Translation > *Any Poetic Form*

Send: Full text
How to send: Submittable

Respected poetry series originally founded by prominent poets in the sixties. New Series continues their editorial policy: translation of good poets by translators who are often themselves poets, fluent in the foreign language, and sometimes working with the original poet. Publishes translations into English only. No original English language poetry. Send submissions via online submission system.

M0347 Monomyth

Magazine
Atlantean Publishing, 4 Pierrot Steps, 71 Kursaal Way, Southend-on-Sea, Essex, SS1 2UY
United Kingdom

atlanteanpublishing@hotmail.com

https://atlanteanpublishing.fandom.com/wiki/Monomyth

Book Publisher / Magazine Publisher: Atlantean Publishing (**P0057**)

Fiction > *Short Fiction*

Poetry > *Any Poetic Form*

Closed to approaches.

Features mostly short fiction, covering a wide variety of genres but often quirky, offbeat or fantastical. Send submissions by email or by post with SAE / email address for response. See website for full guidelines.

Editor: David-John Tyrer

M0348 The Moth

Magazine
Ardan Grange, Milltown, Belturbet, Co. Cavan
Ireland
Tel: 353 (0) 87 2657251

submissions@themothmagazine.com

https://www.themothmagazine.com

Fiction > *Short Fiction*: Literary

Poetry > *Any Poetic Form*

Send: Full text
How to send: Email; Post

Submit up to six poems or up to two short stories by post or by email. Accepts fiction submissions between September and April only. Poetry submissions are open all year. See website for full submission guidelines.

Editor: Rebecca O'Connor

M0349 Motor Boat & Yachting

Magazine
United Kingdom

mby@futurenet.com

https://www.mby.com
https://www.youtube.com/user/ybwtv
https://www.facebook.com/motorboatandyachting
https://twitter.com/mbymagazine
https://www.instagram.com/motorboat_and_yachting/

Magazine Publisher: Future

Nonfiction > *Articles*
Motor Boats; Yachts

Magazine publishing news and features related to motor boats and motor cruising.

Editor: Hugo Andreae

M0350 Motorcaravan Motorhome Monthly (MMM)

Magazine
Warners Group Publications, The Maltings, West Street, Bourne, LINCS, PE10 9PH
United Kingdom

https://www.outandaboutlive.co.uk/motorhomes

Magazine Publisher: Warners Group Publications

Nonfiction > *Articles*
Motorhomes; Travel

Publishes articles on motorhome travel.

Editor: Mike & Jane Jago

Managing Editor: Daniel Atwood

M0351 Mountain Living

Magazine
United States

https://www.mountainliving.com
https://www.facebook.com/mountainlivingmag
https://www.instagram.com/mountainlivingmag/
https://www.pinterest.com/mtnlivingmag/

Nonfiction > *Articles*
Architecture; Interior Design; Luxury Lifestyle; Mountain Lifestyle

Send: Query
How to send: Email

Magazine featuring mountain residences, from luxurious high-country retreats to charming guest cabins, with styles that range from traditional to contemporary. Submit via email and include a brief description of the home with size, location and any distinctive details.

Editor: Irene Rawlings, Editor in Chief

Editor-in-Chief: Darla Worden

M0352 Moving Worlds: A Journal of Transcultural Writings

Magazine
School of English, University of Leeds, Leeds, LS2 9JT
United Kingdom
Tel: +44 (0) 1133 434792
Fax: +44 (0) 1133 434774

mworlds@leeds.ac.uk

http://www.movingworlds.net

Types: Fiction; Poetry; Translations
Formats: Articles; Essays
Subjects: Culture; Experimental; Literary; Literary Criticism
Markets: Academic; Adult

Biannual international magazine for creative work as well as criticism, literary as well as visual texts, writing in scholarly as well as more personal modes, in English and translations into English. It is open to experimentation, and represents work of different kinds and from different cultural traditions. Its central concern is the transcultural.

Editors: Shirley Chew; Stuart Murray

M0353 Mslexia

Magazine
PO Box 656, Newcastle upon Tyne, NE99 1PZ
United Kingdom
Tel: +44 (0) 1912 048860

postbag@mslexia.co.uk

https://mslexia.co.uk

Fiction > *Short Fiction*

Nonfiction
  Articles: Creative Writing
  Essays: Creative Writing; Memoir; Personal
  Essays
  Interviews: Creative Writing

Poetry > *Any Poetic Form*

Send: Full text
How to send: Online submission system; Post

By women, for women who write, who want to
write, who teach creative writing or who have
an interest in women's literature and creativity.
Publishes short stories, flash fiction, poetry,
memoir and life writing, articles, and
interviews.

M0354 Muse

Magazine
United States

Magazine Publisher: Cricket Media, Inc.

M0355 My Weekly

Magazine
D C Thomson & Co Ltd, My Weekly, 2 Albert
Square, Dundee, DD1 1DD
United Kingdom
Tel: +44 (0) 1382 223131
Fax: +44 (0) 1382 452491

sjohnstone@dctmedia.co.uk

https://www.myweekly.co.uk/

Newspaper Publisher / Magazine Publisher:
DC Thomson Media

Types: Fiction; Nonfiction
Formats: Articles
Subjects: Beauty; Cookery; Crafts; Fashion;
Finance; Gardening; Health; Lifestyle; Travel;
Women's Interests
Markets: Adult

Weekly women's magazine aged at the over-
50s, publishing a mix of lifestyle features, true
life stories, and fiction.

Editor: S. Johnstone

M0356 Mystery Weekly Magazine

Magazine
United States

https://www.mysteryweekly.com

Fiction > *Short Fiction*: Mystery

Send: Full text
How to send: Online submission system

Submit mysteries between 2,500 and 7,500
words through online submission system
available on website.

M0357 Mythaxis Review

Online Magazine; Print Magazine
United States

https://mythaxis.com
https://www.youtube.com/channel/
UC4LGvC_n_Fk7jLmoU-KgRag
https://twitter.com/mythaxisreview
https://www.instagram.com/mythaxisreview
https://www.facebook.com/mythaxisreview
https://www.linkedin.com/company/mythaxis-
review
https://www.reddit.com/user/Mythaxis/
https://www.crunchbase.com/organization/
mythaxis-review

Nonfiction
  Articles: Arts; Books; Films; Music; Poetry
  as a Subject; Technology
  Interviews: Arts; Technology

A cutting edge publication that seeks to present
art and artists at the axis of curiosity and the
energetic core of the creative act. Looks at
books, movies, music and more.

M0358 Nailpolish Stories

Magazine
United States

ncmonaghan@gmail.com

https://nailpolishstories.wordpress.com

Types: Fiction
Markets: Adult

Send: Full text
How to send: Email

Online literary journal publishing stories
exactly 25 words long. All stories must use a
nail polish colour as the title. Submit by email.

Editor: Nicole Monaghan

M0359 Nanoism

Online Magazine
United States

editor@nanoism.net

http://nanoism.net

Fiction > *Short Fiction*: Literary

Send: Full text
How to send: In the body of an email
How not to send: Email attachment

Twitterzine publishing short stories up to 140
characters. Also accepts serials of up to 3-7
parts, though each must be able to stand on its
own. Submit no more than once per week, by
email.

M0360 Narrow Gauge World

Magazine
United Kingdom

Magazine Publisher: Warners Group
Publications

M0361 Nashville Review

Magazine
United States

thenashvillereview@gmail.com

https://as.vanderbilt.edu/nashvillereview

Types: Fiction; Nonfiction; Poetry;
Translations
Formats: Essays; Short Fiction
Subjects: Literary
Markets: Adult

Send: Full text

Submit short stories and novel excerpts up to
8,000 words, or three flash fiction pieces
(1,000 words each), 1-3 poems (up to ten pages
total), or creative nonfiction including memoir
excerpts, essays, imaginative meditations, up
to 8,000 words, via online submission system
during the three annual reading periods:
January, May, and September.

M0362 NB Magazine

Magazine
172 Winsley Road, Bradford-on-Avon,
Wiltshire, BA15 1NY
United Kingdom
Tel: +44 (0) 1225 302266

info@nbmagazine.co.uk

https://nbmagazine.co.uk

Nonfiction > *Articles*: Book Publishing

Magazine and online platform for book lovers,
book clubs and all round bibliophiles.
Publishes articles and features on books and
the book trade, as well as extracts from books.

M0363 Neon

Magazine
United Kingdom

subs@neonmagazine.co.uk

https://www.neonmagazine.co.uk

Fiction > *Short Fiction*
  Dark; Literary; Speculative; Surreal

Poetry
  Any Poetic Form: Dark; Literary; Surreal
  Graphic Poems: Dark; Literary; Surreal

Send: Full text
How to send: Email

Quarterly online magazine publishing stylised
poetry and prose, particularly the new,
experimental, and strange. Welcomes genre
fiction. Dark material preferred over humour;
free verse preferred over rhyme. Send work
pasted into the body of an email with a
biographical note and the word "Submission"
in the subject line.

Editor: Krishan Coupland

M0364 Nerve Cowboy

Magazine
PO Box 4973, Austin, Texas 78765
United States

http://www.nervecowboy.com/
https://www.facebook.com/Nerve-Cowboy-240567569317649

Fiction > *Short Fiction*

Nonfiction > *Reviews*: Live Music

Poetry > *Any Poetic Form*

Send: Full text; Self-Addressed Stamped Envelope (SASE)
How to send: Post
How not to send: Email

Send poems, and stories up to five pages in length, with SASE. Contributors are encouraged to have acquired and familiarised themselves with the magazine before submitting. Not a cowboy-themed magazine. No simultaneous submissions or submissions by email.

Editors: Jerry Hagins; Joseph Shields; Elissa Yeates

M0365 The New Accelerator

Online Magazine
United Kingdom

editors@thenewaccelerator.com

https://thenewaccelerator.com
http://twitter.com/newaccelerator
http://facebook.com/TheNewAccelerator

Fiction > *Short Fiction*: Science Fiction

Send: Full text
How to send: Word file email attachment; PDF file email attachment

Online science fiction short story anthology. The aim of the anthology is to bring cutting-edge fiction to an eager and discerning global science fiction audience. Seeks stories that are between 2,500 and 5,000 words long, but in exceptional cases will accept stories up to 10,000 words.

Editor: Andy Coughlan and David Winstanley

M0366 New England Review

Magazine
Middlebury College, Middlebury, VT 05753
United States
Tel: +1 (802) 443-5075

nereview@middlebury.edu

https://www.nereview.com
https://newenglandreview.submittable.com/submit
https://www.facebook.com/NewEnglandReviewMiddlebury/
https://twitter.com/nerweb

Fiction
 Novel Excerpts; *Novellas*; *Short Fiction*
Nonfiction in Translation > *Essays*

Nonfiction
 Essays: Personal Essays
 Short Nonfiction: Arts; Cultural Criticism; Environment; Films; Literary Criticism; Travel
Poetry > *Any Poetic Form*

Scripts > *Theatre Scripts*: Drama

Closed to approaches.

Costs: A fee is charged for online submissions. $3 per submission.

Welcomes submissions in fiction, poetry, nonfiction, drama, and translation. Different submission windows for different categories of work. See website for details.

Editor: Stephen Donadio

M0367 New Orleans Review

Online Magazine
United States

noreview@loyno.edu

https://www.neworleansreview.org
https://www.facebook.com/neworleans.review/
https://twitter.com/NOReview

Fiction > *Short Fiction*: Literary

Nonfiction
 Reviews: Literature
 Short Nonfiction: General

Poetry > *Any Poetic Form*

Send: Full text
How to send: Submittable

Costs: A fee is charged upon submission. $3 per submission.

A journal of contemporary literature and culture. Send one story or piece of nonfiction up to 5,000 words, or up to five poems via online submission system.

Editor: Christopher Chambers

M0368 The New Shetlander

Magazine
United Kingdom

vas@shetland.org

https://www.shetland-communities.org.uk/subsites/vas/the-new-shetlander.htm

Fiction > *Short Fiction*
 Literary; Shetland

Nonfiction > *Articles*
 Arts; Culture; History; Literature; Politics; Shetland

Poetry > *Any Poetic Form*: Shetland

Send: Full text
How to send: Email

Publishes short stories, poetry, and historical articles with a Shetland interest. Contributions and enquiries may be sent by email.

Editors: Laureen Johnson; Brian Smith

M0369 New Theatre Quarterly

Magazine
United Kingdom

M.Shevtsova@gold.ac.uk

https://www.cambridge.org/core/journals/new-theatre-quarterly

ACADEMIC > **Nonfiction**
 Articles: Theatre
 Interviews: Theatre

Send: Full text
How to send: Email

Provides a lively international forum where theatrical scholarship and practice can meet, and where prevailing assumptions can be subjected to vigorous critical questioning. The journal publishes articles, interviews with practitioners, documentation and reference materials covering all aspects of live theatre.

Editors: Maria Shevtsova; Simon Trussler

M0370 New Welsh Reader

Magazine
United Kingdom

editor@newwelshreview.com

https://newwelshreview.com/new-welsh-reader

Fiction > *Short Fiction*: Literary

Nonfiction
 Essays: General
 Short Nonfiction: Creative Nonfiction

Poetry > *Any Poetic Form*

Send: Full text
How to send: Online submission system

Focus is on Welsh writing in English, but has an outlook which is deliberately diverse, encompassing broader UK and international contexts. For feature articles, send 300-word query by email. Submit through online submission system only. Postal submissions will be returned unopened. Full details available on website.

Editor: Gwen Davies

M0371 No.1

Magazine
United Kingdom

Newspaper Publisher / Magazine Publisher: DC Thomson Media

M0372 The North

Magazine
The Poetry Business, Campo House, 54 Campo Lane, Sheffield, S1 2EG
United Kingdom
Tel: +44 (0) 1144 384074

office@poetrybusiness.co.uk

https://poetrybusiness.co.uk

Poetry > *Any Poetic Form*: Contemporary

Send: Full text
How to send: Domestic Post; Overseas online submission system
How not to send: International Post; Domestic online submission system

Send up to 6 poems with SASE / return postage. We publish the best of contemporary poetry. No "genre" or derivative poetry. Submitters should be aware of, should preferably have read, the magazine before submitting. See our website for notes on submitting poems. No submissions by email. Overseas submissions may be made through online submission system.

Editors: Ann Sansom; Peter Sansom

M0373 Nursery World
Magazine
MA Education, St Jude's Church, Dulwich Road, London, SE24 0PB
United Kingdom

https://www.nurseryworld.co.uk

PROFESSIONAL > **Nonfiction** > *Articles*
  Childcare; Preschool

Magazine aimed at professionals dealing with the care of children in nurseries, primary schools, childcare, etc.; nannies and foster parents; and those involved with caring for expectant mothers, babies, and young children.

Editor: Karen Faux

Editor-in-Chief: Liz Roberts

M0374 OBRA / Aftifact
Magazine
United States

editors@obraartifact.com

https://obraartifact.com

Types: Fiction; Nonfiction; Poetry; Translations
Formats: Essays
Subjects: Experimental; Literary
Markets: Adult

Closed to approaches.

Closed to submissions as at September 2019. Check website for current status. Publishes fiction, creative nonfiction, essays, and poetry, for print and online publication. Submit via online submission system.

Editor: Carley Fockler

M0375 Obsidian: Literature in the African Diaspora
Magazine
Illinois State University, Williams Hall Annex, Normal, IL 61790
United States

https://obsidianlit.org
https://obsidian.submittable.com/submit

Fiction > *Short Fiction*: African Diaspora

Poetry > *Any Poetic Form*: African Diaspora

Scripts > *Theatre Scripts*: African Diaspora

Send: Full text
How to send: Submittable

Publishes scripts, fiction, and poetry focused on Africa and her Diaspora. Reading period runs from September 15 to January 15. See website for submission guidelines and to submit via online submission system.

M0376 The Official Jacqueline Wilson Mag
Magazine
United Kingdom

Newspaper Publisher / Magazine Publisher: DC Thomson Media

M0377 OK! Magazine
Magazine
One Canada Square, Canary Wharf, London, E14 5AB
United Kingdom
Tel: +44 (0) 20 8612 7000

https://www.ok.co.uk

Magazine Publisher: Reach Magazines Publishing

Nonfiction
  Articles: Lifestyle; Women's Interests
  Interviews: Celebrity
  News: Celebrity

Celebrity magazine, welcoming ideas for features and interviews/pictures of celebrities.

Editor: Charlotte Seligman

Editor-in-Chief: Karen Cross

M0378 Old Glory
Magazine
United Kingdom
Tel: +44 (0) 7943 021585

colin.tyson@kelseymedia.co.uk

https://www.oldglory.co.uk
https://www.facebook.com/OldGloryMag/

Magazine Publisher: Kelsey Media

Nonfiction > *Articles*
  History; Steam Engines; Steam Power

Publishes articles, features, and news covering industrial and transport heritage in the United Kingdom and overseas, particularly vintage vehicles and the preservation and restoration of steam engines.

Editor: Colin Tyson

M0379 Oor Wullie
Magazine
United Kingdom

Newspaper Publisher / Magazine Publisher: DC Thomson Media

M0380 Orbis International Literary Journal
Magazine
17 Greenhow Avenue, West Kirby, Wirral, CH48 5EL
United Kingdom

carolebaldock@hotmail.com

http://www.orbisjournal.com

Types: Fiction; Nonfiction; Poetry
Formats: Articles; Essays; News; Reviews; Short Fiction
Subjects: Arts; Comedy / Humour; Literary; Women's Interests
Markets: Adult

Send: Full text

One of the longest running UK magazines; established 1969 And one of the most highly regarded; Peter Finch, Chief Executive of the Welsh Academi includes this magazine in his Top 10 publications (The Poetry Business). Around one third of the poems in each issue are from Overseas (and around one fifth of subscribers):read, enjoy, inwardly digest; and improve your chances of being published abroad. One of the few magazines which is also a useful resource. Includes news items, competition listings and magazine reviews. One of the few magazines to provide contributors with proofs and editorial critique. Readers' Award: £50 for the piece receiving the most votes, plus £50 between four runners-up. Submissions by post only, unless overseas.

Editor: Carole Baldock

M0381 The Orchid Review
Magazine
United Kingdom

Magazine Publisher: The Royal Horticultural Society (RHS)

M0382 Our Dogs
Magazine
Northwood House, Greenwood Business Centre, Regent Road, Salford, M5 4QH
United Kingdom
Tel: +44 (0) 1617 094571
Fax: +44 (0) 844 504 9013

alismith@ourdogs.co.uk

http://www.ourdogs.co.uk

Types: Nonfiction
Formats: Articles; News
Subjects: Hobbies; How To
Markets: Adult; Professional

Magazine on the showing and breeding of pedigree dogs.

Editor: Alison Smith

M0383 Outside
Magazine
United States

https://www.outsideonline.com
https://www.facebook.com/outsidemagazine
https://twitter.com/outsidemagazine
https://www.instagram.com/outsidemagazine

Magazine Publisher: Outside Interactive Inc.

Nonfiction > *Articles*
Environment; Fitness; Outdoor Activities;
Sport; Travel

Magazine of the outdoors. Covers travel, sports, gear, and fitness, as well as the personalities, the environment, and the style and culture of the outdoors.

M0384 Oxford Poetry

Magazine
c/o Partus Press, Suite 270, 266 Banbury Road, Oxford, OX2 7DL
United Kingdom

editors@oxfordpoetry.co.uk

http://www.oxfordpoetry.co.uk

Book Publisher / Magazine Publisher: Partus Press

Nonfiction
Articles: Literature
Essays: Literature
Interviews: Literature
Reviews: Literature

Poetry in Translation > *Any Poetic Form*

Poetry > *Any Poetic Form*

Closed to approaches.

Costs: A fee is charged upon submission. £3 submission fee.

Publishes poems, interviews, reviews, and essays. Accepts unpublished poems on any theme and of any length during specific biannual submission windows, which are announced on the website. Send up to four poems by email. See website for full details.

M0385 Pacifica Literary Review

Magazine
Seattle, WA
United States

pacificalitreview@gmail.com

http://www.pacificareview.com

Types: Fiction; Nonfiction; Poetry
Subjects: Literary
Markets: Adult

Send: Full text

Accepts poetry, fiction, and creative nonfiction. Prose should be under 5,000 words. Flash fiction up to 1,000 words. Will consider novel excerpts, but must work as stand alone entities. For poetry and flash fiction submit a maximum of three pieces at a time. Send submissions through online submission system. See website for full guidelines.

Editor: Matt Muth

M0386 pacificREVIEW

Magazine
Dept. of English and Comparative Literature, San Diego State University, 5500 Campanile Dr., San Diego, CA 92182-6020
United States

pacrevjournal@gmail.com

https://pacificreview.sdsu.edu

Types: Fiction; Nonfiction; Poetry
Formats: Essays; Short Fiction
Markets: Adult

Closed to approaches.

Closed as at September 2019. Check website for current status. Publishes poems, fiction (short stories, flash fiction and excerpts that stand alone), memoir, creative non-fiction, essays, comics, visual art, photography, documented performance and hybrid.

M0387 Packingtown Review

Magazine
United States

packingtownreview@gmail.com

http://www.packingtownreview.com

Types: Fiction; Nonfiction; Poetry; Scripts; Translations
Subjects: Drama; Literary; Literary Criticism
Markets: Adult

Send: Full text
How to send: Email

Submit 3-5 poems, fiction, criticism, or creative nonfiction up to 4,000 words, drama up to 15 pages, or translations, with 60-word bio in the third person. Send as attachment by email. See website for full guidelines.

M0388 The Paddock Review

Magazine
United States

https://paddockreview.com

Types: Poetry
Subjects: Literary
Markets: Adult

Send: Full text

Submit 1-3 poems through online submission system. Accepts previously published poems and simultaneous submissions. Include short bio.

M0389 Pain

Magazine
United Kingdom

pain@partuspress.com

https://www.painpoetry.co.uk
https://partus.submittable.com/submit

Book Publisher / Magazine Publisher: Partus Press

Nonfiction
Articles: Literature
Essays: Creative Nonfiction

Poetry > *Any Poetic Form*

Closed to approaches.

Costs: A fee is charged upon submission. £3.00 fee per submission.

Publishes unpublished poems as well as short essays and articles with a literary focus.

M0390 Parchment Craft

Magazine
United Kingdom

Magazine Publisher: Warners Group Publications

M0391 The Paris Review

Magazine
United States
Tel: +1 (212) 343-1333

queries@theparisreview.org

https://www.theparisreview.org
https://www.facebook.com/parisreview
https://twitter.com/parisreview
http://theparisreview.tumblr.com/

Fiction > *Short Fiction*: Literary

Nonfiction
Interviews; *Short Nonfiction*
Poetry > *Any Poetic Form*

Closed to approaches.

Send submissions through online submission system only. Postal submissions are suspended at this time. All submissions must be in English and previously unpublished, though translations are acceptable if accompanied by copy of the original text. Simultaneous submissions accepted as long as immediate notification is given of acceptance elsewhere.

Executive Editor: Brigid Hughes

M0392 Park & Holiday Home Inspiration

Magazine
United Kingdom

Magazine Publisher: Warners Group Publications

M0393 Peace and Freedom

Magazine
United Kingdom

p_rance@yahoo.co.uk

http://pandf.booksmusicfilmstv.com/

Fiction > *Short Fiction*
Environment; Social Issues

Nonfiction

Articles: Environment; Social Issues
Essays: Environment; Social Issues
Poetry > *Any Poetic Form*
Environment; Social Issues

Magazine publishing poetry, fiction, and articles, with an emphasis on social, humanitarian and environmental issues. Also publishes interviews of animal welfare/environmental/human rights campaigners, writers, poets, artists, film, music and TV personalities, up to 1,000 words. Reviews of books / records / events etc. up to 50 words also considered. Email submissions accepted for reviews, short stories, and interviews ONLY.

Editor: Paul Rance

M0394 People's Friend Pocket Novels
Magazine
DC Thomson & Co. Ltd, 2 Albert Square, Dundee, DD1 9QJ
United Kingdom
Tel: +44 (0) 1382 223131

tsteel@dctmedia.co.uk

https://www.thepeoplesfriend.co.uk

Magazine: The People's Friend (**M0395**)

Fiction > *Novellas*
Family Saga; Romance

Send: Query; Synopsis; Writing sample
How to send: Email; Post

Publishes romance and family fiction between 37,000 and 39,000 words, aimed at adults aged over 30. Send query by post or by email (preferred) with synopsis and first two chapters in first instance. See website for more information.

Editor: Tracey Steel

M0395 The People's Friend
Magazine
DC Thomson & Co. Ltd., 2 Albert Square, Dundee, DD1 9QJ
United Kingdom
Tel: +44 (0) 1382 223131

peoplesfriend@dcthomson.co.uk

http://www.thepeoplesfriend.co.uk

Newspaper Publisher / Magazine Publisher: DC Thomson Media

Types: Fiction; Nonfiction; Poetry
Formats: Articles; Short Fiction
Subjects: Adventure; Cookery; Crafts; Crime; Hobbies; Mystery; Nature; Romance; Thrillers; Traditional; Travel; Women's Interests
Markets: Adult

Publishes complete short stories (1,200-3,000 words (4,000 for specials)) and serials, focusing on character development rather than complex plots, plus 10,000-word crime

thrillers. Also considers nonfiction from nature to nostalgia and from holidays to hobbies, and poetry. Guidelines available on website.

Magazine: People's Friend Pocket Novels (**M0394**)

M0396 Period Living
Magazine
Future Publishing Limited, Quay House, The Ambury, Bath, BA1 1UA
United Kingdom

realhomes@futurenet.com

https://www.realhomes.com/period-living

Types: Nonfiction
Formats: Articles
Subjects: Crafts; Design; Gardening
Markets: Adult

Magazine on renovating and decorating period homes, or in a period style.

M0397 Petroleum Geoscience
Magazine
United Kingdom

Book Publisher / Magazine Publisher: The Geological Society Publishing House (**P0322**)

M0398 The Philosopher
Online Magazine
United Kingdom

http://www.the-philosopher.co.uk

Nonfiction > *Articles*: Philosophy

Publishes philosophical articles up to 3,000 words. Articles are considered without discrimination as to subject matter or author. The only criterion is that it must be philosophical in method. See website for submission guidelines.

Editor: Martin Cohen

M0399 The Photographer
Magazine
The British Institute of Professional Photography, The Artistry House, 16 Winckley Square, Preston, PR1 3JJ
United Kingdom
Tel: +44 (0) 1772 367968

admin@bipp.com

https://www.bipp.com

PROFESSIONAL > **Nonfiction** > *Articles*: Photography

Photography magazine for professional photographers.

M0400 Pianist
Magazine
United Kingdom

Magazine Publisher: Warners Group Publications

M0401 Pilot
Magazine
Evolution House, 2-6 Easthampstead Road, Wokingham, RG40 2EG
United Kingdom

philip.whiteman@archant.co.uk

https://www.pilotweb.aero

Magazine Publisher: Archant

ADULT > **Nonfiction** > *Articles*
Air Travel; Piloting

PROFESSIONAL > **Nonfiction** > *Articles*
Air Travel; Piloting

Send: Full text
How to send: Email

Aimed at private, commercial and would-be flyers, including enthusiasts.

Editor: Nick Bloom

M0402 Planet
Magazine
PO Box 44, Aberystwyth, Ceredigion, SY23 3ZZ
United Kingdom
Tel: +44 (0) 1970 611255

submissions@planetmagazine.org.uk

http://www.planetmagazine.org.uk

Types: Fiction; Nonfiction; Poetry
Formats: Articles; Reviews; Short Fiction; Theatre Scripts
Subjects: Arts; Current Affairs; Literary; Literature; Music; Politics
Markets: Adult

Closed to approaches.

Publishes mostly commissioned material, but will accept ideas for articles and reviews, and unsolicited submissions of fiction and poetry. Submit one piece of short fiction between 1,500 and 2,500 words, or 4-6 poems at a time. A range of styles and themes are accepted, but postal submissions will not be considered unless adequate return postage is provided. If you have an idea for a relevant article send a query with brief synopsis.

Editor: Emily Trahair

M0403 The Plant Review
Magazine
United Kingdom

Magazine Publisher: The Royal Horticultural Society (RHS)

M0404 Platinum Magazine
Magazine
United Kingdom

Newspaper Publisher / Magazine Publisher: DC Thomson Media

M0405 PN Review

Magazine
4th Floor, Alliance House, 30 Cross Street,
Manchester, M2 7AQ
United Kingdom
Tel: +44 (0) 161 834 8730
Fax: +44 (0) 161 832 0084

PNRsubmissions@carcanet.co.uk

http://www.pnreview.co.uk

Types: Poetry; Translations
Formats: Articles; Interviews; News; Reviews
Markets: Adult

Send: Query
Don't send: Full text

Send query with synopsis and sample pages,
after having familiarised yourself with the
magazine. Accepts prose up to 15 double-
spaced pages or 4 poems / 5 pages of poetry.
Bimonthly magazine of poetry and poetry
criticism. Includes editorial, letters, news,
articles, interviews, features, poems,
translations, and a substantial book review
section. No short stories, children's prose /
poetry, or non-poetry related work (academic,
biography etc.). Accepts electronic
submissions from individual subscribers only –
otherwise only hard copy submissions are
considered.

Editor: Michael Schmidt

M0406 Poetry Ireland Review

Magazine
11 Parnell Square East, Dublin 1, D01 ND60
Ireland
Tel: +353 (0)1 6789815
Fax: +353 (0)1 6789782

pir@poetryireland.ie
info@poetryireland.ie

https://www.poetryireland.ie

Nonfiction
  Articles: Poetry as a Subject
  Reviews: Poetry as a Subject
Poetry > *Any Poetic Form*

Send: Full text; Proposal
How to send: Post; Submittable

Send up to six poems through online
submission system, or by post. Poetry is
accepted from around the world, but must be
previously unpublished. No sexism or racism.
Articles and reviews are generally
commissioned, however proposals are
welcome. No unsolicited reviews or articles.

Editor: Colette Bryce

M0407 The Poetry Review

Magazine
The Poetry Society, 22 Betterton Street,
London, WC2H 9BX
United Kingdom

Tel: +44 (0) 20 7420 9880
Fax: +44 (0) 20 7240 4818

poetryreview@poetrysociety.org.uk

https://poetrysociety.org.uk/

Nonfiction
  Essays: Poetry as a Subject
  Reviews: Poetry as a Subject
Poetry in Translation > *Any Poetic Form*
Poetry > *Any Poetic Form*

Send: Full text
How to send: Submittable

Describes itself as "one of the liveliest and
most influential literary magazines in the
world", and has been associated with the rise
of the New Generation of British poets – Carol
Ann Duffy, Simon Armitage, Glyn Maxwell,
Don Paterson... though its scope extends
beyond the UK, with special issues focusing on
poetries from around the world. Send up to 6
unpublished poems, or literary translations of
poems, through online submission system.

M0408 Poetry Wales

Magazine
Suite 6, 4 Derwen Road, Bridgend, CF31 1LH
United Kingdom
Tel: +44 (0) 1656 663018

powales.ceditor@gmail.com
info@poetrywales.co.uk

https://poetrywales.co.uk
http://twitter.com/poetrywales
http://facebook.com/poetrywales
http://instagram.com/poetrywales

Nonfiction
  Articles: Poetry as a Subject
  Reviews: Books; Poetry as a Subject
Poetry > *Any Poetic Form*

Closed to approaches.

Publishes poetry, features, and reviews from
Wales and beyond. Submit via online
submission system, or by post. Also runs
competitions.

Editor: Nia Davies

M0409 The Political Quarterly

Magazine
12 Hempland Avenue, York, YO31 1DE
United Kingdom

submissions@politicalquarterly.org.uk

http://www.politicalquarterly.org.uk

Nonfiction > *Articles*: Politics

Send: Full text
How to send: Email

Magazine covering national and international
politics. Accepts unsolicited articles.

M0410 Popshot Quarterly

Magazine
United Kingdom

submit@popshotpopshot.com

https://www.popshotpopshot.com

Fiction > *Short Fiction*: Literary
Poetry > *Any Poetic Form*

Send: Full text
How to send: Email

Publishes flash fiction, short stories, and poetry
on the theme of the current issue (see website).
Submit by email.

M0411 Prac Crit

Magazine
United Kingdom

editors@praccrit.com

http://www.praccrit.com

Types: Nonfiction
Formats: Essays; Interviews
Subjects: Contemporary; Literary; Literary
Criticism
Markets: Adult

Send: Query
Don't send: Full text
How to send: Email

Publishes close analysis of poems; essays;
interviews; and reflections from poets. Most
articles are commissioned, but will accept
proposals for essays or interviews. No direct
submissions of poetry.

M0412 Practical Boat Owner Magazine

Magazine
United Kingdom
Tel: +44 (0) 1252 555213

pbo@futurenet.com

https://www.pbo.co.uk

Magazine Publisher: Future

Nonfiction > *Articles*: Boats

Cruising boats magazine covering both power
and sail. Publishes technical articles on
maintenance, restoration, modifications, etc.

M0413 Practical Caravan

Magazine
Future Publishing Limited, Quay House, The
Ambury, Bath, BA1 1UA
United Kingdom

https://www.practicalcaravan.com

Types: Nonfiction
Formats: Articles; Reviews
Subjects: Leisure; Travel
Markets: Adult

Publishes material relating to caravanning and
touring caravans, including features, reviews,

travel pieces, etc. No static van or motorcaravan stories. Features must be accompanied by photos.

M0414 Practical Fishkeeping

Magazine
The Maltings, West Street, Bourne,
Lincolnshire, PE10 9PH
United Kingdom
Tel: +44 (0) 1778 391194

editorial@practicalfishkeeping.co.uk

https://www.practicalfishkeeping.co.uk
https://www.facebook.com/PFKmag/
https://www.twitter.com/PFKmagazine
https://www.instagram.com/pfkmag/
https://www.youtube.com/channel/UC--fz-
Y9Zn6cZ-XKcIBjeGw

Magazine Publisher: Warners Group
Publications

Nonfiction > *Articles*: Pet Fish

Publishes practical articles on all aspects of keeping fish.

Editor: Karen Youngs

M0415 The Practising Midwife

Magazine
Saturn House, Mercury Rise, Altham Industrial
Park, Altham, Lancashire, BB5 5BY
United Kingdom

info@all4maternity.com

https://www.all4maternity.com
https://twitter.com/all4maternity
https://www.facebook.com/all4maternity/

PROFESSIONAL > **Nonfiction**
 Articles: Midwifery
 News: Midwifery

How to send: Online submission system

Publishes accessible, authoritative and readable information for midwives, students and other professionals in the maternity services.

Editor-in-Chief: Alys Einion

Editors: Claire Feeley; Laura Yeates

M0416 The Practitioner

Magazine
United Kingdom

editor@thepractitioner.co.uk

https://www.thepractitioner.co.uk

PROFESSIONAL > **Nonfiction**
 Articles: Health; Medicine
 News: Health; Medicine

Send: Query; Full text
How to send: Email

Monthly magazine for General Practitioners, covering latest clinical issues. Considers ideas for articles and submissions of case reports.

Editor: Corinne Short

M0417 Preservation Magazine

Magazine
2600 Virginia Avenue NW, Suite 1100,
Washington, DC 20037
United States
Tel: +1 (202) 588-6013

preservation@savingplaces.org

https://savingplaces.org/preservation-magazine

Nonfiction > *Articles*
 History; Travel

Send: Query
How to send: Phone; Email

Magazine publishing material on the preservation of historic buildings and neighbourhoods in the United States.

Editor: Arnold Berke

M0418 Pride

Magazine
1 Garrat Lane, London, SW18 4AQ
United Kingdom
Tel: +44 (0) 20 8871 4443

editor@pridemagazine.com

http://pridemagazine.com
http://www.facebook.com/PrideMagazine
http://www.instagram.com/pridemaguk

Nonfiction
 Articles: Beauty; Career Development;
 Entertainment; Fashion; Hairstyles; Health;
 Lifestyle
 News: Ethnic Groups; Social Issues

Magazine aimed at black women. Publishes news, and articles and features on entertainment, hair, beauty, and fashion.

Editor: CJ Cushnie

M0419 Proceedings of the Yorkshire Geological Society

Magazine
United Kingdom

Book Publisher / Magazine Publisher: The
Geological Society Publishing House (**P0322**)

M0420 Prole

Magazine
United Kingdom

submissionspoetry@prolebooks.co.uk
submissionsprose@prolebooks.co.uk

https://prolebooks.co.uk
https://facebook.com/Prole-236155444300
https://twitter.com/Prolebooks

Fiction > *Short Fiction*: Literary

Nonfiction > *Short Nonfiction*: Creative
Nonfiction

Poetry > *Any Poetic Form*

Send: Full text
How to send: In the body of an email

Publishes accessible literature of high quality, including poetry, short fiction, and creative nonfiction. Seeks to appeal to a wide audience and avoid literary elitism (obscure references and highly stylised structures and forms are unlikely to find favour). No previously published material or simultaneous submissions. Submit one piece of prose or up to five poems (or three longer poems) in the body of an email, with your name, contact details, word count and third person author bio up to 100 words. See website for appropriate email addresses for prose and poetry submissions, and full submission guidelines. No attachments.

M0421 Psychic News

Magazine
Unit 2, Griggs Business Centre, West Street,
Coggeshall, Essex, CO6 1NT
United Kingdom
Tel: +44 (0) 1376 563091

pneditorials@gmail.com

https://www.psychicnews.org.uk
https://www.facebook.com/psychicnews/
https://twitter.com/psychicnewsmag

Nonfiction > *Articles*: Spirituality

Magazine of the paranormal, covering ghosts, spiritual healing, psychic research, etc.

Editor: Tony Ortzen

M0422 Pushing Out the Boat

Magazine
United Kingdom

info@pushingouttheboat.co.uk

https://www.pushingouttheboat.co.uk

Fiction > *Short Fiction*: Literary

Poetry > *Any Poetic Form*

Scripts > *Theatre Scripts*

Closed to approaches.

Magazine of prose, poetry and visual arts, based in North-East Scotland. Welcomes work in English, Doric or Scots. Submit via online submission system during open reading periods. See website for details.

M0423 Qu Literary Magazine

Magazine
United States

qulitmag@queens.edu

http://www.qulitmag.com

Fiction > *Short Fiction*: Literary

Nonfiction > *Essays*

Poetry > *Any Poetic Form*

Scripts
 Film Scripts; *TV Scripts*; *Theatre Scripts*

Closed to approaches.

Submit prose or poems via online submission system. $2 fee. Does not accept international submissions.

M0424 Quail Bell
Magazine
United States

submissions@quailbellmagazine.com

http://www.quailbellmagazine.com

Fiction > *Short Fiction*
Intersectional Feminism; Literary

Nonfiction > *Articles*: Intersectional Feminism

Poetry > *Any Poetic Form*: Intersectional Feminism

Send: Full text
How to send: Email

An intersectional feminist magazine. Send submissions by email. See website for full guidelines.

M0425 Quarter After Eight
Magazine
United States

editor@quarteraftereight.org

http://www.quarteraftereight.org

Types: Fiction; Nonfiction; Poetry; Scripts; Translations
Formats: Interviews; Reviews
Subjects: Drama; Experimental
Markets: Adult

Send: Full text

Publishes fiction, poetry, and nonfiction. Submit one story or essay or up to three flash prose pieces or four poems via online submission system. Accepts online submissions between October 15 and April 15 only.

M0426 Quarterly Journal of Engineering Geology and Hydrogeology
Magazine
United Kingdom

Book Publisher / Magazine Publisher: The Geological Society Publishing House (**P0322**)

M0427 R.kv.r.y. Quarterly Literary Journal
Magazine
United States

r.kv.r.y.editor@gmail.com

http://rkvryquarterly.com

Types: Fiction; Nonfiction; Poetry
Formats: Essays; Short Fiction
Subjects: Literary
Markets: Adult

Closed to approaches.

Closed to submissions as at November 2019. Check website for current status. Literary journal publishing works relating to acts, processes, or instances of recovery. Submit up to 3,000 words for prose, up to 1,000 words for flash fiction, or up to three poems, via online submission system. £3 submission charge. Closed to submissions during the summer months.

M0428 Rabid Oak
Online Magazine
United States

rabidoak@gmail.com

https://rabidoak.com

Fiction > *Short Fiction*

Nonfiction > *Short Nonfiction*

Poetry > *Any Poetic Form*

Send: Full text; Author bio
How to send: Email

Online literary journal. Send up to five poems or two pieces of fiction or nonfiction (up to 1,000 words) in a Word document attachment.

M0429 Race & Class
Magazine
United Kingdom

raceandclass@irr.org.uk

https://journals.sagepub.com/home/rac

Types: Nonfiction
Formats: Articles; Essays
Subjects: Sociology
Markets: Academic

Refereed, ISI-ranked journal on racism and imperialism in the world today.

Editors: Jenny Bourne; Hazel Waters

M0430 Racecar Engineering
Magazine
The Chelsea Magazine Company, Jubilee House, 2 Jubilee Place, London, SW3 3TQ
United Kingdom
Tel: +44 (0) 20 7349 3700

editorial@racecarengineering.com

https://www.racecar-engineering.com
https://www.facebook.com/RacecarEngineering/
https://twitter.com/RacecarEngineer

Magazine Publisher: The Chelsea Magazine Company

Nonfiction
Articles: Engineering; Racecars
News: Engineering; Racecars

Publishes news articles and in-depth features on racing cars and related products and technology. No material on road cars or racing drivers.

Editor: Charles Armstrong-Wilson

M0431 Racing Post
Magazine
Floor 7, Vivo Building, South Bank Central, 30 Stamford Street, London, SE1 9LS
United Kingdom

help@racingpost.com

https://www.racingpost.com

Nonfiction
Articles: Horse Racing
News: Horse Racing

Daily paper of horse racing, plus some general sport.

M0432 The Racket
Magazine
United States

theracketreadingseries@gmail.com

https://theracketsf.com

Fiction > *Short Fiction*

Poetry > *Any Poetic Form*

Send: Full text
How to send: Email

Considers submissions that contain work(s) of poetry and/or prose with a total combined word count of 2,000 words or fewer. See website for full guidelines.

M0433 Radar Poetry
Magazine
United States

radarpoetry@gmail.com

https://www.radarpoetry.com

Poetry > *Any Poetic Form*

Closed to approaches.

Costs: A fee is charged upon submission. $3.

Electronic journal, published quarterly. Submit 3-5 original, previously unpublished poems through online submission system. Accepts submissions November 1 to January 1 (free), and March 1 to May 1 ($3) annually.

Editors: Rachel Marie Patterson; Dara-Lyn Shrager

M0434 Radio User
Magazine
United Kingdom

https://www.radioenthusiast.co.uk/
https://www.facebook.com/radioenthusiasts/
https://twitter.com/renthusiasts

Magazine Publisher: Warners Group Publications

Nonfiction > *Articles*: Radio Technology

Magazine relating to receiving and listening to radio signals, aimed at radio enthusiasts.

Editors: Elaine Richards; Georg Wiessala

M0435 Ramsay's

Magazine
United Kingdom

Magazine Publisher: Warners Group
Publications

M0436 Reach

Magazine
IDP, 24 Forest Houses, Halwill, Beaworthy,
Devon, EX21 5UU
United Kingdom

publishing@indigodreams.co.uk

http://www.indigodreams.co.uk/reach-poetry/
4563791643

Poetry > *Any Poetic Form*: Literary

Send: Full text
How to send: Email

Costs: A subscription is required in order to
submit.

Currently accepting submissions from
subscribers only.

Publishes quality poetry from both experienced
and new poets. Formal or free verse, haiku...
everything is considered. Subscribers can
comment on and vote for poetry from the
previous issue, the winner receiving £50, plus
regular in-house anthologies and competitions.
Receives no external funding and depends
entirely on subscriptions. Submit up to two
poems by email. No simultaneous submissions.

Editor: Ronnie Goodyer

M0437 The Reader

Magazine
The Mansion House, Calderstones Park,
Liverpool, L18 3JB
United Kingdom
Tel: + 44 (0) 1517 292200

magazine@thereader.org.uk

https://www.thereader.org.uk
https://www.thereader.org.uk/what-we-do/the-
reader-magazine/
https://twitter.com/thereaderorg
https://www.facebook.com/thereaderorg
https://www.instagram.com/thereaderorg/

Nonfiction > *Articles*: Literature

Magazine of charity promoting shared reading
through reading aloud groups. No longer
publishes original fiction and poetry.

M0438 Red Magazine

Magazine
30 Panton Street, Leicester Square, London,
SW1Y 4AJ
United Kingdom

https://www.redonline.co.uk

Types: Nonfiction
Formats: Articles; News; Reviews
Subjects: Beauty; Cookery; Design; Fashion;
Lifestyle; Travel; Women's Interests
Markets: Adult

Send: Query
Don't send: Full text

Magazine aimed at women in their thirties.
Usually uses regular contributors, but will
consider queries for ideas.

M0439 Relevant

Magazine
United States

submissions@relevantmediagroup.com

https://relevantmagazine.com

Types: Nonfiction
Formats: Articles
Subjects: Culture; Lifestyle; Religion
Markets: Adult

Send: Full text
How to send: Email

Christian lifestyle magazine aimed at adults in
their 20s and 30s, covering faith, culture, and
"intentional living".

M0440 Resurgence & Ecologist

Magazine
The Resurgence Centre, Fore Street, Hartland,
Bideford, Devon, EX39 6AB
United Kingdom

brendan@theecologist.org

https://theecologist.org

Nonfiction
    Articles: Environment
    News: Environment

Aims to foster a greater connection to nature in
order to enhance personal wellbeing, support
resilient communities and inform social change
towards regenerative societies that enrich
rather than deplete our natural environment.

Editor: Zac Goldsmith

M0441 Right Start Online

Online Magazine
United Kingdom

info@rightstartonline.co.uk

https://www.rightstartonline.co.uk

Nonfiction > *Articles*: Parenting

Magazine covering pre-school children's
health, lifestyle, development, education, etc.
Contact the editor by email to discuss editorial
opportunities.

Editor: Lynette Lowthian

M0442 Riptide

Magazine
The Department of English, The University of
Exeter, Queen's Building, Queen's Drive,
Exeter, EX4 6QH
United Kingdom

editors@riptidejournal.co.uk

http://www.riptidejournal.co.uk
http://twitter.com/#!/RiptideJournal
http://www.facebook.com/pages/Riptide-
Journal/161555683865263

Fiction > *Short Fiction*: Literary

Poetry > *Any Poetic Form*

Closed to approaches.

Bi-annual anthology of new short fiction and
poetry by both established and emerging
writers. Send one unpublished original story up
to 5,000 words or up to five poems up to 40
lines each, by post or as a Word file email
attachment.

M0443 Rising Innovator

Online Magazine
United States

editorial@risinginnovator.com

https://www.risinginnovator.com
https://docs.google.com/document/d/
1_YIzJeFywByFcqOfNEod86dNiAR1MnTQb
tSUXERqDn4/edit
https://facebook.com/risinginnovator/
https://www.linkedin.com/company/rising-
innovator
https://www.instagram.com/risinginnovator/
https://twitter.com/risinginnovate
https://pinterest.com/risinginnovator

ADULT > **Nonfiction** > *Articles*
    Business; Entrepreneurship

CHILDREN'S > **Nonfiction** > *Articles*
    Business; Entrepreneurship

PROFESSIONAL > **Nonfiction** > *Articles*
    Business; Education; Entrepreneurship

Send: Pitch
How to send: Email; Online contact form

A web-only publication to support
entrepreneurship in children. We have three
basic targets: children aged 8 to 18, their
parents, and any school staff that teach
entrepreneurship. We offer news, profiles,
guides, advice, and any articles of interest to
our audience. We also offer a few free online
tools as well, such as a quiz that helps children
select a business idea.

Because of our different targets, sometimes we
solicit the same content to be written for two
different audiences. We keep content
differentiated on our website. If you have
further questions then please refer to the
guidelines above or email us.

M0444 River Styx

Magazine
3301 Washington Ave, Suite 2C, St. Louis,
MO 63103
United States

ManagingEditor@riverstyx.org

http://www.riverstyx.org
https://twitter.com/riverstyxmag/
https://www.facebook.com/
RiverStyxLiteraryMagazine/
https://www.linkedin.com/company/river-styx/
https://www.instagram.com/riverstyxmag/

Fiction > *Short Fiction*

Nonfiction > *Essays*

Poetry > *Any Poetic Form*

Scripts > *Theatre Scripts*

How to send: Submittable; Post
How not to send: Email

Costs: A fee is charged for online submissions; Offers services that writers have to pay for. £3 submission fee for online submissions. Offers critiquing services.

A multicultural magazine of poetry, short fiction, essays, short plays, and art. Seeks to publish work that is striking in its originality, energy, and craft, from both new and established writers.

Editor: Richard Newman

M0445 Rugby World
Magazine
161 Marsh Wall, London, E14 9AP
United Kingdom
Tel: +44 (0) 330 390 6479

sarah.mockford@futurenet.com

https://www.rugbyworld.com
https://www.facebook.com/
rugbyworldmagazine
https://www.youtube.com/user/rugbyworld08
https://twitter.com/rugbyworldmag

Magazine Publisher: Future Media Group

Nonfiction
Articles: Rugby
News: Rugby

Send: Query; Author bio; Synopsis

Magazine publishing news and articles related to rugby. Send idea with coverline, headline, and 50-word synopsis, along with brief resume of your experience.

Editor: Sarah Mockford

M0446 Rural Builder
Magazine
Shield Wall Media LLC, PO Box 255, Iola, WI 54945
United States

https://www.constructionmagnet.com/rural-builder

PROFESSIONAL > Nonfiction
Articles: Architecture; Building / Construction; Design; How To
News: Architecture; Building / Construction; Design; How To

Magazine for builders and suppliers of primarily low-rise agricultural and small retail and municipal structures in cities with populations under 250,000.

Editor: Karen Knapstein

M0447 S/tick
Magazine
Canada

editor@dontdiepress.org

https://www.dontdiepress.org/stickmag/

Types: Fiction; Poetry
Formats: Short Fiction
Subjects: Literary; Women's Interests
Markets: Adult

Send: Full text
How to send: Email

Online magazine publishing feminist prose and poetry. Send up to five poems or up to 2,000 words of prose by email. See website for full guidelines.

Editor: Sarah-Jean Krahn

M0448 Sable
Online Magazine
SAKS Publications, PO Box 33504, London, E9 7YE
United Kingdom

editorial@sablelitmag.org
micro@sablelitmag.org

http://www.sablelitmag.org
https://www.facebook.com/SABLELitmag.org
https://twitter.com/SABLELitMag

Fiction > *Short Fiction*

Nonfiction > *Reviews*

Send: Full text
How to send: Email

A showcase of new creative work by writers of colour. Publishes reviews and flash fiction up to 600 words.

M0449 Saddlebag Dispatches
Magazine
United States

submissions@saddlebagdispatches.com

https://saddlebagdispatches.com

Types: Fiction; Nonfiction; Poetry
Formats: Articles; Short Fiction
Subjects: Westerns
Markets: Adult

Send: Full text
How to send: Email

Publishes fiction, nonfiction, and poetry about the American West. Looks for themes of open country, unforgiving nature, struggles to survive and settle the land, freedom from authority, cooperation with fellow adventurers, and other experiences that human beings

encounter on the frontier. Send submissions by email. See website for full guidelines.

M0450 Saga Magazine
Magazine
Saga Publishing Ltd, The Saga Building, Enbrook Park, Folkestone, Kent, CT20 3SE
United Kingdom
Tel: +44 (0) 1303 771111

https://www.saga.co.uk/magazine

Types: Nonfiction
Formats: Articles; Interviews
Subjects: Lifestyle
Markets: Adult

Send: Query
Don't send: Full text

Magazine for older people.

M0451 SAIL Magazine
Magazine
23a Glendale Street, Salem, MA 01970
United States
Tel: +1 (860) 767-3200
Fax: +1 (860) 767-1048

sailmail@sailmagazine.com

https://www.sailmagazine.com

Types: Nonfiction
Formats: Articles
Subjects: Leisure; Sport; Travel
Markets: Adult

Sailing magazine covering boats, DIY, cruising, racing, equipment, etc.

Editor: Adam Cort

M0452 Sailing Today
Magazine
The Chelsea Magazine Company, Jubilee House, 2 Jubilee Place, London, SW3 3QW
United Kingdom
Tel: +44 (0) 20 7349 3700

editor@sailingtoday.co.uk

https://www.sailingtoday.co.uk
https://www.facebook.com/sailingtoday/
https://twitter.com/SailingTodayMag
https://www.youtube.com/channel/UCah1Wlfp86HD0tpbhW1LP1Q

Nonfiction > *Articles:* Sailing

Practical magazine for cruising sailors. Offers a wealth of practical advice and a dynamic mix of in-depth boat, gear and equipment news.

Editor: Rodger Witt

M0453 Sarasvati
Magazine
24 Forest Houses, Halwill, Beaworthy, Devon, EX21 5UU
United Kingdom

dawnidp@gmail.com

http://www.indigodreams.co.uk/sarasvati/

Types: Fiction; Poetry
Formats: Short Fiction
Markets: Adult

Showcases poetry and prose. Each contributor will have three to four A5 pages available to their work. Submit up to five poems, or prose up to 1,000 words.

Editor: Dawn Bauling

M0454 Scintilla
Magazine
United Kingdom

poetry@vaughanassociation.org

http://www.vaughanassociation.org

Fiction > *Short Fiction*
Contemporary; Metaphysical

Nonfiction > *Essays*
17th Century; Literature; Metaphysical

Poetry > *Any Poetic Form*
Contemporary; Metaphysical

Send: Full text
How to send: Email attachment

An international, peer-reviewed journal of literary criticism, prose, and new poetry in the metaphysical tradition.

Editor: Dr. Kevin Mills

General Editor: Joseph Sterrett

Poetry Editor: Damian Walford Davies

Prose Editor: Erik Ankerberg

M0455 Scottish Caravans & Motorhomes
Magazine
United Kingdom

Newspaper Publisher / Magazine Publisher:
DC Thomson Media

M0456 The Scottish Farmer
Magazine
200 Renfield St, Glasgow, G2 3QB
United Kingdom

https://www.thescottishfarmer.co.uk
https://www.facebook.com/scottishfarmer
https://twitter.com/scottishfarmer
https://www.instagram.com/
scottishfarmernewspaper/
https://www.linkedin.com/company/17949188

Magazine Publisher: Newsquest Media Group

PROFESSIONAL > **Nonfiction**
Articles: Farming; Scotland
News: Farming; Scotland

Agricultural magazine publishing news and features on political, personal, and technological developments in farming, as well as rural and craft items. Approach with ideas by email or fax.

Editors: Alasdair Fletcher; Deputy Editor: Ken Fletcher

M0457 Scottish Field
Magazine
Fettes Park, 496 Ferry Road, Edinburgh, EH5 2DL
United Kingdom
Tel: +44 (0) 1315 511000
Fax: +44 (0) 1315 517901

editor@scottishfield.co.uk

https://www.scottishfield.co.uk
https://www.facebook.com/scottishfield
http://www.twitter.com/scottishfield

Nonfiction > *Articles*
Beauty; Culture; Fashion; Food and Drink; Gardening; Interior Design; Lifestyle; Outdoor Activities; Scotland; Travel

Lifestyle magazine publishing articles and features of general Scottish interest.

Editors: Richard Bath; Claire Grant

M0458 Scottish Journal of Geology
Magazine
United Kingdom

Book Publisher / Magazine Publisher: The Geological Society Publishing House (**P0322**)

M0459 Scottish Wedding
Magazine
United Kingdom

Newspaper Publisher / Magazine Publisher:
DC Thomson Media

M0460 Scout Life
Magazine
1325 West Walnut Hill Lane, PO Box 152079, Irving, TX 75015-2079
United States
Tel: +1 (866) 584-6589

https://scoutlife.org
https://facebook.com/scoutlifemag
https://twitter.com/scoutlifemag
https://www.instagram.com/boyslifemagazine/
https://www.youtube.com/c/boyslife
https://www.pinterest.com/ScoutLifeMag/

CHILDREN'S > **Nonfiction** > *Articles*
Comedy / Humour; Games; Hobbies; Leisure; Outdoor Activities

Magazine aimed at young people aged between 6 and 18. Includes games, jokes, contests, giveaways, and articles on hobbies and outdoor activities.

M0461 Screen International
Magazine
Zetland House, 5-25 Scrutton Street, London, EC2A 4HJ

United Kingdom
Tel: +44 (0) 20 8102 0900

info@mbi.london

https://www.screendaily.com
https://www.facebook.com/ScreenDaily/
https://twitter.com/screendaily
https://www.linkedin.com/company-beta/
2298039/
https://www.youtube.com/channel/
UCKV7nCATTd4LFbD93ScBUoA
https://www.instagram.com/screendaily/?hl=en

Magazine Publisher: Media Business Insights (MBI)

PROFESSIONAL > **Nonfiction** > *Articles*
Cinemas / Movie Theaters; Film Industry; Films; TV

International trade paper for the film and television industries.

Editors: Leo Barraclough; Matt Mueller

M0462 Scribble
Magazine
14 The Park, Stow on the Wold, Cheltenham, Glos., GL54 1DX
United Kingdom
Tel: +44 (0) 1451 831053

enquiries@parkpublications.co.uk

http://www.parkpublications.co.uk/scribble.html

Magazine Publisher: Park Publications

Fiction > *Short Fiction*

Send: Full text
How to send: Email; Post

Costs: A fee is charged upon submission. £3. Free for subscribers.

Accepts short stories on any subject from new and experienced writers. Each quarter prizes of £75, £25, and £15 will be awarded for the best three stories in the edition. These competitions are free to annual subscribers, who also have the option to submit by email. See website for further details.

Editor: David Howarth

M0463 Scribbler Arts and Literary Magazine
Magazine
United States

bookwormpublishinghouse@gmail.com

http://www.scribblerliterarymagazine.com

CHILDREN'S
Fiction > *Short Fiction*
Nonfiction > *Essays*
Poetry > *Any Poetic Form*
Scripts > *Theatre Scripts*

YOUNG ADULT
Fiction > *Short Fiction*
Nonfiction > *Essays*

Poetry > *Any Poetic Form*
Scripts > *Theatre Scripts*

Send: Full text
How to send: Online submission system; Email

Magazine aimed at children and young adults, publishing original work by children aged 7-13. Submit up to 5 poems or up to 3,000 words of prose.

M0464 The Scribbler

Magazine
11 Northgate, Peebles, EH45 8RX
United Kingdom
Tel: +44 (0) 7522 934770

greyladiesOCB@gmail.com

http://www.thescribblerreview.co.uk

Fiction > *Short Fiction*

Nonfiction > *Reviews*: Literature

Each issue contains reviews of much-loved and less well-known fiction for women and children, and a short story.

M0465 Sea Breezes

Magazine
The Office, Strenaby Farm, Lonan Church Road, Laxey, Isle of Man, IM4 7JX
United Kingdom
Tel: +44 (1624) 863672

sb.enquiries@seabreezes.co.im

https://seabreezes.co.im
https://twitter.com/seabreezesmag
https://www.facebook.com/seabreezesmagazine/

PROFESSIONAL > **Nonfiction** > *Articles*: S hipping

Monthly magazine devoted to the worldwide shipping industry.

Editor: Captain Andrew C. Douglas

M0466 Seen and Heard

Magazine
United Kingdom

nagalro@nagalro.com

http://www.nagalro.com/seen-and-heard-journal/seen-and-heard.aspx

Types: Nonfiction
Formats: Articles; News
Subjects: Legal
Markets: Academic; Professional

Association magazine for children's guardians, family court advisers and independent social workers who work with children and parents in family court proceedings. Provided free to members. See website for submission guidelines.

Editor: Rodney Noon

M0467 Sentinel Literary Quarterly

Magazine
120 Warland Road, London, SE18 2ET
United Kingdom
Tel: +44 (0) 7812 755751

editor@sentinelquarterly.com

https://sentinelquarterly.com
http://www.facebook.com/pages/Sentinel-Literary-Quarterly/99050249348
http://twitter.com/sentinelpoetry

Fiction
  Novel Excerpts; *Short Fiction*
Nonfiction
  Essays; *Interviews*; *Reviews*
Poetry > *Any Poetic Form*

Scripts > *Theatre Scripts*

Send: Full text
How to send: Email

Magazine publishing poetry on any subject, short stories and excerpts from novels on any theme, academic essays, reviews, and interviews. Submit by email only; send 6 poems up to 60 lines each, or one long poem up to 200 lines with two shorter poems, or one piece of prose. Turnaround in 6 weeks. No simultaneous submissions.

M0468 Ships Monthly Magazine

Magazine
Kelsey Media, The Granary, Downs Court, Yalding Hil, Yalding, Kent, ME18 6AL
United Kingdom
Tel: +44 (0) 1959 543747

https://shipsmonthly.com

Magazine Publisher: Kelsey Media

ADULT > **Nonfiction** > *Articles*: Ships

PROFESSIONAL > **Nonfiction** > *Articles*
  Shipping; Ships

Magazine aimed at ship enthusiasts and maritime professionals. Publishes news and illustrated articles related to all kinds of ships, including reports on the ferry, cruise, new building and cargo ship scene as well as navies across the world.

Editor: Nicholas Leach

M0469 Shooter Literary Magazine

Magazine
United Kingdom

submissions.shooterlitmag@gmail.com

https://shooterlitmag.com

Fiction > *Short Fiction*

Nonfiction
  Essays: General
  Short Nonfiction: Memoir

Poetry > *Any Poetic Form*

Send: Full text; Author bio
How to send: Email

Publishes literary fiction, poetry, creative nonfiction and memoir relating to specific themes for each issue. See website for current theme and full submission guidelines.

M0470 Shoreline of Infinity

Magazine
United Kingdom

editor@shorelineofinfinity.com

https://www.shorelineofinfinity.com
https://www.facebook.com/ShorelineOfInfinity/
https://twitter.com/shoreinf
https://www.youtube.com/channel/UCm2N3L9V2rvnkS5dCRzttCg
https://www.instagram.com/shoreinf/

Fiction > *Short Fiction*
  Fantasy; Science Fiction

Poetry > *Any Poetic Form*: Science Fiction

Science Fiction magazine from Scotland. We want stories that explore our unknown future. We want to play around with the big ideas and the little ones. We want writers to tell us stories to inspire us, give us hope, provide some laughs. Or to scare the stuffing out of us. We want good stories: we want to be entertained. We want to read how people cope in our exotic new world, we want to be in their minds, in their bodies, in their souls.

Editor: Noel Chidwick

M0471 Shout

Magazine
United Kingdom

Newspaper Publisher / Magazine Publisher: DC Thomson Media

M0472 Skier & Snowboarder Magazine

Magazine
The Lodge, West Heath, Ashgrove Road, Sevenoaks, Kent, TN13 1ST
United Kingdom
Tel: +44 (0) 07768 670158

https://www.skierandsnowboarder.com

Types: Nonfiction
Formats: Articles
Subjects: Sport
Markets: Adult

Magazine publishing features on skiing. Contact via form on website.

M0473 Slime Factory

Magazine
United Kingdom

Newspaper Publisher / Magazine Publisher:
DC Thomson Media

M0474 Smart Retailer
Magazine
PO Box 5000, N7528 Aanstad Road, Iola, WI
54945-5000
United States
Tel: +1 (715) 445-5000
Fax: +1 (715) 445-4053

danb@jonespublishing.com

http://smart-retailer.com

Types: Nonfiction
Formats: Articles; Interviews; News
Subjects: Business; Finance; How To; Legal
Markets: Professional

Send: Full text
How to send: Email

Trade magazine for independent gift retailers.
Send complete ms by email with CV and
published clips.

Editor: Dan Brownell

M0475 Smithsonian Magazine
Magazine
Capital Gallery, Suite 6001, MRC 513, PO
Box 37012, Washington, DC 20013
United States
Tel: +1 (202) 275-2000

smithsonianmagazine@si.edu

http://www.smithsonianmag.com

Magazine Publisher / Book Publisher:
Smithsonian Institution (**P0775**)

Types: Nonfiction
Formats: Articles
Subjects: Anthropology; Archaeology; Arts;
Culture; History; Lifestyle; Nature; Science;
Technology
Markets: Adult

Send: Query
Don't send: Full text

Publishes articles on archaeology, arts,
different lifestyles, cultures and peoples,
nature, science and technology. Submit
proposal through online form on website.

M0476 Smoke
Magazine
1-27 Bridport Street, Liverpool, L3 5QF
United Kingdom
Tel: +44 (0) 7710 644325

windowsproject@btinternet.com

https://smokemagazine.wordpress.com

Writing Group: The Windows Project

Poetry > *Any Poetic Form*

Send: Full text; Self-Addressed Stamped
Envelope (SASE)
How to send: Post

New writing, poetry and graphics by some of
the best established names alongside new work
from Merseyside, from all over the country and
the world.

M0477 SnoWest
Magazine
360 B Street, Idaho Falls, ID 83402
United States
Tel: +1 (208) 524-7000
Fax: +1 (208) 522-5241

https://www.snowest.com

Types: Nonfiction
Formats: Articles
Subjects: Leisure; Sport
Markets: Adult

Send: Query
Don't send: Full text

Snowmobiling magazine. Send query with
published clips.

M0478 Somerset Home
Magazine
22992 Mill Creek Drive, Laguna Hills, CA
92653
United States

somersethome@stampington.com

https://stampington.com/somerset-home

Types: Nonfiction
Formats: Articles
Subjects: Design
Markets: Adult

Send: Query
Don't send: Full text

Home decor magazine.

M0479 South
Magazine
PO Box 9338, Wimborne, BH21 9JA
United Kingdom

south@southpoetry.org

http://www.southpoetry.org

Types: Poetry
Markets: Adult

Send: Full text
How not to send: Email

Submit up to three poems by post (two copies
of each), along with submission form available
on website. No previously published poems
(including poems that have appeared on the
internet). Submissions are not returned. See
website for full details. No translations or
submissions by email.

Editors: Peter Keeble; Anne Peterson; Chrissie
Williams

M0480 Southern Humanities Review
Magazine
9088 Haley Center, Auburn University,
Auburn, AL 36849
United States
Tel: +1 (334) 844-9088

shr@auburn.edu

http://www.southernhumanitiesreview.com
https://www.facebook.com/
southernhumanitiesreview
https://twitter.com/SouthernHReview
https://www.instagram.com/
southernhumanitiesreview/
https://www.youtube.com/channel/
UCnywOlZbBtEX7OFYMUMSQsg

Fiction > *Short Fiction*

Nonfiction > *Essays*
Creative Nonfiction; Literary Journalism;
Literary; Lyric Essays; Memoir; Personal
Essays; Travel

Poetry > *Any Poetic Form*

Send: Full text
How to send: Submittable
How not to send: Post; Email

Submissions for all fiction and nonfiction are
open from August 24 until November 1 in the
fall and from January 15 until March 14 in the
spring. Poetry submissions are open from
August 24 until September 7 in the fall and
from January 15 until March 14 in the spring.
Submissions for online fiction features are
open year-round.

Editors: Anton DiSclafani; Virginia M.
Kouidis; Dan Latimer; Rose McLarney

M0481 The Southern Review
Magazine
Johnston Hall, 3rd Floor, Louisiana State
University, Baton Rouge, LA 70803
United States
Tel: +1 (225) 578-6453
Fax: +1 (225) 578-6461

southernreview@lsu.edu

https://thesouthernreview.org
https://www.facebook.com/lsusouthernreview
https://twitter.com/southern_review
https://soundcloud.com/lsupress_and_tsr

Fiction in Translation > *Short Fiction*

Fiction > *Short Fiction*

Nonfiction in Translation > *Essays*

Nonfiction > *Essays*

Poetry in Translation > *Any Poetic Form*

Poetry > *Any Poetic Form*

Closed to approaches.

Costs: A fee is charged upon submission. $3
per submission.

Strives to discover and promote a diverse array of engaging, relevant, and challenging literature—including fiction, nonfiction, poetry, and translation from literary luminaries as well as the best established and emerging writers.

M0482 Southern Theatre

Magazine
3309 Northampton Drive, Greensboro, NC 27408-5224
United States
Tel: +1 (336) 292-6041
Fax: +1 (336) 294-3292

deanna@setc.org

https://www.setc.org/publications-resources/southern-theatre/

Types: Nonfiction
Formats: Articles; Theatre Scripts
Markets: Adult

Send: Full text
How to send: Email

Theatre magazine focusing on the 10 Southeastern states of the US. Submit by post or email.

Editor: Deanna Thompson

M0483 Southword Journal

Magazine
Frank O'Connor House, 84 Douglas Street, Cork
Ireland
Tel: +353 021 4312955

info@munsterlit.ie

http://www.munsterlit.ie/
Southword%20Journal.html
https://www.facebook.com/Southword.Journal/
https://southword.submittable.com/submit/

Fiction > *Short Fiction*

Poetry > *Any Poetic Form*

Accepts submissions during specific submission windows only. See website for details.

M0484 The Sow's Ear

Magazine
United States

sowsearsubmit@gmail.com

http://www.sowsearpoetry.org
https://www.facebook.com/
SowsEarPoetryReview?ref=hl
https://twitter.com/SowsEarPR

Poetry > *Any Poetic Form*

Send: Full text
How to send: Post; Email

Submissions of fine poetry in any style and length. Wants work that is carefully crafted, keenly felt, and freshly perceived. Like poems

with voice, specificity, delight in language, and a meaning that unfolds.

Art Editor: Kristin Zimet

Editor: Janet Harrison

M0485 Speciality Food

Magazine
Aceville Publications Ltd., 21-23 Phoenix Court, Hawkins Road, Colchester, Essex, CO2 8JY
United Kingdom
Tel: +44 (0) 1206 505981

holly.shackleton@aceville.co.uk

https://www.specialityfoodmagazine.com

Types: Nonfiction
Formats: Articles; News
Subjects: Business; Cookery
Markets: Professional

Trade magazine for the food and drink industry.

Editor: Holly Shackleton

M0486 Specialty Fabrics Review

Magazine
1801 County Road B W, Roseville, MN 55113-4061
United States
Tel: +1 (651) 222-2508

generalinfo@ifai.com

https://specialtyfabricsreview.com

Types: Nonfiction
Formats: Articles
Subjects: Business; Design
Markets: Professional

Magazine covering the industrial textiles industry.

M0487 Spirituality & Health

Magazine
United States
Tel: +1 (844) 375-3755

editors@spiritualityhealth.com

https://spiritualityhealth.com

Types: Nonfiction
Formats: Articles; Interviews; Reviews
Subjects: Health; Lifestyle; Spirituality
Markets: Adult

Send: Full text
How to send: Email

Magazine that aims to help people improve their lives both physically and spiritually. Send submissions by email. No attachments. Response not guaranteed. See website for full guidelines.

M0488 Sports Afield

Magazine
P.O. Box 271305, Fort Collins, CO 80527
United States

editorinchief@sportsafield.com

http://sportsafield.com

Types: Nonfiction
Formats: Articles
Subjects: Adventure; Nature; Sport
Markets: Adult

Send: Full text
How to send: Email

Hunting adventure magazine. Publishes articles on high-end hunting and shooting, and coverage of guns, optics, clothing, and other equipment. Send complete ms by email only. See website for full guidelines.

M0489 Stamp Collector

Magazine
United Kingdom

Magazine Publisher: Warners Group Publications

M0490 Stand Magazine

Magazine
School of English, Leeds University, Leeds, LS2 9JT
United Kingdom
Tel: +44 (0) 113 233 4794

engstand@leeds.ac.uk
enquiries@standmagazine.org

https://standmagazine.org
https://www.facebook.com/pages/Stand-Magazine/270598523017007
https://twitter.com/Stand_poetry

Fiction > *Short Fiction*: Literary

Poetry > *Any Poetic Form*

Send: Full text
How to send: Email

A well established magazine of poetry and literary fiction. Has previously published the work of, among others, Samuel Beckett, Angela Carter, Seamus Heaney, Geoffrey Hill, and Andrew Motion.

M0491 Stanford Magazine

Magazine
United States

stanford.magazine@stanford.edu

https://stanfordmag.org

Types: Nonfiction
Formats: Articles; Essays
Markets: Academic; Adult

University alumni magazine.

M0492 Stickman Review

Online Magazine
United States

fiction@stickmanreview.com
nonfiction@stickmanreview.com
poetry@stickmanreview.com

http://www.stickmanreview.com

Fiction > *Short Fiction*: Literary

Nonfiction > *Essays*: Literary

Poetry > *Any Poetic Form*

Send: Full text
How to send: Email

Publishes literary fiction, poetry, and literary nonfiction. Accepts submissions February to April and August to October.

M0493 The Stinging Fly

Magazine
PO Box 6016, Dublin 1
Ireland

stingingfly@gmail.com

http://www.stingingfly.org

Types: Fiction; Nonfiction; Poetry
Formats: Essays; Interviews; Reviews; Short Fiction
Subjects: Literary
Markets: Adult

Closed to approaches.

Send submissions with SAE or international reply coupons sufficient for return of MS. Submit one story or up to four poems at a time. Poems and short stories should be as long or as short as they need to be. Has published stories over 5,000 words and as short as 600. Await response before making further submissions. For reviews, email editor with sample review as attachment. No submissions by email. Accepts submissions during specific months only. See website for details.

Publisher: Declan Meade

M0494 Stitch

Magazine
United Kingdom

Magazine Publisher: Warners Group Publications

M0495 Strand Magazine

Magazine
33228 West 12 Mile Rd. #285, Farmington Hills, MI 48334
United States
Tel: +1 (800) 300-6652

strandmag@strandmag.com

https://strandmag.com
https://www.facebook.com/strandmagazine/
https://twitter.com/StrandMag

https://www.instagram.com/strandmag/?hl=en
https://www.pinterest.com/strandmag/

Fiction > *Short Fiction*: Mystery

Nonfiction
   Articles: Creative Writing; Mystery
   Interviews: Mystery
   Reviews: Mystery; Thrillers

Originally founded in 1891 in England, but closed due to economic difficulties in the 1950s. Publishes mystery stories, and articles, interviews, and reviews related to the genre.

Editor: A.F. Gulli

M0496 Strategic Finance

Magazine
United States

aschulman@imanet.org

https://sfmagazine.com

Types: Nonfiction
Formats: Articles
Subjects: Finance
Markets: Professional

Send: Full text

Publishes articles that help financial professionals perform their jobs more effectively, advance their careers, grow personally and professionally, and make their organisations more profitable.

M0497 Stylist

Magazine
26-34 Emerald Street, London, WC1N 3QA
United Kingdom
Tel: +44 (0) 20 7611 9700

reception@stylist.co.uk

https://www.thestylistgroup.com

Types: Nonfiction
Formats: Articles; News
Subjects: Beauty; Entertainment; Fashion; Lifestyle; Women's Interests
Markets: Adult

Magazine of feminism, fashion, beauty, lifestyle trends, and news.

M0498 Subtropics

Magazine
PO Box 112075, 4008 Turlington Hall, University of Florida, Gainesville, FL 32611-2075
United States

subtropics@english.ufl.edu

http://subtropics.english.ufl.edu
http://www.facebook.com/subtropicsmag/
https://twitter.com/subtropicsmag/

Fiction > *Short Fiction*: Literary

Nonfiction > *Essays*

Poetry > *Any Poetic Form*

Closed to approaches.

Costs: A fee is charged upon submission. $3.00 for each submission.

Publishes literary fiction, essays, and poetry, of any length. Submit via online submission system during open windows. $3 charge per submission.

Editor: David Leavitt

Managing Editor: Mark Mitchell

Poetry Editors: Ange Mlinko; Sidney Wade

M0499 Successful Meetings

Magazine
100 Lighting Way, Secaucus, NJ 07094-3626
United States
Tel: +1 (201) 902-1978

ledelstein@ntmllc.com

http://www.successfulmeetings.com

Formats: Articles
Subjects: Business
Markets: Professional

Magazine for multi-tasking meeting planners.

Editor: Loren Edelstein

M0500 Sunshine Artist

Magazine
United States

https://sunshineartist.com

Magazine Publisher: JP Media LLC

PROFESSIONAL > **Nonfiction** > *Reviews*
   Arts; Crafts

Publishes reviews of fine art fairs, festivals, events, and small craft shows around the country, for professionals making a living through art shows.

Editor: Joyce Greenholdt

Managing Editor: Melissa Jones

M0501 The Supplement

Magazine
Atlantean Publishing, 4 Pierrot Steps, 71 Kursaal Way, Southend-on-Sea, Essex, SS1 2UY
United Kingdom

atlanteanpublishing@hotmail.com

https://atlanteanpublishing.wordpress.com/
https://atlanteanpublishing.fandom.com/wiki/The_Supplement

Book Publisher / Magazine Publisher: Atlantean Publishing (**P0057**)

Fiction > *Short Fiction*

Nonfiction
   Articles: General
   News: Small Press
   Reviews: Books; Films
Poetry > *Any Poetic Form*

Closed to approaches.

Publishes small-press news and advertisements, reviews covering new publications from small presses, independent and mainstream books, films and much more beside, and various articles on an equally wide variety of topics — as well as the occasional poem or very short piece of fiction, often related to the non-fiction content.

Editor: David-John Tyrer

M0502 Surface
Magazine
3921 Alton Road, Suite 413, Miami Beach, FL 33140
United States
Tel: +1 (212) 229-1500

editorial@surfacemag.com

https://www.surfacemag.com
https://twitter.com/SurfaceMag
https://www.instagram.com/surfacemag/
https://www.facebook.com/surfacemag
https://www.pinterest.com/surfacemag/
https://www.youtube.com/surfacemedia/videos

Magazine Publisher: Future Media Group

Nonfiction > *Articles*
  Architecture; Arts; Contemporary Culture; Design; Fashion; Travel

American magazine of global contemporary design. Covers architecture, art, design, fashion, and travel, with a focus on how these fields shape and are shaped by contemporary culture.

M0503 Sweet Princess Magic
Magazine
United Kingdom

Newspaper Publisher / Magazine Publisher: DC Thomson Media

M0504 Tabletop Gaming
Magazine
United Kingdom

Magazine Publisher: Warners Group Publications

M0505 Tagvverk
Magazine
United States

tagvverk@gmail.com

http://tagvverk.info

Types: Fiction; Nonfiction; Poetry
Formats: Essays; Reviews
Subjects: Literary; Literary Criticism
Markets: Adult

Closed to approaches.

Online magazine publishing poetry, fiction, essays, reviews, criticisms, visual poems and

multimedia projects. Send submissions by email.

Editors: Miriam Karraker; Barrett White

M0506 Tahoma Literary Review
Magazine
United States

poetry@tahomaliteraryreview.com
fiction@tahomaliteraryreview.com
nonfiction@tahomaliteraryreview.com

https://tahomaliteraryreview.com

Fiction > *Short Fiction*
  Experimental; Literary

Nonfiction
  Essays: General, and in particular: Experimental; Lyric Essays
  Short Nonfiction: Narrative Nonfiction

Poetry
  Formal Poetry; *Free Verse*; *Long Form Poetry*

Closed to approaches.

Costs: A fee is charged upon submission; Offers services that writers have to pay for. $4 for poetry and flash prose; $5 for longer prose. Critiques available for an additional fee.

Publishes poetry, fiction, and nonfiction. Charges $4 submission fee for short works; $5 submission fee for long works. Submit online through online submission system.

M0507 Takahe
Magazine
PO Box 13 335, Christchurch 8141
New Zealand

secretary@takahe.org.nz

https://www.takahe.org.nz
https://twitter.com/takahemagazine

Fiction > *Short Fiction*: Literary

Nonfiction
  Essays: Cultural Criticism; New Zealand; South Pacific
  Reviews: Books

Poetry > *Any Poetic Form*

Send: Full text; Author bio
How to send: Email attachment; Domestic Post

Submit up to four poems, or short stories up to 3,000 words, by email (preferred) or hard copy by post (New Zealand submissions only). See website for full details.

Art Editor / Essays Editor: Andrew Paul Wood

Fiction Editor: Zoë Meager

Poetry Editors: Jeni Curtis; Gail Ingram

Reviews Editor: Michelle Elvy

M0508 Take a Break
Magazine
United Kingdom

feedback@takeabreak.co.uk

https://takeabreak.co.uk
http://www.facebook.com/takeabreakmag
http://instagram.com/takeabreak.mag
https://twitter.com/takeabreakmag
https://www.youtube.com/channel/UCWNCQhPiJ5WXsMi0Fnpmuag

Magazine Publisher: Bauer Media Group

Nonfiction > *Articles*
  Beauty; Cookery; Fashion; Health; Pets; Real Life Stories; Travel

Weekly magazine publishing compelling true-life stories, the latest health, fashion and beauty tips, plus cookery and travel.

Editor: John Dale

M0509 Tammy Journal
Print Magazine
United States

thetjournal@gmail.com

https://www.tammyjournal.com

Book Publisher / Magazine Publisher: Tammy Chapbooks

Fiction > *Short Fiction*: Literary

Poetry > *Any Poetic Form*

How to send: Submittable

Costs: A fee is charged upon submission. $3 per submission. $15 to submit and receive a copy of the journal. $20 for expedited response.

Submit poetry up to to 10 pages, or fiction up to 20 pages.

M0510 Tampa Review
Magazine
University of Tampa Press, The University of Tampa, 401 West Kennedy Blvd., Tampa, FL 33606-1490, Box 19F
United States
Tel: (813) 253-6266
Fax: (813) 253-6266

utpress@ut.edu

https://tampareview.ut.edu

Types: Fiction; Nonfiction; Poetry; Translations
Formats: Essays; Interviews; Short Fiction
Subjects: Commercial; Culture; Experimental; Fantasy; History; Literary
Markets: Adult

Closed to approaches.

Submit 3-6 poems or one piece of prose up to 5,000 words with SASE between September and December only. Submissions received prior to August are returned unread. No submissions by email or simultaneous submissions.

Editor: Richard Mathews

Fiction Editor: Lisa Birnbaum and Kathleen Ochshorn

Nonfiction Editor: Elizabeth Winston

Poetry Editor: Donald Morrill and Martha Serpas

M0511 Tate Etc.
Magazine
Tate, Millbank, London, SW1P 4RG
United Kingdom
Tel: +44 (0) 20 7887 8606

https://www.tate.org.uk/tate-etc

Types: Nonfiction
Formats: Articles
Subjects: Arts; Contemporary; History
Markets: Adult

Magazine of the visual arts, aiming to blend the historic with the contemporary.

Assistant Editor: Enrico Tassi

Editor: Aaron Juneau, Assistant Editor

M0512 TD Magazine
Magazine
United States
Tel: +1 (703) 299-8723

submissions@td.org

https://www.td.org/td-magazine

Types: Nonfiction
Formats: Articles
Subjects: Business
Markets: Professional

Send: Query
Don't send: Full text
How to send: Email

Magazine for talent development professionals. No unsolicited mss. Send query with outline up to 100 words.

M0513 Tears in the Fence
Magazine
Flats, Durweston Mill, Mill Lane, Durweston, Blandford Forum, Dorset, DT11 0QD
United Kingdom
Tel: +44 (0) 7824 618708

tearsinthefence@gmail.com

https://tearsinthefence.com

Fiction > *Short Fiction*

Nonfiction
  Essays: General
  Interviews: General
  Reviews: General
  Short Nonfiction: Creative Nonfiction

Poetry
  Any Poetic Form; *Prose Poetry*

Send: Full text
How to send: Email attachment; In the body of an email

International literary magazine publishing poetry, fiction, prose poems, essays, translations, interviews and reviews. Publishes fiction as short as 100 words or as long as 3,500. Maximum 6 poems per poet per issue. No simultaneous submissions or previously published material. Send submissions by email as both an attachment and in the body of the email.

Editor: David Caddy

M0514 Teen Breathe
Magazine
GMC Publications Ltd, 86 High Street, Lewes, BN7 1XU
United Kingdom
Tel: +44 (0) 1273 477374

hello@breathemagazine.com

https://www.teenbreathe.co.uk

YOUNG ADULT > **Nonfiction** > *Articles*
  Health; Lifestyle

Send: Full text

Magazine for young people who want to find time for themselves. Focuses on Wellbeing, Mindfulness, Creativity and Escaping. Experienced writers should send ideas with examples of previous work. New writers should submit complete articles. Submit using forms on website.

M0515 The Temz Review
Online Magazine
London, ON
Canada

thetemzreview@gmail.com

https://www.thetemzreview.com

Fiction > *Short Fiction*: Literary

Nonfiction > *Reviews*: Literature

Poetry > *Any Poetic Form*

Closed to approaches.

Quarterly online magazine. Submit one piece of fiction or creative nonfiction (or more than one if under 1,000 words) or 1-8 poems via online submission system. For reviews, send query by email.

M0516 Texas Monthly
Magazine
PO Box 1569, Austin, TX 78767-1569
United States
Tel: +1 (512) 320-6900
Fax: +1 (512) 476-9007

news@texasmonthly.com

https://www.texasmonthly.com

Formats: Articles; Film Scripts; News; TV Scripts
Subjects: Culture; Lifestyle; Music; Politics; Travel
Markets: Adult

Monthly magazine covering Texas.

M0517 That's Life!
Magazine
FREEPOST LON12043, H Bauer Publishing, London, NW1 1YU
United Kingdom

stories@thatslife.co.uk

http://www.thatslife.co.uk

Types: Nonfiction
Formats: Articles; News
Subjects: Lifestyle
Markets: Adult

Publishes nonfiction true life stories. See website for details.

M0518 This Is
Magazine
United Kingdom

Newspaper Publisher / Magazine Publisher: DC Thomson Media

M0519 This Is Little Baby Bum
Magazine
United Kingdom

Newspaper Publisher / Magazine Publisher: DC Thomson Media

M0520 The Threepenny Review
Magazine
PO Box 9131, Berkeley, CA 94709
United States
Tel: +1 (510) 849-4545

wlesser@threepennyreview.com

http://www.threepennyreview.com

Fiction > *Short Fiction*: Literary

Nonfiction > *Articles*
  Arts; Culture; Literature

Poetry > *Any Poetic Form*

Closed to approaches.

National literary magazine with coverage of the visual and performing arts. Send complete MS by post with SASE or by email as a single Word file attachment. No previously published material, simultaneous submissions, or submissions from May to December. Prospective contributors are advised to read the magazine before submitting.

Editor: Wendy Lesser

M0521 The Times Literary Supplement (TLS)

Magazine
1 London Bridge Street, London, SE1 9GF
United Kingdom
Tel: +44 (0) 20 7782 5000

letters@the-tls.co.uk

https://www.the-tls.co.uk

Types: Nonfiction; Poetry
Formats: Articles; Film Scripts; News; Reviews; Theatre Scripts
Subjects: Arts; History; Literature; Philosophy; Science
Markets: Adult

Send: Query
Don't send: Full text

Publishes coverage of the latest and most important publications, as well as current theatre, opera, exhibitions and film. Also publishes letters to the editor and poetry. Send books for review by post. For poetry, submit up to six poems with SASE. Letters to the Editor may be sent by post or by email to the address provided on the website.

Editor: Stig Abell

M0522 Tin House Magazine

Magazine
United States

alana@tinhouse.com

http://www.tinhouse.com

Types: Fiction; Nonfiction; Poetry
Formats: Essays; Short Fiction
Subjects: Literary
Markets: Adult

Closed to approaches.

Publishes unpublished fiction, nonfiction, and poetry through daily blog. Submit via online submission system.

Editor: Alana Csaposs

M0523 Tocher

Magazine
School of Scottish Studies Archives, University of Edinburgh, 29 George Square, Edinburgh, EH8 9LD
United Kingdom

scottish.studies.arhives@ed.ac.uk

https://www.ed.ac.uk/literatures-languages-cultures/celtic-scottish-studies/research/publications/in-house/tocher

ACADEMIC > **Nonfiction** > *Articles*
    Culture; Folklore, Myths, and Legends; Music; Scotland

ADULT
    Fiction in Translation > *Short Fiction*: Scotland

    Fiction > *Short Fiction*: Scotland

The journal contains traditional Scottish songs, stories, music, customs, beliefs, local history, rhymes and riddles transcribed from tapes held in the sound archive.

M0524 Tolka

Magazine
Ireland

https://www.tolkajournal.org
https://www.instagram.com/tolkajournal/
https://twitter.com/tolkajournal

Fiction > *Short Fiction*: Autofiction

Nonfiction
    Essays: Personal Essays
    Short Nonfiction: Memoir; Travel

Closed to approaches.

Biannual literary journal of non-fiction: publishing essays, reportage, travel writing, auto-fiction, individual stories and the writing that flows in between.

M0525 Total Film

Magazine
Future Publishing Limited, Quay House, The Ambury, Bath, BA1 1UA
United Kingdom
Tel: +44 (0) 1225 442244

jane.crowther@futurenet.com

https://www.futureplc.com/brand/total-film/

Types: Nonfiction
Formats: Articles; Film Scripts; Interviews; Reviews
Subjects: Comedy / Humour
Markets: Adult

"A cheeky, irreverent but always passionate and authoritative look at every part of the film world".

M0526 Toy Collectors Price Guide

Magazine
United Kingdom

Magazine Publisher: Warners Group Publications

M0527 Traction

Magazine
United Kingdom

Magazine Publisher: Warners Group Publications

M0528 The Tusculum Review

Magazine
60 Shiloh Road, Greeneville, TN 37745
United States

review@tusculum.edu

https://ttr.tusculum.edu

Fiction > *Short Fiction*: Literary

Nonfiction > *Essays*

Poetry > *Any Poetic Form*

Scripts > *Theatre Scripts*: Drama

Send: Full text
How to send: Submittable

Costs: A fee is charged upon submission. $2.

We seek well-crafted writing that takes risks. We publish work in and between all genres: poetry, fiction, essays, and plays--we appreciate work in experimental and traditional modes. We accept prose submissions of less than 6,000 words (24 double-spaced pages) and poetry submissions under 10 pages. We publish scripts in the 10-minute format (10 pages).

M0529 TV Times

Magazine
United Kingdom

robert.hiley@futurenet.com

https://www.futureplc.com/brand/tv-times/

Magazine Publisher: Future

Nonfiction > *Articles*
    Entertainment; TV

Magazine publishing television news, listings, and articles.

M0530 UCity Review

Magazine
United States

editors@ucityreview.com

http://www.ucityreview.com

Types: Poetry
Subjects: Literary
Markets: Adult

Send: Full text
How to send: Email

Online magazine accepting submissions of poetry year-round. Submit up to six poems in .doc or .docx format, by email.

M0531 Ulster Tatler

Magazine
39 Boucher Road, Belfast, BT12 6UT
United Kingdom
Tel: +44 (0) 28 9066 3311

edit@ulstertatler.com
info@ulstertatler.com

https://www.ulstertatler.com
https://www.facebook.com/ulstertatlermag
https://twitter.com/ulstertatlermag
https://www.youtube.com/channel/UCHH_sMGsPuy8i0VUj5L0_kA
https://www.instagram.com/ulstertatler/

Nonfiction > *Articles*
    Fashion; High Society; Lifestyle

Lifestyle and society magazine based in Northern Ireland, covering Northern Ireland social events and local fashions.

Editor: Chris Sherry

Features Editor: James Sherry

Fiction Editor: Richard Sherry

M0532 Umbrella Factory

Magazine
United States

https://umbrellafactorymagazine.com

Types: Fiction; Nonfiction; Poetry
Formats: Short Fiction
Subjects: Literary
Markets: Adult

Send: Full text

Submit fiction between 1,000 and 5,000 words, three poems, or a piece of nonfiction. Submit through online submission system. See website for full guidelines.

Editors: Anthony ILacqua; Sharyce Winters

M0533 The Undercommons

Online Magazine
United States

https://www.commontonguezine.com

Online Magazine: The Common Tongue Magazine (**M0126**)

Fiction
Novellas: Dark Fantasy
Short Fiction: Dark Fantasy

Poetry > *Any Poetic Form*: Dark Fantasy

How to send: Online submission system

Dark fantasy magazine. Each issue includes one novella, one short story, and one poem.

M0534 Understorey Magazine

Magazine
Alexa McDonough Institute for Women, Gender and Social Justice, Mount Saint Vincent University, 166 Bedford Highway, Halifax, NS, B3M 2J6
Canada

editor@understoreymagazine.ca

https://understoreymagazine.ca

Fiction > *Short Fiction*
Feminism; Women's Issues; Women

Nonfiction > *Short Nonfiction*
Creative Nonfiction; Feminism; Women's Issues; Women

Poetry > *Any Poetic Form*
Feminism; Women's Issues; Women

Closed to approaches.

Publishes fiction, poetry, and creative nonfiction by Canadian women. Send prose up

to 1,500 words or up to five poems by email. See website for full guidelines.

M0535 Unfit Magazine

Magazine
Eugene, OR 97401
United States

contact@unfitmag.com

http://unfitmag.com

Magazine Publisher: Longshot Press

Fiction > *Short Fiction*
Adventure; Alien Invasion; Alternative History; Cyberpunk; Genetics; Military; Post-Apocalyptic; Science Fiction; Space Opera; Time Travel

Send: Full text
How to send: Online submission system

This magazine is about fiction that isn't fit for "them". What do I mean by "them"? Who in particular are "they"? They are the government. They are your parents. They are your teachers. They are everywhere.

Editor: Daniel Scott White

M0536 Unicorn Universe

Magazine
United Kingdom

Newspaper Publisher / Magazine Publisher: DC Thomson Media

M0537 Unreal Magazine

Magazine
United States

contact@unrealmag.com

https://unrealmag.com

Magazine Publisher: Longshot Press

Fiction > *Short Fiction*
Adventure; Alternative History; Comedy / Humour; Experimental; Fairy Tales; Fantasy; Folklore, Myths, and Legends; Gaslamp Fantasy; High / Epic Fantasy; Historical Fiction; Magical Realism; Military; Superhero Fantasy; Sword and Sorcery

Nonfiction > *Articles*
Fantasy; Magical Realism

Send: Full text
How to send: Online submission system

We want stories that are well written, intelligent, and enjoyable to read. We are looking for stories with metaphors and emotional ambience and imaginative descriptive writing.

M0538 Unthology

Magazine
Unthank Submissions (Unthology), PO Box 3506, Norwich, NR7 7QP
United Kingdom

unthology@unthankbooks.com

http://www.unthankbooks.com

Types: Fiction; Nonfiction
Formats: Essays; Short Fiction
Subjects: Experimental; Literary; Traditional
Markets: Adult

Closed to approaches.

Publishes the work of new or established writers and can include short stories of any length, reportage, essays or novel extracts from anywhere in the world. Allows space for stories of different styles and subjects to rub up against each other, featuring classic slice-of-life alongside the experimental, the shocking and strange. Submit by post with SAE and personal contact details, or by email.

M0539 Urthona

Magazine
Old Abbey House, Abbey Road, Cambridge, CB5 8HQ
United Kingdom
Tel: +44 (0) 7443 499384

urthonamag@gmail.com

https://urthona.com

Nonfiction > *Essays*
Arts; Buddhism; Contemporary; Culture

Poetry > *Any Poetic Form*

How to send: Email

Magazine of Buddhism and the Arts, linking Buddhism and Western culture.

M0540 US Equestrian Magazine

Magazine
United States Equestrian Federation (USEF), 4047 Iron Works Parkway, Lexington, KY 40511
United States
Tel: +1 (859) 258-2472
Fax: +1 (859) 231-6662

goakford@usef.org

http://www.usef.org
https://www.usef.org/media/equestrian-magazine

Nonfiction > *Articles*
Equestrian; Horses

Send: Query
How to send: Email

Magazine publishing articles, features, and interviews about horses and people related to them.

Editors: Glenye Oakford; Brian Sosby

M0541 Vagabond City

Online Magazine
United States

vagabondcitypoetry@gmail.com
vagabondcitynonfic@gmail.com
vagabondcityliterary@gmail.com

https://vagabondcitylit.com

Nonfiction
Essays: Creative Nonfiction
Interviews: General
Reviews: Books

Poetry > *Any Poetic Form*

Send: Full text
How to send: Email

Electronic magazine featuring poetry, art, creative nonfiction and essays by marginalised creators. Also publishes book reviews and interviews. Submit up to five pieces at a time in the body of an email or as a Word file attachment. See website for full guidelines.

M0542 Vallum

Magazine
5038 Sherbrooke West, PO Box 23077 CP
Vendome Station, Montreal, Quebec, H4A 1S7
Canada
Tel: +1 (514) 937-8946

editors@vallummag.com

http://www.vallummag.com

Nonfiction
Essays; *Interviews*; *Reviews*
Poetry > *Any Poetic Form*: Contemporary

Closed to approaches.

Send 4-7 poems, essays of 4-6 pages, interviews of 3-5 pages, reviews of 1-3 pages, through online submission system only. No fiction, plays, movie scripts, memoir, or creative nonfiction. Check website for submission windows and themes.

M0543 Veggie

Magazine
United Kingdom

https://www.vegetarianrecipesmag.com

Nonfiction > *Articles*
Health; Vegetarian Cooking; Vegetarian Food; Vegetarianism

Magazine of vegetarian food, wellness, and lifestyle.

Editors: Sian Bunney; Rachael Perrett

M0544 Verbicide

Magazine
United States

info@scissorpress.com

https://www.verbicidemagazine.com

Types: Fiction; Nonfiction
Formats: Articles; Interviews; Reviews; Short Fiction
Subjects: Entertainment; Music
Markets: Adult

Send: Full text
How to send: Email

Entertainment periodical, online-only since 2009. Accepts short stories between 500 and 3,000 words. For features or music reviews contact by email in advance. See website for specific email addresses and full submission guidelines.

M0545 Vestal Review

Online Magazine
United States

info@vestalreview.org

https://www.vestalreview.net
https://vestalreview.submittable.com/submit
https://www.facebook.com/VestalReview/
https://www.instagram.com/vestalreview/
https://twitter.com/VestalReview

Fiction > *Short Fiction*

Nonfiction
Interviews; *Reviews*

Send: Full text
How to send: Submittable

Publishes flash fiction up to 500 words. Accepts submissions between February 1 and May 31, and between August 1 and November 30. Also accepts proposals for interviews and reviews.

Editor: Mark Budman

M0546 Vietnam

Magazine
United States

Magazine Publisher: HistoryNet LLC

M0547 The Virginia Quarterly Review

Magazine
5 Boar's Head Lane, PO Box 400223,
Charlottesville, VA 22904
United States
Tel: +1 (434) 924-3675
Fax: +1 (434) 924-1397

editors@vqronline.org

https://www.vqronline.org
https://www.facebook.com/vqreview
https://twitter.com/vqr

Fiction > *Short Fiction*

Nonfiction > *Short Nonfiction*
Arts; Creative Nonfiction; Cultural Criticism; History; Literary Criticism; Politics

Poetry > *Any Poetic Form*

Does not want:

Fiction > *Short Fiction*
Fantasy; Romance; Science Fiction

Closed to approaches.

Strives to publish the best writing they can find. Has a long history of publishing accomplished and award-winning authors, but they also seek and support emerging writers.

Editor: Ted Genoways

M0548 Viz

Magazine
31-32 Alfred Place, London, WC1E 7DP
United Kingdom

http://viz.co.uk
https://www.facebook.com/VizComic/
https://twitter.com/vizcomic

Magazine Publisher: Dennis Publishing

Fiction > *Cartoons*: Comedy / Humour

Nonfiction > *Articles*
Comedy / Humour; Satire

Magazine of adult humour, including cartoons, spoof articles, etc.

M0549 Waccamaw

Online Magazine
United States

http://waccamawjournal.com
https://www.facebook.com/Waccamaw-A-Journal-of-Contemporary-Literature-164290950299653/
https://twitter.com/waccamawjournal
https://www.instagram.com/waccamawjournal/

Book Publisher: Athenaeum Press (**P0055**)

Fiction > *Short Fiction*: Literary

Nonfiction > *Essays*

Poetry > *Any Poetic Form*

Send: Full text
How to send: Submittable

Online literary journal publishing poems, stories, and essays. Submit prose up to 6,000 words or 3-5 poems between August 1 and September 8 annually. Submit via online submission system only.

M0550 The Wallace Stevens Journal

Magazine
University of Antwerp, Prinsstraat 13, 2000 Antwerp
Belgium

bart.eeckhout@uantwerp.be

https://www.press.jhu.edu/journals/wallace-stevens-journal

Types: Nonfiction; Poetry
Formats: Articles; Essays
Subjects: Literary; Literary Criticism
Markets: Academic; Adult

Send: Full text
How to send: Email

Publishes articles and essays on all aspects of Wallace Stevens' poetry and life. Also accepts poetry inspired by the poet. See website for full submission guidelines.

Editor: Bart Eeckhout

M0551 Walloon Writers Review

Magazine
United States

https://walloonwriters.com

Types: Fiction; Nonfiction; Poetry
Formats: Essays
Subjects: Literary
Markets: Adult

Publishes stories, poetry, and creative writing inspired by or about Northern Michigan and the Upper Peninsula.

M0552 Wasafiri

Magazine
c/o School of English and Drama, Queen Mary, University of London, Mile End Road, London, E1 4NS
United Kingdom
Tel: +44 (0) 20 7882 2686

wasafiri@qmul.ac.uk

https://www.wasafiri.org
https://www.facebook.com/wasafiri.magazine
https://twitter.com/Wasafirimag
https://www.youtube.com/channel/UC4J-lxAIL8iBiaRR2AOpGFg
https://www.linkedin.com/groups/8343914/profile

Fiction > *Short Fiction*: Literary

Nonfiction
  Articles: Culture; Literature
  Essays: Culture; Literature
Poetry > *Any Poetic Form*

Send: Full text
How to send: Online submission system

The indispensable journal of contemporary African, Asian Black British, Caribbean and transnational literatures.

In over fifteen years of publishing, this magazine has changed the face of contemporary writing in Britain. As a literary magazine primarily concerned with new and postcolonial writers, it continues to stress the diversity and range of black and diasporic writers world-wide. It remains committed to its original aims: to create a definitive forum for the voices of new writers and to open up lively spaces for serious critical discussion not available elsewhere. It is Britain's only international magazine for Black British, African, Asian and Caribbean literatures. Get the whole picture, get the magazine at the core of contemporary international literature today.

Submit via online submissions portal only (see website).

Editor: Malachi McIntosh

M0553 Weber—The Contemporary West

Magazine
Weber State University, 1395 Edvalson Street, Dept. 1405, Ogden, Utah 84408-1405
United States

weberjournal@weber.edu

https://www.weber.edu/weberjournal
https://www.facebook.com/weberjournal
https://twitter.com/WeberJournal

Fiction > *Short Fiction*
  American West; Culture; Environment

Nonfiction
  Essays: Personal Essays
  Short Nonfiction: Commentary; Creative Nonfiction
Poetry > *Any Poetic Form*
  American West; Culture; Environment

Send: Full text
How to send: Email

Invites submissions in the genres of personal narrative, critical commentary, fiction, creative non-fiction, and poetry that offer insight into the environment and culture (both broadly defined) of the contemporary western United States.

Editor: Brad L. Roghaar

M0554 Welsh Country

Magazine
Aberbanc, Llandysul, Ceredigion, SA44 5NP
United Kingdom
Tel: +44 (0) 1559 372010

info@welshcountry.co.uk

http://www.welshcountry.co.uk

Nonfiction
  Articles: Arts; Business; Crafts; Culture; Fishing; Gardening; History; Nature; Wales; Walking
  News: Wales

Magazine covering Welsh villages, history, wildlife, walking, gardening, fishing, business news, places to stay, local artisan Welsh food producers, and the Welsh arts and crafts scene.

Editor: Kath Rhodes

M0555 West Branch

Magazine
Stadler Center, Bucknell University, 1 Dent Drive, Lewisburg, PA 17837
United States

westbranch@bucknell.edu

https://westbranch.blogs.bucknell.edu

Fiction > *Short Fiction*

Nonfiction
  Essays; *Reviews*

Poetry > *Any Poetic Form*

Send: Full text
How to send: Online submission system

Send all submissions via online submission system, between August 1 and April 1 annually.

Editor: Paula Closson Buck

Fiction Editor: Ron Mohring

M0556 Western Humanities Review

Magazine
Department of English, Languages & Communication BLDG, 255 S Central Campus Drive, Room 3500, SLC, UT 84112-0494
United States
Tel: +1 (801) 581-6168
Fax: +1 (801) 585-5167

managingeditor.whr@gmail.com

http://www.westernhumanitiesreview.com
https://www.facebook.com/WHReview/
https://whr.submittable.com/submit

Fiction > *Short Fiction*

Nonfiction
  Essays: General
  Reviews: Books

Poetry > *Any Poetic Form*

Send: Full text
How to send: Submittable

Costs: A fee is charged upon submission. $2 for poetry and prose submissions.

Send one story or essay, or up to five poems, via online submission system. Also accepts book reviews.

M0557 What Motorhome

Magazine
United Kingdom

Magazine Publisher: Warners Group Publications

M0558 The White Review

Magazine
A.104 Fuel Tank, 8-12 Creekside, London, SE8 3DX
United Kingdom

submissions@thewhitereview.org

http://www.thewhitereview.org

Types: Fiction; Nonfiction; Poetry
Formats: Essays; Reviews; Short Fiction
Subjects: Arts; Culture; Literary; Literature
Markets: Adult

Send: Full text
How to send: Email

Print and online arts and literature magazine. Publishes cultural analysis, reviews, and new fiction and poetry. Accepts nonfiction year-round but only accepts poetry and fiction in specific submission windows. Prose submissions should be a minimum of 1,500 words. See website for guidelines and submit by email.

M0559 WI Life

Magazine
104 New Kings Road, London, SW6 4LY
United Kingdom
Tel: +44 (0) 20 7731 5777 ext 217

wilife@nfwi.org.uk

https://www.thewi.org.uk/wie-and-wi-life

Types: Nonfiction
Formats: Articles
Subjects: Cookery; Crafts; Gardening; Nature; Women's Interests
Markets: Adult

Magazine for Women's Institute membership. Welcomes contributions from WI members.

M0560 Willow Springs

Magazine
United States

willowspringsewu@gmail.com

http://willowspringsmagazine.org
https://willowsprings.submittable.com/submit

Fiction > *Short Fiction*

Nonfiction
 Essays; *Interviews*
Poetry > *Any Poetic Form*

How to send: Submittable

Costs: A fee is charged upon submission. $3 reading fee per submission. Writers who cannot afford the reading fee should contact by email to have the fee waived.

Publishes each spring and fall. Accepts fiction and poetry submissions between September 1 and May 31. Nonfiction is open year-round. Submit one packet of work at a time and wait to receive a response before submitting again.

Editor: Samuel Ligon

Managing Editor: Adam O'Connor Rodriguez

M0561 Woman & Home

Magazine
161 Marsh Wall, London, E14 9AP
United Kingdom
Tel: +44 (0) 20 3148 5000

https://www.womanandhome.com

Magazine Publisher: Future

Nonfiction > *Articles*
 Beauty; Fashion; Food; Health; Lifestyle; Travel; Wellbeing; Women's Interests

Our mission is to keep 40+ women informed on the subjects that matter to them, so they can live smarter, healthier and happier lives. We publish celebrity news for grown-ups, as well

as informative, no-nonsense health and wellbeing features about subjects like the menopause. We speak to internationally renown experts to give up-to-date advice on dieting and weight-loss plans. We aim to delight you with delicious – and healthy – recipes. And to inspire your next holiday destinations with travel recommendations both near and far. We filter through the latest fashion and beauty noise to offer you advice on the trends you'll want to try, because they're flattering as well as stylish.

Editor: Catherine Westwood

M0562 Woman's Weekly

Magazine
Time Inc (UK), 161 Marsh Wall, London, E14 9AP
United Kingdom

womansweeklypostbag@timeinc.com

http://www.womansweekly.com

Types: Fiction; Nonfiction
Formats: Articles; News; Short Fiction
Subjects: Beauty; Contemporary; Cookery; Crafts; Fashion; Gardening; Health; Travel; Women's Interests
Markets: Adult

Send: Query
Don't send: Full text
How not to send: Email

Publishes features of interest to women over forty, plus fiction between 1,000 and 2,000 words and serials in four or five parts of 3,400 words each. Only uses experienced journalists for nonfiction. No submissions by email. Submit by post with SAE.

Editor: Diane Kenwood

Features Editor: Sue Pilkington

Fiction Editor: Gaynor Davies

M0563 Woman's Weekly Fiction Special

Magazine
Time Inc (UK), 161 Marsh Wall, London, E14 9AP
United Kingdom

womansweeklypostbag@timeinc.com

https://www.womansweekly.com

Types: Fiction
Formats: Short Fiction
Subjects: Women's Interests
Markets: Adult

Publishes short stories for women between 1,000 and 8,000 words. Send stories by post with SAE – no correspondence by email.

Editor: Gaynor Davies

M0564 Xavier Review

Magazine
United States

radamo@xula.edu

http://www.xavierreview.com

Types: Fiction; Nonfiction; Poetry
Formats: Essays; Interviews; Reviews; Short Fiction
Subjects: Literary; Literary Criticism; Religion
Markets: Adult

Send: Full text
How to send: Email

Publishes poetry, fiction, essays, reviews, and interviews. Prefers email submissions with attachments to postal submissions. Send 3-6 poems, or one piece of prose.

Editor: Ralph Adamo

M0565 Yachting World

Magazine
United Kingdom

yachting.world@timeinc.com

https://www.yachtingworld.com

Types: Nonfiction
Formats: Articles; News
Subjects: Leisure; Sport
Markets: Adult

Publishes news and features relating to yacht racing, yachting events, and cruising.

Editor: Elaine Bunting

M0566 The Yale Review

Magazine
United States

theyalereview@gmail.com

https://yalereview.yale.edu
https://www.facebook.com/YaleReview/
https://www.instagram.com/yalereview/
https://twitter.com/YaleReview

Fiction > *Short Fiction*: Literary

Nonfiction > *Essays*
 Arts; Cultural Criticism; Films; History; Literary Criticism; Memoir; Music; Politics; TV

Poetry > *Any Poetic Form*

Closed to approaches.

Open for submissions of poetry, nonfiction, and fiction from October 5 to November 3, 2020.

Editor: Meghan O'Rourke

M0567 The Yalobusha Review

Magazine
United States

yreditors@gmail.com

https://yr.olemiss.edu

Types: Fiction; Poetry
Formats: Short Fiction
Subjects: Literary; Literature
Markets: Adult

Send: Full text

Submit 3-5 poems, one short story up to 5,000 words, or up to three shorter stories up to 1,000 words each. Accepts a certain number of free entries per month. Once the limit has been reached writers can wait till the next month, or make payment to submit.

Editors: Helene Achanzar; Lara Avery; Linda Masi; Nicholas Sabo

Fiction Editor: Victoria Hulbert

Poetry Editor: Mason Wray

Senior Editors: Sarah Heying; Andy Sia

M0568 Yellow Mama Webzine
Magazine
United States

crosmus@hotmail.com

http://blackpetalsks.tripod.com/yellowmama

Types: Fiction
Subjects: Horror; Literary
Markets: Adult

Send: Full text
How to send: Email

Webzine publishing fiction and poetry. Seeks cutting edge, hardboiled, horror, literary, noir, psychological / horror. No fanfiction, romance, swords & sorcery, fantasy, or erotica. Send submissions by email. See website for full guidelines.

M0569 Yemassee
Magazine
Department of English, University of South Carolina, Columbia, SC 29208
United States

editor@yemasseejournal.org

http://yemasseejournal.org

Types: Fiction; Nonfiction; Poetry
Formats: Essays; Reviews; Short Fiction
Subjects: Literary
Markets: Adult

Publishes poetry, fiction, and nonfiction. Submit 3-5 poems or pieces of flash fiction up to 1,000 words, or a longer short story up to 8,000 words (1,000 words to 5,000 words preferred), via online submission system. See website for full guidelines. $3 submission fee. $6 for expedited submissions.

Editors: Cody Hosek; Dylan Nutter; Victoria Romero

M0570 Yes Poetry Magazine
Online Magazine
United States

editor@yespoetry.com

https://www.yespoetry.com
https://twitter.com/yespoetry
https://yespoetry.tumblr.com/

Fiction > *Short Fiction*

Nonfiction
  Essays; *Interviews*; *Reviews*
Poetry > *Any Poetic Form*

Closed to approaches.

A lifestyle art publication that encourages deep analysis and thought, pushing for progressive change and identification.

Book Publisher: Yes Poetry Chapbooks (**P0946**)

M0571 Your Best Ever Christmas
Magazine
United Kingdom

Newspaper Publisher / Magazine Publisher: DC Thomson Media

M0572 Your Cat
Magazine
Warners Group Publications Plc, The Maltings, West Street, Bourne, Lincolnshire, PE10 9PH
United Kingdom
Tel: +44 (0) 1778 395070

editorial@yourcat.co.uk

https://www.yourcat.co.uk

Magazine Publisher: Warners Group Publications

Types: Fiction; Nonfiction
Formats: Articles; Short Fiction
Subjects: How To
Markets: Adult

Practical magazine covering the care of cats and kittens.

Editor:

M0573 Your Dog
Magazine
The Maltings, West Street, Bourne, Lincolnshire, PE10 9PH
United Kingdom
Tel: +44 (0) 1778 395070

editorial@yourdog.co.uk

https://www.yourdog.co.uk

Magazine Publisher: Warners Group Publications

Nonfiction
  Articles: Dogs
  News: Dogs

Publishes news and articles aimed at dog owners, offering practical advice and some personal experience pieces.

Editor: Sarah Wright

M0574 Yours
Magazine
Media House, Peterborough Business Park, Peterborough, PE2 6EA
United Kingdom

yours@bauermedia.co.uk

https://www.yours.co.uk
https://www.facebook.com/Yoursmagazine
https://twitter.com/yoursmagazine
https://www.pinterest.com/yoursmagazine/

Magazine Publisher: Bauer Media Group

Nonfiction
  Articles: Beauty; Fashion; Finance; Health; Recipes; Travel; Women's Interests
  Interviews: Celebrity

Magazine for women over 50. Publishes tips and expert advice on a range of topics from travel to financial guidance as well as discovering the latest fashion trends, beauty, and health tips. Also exclusive celebrity interviews and recipes for healthy meals or hearty treats.

Editor: Sharon Reid

M0575 Zetetic: A Record of Unusual Inquiry
Magazine
United States

http://zeteticrecord.org

Types: Fiction; Nonfiction; Poetry
Formats: Short Fiction
Subjects: Literary
Markets: Adult

Online magazine publishing fiction, nonfiction, and poetry. Accepts prose between 100 and 2,500 words, or up to three poems between three and 100 lines.

M0576 Zone 3
Magazine
APSU Box 4565, Clarksville, TN 37044
United States
Tel: +1 (931) 221-7031

https://www.zone3press.com

Book Publisher / Magazine Publisher: Zone 3 Press

Fiction > *Short Fiction*
  Contemporary; Literary

Nonfiction > *Short Nonfiction*
  Contemporary; Creative Nonfiction; Literary

Poetry > *Any Poetic Form*

Send: Full text
How to send: Submittable
How not to send: Email

Costs: A fee is charged upon submission. $3.

Publishes fiction, poetry, and creative nonfiction. Accepts submissions through online submission system between August 1 and April 1 annually. $3 submission fee.

Editor: Susan Wallace

Book Publishers

For the most up-to-date listings of these and hundreds of other book publishers, visit https://www.firstwriter.com/publishers

To claim your free access to the site, please see the back of this book.

P0001 4 Color Books
Publishing Imprint
United States

http://www.randomhousebooks.com/imprints/

Book Publisher: Random House (**P0690**)

Nonfiction > *Nonfiction Books*
Arts; Contemporary Politics; Cookery;
Health; Sustainable Living

Collaborates with the most forward-thinking and groundbreaking BIPOC chefs, writers, artists, activists, and innovators to craft visually stunning nonfiction books that inspire readers and give rise to a more healthy, just, and sustainable world for all.

P0002 42 Miles Press
Book Publisher
English Department, Indiana University South Bend, 1700 Mishawaka Avenue, P.O. Box 7111, South Bend, IN 46634-7111
United States

42milespress@gmail.com

https://42milespress.com

Types: Poetry
Subjects: Literary
Markets: Adult

Closed to approaches.

Publishes books and chapbooks of poetry. Currently only accepts submissions via its annual poetry competition, which runs from December 1 to March 15 and costs $25 to enter.

Editor: David Dodd Lee

P0003 4RV Biblical Based
Publishing Imprint
United States

Book Publisher: 4RV Publishing (**P0007**)

Fiction > *Novels:* Christianity

Nonfiction > *Nonfiction Books:* Christianity

Publishes fiction and nonfiction based on the Bible, including Christian works.

P0004 4RV Children's Corner
Publishing Imprint
United States

Book Publisher: 4RV Publishing (**P0007**)

CHILDREN'S > **Fiction**
Chapter Books; Early Readers; Picture Books

Closed to approaches.

Publishes books for any aged reader below 5th grade.

P0005 4RV Fiction
Publishing Imprint
United States

Book Publisher: 4RV Publishing (**P0007**)

ADULT > **Fiction** > *Novels*
General, and in particular: Fantasy;
Romance; Science Fiction

NEW ADULT > **Fiction** > *Novels*

Does not want:

Fiction > *Novels*: Erotic

Publishes novels for adults or young people with high reading abilities.

P0006 4RV Nonfiction
Publishing Imprint
United States

Book Publisher: 4RV Publishing (**P0007**)

Nonfiction > *Nonfiction Books*

Publishes nonfiction works above Young Adult.

P0007 4RV Publishing
Book Publisher
35427 State Highway 58, Hydro, OK 73048
United States
Tel: +1 (405) 820-9640

President@4rvpublishingllc.com
vp_operations@4rvpublishingllc.com
art_director@4rvpublishingllc.com

https://www.4rvpublishing.com
https://www.facebook.com/4RV-Publishing-LLC-20479523692/

https://twitter.com/4RV
https://www.youtube.com/user/4RVPublishingLLC

ADULT
Fiction > *Novels*
General, and in particular: Christianity;
Fantasy; Romance; Science Fiction

Nonfiction > *Nonfiction Books*

Poetry > *Poetry Collections*

CHILDREN'S > **Fiction**
Chapter Books; Early Readers; Middle Grade; Picture Books
TEEN > **Fiction** > *Novels*

YOUNG ADULT > **Fiction** > *Novels*

Does not want:

Fiction > *Novels*: Erotic

Send: Query; Synopsis; Writing sample
How to send: Email attachment

Accepts most genres of fiction and nonfiction books for all ages, including nonfiction, mystery, romance, mainstream, western, Christian, and science-fiction, as well as children's books, middle grade and young adult novels. No poetry or graphic sex or violence. Language should not be overly profane or vulgar. Accepts submissions by email from the US, UK, and Australia. Not accepting children's books as at September 2020. See website for current status and full guidelines.

Publishing Imprints: 4RV Biblical Based (**P0003**); 4RV Children's Corner (**P0004**); 4RV Fiction (**P0005**); 4RV Nonfiction (**P0006**); 4RV Tweens & Teens (**P0008**); 4RV Young Adult (**P0009**)

P0008 4RV Tweens & Teens
Publishing Imprint
United States

Book Publisher: 4RV Publishing (**P0007**)

CHILDREN'S > **Fiction** > *Middle Grade*

TEEN > **Fiction** > *Novels*

Publishes books for teens and tweens grades 5-8.

P0009 4RV Young Adult
Publishing Imprint
United States

Book Publisher: 4RV Publishing (**P0007**)

YOUNG ADULT > **Fiction** > *Novels*

Publishes books for young adults aged 14-18.

P0010 4th Estate
Publishing Imprint
The News Building, 1 London Bridge Street,
London, SE1 9GF
United Kingdom
Tel: +44 (0) 20 8741 7070

4thestate.marketing@harpercollins.co.uk

http://www.4thestate.co.uk

Book Publisher: HarperCollins UK (**P0382**)

Types: Fiction; Nonfiction
Formats: Reference
Subjects: Biography; Comedy / Humour;
Current Affairs; Literary; Science; Travel
Markets: Adult

Closed to approaches.

Strong reputation for Literary and nonfiction.
No unsolicited mss.

P0011 6th
Publishing Imprint

Publishing Imprint: O-Books

P0012 A-R Editions
Book Publisher
1600 Aspen Cmns, Suite 100, Middleton WI
53562
United States
Tel: +1 (608) 836-9000

info@areditions.com

https://www.areditions.com
https://www.facebook.com/areditions

Nonfiction > *Nonfiction Books*: Music

Send: Query; Proposal
How to send: Email; File sharing service

Publisher of modern critical editions of music
based on current musicological research, aimed
at scholars and performers. See website for
submission guidelines.

Managing Editor: Paul L. Ranzini

Publishing Imprint: Greenway Music Press
(**P0342**)

P0013 a...p press
Book Publisher
United States

afterthepause@gmail.com

https://afterthepause.com/a-p-press/

Types: Fiction; Poetry
Formats: Short Fiction

Subjects: Experimental
Markets: Adult

Send: Full text

Publishes poetry, flash fiction, visual poetry,
experimental poetry, and any combination
thereof. Manuscripts must be at least 50 pages.
Send submissions by email.

P0014 Abacus
Publishing Imprint

Publishing Imprint: Little, Brown Book Group
(**P0502**)

P0015 ABC-CLIO
Book Publisher
147 Castilian Drive, Santa Barbara, CA 93117
United States
Tel: +1 (800) 368-6868
Fax: +1 (805) 968-1911

CustomerService@abc-clio.com

https://www.abc-clio.com/
https://www.facebook.com/ABCCLIO
https://twitter.com/ABC_CLIO
https://www.youtube.com/user/ABCCLIOLive
https://www.linkedin.com/company/abc-clio/

ACADEMIC > **Nonfiction** > *Reference*
General, and in particular: History;
Sociology

Publishes academic reference works and
periodicals primarily on topics such as history
and social sciences for educational and public
library settings.

Publishing Imprints: ABC-CLIO / Greenwood
(**P0016**); Libraries Unlimited (*P0491*); Praeger
(*P0664*)

P0016 ABC-CLIO / Greenwood
Publishing Imprint
Acquisitions Department, ABC-
CLIO/Greenwood, ABC-CLIO, PO Box 1911,
Santa Barbara, CA 93116-1911
United States
Tel: +1 (800) 368-6868

acquisition_inquiries@abc-clio.com

http://www.abc-clio.com

Book Publisher: ABC-CLIO (**P0015**)

Types: Nonfiction
Formats: Reference
Subjects: Arts; Biography; Business; Crime;
Culture; Current Affairs; Finance; Health;
History; Legal; Nature; Politics; Psychology;
Religion; Science; Sociology; Technology;
Warfare; Women's Interests
Markets: Academic; Adult

Send: Query
Don't send: Full text

Publisher of general nonfiction and reference
covering history, humanities, and general
interest topics across the secondary and higher

education curriculum. No fiction, poetry, or
drama. Welcomes proposals in appropriate
areas. See website for specific imprint / editor
contact details.

P0017 Abdo Publishing Co
Book Publisher
1920 Lookout Drive, North Mankato MN
56003
United States
Tel: +1 (800) 800-1312
Fax: +1 (800) 862-3480

fiction@abdobooks.com

http://abdopublishing.com

Types: Fiction; Nonfiction
Subjects: Anthropology; Arts; Biography;
Cookery; Crafts; Culture; Current Affairs;
Design; Entertainment; History; Hobbies;
Medicine; Politics; Religion; Science;
Sociology; Sport; Technology; Travel; Warfare
Markets: Children's

Closed to approaches.

Publishes nonfiction, educational material for
children up to the 12th grade, plus fiction
series for children. Not accepting nonfiction
submissions as at May 2017 (see website for
current situation). Writers with a concept for a
fiction series should send samples of
manuscripts by email.

Editor: Paul Abdo

P0018 Abson Books London
Book Publisher
5 Sidney Square, London, E1 2EY
United Kingdom
Tel: +44 (0) 20 7790 4737
Fax: +44 (0) 20 7790 7346

book.sales@absonbooks.co.uk

http://www.absonbooks.co.uk

Nonfiction > *Nonfiction Books*
Dialects; Slang

Publisher of pocket-size books on dialect and
slang.

Publisher: M.J. Ellison

P0019 Abuzz Press
Book Publisher
United States

https://www.abuzzpress.com

Fiction > *Novels*

Nonfiction
Colouring Books: General
Nonfiction Books: How To; New Age

How to send: Online submission system

Publishes nonfiction, adult colouring books,
how-to, new age, and exceptional fiction. No
poetry, short story collections, books with

colour interiors, or illegal material. Send submissions via form on website.

P0020 Acair Ltd
Book Publisher
An Tosgan, 54 Seaforth Road, Stornoway, Isle of Lewis, HS1 2SD
United Kingdom
Tel: +44 (0) 1851 703020

info@acairbooks.com

https://www.acairbooks.com
https://www.facebook.com/acairbooks
https://twitter.com/AcairBooks
https://www.pinterest.co.uk/acairbooks/

ADULT
Fiction in Translation > *Novels*: Gaelic

Nonfiction in Translation > *Nonfiction Books*: Gaelic

Nonfiction > *Nonfiction Books*

Poetry in Translation > *Any Poetic Form*: Gaelic

CHILDREN'S > **Fiction in Translation**
Novels: Gaelic
Picture Books: Gaelic

Publishes a wide range of Gaelic, English and Bilingual books, including children's fiction. 75% of children's books published are exclusively Gaelic.

P0021 Adams Media
Publishing Imprint

Book Publisher: Simon & Schuster Adult Publishing (**P0766**)

P0022 Addison Wesley
Publishing Imprint
United States

Book Publisher: Pearson

ACADEMIC > **Nonfiction** > *Nonfiction Books*
Computer Science; Finance; Mathematics; Statistics

Publishes academic textbooks, learning programs, and multimedia in the areas of computer science, economics, finance, mathematics and statistics.

P0023 Adonis and Abbey Publishing
Book Publisher
Adonis & Abbey Publishers Ltd, P.O. Box 43418, London, SE11 4XZ, United Kingdom
United Kingdom
Tel: +44 (0) 20 7793 8893

editor@adonis-abbey.com

http://www.adonisandabbey.com

Types: Nonfiction
Formats: Reference

Subjects: Anthropology; Culture; Current Affairs; History; Lifestyle; Literary; Traditional
Markets: Academic; Adult

Send: Full text

This press is actively seeking personal material from an experiential point of view while employing a vocabulary that will educate the reader with a real sense of presence. They are also seeking highly academic books on current events and history. Manuscripts with an African or African American view point are also sought. Query first.

P0024 AFK
Publishing Imprint

Book Publisher: Scholastic (**P0740**)

P0025 Agora Books
Book Publisher
55 New Oxford Street, London, WC1A 1BS
United Kingdom
Tel: +44 (0) 20 7344 1000

submissions@agorabooks.co

https://www.agorabooks.co

Literary Agency: Peters Fraser + Dunlop

Types: Fiction
Subjects: Crime; History; Mystery; Suspense; Women's Interests
Markets: Adult

Send: Query
Don't send: Full text

Send synopsis and first three chapters (or 50 pages) as Word document attachments by email. See website for full guidelines.

P0026 Aladdin
Publishing Imprint

Book Publisher: Simon & Schuster Children's Publishing (**P0768**)

P0027 Albert Whitman & Company
Book Publisher
250 South Northwest Highway, Suite 320, Park Ridge, Illinois 60068
United States
Tel: +1 (800) 255-7675
Fax: +1 (847) 581-0039

submissions@albertwhitman.com

http://www.albertwhitman.com

Types: Fiction; Nonfiction
Markets: Children's; Young Adult

Publishes picture books, middle-grade fiction, and young adult novels. Will consider fiction and nonfiction manuscripts for picture books for children ages 1 to 8, up to 1,000 words; middle-grade novels up to 35,000 words for children up to the age of 12; and young adult

novels up to 70,000 words for ages 12-18. See website for full submission guidelines.

Editor-in-Chief: Kathleen Tucker

P0028 Alfred A. Knopf
Publishing Imprint
United States

Book Publisher: Knopf Doubleday Publishing Group (**P0475**)

P0029 Allison & Busby Ltd
Book Publisher
11 Wardour Mews, London, W1F 8AN
United Kingdom
Tel: +44 (0) 20 3950 7834

susie@allisonandbusby.com

http://www.allisonandbusby.com

Types: Fiction
Formats: Short Fiction
Subjects: Autobiography; Contemporary; Cookery; Crime; Culture; Fantasy; History; Literary; Mystery; Romance; Science Fiction; Self Help; Thrillers; Travel; Warfare; Women's Interests
Markets: Adult; Young Adult

How to send: Through a literary agent

Accepts approaches via a literary agent only. No unsolicited MSS or queries from authors.

Publishing Director: Susie Dunlop

P0030 Allworth Press
Book Publisher
307 West 36th Street, 11th Floor, New York, NY 10018
United States
Tel: +1 (212) 643-6816
Fax: +1 (212) 643-6819

allworthsubmissions@skyhorsepublishing.com

https://www.skyhorsepublishing.com/allworth-press/

Book Publisher: Skyhorse Publishing, Inc. (**P0771**)

Types: Nonfiction
Formats: Theatre Scripts
Subjects: Arts; Business; Crafts; Design; Photography
Markets: Adult

Send: Query
Don't send: Full text

Send query with 1-2 page synopsis, annotated chapter outline, market analysis, one or two sample chapters, and author CV. See website for full guidelines.

P0031 Alma Books Ltd
Book Publisher
Thornton House, Thornton Road, Wimbledon, London, SW19 4NG
United Kingdom

info@almabooks.com

https://www.almabooks.com
https://www.facebook.com/AlmaPublishing/
https://twitter.com/almabooks
https://www.pinterest.co.uk/almabooks/
https://www.instagram.com/almapublishing/

Fiction in Translation > *Novels*

Fiction > *Novels*

Nonfiction in Translation > *Nonfiction Books*

Nonfiction > *Nonfiction Books*

Send: Query
How to send: Email

Closed to submissions of contemporary fiction. Accepts proposals for translations of classic literature, and welcomes proposals and ideas for the Classics list.

Publishing Imprints: Alma Classics; Calder Publications Ltd (**P0142**)

P0032 AMACOM Books
Book Publisher
United States
Tel: +1 (800) 250-5308

harpercollinsleadershipcc@harpercollins.com

https://www.harpercollinsleadership.com/amacombooks/

Book Publisher: HarperCollins Leadership (**P0381**)

PROFESSIONAL > **Nonfiction** > *Nonfiction Books*
  Business; Finance; Leadership; Management

Publishes business books only, covering such topics as finance, management, sales, marketing, human resources, customer services, quality control, career growth, etc.

P0033 Amber Books Ltd
Book Publisher
United House, North Road, London, N7 9DP
United Kingdom
Tel: +44 (0) 20 7520 7600

editorial@amberbooks.co.uk

https://www.amberbooks.co.uk

Types: Nonfiction
Formats: Reference
Subjects: History; Warfare
Markets: Adult

Send: Query
Don't send: Full text

Publishes illustrated nonfiction in a wide range of subject areas, particularly military. No fiction, biography or poetry. Send query with synopsis, contents lists, author CV, and one or two sample chapters by post or by email. Do not send SASE or IRCs or cash. Response not guaranteed.

P0034 American Catholic Press
Book Publisher
16565 S. State Street, South Holland, Illinois 60473
United States
Tel: +1 (708) 331-5485
Fax: +1 (708) 331-5484

acp@acpress.org

http://www.americancatholicpress.org

Nonfiction > *Nonfiction Books*
  Christianity; Church Music

Publishes books on the Roman Catholic liturgy, including new music for use in church services. No religious poetry.

Editorial Director: Rev. Michael Gilligan PhD

P0035 Amistad
Publishing Imprint

Book Publisher: HarperCollins

P0036 Anchor Books
Publishing Imprint
United States

Book Publisher: Knopf Doubleday Publishing Group (**P0475**)

P0037 Andersen Press Ltd
Book Publisher
20 Vauxhall Bridge Road, London, SW1V 2SA
United Kingdom

anderseneditorial@penguinrandomhouse.co.uk

https://www.andersenpress.co.uk
https://twitter.com/andersenpresshttps://twitter.com/andersenpress
https://www.facebook.com/andersenpress

CHILDREN'S > **Fiction** > *Picture Books*

How to send: Through a literary agent

Publishes rhyming stories, but no poetry, adult fiction, fiction for older children, nonfiction, or short story collections. Accepts submissions through literary agents only.

P0038 Angry Robot
Book Publisher
Unit 11, Shepperton House, 89 Shepperton Road, London, N1 3DF
United Kingdom
Tel: +44 (0) 20 3813 6940

incoming@angryrobotbooks.com

https://www.angryrobotbooks.com

Book Publisher: Watkins Media (**P0907**)

Types: Fiction
Subjects: Fantasy; Science Fiction
Markets: Adult

How to send: Through a literary agent

Publisher of science fiction and fantasy. Accepts submissions through literary agents only, apart from a specific open door period held each year. See the company's social media for updates.

P0039 Anness Publishing Ltd
Book Publisher
Algores Way, Wisbech, Cambridgeshire, PE13 2TQ
United Kingdom

info@anness.com

http://www.aquamarinebooks.com

Types: Nonfiction; Poetry
Formats: Reference
Subjects: Arts; Cookery; Crafts; Design; Gardening; Health; History; Leisure; Lifestyle; Music; Nature; New Age; Photography; Religion; Science; Sport; Travel; Warfare
Markets: Adult; Children's

Describes itself as one of the largest independent book publishers in the UK.

Publishing Imprints: Armadillo (*P0052*); Lorenz Books (*P0507*); Peony Press (*P0640*); Southwater. (*P0780*)

P0040 Anthony Bourdain Books
Publishing Imprint

Book Publisher: HarperCollins

P0041 Anvil Press Publishers
Book Publisher
P.O. Box 3008, MPO, Vancouver, B.C., V6B 3X5
Canada
Tel: +1 (604) 876-8710

info@anvilpress.com

https://www.anvilpress.com
https://www.facebook.com/Anvil-Press-115437275199047/
https://www.twitter.com/anvilpress
https://www.instagram.com/anvilpress_publishers/

Fiction > *Novels*

Nonfiction > *Nonfiction Books*
  Arts; Photography

Poetry > *Poetry Collections*

Scripts > *Theatre Scripts*: Drama

Closed to approaches.

Publisher designed to discover and nurture Canadian literary talent. Considers work from Canadian authors with SASE only. For prose, send query with synopsis and 20-30 pages; for poetry send 8-12 poems; and for drama send entire MS, unless excessively long. No submissions by email.

Editor: Brian Kaufman

P0042 Apex Publishing Ltd
Book Publisher
307 Holland Road, Holland on Sea, Essex,
CO15 6PD
United Kingdom
Tel: +44 (0) 1255 812555

mail@apexpublishing.co.uk

http://www.apexpublishing.co.uk

Fiction > *Novels*: Contemporary

Nonfiction > *Nonfiction Books*
Biography; Entertainment; Lifestyle;
Memoir; Real Life Stories; Sport

Send: Submission Form
How to send: Post

Will consider publishing a wide range of high-quality non-fiction and also well-written works of contemporary fiction. Has a particular interest in real-life stories, biographies, memoirs, entertainment and lifestyle and sport.

Editor: Chris Cowlin

P0043 Aphrodisia
Publishing Imprint

Book Publisher: Kensington Publishing Corp.
(**P0469**)

P0044 Applause
Publishing Imprint
United States

Book Publisher: The Globe Pequot Press
(**P0329**)

P0045 April Gloaming
Book Publisher
United States

inquiries.aprilgloaming@gmail.com

http://www.aprilgloaming.com

Types: Fiction; Nonfiction; Poetry
Subjects: Literary
Markets: Adult

Send: Query
Don't send: Full text

Nashville-based independent press that aims to capture and better understand the Southern soul, Southern writing, and the Southern holler. Send submissions of poetry, fiction, creative nonfiction, or graphic novels to the specific email addresses given on the website.

P0046 Arabelle Publishing
Book Publisher
United States
Tel: +1 (804) 298-5082

http://www.arabellepublishing.com

Types: Nonfiction
Subjects: Autobiography; Business; Cookery;
Health; How To; Lifestyle; Religion; Women's

Interests
Markets: Adult; Children's; Professional

We are dedicated to glorifying God by celebrating life through stories that reveal His grace and love. We publish high-quality, nonfiction books that inspire, impact, and instruct. We bring communities and cultures together by celebrating the regional history, and the beauty found in the lives of ordinary people who impact the communities in which they live. As at November 2019, we are accepting query submissions for the 2020 publication. Although we will consider all great books, we are specifically accepting queries for Health and Wellness books that are biblically based, Christian Living, and Bible Studies and Devotionals.

P0047 Arc Music
Publishing Imprint

Book Publisher: Arc Publications (**P0048**)

P0048 Arc Publications
Book Publisher
Nanholme Mill, Shaw Wood Road,
Todmorden, Lancs, OL14 6DA
United Kingdom
Tel: +44 (0) 1706 812338

info@arcpublications.co.uk

https://www.arcpublications.co.uk

Types: Poetry; Translations
Subjects: Contemporary; Music
Markets: Adult

Send: Full text

Send 16-24 poems by email as a Word / PDF attachment, maximum one poem per page, during December only. Submissions from outside the UK and Ireland should be sent to specific address for international submissions, available on website. Cover letter should include short bio and details of the contemporary poets you read. See website for full guidelines.

Publishing Imprint: Arc Music (*P0047*)

P0049 Arcadia Books
Book Publisher
139 Highlever Road, London, W10 6PH
United Kingdom
Tel: +44 (0) 20 8960 4967

http://arcadiabooks.co.uk
https://twitter.com/arcadiabooks

Fiction in Translation > *Novels*

Fiction > *Novels*
Crime; Literary

Closed to approaches.

Publisher of translated fiction, literary fiction and crime.

P0050 Arcana
Publishing Imprint

Book Publisher: Aurelia Leo (**P0062**)

P0051 Arcturus Publishing Ltd
Book Publisher
26/27 Bickels Yard, 151-153 Bermondsey
Street, London, SE1 3HA
United Kingdom
Tel: +44 (0) 20 7407 9400
Fax: +44 (0) 20 7407 9444

info@arcturuspublishing.com

https://arcturuspublishing.com
https://www.facebook.com/
ArcturusPublishing/
https://twitter.com/arcturusbooks
https://www.instagram.com/arcturusbooks/

ADULT > **Nonfiction**
Nonfiction Books: Classics / Ancient World;
New Age; Practical Art
Puzzle Books: General
Reference: General

CHILDREN'S > **Nonfiction** > *Nonfiction
Books*

Non-fiction ranges cover reference, practical art, new age, classics, puzzles and children's books.

P0052 Armadillo
Publishing Imprint

Book Publisher: Anness Publishing Ltd
(**P0039**)

P0053 Arsenal Pulp Press
Book Publisher
202-211 East Georgia Street, Vancouver, BC,
V6A 1Z6
Canada
Tel: +1 (604) 687-4233
Fax: +1 (604) 687-4283

info@arsenalpulp.com

https://arsenalpulp.com

ADULT
Fiction > *Novels*
LGBTQIA; Literary

Nonfiction > *Nonfiction Books*
British Columbia; Culture; LGBTQIA;
Literary; Politics; Regional; Sociology;
Youth Culture

CHILDREN'S
Fiction > *Novels*
Diversity; LGBTQIA

Nonfiction > *Nonfiction Books*
Diversity; LGBTQIA

YOUNG ADULT
Fiction > *Novels*: LGBTQIA

Nonfiction > *Nonfiction Books*: LGBTQIA

Send: Synopsis; Outline; Writing sample;
Market info; Self-Addressed Stamped
Envelope (SASE)
How to send: Post
How not to send: Fax; Email; Phone

Publishes Cultural studies,
Political/sociological studies, Regional studies
and guides, in particular for British Columbia,
Cookbooks, Gay and lesbian fiction and
nonfiction (including young adult and
children's), Visual art, Multicultural fiction
and nonfiction, Literary fiction and nonfiction
(no genre fiction, such as mysteries, thriller, or
romance), Youth culture, Health, and books for
children (especially those that emphasise
diversity). Send query with synopsis, chapter
by chapter outline for nonfiction, writing
credentials, 50-page excerpt, and marketing
analysis. Include self-addressed envelope and
appropriate return postage (either Canadian
postage or IRCs), or email address for
response. See website for full details. No
submissions by fax or email, or queries by
phone.

P0054 **Ashley Drake
Publishing Ltd**
Book Publisher
PO Box 733, Cardiff, CF14 7ZY
United Kingdom

post@ashleydrake.com

http://www.ashleydrake.com

ACADEMIC > **Nonfiction** > *Nonfiction
Books*
    Education; History; Medieval Literature;
    Politics; Scandinavia

ADULT > **Nonfiction**
    Nonfiction Books: Leisure; Sport
    Reference: Popular

Send: Proposal

Publishes English and Welsh language trade
and academic books. Welcomes proposals.
Forms for proposals can be found on the
website.

Publishing Imprints: Gwasg Addysgol Cymru;
Morgan Publishing; Scandinavian Academic
Press; St David's Press; Welsh Academic
Press; YDdraig Fach

P0055 **Athenaeum Press**
Book Publisher
United States

https://theathenaeumpress.com
https://www.facebook.com/theathenaeumpress/
https://www.instagram.com/athenaeumpress/
https://twitter.com/athenaeum_press
http://www.amazon.com/shops/
athenaeumpress

Closed to approaches.

Online Magazine: Waccamaw (**M0549**)

P0056 **Atheneum**
Publishing Imprint

Book Publisher: Simon & Schuster Children's
Publishing (**P0768**)

P0057 **Atlantean Publishing**
Book Publisher; Magazine Publisher
4 Pierrot Steps, 71 Kursaal Way, Southend-on-
Sea, Essex, SS1 2UY
United Kingdom

atlanteanpublishing@hotmail.com

https://atlanteanpublishing.fandom.com/wiki/
Atlantean_Publishing
https://atlanteanpublishing.wordpress.com/
https://www.facebook.com/Atlantean.
Publishing

Fiction > *Short Fiction*

Poetry > *Any Poetic Form*

Non-profit-making small press. Produces
several serial publications and numerous one-
off releases, specialising in poetry and short
fiction, both 'general' and 'genre'.

Editor: David-John Tyrer

Magazines: Awen (**M0050**); Bard (**M0056**);
Monomyth (**M0347**); The Supplement
(**M0501**)

P0058 **Atlantic Books**
Book Publisher
Ormond House, 26-27 Boswell Street, London,
WC1N 3JZ
United Kingdom
Tel: +44 (0) 20 7269 1610
Fax: +44 (0) 20 7430 0916

enquiries@atlantic-books.co.uk

https://atlantic-books.co.uk

Types: Fiction; Nonfiction
Subjects: Autobiography; Current Affairs;
History; Literary; Politics
Markets: Adult

Send: Query
Don't send: Full text

Open to submissions of complete novels,
extensive partials, or short stories, within the
literary genre. Send submissions with a one
line pitch and a one paragraph pitch, outlining
the submission.

P0059 **Atlantic Monthly Press**
Publishing Imprint
United States

Book Publisher: Grove Atlantic Inc. (**P0345**)

P0060 **Atom**
Publishing Imprint

Publishing Imprint: Little, Brown Book Group
(**P0502**)

P0061 **Atria**
Publishing Imprint

Book Publisher: Simon & Schuster Adult
Publishing (**P0766**)

P0062 **Aurelia Leo**
Book Publisher
4212 Algonquin Parkway, Louisville, KY
40211-2402
United States

subs@aurelialeo.com

https://aurelialeo.com

Fiction > *Short Fiction*
    Erotic Romance; Fantasy; LGBTQIA;
    Science Fiction

Closed to approaches.

Currently looking for lesbian, gay, bisexual,
and transgender erotic romance with elements
of sci-fi and fantasy for a themed anthology.
1,000 to 17,500 words.

Editor: Zelda Knight

Publishing Imprint: Arcana (*P0050*)

P0063 **Aurora Metro Press**
Book Publisher
67 Grove Avenue, Twickenham, TW1 4HX
United Kingdom
Tel: +44 (0) 20 3261 0000

submissions@aurorametro.com

https://aurorametro.com

ADULT
    Fiction
        Novels; Short Fiction
    Nonfiction > *Nonfiction Books*
        Arts; Biography; History; Popular Culture;
        Travel; Wellbeing

    Scripts
        Film Scripts; Theatre Scripts
YOUNG ADULT > *Fiction* > *Novels*

Send: Query; Synopsis; Author bio; Writing
sample

Publishes adult fiction, YA fiction, drama, and
non-fiction biography and books about the arts
and popular culture.

P0064 **The Authority Guides**
Book Publisher
SRA Books, Unit 3, Spike Island, 133
Cumberland Road, Bristol, BS1 6UX
United Kingdom
Tel: +44 (0) 1789 761345

http://authorityguides.co.uk

Types: Nonfiction
Subjects: Business
Markets: Professional

Publishes pocket-sized business books for
entrepreneurs and business professionals.

P0065 Autumn Publishing Ltd
Book Publisher
Cottage Farm, Mears Ashby Road, Sywell,
Northants, NN6 0BJ
United Kingdom
Tel: +44 (0) 1604 741116
Fax: +44 (0) 1604 670495

customerservice@igloobooks.com

https://autumnpublishing.co.uk

Book Publisher: Bonnier Books (UK) (**P0122**)

CHILDREN'S > **Nonfiction**
Activity Books: General
Nonfiction Books: English; Health;
Mathematics; Nature; Science

Deals in books for babies and toddlers, activity
books, early learning books, and sticker books.
Publisher's philosophy is that children should
enjoy learning with books, and to this end
combines activity and learning by turning
simple workbooks into activity books,
allowing children to learn whilst they play.

Editorial Director: Lyn Coutts

Publishing Imprint: Byeway Books

P0066 Avalon Travel
Publishing Imprint
United States

Book Publisher: Perseus Books (**P0641**)

P0067 Avery
Publishing Imprint

Book Publisher: Penguin Publishing Group
(**P0633**)

P0068 Avid Reader Press
Publishing Imprint

Book Publisher: Simon & Schuster Adult
Publishing (**P0766**)

P0069 Avon
Publishing Imprint
United Kingdom

Book Publisher: HarperCollins UK (**P0382**)

P0070 Avon Books
Publishing Imprint
United States

https://www.harpercollins.com
https://www.harpercollins.com/pages/
avonromance
https://twitter.com/avonbooks
https://www.instagram.com/avonbooks/
https://www.facebook.com/avonromance

Book Publisher: HarperCollins

Fiction > *Novels*
Contemporary Romance; Historical
Romance; Romance; Romantic Comedy;
Supernatural / Paranormal Romance

Closed to approaches.

Publishing award-winning romance since
1941. Recognized for having pioneered the
historical romance category and continues to
publish in wide variety of other genres,
including paranormal, urban fantasy,
contemporary and regency.

P0071 Award Publications Limited
Book Publisher
The Old Riding School, The Welbeck Estate,
Worksop, Nottinghamshire, S80 3LR
United Kingdom
Tel: +44 (0) 1909 478170

info@awardpublications.co.uk

http://www.awardpublications.co.uk

Types: Fiction; Nonfiction
Formats: Reference
Markets: Children's

Publishes children's fiction, nonfiction, and
reference.

P0072 Axis Mundi
Publishing Imprint

Publishing Imprint: O-Books

P0073 Backbeat
Publishing Imprint
United States

Book Publisher: The Globe Pequot Press
(**P0329**)

P0074 Bad Press Ink
Book Publisher
United Kingdom

enquiries@badpress.ink

https://badpress.ink

Types: Fiction
Markets: Adult

Publishes alternative books and niche lifestyle
fiction. Complete online submission process on
website.

Editors: Pat Blayney; Iain Parke

P0075 Badger Learning
Book Publisher
Unit 55 Oldmedow Road, Hardwick Industrial
Estate, King's Lynn, Norfolk, PE30 4JJ
United Kingdom
Tel: +44 (0) 1553 816082
Fax: +44 (0) 1553 768646

info@badger-publishing.co.uk

https://www.badgerlearning.co.uk
https://twitter.com/@BadgerLearning
https://en-gb.facebook.com/badger.learning

ACADEMIC > **Nonfiction** > *Nonfiction
Books*

English; History; Mathematics; Science

CHILDREN'S
Fiction
Chapter Books; *Early Readers*; *Middle
Grade*
Nonfiction > *Nonfiction Books*

TEEN
Fiction > *Novels*
Nonfiction > *Nonfiction Books*

YOUNG ADULT
Fiction > *Novels*
Nonfiction > *Nonfiction Books*

Publishes books for UK schools, particularly
books to engage reluctant and struggling
readers.

P0076 Baker Publishing Group
Book Publisher
6030 East Fulton Road, Ada, MI 49301
United States
Tel: +1 (616) 676-9185
Fax: +1 (616) 676-9573

http://bakerpublishinggroup.com

Fiction > *Novels*: Christianity

Nonfiction > *Nonfiction Books*: Christianity

Publishes high-quality writings that represent
historic Christianity and serve the diverse
interests and concerns of evangelical readers.

Book Publishers: Baker Academic; Baker
Books; Brazos Press; Chosen Books; Fleming
H. Revell

P0077 Ballantine
Publishing Imprint

Book Publisher: Random House (**P0690**)

P0078 Balzer + Bray
Publishing Imprint

Book Publisher: HarperCollins

P0079 Bantam
Publishing Imprint
United States

http://www.randomhousebooks.com/imprints/

Book Publisher: Random House (**P0690**)

Fiction > *Novels*

Nonfiction > *Nonfiction Books*

How to send: Through a literary agent

Publishes original works of fiction and
nonfiction in all formats.

Magazine: island

P0080 Bantam Books
Publishing Imprint

Book Publisher: Transworld Publishers
(**P0835**)

P0081 Bantam Press
Publishing Imprint

Book Publisher: Transworld Publishers
(**P0835**)

P0082 Baobab Press
Book Publisher
121 California Avenue, Reno, NV 89503
United States
Tel: +1 (775) 786-1188

info@baobabpress.com

https://baobabpress.com

ADULT
 Fiction
  Graphic Novels: General
  Novels: Contemporary; Literary
  Short Fiction: Contemporary; Literary
 Nonfiction
  Essays: General
  Short Nonfiction: Memoir

 Poetry > *Poetry Collections*

CHILDREN'S > **Fiction**
 Board Books; Picture Books

How to send: Submittable

Constantly strives to discover, cultivate, and nurture authors working in all genres. Publishes Creative Nonfiction, Short-Story, Novel, and Comic/Visual Narrative manuscripts (Comic/Visual Narrative manuscripts will not be considered without artwork). Also publishes children's picture and board books (send text with or without artwork). Submit via online submission system.

P0083 Barricade Books
Book Publisher
2005 Palmer Ave, Ste 800, Larchmont, NY 10538
United States

Info@barricadebooks.com

http://www.barricadebooks.com

Nonfiction > *Nonfiction Books*

Editor: Carole Stuart

P0084 Barrington Stoke
Book Publisher
18 Walker Street, Edinburgh, EH3 7LP
United Kingdom
Tel: +44 (0) 131 225 4113

info@barringtonstoke.co.uk

https://www.barringtonstoke.co.uk

Types: Fiction; Nonfiction
Formats: Reference
Markets: Children's; Professional

Closed to approaches.

Commissions books via literary agents only. No unsolicited material. Publishes books for

"reluctant, dyslexic, disenchanted and under-confident" readers and their teachers.

P0085 BatCat Press
Book Publisher
c/o Lincoln Park Performing Arts Charter School, One Lincoln Park, Midland, PA 15059
United States

batcatpress@gmail.com

https://batcatpress.com

Types: Fiction; Nonfiction; Poetry
Formats: Short Fiction
Subjects: Literary
Markets: Adult

Closed to approaches.

Publishes literary fiction, poetry, and creative nonfiction. Submit via online submission system.

P0086 Batsford
Publishing Imprint

Book Publisher: Pavilion Books Group Limited (**P0620**)

P0087 BBC Books
Publishing Imprint
United Kingdom

https://www.penguin.co.uk/company/publishers/ebury/bbc-books.html

Book Publisher: Ebury (**P0247**)

Nonfiction > *Nonfiction Books*
 General, and in particular: Entertainment; Food and Drink; Nature; Popular Culture; TV

Specialises in TV and radio tie-ins, as well as food and drink, nature, and history, etc.

Editor: Stuart Biles

P0088 BCS (British Computer Society)
Book Publisher
United Kingdom
Tel: +44 (0) 1793 417417

publishing@bcs.uk

https://www.bcs.org/

PROFESSIONAL > **Nonfiction** > *Nonfiction Books*
 Business; Cyber Security; Data and Information Systems; Finance; Leadership; Legal; Management; Procurement; Project Management; Service Management; Software Development

Publishes books for business and technology professionals.

Editor: Matthew Flynn

P0089 Be About It Press
Book Publisher
United States

zinebeaboutit@gmail.com

http://beaboutitpress.tumblr.com

Types: Fiction; Poetry
Formats: Short Fiction
Subjects: Literary
Markets: Adult

Publishes zines, ebooks, chapbooks, and other short form creative literature online and in print. Print chapbooks by solicitation only. Ebooks by solicitation or during an announced contest. See website for full details.

P0090 Beach Lane Books
Publishing Imprint

Book Publisher: Simon & Schuster Children's Publishing (**P0768**)

P0091 becker&mayer! books
Publishing Imprint
11120 NE 33rd Place Suite 101, Bellevue, WA 98004
United States
Tel: +1 (425) 827-7120
Fax: +1 (425) 828-9659

mike.oprins@quarto.com

https://www.quartoknows.com/brand/2113/becker-mayer/

Book Publisher: The Quarto Group, Inc. (**P0679**)

Types: Nonfiction
Markets: Adult; Children's

Publishes illustrated nonfiction for adults and children.

Editor: Mike Oprins

P0092 becker&mayer! kids
Publishing Imprint

Book Publisher: The Quarto Group, Inc. (**P0679**)

P0093 Berghahn Books Ltd
Book Publisher
3 Newtec Place, Magdalen Rd, Oxford, OX4 1RE
United Kingdom
Tel: +44 (0) 1865 250011
Fax: +44 (0) 1865 250056

editorial@berghahnbooks.com

https://www.berghahnbooks.com
https://www.facebook.com/BerghahnBooks
https://twitter.com/berghahnbooks
https://www.youtube.com/channel/UCuh-JFDwm_HfzX1zJ92tzcw
https://www.instagram.com/berghahnbooks/

ACADEMIC > **Nonfiction** > *Nonfiction Books*
Anthropology; Archaeology; Culture; Education; Environment; Films; Gender; History; Politics; Sociology; TV; Warfare

Send: Query; Submission Form; Outline
How to send: Email attachment

Academic publisher of books and journals covering the social sciences. Download New Book Outline form from website, complete, and submit by email with an outline and/or chapter summary.

Editor: Marion Berghahn

P0094 **Berkley**
Publishing Imprint

Book Publisher: Penguin Publishing Group (**P0633**)

P0095 **Berrett-Koehler Publishers**
Book Publisher
1333 Broadway, Suite 1000, Oakland, CA 94612
United States
Tel: +1 (510) 817-2277
Fax: +1 (510) 817-2278

bkpub@bkpub.com

https://www.bkconnection.com
https://www.facebook.com/BerrettKoehler
https://twitter.com/Bkpub
https://www.linkedin.com/company/berrett-koehler-publishers/
https://www.pinterest.com/berrettkoehler/
https://www.youtube.com/berrettkoehler

Nonfiction > *Nonfiction Books*
Business; Career Development; Communication; Creativity; Economics; Equality; Leadership; Management

Send: Proposal; Outline; Writing sample; Market info
How to send: PDF file email attachment

Connecting people and ideas to create a world that works for all. Publishes titles that promote positive change at personal, organizational, and societal levels.

Senior Editor: Jeevan Sivasubramaniam

P0096 **Bess Press**
Book Publisher
3565 Harding Avenue, Honolulu, HI 96816
United States
Tel: +1 (808) 734-7159
Fax: +1 (808) 732-3627

submission@besspress.com

https://www.besspress.com

ACADEMIC > **Nonfiction** > *Nonfiction Books*
Hawai'i; Pacific

ADULT
Fiction > *Novels*
Hawai'i; Pacific

Nonfiction > *Nonfiction Books*
Biography; Hawai'i; Memoir; Pacific

CHILDREN'S > **Fiction**
Activity Books: Hawai'i; Pacific
Board Books: Hawai'i; Pacific
Picture Books: Hawai'i; Pacific

Send: Query
How to send: Email

Publishes books about Hawai'i and the Pacific. All submissions should be sent by email. See website for full guidelines.

P0097 **Between the Lines**
Book Publisher
401 Richmond Street West, Studio 281, Toronto, Ontario M5V 3A8
Canada
Tel: +1 (416) 535-9914

info@btlbooks.com
submissions@btlbooks.com

https://btlbooks.com
http://twitter.com/readBTLbooks
http://facebook.com/BTLbooks
https://www.instagram.com/btlbooks

Nonfiction > *Nonfiction Books*
Politics; Social Issues

How to send: Email

We publish nonfiction books that expose and challenge oppression in our society. We aim to amplify the struggles of Black, Indigenous, and racialized communities; migrants; women; queer folks; and working-class people. We are proudly left-wing and the books we publish reflect our activist roots and our commitment to social justice struggles. Our authors are academics, journalists, artists, and activists—all our authors hope their books will spark political and social change.

Acquisitions Editor: Paul Eprile

P0098 **Birlinn Ltd**
Book Publisher
West Newington House, 10 Newington Road, Edinburgh, EH9 1QS
United Kingdom

info@birlinn.co.uk

http://birlinn.co.uk
https://www.facebook.com/birlinnbooks/
https://twitter.com/BirlinnBooks
https://www.youtube.com/channel/UChVAhFnMniUb_3XiVmXPT7Q
https://www.instagram.com/birlinnbooks/

Fiction
Novels: Comedy / Humour; Crime; Historical Fiction; Thrillers
Short Fiction Collections: General

Nonfiction > *Nonfiction Books*

Art History; Arts; Biography; Business; Comedy / Humour; Crime; Current Affairs; Folklore, Myths, and Legends; Food; Gaelic; Gardening; Geology; Local History; Memoir; Nature; Photography; Politics; Scotland; Sport; Traditional Music; Travel

Send: Query; Synopsis; Writing sample
How to send: Email
How not to send: Post

Focuses on Scottish material: local, military, and Highland history; humour, adventure; reference, guidebooks, and folklore. No longer accepting submissions for fiction, poetry, or children's books. Submissions for these areas must be made through a literary agent. Continues to accept direct submissions for nonfiction.

P0099 **Bitter Lemon Press**
Book Publisher
47 Wilmington Square, London, WC1X 0ET
United Kingdom
Tel: +44 (0) 20 7278 3738

books@bitterlemonpress.com

http://www.bitterlemonpress.com

Types: Fiction
Subjects: Crime; Literary; Thrillers
Markets: Adult

How to send: Through a literary agent

Accepts submissions in the literary crime and thriller genres. Submissions may be sent by email and must come through a literary agent.

P0100 **The Bitter Oleander Press**
Book Publisher; Magazine Publisher
4983 Tall Oaks Drive, Fayetteville, NY 13066-9776
United States

info@bitteroleander.com

https://www.bitteroleander.com

Poetry > *Any Poetic Form*

Closed to approaches.

Publishes poetry collections and a journal of poetry and short fiction.

Magazine: The Bitter Oleander

P0101 **Black & White Publishing Ltd**
Book Publisher
Nautical House, 104 Commercial Street, Edinburgh, EH6 6NF
United Kingdom
Tel: +44 (0) 1316 254500
Fax: +44 (0) 1316 254501

submissions@blackandwhitepublishing.com
mail@blackandwhitepublishing.com

https://blackandwhitepublishing.com
https://twitter.com/bwpublishing
https://www.facebook.com/
blackandwhitepublishing/
https://www.instagram.com/bwpublishing/
https://www.youtube.com/user/
blackandwhitePub

Fiction > *Novels*

Nonfiction > *Nonfiction Books*
Celebrity Memoir; Comedy / Humour; Food
and Drink; Ireland; Lifestyle; Nature;
Scotland; Sport

Send: Query; Proposal
How to send: Email; Through a literary agent

Publisher of general fiction and nonfiction. See
website for an idea of the kind of books
normally published. Accepts fiction
submissions during specific submission
windows only, or through a literary agent year-
round. Check website for details and to submit
via online submission system. No poetry, short
stories, or work in languages other than
English.

Editors: Campbell Brown; Alison McBride

Publishing Imprints: Ink Road (*P0437*); Itchy
Coo (*P0445*)

P0102 **Black Cat**
Publishing Imprint
United States

Book Publisher: Grove Atlantic Inc. (**P0345**)

P0103 **Black Coffey Publishing**
Book Publisher
23 Cromwell rd, Warley, Brentwood, Essex,
CM14 5DT
United Kingdom

Paul@blackcoffeypublishing.com

http://www.blackcoffeypublishing.com

Types: Fiction
Formats: Short Fiction
Subjects: Adventure; Comedy / Humour;
Commercial; Contemporary; Crime; Drama;
Fantasy; Mystery; Satire; Science Fiction;
Suspense; Thrillers; Westerns
Markets: Adult; Young Adult

Closed to approaches.

**Not accepting submissions as at January
2019. Check website for current
status.** Specialist digital publisher actively
looking for short stories in our 2012 release
schedule. We scheduled to publish humorous
short story collections on: + 'Office life' +
'Growing up in the 1970s' + 'Leaving home
for the first time' Submissions can be made via
our website.

Editor: Paul Coffey

P0104 **Black Dog & Leventhal**
Publishing Imprint
United States

Book Publisher: Perseus Books (**P0641**)

P0105 **Black Heron Press**
Book Publisher
PO Box 614, Anacortes, WA 98221
United States

https://blackheronpress.com

Fiction > *Novels:* Literary

Send: Query; Writing sample; Self-Addressed
Stamped Envelope (SASE)
How to send: Post

Publisher of literary fiction. No submissions or
queries by email. Send query with first 30-40
pages by post with SASE.

Publisher: Jerry Gold

P0106 **Black Lizard**
Publishing Imprint
United States

Book Publisher: Knopf Doubleday Publishing
Group (**P0475**)

P0107 **Black Swan**
Publishing Imprint

Book Publisher: Transworld Publishers
(**P0835**)

P0108 **Black Velvet
Seductions**
Book Publisher
United States

https://blackvelvetseductions.com
https://www.facebook.com/
blackvelvetseductions/
https://twitter.com/BVSBooks
https://www.instagram.com/bvsbooks/
https://www.pinterest.com/BVSPublishing/

Fiction > *Novels*
Adventure; Contemporary; Erotic; Fantasy;
Historical Fiction; Supernatural /
Paranormal; Thrillers; Westerns

Send: Full text; Synopsis
How to send: Online submission system

We are looking for a marriage of the romance
genre (think Harlequin, Silhouette, MIRA)
with a much higher degree of eroticism. We
want all of the emotional impact, all the angst,
all the character development, and all the
conflict you would find in any traditional
romance novel. But we want it to go several
steps beyond the normal romance when it
comes to sexual content and eroticism.

Stories may include any of the tried and true
plot elements that have worked in romance
novels for years. For example, authors can use
secret baby, forced marriage, marriage of

convenience, revenge, etc. as elements of their
stories.

While we want a higher level of eroticism and
a greater diversity of sexual activity in our
books we do not want books that sacrifice the
romance's story line in an effort to force a
quick sexual pace. We believe the specific
story and the make-up of the characters should
decide the placement and frequency of sex
scenes and we give authors wide latitude.

There are very few taboos in our line but the
following are very firm. We do not want to see
material containing bestiality, necrophilia or
paedophilia.

Editor: Laurie Sanders

P0109 **Blackfriars**
Publishing Imprint

Publishing Imprint: Little, Brown Book Group
(**P0502**)

P0110 **Blackstaff Press**
Book Publisher
Jubilee Business Park, 21 Jubilee Road,
Newtownards, BT23 4YH
United Kingdom
Tel: +44 (0) 28 9182 6339

info@blackstaffpress.com

https://blackstaffpress.com
https://facebook.com/Blackstaffpressni
https://twitter.com/BlackstaffNI

Fiction > *Novels*

Nonfiction > *Nonfiction Books*
General, and in particular: Biography;
History; Ireland; Memoir; Northern Ireland;
Politics; Sport

Closed to approaches.

Focuses on subjects of interest to the Irish
market, both north and south. However, will
consider other proposals if they are strong
enough to generate interest from farther afield
and specially if there is a connection to Ireland.

Editor: Patsy Horton

Publishing Imprint: Beeline

P0111 **Bloodaxe Books Ltd**
Book Publisher
Eastburn, South Park, Hexham,
Northumberland, NE46 1BS
United Kingdom
Tel: +44 (0) 01434 611581

editor@bloodaxebooks.com
submissions@bloodaxebooks.com

https://www.bloodaxebooks.com

Poetry > *Poetry Collections*

Send: Writing sample; Self-Addressed
Stamped Envelope (SASE)

How to send: Post
How not to send: Email

Submit poetry only if you have a track record of publication in magazines. If so, send sample of up to a dozen poems with SAE. No submissions by email or on disk. Poems from the UK sent without return postage will be recycled unread; submissions by email will be deleted unread. No longer accepting poets who have already published a full-length collection with another publisher. Considers North American poets by invitation or recommendation only. See website for full details.

Editorial Director: Neil Astley

P0112 Bloomsbury Publishing Plc

Book Publisher
50 Bedford Square, London, WC1B 3DP
United Kingdom

https://www.bloomsbury.com
https://www.facebook.com/BloomsburyPublishing/
https://www.instagram.com/bloomsburypublishing/
https://twitter.com/BloomsburyBooks
https://www.youtube.com/bloomsburypublishing

ACADEMIC > **Nonfiction** > *Nonfiction Books*

ADULT
  Fiction > *Novels*
  Nonfiction > *Nonfiction Books*

CHILDREN'S > **Fiction** > *Novels*

PROFESSIONAL > **Nonfiction** > *Nonfiction Books*

YOUNG ADULT > **Fiction** > *Novels*

Publishes books for the adult, academic, professional, children's, and young adult markets.

Book Publishers: A & C Black Publishers Limited; Bloomsbury Spark; Walker & Company

Publishing Imprint: Absolute Press

P0113 Blue Guides Limited
Book Publisher
Winchester House, Dean Gate Avenue, Taunton, Somerset, TA1 2UH
United Kingdom

editorial@blueguides.com

http://blueguides.com

Types: Nonfiction
Subjects: Culture; Travel
Markets: Adult

Publishes travel guides. Always on the lookout for new authors. Contact by email in first instance, giving an indication of your areas of interest.

P0114 Blue Lamp Books
Publishing Imprint
United Kingdom

https://mangobooks.co.uk/pages/about-mango-books

Book Publisher: Mango Books (**P0526**)

Nonfiction > *Nonfiction Books*: Police History

Publishes nonfiction books on police history.

P0115 Blue Rider Press
Publishing Imprint
United States

Book Publisher: Penguin Publishing Group (**P0633**)

P0116 Blue Star Press
Book Publisher
Bend, OR
United States

brenna@bluestarpress.com
contact@bluestarpress.com

https://www.bluestarpress.com

Nonfiction > *Nonfiction Books*
  Arts; Comedy / Humour; Creativity; Wellbeing

Send: Submission Form
How to send: Email

Focuses on the arts, creative processes, wellness, and witty non-fiction.

P0117 Bluemoose Books Ltd
Book Publisher
25 Sackville Street, Hebden Bridge, HX7 7DJ
United Kingdom

kevin@bluemoosebooks.com

http://www.bluemoosebooks.com

Types: Fiction
Markets: Adult

Send: Query
Don't send: Full text

Send query with synopsis and first three chapters by email. No unsolicited MSS, children's books, or young adult.

Editors: Hetha Duffy; Kevin Duffy

P0118 BMM
Publishing Imprint

Book Publisher: SportsBooks Limited (**P0784**)

P0119 BOA Editions, Ltd
Book Publisher
250 North Goodman Street, Suite 306, Rochester, NY 14607
United States
Tel: +1 (585) 546-3410

contact@boaeditions.org

https://www.boaeditions.org

Fiction > *Short Fiction Collections*: Literary

Nonfiction > *Nonfiction Books*
  Literature; Poetry as a Subject

Poetry in Translation > *Poetry Collections*

Poetry > *Poetry Collections*

Closed to approaches.

Publisher of literary fiction, poetry, and prose about poetry and poetics. Specific reading periods (see website). Also runs annual poetry and fiction competitions. See website for more details.

Editors: Peter Conners; Nora A. Jones; Thom Ward

P0120 The Bodley Head
Publishing Imprint
United Kingdom

Book Publisher: Vintage (**P0891**)

P0121 Bonneville Books
Publishing Imprint

Book Publisher: Cedar Fort (**P0156**)

P0122 Bonnier Books (UK)
Book Publisher
4th Floor, Victoria House, Bloomsbury Square, London, WC1B 4DA
United Kingdom
Tel: +44 (0) 20 3770 8883

hello@bonnierbooks.co.uk

https://www.bonnierbooks.co.uk

ADULT
  Fiction > *Novels*
  Nonfiction > *Nonfiction Books*

CHILDREN'S
  Fiction
    Chapter Books; Early Readers; Picture Books
  Nonfiction > *Nonfiction Books*

How to send: Through a literary agent

Publishes adult fiction and nonfiction, and children's books. Accepts approaches through a literary agent only.

Book Publishers: Autumn Publishing Ltd (**P0065**); Hot Key Books (**P0417**)

Publishing Imprint: Templar Books (**P0815**)

P0123 Book House
Publishing Imprint

Book Publisher: The Salariya Book Company (**P0729**)

P0124 Book Sales
Publishing Imprint

Book Publisher: The Quarto Group, Inc. (**P0679**)

P0125 Bookouture
Book Publisher
United Kingdom

http://www.bookouture.com
https://twitter.com/bookouture

Book Publisher: Hachette UK (**P0354**)

Fiction > *Novels*
Book Club Fiction; Chick Lit; Commercial; Contemporary Romance; Cozy Mysteries; Crime; Domestic Suspense; Historical Fiction; Multicultural; Police Procedural; Psychological Thrillers; Romantic Comedy; Thrillers; Women's Fiction

Nonfiction > *Nonfiction Books*

Send: Full text
How to send: Online submission system

Publishes commercial fiction and some text-lead nonfiction.

For most authors outside the bestseller lists, traditional publishers simply aren't adding enough value to justify low royalty rates. And because authors aren't all experts in editing, design, or marketing, self-publishing doesn't get the most out of their books or time. Digital publishing offers incredible opportunities to connect with readers all over the world – but finding the help you need to make the most of them can be tricky.

That's why we bring both big publisher experience and small team creativity. We genuinely understand and invest in brands – developing long-term strategies, marketing plans and websites for each of our authors.

And we work with the most brilliant editorial, design and marketing professionals in the business to make sure that everything we do is perfectly tailored to you and ridiculously good.

Combine all of that with an incredible 45% royalty rate we think we're simply the perfect combination of high returns and inspirational publishing.

P0126 The Borough Press
Publishing Imprint
United Kingdom

Book Publisher: HarperCollins UK (**P0382**)

P0127 Brava
Publishing Imprint

Book Publisher: Kensington Publishing Corp. (**P0469**)

P0128 Breedon Books
Publishing Imprint
United Kingdom

Book Publisher: Brewin Books Ltd (**P0129**)

P0129 Brewin Books Ltd
Book Publisher
19 Enfield Ind. Estate, Redditch, Worcestershire, B97 6BY
United Kingdom
Tel: +44 (0) 1527 854228
Fax: +44 (0) 1527 60451

admin@brewinbooks.com

https://www.brewinbooks.com
http://www.facebook.com/brewinbooks
http://www.twitter.com/brewinbooks

ADULT
Fiction > *Novels*
Contemporary; Ghost Stories

Nonfiction > *Nonfiction Books*
Arts; Biography; Comedy / Humour; Creativity; Family; Health; History; Memoir; Military History; Military; Music; Police; Social History; Sport; The Midlands; Transport; Wellbeing

CHILDREN'S
Fiction
Novels; Picture Books
Nonfiction > *Nonfiction Books*

Send: Query; Synopsis; Author bio
How to send: Email; Post

Publishes regional books on Midland history in the areas of the police, hospitals, the military, family, social and biographies. Also publishes contemporary fiction and books for children. Welcomes submissions from aspiring authors.

Authors: Rob Blakeman; Carl Chinn; Alton Douglas; Brian Drew; Audrey Duggan; Jean Field; Jill Fraser; Gwen Freeman; Patrick Hayes; Nick Owen; Shirley Thompson

Publishing Imprints: Breedon Books (*P0128*); Brewin Books; History into Print; Hunt End Books (*P0423*); Richards Publishing (*P0704*)

P0130 Bridge House Publishing LLP
Book Publisher
United Kingdom

editor@bridgehousepublishing.co.uk

http://www.bridgehousepublishing.co.uk

Fiction > *Short Fiction*

An independent publishing house that specialises in fiction which is a little bit different. We focus mainly on short story collections. Run by writers for writers we do it all for love but we like to give new writers a voice.

Editor: Debz Hobbs-Wyatt

P0131 Bright Press
Publishing Imprint

Book Publisher: The Quarto Group, Inc. (**P0679**)

P0132 Bristol University Press
Book Publisher
1-9 Old Park Hill, Bristol, BS2 8BB
United Kingdom
Tel: +44 (0) 1179 545940

bup-info@bristol.ac.uk

http://bristoluniversitypress.co.uk

Types: Nonfiction
Subjects: Business; Current Affairs; Finance; Legal; Nature; Politics; Sociology
Markets: Academic

Send: Query
Don't send: Full text

Publishes scholarship and education in the social sciences. Send query with proposal by email.

Publishing Imprint: Policy Press (*P0659*)

P0133 The British Academy
Book Publisher
10–11 Carlton House Terrace, London, SW1Y 5AH
United Kingdom
Tel: +44 (0) 20 7969 5200

pubs@thebritishacademy.ac.uk

https://www.thebritishacademy.ac.uk
https://www.thebritishacademy.ac.uk/publishing/

ACADEMIC > **Nonfiction** > *Nonfiction Books*
Archaeology; Culture; History; Philosophy; Society

Registered charity publishing not for profit. Publishes humanities and social sciences, particularly history, philosophy, and archaeology.

P0134 The British Museum Press
Book Publisher
British Museum, Great Russell Street, London, WC1B 3DG
United Kingdom
Tel: +44 (0) 20 7323 8528

publicity@britishmuseum.org

https://www.britishmuseum.org/about_us/services/the_british_museum_press.aspx

Types: Nonfiction
Subjects: Archaeology; Arts; Culture; History
Markets: Academic; Adult; Children's

Publishes books inspired by the collections of the British Museum, covering fine and decorative arts, history, archaeology and world cultures.

P0135 Broadside Books
Publishing Imprint

Book Publisher: HarperCollins

P0136 Bromley House Editions
Publishing Imprint

Book Publisher: Five Leaves Publications (**P0295**)

P0137 Brow Books
Book Publisher
Australia

info@browbooks.com

http://www.browbooks.com

Types: Fiction; Nonfiction; Translations
Formats: Short Fiction
Subjects: Literary
Markets: Adult

Send: Full text

Publishes literary fiction and nonfiction, including translations. Accepts submissions from anyone who identifies as Australian, particularly those who "identify as queer and/or trans and/or intersex and/or are of any colour, religion, or gender, and/or have a disability" [sic]. Submit via online submission system.

P0138 Burgess Lea Press
Publishing Imprint

Book Publisher: The Quarto Group, Inc. (**P0679**)

P0139 Burning Chair
Book Publisher
United Kingdom

info@burningchairpublishing.com

https://burningchairpublishing.com

Fiction > *Novels*
  Adventure; Commercial; Crime; Historical Fiction; Horror; Mystery; Supernatural / Paranormal; Suspense; Thrillers

Closed to approaches.

We promise to always put our authors and their books first with: an open, supportive and collaborative approach; fair royalties; tailored, cutting edge production, marketing and promotion.

P0140 C&T Publishing
Book Publisher
1651 Challenge Drive, Concord, CA 94520-5206
United States

support@ctpub.com

https://www.ctpub.com

Nonfiction > *Nonfiction Books*
  Embroidery; Quilting; Sewing

Publishes books on sewing and related crafts.

Publishing Imprints: Crosley-Griffith (*P0200*); FunStitch Studio (*P0311*); Kansas City Star Quilts; Stash Books (*P0797*)

P0141 Caitlin Press Inc.
Book Publisher; Ebook Publisher
3375 Ponderosa Way, Qualicum Beach, BC, V9K 2J8
Canada
Tel: +1 (604) 741-4200

vici@caitlin-press.com

https://caitlin-press.com
http://facebook.com/caitlinbooks
http://twitter.com/caitlinpress
http://instagram.com/caitlinpress.
daggereditions

ADULT
Fiction
  Novels: General, and in particular: Adventure
  Short Fiction Collections: General

Nonfiction
  Essays: General
  Nonfiction Books: General, and in particular: Arts; Biography; British Columbia; Comedy / Humour; Cookery; History; Memoir; Nature; Outdoor Activities; Photography; Politics; Sport; Travel; Women's Issues; Women's Studies
Poetry > *Poetry Collections*

CHILDREN'S > **Fiction** > *Novels*

Send: Query; Outline; Author bio; Writing sample
Don't send: Full text
How to send: Post
How not to send: Email

Publishes books on topics concerning or by writers from the British Columbia Interior and stories about and by British Columbia women. No submissions by email. See website for full guidelines.

Editors: Sarah Corsie; Vici Johnstone; Holly Vestad

P0142 Calder Publications Ltd
Publishing Imprint
3 Castle Yard, Richmond TW10 6TF
United Kingdom
Tel: +44 (0) 20 8940 6917

info@almabooks.com

https://almabooks.com/product-category/calder-collection/?imprint=4

Book Publisher: Alma Books Ltd (**P0031**)

Types: Fiction; Nonfiction; Poetry; Scripts
Formats: Theatre Scripts
Subjects: Autobiography; Drama; Fantasy; Literary; Literary Criticism; Music; Politics; Sociology
Markets: Adult

Closed to approaches.

Publishes a wide range of material, with a reputation for being controversial. Not accepting any new material.

P0143 Cambridge University Press
Book Publisher
Shaftesbury Road, Cambridge, CB2 8EA
United Kingdom
Tel: +44 (0) 1223 553311

directcs@cambridge.org

https://www.cambridge.org
https://www.facebook.com/CambridgeUniversityPress
https://twitter.com/CambridgeUP
https://www.youtube.com/CambridgeUP
https://www.linkedin.com/company/cambridge-university-press
https://instagram.com/cambridgeuniversitypress

ACADEMIC > **Nonfiction** > *Nonfiction Books*
  Animals; Anthropology; Archaeology; Arts; Astronomy; Biology; Chemistry; Classics / Ancient World; Computer Science; Culture; Economics; Education; Engineering; Environment; Geography; History; Language; Legal; Literature; Management; Mathematics; Medicine; Music; Philosophy; Physics; Politics; Psychology; Religion; Science; Sociology; Statistics; Theatre

World's oldest publisher, with offices around the world. Publishes nonfiction, reference, academic textbooks, educational material, and academic journals. No fiction or poetry.

P0144 Candlemark & Gleam
Book Publisher
United States

eloi@candlemarkandgleam.com

https://www.candlemarkandgleam.com

Types: Fiction
Subjects: Fantasy; Science Fiction
Markets: Adult

Publishes mainly science fiction, but also speculative fiction, broadly defined. Cross-genre/interstitial and SF/F hybrid works are fine; ones with mythic/historical echoes even better. Send query by email with one-page synopsis and 10 pages (or, for medium works (12-42K), the complete ms) as attachments. See website for full guidelines.

P0145 Candy Jar Books
Book Publisher
Mackintosh House, 136 Newport Road,
Cardiff, CF24 1DJ
United Kingdom
Tel: +44 (0) 29 2115 7202

shaun@candyjarbooks.co.uk

http://www.candyjarbooks.co.uk

Types: Fiction; Nonfiction
Markets: Adult; Young Adult

Send: Full text

Award-winning independent book publisher,
publishing a wide variety of books, from
nonfiction, general fiction and children's,
through to a range of cult TV books. Submit by
post or using online submission form. No
children's picture books. See website for full
guidelines.

Publishing Director: Shaun Russell

P0146 Canongate Books
Book Publisher
14 High Street, Edinburgh, EH1 1TE
United Kingdom
Tel: +44 (0) 1315 575111

info@canongate.co.uk

https://canongate.co.uk

Types: Fiction; Nonfiction; Translations
Subjects: Autobiography; Comedy / Humour;
Culture; History; Literary; Politics; Science;
Travel
Markets: Adult

How to send: Through a literary agent

Publisher of a wide range of literary fiction and
nonfiction, with a traditionally Scottish slant
but becoming increasingly international.
Publishes fiction in translation under its
international imprint. No children's books,
poetry, or drama. Accepts submissions through
literary agents only.

Publishing Imprints: Canongate Classics
(*P0147*); Canongate International (*P0148*)

P0147 Canongate Classics
Publishing Imprint

Book Publisher: Canongate Books (**P0146**)

P0148 Canongate International
Publishing Imprint

Book Publisher: Canongate Books (**P0146**)

P0149 Canopus Publishing Ltd
Book Publisher
United Kingdom

robin@canopusbooks.com

http://www.canopusbooks.com

Types: Nonfiction
Subjects: Arts; Science; Technology
Markets: Academic; Adult

Publishes books spanning the arts and sciences,
including physics, astronomy, and engineering.

Editor: Robin Rees

P0150 Carina Press
Publishing Imprint
United States

submissions@carinapress.com
CustomerService@Harlequin.com

https://www.carinapress.com
https://www.writeforharlequin.com/carina-
press-submission-guidelines/
https://www.facebook.com/CarinaPress
https://carinapress.submittable.com/submit

Book Publisher: Harlequin Enterprises (**P0361**)

Fiction > *Novels*
Contemporary Romance; Erotic Romance;
Fantasy Romance; Historical Romance;
Mystery; Romantic Suspense; Science
Fiction; Supernatural / Paranormal Romance;
Urban Fantasy

Send: Query; Full text; Synopsis
How to send: Submittable
How not to send: Email

Digital-first adult fiction imprint. See website
for details submission guidelines and to submit
via online submission system.

Editors: Kerri Buckley; Stephanie Doig

P0151 Carolrhoda Lab
Publishing Imprint

Book Publisher: Lerner Publishing Group
(**P0487**)

P0152 Cartwheel Books
Publishing Imprint

Book Publisher: Scholastic (**P0740**)

P0153 Castle Point Books
Publishing Imprint

Publishing Imprint: St Martin's Press (**P0789**)

P0154 The Catholic University of America Press
Book Publisher
620 Michigan Ave NE, 240 Leahy Hall,
Washington, DC 20064
United States

https://www.cuapress.org
https://www.facebook.com/CUAPR/
https://twitter.com/CUAPress

ACADEMIC > **Nonfiction** > *Nonfiction Books*
Christianity; History; Language; Literature;
Medieval; Philosophy; Politics; Religion

ADULT > **Nonfiction** > *Nonfiction Books*
Christianity; History; Language; Literature;
Medieval; Philosophy; Politics; Religion

Send: Query; Proposal; Table of Contents;
Author bio; Market info; Self-Addressed
Stamped Envelope (SASE)
How to send: Post; Email

Publishes books disseminating scholarship in
the areas of theology, philosophy, church
history, and medieval studies. Send query with
outline, CV, sample chapter, and publishing
history.

Acquisitions Editor: John Martino

Editorial Director: Trevor Lipscombe

P0155 Catnip Publishing Ltd
Book Publisher
Hathaway House, Popes Drive, London, N3
1QF
United Kingdom

http://www.catnippublishing.co.uk
https://www.facebook.com/catnipbooks/

CHILDREN'S > **Fiction**
Novels; Picture Books
TEEN > **Fiction** > *Novels*

YOUNG ADULT > **Fiction** > *Novels*

Publishes fiction for children of all ages, from
picture books to teen.

Editor: Non Pratt

Publishing Imprints: Happy Cat; Happy Cat
First Readers

P0156 Cedar Fort
Book Publisher
2373 W. 700, S. Springville, UT 84663
United States
Tel: +1 (801) 489-4084

http://www.cedarfort.com

Types: Fiction; Nonfiction
Formats: Short Fiction
Subjects: Adventure; Comedy / Humour;
Fantasy; History; Mystery; Religion;
Romance; Science Fiction; Self Help; Thrillers
Markets: Adult; Children's; Young Adult

Send: Full text

Publishes books with strong moral or religious
values that inspire readers to be better people.
No poetry, short stories, or erotica. See website
for full submission guidelines, and to submit
using online submission system.

Publishing Imprints: Bonneville Books
(*P0121*); CFI (*P0159*); Council Press (*P0193*);
Front Table Books (*P0308*); Hobble Creek
Press (*P0407*); Horizon Publishers (*P0416*);
King Dragon Press (*P0472*); Pioneer Plus
(*P0654*); Plain Sight Publishing (*P0655*);
Sweetwater Books (*P0807*)

P0157 Cengage

Book Publisher
Cheriton House, North Way, Andover, SP10 5BE
United Kingdom
Tel: +44 (0)1264 332424
Fax: +44 (0)1264 342745

EMEAHEPublishing@cengage.com

http://www.cengage.co.uk

Types: Nonfiction
Markets: Academic

Send: Query
Don't send: Full text

Welcomes unsolicited material aimed at students. Send query by email in first instance. See website for full guidelines.

Book Publishers: Gale (**P0314**); KidHaven Press; Zero to Ten Limited

P0158 CF4K

Publishing Imprint
United Kingdom

https://www.christianfocus.com

Book Publisher: Christian Focus Publications (**P0171**)

CHILDREN'S
   Fiction
      Board Books: Christianity; Evangelism
      Chapter Books: Christianity; Evangelism
      Early Readers: Christianity; Evangelism
      Middle Grade: Christianity; Evangelism
      Picture Books: Christianity; Evangelism
   Nonfiction > *Nonfiction Books*
      Christianity; Evangelism

Books for children, including Sunday school and Home school titles.

P0159 CFI

Publishing Imprint

Book Publisher: Cedar Fort (**P0156**)

P0160 Chambers

Publishing Imprint
United Kingdom

enquiries@chambers.co.uk

https://chambers.co.uk
https://www.facebook.com/wordlovers/
https://twitter.com/chamberswords

Book Publisher: John Murray (Publishers) Ltd

Nonfiction
   Puzzle Books: General
   Reference: Language

Publishes dictionaries, thesauruses, and puzzle books, including crosswords.

P0161 Changemakers

Book Publisher
Maryland
United States

office1@jhpbooks.net

https://www.johnhuntpublishing.com/changemakers-books/

Types: Nonfiction
Subjects: Adventure; Anthropology; Archaeology; Autobiography; Business; Commercial; Current Affairs; Lifestyle; Men's Interests; Nature; Philosophy; Psychology; Self Help; Spirituality
Markets: Adult

Send: Full text

Transform your life, transform your world. We publish for individuals committed to transforming their lives and transforming the world. Our readers seek to become positive, powerful agents of change. We inform, inspire, and provide practical wisdom and skills to empower us to write the next chapter of humanity's future.

Authors: Mark Hawthorne; P T Mistleberger; Jayne Morris; Michelle Ray; Neil Richardson; Gleb Tsipursky; Nicholas Vesey; Tim Ward

P0162 Charisma House

Book Publisher
600 Rinehart Rd, Lake Mary, FL 32746
United States
Tel: +1 (407) 333-0600

info@charismamedia.com

https://charismahouse.com
https://www.facebook.com/CharismaHouse/
https://twitter.com/charismahouse
https://www.instagram.com/charismahousebooks/

Media Company: Charisma Media

Fiction > *Novels:* Christianity

Nonfiction > *Nonfiction Books*
   Christian Living; Christianity; Politics

Through the power of the Holy Spirit we inspire people to radically change their world. Providing Spirit-Filled Christians globally with resources to empower them to change their world through the power of the Holy Spirit.

Publishing Imprints: CharismaKids; Creation House Press; Siloam.

P0163 Charles River Press

Book Publisher
United States
Tel: +1 (508) 364-9851

info@charlesriverpress.com

http://www.charlesriverpress.com
https://www.facebook.com/charles.r.press/
https://twitter.com/CharlesRiverLLC

https://www.youtube.com/user/CharlesRiverPress/

ADULT
   Fiction > *Novels:* Erotic
   Nonfiction > *Nonfiction Books:* Sport

YOUNG ADULT > **Fiction** > *Novels*

Send: Author bio; Market info; Synopsis; Full text

Costs: Offers services that writers have to pay for. Also offers editing and design services.

Currently accepting young adult, sports, and erotica manuscripts.

Authors: Richard Herrick; John McMullen; Mike Ryan; Tony Schiavone; Jonathan Womack; Rowena Womack

Editor: Jonathan Womack

P0164 Charlesbridge Publishing

Book Publisher
9 Galen Street, Watertown, MA 02472
United States
Tel: +1 (617) 926-0329
Fax: +1 (800) 926-5775

tradeeditorial@charlesbridge.com

https://www.charlesbridge.com
https://twitter.com/charlesbridge
https://www.facebook.com/CharlesbridgePublishingInc
https://www.pinterest.com/charlesbridge/
https://www.instagram.com/charlesbridgepublishing/
https://charlesbridgebooks.tumblr.com/
https://www.youtube.com/user/Charlesbridge1

CHILDREN'S
   Fiction
      Board Books; *Early Readers*; *Middle Grade*; *Picture Books*
   Nonfiction
      Board Books: General
      Early Readers: General
      Middle Grade: Arts; Biography; History; Mathematics; Nature; Science; Social Issues
      Picture Books: General

Send: Full text
How to send: Word file email attachment; PDF file email attachment
How not to send: In the body of an email

Publishes books for children, with teen and adult imprints.

Publishing Imprints: Charlesbridge Teen (**P0165**); Imagine Publishing (**P0431**)

P0165 Charlesbridge Teen

Publishing Imprint
9 Galen Street, Watertown, MA 02472
United States

Tel: +1 (800) 225-3214
Fax: +1 (800) 926-5775

ya.submissions@charlesbridge.com

https://charlesbridgeteen.com
https://twitter.com/CharlesbridgeYA
https://www.facebook.com/
CharlesbridgePublishingInc/
https://www.pinterest.com/charlesbridge/
https://www.instagram.com/charlesbridgeteen/
http://charlesbridgebooks.tumblr.com/

Book Publisher: Charlesbridge Publishing
(**P0164**)

YOUNG ADULT
Fiction > *Novels*
Nonfiction > *Nonfiction Books*

Send: Query; Synopsis; Writing sample;
Proposal; Outline
How to send: Email attachment

Features storytelling that presents new ideas
and an evolving world. Our carefully curated
stories give voice to unforgettable characters
with unique perspectives. We publish books
that inspire teens to cheer or sigh, laugh or
reflect, reread or share with a friend, and
ultimately, pick up another book. Our mission
– to make reading irresistible!

P0166 Chatto & Windus
Publishing Imprint
United Kingdom

Book Publisher: Vintage (**P0891**)

P0167 Child's Play (International) Ltd
Book Publisher
United Kingdom

office@childs-play.com

http://www.childs-play.com
https://www.facebook.com/ChildsPlayBooks/
https://twitter.com/ChildsPlayBooks
http://pinterest.com/childsplaybooks/
http://www.instagram.com/childsplaybooks/
https://www.youtube.com/channel/
UCik8Eew5rGc2LfpggFgX4Qg

CHILDREN'S
Fiction
Activity Books; *Board Books*; *Picture
Books*
Poetry > *Picture Books*

Closed to approaches.

Specialises in publishing books that allow
children to learn through play. No novels.

Editor: Sue Baker

P0168 Childswork / ChildsPLAY, LLC
Book Publisher
40 Aero Road, Unit #2, Bohemia, NY 11716

United States
Tel: +1 (800) 962-1141

https://childswork.com
https://www.facebook.com/
childsworkchildsplay
https://twitter.com/childswork
https://www.pinterest.com/childswork/
https://www.instagram.com/
childsworkchildsplay/
https://www.youtube.com/
childsworkchildsplay
https://www.linkedin.com/company/
child%27s-work

PROFESSIONAL > **Nonfiction** > *Nonfiction
Books*
Child Psychotherapy; Education; Psychology

How not to send: Post

A leading provider in child therapy resources,
focusing on therapeutic tools used by
counselors, teachers and therapists.

P0169 Choc Lit
Book Publisher
Penrose House, Camberley, Surrey, GU15
2AB
United Kingdom
Tel: +44 (0) 1276 586367

info@choc-lit.com
submissions@choc-lit.com

https://www.choc-lit.com
https://twitter.com/choclituk
https://www.facebook.com/Choc-Lit-
30680012481/
https://www.instagram.com/choclituk/
https://www.youtube.com/channel/
UCLZBZ2qeR5gtOyDoqEjMbQw

Fiction > *Novels*
Contemporary Romance; Fantasy Romance;
Historical Romance; Romance; Romantic
Suspense; Timeslip Romance

Send: Query; Synopsis
How to send: Online submission system

Publishes romance suitable for an adult
audience, between 60,000 and 100,000 words
in length.

Author: Juliet Archer

Publishing Imprint: Ruby Fiction (**P0716**)

P0170 Chris Andrews Publications
Book Publisher
15 Curtis Yard, North Hinksey Lane, Oxford,
OX2 0LX
United Kingdom
Tel: +44 (0) 1865 723404
Fax: +44 (0) 1865 244243

enquiries@cap-ox.com

https://cap-ox.com
https://www.facebook.com/
ChrisAndrewsPublications/

https://twitter.com/capoxford
https://www.instagram.com/capoxford/

Nonfiction > *Coffee Table Books*
Photography; Travel

Publishes souvenir books with photography of
various locations.

Book Publisher: Oxford Picture Library

Publisher: Chris Andrews

P0171 Christian Focus Publications
Book Publisher
Geanies House, Fearn by Tain, Ross-shire,
IV20 1TW
United Kingdom
Tel: +44 (0) 1862 871011

info@christianfocus.com

https://www.christianfocus.com
https://twitter.com/christian_focus
https://www.facebook.com/christianfocus
https://www.linkedin.com/company/
christian%E2%80%93focus%E2%80%93publi
cations-limited

Nonfiction > *Nonfiction Books*: Evangelism

Send: Synopsis; Table of Contents; Writing
sample; Author bio; Submission Form
How to send: Email; Post

A conservative, evangelical publishing house.

Publishing Imprints: CF4K (**P0158**); Christian
Focus; Christian Heritage; Mentor

P0172 Chronicle Books LLC
Book Publisher
680 Second Street, San Francisco, California
94107
United States
Tel: +1 (415) 537 4200

submissions@chroniclebooks.com

https://www.chroniclebooks.com
https://facebook.com/ChronicleBooks
https://twitter.com/ChronicleBooks
https://pinterest.com/ChronicleBooks
https://instagram.com/ChronicleBooks

ADULT > **Nonfiction** > *Nonfiction Books*
Arts; Beauty; Cookery; Design; Fashion;
Interior Design; Photography; Popular
Culture; Relationships

CHILDREN'S
Fiction
Activity Books; *Board Books*; *Chapter
Books*; *Early Readers*; *Middle Grade*;
Picture Books
Nonfiction
Activity Books; *Board Books*; *Chapter
Books*; *Early Readers*; *Middle Grade*;
Picture Books

Send: Query; Outline; Writing sample; Market
info; Author bio
How to send: Email; Post

Publishes nonfiction for adults, and fiction and nonfiction for children. Children submissions must be sent by post; adult submission should be sent by email. See website for full guidelines.

P0173 Church House Publishing
Publishing Imprint

Book Publisher: Hymns Ancient & Modern Ltd (**P0424**)

P0174 Cinnamon Press
Book Publisher
Office 49019, PO Box 92, Cardiff, CF11 1NB
United Kingdom

jan@cinnamonpress.com

https://www.cinnamonpress.com

Fiction > *Novels*

Nonfiction > *Nonfiction Books*

Poetry > *Poetry Collections*

Closed to approaches.

Small-press publisher of full length poetry collections, unique and imaginative novels, and practical and informative nonfiction with wide appeal. Willing to consider most genres as long as writing is thought-provoking, enjoyable, and accessible; but does not publish genre fiction (romantic, erotica, horror or crime), biography, autobiography, academic, technical or how-to. No unsolicited MSS. See website for submission details.

Editor: Jan Fortune

P0175 Citadel Press
Publishing Imprint

Book Publisher: Kensington Publishing Corp. (**P0469**)

P0176 Clairview Books
Book Publisher
Russet, Sandy Lane, West Hoathly, West Sussex, RH19 4QQ
United Kingdom

office@clairviewbooks.com

https://www.clairviewbooks.com
https://www.facebook.com/Clairview-Books-190962737588974/

Nonfiction > *Nonfiction Books*
Arts; Current Affairs; History; Politics; Science; Spirituality

Send: Query; Proposal; Table of Contents; Writing sample
Don't send: Full text
How to send: Email; Post

Publishes nonfiction books which challenge conventional thinking. Send query by post or by email, with outline of around 200 words,

list of chapters, and a sample chapter. No unsolicited MSS.

Authors: Wendy Cook; Howard Storm; Gore Vidal

Managing Director: Mr S. Gulbekian

P0177 Clarion Books
Publishing Imprint
United States

https://www.hmhbooks.com/imprints/clarion

Book Publisher: Houghton Mifflin Harcourt Books for Young Readers Division (**P0418**)

CHILDREN'S
Fiction
Chapter Books; *Middle Grade*; *Picture Books*
Nonfiction > *Nonfiction Books*

Publishes fiction for children (including picture books) and nonfiction for all ages. Began publishing children's fiction and picture books in 1965 and has published many award-winning titles throughout the years. Its distinguished author list includes National Book Award winners, Caldecott, Newbery, Printz, and Sibert Medal and Honor recipients.

Authors: Eve Bunting; Eileen Christelow; Russell Freedman; Mary Downing Hahn; Kate Milford; Linda Sue Park; Catherine Reef; Marilyn Singer

P0178 Clarkson Potter
Publishing Imprint
1745 Broadway, New York, NY 10019
United States
Tel: +1 (212) 782-9000

http://crownpublishing.com/archives/imprint/clarkson-potter

Book Publisher: Random House (**P0690**)

Types: Nonfiction
Subjects: Arts; Commercial; Cookery; Design; Lifestyle; Literary
Markets: Adult

How to send: Through a literary agent

Imprint dedicated to lifestyle, publishing books by chefs, cooks, designers, artists, and writers. Accepts approaches via literary agents only.

P0179 Cleis Press
Book Publisher
221 River St, 9th Fl, Hoboken, NJ 07030
United States
Tel: +1 (212) 431-5455

cleis@cleispress.com
acquisitions@cleispress.com

https://cleispress.com
https://instagram.com/cleis_press
https://twitter.com/cleispress
https://www.facebook.com/CleisPress.Page

https://www.pinterest.com/cleispress/
https://cleispress.tumblr.com/

Fiction > *Novels*
Erotic Romance; Erotic

Nonfiction > *Nonfiction Books*
Feminism; Health; LGBTQIA; Memoir; Relationships; Self Help; Sex; Sexuality; Women's Studies

Send: Query; Author bio; Writing sample
How to send: Email

The largest independent sexuality publishing company in the United States. With a focus on LGBTQ, BDSM, romance, and erotic writing for all sexual preferences.

Publisher: Fr�d�rique Delacoste

P0180 Colin Smythe Ltd
Book Publisher
38 Mill Lane, Gerrards Cross, Buckinghamshire, SL9 8BA
United Kingdom
Tel: +44 (0) 1753 886000
Fax: +44 (0) 1753 886469

info@colinsmythe.co.uk

http://www.colinsmythe.co.uk

Types: Fiction; Nonfiction; Poetry; Scripts
Formats: Theatre Scripts
Subjects: Biography; Drama; Fantasy; History; Hobbies; Literary Criticism; Science Fiction
Markets: Adult

Publishes fiction, nonfiction, drama, and poetry. Particular interest in Irish literature. No unsolicited MSS.

Authors: Hugh Cook; Peter Bander van Duren; James Joyce; Terry Pratchett; Oscar Wilde

Editor: Colin Smythe

P0181 College Press Publishing
Book Publisher
2111 N. Main Street, Suite C, Joplin, MO 64801, PO Box 1132, Joplin, MO 64801
United States
Tel: +1 (800) 289-3300

collpressbooks@gmail.com

https://collegepress.com

Types: Nonfiction
Subjects: Biography; History; Religion
Markets: Adult

Send: Query
Don't send: Full text

Publishes Bible studies, topical studies (biblically based), apologetic studies, historical biographies of Christians, Sunday/Bible School curriculum (adult electives). No poetry, game or puzzle books, books on prophecy from a premillennial or dispensational viewpoint, or any books that do not contain a Christian message. Send query by email or by post with SASE. See website for required contents.

Publishing Imprint: HeartSpring Publishing (*P0398*)

P0182 Collins
Publishing Imprint
United Kingdom

Book Publisher: HarperCollins UK (**P0382**)

P0183 Colourpoint Educational
Book Publisher
Colourpoint House, Jubilee Business Park, 21 Jubilee Road, Newtownards, Northern Ireland, BT23 4YH
United Kingdom
Tel: +44 (0) 28 9182 0505

sales@colourpoint.co.uk

https://colourpointeducational.com
https://twitter.com/ColourpointEdu

ACADEMIC > **Nonfiction** > *Nonfiction Books*
Biology; Business; Chemistry; Design; Digital Technology; English; French; Gaelic; Geography; Health; History; Home Economics / Domestic Science; Legal; Lifestyle; Mathematics; Physical Education; Physics; Politics; Religion; Technology

Send: Query
How to send: Email

Provides textbooks, ebooks and digital resources for Northern Ireland students at Key Stage 3 level, and the CCEA revised specification at GCSE and AS/A2/A-level.

Editor: Wesley Johnston

P0184 Columbia University Press
Book Publisher
61 West 62nd Street, New York, NY 10023
United States
Tel: +1 (212) 459 0600

https://cup.columbia.edu
https://www.facebook.com/ColumbiaUniversityPress
https://twitter.com/Columbiaup
http://www.pinterest.com/columbiaup
http://www.cupblog.org/

ACADEMIC > **Nonfiction** > *Nonfiction Books*
African American; African Diaspora; Animals; Arts; Biography; Business; Climate Science; Economics; Films; Finance; Food; Gender; History; Journalism; Language; Literature; Media; Memoir; Middle East; New York City; Philosophy; Politics; Psychology; Religion; Science; Sexuality; Sociology

Send: Proposal; Table of Contents; Market info; Author bio
How to send: Email

American scholarly publisher based in New York.

Editorial Director: Jennifer Crewe

Publishing Imprint: Wallflower Press

P0185 Concord Theatricals
Literary Agency; Book Publisher
250 W. 57th Street, 6th Floor, New York, NY 10107-0102
United States
Tel: +1 (866) 979-0447

info@concordtheatricals.com

https://www.concordtheatricals.com/

Scripts > *Theatre Scripts*

Closed to approaches.

Publishes plays and represents writers of plays. Deals in well-known plays from Broadway and London's West End.

P0186 Concord Theatricals Ltd
Book Publisher
Aldwych House, 71 – 91 Aldwych, London, WC2B 4HN
United Kingdom
Tel: +44 (0) 20 7054 7298

acquisitions@concordtheatricals.co.uk

https://www.concordtheatricals.co.uk

Scripts > *Theatre Scripts*
Drama; Musicals

Closed to approaches.

Publishes plays only. Send submissions by email only, following the guidelines on the website.

P0187 Constable & Robinson
Publishing Imprint

Publishing Imprint: Little, Brown Book Group (**P0502**)

P0188 Convergent Books
Publishing Imprint

Book Publisher: Random House (**P0690**)

P0189 Cool Springs Press
Publishing Imprint

Book Publisher: The Quarto Group, Inc. (**P0679**)

P0190 Corgi
Publishing Imprint

Book Publisher: Transworld Publishers (**P0835**)

P0191 Cornerstone
Book Publisher

Book Publisher: Penguin Random House UK (**P0635**)

P0192 Corsair
Publishing Imprint

Publishing Imprint: Little, Brown Book Group (**P0502**)

P0193 Council Press
Publishing Imprint

Book Publisher: Cedar Fort (**P0156**)

P0194 Coyote Arts
Book Publisher
PO Box 6690, Albuquerque, NM 87197-6690
United States

jordan@coyote-arts.com

https://coyote-arts.com
https://www.facebook.com/coyoteartsllc/
https://twitter.com/coyoteartsllc
https://instagram.com/coyoteartsllc
https://www.pinterest.com/coyoteartsllc/

Fiction > *Novels*
Arts; Literary

Nonfiction > *Nonfiction Books*: Arts

Poetry > *Any Poetic Form*

A literary arts publisher dedicated to the power of words and images to transform human lives and the environment we inhabit. Publishes works in the genres of poetry, fiction, non-fiction, and drama that engage the sense of wonder and possibility.

P0195 Crabtree Publishing
Book Publisher
347 Fifth Ave, Suite 1402-145, New York, NY 10016
United States
Tel: +1 (212) 496-5040
Fax: +1 (800) 355-7166

http://www.crabtreebooks.com

Types: Nonfiction
Subjects: History; Science; Sociology
Markets: Academic; Children's

Closed to approaches.

Publishes educational books for children. No unsolicited mss -- all material is generated in-house.

P0196 Creative Essentials
Publishing Imprint
United Kingdom

Book Publisher: Oldcastle Books Group (**P0592**)

P0197 Crime & Mystery Club
Publishing Imprint
United Kingdom

Book Publisher: Oldcastle Books Group
(**P0592**)

P0198 Crime Express
Publishing Imprint

Book Publisher: Five Leaves Publications
(**P0295**)

P0199 Croner-i Limited
Book Publisher
240 Blackfriars Road, London, SE1 8NW
United Kingdom
Tel: +44 (0) 800 231 5199

sales@croneri.co.uk

https://www.croneri.co.uk

Types: Nonfiction
Subjects: Business
Markets: Professional

Publishes books and resources for business professionals covering tax and accounting, human resources, health and safety, and compliance.

P0200 Crosley-Griffith
Publishing Imprint
United States

Book Publisher: C&T Publishing (**P0140**)

P0201 Crowerotica Fantasies
Publishing Imprint

Publishing Imprint: Emerentsia Publications
(**P0262**)

P0202 Crown Archetype
Publishing Imprint

Book Publisher: Random House (**P0690**)

P0203 Crown Forum
Publishing Imprint

Book Publisher: Random House (**P0690**)

P0204 The Crowood Press
Book Publisher
The Stable Block, Crowood Lane, Ramsbury, Marlborough, Wiltshire, SN8 2HR
United Kingdom
Tel: +44 (0) 1672 520320

enquiries@crowood.com
submissions@crowood.com

https://www.crowood.com
https://twitter.com/crowoodpress
http://www.facebook.com/TheCrowoodPress
https://www.instagram.com/thecrowoodpress/

Nonfiction > *Nonfiction Books*

Architecture; Arts; Aviation; Cars; Crafts; Crocheting; Cycling; Dance; Dogs; Embroidery; Engineering; Equestrian; Films; Gardening; Home Improvement; Knitting; Lacemaking; Martial Arts; Military History; Model Making; Nature; Performing Arts; Photography; Railways; Sport; Theatre; Transport; Walking

Send: Query; Synopsis; Writing sample; Author bio
Don't send: Full text
How to send: Email; Post

Publishes high-quality books packed with detailed information on specialist interests. Send proposals by post or by email.

Book Publisher: Robert Hale Publishers

Publishing Imprint: J.A. Allen

P0205 Currock Press
Book Publisher
United Kingdom

john.i.clarke@btinternet.com

https://www.currockpress.com

Poetry > *Poetry Collections*

Closed to approaches.

No current plans for any further publications.

Editor: John Clarke

P0206 Custom House
Publishing Imprint

Book Publisher: HarperCollins

P0207 D&B Publishing
Book Publisher
80 Walsingham Road, Hove, BN3 4FF
United Kingdom
Tel: +44 (0) 1273 711443

info@dandbpublishing.com

http://www.dandbpublishing.com

Nonfiction
  Nonfiction Books: Fitness; Health; Mind, Body, Spirit; Running
  Puzzle Books: General

Publishes books related to the body and mind – with books on the Alexander Technique, running and also a highly successful range of puzzle books and bridge books.

Editors: Dan Addelman; Byron Jacobs

P0208 Dafina
Publishing Imprint

Book Publisher: Kensington Publishing Corp.
(**P0469**)

P0209 Dalesman Publishing Co. Ltd
Book Publisher; Magazine Publisher
The Gatehouse, Skipton Castle, Skipton, North Yorkshire, BD23 1AL
United Kingdom
Tel: +44 (0) 1756 693479

jon@dalesman.co.uk

https://www.dalesman.co.uk

Types: Nonfiction
Subjects: Comedy / Humour; Crafts; History; Hobbies; Travel

Publishes regional books covering Yorkshire, and the Lake and Peak districts. Considers unsolicited MSS on relevant topics.

Editor: Jon Stokoe

Magazine: Dalesman (**M0152**)

P0210 Dalkey Archive Press
Book Publisher
6271 E 535 North Road, McLean, IL 61754
United States

subeditor@dalkeyarchive.com

http://www.dalkeyarchive.com

Types: Fiction; Nonfiction; Poetry; Scripts
Subjects: Autobiography; Experimental; Literary; Literary Criticism
Markets: Adult

Publishes primarily literary fiction, with an emphasis on fiction that belongs to the experimental tradition of Sterne, Joyce, Rabelais, Flann O'Brien, Beckett, Gertrude Stein, and Djuna Barnes. Occasionally publishes poetry or nonfiction. Send submissions by email. See website for full guidelines.

P0211 Damaged Goods Press
Book Publisher
United States

editor@damagedgoodspress.com

http://www.damagedgoodspress.com

Types: Nonfiction; Poetry
Subjects: Autobiography
Markets: Adult

Small press specialising in books by queer and trans people. Publishes chapbooks and full-length manuscripts of poetry, micro-memoir, lyric essay, prose poetry, and hybrid nonfiction. Content does not need to be queer or trans related.

P0212 Dancing Girl Press
Book Publisher
United States

dancinggirlpress@yahoo.com

http://www.dancinggirlpress.com

Poetry > *Chapbook*

Send: Full text

Publishes chapbooks by female poets between 12 and 32 pages. No payment, but free 10 copies and 40% discount on further copies.

P0213 Dancing Star Press
Book Publisher
United States

submissions@dancingstarpress.com

https://www.dancingstarpress.com

Types: Fiction
Subjects: Fantasy; Science Fiction
Markets: Adult

Send: Full text

Publishes speculative fiction novellas between 17,500 and 40,000 words in length. Accepts manuscripts by email between April 1 and June 30, and between October 1 and December 31.

P0214 Darby Creek
Publishing Imprint
United States

https://lernerbooks.com/pages/our-imprints

Book Publisher: Lerner Publishing Group
(**P0487**)

CHILDREN'S > Fiction
  Chapter Books; Middle Grade
YOUNG ADULT > Fiction > *Novels*

How to send: Through a literary agent; By referral

Publishes series fiction for emerging, striving, and reluctant readers ages 8 to 18 (grades 4–12). From chapter books to page-turning YA novels, aims to engage readers with strong characters, exciting premises, and accessible formats. Makes reading an adventure instead of a challenge or a chore.

P0215 Darf Publishers
Book Publisher
277 West End Lane, London, NW6 1QS
United Kingdom
Tel: +44 (0) 20 7431 7009
Fax: +44 (0) 20 7431 7655

submissions@darfpublishers.co.uk

https://darfpublishers.co.uk

Types: Fiction; Nonfiction; Translations
Markets: Adult; Children's

Publisher of new and emerging writers from around the world, translated into English. Accepts submissions in any genre. Send query by email with synopsis, three sample chapters, and a brief outline of your background and what qualifies you to write your book.

P0216 Darton, Longman & Todd Ltd
Book Publisher
1 Spencer Court, 140-142 Wandsworth High Street, London, SW18 4JJ
United Kingdom

editorial@darton-longman-todd.co.uk

http://www.darton-longman-todd.co.uk

Types: Fiction; Nonfiction
Formats: Film Scripts; TV Scripts
Subjects: Arts; Autobiography; Comedy / Humour; Cookery; Literature; Religion; Self Help; Sport; Women's Interests
Markets: Adult; Young Adult

Send: Full text

Publishes spritual and theological books – mainly Christian. Send query by email with proposal and sample chapter. See website for full guidelines.

P0217 DAW
Publishing Imprint

Book Publisher: Penguin Publishing Group
(**P0633**)

P0218 Dawn Publications
Publishing Imprint
United States

https://www.sourcebooks.com/dawn-publications.html

Book Publisher: Sourcebooks (**P0779**)

CHILDREN'S > Nonfiction > *Nonfiction Books:* Nature

Publishes creative nonfiction manuscripts for children that relate to nature and science.

P0219 dbS Productions
Book Publisher
PO Box 94, Charlottesville, VA 22902-0094
United States
Tel: +1 (800) 745-1581
Fax: +1 (434) 293-5502

info@dbs-sar.com

http://www.dbs-sar.com

PROFESSIONAL > Nonfiction > *Nonfiction Books:* Search and Rescue

Describes itself as the leader in research and education in behavioral profiles of lost subjects. Always looking for new and interesting publications related to the field of search and rescue. Authors are encouraged to make contact early in the development of their projects.

Editor: Bob Adams

P0220 DC Thomson
Book Publisher
2 Albert Square, Dundee, DD1 9QJ
United Kingdom

innovation@dcthomson.co.uk

http://www.dcthomson.co.uk

Types: Fiction; Nonfiction
Markets: Adult; Children's

Publisher of newspapers, magazines, comics, and books, with offices in Dundee, Aberdeen, Glasgow, and London. For fiction guidelines send large SAE marked for the attention of the Central Fiction Department.

P0221 Dead End Street
Book Publisher
320 North Carson Street, Carson City, Nevada 89701
United States

https://www.deadendstreet.com

Fiction > *Novels*

Nonfiction > *Nonfiction Books*

Formed in 1997 by three lifelong friends to pioneer the still-nascent field of electronic publishing. Through fits and starts and ups and downs, the company continues to successfully publish compelling reads long after its original competitors folded.

Editor: John P. Rutledge

P0222 Deep Overstock Publishing
Book Publisher; Magazine Publisher
Portland, OR
United States

dop@deepoverstock.com
submissions@deepoverstock.com
editors@deepoverstock.com

https://deepoverstock.com
https://www.facebook.com/deepoverstock
https://www.instagram.com/deepoverstock
https://www.twitter.com/deepoverstock

Fiction > *Novels*

Nonfiction > *Nonfiction Books*

Poetry > *Poetry Collections*

Send: Pitch; Author bio
How to send: In the body of an email

Publishes full-length novels and longer works by booksellers and book industry workers.

Magazine: Deep Overstock Magazine (**M0162**)

P0223 Del Rey
Publishing Imprint
United Kingdom

Book Publishers: Ebury (**P0247**); Random House (**P0690**)

P0224 Del Rey/LucasBooks
Publishing Imprint

Book Publisher: Random House (**P0690**)

P0225 Denene Millner Books
Publishing Imprint

Book Publisher: Simon & Schuster Children's Publishing (**P0768**)

CHILDREN'S > **Fiction** > *Picture Books*

P0226 DeVorss & Company
Book Publisher
PO Box 1389, Camarillo, CA 93011-1389
United States

editorial@devorss.com

https://www.devorss.com

Nonfiction > *Nonfiction Books*
Alternative Health; Inspirational; Lifestyle; Mind, Body, Spirit; Religion; Self Help; Spirituality

Send: Query; Outline; Table of Contents; Market info; Author bio; Self-Addressed Stamped Envelope (SASE)
How to send: Email; Post

A book publisher and distributor of Metaphysical, Inspirational, Spiritual, Self-Help, and New Thought titles.

P0227 Dewi Lewis Publishing
Book Publisher
8 Broomfield Road, Heaton Moor, Stockport, SK4 4ND
United Kingdom
Tel: +44 (0) 1614 429450
Fax: +44 (0) 1614 429450

mail@dewilewispublishing.com
dewi.lewis@btconnect.com

https://www.dewilewis.com

Nonfiction > *Illustrated Books*: Photography

Closed to approaches.

Publishes books of photography.

Editors: Dewi Lewis; Caroline Warhurst

P0228 Dey Street Books
Publishing Imprint

Book Publisher: HarperCollins

P0229 Dial Books for Young Readers
Publishing Imprint
United States

Book Publisher: Penguin Young Readers Group (**P0638**)

CHILDREN'S
Fiction
Chapter Books; *Early Readers*; *Middle Grade*; *Picture Books*

Nonfiction
Chapter Books; *Early Readers*; *Middle Grade*; *Picture Books*
YOUNG ADULT
Fiction > *Novels*
Nonfiction > *Nonfiction Books*

Closed to approaches.

Publishes books for children, from beginner readers and picture books, to fiction and nonfiction for middle-grade and young adults. No unsolicited MSS.

Publishing Imprint: Dial Easy-to-Read

P0230 The Dial Press
Publishing Imprint

Book Publisher: Random House (**P0690**)

P0231 Dialogue Books
Publishing Imprint

Publishing Imprint: Little, Brown Book Group (**P0502**)

P0232 Discovery Walking Guides Ltd
Book Publisher
United Kingdom

ask.discovery@ntlworld.com

http://www.dwgwalking.co.uk

Types: Nonfiction
Subjects: Travel
Markets: Adult

Send: Query
Don't send: Full text

Publishes walking guidebooks and maps. Welcomes proposals for new projects. Send query by email. No attachments.

P0233 Diversion Books
Book Publisher
United States
Tel: +1 (212) 961-6390

info@diversionbooks.com
submit@diversionbooks.com

http://www.diversionbooks.com

Nonfiction > *Nonfiction Books*
Business; Crime; Current Affairs; History; Music; Sport

How to send: Through a literary agent

Currently accepting submissions through literary agents only.

Editors: Melanie Madden; Keith Wallman; Mark Weinstein

P0234 DK (Dorling Kindersley Ltd)
Book Publisher
One Embassy Gardens, 8 Viaduct Gardens,

London, SW11 7BW
United Kingdom
Tel: +44 (0) 1206 255678

adulteditorial@uk.dk.com
childreneditorial@uk.dk.com
travelguides@uk.dk.com

https://www.dk.com
https://www.facebook.com/dkbooks.uk
https://twitter.com/DKbooks
https://www.instagram.com/DKbooks/
https://www.youtube.com/user/DKinVideo
https://www.pinterest.co.uk/dkpublishing/

Book Publisher: Penguin Random House

ADULT > **Nonfiction**
Nonfiction Books: Arts; Beauty; Business; Career Development; Comic Books; Crafts; Culture; Education; Films; Fitness; Food and Drink; Gardening; Health; History; Hobbies; Language; Medicine; Nature; Parenting; Photography; Pregnancy; Relationships; Religion; Science; Sport; TV; Transport; Travel
Reference: General

CHILDREN'S > **Nonfiction** > *Nonfiction Books*

How to send: Through a literary agent

Publishes illustrated adult nonfiction and nonfiction for children. No unsolicited MSS. Approach via a literary agent only.

Book Publisher: DK Publishing (**P0235**)

Publishing Imprints: Eyewitness Guides; Eyewitness Travel Guides; Funfax

P0235 DK Publishing
Book Publisher
1450 Broadway, Suite 801, New York, NY 10018
United States

ecustomerservice@randomhouse.com

http://www.dk.com

Book Publisher: DK (Dorling Kindersley Ltd) (**P0234**)

Types: Nonfiction
Subjects: Culture; History; Nature; Science; Travel
Markets: Children's

How to send: Through a literary agent

Publishes highly visual nonfiction for children. Assumes no responsibility for unsolicited mss. Approach through an established literary agent.

P0236 Dodo Ink
Book Publisher
United Kingdom

dodopublishingco@gmail.com

http://www.dodoink.com

Types: Fiction
Subjects: Literary
Markets: Adult

Closed to approaches.

Independent UK publisher aiming to publish three novels per year, in paperback and digital formats. Publishes risk-taking, imaginative novels, that don't fall into easy marketing categories. Closed to submissions as at June 2017.

Editor: Sam Mills

P0237 Dodona
Publishing Imprint

Publishing Imprint: O-Books

P0238 DogHorn Publishing
Book Publisher
United Kingdom

https://www.doghornpublishing.com

Fiction > *Novels*

Nonfiction > *Nonfiction Books*

Poetry > *Poetry Collections*

Scripts > *Theatre Scripts*: Drama

A boutique publisher of challenging and exciting fiction, nonfiction, drama and poetry.

Publishing Imprints: Fruit Bruise Press (*P0310*); Superbia Books (*P0804*)

P0239 Dollarbooks PTY LTD
Book Publisher
20 Langerman Avenue, Milnerton, 7441
South Africa

info@thedollarbooks.com

https://thedollarbooks.com

Types: Fiction; Nonfiction; Poetry; Scripts; Translations
Formats: Film Scripts; Radio Scripts; Reference; Short Fiction; TV Scripts; Theatre Scripts
Subjects: Adventure; Anthropology; Antiques; Archaeology; Architecture; Arts; Autobiography; Beauty; Business; Comedy / Humour; Commercial; Contemporary; Cookery; Crafts; Crime; Culture; Current Affairs; Design; Drama; Entertainment; Erotic; Experimental; Fantasy; Fashion; Finance; Gardening; Gothic; Health; History; How To; Legal; Leisure; Lifestyle; Literary; Literary Criticism; Media; Medicine; Men's Interests; Music; Mystery; Nature; New Age; Philosophy; Photography; Politics; Psychology; Religion; Romance; Satire; Science; Science Fiction; Self Help; Sociology; Sport; Suspense; Technology; Thrillers; Traditional; Travel; Warfare; Westerns; Women's Interests
Markets: Academic; Adult; Children's; Professional; Young Adult

Send: Full text

Revolutionising the publishing industry and this is how it works. You, as an author, simply upload your book content, your cover and your biography, and we sell your work to the world for one US Dollar. We take 30% and you take 70% in royalties. Nobody can sell for less or more than you. You may think that a dollar for a book is very cheap, and you are perfectly correct. This is all about giving and receiving. Would you not rather sell 10 000 copies of your book for 1$ each instead of only a 100 or so copies at $6?

Authors: Craig Anthony Ferreira; Bandana Ojha; Scott Skipper

Editor: Craig Ferreira

P0240 Doubleday
Publishing Imprint
United States

Book Publisher: Knopf Doubleday Publishing Group (**P0475**)

P0241 Down East Books
Publishing Imprint
United States

Book Publisher: The Globe Pequot Press (**P0329**)

P0242 Duncan Petersen Publishing Limited
Book Publisher
Studio 6 82, Silverthorne Road, London, SW8 3HE
United Kingdom
Tel: +44 (0) 20 0147 8220

duncan.petersen@zen.co.uk

http://duncanpetersen.blogspot.com/

Types: Nonfiction
Subjects: Antiques; Travel

Travel publishing house based in London.Publishes Hotel Guides, along with a variety of walking and cycling guides for Britain.

P0243 Dutton
Publishing Imprint
United States

Book Publisher: Penguin Publishing Group (**P0633**)

P0244 Dutton Children's Books
Publishing Imprint
United States

Book Publisher: Penguin Young Readers Group (**P0638**)

P0245 Dynasty Press
Book Publisher
36 Ravensdon Street, Kennington, London, SE11 4AR
United Kingdom
Tel: +44 (0) 7970 066894

admin@dynastypress.co.uk

http://www.dynastypress.co.uk

Types: Nonfiction
Subjects: Biography; History
Markets: Adult

Publishes books connected to royalty, dynasties and people of influence.

P0246 Eastland Press
Book Publisher
PO Box 99749, Seattle, WA 98139
United States
Tel: +1 (206) 931-6957
Fax: +1 (206) 283-7084

info@eastlandpress.com

http://www.eastlandpress.com

Types: Nonfiction
Subjects: Health; Medicine
Markets: Professional

Send: Query
Don't send: Full text

Publishes textbooks for practitioners of Chinese medicine, osteopathy, and other forms of bodywork.

P0247 Ebury
Book Publisher
United Kingdom

Book Publisher: Penguin Random House UK (**P0635**)

Publishing Imprints: BBC Books (**P0087**); Del Rey (*P0223*); Ebury Enterprises (*P0248*); Ebury Press (*P0249*); Pop Press (*P0660*); Rider Books (*P0705*); Vermilion (*P0885*); Virgin Books (*P0896*); WH Allen (*P0922*)

P0248 Ebury Enterprises
Publishing Imprint
United Kingdom

Book Publisher: Ebury (**P0247**)

P0249 Ebury Press
Publishing Imprint
United Kingdom

Book Publisher: Ebury (**P0247**)

P0250 Ecco
Publishing Imprint

Book Publisher: HarperCollins

P0251 Economist Books.
Publishing Imprint

Publishing Imprint: Profile Books (**P0666**)

P0252 Ediciones Lerner
Publishing Imprint

Book Publisher: Lerner Publishing Group
(**P0487**)

P0253 Educator's International Press
Book Publisher
756 Linderman Avenue, Kingston, NY 12401
United States
Tel: +1 (518) 334-0276
Fax: +1 (703) 661-1547

info@edint.com
submissions@edint.com

https://edint.presswarehouse.com

ACADEMIC > **Nonfiction** > *Nonfiction Books*

Send: Query; Synopsis; Author bio; Outline
How to send: Email

Main mission was initially to keep scholarly and educations content in print and to assist established educational authors in keeping their published books in print at a time when many publishers typically put out of print those books that had annual sales totalling less than 500 copies.

Publisher: William Clockel

P0254 Educe Press
Book Publisher
Butte, MT
United States

editor@educepress.com

https://educepress.com

Types: Fiction; Nonfiction; Poetry
Formats: Short Fiction
Subjects: Literary
Markets: Adult

Closed to approaches.

Publishes literary fiction, nonfiction, and poetry. Closed to submissions as at April 2019. Check website for current status.

Editors: Colin Cote; Carrie Seymour

Publisher: Matthew R. K. Haynes

P0255 Egmont Books
Publishing Imprint
United Kingdom

Book Publisher: HarperCollins UK (**P0382**)

P0256 Ekstasis Editions
Book Publisher
United States

ekstasis@islandnet.com

http://www.ekstasiseditions.com

Types: Fiction; Nonfiction; Poetry
Formats: Short Fiction
Subjects: Literary; Spirituality
Markets: Adult; Children's

Send: Query
Don't send: Full text

Usually accepts submissions from Canadian authors only. Send query by post with SAE with sufficient Canadian postage for return, with author bio, synopsis, and first three chapters up to a maximum of 50 pages.

P0257 Electio Publishing
Book Publisher
United States

info@electiopublishing.com

http://www.electiopublishing.com

Types: Fiction
Subjects: Adventure; Autobiography; Fantasy; History; Horror; Literary; Mystery; Religion; Romance; Science Fiction
Markets: Academic; Adult

Closed to approaches.

First and foremost a faith-based publisher, but will consider anything that is marketable to a wide audience, whether it is fiction or nonfiction.

P0258 Eleusinian Press
Book Publisher
United Kingdom

shop@eleusinianpress.co.uk

http://www.eleusinianpress.co.uk
https://www.facebook.com/eleusinianpress

Nonfiction > *Nonfiction Books*
  Music; Politics

A small publisher specialising in madness, music and radical politics.

Authors: Tristam Vivian Adams; Liz Albl; Graham Askey; Michael Burnett; Thomas D'Angelo; Zenon Gradkowski; Esther Leslie; Andrew Roberts; Richard Shrubb; Daniel Spicer; Jan Tchamani; Ben Watson; Kit Withnail; Dave Wood

Editor: Alastair Kemp

P0259 Elliott & Thompson
Book Publisher
2 John Street, London, WC1N 2ES
United Kingdom
Tel: +44 (0) 7973 956107

info@eandtbooks.com
sarah@eandtbooks.com

http://www.eandtbooks.com
https://twitter.com/eandtbooks
https://www.instagram.com/elliottandthompson/

Fiction > *Novels*

Nonfiction
  Gift Books: General
  Nonfiction Books: Arts; Biography; Business; Comedy / Humour; Economics; History; Language; Music; Nature; Politics; Science; Sport

Publishes original and bestselling nonfiction and carefully selected fiction.

P0260 Elm Books
Book Publisher
United States

Leila.ElmBooks@gmail.com

https://www.elm-books.com
https://www.facebook.com/ElmBooks
https://twitter.com/elmbooks

ACADEMIC > **Nonfiction** > *Nonfiction Books*
  Anthropology; History

ADULT
  Fiction > *Novels*
    Fantasy; Mystery; Romance; Science Fiction

  Poetry > *Poetry Collections*

CHILDREN'S > **Fiction**
  Chapter Books; *Early Readers*; *Middle Grade*

Send: Query; Outline; Writing sample
How to send: Email

Small, independent publisher and distributor. Publishes mysteries, romance, science fiction, disability literature, short story anthologies, scholarly publications in history and anthropology, poetry, and multicultural children's books. No picture books. See website for current open calls.

P0261 Elsevier Ltd
Book Publisher
The Boulevard, Langford Lane, Kidlington, Oxford, OX5 1GB
United Kingdom
Tel: +44 (0) 1865 843000
Fax: +44 (0) 1865 843010

https://www.elsevier.com

Types: Nonfiction
Formats: Reference
Subjects: Health; Medicine; Science; Technology
Markets: Academic; Professional

Send: Query
Don't send: Full text

Publisher of medical, scientific, and technical books for the professional and academic markets.

Book Publishers: Morgan Kaufmann Publishers; Reed Business Information (RBI)

P0262 Emerentsia Publications
Publishing Imprint
Sweden

emerentsia.publications@gmail.com

http://www.emerentsiabooks.com

Publishing Imprint: Emerentsia Publications
(**P0262**)

Types: Fiction; Nonfiction
Formats: Short Fiction
Subjects: Erotic; Fantasy; Mystery; Romance;
Science Fiction; Self Help
Markets: Adult

Send: Full text

We write and publish primarily epic fantasy,
science fiction, mystery fiction, urban fantasy
and fairy retellings, but we're working on
expanding our publications as we become
more established.

Authors: Liz Crowe; N. Lee; Nathalie M.L.
Romer

Publishing Imprints: Crowerotica Fantasies
(*P0201*); Emerentsia Publications (**P0262**);
Oh! With Dots (*P0587*)

P0263 Emily Bestler Books
Publishing Imprint

Book Publisher: Simon & Schuster Adult
Publishing (**P0766**)

P0264 Emperor's New Clothes Press
Book Publisher; Consultancy
United States

http://www.encpress.com
https://www.facebook.com/ENCPress/

Fiction > *Novels*

Closed to approaches.

Costs: Offers services that writers have to pay
for.

Submissions on hold, but continue to act as
consultants to those wishing to self-publish.

Editor: Olga Gardner Galvin

P0265 Encyclopedia Britannica (UK) Ltd
Book Publisher
2nd Floor, Unity Wharf, Mill Street, London,
SE1 2BH
United Kingdom
Tel: +44 (0) 20 7500 7800
Fax: +44 (0) 20 7500 7878

enquire@britannica.co.uk

https://britannica.co.uk

ACADEMIC > **Nonfiction** > *Reference*

ADULT > **Nonfiction** > *Reference*

Global digital educational publisher,
publishing information and instructional
products used in schools, universities, homes,
libraries and workplaces throughout the world.

P0266 Enliven
Publishing Imprint

Book Publisher: Simon & Schuster Adult
Publishing (**P0766**)

P0267 Enthusiast Books
Book Publisher
PO Box 352, Pepin, WI 54759
United States
Tel: +1 (715) 381-9755

info@iconobooks.com

http://www.enthusiastbooks.com

Types: Nonfiction
Subjects: History; Hobbies; Travel; Warfare
Markets: Adult

Send: Query
Don't send: Full text

Publishes books for transportation enthusiasts.
Send query with SASE and outline.

P0268 Entrepreneur Press
Book Publisher
United States

books@entrepreneur.com

https://www.entrepreneur.com/press

PROFESSIONAL > **Nonfiction** > *Nonfiction
Books*
   Business; Entrepreneurship; Finance

Send: Outline; Table of Contents; Writing
sample; Market info; Author bio
How to send: Online submission system

An independent publishing company that
publishes titles focusing on starting and
growing a business, personal finance, real
estate and careers. Submit proposals online via
online submission system.

Publisher: Justin Koenigsberger

P0269 Epic Ink
Publishing Imprint

Book Publisher: The Quarto Group, Inc.
(**P0679**)

P0270 Essex Publications
Publishing Imprint
United Kingdom

http://www.uhpress.co.uk/subject-areas/essex-
publications

Book Publisher: University of Hertfordshire
Press (**P0864**)

ACADEMIC > **Nonfiction** > *Nonfiction
Books*: Local History

This series aims to publish important scholarly
studies on the historic county of Essex in
attractive and well-illustrated volumes.

P0271 Everyman Chess
Publishing Imprint
United Kingdom

info@everymanchess.com

https://everymanchess.com
https://www.facebook.com/everymanchess
https://www.twitter.com/everymanchess
https://www.youtube.com/user/
EverymanChessChannel
https://vimeo.com/everymanchess

Book Publisher: Gloucester Publishers (**P0330**)

Nonfiction > *Nonfiction Books*: Chess

Describes itself as the world's preeminent
chess book publisher.

P0272 Everyman's Library
Publishing Imprint
United States

Book Publisher: Knopf Doubleday Publishing
Group (**P0475**)

P0273 Everything With Words
Book Publisher
United Kingdom

info@everythingwithwords.com

http://www.everythingwithwords.com

ADULT > **Fiction** > *Novels*: Literary

CHILDREN'S > **Fiction** > *Novels*

How to send: Email

Publishes fiction for adults and children,
including short story anthologies. No picture
books or stories in rhyme for young children.
Looks for good stories rather than didactic
tales. No crime or fantasy.

P0274 Exley Publications
Book Publisher
16 Chalk Hill, Watford, WD19 4BG
United Kingdom
Tel: +44 (0) 1923 474480

https://www.helenexley.com

Types: Nonfiction
Markets: Adult

Publishes gift books.

P0275 F. Warne & Co.
Publishing Imprint
United States

Book Publisher: Penguin Young Readers
Group (**P0638**)

P0276 Facet Publishing

Book Publisher
7 Ridgmount Street, London, WC1E 7AE
United Kingdom
Tel: +44 (0) 20 7255 0590

info@facetpublishing.co.uk

https://www.facetpublishing.co.uk
https://www.facebook.com/facetpublishing
https://twitter.com/facetpublishing
https://www.youtube.com/user/facetpublishing
https://www.linkedin.com/company/facet-publishing

PROFESSIONAL > **Nonfiction** > *Nonfiction Books*
  Data and Information Systems; Information Science

Describes itself as the leading publisher of books for library, information and heritage professionals worldwide.

: Sarah Busby

Publishing Imprints: Clive Bingley Books; Library Association Publishing.

P0277 Fahrenheit Press

Book Publisher
United States

submissions@fahrenheit-press.com

http://www.fahrenheit-press.com

Types: Fiction
Subjects: Commercial; Crime; Thrillers
Markets: Adult

Publishes crime and thriller print and ebooks. Send submissions by email.

P0278 Fair Winds Press

Publishing Imprint

Book Publisher: The Quarto Group, Inc. **(P0679)**

P0279 Falstaff Books

Book Publisher
United States

info@falstaffbooks.com

http://falstaffbooks.com

Types: Fiction
Subjects: Fantasy; Horror; Romance; Science Fiction
Markets: Adult

Closed to approaches.

Publishes novels and novellas in the following genres: Fantasy, Urban Fantasy, Science Fiction, Horror, Romance, Weird West, and misfit toys.

P0280 Familius

Book Publisher
United States

bookideas@familius.com

https://www.familius.com
https://www.facebook.com/familiustalk
https://www.instagram.com/familiustalk/?hl=en
https://twitter.com/familiustalk
https://www.pinterest.com/familius/
https://www.youtube.com/channel/UCe0DyumvESLsKkVQ86xQfAg?feature=emb_ch_name_ex

ADULT > **Nonfiction** > *Nonfiction Books*
  Cookery; Education; Family; Health; Parenting; Relationships; Self Help; Wellbeing

CHILDREN'S > **Fiction**
  Board Books: Family
  Picture Books: Family

YOUNG ADULT > **Nonfiction** > *Nonfiction Books*
  Health; Wellbeing

Send: Query; Outline; Writing sample; Market info; Author bio
Don't send: Full text
How to send: Email

Publishes nonfiction for adults, young adults, and children, focused on family as the fundamental unit of society. Submit by email or if necessary by post.

P0281 Family Tree Books

Publishing Imprint
United States

Book Publisher: Penguin Publishing Group **(P0633)**

P0282 Fand Music Press

Book Publisher
Glenelg , 10 Avon Close , Petersfield , Hampshire , GU31 4LG
United Kingdom
Tel: +44 (0) 1730 267341

contact@fandmusic.com

https://fandmusic.com

Fiction > *Short Fiction:* Music

Nonfiction > *Nonfiction Books:* Music

Poetry > *Any Poetic Form:* Music

Publisher of sheet music, now also publishing books about music, CD recordings, and poetry and short stories.

Managing Editor: Peter Thompson

P0283 Farrar, Straus & Giroux, Inc.

Book Publisher
120 Broadway, New York, NY 10271
United States
Tel: +1 (212) 741-6900

sales@fsgbooks.com

https://us.macmillan.com/fsg

Types: Fiction; Nonfiction; Poetry
Markets: Adult; Children's; Young Adult

Closed to approaches.

Not accepting submissions.

Publishing Imprint: Hill and Wang

P0284 Farrar, Straus and Giroux Books for Younger Readers

Book Publisher
175 Fifth Avenue, New York, NY 10010
United States

childrens.editorial@fsgbooks.com

http://us.macmillan.com/publishers/farrar-straus-giroux#FYR

Types: Fiction; Nonfiction
Markets: Children's; Young Adult

Closed to approaches.

Publishes fiction, nonfiction, and picture books for children and teenagers. No unsolicited mss.

P0285 Fathom Books

Book Publisher
United States

editor@fathombooks.org

http://fathombooks.org
https://sharkpackpoetry.com/fathom-books/
https://spr.submittable.com/submit

Fiction > *Novels*
  Experimental; LGBTQIA; Literary; Philosophy; Women

Poetry > *Any Poetic Form*

Closed to approaches.

Costs: Offers services that writers have to pay for. Free to submit, but fee for expedited response.

Independent small press publishing volumes of poetry, very experimental fiction, hybrids, poetics, speculation, etc. Primary interest is text by women and queers. Accepts submissions via online submission system during specific windows only.

P0286 Favorite World Press

Book Publisher
United States

info@favoriteworldpress.com

https://www.favoriteworldpress.com

ADULT
  Fiction > *Novels*
    Animals; Environment; Nature; Sustainable Living

  Nonfiction > *Nonfiction Books*
    Animals; Environment; Nature; Sustainable Living

Poetry > *Any Poetic Form*
  Animals; Environment; Nature; Sustainable
  Living
CHILDREN'S
  Fiction
    Middle Grade: Nature
    Picture Books: Nature

  Nonfiction > *Nonfiction Books*: Nature
YOUNG ADULT
  Fiction > *Novels*
    Animals; Environment; Nature; Sustainable
    Living

  Nonfiction > *Nonfiction Books*
    Animals; Environment; Nature; Sustainable
    Living

Send: Query; Author bio; Synopsis; Writing
sample
How to send: Online contact form

An independent publisher based in New York
City. We believe that one of the best ways to
help change the world is to start small. Our
primary mission is to educate, entertain, and
inspire young readers with books that focus on
nature, wildlife, green living, and
compassionate action. Our titles are
specifically chosen to encourage creativity,
critical thinking, and the confidence to show
caring. By fostering an appreciation for the
wild and the wondrous and an understanding of
the importance of being kind towards both
people and the planet, we aim to help shape the
next generation of brave, big-hearted, planetary
stewards. We help shape them – they help
shape the world!

We also focus on young adult and adult fiction
and nonfiction books for a general audience
that illuminate and celebrate the splendor of
nature, demystify the functioning of the
environment, and promote biodiversity
conservation and sustainable living.

We globally distribute high-quality hardcover,
paperback, and electronic books through all
major outlets, including Amazon, Barnes &
Noble, WHSmith, and Booktopia.

For a complete list of genres and submission
guidelines please see our website.

P0287 The Feminist Press
Book Publisher
365 Fifth Avenue, Suite 5406, New York, NY
10016
United States

editor@feministpress.org

https://www.feministpress.org
https://www.facebook.com/FeministPress/
http://thefeministpress.tumblr.com/
https://www.youtube.com/channel/
UCClCd_SsorK5JGKCE7rD7vw
https://twitter.com/FeministPress
https://www.instagram.com/feministpress/
ADULT

Fiction
  Graphic Novels: Feminism
  Novels: Contemporary; Fantasy; Feminism;
  Mystery; Science Fiction
Nonfiction > *Nonfiction Books*
  Activism; Africa; African American; Arts;
  Asia; Asian American; Biography;
  Education; Feminism; Films; Health;
  History; Italian American; Italy;
  Journalism; Judaism; LGBTQIA; Legal;
  Media; Medicine; Memoir; Middle East;
  Popular Culture; Postcolonialism; Science;
  Sexuality; South America

Poetry > *Poetry Collections*: Feminism

CHILDREN'S > **Fiction** > *Novels*: Feminism

Send: Query; Synopsis; Writing sample;
Author bio; Marketing Plan
How to send: Email; Post

Feminist publisher, publishing an array of
genres including cutting-edge fiction, activist
nonfiction, literature in translation, hybrid
memoirs, children's books, and more.

Editor: Florence Howe

P0288 Fernwood Publishing
Book Publisher
32 Oceanvista Lane, Site 2A, Box 5, Black
Point, NS B0J 1B0
Canada
Tel: +1 (902) 857-1388
Fax: +1 (902) 857-1328

editorial@fernpub.ca

http://www.fernwoodbooks.ca

Types: Nonfiction; Translations
Formats: Reference
Subjects: Anthropology; Archaeology;
Business; Culture; Current Affairs; Finance;
Health; History; Literary Criticism; Medicine;
Nature; Philosophy; Politics; Sociology; Sport;
Women's Interests
Markets: Academic; Adult

Send: Query
Don't send: Full text

Social justice publisher. Publishes both for a
general and academic audience, including
reference books, for use in college and
university courses. Concentrates on social
sciences, humanities, gender studies, literary
criticism, politics, and cultural studies. Send 5-
8 page proposal including tentative table of
contents; the theoretical framework of the
book, and how it relates to the subject matter;
market analysis; level (college / university);
and estimated length and completion date. See
website for full details.

Editor: Wayne Antony

Publisher: Errol Sharpe

P0289 Fidra Books
Book Publisher
United Kingdom

info@fidrabooks.co.uk

http://www.fidrabooks.co.uk

Types: Fiction
Markets: Children's

Ssmall independent publisher specialising in
reprinting children's books that have been
unfairly neglected and deserve to be back in
print. Books range from 1930s adventure
stories to iconic 1960s fantasy novels and from
pony books by Carnegie medal winning
authors to contemporary boarding school
stories.

Editors: Malcolm Robertson; Vanessa
Robertson

P0290 Fircone Books Ltd
Publishing Imprint
The Holme, Church Road, Eardisley,
Herefordshire, HR3 6NJ
United Kingdom
Tel: +44 (0) 1544 327182

info@logastonpress.co.uk

https://logastonpress.co.uk/product-category/
firconebooks/

Book Publisher: Logaston Press

Nonfiction > *Nonfiction Books*
  Church Architecture; Church Art

Publishes books on church art and architecture,
and children's illustrated books.

P0291 Firebird
Publishing Imprint
United States

Book Publisher: Penguin Young Readers
Group (**P0638**)

P0292 Firefly
Book Publisher
D.20, Cardiff Metropolitan University,
Cyncoed Road, Cyncoed, Cardiff, CF23 6XD
United Kingdom

submissions@fireflypress.co.uk
hello@fireflypress.co.uk

https://fireflypress.co.uk
https://www.facebook.com/FireflyPress/
https://twitter.com/FireflyPress
https://www.instagram.com/fireflypress/
https://www.youtube.com/channel/
UCqzaLmXCoGJEQuaooZcnb4Q

CHILDREN'S > **Fiction**
  Early Readers; *Middle Grade*
TEEN > **Fiction** > *Novels*

YOUNG ADULT > **Fiction** > *Novels*

How to send: Through a literary agent

Publishes fiction and nonfiction for children
and young adults aged 5-19. Not currently
accepting nonfiction submissions. Fiction
submissions through agents only. Not currently

publishing any picture books or colour illustrated book for any age group.

Editor: Janet Thomas

P0293 Fiscal Publications
Book Publisher
Unit 100, The Guildhall, Edgbaston Park Road, Birmingham, B15 2TU
United Kingdom
Tel: +44 (0) 800 678 5934

info@fiscalpublications.com

https://www.fiscalpublications.com

ACADEMIC > **Nonfiction** > *Nonfiction Books*
  Economics; Finance; Taxation

PROFESSIONAL > **Nonfiction** > *Nonfiction Books*
  Economics; Finance; Taxation

Send: Query
How to send: Email

Publishes academic and professional books specialising in taxation, public finance and public economics. Materials are relevant worldwide to policy-makers, administrators, lecturers and students of the economics, politics, law and practice of taxation.

Editor: Andy Lymer

P0294 Five Leaves Bookshop
Publishing Imprint

Book Publisher: Five Leaves Publications (**P0295**)

P0295 Five Leaves Publications
Book Publisher
14a Long Row, Nottingham, NG1 2DH
United Kingdom
Tel: +44 (0) 1158 373097

info@fiveleaves.co.uk

https://fiveleaves.co.uk/

Types: Fiction; Nonfiction; Poetry; Scripts
Formats: Short Fiction
Subjects: Arts; Biography; Crime; History; Literature; Politics; Religion; Sociology
Markets: Adult; Young Adult

Closed to approaches.

Small publisher with interests including social history, Jewish culture, politics, poetry, and fiction. Publishes both commercial and non-commercial work. No unsolicited mss.

Editor: Ross Bradshaw

Publishing Imprints: Bromley House Editions (*P0136*); Crime Express (*P0198*); Five Leaves Bookshop (*P0294*); More Shoots More Leaves (*P0554*); New London Editions (*P0577*); Richard Hollis (*P0703*)

P0296 Flame Of The Forest Publishing Pte Ltd
Book Publisher
Blk 5 Ang Mo Kio Industrial Park 2A, #07-22/23, AMK Tech II, 567760
Singapore
Tel: (65) 6484 8887

editor@flameoftheforest.com

https://www.flameoftheforest.com

ADULT
  Fiction > *Novels*
  Nonfiction > *Nonfiction Books*

CHILDREN'S > **Fiction** > *Early Readers*

Send: Query; Synopsis; Writing sample
How to send: Email; Post

Submit a synopsis with a couple of sample chapters by email or by post. Submissions by post will not be returned.

Publishing Imprints: Angsana Books; Bamboo Books; Chiku Books

P0297 Fleet
Publishing Imprint

Publishing Imprint: Little, Brown Book Group (**P0502**)

P0298 Floris Books
Book Publisher
Canal Court, 40 Craiglockhart Avenue, Edinburgh, EH14 1LT
United Kingdom
Tel: +44 (0) 1313 372372

editorial@florisbooks.co.uk
floris@florisbooks.co.uk

https://www.florisbooks.co.uk
http://www.facebook.com/FlorisBooks
https://twitter.com/FlorisBooks
http://www.youtube.com/user/FlorisBooks
http://pinterest.com/florisbooks/

ADULT > **Nonfiction** > *Nonfiction Books*
  Arts; Astrology; Health; Holistic Health; Literature; Mind, Body, Spirit; Parenting; Philosophy; Religion; Space; Spirituality

CHILDREN'S
  Fiction
    Board Books; *Early Readers*; *Middle Grade*; *Novels*; *Picture Books*; *Short Fiction*
  Nonfiction > *Nonfiction Books*
    Activities; Crafts

Send: Synopsis; Writing sample; Table of Contents; Author bio
How to send: Online submission system
How not to send: Post

Publishes a wide range of books including adult nonfiction, picture books and children's novels. No poetry or verse, fiction for people over the age of 14, or autobiography, unless it specifically relates to a relevant nonfiction

subject area. No submissions by email. Send via online form. See website for full details of areas covered and submission guidelines.

Publishing Imprint: Kelpies (**P0465**)

P0299 Folens Ltd
Book Publisher
Hibernian Industrial Estate, Greenhills Road, Tallaght, Dublin 24, D24 DH05
Ireland

proposals@folens.ie

https://www.folens.ie

Types: Nonfiction
Markets: Academic

Send: Full text

Publishes educational books and digital content for Primary and Post-Primary teachers and students in Ireland.

P0300 Folger Shakespeare Library
Publishing Imprint

Book Publisher: Simon & Schuster Adult Publishing (**P0766**)

P0301 Forever
Publishing Imprint

Book Publisher: Grand Central Publishing (**P0337**)

P0302 Fort Publishing
Book Publisher
Old Belmont House, 12 Robsland Avenue, Ayr, KA7 2RW
United Kingdom
Tel: +44 (0) 1292 880693
Fax: +44 (0) 1292 270134

fortpublishing@aol.com

http://www.fortpublishing.co.uk

Nonfiction > *Nonfiction Books*
  History; Scotland; Sport

One of Scotland's leading independent publishers, specialising in sport, history and local interest.

Editor: James McCarroll

P0303 The Foundry Publishing Company
Book Publisher
PO Box 419527, Kansas City, MO 64141-6527
United States
Tel: +1 (816) 931-1900
Fax: +1 (816) 531-0923

rmcfarland@thefoundrypublishing.com

https://www.thefoundrypublishing.com
https://www.facebook.com/TheFoundryPublishing/
https://twitter.com/WeAreTheFoundry

https://www.youtube.com/c/
TheFoundryPublishing
https://www.instagram.com/
thefoundrycommunity/

Nonfiction > *Nonfiction Books*
Christianity; Evangelism

Poetry > *Any Poetic Form*: Christianity

Send: Table of Contents; Synopsis; Writing
sample
How to send: Word file email attachment

Publishes Christian books that reflect an
evangelical Wesleyan stance in accord with the
Church of the Nazarene. Also poems and
anecdotes. Send submissions by email.

P0304 Frances Lincoln Children's Books
Publishing Imprint
74-77 White Lion Street, London, N1 9PF
United Kingdom
Tel: +44 (0) 20 7284 9300
Fax: +44 (0) 20 7485 0490

QuartoKidsSubmissions@Quarto.com

http://www.quartoknows.com/Frances-
Lincoln-Childrens-Books

Book Publisher: The Quarto Group, Inc.
(**P0679**)

Types: Fiction; Nonfiction; Poetry
Subjects: Culture
Markets: Children's

Publishes picture books, multicultural books,
poetry, picture books and information books.
Submit by email. See website for full
guidelines.

Editor: Katie Cotton

Publishers: Janetta Otter-Barry; Rachel
Williams

P0305 Free Association Books Ltd
Book Publisher
1 Angel Cottages, Milespit Hill, London, NW7
1RD
United Kingdom

contact@freeassociationpublishing.com

https://freeassociationpublishing.com

Types: Nonfiction
Subjects: Health; History; Politics;
Psychology; Sociology
Markets: Adult

Send: Query
Don't send: Full text

Send submissions by post or by email.
Publishes books on a wide range of topics
including psychotherapy, social work, health
studies, history, public policy and more.

P0306 Free Press
Publishing Imprint

Book Publisher: Simon & Schuster Adult
Publishing (**P0766**)

P0307 Free Spirit Publishing
Book Publisher
6325 Sandburg Road, Suite 100, Minneapolis,
MN 55427-3674
United States
Tel: +1 (612) 338-2068
Fax: +1 (612) 337-5050

help4kids@freespirit.com

http://www.freespirit.com

Types: Fiction; Nonfiction
Subjects: How To; Lifestyle; Self Help;
Sociology
Markets: Academic; Adult; Children's; Young
Adult

Send: Query
Don't send: Full text

Publishes nonfiction books and learning
materials for children and teens, parents,
educators, counselors, and others who live and
work with young people. Also publishes fiction
relevant to the mission of providing children
and teens with the tools they need to succeed in
life, e.g.: self-esteem; conflict resolution, etc.
No general fiction or storybooks; books with
animal or mythical characters; books with
religious or New Age content; or single
biographies, autobiographies, or memoirs.
Submit by proposals by post or through online
submission system. No submissions by fax or
email. See website for full submission
guidelines.

P0308 Front Table Books
Publishing Imprint

Book Publisher: Cedar Fort (**P0156**)

P0309 Frontline Books
Publishing Imprint
47 Church Street, Barnsley, South Yorkshire,
S70 2AS
United Kingdom
Tel: +44 (0) 1226 734555
Fax: +44 (0) 1226 734438

info@frontline-books.com

https://www.frontline-books.com
https://twitter.com/frontline_books

Book Publisher: Pen & Sword Books Ltd
(**P0626**)

Nonfiction > *Nonfiction Books*
History; Warfare

Send: Query

Military history publisher. Publishes on a wide
range of military history topics and periods,
from Ancient Greece and Rome to the present
day. Welcomes submissions.

P0310 Fruit Bruise Press
Publishing Imprint
United Kingdom

Book Publisher: DogHorn Publishing (**P0238**)

P0311 FunStitch Studio
Publishing Imprint
United States

Book Publisher: C&T Publishing (**P0140**)

P0312 G.P. Putnam's Sons
Publishing Imprint
United States

Book Publisher: Penguin Publishing Group
(**P0633**)

P0313 G.P. Putnam's Sons Books for Young Readers
Publishing Imprint
United States

consumerservices@penguinrandomhouse.com

https://www.penguin.com/publishers/
gpputnamssonsbooksforyoungread/

Book Publisher: Penguin Young Readers
Group (**P0638**)

CHILDREN'S > **Fiction**
Novels; *Picture Books*

How to send: Through a literary agent

Publishes approximately fifty trade hardcover
books a year for children, including lively,
accessible picture books and some of today's
strongest voices in fiction.

P0314 Gale
Book Publisher
27500 Drake Road, Farmington Hills, MI
48331
United States
Tel: +1 (800) 877-4253
Fax: +1 (877) 363-4253

gale.customerservice@cengage.com

https://www.gale.com
https://www.facebook.com/GaleCengage/
https://www.linkedin.com/company/gale
https://twitter.com/galecengage
https://www.youtube.com/user/GaleCengage

Book Publisher: Cengage (**P0157**)

ACADEMIC > **Nonfiction**
Nonfiction Books: Business; Education;
Finance; Health; History; Legal; Literature;
Medicine; Science; Sociology; Technology
Reference: General

ADULT > **Nonfiction**
Nonfiction Books: Business; Education;
Finance; Health; History; Hobbies; Legal;
Literature; Medicine; Science; Sociology;
Technology
Reference: General

PROFESSIONAL > Nonfiction
 Nonfiction Books: Business; Education;
 Finance; Health; Legal; Medicine; Science;
 Technology
 Reference: General

Supplies businesses, schools, and libraries with books and electronic reference materials.

Book Publisher: KidHaven Press

Publishing Imprints: The Taft Group;
Blackbird Press; Charles Scribner & Sons;
Five Star; G.K. Hall & Co.; Graham &
Whiteside Ltd; Greenhaven Publishing; KG
Saur Verlag GmbH & Co. KG; Lucent Books;
Macmillan Reference USA; Primary Source
Media; Schirmer Reference; St James Press;
Thorndike Press; Twayne Publishers; UXL;
Wheeler Publishing

P0315 Gallery
Publishing Imprint

Book Publisher: Simon & Schuster Adult
Publishing (**P0766**)

P0316 Galley Beggar Press
Book Publisher
United Kingdom

submissions@galleybeggar.co.uk

http://galleybeggar.co.uk

Types: Fiction; Nonfiction
Formats: Short Fiction
Subjects: Literary
Markets: Adult

Closed to approaches.

Publishes adult literary fiction (novels and short story collections) and narrative nonfiction only. Open to submissions by email during specific submission windows. See website for full details.

P0317 Galore Park Publishing
Book Publisher
United Kingdom

https://www.galorepark.co.uk
https://twitter.com/Galore_Park
https://www.facebook.com/Galore1Park/

Publishing Imprint: Hodder Education Group

**ACADEMIC > Nonfiction > *Nonfiction
Books*:** Education

How to send: Online submission system

Specialises in preparation for 11+, pre-test and 13+ Common Entrance exams and leads the market in textbooks for pupils studying at independent schools.

P0318 Garden-Door Press
Book Publisher
Ithaca, NY
United States

gardendoorpress@gmail.com

http://www.garden-doorpress.com

Types: Poetry
Subjects: Experimental; Literary
Markets: Adult

Closed to approaches.

Micro-press based in Ithaca, New York.
Publishes poetry chapbooks. Closed to submissions as at April 2019. Check website for current status.

P0319 Gazing Grain Press
Book Publisher
United States

gazinggrainpress@gmail.com

https://www.gazinggrainpress.com

Types: Fiction; Nonfiction; Poetry
Subjects: Women's Interests
Markets: Adult

Inclusive feminist literary press. Publishes poetry, fiction, and nonfiction chapbook contests, and book reviews. Accepts submissions for chapbooks through annual contest only ($15 entry fee). See website for details.

P0320 Gemstone Publishing
Book Publisher
1940 Greenspring Drive, Suite I-L, Timonium, MD 21093
United States
Tel: +1 (443) 318-8467
Fax: +1 (443) 318-8411

humark@gemstonepub.com

https://www.gemstonepub.com

Types: Nonfiction
Formats: Reference
Subjects: Hobbies
Markets: Adult

Publishes nonfiction and reference works such as price guides relating to comics and other collectables.

P0321 Genealogical Publishing Company
Book Publisher
3600 Clipper Mill Road, Suite 260, Baltimore, Maryland 21211
United States
Tel: +1 (410) 837-8271
Fax: +1 (410) 752-8492

web@genealogical.com

https://genealogical.com

Types: Nonfiction
Subjects: History; Hobbies; How To
Markets: Adult

Publishes books for amateur genealogists.

P0322 The Geological Society Publishing House
Book Publisher; Magazine Publisher
Unit 7, Brassmill Enterprise Centre, Brassmill Lane, Bath, BA1 3JN
United Kingdom

https://www.geolsoc.org.uk/publications

ACADEMIC > Nonfiction
 Articles: Earth Science; Geology
 Nonfiction Books: Earth Science; Geology;
 Memoir

Publishes postgraduate books and journals on the earth sciences.

: Angharad Hills

Magazines: Geochemistry: Exploration,
Environment, Analysis (*M0230*); Journal of the
Geological Society (*M0295*); Petroleum
Geoscience (*M0397*); Proceedings of the
Yorkshire Geological Society (*M0419*);
Quarterly Journal of Engineering Geology and
Hydrogeology (*M0426*); Scottish Journal of
Geology (*M0458*)

P0323 George Ronald Publisher
Book Publisher
United Kingdom

sales@grbooks.com

http://grbooks.com
http://www.facebook.com/pages/George-Ronald-Books/25850856123

Nonfiction > *Nonfiction Books*: Religion

Send: Query
How to send: Email

Religious publisher, concentrating solely on books of interest to Baha'is. Send email for copy of submission guidelines.

P0324 Ghostwoods Books
Book Publisher
United Kingdom

ghostwoodsbooks@gmail.com

http://gwdbooks.com
https://www.facebook.com/GhostwoodsBooks/

Fiction > *Short Fiction*

Closed to approaches.

A small, fair-trade publishing company.
Publishes collections of short stories. Accepts submissions to specific calls only.

Editors: Tim Dedopulos; Salome Jones

P0325 Gifted Unlimited, LLC
Book Publisher
12340 U.S. Highway 42, No. 453, Goshen, KY 40026
United States
Tel: +1 (502) 715-6306

info@giftedunlimitedllc.com

https://www.giftedunlimitedllc.com

Types: Nonfiction
Markets: Academic; Adult; Children's

Send: Query
Don't send: Full text

Publishes books that support the academic, social, or emotional needs of gifted children and adults. No fiction, poetry, or K-12 classroom materials. Approach via proposal submission form on website.

P0326 Gill Books
Book Publisher
Hume Avenue, Park West, Dublin, D12 YV96
Ireland
Tel: +353 (01) 500 9500

submissions@gill.ie

https://www.gillbooks.ie
http://www.facebook.com/GillBooks
http://www.twitter.com/Gill_Books
http://www.instagram.com/GillBooks

ADULT > Nonfiction
  Gift Books: Ireland
  Nonfiction Books: Biography; Comedy / Humour; Crafts; Crime; Current Affairs; Food and Drink; History; Hobbies; Ireland; Lifestyle; Mind, Body, Spirit; Nature; Parenting; Politics; Sport
  Reference: General, and in particular: Ireland
CHILDREN'S
  Fiction > *Novels*
  Nonfiction > *Nonfiction Books*

Send: Query; Outline; Synopsis; Table of Contents; Writing sample; Author bio
How to send: Email

Publishes adult nonfiction and children's fiction and nonfiction. No adult fiction, poetry, short stories or plays. In general, focuses on books of Irish interest. Prefers proposals by email, but will also accept proposals by post. See website for full submission guidelines.

Editor: Deborah Marsh

P0327 GL Assessment
Book Publisher
1st Floor Vantage London, Great West Road, Brentford, TW8 9AG
United Kingdom
Tel: +44 (0) 3301 235375

info@gl-assessment.co.uk

https://www.gl-assessment.co.uk

ACADEMIC > **Nonfiction** > *Nonfiction Books*

Publishes educational testing and assessment material.

P0328 Glass Poetry Press
Book Publisher
United States

editor@glass-poetry.com

http://www.glass-poetry.com/submissions.html

Types: Poetry
Markets: Adult

Closed to approaches.

Publishes poetry manuscripts between 15 and 25 pages. Currently closed to submissions.

P0329 The Globe Pequot Press
Book Publisher
246 Goose Lane, 2nd Floor, Guilford, CT 06437
United States

GPSubmissions@rowman.com

http://www.globepequot.com
https://rowman.com/Page/GlobePequot
https://www.facebook.com/globepequot/
https://twitter.com/globepequot

Book Publisher: Rowman & Littlefield Publishing Group

Nonfiction > *Nonfiction Books*
  Biography; Business; Cookery; Gardening; History; Mind, Body, Spirit; Nature; Travel

Send: Outline; Table of Contents; Writing sample; Author bio; Market info
How to send: Email; Post

Publishes books about iconic brands and people, regional interest, history, lifestyle, cooking and food culture, and folklore – books that hit the intersection of a reader's interest in a specific place and their passion for a specific topic.

Publishing Imprints: Applause (*P0044*); Astragal Press; Backbeat (*P0073*); Down East Books (*P0241*); FalconGuides; Lyons Press (*P0515*); Mcbooks Press (*P0538*); Muddy Boots (*P0558*); Pineapple Press (**P0652**); Prometheus (*P0667*); Skip Jack Press (*P0770*); Stackpole Books (**P0792**); TwoDot (*P0846*); Union Park Press (*P0856*)

P0330 Gloucester Publishers
Book Publisher
36 Chapel Road, London, SE27 0TY
United Kingdom

https://find-and-update.company-information.
service.gov.uk/company/04680814

Publishing Imprint: Everyman Chess (**P0271**)

P0331 Gnome On Pig Productions Incorporated
Book Publisher
Canada

booksubmissions@
gnomeonpigproductions.com

https://www.gnomeonpigproductions.com

Types: Fiction; Nonfiction
Subjects: Drama; Erotic; Fantasy; Horror; Science Fiction
Markets: Adult; Children's; Young Adult

Closed to approaches.

Publishes fiction for children, teens, new adults, and adults. Also occasional nonfiction. Closed to submissions as at February 2020. Check website for current status.

P0332 Godstow Press
Book Publisher
60 Godstow Road, Wolvercote, Oxford, OX2 8NY
United Kingdom
Tel: +44 (0) 1865 556215

info@godstowpress.co.uk

http://www.godstowpress.co.uk

Fiction > *Novels*
  Historical Fiction; Philosophy; Spirituality

Poetry > *Any Poetic Form*
  Philosophy; Spirituality

Small publisher of creative work with a spiritual / philosophical content, particularly historical fiction.

Editors: David Smith; Linda Smith

P0333 Goldsmiths Press
Book Publisher
Room 2, 33 Laurie Grove, New Cross, London, SE14 6NW
United Kingdom

goldsmithspress@gold.ac.uk

https://www.gold.ac.uk/goldsmiths-press

Types: Fiction; Nonfiction; Poetry
Markets: Academic; Adult

Send: Query
Don't send: Full text

University press aiming to cut across disciplinary boundaries and blur the distinctions between theory, practice, fiction and nonfiction. See website for proposal forms and submit by email.

Editors: Adrian Driscoll; Sarah Kember; Ellen Parnavelas; Guy Sewell

P0334 Goop Press
Publishing Imprint

Book Publisher: Grand Central Publishing (**P0337**)

P0335 Government Publications
Book Publisher
Ireland

publications@opw.ie

https://www.opw.ie/en/
governmentpublications/

Types: Nonfiction
Formats: Reference
Subjects: Architecture; Legal
Markets: Adult; Professional

Publishes Irish government publications.

P0336 Grand Central Life & Style
Publishing Imprint

Book Publisher: Grand Central Publishing
(**P0337**)

P0337 Grand Central Publishing
Book Publisher
United States

https://www.grandcentralpublishing.com

Book Publisher: Hachette Book Group (**P0348**)

Types: Fiction; Nonfiction
Subjects: Beauty; Comedy / Humour; Culture;
Fashion; Lifestyle; Mystery; Romance;
Thrillers
Markets: Adult

How to send: Through a literary agent

Publishes a wide variety of fiction, nonfiction,
humour, beauty, fashion, romance, lifestyle,
mystery/thrillers, and pop culture books.
Approaches from literary agents only.

Publishing Imprints: Forever (*P0301*); Goop
Press (*P0334*); Grand Central Life & Style
(*P0336*); Twelve (*P0843*)

P0338 Grant Books
Book Publisher
Pershore, Worcestershire
United Kingdom
Tel: +44 (0) 1386 803803

golf@grantbooks.co.uk

https://www.grantbooks.co.uk

Nonfiction > *Nonfiction Books*: Golf

Publishes golf-related books covering history,
biography, course architecture, etc. No fiction,
humour, or instructional.

Editor: H.R.J. Grant

P0339 Granta Books
Book Publisher
12 Addison Avenue, London, W11 4QR
United Kingdom

Tel: +44 (0) 20 7605 1360
Fax: +44 (0) 20 7605 1361

info@granta.com

https://granta.com/books/

Types: Fiction; Nonfiction
Subjects: Autobiography; Culture; History;
Literary; Literary Criticism; Nature; Politics;
Sociology; Travel
Markets: Adult

Closed to approaches.

Publishes around 70% nonfiction / 30% fiction.
In nonfiction publishes serious cultural,
political and social history, narrative history, or
memoir. Rarely publishes straightforward
biographies. No genre fiction. Not accepting
unsolicited submissions.

P0340 Graphic Universe
Publishing Imprint

Book Publisher: Lerner Publishing Group
(**P0487**)

P0341 Graphix
Publishing Imprint

Book Publisher: Scholastic (**P0740**)

P0342 Greenway Music Press
Publishing Imprint
United States

https://www.areditions.com/gmp/shop.html

Book Publisher: A-R Editions (**P0012**)

Nonfiction > *Nonfiction Books*: Music

Brings important but under-appreciated
compositions to a larger audience. Focuses on
music for standard chamber ensembles, solo
instruments and voices, and keyboard.

P0343 Greenwillow Books
Publishing Imprint

Book Publisher: HarperCollins

P0344 Griffin
Publishing Imprint

Publishing Imprint: St Martin's Press (**P0789**)

P0345 Grove Atlantic Inc.
Book Publisher
154 West 14th Street, 12th Floor, New York,
NY 10011
United States
Tel: +1 (212) 614-7850
Fax: +1 (212) 614-7886

info@groveatlantic.com

https://groveatlantic.com

Fiction > *Novels*

Nonfiction > *Nonfiction Books*

How to send: Through a literary agent

Approach through an agent only. Publishes
general fiction and nonfiction.

Publishing Imprints: Atlantic Monthly Press
(*P0059*); Black Cat (*P0102*); Grove Press
(*P0346*); The Mysterious Press (*P0563*)

P0346 Grove Press
Publishing Imprint
United States

Book Publisher: Grove Atlantic Inc. (**P0345**)

P0347 Gryphon House, Inc.
Book Publisher
PO Box 10, 6848 Leons Way, Lewisville, NC
27023
United States
Tel: +1 (336) 712-3490
Fax: +1 (877) 638-7576

info@ghbooks.com

https://www.gryphonhouse.com

ADULT > **Nonfiction** > *Nonfiction
Books*: Parenting

PROFESSIONAL > **Nonfiction** > *Nonfiction
Books*: Education

Send: Query; Market info; Table of Contents;
Writing sample; Author bio

Publishes books intended to help teachers and
parents enrich the lives of children from birth
to age eight. See website for proposal
submission guidelines.

P0348 Hachette Book Group
Book Publisher
United States

https://www.hachettebookgroup.com

Book Publisher: Hachette Livre (**P0353**)

Types: Fiction; Nonfiction
Subjects: Contemporary; Literary
Markets: Adult

Includes 24 imprints covering the entire array
of contemporary fiction and nonfiction, from
the most popular to the most literary.

Book Publishers: Grand Central Publishing
(**P0337**); Little, Brown and Company (**P0501**);
Perseus Books (**P0641**)

P0349 Hachette Books
Publishing Imprint
United States

Book Publisher: Perseus Books (**P0641**)

P0350 Hachette Children's Group
Book Publisher
3rd Floor, Carmelite House, 50 Victoria
Embankment, London, EC4Y 0DZ
United Kingdom

editorial@hachettechildrens.co.uk

https://www.hachettechildrens.co.uk
https://www.facebook.com/hachettekids/
https://twitter.com/hachettekids
https://www.instagram.com/hachettekids/

Book Publisher: Hachette UK (**P0354**)

CHILDREN'S
Fiction
Board Books; *Chapter Books*; *Early
Readers*; *Gift Books*; *Middle Grade*;
Picture Books
Nonfiction
Board Books; *Gift Books*; *Nonfiction Books*

How to send: Through a literary agent

Aims to cater for every child, with baby and
pre-school books, picture books, gift, fiction,
non-fiction, series fiction, books for the school
and library market and licensed publishing.

Publishing Imprints: Franklin Watts; Hodder
Children's Books (*P0409*); Little, Brown
Books for Young Readers (*P0503*); Orchard
Books; Orion Children's Books (*P0602*); Pat-
a-Cake (*P0617*); Quercus Children's Books
(*P0683*); Wayland Books (*P0912*); Wren &
Rook (*P0940*)

P0351 **Hachette Digital**
Publishing Imprint

Publishing Imprint: Little, Brown Book Group
(**P0502**)

P0352 **Hachette Go!**
Publishing Imprint
United States

Book Publisher: Perseus Books (**P0641**)

P0353 **Hachette Livre**
Book Publisher
France

https://www.hachette.com

Types: Fiction; Nonfiction
Markets: Academic; Adult; Children's

International publishing group with operations
in all English speaking markets.

Book Publishers: Hachette Book Group
(**P0348**); Hachette UK (**P0354**); Quercus
Books (**P0682**)

Publishing Imprint: Headline Publishing
Group

P0354 **Hachette UK**
Book Publisher
Carmelite House, 50 Victoria Embankment,
London, EC4Y 0DZ
United Kingdom
Tel: +44 (0) 20 3122 6000

enquiries@hachette.co.uk

https://www.hachette.co.uk
https://www.facebook.com/HachetteBooksUK/

https://twitter.com/hachetteuk
https://www.instagram.com/hachetteuk/

Book Publisher: Hachette Livre (**P0353**)

Fiction > *Novels*

Nonfiction > *Nonfiction Books*

How to send: Through a literary agent

Publishing group made up of ten autonomous
publishing divisions and over fifty imprints
with a rich and diverse history. Accepts
submissions via literary agents only.

Book Publishers: Bookouture (**P0125**);
Hachette Children's Group (**P0350**); Laurence
King Publishing Ltd (**P0482**)

Publishing Imprints: Headline Publishing
Group; Hodder & Stoughton; Hodder
Education Group; John Murray; Little, Brown
Book Group (**P0502**); Octopus Publishing
Group; Orion Publishing Group

P0355 **Halban Publishers**
Book Publisher
United Kingdom
Tel: +44 (0) 20 7692 5541

books@halbanpublishers.com

http://www.halbanpublishers.com

Types: Fiction; Nonfiction
Subjects: Autobiography; History; Literary
Criticism; Philosophy; Politics; Religion
Markets: Adult

Closed to approaches.

**Closed to submissions as at March 30, 2019.
Check website for current
status.** Independent publisher of fiction,
memoirs, history, biography, and books of
Jewish interest. Send query with synopsis by
email only. No unsolicited MSS.

Editors: Martine Halban; Peter Halban

P0356 **Half Mystic Press**
Book Publisher
United States

hello@halfmystic.com

https://www.halfmystic.com
https://halfmystic.submittable.com/submit

Fiction
Novellas; *Novels*; *Short Fiction Collections*
Nonfiction > *Nonfiction Books*
Memoir; Music

Poetry > *Poetry Collections*

Send: Query; Author bio
How to send: Submittable

Publishes poetry, essay, and short story
collections; drama; memoirs; novellas; full-
length novels; experimental work. See website
for full submission guidelines.

P0357 **Halsgrove**
Book Publisher
Halsgrove House, Ryelands Business Park,
Bagley Road, Wellington, Somerset, TA21
9PZ
United Kingdom
Tel: +44 (0) 1823 653777
Fax: +44 (0) 1823 216796

sales@halsgrove.com

http://www.halsgrove.com

Types: Nonfiction
Subjects: Arts; Biography; History;
Photography
Markets: Adult

Send: Full text

Publishes regional material covering various
regions in the areas of history, biography,
photography, and art. No fiction or poetry.
Send query by email with brief synopsis in first
instance.

P0358 **Hampton Roads
Publishing**
Publishing Imprint
65 Parker Street, Suite 7, Newburyport, MA
01950
United States
Tel: +1 (978) 465-0504
Fax: +1 (978) 465-0243

submissions@rwwbooks.com

http://redwheelweiser.com

Publishing Imprint: Red Wheel

Types: Nonfiction
Subjects: Health; Spirituality
Markets: Adult

Send: Query
Don't send: Full text

Publishes books on metaphysics, spirituality,
and health. Send query by email with author
info and proposal. See website for full
guidelines.

P0359 **Handtype Press**
Book Publisher
United States

handtype@gmail.com

http://handtype.com

Types: Fiction; Nonfiction; Translations
Subjects: Autobiography
Markets: Adult

Send: Query
Don't send: Full text

Showcases literature and art created by signers
(both deaf and hearing) or about the deaf or
signing experience. Will consider fiction,
essays, memoirs, and translations into English
of signed and written works in other languages.
Send query with a brief summary of your

project, your publishing history, and a sample of your work (preferably the first 20 pages of prose) in a Word file.

P0360 HappenStance Press
Book Publisher
21 Hatton Green, Glenrothes, Fife, KY7 4SD
United Kingdom

https://www.happenstancepress.com
https://twitter.com/Nell_Nelson
https://www.facebook.com/HappenStance-Press-114680661902101/

Poetry > *Any Poetic Form*

Closed to approaches.

Small publisher of poetry chapbooks by both new and established poets. Unlikely to publish poets with no track record.

Editor: Helena Nelson

P0361 Harlequin Enterprises
Book Publisher
Bay Adelaide Centre, East Tower, 22 Adelaide Street West, 41st Floor, Toronto, ON M5H 4E3
Canada
Tel: +1 (888) 432-4879

https://www.harlequin.com
https://harlequin.submittable.com/submit
https://www.facebook.com/HarlequinBooks
https://twitter.com/HarlequinBooks
https://www.pinterest.com/harlequinbooks/
https://www.youtube.com/user/harlequinbooks
https://www.instagram.com/harlequinbooks/

Book Publisher: HarperCollins

ADULT > **Fiction** > *Novels*: Romance

YOUNG ADULT > **Fiction** > *Novels*: Romance

How to send: Submittable

International publisher of romance fiction. See website for current needs, and appropriate imprints or series to submit to. Also offers manuscript critiquing service.

Book Publisher: Harlequin American Romance

Publishing Imprints: Carina Press (**P0150**); HQN Books; Harlequin Books; Harlequin Dare; Luna; MIRA; Mills & Boon; Red Dress Ink; Silhouette; Steeple Hill Books;

P0362 Harmony Books
Publishing Imprint

Book Publishers: The Crown Publishing Group; Random House (**P0690**)

P0363 Harmony Ink Press
Book Publisher
5032 Capital Circle SW, Ste 2 PMB 279, Tallahassee, FL 32305-7886
United States

Tel: +1 (800) 970-3759
Fax: +1 (888) 308-3739

submissions@harmonyinkpress.com

https://www.harmonyinkpress.com

Types: Fiction
Subjects: Fantasy; Mystery; Romance; Science Fiction
Markets: Young Adult

Closed to approaches.

Publishes Teen and New Adult fiction featuring significant personal growth of unforgettable characters across the LGBTQ+ spectrum. Closed to general submissions as at November 2019.

P0364 Harper Audio (UK)
Publishing Imprint
United Kingdom

Book Publisher: HarperCollins UK (**P0382**)

P0365 Harper Books
Publishing Imprint

Book Publisher: HarperCollins

P0366 Harper Business
Publishing Imprint
195 Broadway, New York, NY 10007
United States
Tel: +1 (212) 207-7000

http://www.harperbusiness.com

Book Publisher: HarperCollins

Types: Nonfiction
Subjects: Business
Markets: Adult; Professional

How to send: Through a literary agent

Publishes innovative, authoritative, and creative business books from world-class thinkers. Accepts approaches through literary agents only.

P0367 Harper Design
Publishing Imprint

Book Publisher: HarperCollins

P0368 Harper Inspire
Publishing Imprint
United Kingdom

Book Publisher: HarperCollins UK (**P0382**)

P0369 Harper Luxe
Publishing Imprint

Book Publisher: HarperCollins

P0370 Harper North
Publishing Imprint
United Kingdom

Book Publisher: HarperCollins UK (**P0382**)

P0371 Harper Perennial
Publishing Imprint

Book Publisher: HarperCollins

P0372 Harper Voyager
Publishing Imprint
United Kingdom

Book Publishers: HarperCollins; HarperCollins UK (**P0382**)

P0373 Harper Wave
Publishing Imprint

Book Publisher: HarperCollins

P0374 Harper360
Publishing Imprint
United Kingdom

Book Publisher: HarperCollins UK (**P0382**)

P0375 HarperAudio
Publishing Imprint

Book Publisher: HarperCollins

P0376 HarperChildren's Audio
Publishing Imprint

Book Publisher: HarperCollins

P0377 HarperCollins 360
Publishing Imprint

Book Publisher: HarperCollins

P0378 HarperCollins Children's Books
Publishing Imprint
United Kingdom

Book Publishers: HarperCollins; HarperCollins UK (**P0382**)

P0379 HarperCollins Focus
Book Publisher

focuscc@harpercollins.com

https://www.harpercollinsfocus.com

Book Publisher: HarperCollins

Book Publisher: HarperCollins Leadership (**P0381**)

P0380 HarperCollins Ireland
Publishing Imprint
United Kingdom

Book Publisher: HarperCollins UK (**P0382**)

P0381 HarperCollins Leadership
Book Publisher

hcleadership@harpercollins.com

https://www.harpercollinsleadership.com
https://www.facebook.com/
harpercollinsleadership/
https://twitter.com/hcleadership
https://www.instagram.com/hcleadership/

Book Publisher: HarperCollins Focus (**P0379**)

PROFESSIONAL > **Nonfiction** > *Nonfiction Books*: Leadership

Feeds your inner drive to grow as a leader with integrated, values-based development experiences that give you the inspiration and insights you need to thrive in your current role—and your next.

Book Publisher: AMACOM Books (**P0032**)

P0382 **HarperCollins UK**
Book Publisher
The News Building, 1 London Bridge Street, London, SE1 9GF, GLASGOW OFFICE:, 103 Westerhill Road, Bishopbriggs, Glasgow, G64 2QT
United Kingdom
Tel: +44 (0) 20 8741 7070
Fax: +44 (0) 20 8307 4440

enquiries@harpercollins.co.uk

https://www.harpercollins.co.uk

Book Publisher: HarperCollins

Types: Fiction; Nonfiction
Formats: Film Scripts; Reference
Subjects: Autobiography; Cookery; Crafts; Crime; Entertainment; Fantasy; Gardening; Health; History; Leisure; Lifestyle; Literary; Media; Science; Science Fiction; Sport; Thrillers; Warfare
Markets: Adult; Children's

How to send: Through a literary agent

One of the UK's three largest publishers, with one of the broadest ranges of material published. All approaches must come through an agent. No unsolicited MSS.

Authors: Cecelia Ahern; Agatha Christie; Patricia Cornwell; Lindsey Kelk; Derek Landy

Book Publisher: HarperPress

Publishing Imprints: 4th Estate (**P0010**); Avon (*P0069*); The Borough Press (*P0126*); Collins (*P0182*); Egmont Books (*P0255*); HQ (*P0420*); HQ Digital (*P0421*); Harper Audio (UK) (*P0364*); Harper Inspire (*P0368*); Harper North (*P0370*); Harper Voyager (*P0372*); Harper360 (*P0374*); HarperCollins Children's Books (*P0378*); HarperCollins Ireland (*P0380*); HarperFiction (*P0384*); HarperNonFiction (*P0385*); Mills & Boon; Mudlark (*P0559*); One More Chapter (*P0595*); Times Books (*P0825*); William Collins (*P0931*)

P0383 **HarperFestival**
Publishing Imprint

Book Publisher: HarperCollins

P0384 **HarperFiction**
Publishing Imprint
United Kingdom

Book Publisher: HarperCollins UK (**P0382**)

P0385 **HarperNonFiction**
Publishing Imprint
United Kingdom

Book Publisher: HarperCollins UK (**P0382**)

P0386 **HarperOne**
Publishing Imprint

Book Publisher: HarperCollins

P0387 **HarperTeen**
Publishing Imprint

Book Publisher: HarperCollins

P0388 **HarperTeen Impulse**
Publishing Imprint

Book Publisher: HarperCollins

P0389 **HarperVia**
Publishing Imprint

Book Publisher: HarperCollins

P0390 **Harvard Business Publishing**
Book Publisher
United States
Tel: +1 (800) 545-7685
Fax: +1 (617) 783-7666

custserv@hbsp.harvard.edu

https://hbsp.harvard.edu
https://www.facebook.com/HarvardBizEdu/
https://twitter.com/HarvardBizEdu
https://www.linkedin.com/company/harvardbizedu
https://www.youtube.com/channel/UCRp-04NDMZh_61j-HszFbSg

ACADEMIC > **Nonfiction** > *Nonfiction Books*
Business; Management

PROFESSIONAL > **Nonfiction** > *Nonfiction Books*
Business; Management

Publishes business books for the professional and academic markets.

Editor: Astrid Sandoval

P0391 **Harvard Common Press**
Publishing Imprint
100 Cummings Center, Suite 253C, Beverly, MA 01915
United States
Tel: +1 (978) 282-9590
Fax: +1 (978) 282-7765

dan.rosenberg@quarto.com

http://www.harvardcommonpress.com

Book Publisher: The Quarto Group, Inc. (**P0679**)

Types: Nonfiction
Subjects: Cookery; Lifestyle
Markets: Adult

Send: Query
Don't send: Full text

Publishes books on cookery and parenting. See website for full guidelines.

Editorial Director: Dan Rosenberg

Publishing Imprint: Gambit Books

P0392 **Harvard Square Editions (HSE)**
Book Publisher
United States

https://harvardsquareeditions.org

Types: Fiction
Subjects: Literary; Nature; Sociology
Markets: Adult

Accepts novel and novella submissions with environmental and social themes. Send query with brief synopsis, first chapter, author's name and contact info and a one-paragraph bio in third person via online form on website.

P0393 **Harvill Secker**
Publishing Imprint
United Kingdom

Book Publisher: Vintage (**P0891**)

P0394 **Hawthorn Press**
Book Publisher
1 Lansdown Lane, Stroud, Gloucestershire, GL5 1BJ
United Kingdom
Tel: +44 (0) 1453 757040

info@hawthornpress.com

http://www.hawthornpress.com

Nonfiction > *Nonfiction Books*
Lifestyle; Self Help

Send: Query; Table of Contents; Author bio; Self-Addressed Stamped Envelope (SASE); Submission Form
How to send: Post

Publisher aiming to contribute to a more creative, peaceful and sustainable world through its publishing. Publishes mainly commissioned work, but will consider approaches. Send first two chapters with introduction, full table of contents/book plan, brief author biography and/or CV. Allow at least 2-4 months for response.

P0395 **Hawthorne Books**
Book Publisher
2201 NE 23rd Avenue Third Floor, Portland,

OR 97212
United States
Tel: +1 (503) 327-8849

rhughes@hawthornebooks.com

http://www.hawthornebooks.com
https://www.facebook.com/HawthorneBooks
http://twitter.com//hawthornebooks
http://pinterest.com/hawthornebooks/

Fiction > *Novels*: Literary

Nonfiction > *Nonfiction Books*
  Memoir; Narrative Essays

How to send: Through a literary agent

An independent literary press based in Portland, Oregon, with a national scope and deep regional roots. Focuses on literary fiction and nonfiction with innovative and varied approaches to the relationships between essay, memoir, and narrative.

Associate Editor: Adam O'Connor Rodriguez

Authors: Kassten Alonso; Poe Ballantine; Peter Donahue; Monica Drake; D'Arcy Fallon; Peter Fogtdal; Jeff Meyers; Mark Mordue; Scott Nadelson; Toby Olson; Gin Phillips; Lynne Sharon Schwartz; Tom Spanbauer; Michael Strelow; Richard Wiley

P0396 Hay House Publishers
Book Publisher
The Sixth Floor, Watson House, 54 Baker Street, London, W1U 7BU
United Kingdom
Tel: +44 (0) 20 3675 2450
Fax: +44 (0) 20 3675 2451

submissions@hayhouse.co.uk

http://www.hayhouse.co.uk

Types: Nonfiction
Subjects: Biography; Business; Current Affairs; Finance; Health; Lifestyle; Medicine; Men's Interests; Nature; Philosophy; Psychology; Religion; Self Help; Sociology; Women's Interests
Markets: Adult

Send: Query
Don't send: Full text

Describes itself as the world's leading mind body and spirit publisher. Approach via form on website. See website for full submission guidelines.

P0397 Haynes Publishing
Book Publisher
Sparkford, Near Yeovil, Somerset, BA22 7JJ
United Kingdom
Tel: +44 (0) 1963 440635

bookseditorial@haynes.co.uk

http://www.haynes.co.uk

Types: Nonfiction
Formats: Reference

Subjects: How To; Leisure; Sport; Technology
Markets: Adult

Mostly publishes motoring and transport titles, including DIY service and repair manuals for cars and motorbikes, motoring in general (including Motor Sports), but also home, DIY, and leisure titles. Unsolicited MSS welcome, if on one of the above areas of interest.

P0398 HeartSpring Publishing
Publishing Imprint

Book Publisher: College Press Publishing **(P0181)**

P0399 Hellgate Press
Book Publisher
United States
Tel: +1 (800) 795-4059

harley@hellgatepress.com

http://www.hellgatepress.com

Types: Fiction; Nonfiction
Subjects: Adventure; Autobiography; History; Travel; Warfare
Markets: Adult; Children's; Young Adult

Send: Query
Don't send: Full text

Publishes nonfiction titles on military history and experiences, and fast-paced Historical or Adventure Fiction Books for Children, Teens and Young Adults. Primarily interested in American soldiers and their battles, but will also consider books on other armies (including the ancient world) and travel/adventure books. Send query with synopsis by email or post.

P0400 Helter Skelter Publishing
Book Publisher
United Kingdom

sales@helterskelterpublishing.com

http://www.helterskelterpublishing.com

Nonfiction > *Nonfiction Books*: Music

Publishes books on music.

Editor: Sean Body

Publishing Imprint: Firefly Publishing

P0401 Henry Holt Books for Young Readers
Publishing Imprint
United States

press.inquiries@macmillan.com

https://us.macmillan.com/mackids/

Book Publisher: Macmillan Children's Publishing Group **(P0522)**

CHILDREN'S > **Fiction**
  Chapter Books; *Novels*; *Picture Books*

Publishes quality picture books, chapter books, and novels for preschoolers through young adults.

P0402 Heritage House
Book Publisher
103 – 1075 Pendergast Street, Victoria, BC, V8V 0A1
Canada

books@heritagehouse.ca
info@heritagehouse.ca

http://www.heritagehouse.ca
https://www.facebook.com/HeritageHouseBooks/
https://twitter.com/HHPublishing
https://www.instagram.com/heritagehousepublishing/

ADULT > **Nonfiction** > *Nonfiction Books*
  Animals; Arts; Biography; British Columbia; Comedy / Humour; Crime; History; Legal; Leisure; Memoir; Military; Nature; Nautical; Outdoor Activities; Photography; Politics; Sport; Travel; Yukon

CHILDREN'S
  Fiction
    Board Books; *Early Readers*; *Picture Books*
  Nonfiction > *Nonfiction Books*
    Nature; Science

YOUNG ADULT > **Fiction** > *Novels*

Send: Synopsis; Author bio; Market info; Outline; Writing sample
How to send: Email
How not to send: Post

Committed to amplifying the stories and voices of the extraordinary people who have helped shape the diverse cultural landscape of Western Canada. Also publishes humour, contemporary art and photography, Indigenous studies, politics and contemporary issues, nature guides, and children's books.

P0403 Heroic Books
Book Publisher; Editorial Service
United Kingdom

info@heroicbooks.com

http://www.heroicbooks.com
https://www.facebook.com/HeroicBooks/
https://twitter.com/HeroicBooks
https://www.instagram.com/heroicbooks/

ADULT > **Fiction** > *Novels*
  Fantasy; Science Fiction

YOUNG ADULT > **Fiction** > *Novels*
  Fantasy; Science Fiction

How to send: Online submission system

Costs: Offers services that writers have to pay for.

We are an innovative publisher across the fantasy and science fiction genre. We are committed to finding the most exciting authors and publishing their work to the highest possible quality. Experienced in media and business beyond the traditional, we are committed to breaking new ground for our authors. Working with illustrators, narrators, and other creatives, we aim to make sure every novel reaches its full potential. So, if you are an author, an artist, a narrator, a reader – please join us.

Author: Davis Ashura

Book: A Testament of Steel

Editor: Zoe George

P0404 Hertfordshire Publications
Publishing Imprint
United Kingdom

http://www.uhpress.co.uk/subject-areas/hertfordshire-publications

Book Publisher: University of Hertfordshire Press (**P0864**)

ACADEMIC > **Nonfiction** > *Nonfiction Books*: Local History

P0405 Hippocrene Books, Inc.
Book Publisher
171 Madison Avenue, New York NY 10016
United States
Tel: +1 (212) 685-4371
Fax: +1 (718) 228-6355

editorial@hippocrenebooks.com

https://www.hippocrenebooks.com

Types: Nonfiction
Formats: Reference
Subjects: Cookery; History
Markets: Adult

Publishes general nonfiction, particularly foreign language reference books and ethnic cookbooks. No fiction. Send submissions by email.

P0406 The History Press
Book Publisher
97 St George's Place, Cheltenham, Gloucestershire, GL50 3QB
United Kingdom
Tel: +44 (0) 1242 895310
Fax: +44 (0) 1453 883233

web@thehistorypress.co.uk

https://www.thehistorypress.co.uk
https://www.facebook.com/thehistorypressuk/
https://twitter.com/TheHistoryPress/
https://www.pinterest.com/thehistorypress/

Nonfiction > *Nonfiction Books*: History

Send: Query; Synopsis; Author bio; Market info; Proposal
Don't send: Full text
How to send: Email

Publishes books on history, from local to international. Welcomes submissions from both new and established authors. Send query by email. No unsolicited mss. See website for full guidelines.

Publishing Imprint: Phillimore (**P0645**)

P0407 Hobble Creek Press
Publishing Imprint

Book Publisher: Cedar Fort (**P0156**)

P0408 Hodder & Stoughton Ltd
Book Publisher
Carmelite House, 50 Victoria Embankment, London, EC4Y 0DZ
United Kingdom
Tel: +44 (0) 20 3122 6000

enquiries@hachette.co.uk

https://www.hodder.co.uk

Types: Fiction; Nonfiction
Subjects: Autobiography; Comedy / Humour; Commercial; Cookery; History; Lifestyle; Literary; Spirituality; Travel
Markets: Adult

How to send: Through a literary agent

Large London-based publisher of nonfiction and commercial and literary fiction.

Book Publishers: Hodder Faith; John Murray (Publishers) Ltd

Publishing Imprint: Nicholas Brealey Publishing

P0409 Hodder Children's Books
Publishing Imprint

Book Publisher: Hachette Children's Group (**P0350**)

P0410 Hodder Education
Book Publisher
Carmelite House, 50 Victoria Embankment, London, EC4Y 0DZ
United Kingdom
Tel: +44 (0) 1235 827720
Fax: +44 (0) 1235 400450

educationenquiries@hodder.co.uk

http://www.hoddereducation.co.uk

Types: Nonfiction
Formats: Reference
Subjects: Health; Medicine; Science; Self Help
Markets: Academic; Adult

Send: Query
Don't send: Full text

Publishes educational and reference books including home learning and school textbooks. See website for more details and for specific

submission addresses for different types of books.

Book Publisher: Rising Stars (**P0706**)

P0411 Hogarth
Publishing Imprint

Book Publisher: Random House (**P0690**)

P0412 Hogarth Press
Publishing Imprint
United Kingdom

Book Publisher: Vintage (**P0891**)

P0413 Hogs Back Books
Book Publisher
34 Long Street, Devizes, Wiltshire, SN10 1NT
United Kingdom

enquiries@hogsbackbooks.com
submissions@hogsbackbooks.com

http://www.hogsbackbooks.com

CHILDREN'S
  Fiction
    Early Readers; *Picture Books*
  Nonfiction > *Nonfiction Books*

TEEN > **Fiction** > *Novels*

YOUNG ADULT
  Fiction > *Novels*
  Nonfiction > *Nonfiction Books*

Send: Full text; Synopsis; Writing sample
How to send: Email; Post

Publishes picture books and nonfiction for children up to 10, early readers for children up to 14, teenage fiction and young adult fiction and nonfiction. Send submissions by email or by post to an address in France (see website for details). All responses are by email.

P0414 Holloway House
Publishing Imprint

Book Publisher: Kensington Publishing Corp. (**P0469**)

P0415 Honest Publishing
Book Publisher
United Kingdom

info@honestpublishing.com

https://www.honestpublishing.com
https://www.facebook.com/HonestPublishing
https://twitter.com/HonestPublisher

Fiction
  Novels; *Short Fiction*
Poetry > *Poetry Collections*

Closed to approaches.

A British independent book publisher of both fiction and nonfiction. Founded by three friends in 2010, the company strives to publish alternative, original voices, and to provide an audience for unique writers neglected by the mainstream.

Author: Bogdan Tiganov

P0416 Horizon Publishers
Publishing Imprint

Book Publisher: Cedar Fort (**P0156**)

P0417 Hot Key Books
Book Publisher
4th Floor, Victoria House, Bloomsbury Square, London, WC1B 4DA
United Kingdom
Tel: +44 (0) 20 3770 8883

hello@bonnierbooks.co.uk

http://hotkeybooks.com
https://twitter.com/HotKeyBooks
https://instagram.com/hotkeybooks/
https://www.facebook.com/HotKeyBooks

Book Publisher: Bonnier Books (UK) (**P0122**)

TEEN > **Fiction** > *Novels*

YOUNG ADULT > **Fiction** > *Novels*

How to send: Through a literary agent

Publishes fiction and nonfiction for teens and young adults. Accepts approaches through literary agents only.

P0418 Houghton Mifflin Harcourt Books for Young Readers Division
Book Publisher

Book Publisher: Houghton Mifflin Harcourt

Publishing Imprint: Clarion Books (**P0177**)

P0419 Howard
Publishing Imprint

Book Publisher: Simon & Schuster Adult Publishing (**P0766**)

P0420 HQ
Publishing Imprint
United Kingdom

Book Publisher: HarperCollins UK (**P0382**)

P0421 HQ Digital
Publishing Imprint
United Kingdom

Book Publisher: HarperCollins UK (**P0382**)

P0422 Human Kinetics
Book Publisher
1607 N Market Street, Champaign, Illinois 61825
United States
Tel: +1 (800) 747-4457
Fax: +1 (217) 351-1549

acquisitions@hkusa.com

https://us.humankinetics.com
https://www.facebook.com/HumanKinetics

ACADEMIC > **Nonfiction** > *Nonfiction Books*
 Fitness; Health; Nutrition; Sport

ADULT > **Nonfiction** > *Nonfiction Books*
 Fitness; Health; Nutrition; Sport

PROFESSIONAL > **Nonfiction** > *Nonfiction Books*
 Fitness; Health; Nutrition; Sport

Send: Query; Table of Contents
How to send: Post; Email

Publishes books on health, fitness, and sport, aimed at the academic market, professionals in the field, and the general public. Send query by post or email.

P0423 Hunt End Books
Publishing Imprint
United Kingdom

Book Publisher: Brewin Books Ltd (**P0129**)

P0424 Hymns Ancient & Modern Ltd
Book Publisher
13a Hellesdon Park Road, Norwich, NR6 5DR
United Kingdom

https://www.hymnsam.co.uk

Types: Nonfiction
Formats: Reference
Subjects: Biography; Comedy / Humour; Music; Religion
Markets: Academic; Adult

Send: Query
Don't send: Full text

Publishes religious books including hymn books, liturgical material, and schoolbooks.

Publishing Imprints: Canterbury Press; Church House Publishing (*P0173*); SCM Press; Saint Andrew Press (**P0726**)

P0425 Ian Allan Publishing Ltd
Book Publisher
Terminal House, Shepperton, TW17 8AS
United Kingdom

https://www.ianallanpublishing.com

Types: Nonfiction
Formats: Reference
Subjects: History; Hobbies; Travel; Warfare
Markets: Adult

Former publisher of nonfiction and reference books relating to transport, now publishes Masonic books and magazine.

Publishing Imprints: Lewis Masonic (*P0490*); Midland Publishing

P0426 Ibbetson Street Press
Book Publisher
25 School Street, Somerville, MA 02143
United States
Tel: +1 (617) 628-2313

tapestryofvoices@yahoo.com

http://ibbetsonpress.com

Types: Poetry
Subjects: Literary
Markets: Adult

Send: Full text

Poetry press publishing a regular journal and poetry books. Send query by email with brief bio and 3-5 poems in the body of the email. No attachments.

Editors: Harris Gardner; Lawrence Kessenich; Emily Pineau

P0427 Icon Books Ltd
Book Publisher
Omnibus Business Centre, 39-41 North Road, London, N7 9DP
United Kingdom
Tel: +44 (0) 20 7697 9695
Fax: +44 (0) 20 7697 9501

submissions@iconbooks.com

http://www.iconbooks.co.uk

Types: Nonfiction
Subjects: Arts; Comedy / Humour; History; Philosophy; Politics; Psychology; Religion; Science; Sport
Markets: Adult

Send: Query
Don't send: Full text

Submit by email only. See website for full guidelines. Has in the past tended to publish series of books, including an ongoing series of graphic introductions to key figure and ideas in history, science, psychology, philosophy, religion, and the arts, but increasingly publishing individual nonfiction titles in such areas as politics, popular philosophy and psychology, history, sport, humour and, especially, popular science.

P0428 Idyll Arbor
Book Publisher
39129 264th Ave SE, Enumclaw, WA 98022
United States
Tel: +1 (360) 825-7797
Fax: +1 (360) 825-5670

sales@idyllarbor.com

http://www.idyllarbor.com

Types: Nonfiction
Subjects: Health; How To; Leisure; Medicine; Psychology
Markets: Adult; Professional

Send: Full text

Publishes practical books on healthcare and therapies aimed at people or families dealing with a condition and activity directors. Will accept completed mss or queries, but prefers to receive query with outline and sample chapter by email.

P0429 Ig Publishing
Book Publisher
PO Box 2547, New York, NY 10163
United States
Tel: +1 (718) 797-0676
Fax: +1 (718) 797-0676

robert@igpub.com

http://igpub.com

Types: Fiction; Nonfiction
Subjects: Culture; Literary
Markets: Adult; Young Adult

Send: Query
Don't send: Full text

Publishes original literary fiction from writers who are perceived to have been overlooked by the mainstream publishing establishment, plus political and cultural nonfiction. Young adult imprint is devoted to bringing back young adult literature from as far back as the '30s and '40s and as recently as the '70s and '80s. No unsolicited mss. Send query by email only.

Editor-in-Chief: Robert Lasner

P0430 Image Books
Publishing Imprint

Book Publisher: Random House (**P0690**)

P0431 Imagine Publishing
Publishing Imprint
United States

adult.submissions@charlesbridge.com

https://www.imaginebooks.net
https://twitter.com/Imagine_CB
https://www.facebook.com/ImaginePress/
https://www.pinterest.com/charlesbridge/adult-books-from-imagine-publishing/
https://www.instagram.com/imagine_cb/

Book Publisher: Charlesbridge Publishing (**P0164**)

Nonfiction
Coffee Table Books: General
Nonfiction Books: Arts; Comedy / Humour; Cookery; History; Nature; Politics; Women's Studies
Puzzle Books: General

Send: Full text; Writing sample
How to send: Email

Publishes 8-10 titles a year, primarily focused on history, politics, women's studies, and nature.

P0432 Imagine That Publishing
Book Publisher
Marine House, Tide Mill Way, Woodbridge, Suffolk, IP12 1AP
United Kingdom
Tel: +44 (0) 1394 386651

customerservice@topthatpublishing.com

https://www.imaginethat.com
https://www.facebook.com/ImagineThatPublishing/
https://twitter.com/imaginethatbook
https://www.instagram.com/imaginethatbook/

CHILDREN'S
Fiction > *Novels*
Nonfiction > *Nonfiction Books*

Closed to approaches.

Publishes Activity Books, Board Books, Fiction, Magnetic Books, Novelty Books, Picture Storybooks, Press Out & Play, and Sticker Books. Does not currently publish "regular" children's or adults fiction. See online book catalogue for the kinds of books published. If suitable for the list, send submissions by email (preferred), ideally under 1MB, or by post (mss not returned). See website for full guidelines. Responds within 8 weeks if interested. No simultaneous submissions.

Editors: Dan Graham; Josh Simpkin-Betts

P0433 Immanion Press
Book Publisher
United Kingdom

editorial@immanion-press.com

https://www.immanion-press.com/

Types: Fiction; Nonfiction
Subjects: Comedy / Humour; Fantasy; Horror; Literary; Science Fiction; Spirituality
Markets: Adult

Send: Query
Don't send: Full text

Closed to fiction submissions as at April 2020. Publishes innovative and intelligent dark fantasy, literary fantasy, science fiction, horror, slipstream, magic realism, and black comedies. Also publishes nonfiction on magic, qabala, Tarot and associated thematic subjects. No derivative or "twee" high fantasy, overly technical, non-character driven science fiction, or visceral gore horror. Send synopsis with first 30 pages and author bio by post or by email as Word, PDF, or plain text attachment. Full submission details on website.

P0434 Impact
Publishing Imprint
United States

http://www.impact-books.com

Book Publisher: Penguin Publishing Group (**P0633**)

Types: Nonfiction
Formats: Reference
Subjects: Arts; How To
Markets: Adult

Publishes books to assist artists drawing comics, superheroes, Japanese-style manga, fantasy, creatures, action, caricature, anime, etc.

Acquisitions Editor: Pamela Wissman

P0435 Impress Books Limited
Book Publisher
13-14 Crook Business Centre, New Road, Crook, County Durham, DL15 8QX
United Kingdom

contact@impress-books.co.uk

http://www.impress-books.co.uk
http://instagram.com/impress_books
https://twitter.com/impressBooks1
https://www.facebook.com/Impress-Books-1623623654535795/

Fiction > *Novels*
Crime; Historical Fiction; Literary

Nonfiction > *Nonfiction Books*

Send: Writing sample; Synopsis
How to send: Word file email attachment; Online contact form

Interested in quality, thought-provoking titles for the enquiring general reader. Specialises in discovering and nurturing fresh voices in crime, historical and literary fiction.

P0436 Indiana University Press
Book Publisher
IU Office of Scholarly Publishing, Herman B Wells Library E350, 1320 E 10th Street E4, Bloomington, IN 47405-3907
United States
Tel: +1 (812) 855-8817

iuporder@indiana.edu

https://iupress.org
https://www.facebook.com/iupress
https://twitter.com/iupress
https://www.instagram.com/iu.press/
https://www.youtube.com/c/IndianaUniversityPress/videos

ACADEMIC > **Nonfiction** > *Nonfiction Books*
Africa; American Civil War; American Midwest; Eastern Europe; Films; Folklore, Myths, and Legends; Gender; Holocaust Studies; International; Ireland; Judaism; Media; Middle East; Military History; Music; Paleontology; Performing Arts; Philosophy; Railways; Refugees; Regional; Religion; Russia; Sexuality; Transport

Send: Proposal; Outline; Table of Contents; Writing sample; Author bio
How to send: Online submission system

Submit proposals via online proposal submission form.

P0437 Ink Road
Publishing Imprint

Book Publisher: Black & White Publishing Ltd (**P0101**)

P0438 The Innovation Press
Book Publisher
United States

submissions@theinnovationpress.com
info@theinnovationpress.com

https://www.theinnovationpress.com
http://www.facebook.com/theinnovationpress
https://twitter.com/InnovationPress
http://instagram.com/theinnovationpress

CHILDREN'S
  Fiction
    Chapter Books; *Graphic Novels*; *Middle Grade*; *Picture Books*
  Nonfiction
    Activity Books; *Chapter Books*; *Middle Grade*; *Picture Books*

Send: Synopsis; Writing sample; Author bio
How to send: Email

Publishes memorable children's books that inspire learning, enliven creative thinking, and spark imaginations. From innovative activity books to clever fiction.

P0439 Insomniac Press
Book Publisher
520 Princess Avenue, London, ON N6B 2B8
Canada
Tel: +1 (519) 266-3556

http://www.insomniacpress.com

Types: Fiction; Nonfiction; Poetry
Formats: Reference; Short Fiction
Subjects: Business; Comedy / Humour; Commercial; Crime; Culture; Experimental; Finance; Gardening; Health; Legal; Lifestyle; Literary; Literary Criticism; Medicine; Music; Mystery; Politics; Religion; Self Help; Sport; Suspense; Travel
Markets: Adult

Send: Query
Don't send: Full text

Particularly interested in creative nonfiction on business / personal finance; gay and lesbian studies; black Canadian studies and others. No science fiction, cookbooks, romance, or children's books. Send query by email or post in first instance. Approaches by authors who have had work published elsewhere (e.g. short stories in magazines) will receive closer attention.

P0440 International Publishers
Book Publisher
235 W 23rd Street, New York, NY 10011-2302
United States
Tel: +1 (212) 366-9816
Fax: +1 (212) 366-9820

service@intpubnyc.com

https://www.intpubnyc.com

Nonfiction > *Nonfiction Books*
  Culture; Gender Issues; History; Marxism; Philosophy; Politics; Social Issues

Marxist publishers of books on labour rights, race and gender issues, Marxist science, etc.

P0441 InterVarsity Press (IVP)
Book Publisher
36 Causton Street, London, SW1P 4ST
United Kingdom
Tel: +44 (0) 20 7592 3900

submissions@ivpbooks.com

https://ivpbooks.com
https://www.facebook.com/ivpbooks
https://www.instagram.com/ivpbooks/
https://twitter.com/IVPbookcentre

ACADEMIC > **Nonfiction** > *Nonfiction Books*: Religion

ADULT > **Nonfiction** > *Nonfiction Books*
  Biography; Christian Living; Church History; Contemporary Culture; Religion

Send: Query
How to send: Online contact form

Aims to produce quality, Evangelical books for the digital age. Send query through form on website.

P0442 Interweave
Publishing Imprint
United States

Book Publisher: Penguin Publishing Group (**P0633**)

Types: Nonfiction
Subjects: Crafts; Hobbies
Markets: Adult

Editor: Kerry Bogert

P0443 IOP Publishing
Book Publisher
Temple Circus, Temple Way, Bristol, BS1 6HG
United Kingdom
Tel: +44 (0) 1179 297481
Fax: +44 (0) 1179 294318

ebooks@ioppublishing.org

https://ioppublishing.org

Types: Nonfiction
Subjects: Science
Markets: Academic; Professional

Send: Query
Don't send: Full text

Publishes books in physics and related areas such as mathematical physics, medical physics, astronomy, materials science, nanoscience, electronic materials and instrumentation. Continually looking to add new high-quality books. If you have an idea for an advanced textbook, monograph, review or handbook submit according to guidelines on website.

P0444 Iqon Editions
Publishing Imprint

Book Publisher: The Quarto Group, Inc. (**P0679**)

P0445 Itchy Coo
Publishing Imprint

Book Publisher: Black & White Publishing Ltd (**P0101**)

P0446 Ivy Kids
Publishing Imprint

Book Publisher: The Quarto Group, Inc. (**P0679**)

P0447 Ivy Press
Publishing Imprint

Book Publisher: The Quarto Group, Inc. (**P0679**)

P0448 Jacar Press
Book Publisher
6617 Deerview Trl, Durham, NC 27712
United States
Tel: +1 (919) 810-2863

jacarassist@gmail.com

http://jacarpress.com

Types: Poetry
Subjects: Literary
Markets: Adult

Send: Full text

Publisher of full-length and chapbook collections of poetry. Accepts submissions through annual competitions only ($15 submission fee). Also publishes online magazine.

P0449 Jacaranda Books Art Music Ltd
Book Publisher
27 Old Gloucester Street, London, WC1N 3AX
United Kingdom

office@jacarandabooksartmusic.co.uk

https://www.jacarandabooksartmusic.co.uk

Types: Fiction
Subjects: Arts; Autobiography; Beauty; Commercial; Crime; Fashion; History;

Literary; Music; Photography; Science Fiction; Women's Interests
Markets: Adult

Send: Query
Don't send: Full text

Publishes adult fiction and nonfiction, including crime, romance, illustrated books, biography, memoir, and autobiography. Particularly interested in books where the central character or theme relates to minority groups and/or has strong female protagonists. Also interested in original works from or about African, African-American, Caribbean and black British artists working in the fields of photography, fine art, fashion, and contemporary and modern art, and artists of calibre from the soul, blues, R&B and reggae traditions. Send query with writer CV, detailed synopsis, and 20-30 pages of consecutive text. See website for full submission guidelines.

Publisher: Valerie Brandes

P0450 Jane's Information Group
Book Publisher
Sentinel House, 163 Brighton Road, Coulsdon, Surrey, CR5 2YH
United Kingdom

https://www.janes.com

Types: Nonfiction
Formats: Reference
Subjects: Warfare
Markets: Adult

Publisher of magazines, books, reference works, online material, and yearbooks related to defence, aerospace, security, and transport topics.

P0451 Jeter Publishing
Publishing Imprint

Book Publisher: Simon & Schuster Adult Publishing (**P0766**)

P0452 Jewish Lights Publishing
Publishing Imprint
4507 Charlotte Ave, Suite 100, Nashville, TN 37209
United States
Tel: +1 (615) 255-2665
Fax: +1 (615) 255-5081

submissions@turnerpublishing.com

http://jewishlights.com

Book Publisher: Turner Publishing (**P0840**)

Types: Fiction; Nonfiction
Subjects: Crime; History; Men's Interests; Mystery; Philosophy; Religion; Science Fiction; Women's Interests
Markets: Adult; Children's; Young Adult

Publishes work about the unity and community of the Jewish People and the relevance of Judaism to everyday life. Send submissions by email.

P0453 Jo Fletcher Books
Publishing Imprint
United Kingdom

info@jofletcherbooks.co.uk
submissions@jofletcherbooks.co.uk

https://www.jofletcherbooks.com
https://www.facebook.com/jofletcherbooks
https://twitter.com/JoFletcherBooks
https://www.youtube.com/channel/UCU2vJMMmmWwI-B5cHwKKSFQ

Book Publisher: Quercus Books (**P0682**)

Fiction > *Novels*
Fantasy; Horror; Science Fiction

Send: Query; Synopsis; Writing sample
How to send: Word file email attachment

Specialist science fiction, fantasy and horror imprint. Send query by email with synopsis and first three chapters or first 10,000 words.

Editor: Nicola Budd

P0454 Joffe Books Ltd
Book Publisher
United Kingdom

submissions@joffebooks.com

http://www.joffebooks.com

Types: Fiction
Subjects: Crime; Mystery; Suspense; Thrillers
Markets: Adult

Send: Full text

Publishes full-length crime fiction, mysteries, and thrillers. No kids books, sci-fi, nonfiction, conspiracy theories, or erotic. Send query by email with complete ms as an attachment, a synopsis in the body of the email, and 100 words about yourself. Include "submission" in the subject line. Reply not guaranteed unless interested. See website for full guidelines.

Editor: Jasper Joffe

P0455 John Scognamiglio Books
Publishing Imprint

Book Publisher: Kensington Publishing Corp. (**P0469**)

P0456 Jolly Learning
Book Publisher
Tailours House, High Road, Chigwell, Essex, IG7 6DL
United Kingdom
Tel: +44 (0) 20 8501 0405
Fax: +44 (0) 20 8500 1696

info@jollylearning.co.uk

https://www.jollylearning.co.uk
https://www.facebook.com/Jolly-Learning-195770143786043/
http://www.twitter.com/jollylearning
https://www.youtube.com/user/jollylearning/videos

CHILDREN'S
  Fiction > *Early Readers*
  Nonfiction > *Early Readers*

PROFESSIONAL > **Nonfiction** > *Nonfiction Books:* Education

Publishes books for children to help with reading, using the synthetic phonics method of teaching the letter sounds in a way that aims to be fun and multi-sensory.

P0457 Jonathan Cape
Publishing Imprint
United Kingdom

https://www.penguin.co.uk/company/publishers/vintage/jonathan-cape.html

Book Publisher: Vintage (**P0891**)

Types: Fiction; Nonfiction; Poetry
Markets: Adult

Send: Query
Don't send: Full text

Renowned for its prizewinning fiction, nonfiction, poetry and graphic novels.

P0458 Josef Weinberger Ltd
Book Publisher
12-14 Mortimer Street, London, W1T 3JJ
United Kingdom
Tel: +44 (0) 20 7580 2827
Fax: +44 (0) 20 7436 9616

general.info@jwmail.co.uk

http://www.josef-weinberger.com

Types: Scripts
Formats: Theatre Scripts
Markets: Adult

Publishes theatre scripts for musicals, plays, pantomimes, operas, and operettas.

P0459 JournalStone Publishing
Book Publisher
United States

journalstone.submissions@gmail.com

https://journalstone.com

Types: Fiction
Subjects: Commercial; Gothic; Literary
Markets: Adult

Closed to approaches.

Publishes horror in all its forms – from literary to weird, Gothic to psychological, and (almost) everything in between.

P0460 Kamera Books
Publishing Imprint
United Kingdom

Book Publisher: Oldcastle Books Group
(**P0592**)

P0461 Karnak House
Book Publisher
United Kingdom

karnakhouse@aol.com

https://www.karnakhouse.co.uk

Types: Fiction; Nonfiction; Poetry
Subjects: Anthropology; Culture; History;
Literary Criticism; Music; Philosophy;
Politics; Religion; Science; Women's Interests
Markets: Adult; Children's

Publisher of books on the culture and history
of African civilisations and cultures
worldwide.

P0462 The Kates Hill Press
Book Publisher
39 Cowley Drive, Dudley, West Midlands,
DY1 2SS
United Kingdom
Tel: +44 (0) 1384 254719

kateshillpress1992@gmail.com

https://kateshillpress.com

Types: Fiction; Nonfiction; Poetry
Formats: Short Fiction
Subjects: Autobiography; Comedy / Humour;
Crime; History; Sociology; Sport
Markets: Adult

Small independent publisher producing short
runs of fiction and social history books with a
west midlands theme or by a west midlands
writer. Also publishes booklets of poetry and
dialect verse by Black Country/West Midlands
poets.

P0463 Katherine Tegen Books
Publishing Imprint

Book Publisher: HarperCollins

P0464 Kathy Dawson Books
Publishing Imprint
Penguin Group, 375 Hudson Street, New York,
NY 10014
United States

http://kathydawsonbooks.tumblr.com

Book Publishers: Penguin Group (USA);
Penguin Young Readers Group (**P0638**)

Types: Fiction
Markets: Children's; Young Adult

Send: Query
Don't send: Full text

Publishes middle grade and young adult
fiction. Submit query by post only, with first

10 pages and details of any relevant publishing
history. Do not include SASE – all
submissions are recycled. Response only if
interested.

P0465 Kelpies
Publishing Imprint
United Kingdom

floris@florisbooks.co.uk

https://discoverkelpies.co.uk
https://www.facebook.com/DiscoverKelpies/
https://twitter.com/DiscoverKelpies

Book Publisher: Floris Books (**P0298**)

CHILDREN'S
Fiction
    Novels: Adventure; Comedy / Humour;
    Fantasy; Ghost Stories; Magic; Romance;
    Science Fiction; Scotland; Thrillers;
    Traditional
    Picture Books: General, and in
    particular: Scotland
Nonfiction
    Nonfiction Books: Education; History;
    Scotland; Sport
    Picture Books: General, and in
    particular: Animals; Scotland

Publishes Scottish books for children
everywhere. Does not accept unsolicited
submissions direct from authors, unless they
are from under-represented communities.
Welcomes submissions from literary agents.

P0466 Kenilworth Press
Publishing Imprint
Quiller Publishing, Wykey House, Wykey,
Shrewsbury, Shropshire, SY4 1JA
United Kingdom
Tel: +44 (0) 1939 261616

info@quillerbooks.com

https://www.quillerpublishing.com/product-
category/equestrian-kenilworth-press

Book Publisher: Quiller Publishing Ltd
(**P0685**)

Nonfiction > *Nonfiction Books*
    Equestrian; Horses

Send: Synopsis; Writing sample; Market info;
Author bio; Self-Addressed Stamped Envelope
(SASE)
How to send: Email; Post

Equestrian publisher publishing nonfiction.
Not accepting poetry or novels.

Editor: John Beaton

P0467 Kensington Hardcover
Publishing Imprint

Book Publisher: Kensington Publishing Corp.
(**P0469**)

P0468 Kensington Mass-Market
Publishing Imprint

Book Publisher: Kensington Publishing Corp.
(**P0469**)

P0469 Kensington Publishing Corp.
Book Publisher
119 West 40th Street, New York, NY 10018
United States
Tel: +1 (800) 221-2647

jscognamiglio@kensingtonbooks.com

http://www.kensingtonbooks.com

Types: Fiction; Nonfiction
Subjects: Autobiography; Business;
Commercial; Contemporary; Crime; Fantasy;
Health; History; Lifestyle; Literary; Mystery;
Romance; Science Fiction; Self Help;
Suspense; Thrillers; Warfare; Women's
Interests
Markets: Adult

Send: Query
Don't send: Full text

No children's, young adult, or poetry. Send
query only, in the body of the email. No
attachments. See website for full guidelines.

Editor: John Scognamiglio

Publishing Imprints: Aphrodisia (*P0043*);
Brava (*P0127*); Citadel Press (*P0175*); Dafina
(*P0208*); Holloway House (*P0414*); John
Scognamiglio Books (*P0455*); KTeen (*P0479*);
KTeen Dafina (*P0480*); Kensington Hardcover
(*P0467*); Kensington Mass-Market (*P0468*);
Kensington Trade Paperback (*P0470*); Lyle
Stuart Books (*P0514*); Lyrical Caress (*P0516*);
Lyrical Liaison (*P0517*); Lyrical Press
(**P0518**); Lyrical Shine (*P0519*); Lyrical
Underground (*P0520*); Pinnacle (*P0653*);
Rebel Base Books (*P0697*); Zebra; Zebra
Shout (*P0948*)

P0470 Kensington Trade Paperback
Publishing Imprint

Book Publisher: Kensington Publishing Corp.
(**P0469**)

P0471 Kernpunkt Press
Book Publisher
United States

http://www.kernpunktpress.com

Types: Fiction; Nonfiction
Formats: Short Fiction
Subjects: History; Literary; Science Fiction
Markets: Adult

Send: Query
Don't send: Full text

Independent publisher of literary fiction. Values art over entertainment. Send submission through online submission system. $10 submission fee.

Editor-in-Chief: Jesi Buell

P0472 King Dragon Press
Publishing Imprint

Book Publisher: Cedar Fort (**P0156**)

P0473 Klutz
Publishing Imprint

Book Publisher: Scholastic (**P0740**)

P0474 Kluwer Law International
Book Publisher
25 Canada Square, Canary Wharf, London, E14 5LQ
United Kingdom

https://kluwerlawonline.com

Book Publisher: Wolters Kluwer (**P0937**)

PROFESSIONAL > **Nonfiction** > *Nonfiction Books*: Legal

Send: Query
Don't send: Full text

Publisher of international law titles, including looseleafs and journals. Welcomes unsolicited synopses and ideas on relevant topics.

P0475 Knopf Doubleday Publishing Group
Book Publisher
United States

http://knopfdoubleday.com

Book Publisher: Penguin Random House

Fiction > *Novels*

Nonfiction > *Nonfiction Books*

Publishing Imprints: Alfred A. Knopf (*P0028*); Anchor Books (*P0036*); Black Lizard (*P0106*); Doubleday (*P0240*); Everyman's Library (*P0272*); Nan A. Talese (**P0564**); Pantheon (*P0612*); Schocken Books (*P0739*); Vintage Books (*P0892*)

P0476 Kokila
Publishing Imprint
United States

Book Publisher: Penguin Young Readers Group (**P0638**)

P0477 Kore Press
Book Publisher
4207 E. Waverly Street, Tucson, AZ 85712
United States
Tel: +1 (520) 261-2438

https://korepress.org

Types: Fiction; Nonfiction; Poetry
Subjects: Autobiography; Culture; Literary; Literary Criticism
Markets: Adult

Closed to approaches.

Publishes fiction, poetry, nonfiction, hybrid, and cultural criticism. Accepts submissions both through open submission windows and competitions.

Managing Editor: Ann Dernier

P0478 Krause Publications
Publishing Imprint
United States

Book Publisher: Penguin Publishing Group (**P0633**)

Types: Nonfiction
Formats: Reference
Subjects: Antiques; Hobbies; How To; Sport
Markets: Adult

Largest publisher of material on hobbies and collectibles in the world. Send query with outline, sample chapter, and description of how your book will make a unique contribution.

P0479 KTeen
Publishing Imprint

Book Publisher: Kensington Publishing Corp. (**P0469**)

P0480 KTeen Dafina
Publishing Imprint

Book Publisher: Kensington Publishing Corp. (**P0469**)

P0481 Lantana Publishing
Book Publisher
The Oxford Foundry, 3-5 Hythe Bridge Street, Oxford, OX1 2EW
United Kingdom

submissions@lantanapublishing.com

http://www.lantanapublishing.com

Types: Fiction; Nonfiction
Subjects: Contemporary; Culture
Markets: Children's

Send: Full text

Publishes picture books and narrative nonfiction focused on diversity for 4 to 8 year olds up to 500 words (prefers 200-400 words). Particularly interested in contemporary writing with modern-day settings, especially if they feature Black, Asian and Minority Ethnic families. Publishes almost exclusively authors of Black, Asian and Minority Ethnic backgrounds.

P0482 Laurence King Publishing Ltd
Book Publisher
Carmelite House, 50 Victoria Embankment, London, EC4Y 0DZ
United Kingdom
Tel: +44 (0) 20 7841 6900

commissioning@laurenceking.com

https://www.laurenceking.com
https://twitter.com/LaurenceKingPub
https://www.instagram.com/LaurenceKingPub/
https://www.facebook.com/LaurenceKingPublishing
https://www.pinterest.co.uk/LaurenceKingPub/
https://vimeo.com/laurencekingpublishing
https://www.youtube.com/user/laurencekingpub

Book Publisher: Hachette UK (**P0354**)

ACADEMIC > **Nonfiction** > *Nonfiction Books*
 Architecture; Arts; Beauty; Design; Fashion; Films; Music; Nature; Photography; Popular Culture; Popular Science

ADULT > **Nonfiction** > *Nonfiction Books*
 Architecture; Arts; Beauty; Design; Fashion; Films; Music; Nature; Photography; Popular Culture; Popular Science

CHILDREN'S > **Nonfiction** > *Illustrated Books*

Send: Query; Synopsis; Market info; Author bio
How to send: Email

Publisher of books on the creative arts. Send proposal by email.

P0483 Leapfrog Press
Book Publisher
PO Box 505, Fredonia, NY 14063
United States

leapfrog@leapfrogpress.com

https://leapfrogpress.com
https://www.facebook.com/Leapfrogpress
https://twitter.com/leapfrogpress1
https://instagram.com/leapfrogpress

ADULT
 Fiction > *Novels*
 Nonfiction > *Nonfiction Books*
 Poetry > *Poetry Collections*

CHILDREN'S > **Fiction** > *Middle Grade*

YOUNG ADULT > **Fiction** > *Novels*

Closed to approaches.

Publisher with an eclectic list of fiction, poetry, and nonfiction, including paperback originals of adult, young adult and middle-grade fiction, and nonfiction.

P0484 Leaping Hare Press
Publishing Imprint

Book Publisher: The Quarto Group, Inc.
(**P0679**)

P0485 Leo Cooper
Publishing Imprint

Book Publisher: Pen & Sword Books Ltd
(**P0626**)

P0486 Lerner Digital
Publishing Imprint

Book Publisher: Lerner Publishing Group
(**P0487**)

P0487 Lerner Publishing Group
Book Publisher
241 First Avenue North, Minneapolis, MN
55401-1607
United States
Tel: +1 (800) 328-4929
Fax: +1 (800) 332-1132

custserve@lernerbooks.com

https://lernerbooks.com
https://www.facebook.com/lernerbooks
https://twitter.com/lernerbooks

CHILDREN'S
 Fiction
  Audiobooks; *Ebooks*; *Graphic Novels*;
  Middle Grade; *Novels*; *Picture Books*
 Nonfiction
  Audiobooks; *Ebooks*; *Nonfiction Books*
YOUNG ADULT
 Fiction
  Audiobooks; *Ebooks*; *Novels*
 Nonfiction
  Audiobooks; *Ebooks*; *Nonfiction Books*

How to send: Through a literary agent; By
referral

Publishes fiction and nonfiction for children
and young adults. No submissions or queries
from unagented or unreferred authors.

: Zelda Wagner

Publishing Imprints: Carolrhoda Books;
Carolrhoda Lab (*P0151*); Darby Creek
(**P0214**); Ediciones Lerner (*P0252*); First
Avenue Editions; Graphic Universe (*P0340*);
Kar-Ben Publishing; Lerner Digital (*P0486*);
Lerner Publications; LernerClassroom
(*P0488*); Millbrook Press (*P0546*); Twenty-
First Century Books (*P0844*); Zest Books
(*P0951*)

P0488 LernerClassroom
Publishing Imprint

Book Publisher: Lerner Publishing Group
(**P0487**)

P0489 Les Figues Press
Book Publisher
6671 Sunset Blvd., Suite 1521, Los Angeles,

CA 90028
United States
Tel: +1 (323) 734-4732

info@lesfigues.com

http://www.lesfigues.com

Types: Fiction; Poetry
Formats: Short Fiction
Markets: Adult

Send: Full text

Publishes fiction and poetry. Accepts
submissions through its annual contest only
($25 entry fee). Accepts poetry, novellas,
innovative novels, anti-novels, short story
collections, lyric essays, hybrids, and all forms
not otherwise specified. Submit via form on
website.

P0490 Lewis Masonic
Publishing Imprint

Book Publisher: Ian Allan Publishing Ltd
(**P0425**)

P0491 Libraries Unlimited
Publishing Imprint
United States

Book Publisher: ABC-CLIO (**P0015**)

P0492 Lighthouse Trails Publishing
Book Publisher
PO Box 908, Eureka, MT 59917
United States
Tel: +1 (406) 889-3610
Fax: +1 (406) 889-3633

editors@lighthousetrails.com
david@lighthousetrails.com

https://www.lighthousetrails.com
https://www.facebook.com/
LighthouseTrailsResearch
http://www.twitter.com/LTrails
http://www.youtube.com/joiful77

ADULT
 Fiction > *Novels*: Christianity

 Nonfiction > *Nonfiction Books*: Christianity

CHILDREN'S > **Nonfiction**
 Activity Books: Christianity
 Nonfiction Books: Christianity
 Picture Books: Christianity
 Puzzle Books: Christianity

Publishes Christian books that promote Jesus
Christ.

Acquisitions Editor: David Dombrowski

P0493 Lillenas Music
Book Publisher
501 E Third St, Dayton, OH 45402
United States
Tel: +1 (800) 363-2122
Fax: +1 (800) 363-2122

info@lillenas.com

https://lillenas.com

ADULT > **Nonfiction** > *Nonfiction Books*
 Choral Music; Church Music; Hymns

CHILDREN'S > **Nonfiction** > *Nonfiction
Books*
 Choral Music; Church Music; Hymns

YOUNG ADULT > **Nonfiction** > *Nonfiction
Books*
 Choral Music; Church Music; Hymns

Closed to approaches.

Publishes religious music books.

P0494 The Lilliput Press
Book Publisher
62-63 Sitric Road, Arbour Hill, Dublin 7
Ireland

editorial@lilliputpress.ie
contact@lilliputpress.ie

http://www.lilliputpress.ie

Fiction > *Novels*: Ireland

Nonfiction
 Nonfiction Books: Architecture; Arts;
 Biography; Cultural Criticism; Environment;
 Food; Genealogy; History; Ireland; Literary
 Criticism; Literature; Local History; Memoir;
 Mind, Body, Spirit; Music; Nature;
 Philosophy; Photography; Travel
 Reference: Ireland

Poetry > *Any Poetic Form*: Ireland

Closed to approaches.

Publishes books broadly focused on Irish
themes. Send query by email with one-page
synopsis and cthree sample chapters. See
website for full guidelines.

P0495 Limitless Publishing
Book Publisher
United States

submissions@limitlesspublishing.com

http://www.limitlesspublishing.net

Types: Fiction; Nonfiction
Subjects: Fantasy; Mystery; Romance; Science
Fiction; Suspense; Thrillers; Warfare
Markets: Adult; Young Adult

Closed to approaches.

Send submissions by email with brief bio,
writing background and publishing history,
social networks used, description of your book,
and the first four chapters as a Microsoft Word
attachment.

P0496 Lincoln First Editions
Publishing Imprint

Book Publisher: The Quarto Group, Inc.
(**P0679**)

P0497 Liquid Light Press
Book Publisher
United States

editor@liquidlightpress.com

http://www.liquidlightpress.com

Types: Poetry
Subjects: Literary
Markets: Adult

Publishes poetry chapbooks. Send submissions by email. $25 reading fee per submission.

Editor: Markiah Friedman

P0498 Little Bigfoot
Publishing Imprint
United States

Book Publisher: Sasquatch Books (**P0737**)

CHILDREN'S
 Fiction > *Picture Books*
  General, and in particular: American West; Nature; Pacific Northwest

 Nonfiction > *Nonfiction Books*
  General, and in particular: American West; Nature; Pacific Northwest

P0499 Little Wing
Publishing Imprint
United Kingdom

https://mangobooks.co.uk/pages/about-mango-books

Book Publisher: Mango Books (**P0526**)

Nonfiction > *Nonfiction Books*: Entertainment

Publishes titles in the entertainment genre.

P0500 Little, Brown
Publishing Imprint

Publishing Imprint: Little, Brown Book Group (**P0502**)

P0501 Little, Brown and Company
Book Publisher
1290 Avenue of the Americas, New York, NY 10104
United States

https://www.littlebrown.com

Book Publisher: Hachette Book Group (**P0348**)

Types: Fiction; Nonfiction
Markets: Adult; Children's

How to send: Through a literary agent

Publishes general fiction and nonfiction for the adult and children's markets. No unsolicited MSS or approaches direct from authors – will only consider approaches from literary agents.

P0502 Little, Brown Book Group
Publishing Imprint
Carmelite House, 50 Victoria Embankment, LONDON, EC4Y 0DZ
United Kingdom
Tel: +44 (0) 20 3122 7000

info@littlebrown.co.uk

http://www.littlebrown.co.uk

Book Publisher: Hachette UK (**P0354**)

Types: Fiction; Nonfiction
Subjects: Autobiography; Comedy / Humour; Crime; Entertainment; Fantasy; History; How To; Literary; Literature; Science Fiction; Thrillers
Markets: Adult; Young Adult

How to send: Through a literary agent

Accepts submissions via agents only.

Book Publisher: Virago Press

Publishing Imprints: Abacus (*P0014*); Atom (*P0060*); Blackfriars (*P0109*); Constable & Robinson (*P0187*); Corsair (*P0192*); Dialogue Books (*P0231*); Fleet (*P0297*); Hachette Digital (*P0351*); Little, Brown (*P0500*); Orbit; Piatkus Books (**P0647**); Piatkus Constable & Robinson (**P0648**); Sphere (*P0783*); Virago (*P0895*)

P0503 Little, Brown Books for Young Readers
Publishing Imprint

Book Publisher: Hachette Children's Group (**P0350**)

P0504 Liverpool University Press
Book Publisher
4 Cambridge Street, Liverpool, L69 7ZU
United Kingdom
Tel: +44 (0) 1517 942233

lup@liv.ac.uk

https://www.liverpooluniversitypress.co.uk

Types: Nonfiction
Subjects: Archaeology; Architecture; Arts; Culture; History; Literature; Politics; Science Fiction; Sociology
Markets: Academic

Send: Query
Don't send: Full text

Publishes books and journals, specialising in Modern Languages, Postcolonial, Slavery and Migration Studies, Irish History, Labour History, Science Fiction Studies and Art History. Download proposal submission form from website.

Editors: Anthony Cond; Alison Welsby

P0505 Lonely Planet
Book Publisher
302 DLF City Court, Sikanderpur|Gurgaon 122002
India

https://www.lonelyplanet.com

Types: Nonfiction
Formats: Reference
Subjects: Travel
Markets: Adult

Publishes travel guides.

P0506 Lorena Jones Books
Publishing Imprint

Book Publisher: Random House (**P0690**)

P0507 Lorenz Books
Publishing Imprint

Book Publisher: Anness Publishing Ltd (**P0039**)

P0508 Lost Lake Folk Art
Publishing Imprint

Book Publisher: Shipwreckt Books Publishing Company (**P0762**)

P0509 Louisiana State University Press
Book Publisher
338 Johnston Hall, Louisiana State University, Baton Rouge, LA 7080
United States

https://lsupress.org
https://blog.lsupress.org/
https://www.facebook.com/pages/LSU-Press/38236386996
https://twitter.com/lsupress
https://soundcloud.com/lsupress_and_tsr

ACADEMIC > **Nonfiction** > *Nonfiction Books*
 African American; American Civil War; American History; Archaeology; Architecture; Caribbean History; Culture; Environment; History; Literature; Louisiana; Media; Poetry as a Subject; Roots Music; Social Justice; US Southern States; World War II

ADULT
 Nonfiction > *Nonfiction Books*
  Louisiana; US Southern States

 Poetry > *Any Poetic Form*

Send: Query; Writing sample; Outline; Author bio; Table of Contents; Market info
How to send: Email attachment

Publishes scholarly monographs and general interest books about Louisiana and the South.

Poetry proposals should include a cover letter, a one-page summary of the work, few sample poems from the work, and a current resume or curriculum vitae.

Proposals for everything except poetry should include a cover letter, working title, table of contents, sample chapters, information about competitive titles, and a resume or curriculum vitae.

P0510 Loyola Classics
Publishing Imprint

Book Publisher: Loyola Press (**P0511**)

P0511 Loyola Press
Book Publisher
3441 North Ashland Avenue, Chicago, IL 60657
United States
Tel: +1 (773) 281-1818
Fax: +1 (773) 281-0152

submissions@loyolapress.com

http://www.loyolapress.org

Types: Nonfiction
Subjects: Religion
Markets: Adult

Send: Query
Don't send: Full text

Catholic publisher of books on Catholic tradition, prayer, and spirituality. Send one-page query email or by post. See website for full guidelines.

Publishing Imprint: Loyola Classics (*P0510*)

P0512 Luna Press Publishing
Book Publisher
149/4 Morrison Street, Edinburgh, EH3 8AG
United Kingdom

lunapress@outlook.com

http://www.lunapresspublishing.com

Types: Fiction; Nonfiction
Formats: Short Fiction
Subjects: Fantasy; Science Fiction
Markets: Academic; Adult

Send: Query
Don't send: Full text

Publishes Science Fiction, Fantasy, and Dark Fantasy (including their sub-genres). Will consider short stories, novelettes, novellas, novels, graphic novels, academic material. See website for submission guidelines.

P0513 The Lutterworth Press
Publishing Imprint
PO Box 60, Cambridge, CB1 2NT
United Kingdom
Tel: +44 (0) 1223 350865
Fax: +44 (0) 1223 366951

publishing@lutterworth.com

https://www.lutterworth.com
https://lutterworthpress.wordpress.com

https://twitter.com/LuttPress
https://www.facebook.com/JamesClarkeandCo
https://www.instagram.com/lutterworthpress

Book Publisher: James Clarke & Co.

ADULT > **Nonfiction** > *Nonfiction Books*
Antiques; Archaeology; Architecture; Arts; Biography; Crafts; Education; Environment; Games; History; Leisure; Literature; Nature; Philosophy; Religion; Science; Sport; Technology

CHILDREN'S
Fiction > *Novels*

Nonfiction > *Nonfiction Books*: Religion

Send: Submission Form
How to send: Post; Fax; Email

Publisher of religious books. Handles nonfiction for adults, and fiction and nonfiction for children. No adult fiction, cookery books, or drama or poetry.

Not currently accepting children's books.

P0514 Lyle Stuart Books
Publishing Imprint

Book Publisher: Kensington Publishing Corp. (**P0469**)

P0515 Lyons Press
Publishing Imprint
United States

Book Publisher: The Globe Pequot Press (**P0329**)

P0516 Lyrical Caress
Publishing Imprint

Book Publisher: Kensington Publishing Corp. (**P0469**)

P0517 Lyrical Liaison
Publishing Imprint

Book Publisher: Kensington Publishing Corp. (**P0469**)

P0518 Lyrical Press
Publishing Imprint
Kensington Publishing Corp., 119 West 40th Street, New York, NY 10018
United States

jscognamiglio@kensingtonbooks.com

https://www.kensingtonbooks.com

Book Publisher: Kensington Publishing Corp. (**P0469**)

Types: Fiction
Subjects: Mystery; Romance; Suspense; Thrillers; Women's Interests
Markets: Adult

Send: Query
Don't send: Full text

Send query by email with synopsis as attachment. See website for full list of editors' emails and interests and approach one editor only.

Editor: John Scognamiglio

P0519 Lyrical Shine
Publishing Imprint

Book Publisher: Kensington Publishing Corp. (**P0469**)

P0520 Lyrical Underground
Publishing Imprint

Book Publisher: Kensington Publishing Corp. (**P0469**)

P0521 Mabecron Books Ltd
Book Publisher
3 Briston Orchard, St Mellion, Saltash, Cornwall, PL12 6RQ
United Kingdom

sales@mabecronbooks.co.uk

https://mabecronbooks.co.uk

Types: Fiction; Nonfiction
Subjects: Cookery
Markets: Adult; Children's

Send: Full text

Welcomes submissions of books with quality, style, and saleability. Favours books with a Cornish theme. Absence of a Cornish theme will not mean a book is necessarily rejected, but makes the decision more difficult. Particularly interested in children's picture books, cookery, and children's fiction. Send submissions by post only, with SAE.

P0522 Macmillan Children's Publishing Group
Book Publisher

Book Publisher: Macmillan

Publishing Imprint: Henry Holt Books for Young Readers (**P0401**)

P0523 Macmillan Education
Book Publisher
United Kingdom

https://www.springernature.com/gp/macmillaneducation

Book Publisher: Springer Nature (**P0785**)

ACADEMIC > **Nonfiction** > *Nonfiction Books*: Education

Publishes a wide range of educational materials for the international market.

P0524 Macmillan Publishers
Book Publisher
175 Fifth Avenue, New York, NY 10010
United States

press.inquiries@macmillan.com

https://us.macmillan.com

Types: Fiction; Nonfiction
Markets: Adult; Children's; Young Adult

How to send: Through a literary agent

US office of international publisher of
hardcover, trade paperback, and paperback
books for adults, children, and teens.

Book Publisher: Macmillan New Writing

Publishing Imprint: St Martin's Press (**P0789**)

P0525 Mad Gleam Press
Book Publisher
482 Alvarado St, Monterey, CA 93940
United States

madgleampress@gmail.com

https://www.madgleampress.com

Types: Fiction; Poetry
Subjects: Literary
Markets: Adult

Closed to approaches.

**Closed to submissions as at June 2019.
Check website for current status.** Publishes
fiction and poetry collections. Particularly
interested in collaborative / transmedia pieces.
Send submissions by email with author bio /
resume.

P0526 Mango Books
Book Publisher
United Kingdom

https://mangobooks.co.uk

Nonfiction > *Nonfiction Books*
   Crime; Mystery

How to send: Email

Publishes nonfiction on crime, detection, and
mystery. Welcomes submissions.

Publishing Imprints: Blue Lamp Books
(**P0114**); Little Wing (**P0499**)

P0527 Mango Publishing Group
Book Publisher
2850 Douglas Road, 2nd Floor, Coral Gables,
FL 33134
United States
Tel: +1 (305) 428-2299

support@mangopublishinggroup.com

https://mangopublishinggroup.com
https://www.facebook.com/mangopublishing
https://twitter.com/MangoPublishing
https://www.instagram.com/mangopublishing/
https://www.pinterest.com/mangomediainc/
https://www.linkedin.com/company/
mangopublishing/

ADULT
   Fiction > *Novels*

Nonfiction
   Nonfiction Books: Adventure; Business;
   Cookery; Crafts; Entertainment;
   Environment; Feminism; Films; Finance;
   Health; Hobbies; LGBTQIA; Science; Self
   Help; Spirituality; Technology; Veganism
   Reference: General

   Poetry > *Poetry Collections*

CHILDREN'S > **Nonfiction** > *Nonfiction
Books*

YOUNG ADULT > **Nonfiction** > *Nonfiction
Books*

An innovative independent publisher based in
Miami. Publishes books from the freshest,
most distinctive voices of our time, and seeks
to stretch the boundaries of our online culture,
social media and ideas.

P0528 Manic D Press
Book Publisher
PO Box 410804, San Francisco, CA 94141
United States

mss@manicdpress.com

https://www.manicdpress.com

Types: Fiction; Poetry
Formats: Short Fiction
Markets: Adult; Children's

Send: Query
Don't send: Full text

Before submitting, you must have read at least
one of the publisher's books. You do not need
to have bought one -- they can be borrowed
from libraries -- but you need to have read one.
Prefers email submissions. Send 5-10 poems,
3-5 short stories, a synopsis and one chapter
for novels, a representative sample for graphic
novels, visual art, or children's books.

P0529 Manor House Publishing
Book Publisher
452 Cottingham Crescent, Ancaster ON L9G
3V6
Canada

mbdavie@manor-house.biz

https://manor-house-publishing.com

Types: Fiction; Nonfiction; Poetry
Formats: Short Fiction
Subjects: Biography; Business; Fantasy; New
Age; Politics
Markets: Adult; Young Adult

Send: Query
Don't send: Full text

Send query by email only. See website for full
guidelines. Response only if interested.

P0530 Mantra
Publishing Imprint

Publishing Imprint: O-Books

P0531 Margaret K. McElderry
Publishing Imprint

Book Publisher: Simon & Schuster Children's
Publishing (**P0768**)

P0532 Margaret River Press
Book Publisher
PO Box 47, Witchcliffe, WA 6286
Australia
Tel: +61 (0) 8 9757 6009

info@margaretriverpress.com

https://margaretriverpress.com

Types: Fiction; Nonfiction; Poetry
Formats: Short Fiction
Subjects: Autobiography; Leisure; Lifestyle
Markets: Adult

Closed to approaches.

Small press based in Australia. Closed to
submissions as at December 2019.

P0533 Marion Boyars Publishers
Book Publisher
26 Parke Road, London, SW13 9NG
United Kingdom

catheryn@marionboyars.com

http://www.marionboyars.co.uk

Types: Fiction; Nonfiction
Formats: Film Scripts; Theatre Scripts
Subjects: Anthropology; Autobiography;
Culture; Drama; Literary Criticism; Music;
Philosophy; Psychology; Sociology; Women's
Interests
Markets: Adult; Children's

Not accepting new submissions as at March
2020. Check website for current status.

Editor: Catheryn Kilgarriff

P0534 Marsh Hawk Press
Book Publisher
PO Box 206, East Rockway, NY 11518-0206
United States

https://marshhawkpress.org

Types: Poetry
Subjects: Literary
Markets: Adult

Send: Full text

Publishes poetry chapbooks submitted through
its three national poetry prizes (submission
fees apply).

P0535 Martin Books
Book Publisher

Book Publisher: Simon & Schuster UK
Limited (**P0769**)

P0536 **Marvel Comics**
Book Publisher
1290 Avenue of the Americas, New York, NY
10104
United States
Tel: +1 (212) 576-4000

https://www.marvel.com

Types: Fiction
Subjects: Adventure; Comedy / Humour;
Fantasy; Horror; Science Fiction
Markets: Adult; Children's; Young Adult

Publisher of action comics.

P0537 **Maryland Historical
Society Press**
Book Publisher
Maryland Center for History and Culture, 610
Park Ave., Baltimore, MD 21201
United States

mkado@mdhistory.org

https://www.mdhistory.org/publications/book-
publishing/

Nonfiction > *Nonfiction Books*
History; Maryland

Send: Query
How to send: Post; Email

Publishes books on the history and people of
Maryland. Send query by post or by email. See
website for full guidelines.

Editors: Patricia Dockman Anderson; Robert
Cottom

P0538 **Mcbooks Press**
Publishing Imprint
United States

Book Publisher: The Globe Pequot Press
(**P0329**)

P0539 **Mentor Books**
Book Publisher
43 Furze Road, Sandyford Industrial Estate,
Dublin 18
Ireland
Tel: 01 2952112
Fax: 01 295 2114

admin@mentorbooks.ie

http://www.mentorbooks.ie

Types: Nonfiction
Subjects: Biography; Business; Comedy /
Humour; Crime; History; Politics; Science;
Sport
Markets: Academic; Adult

Publishes educational books and general
nonfiction of Irish interest.

P0540 **Menus and Music**
Book Publisher
1462 66th Street, Emeryville, CA 94608

United States
Tel: +1 (510) 658-9100

info@menusandmusic.com

https://www.menusandmusic.com
https://www.facebook.com/menusandmusic
https://twitter.com/menusandmusic
https://www.pinterest.com/menusandmusic/
https://www.instagram.com/menusandmusic/

Nonfiction > *Nonfiction Books*
Arts; Food; Music; Travel

Publishes books combining inspiring food,
music, art and travel.

Editor: Sharon O'Connor

P0541 **Merlin Unwin Books**
Book Publisher
Palmers House, 7 Corve Street, Ludlow,
Shropshire, SY8 1DB
United Kingdom
Tel: +44 (0) 1584 877456

books@merlinunwin.co.uk

http://www.merlinunwin.co.uk

Types: Nonfiction
Subjects: Autobiography; Comedy / Humour;
Cookery; Leisure; Nature; Sport
Markets: Adult

Publishes books on the countryside and
countryside pursuits, covering such topics as
nature, fishing, shooting, etc.

P0542 **Messianic Jewish
Publishers**
Book Publisher
6120 Day Long Lane, Clarksville, MD 21029
United States
Tel: +1 (410) 531-6644

Lisa@MessianicJewish.net

http://www.messianicjewish.net

Types: Fiction; Nonfiction
Subjects: Religion
Markets: Adult

Send: Query
Don't send: Full text

Publishes books which address Jewish
evangelism; the Jewish roots of Christianity;
Messianic Judaism; Israel; the Jewish People.
Publishes mainly nonfiction, but some fiction.
See website for full submission guidelines.

P0543 **Methuen Publishing Ltd**
Book Publisher
Orchard House, Railway Street, Slingsby,
York, YO62 4AN
United Kingdom
Tel: +44 (0) 1653 628152
Fax: +44 (0) 1653 628195

editorial@methuen.co.uk

http://www.methuen.co.uk
https://twitter.com/MethuenandCo

Fiction > *Novels*

Nonfiction
Essays: General
Nonfiction Books: Autobiography;
Biography; Classics / Ancient World;
Literature; Politics; Sport; Theatre; Travel;
World War II

Send: Query
How to send: Email
How not to send: Phone

No unsolicited submissions. Send query by
email only, stating the subject area of your
manuscript. No phone calls regarding
submissions.

P0544 **Michael Joseph**
Book Publisher
80 Strand, London, WC2R 0RL
United Kingdom
Tel: +44 (0) 20 7139 3000

https://www.penguin.co.uk/company/
publishers/michael-joseph.html

Book Publishers: Penguin Random House;
Penguin Random House UK (**P0635**)

Types: Fiction; Nonfiction
Subjects: Autobiography; Commercial;
Cookery; Crime; Lifestyle; Thrillers; Women's
Interests
Markets: Adult

How to send: Through a literary agent

Publishes women's fiction, crime, thrillers,
cookery, memoirs and lifestyle books. Accepts
submissions through literary agents only.

P0545 **Milkweed Editions**
Book Publisher
1011 Washington Avenue South, Open Book,
Suite 300, Minneapolis, MN 55415
United States
Tel: +1 (612) 332-3192

thanks@milkweed.org

https://milkweed.org
http://www.facebook.com/milkweed.books
http://twitter.com/#!/Milkweed_Books
https://www.instagram.com/milkweed_books/
http://www.youtube.com/MilkweedEditions
https://www.pinterest.com/Milkfolk/

Fiction > *Novels*

Nonfiction > *Nonfiction Books*

Poetry > *Poetry Collections*

Closed to approaches.

An independent publisher of fiction,
nonfiction, and poetry.

P0546 **Millbrook Press**
Publishing Imprint

Book Publisher: Lerner Publishing Group
(**P0487**)

P0547 Minotaur
Publishing Imprint

Publishing Imprint: St Martin's Press (**P0789**)

P0548 Mirror Books
Book Publisher
Northern & Shell Building, 10 Lower Thames
Street, London, EC3R 6EN
United Kingdom

submissions@mirrorbooks.co.uk

https://mirrorbooks.co.uk

Nonfiction > *Nonfiction Books*
Celebrity; Crime; Memoir; Nostalgia

How to send: Email

Currently accepting submissions with a focus
on nonfiction real-life (memoir, crime,
nostalgia, personalities and celebrities). Send
submissions by email.

P0549 The MIT Press
Book Publisher
One Rogers Street, Cambridge, MA 02142-
1209
United States
Tel: +1 (617) 253-5646

https://mitpress.mit.edu
https://www.facebook.com/mitpress
https://twitter.com/mitpress
https://www.linkedin.com/company/11587565/
https://www.pinterest.com/mitpress/
https://www.instagram.com/mitpress/
https://www.youtube.com/c/TheMITPress

ACADEMIC > **Nonfiction** > *Nonfiction
Books*
Arts; Design; Science; Sociology;
Technology

University press publishing books and journals
at the intersection of science, technology, art,
social science, and design.

Acquisitions Editors: Matthew Browne; Susan
Buckley; Beth Clevenger; Katie Helke;
Victoria Hindley; Justin Kehoe; Philip
Laughlin; Marc Lowenthal; Gita Manaktala;
Jermey Matthews; Robert Prior; Elizabeth
Swayze; Emily Taber; Thomas Weaver

Publishing Imprint: Bradford Books

P0550 Modern Library
Publishing Imprint

Book Publisher: Random House (**P0690**)

P0551 The Monacelli Press
Publishing Imprint
Attn: Acquisitions, 65 Bleecker Street, 8th
Floor, New York, New York 10012
United States

submissions@themonacellipress.com

https://www.phaidon.com/store/the-monacelli-
press/

Book Publisher: Phaidon Press (**P0644**)

Nonfiction > *Nonfiction Books*
Architecture; Arts; Gardening; Interior
Design; Photography

How to send: Post; Email

Will review book proposals in the fields of
architecture and landscape architecture, fine
and decorative arts, design, and photography.

P0552 Monday Books
Book Publisher
Festival House, Jessop Avenue, Cheltenham,
GL50 3SH
United Kingdom
Tel: +44 (0) 1242 633717

info@mondaybooks.com

http://www.mondaybooks.com

Nonfiction > *Nonfiction Books*

Closed to approaches.

Independent publisher of strongly written
nonfiction covering a range of subjects.

P0553 Moon Books
Publishing Imprint
Worthing, UK
United Kingdom

office1@jhpbooks.net

https://www.johnhuntpublishing.com/moon-
books/

Book Publisher: John Hunt Publishing Ltd

Types: Nonfiction
Subjects: Religion
Markets: Adult

Send: Full text

What is Paganism? A religion, a spirituality, an
alternative belief system, nature worship? You
can find support for all these definitions (and
many more) in dictionaries, encyclopedias, and
text books of religion, but subscribe to any one
and the truth will evade you. Above all
Paganism is a creative pursuit, an encounter
with reality, an exploration of meaning and an
expression of the soul. Druids, Heathens,
Wiccans and others, all contribute their
insights and literary riches to the Pagan
tradition. We invite you to begin or to deepen
your own encounter, right here, right now.

Authors: Cyndi Brannen; Morgan Daimler;
Melusine Draco; Jane Meredith; Rachel
Patterson; Emma Restall-Orr; Llyn Roberts;
Elen Sentier

P0554 More Shoots More Leaves
Publishing Imprint

Book Publisher: Five Leaves Publications
(**P0295**)

P0555 Morrow Gift
Publishing Imprint

Book Publisher: HarperCollins

P0556 Motorbooks
Publishing Imprint

Book Publisher: The Quarto Group, Inc.
(**P0679**)

P0557 Mud Pie Books
Book Publisher
Oxford, OX2 6HY
United Kingdom
Tel: +44 (0) 7985 935320

info@mudpiebooks.com

https://mudpiebooks.com

Fiction > *Novels*: Buddhism

Nonfiction > *Nonfiction Books*: Buddhism

Poetry > *Poetry Collections*: Buddhism

Publishes books about Buddhism, and books
for Buddhists.

P0558 Muddy Boots
Publishing Imprint
United States

Book Publisher: The Globe Pequot Press
(**P0329**)

P0559 Mudlark
Publishing Imprint
United Kingdom

Book Publisher: HarperCollins UK (**P0382**)

P0560 Murdoch Books UK Ltd
Book Publisher
United Kingdom
Tel: +44 (0) 20 8785 5995
Fax: +44 (0) 20 8785 5985

http://www.murdochbooks.co.uk

Book Publisher: Murdoch Books Pty Limited
Australia

Types: Nonfiction
Subjects: Cookery; Crafts; Design; Gardening;
Lifestyle
Markets: Adult

Publishers of full-colour nonfiction.

P0561 Myriad Editions
Book Publisher
United Kingdom

submissions@myriadeditions.com

https://myriadeditions.com

Types: Fiction; Nonfiction
Subjects: Autobiography; Contemporary;

Crime; History; Literary; Medicine; Politics; Thrillers
Markets: Adult
Closed to approaches.

Publishes literary fiction: contemporary and historical; crime fiction: psychological and political thrillers with strong female characters; graphic novels: documentary comics, graphic reportage, fiction, memoir and life writing, graphic medicine; and literary or political nonfiction: feminist, literary nonfiction, memoir. No young adult fiction, children's books, horror, science fiction, fantasy, plays or poetry, or books that have been previously published or self-published (in print or as ebooks) unless you are a graphic novelist. Do not send proposals – send complete manuscript by email. See website for full guidelines.

P0562 Myrmidon Books Ltd
Book Publisher
Rotterdam House, 116 Quayside, Newcastle upon Tyne, NE1 3DY
United Kingdom
Tel: +44 (0) 1912 064005
Fax: +44 (0) 1912 064001

ed@myrmidonbooks.com

http://www.myrmidonbooks.com

Fiction > *Novels*
Commercial; Literary

Send: Query; Writing sample; Author bio
How to send: Post
How not to send: Email; Fax

Submit your initial three chapters and a one-page covering letter providing information about yourself and your work. A synopsis or structure plan may be useful for a non-fiction proposal, but a synopsis is not required for fiction submissions and will not be read.

P0563 The Mysterious Press
Publishing Imprint
United States

Book Publisher: Grove Atlantic Inc. (**P0345**)

P0564 Nan A. Talese
Publishing Imprint
1745 Broadway, 22nd floor, New York, NY 10019
United States
Tel: +1 (212) 782-8918
Fax: +1 (212) 782-8448

ntalese@randomhouse.com

http://www.randomhouse.com/nanatalese

Book Publisher: Knopf Doubleday Publishing Group (**P0475**)

Types: Fiction; Nonfiction
Subjects: Culture; History; Literary; Philosophy; Sociology
Markets: Adult

How to send: Through a literary agent
Publishes nonfiction and literary fiction with a compelling storyline, good characterisation and use of language. Accepts approaches via a literary agent only.

Editorial Director / Publisher: Nan Talese

P0565 Nancy Paulsen Books
Publishing Imprint
United States

Book Publisher: Penguin Young Readers Group (**P0638**)

P0566 National Museums Scotland Enterprises
Book Publisher
National Museums of Scotland, Chambers Street, Edinburgh, EH1 1JF
United Kingdom
Tel: +44 (0) 1312 474026
Fax: +44 (0) 1312 474012

publishing@nms.ac.uk

https://www.nms.ac.uk/about-us/our-organisation/nms-enterprises/

Types: Nonfiction
Subjects: Archaeology; Arts; Culture; History; Literature; Nature
Markets: Academic; Adult; Children's

Publishes books reflecting the range and international importance of the museum's collections., from catalogues to children's books, academic monographs, biographies, and souvenir booklets.

P0567 National Trust
Publishing Imprint

Book Publisher: Pavilion Books Group Limited (**P0620**)

P0568 Natural History Museum Publishing
Book Publisher
The Natural History Museum, Cromwell Road, London, SW7 5BD
United Kingdom
Tel: +44 (0) 20 7942 5336

publishing@nhm.ac.uk

http://www.nhm.ac.uk/business-services/publishing.html

Types: Nonfiction
Subjects: Arts; Nature; Science
Markets: Adult

Publishes accessible, fully illustrated books about the natural world.

P0569 Naturegraph & Keven Brown Publications
Book Publisher
4855 Scotch Court, Carmichael, CA 95608
United States

naturegraph@gmail.com

http://www.naturegraph.com

Nonfiction in Translation > *Nonfiction*
Books: Islamic Philosophy

Nonfiction > *Nonfiction Books*
California; Native Americans; Nature

Publishes mainly books on nature, Native American subjects, and translations of Islamic philosophy.

Editors: Barbara Brown; Keven Brown

P0570 Naughty Nights Press
Book Publisher
Canada

submissions@naughtynightspress.com

http://naughtynightspress.blogspot.com

Types: Fiction
Subjects: Erotic; Fantasy; Romance
Markets: Adult

Publishes erotic and paranormal romance ebooks. See website for full submission guidelines.

P0571 NBM Publishing
Book Publisher
160 Broadway, Suite 700 East Wing, New York, NY 10038
United States

tnantier@nbmpub.com

http://nbmpub.com

Types: Fiction
Subjects: Comedy / Humour; Fantasy; Horror; Mystery; Satire; Science Fiction
Markets: Adult; Young Adult

Send: Query
Don't send: Full text

Publisher of graphic novels, interested in general fiction, humour, satire of fantasy and horror, and mystery. No superheroes. Accepting approaches from previously published authors only (including those with proven success in online comics). No submissions from authors outside North America. See website for full submission guidelines.

Editor: Terry Nantier

P0572 Necro Publications
Book Publisher
United States

https://necropublications.com
http://www.twitter.com/necrodave
http://www.facebook.com/necropublications

Fiction > Novels
   Dark; Horror; Noir; Science Fiction; Urban Fantasy

Closed to approaches.

Small press publishing modern dark horror, science fiction, urban fantasy, noir, and more.

P0573 Negative Capability Press
Book Publisher
United States

swalker@negativecapabilitypress.org

http://www.negativecapabilitypress.org

Types: Fiction; Nonfiction; Poetry
Subjects: Literary
Markets: Adult

Send: Full text

Publishes books of literary fiction, nonfiction, and poetry. Accepts submissions through competitions and open submissions ($25 submission fee) via online submission system.

P0574 Nell James Publishers
Book Publisher
United Kingdom

info@nelljames.co.uk

https://nelljames.co.uk
https://twitter.com/NJamesPublisher

Nonfiction > Nonfiction Books
   Contemporary; Social Issues

Send: Outline; Synopsis; Pitch; Market info; Author bio; Submission Form
How to send: Email

An independent publisher of nonfiction books, bringing awareness to issues in modern society. Download submission form from website and return by email.

P0575 Nelson Books
Publishing Imprint

Book Publisher: HarperCollins

P0576 New Holland Publishers Australia
Book Publisher
Level 1, 178 Fox Valley Road, Wahroonga, NSW, 2076
Australia
Tel: +61 2 8986 4700

orders@newholland.com.au

http://au.newhollandpublishers.com

Nonfiction > Nonfiction Books
   General, and in particular: Arts; Autobiography; Biography; Cookery; Crafts; Drinks; Gardening; Health; Memoir; Military; Nature; Pets; Sport

Send: Query; Author bio; Market info; Synopsis; Writing sample; Full text
How to send: Post

Publisher with offices in Australia and New Zealand. Welcomes all manuscript submissions from authors wishing to be published. However, primarily deals with non-fiction categories.

P0577 New London Editions
Publishing Imprint

Book Publisher: Five Leaves Publications (**P0295**)

P0578 New Walk Editions
Book Publisher
c/o Nick Everett, School of English, Leicester University, University Road, Leicester, LE1 7RH
United Kingdom

newwalkmagazine@gmail.com

https://newwalkmagazine.com

Poetry > Poetry Collections

Send: Full text; Author bio
How to send: Word file email attachment; Post

A small press specialising in extremely high quality poetry pamphlets. Interested in poetic plurality: equally interested in established and new poets, and a broad church stylistically and thematically. Send 12-20 pages of poems by email or by post.

Editor: Nick Everett

P0579 North Light Books
Publishing Imprint
United States

Book Publisher: Penguin Publishing Group (**P0633**)

P0580 Northern Eye Books
Book Publisher
22 Crosland Terrace, Helsby, Frodsham, Cheshire, WA6 9LY
United Kingdom
Tel: +44 (0) 1829 770309

tony@northerneyebooks.com

https://www.northerneyebooks.co.uk
https://www.facebook.com/NorthernEyeBooks/
https://twitter.com/northerneyeboo
https://www.pinterest.co.uk/tony9709/

Nonfiction > Nonfiction Books: Walking Guides

Send: Query

Publishes walking books for the Lake District, Peak District, Yorkshire Dales, other UK National Parks, the Wales Coast Path, South West Coast Path, Wales and Cheshire. Most

books are commissioned, but willing to consider ideas or a sample chapter.

Authors: Jen Darling; Roger Redfern; Carl Rogers

Editor: Tony Bowerman

Publishing Imprint: Marabooks

P0581 Northern Illinois University Press
Publishing Imprint
Sage House, 512 East State Street, Ithaca, NY 14850
United States
Tel: +1 (607)253-2338

cupressinfo@cornell.edu

https://www.cornellpress.cornell.edu/imprints/northern-illinois-university-press/

Book Publisher: Cornell University Press

ACADEMIC > Nonfiction > Nonfiction Books
   American Midwest; Christianity; Culture; European History; History; Philosophy; Politics; Religion; Russia; South-East Asia

ADULT > Nonfiction > Nonfiction Books
   American Midwest; Christianity; Culture; European History; History; Philosophy; Politics; Religion; Russia; South-East Asia

Publishes scholarly and trade books in the humanities and social sciences for both specialists and general readers. The Press has long published major works in Russian and Eurasian studies and has additional series in Orthodox Christianity and Southeast Asian studies. Also publishes books on politics, philosophy, religion, European history, and American Midwest history and culture.

Acquisitions Editor: Melody Herr

Editorial Director: Mary Lincoln

P0582 NorthSouth Books
Book Publisher
600 Third Avenue, 2nd Floor, NY, NY 10016
United States
Tel: +1 (917) 699-2079

info@northsouth.com
submissionsnsb@gmail.com

https://northsouth.com

CHILDREN'S > Fiction
   Board Books; Picture Books

Closed to approaches.

Publishes picture books for children up to 1,000 words. Seeks fresh, original fiction on universal themes that would appeal to children aged 3-8. Generally does not acquire rhyming texts, as must also be translated into German. Send submissions by email as Word document or pasted directly into the body of the email. Authors do not need to include illustrations, but if the author is also an illustrator sample sketches can be included in PDF or JPEG form.

P0583 Nosy Crow
Book Publisher
The Crow's Nest, 14 Baden Place, Crosby Row, London, SE1 1YW
United Kingdom
Tel: +44 (0) 20 7089 7575

hello@nosycrow.com

https://nosycrow.com
https://www.facebook.com/NosyCrow
https://www.instagram.com/nosycrow/
https://twitter.com/nosycrow
https://www.youtube.com/user/NosyCrow

CHILDREN'S
  Fiction
    Board Books; *Chapter Books*; *Middle Grade*; *Picture Books*
  Nonfiction > *Nonfiction Books*

Publishes child-focused, parent-friendly children's books for ages 0-12. No submissions from white people.

Editor: Adrian Soar

P0584 Oak Tree Press
Book Publisher
33 Rochestown Rise, Rochestown, Cork
Ireland
Tel: +353 86 244 1633
Fax: +353 86 330 7694

info@oaktreepress.com

https://oaktreepress.eu

Types: Nonfiction
Subjects: Business; Finance; Legal
Markets: Professional

Publishes books on business, particularly for small business owners and managers.

P0585 Oberon Press
Book Publisher
205–145 Spruce Street, Ottawa, Ontario, K1R 6P1
Canada
Tel: +1 (613) 238-3275
Fax: +1 (613) 238-3275

oberon@sympatico.ca

http://www.oberonpress.ca

Types: Fiction; Nonfiction; Poetry
Markets: Adult

Closed to approaches.

No longer accepting new manuscript submissions.

P0586 Oghma Creative Media
Book Publisher
United States

submissions@oghmacreative.net

https://oghmacreative.com

ADULT
  Fiction > *Novels*
    Contemporary Romance; Contemporary; Crime; Diversity; Environment; Fantasy; High / Epic Fantasy; Historical Fiction; Historical Romance; Horror; LGBTQIA; Mainstream; Military; Mystery; Nautical; Police Procedural; Romance; Romantic Comedy; Romantic Thrillers; Science Fiction; Secret Intelligence; Space Opera; Supernatural / Paranormal; Thrillers; Traditional; Westerns

  Nonfiction > *Nonfiction Books*
    Biography; Entertainment; History; Military; Mind, Body, Spirit; Music; TV

CHILDREN'S > **Fiction**
  Chapter Books; *Middle Grade*; *Picture Books*
NEW
ADULT > **Fiction** > *Novels*: Contemporary Romance

YOUNG ADULT > **Fiction** > *Novels*

A traditional publisher reaching out to authors who don't want to take the self-publishing route. Provides a team of editors, designers, and marketers to help bring your work to its finished form. Aims to develop long-term relationships with authors and artists. Closed to submissions between November 1 and April 1.

P0587 Oh! With Dots
Publishing Imprint

Publishing Imprint: Emerentsia Publications (**P0262**)

P0588 The Ohio State University Press
Book Publisher
180 Pressey Hall, 1070 Carmack Road, Columbus, OH 43210-1002
United States
Tel: +1 (614) 292-8256
Fax: +1 (614) 292-2065

info@osupress.org

https://ohiostatepress.org

Types: Fiction; Nonfiction; Poetry
Formats: Film Scripts
Subjects: Business; Crime; Culture; Finance; Health; History; Literary Criticism; Media; Politics; Sociology; Women's Interests
Markets: Academic

Send: Query
Don't send: Full text

Publishes mainly academic nonfiction. Check website for appropriate editor to submit your work to and details of the appropriate material to submit.

Editors: Becca Bostock-Holtzman; Tara Cyphers; Ana Jimenez-Moreno; Kristen Elias Rowley; Tony Sanfilippo

P0589 Ohio University Press
Book Publisher
30 Park Place, Suite 101, Athens, OH 45701-2909
United States

huard@ohio.edu

https://www.ohioswallow.com

ACADEMIC > **Nonfiction** > *Nonfiction Books*
    Africa; American History; American Midwest; Anthropology; Appalachia; Art History; Arts; Asia; Central America; Environment; Europe; Films; Food; Gender; Health; History; Journalism; Legal; Literature; Media; North America; Ohio; Performing Arts; Philosophy; Politics; Religion; South America; Sport; TV; Women

Send: Query; Table of Contents; Writing sample; Author bio
Don't send: Full text

Publishes primarily nonfiction. See website for full guidelines.

Editor: Ricky S. Huard

Publishing Imprint: Swallow Press (*P0805*)

P0590 Old Street Publishing Ltd
Book Publisher
8 Hurlingham Business Park, Sulivan Road, London, SW6 3DU
United Kingdom
Tel: +44 (0) 20 8787 5812

info@oldstreetpublishing.co.uk

http://www.oldstreetpublishing.co.uk
https://twitter.com/oldstpublishing

Fiction > *Novels*

Nonfiction > *Nonfiction Books*

Send: Query; Outline
Don't send: Full text
How to send: Email

Independent British publisher of fiction and nonfiction.

Chair: David Reynolds

Managing Director: Ben Yarde-Buller

P0591 Oldcastle Books
Publishing Imprint
United Kingdom

Book Publisher: Oldcastle Books Group (**P0592**)

P0592 Oldcastle Books Group
Book Publisher
18 Coleswood Road, Harpenden,

Hertfordshire, AL5 1EQ
United Kingdom
Tel: +44 (0) 1582 766348

publicity@oldcastlebooks.com

http://www.oldcastlebooks.co.uk

Fiction > *Novels*

Nonfiction > *Nonfiction Books*

How to send: Through a literary agent

Accepts submissions through literary agents only.

Managing Director: Ion S. Mills

Publishing Imprints: Creative Essentials (*P0196*); Crime & Mystery Club (*P0197*); High Stakes Publishing; Kamera Books (*P0460*); No Exit Press; Oldcastle Books (*P0591*); Pocketessentials; Pulp! The Classics (*P0673*)

P0593 Oleander Press
Book Publisher
16 Orchard Street, Cambridge, CB1 1JT
United Kingdom

editor@oleanderpress.com

http://www.oleanderpress.com

Types: Fiction; Nonfiction; Poetry
Formats: Reference
Subjects: Biography; History; Horror; Literature; Travel
Markets: Adult; Children's

Closed to approaches.

Closed to submissions as at June 2020.

Publishes biography, Cambridge / local, children's, classic horror, language and literature, fiction, games and pastimes, modern poets, Arabia, and Libya. Looking for nonfiction – in particular children's nonfiction. Send submissions by email or by post.

Editor: Jon Gifford

P0594 Omnibus Press
Book Publisher
14/15 Berners Street, London, W1T 3LJ
United Kingdom
Tel: +44 (0) 20 7612 7400

omniinfo@wisemusic.com

https://omnibuspress.com

Book Publisher: Wise Music Group (**P0934**)

Types: Nonfiction
Subjects: Biography; Music
Markets: Adult

Publisher of music books, including song sheets and rock and pop biographies.

P0595 One More Chapter
Publishing Imprint
United Kingdom

Book Publisher: HarperCollins UK (**P0382**)

P0596 One Signal
Publishing Imprint

Book Publisher: Simon & Schuster Adult Publishing (**P0766**)

P0597 One World
Publishing Imprint

Book Publisher: Random House (**P0690**)

P0598 Ooligan Press
Book Publisher
PO Box 751, Portland, OR 97207
United States
Tel: +1 (503) 725-9748
Fax: +1 (503) 725-3561

https://ooligan.pdx.edu

Types: Fiction; Nonfiction; Poetry
Subjects: Autobiography; History; Literary; Sociology
Markets: Adult; Young Adult

Send: Query
Don't send: Full text

Publishes works of historical and social value, or significance to the Pacific Northwest region (Northern California, Oregon, Idaho, Washington, British Columbia, and Alaska). Accepts queries by email and proposals via online submission system. See website for full details.

P0599 Open University Press
Book Publisher
United Kingdom

Laura.Pacey@mheducation.com

https://www.mheducation.co.uk/professionals/open-university-press

Book Publisher: McGraw-Hill Education

Types: Nonfiction
Subjects: Health; Psychology; Sociology
Markets: Academic; Professional

Publishes books on social sciences only.

P0600 Orchard Books
Publishing Imprint
United States

Book Publisher: Scholastic (**P0740**)

P0601 Orenda Books
Book Publisher
16 Carson Road, West Dulwich, London, SE21 8HU
United Kingdom

westcamel@orendabooks.co.uk

http://orendabooks.co.uk

Types: Fiction
Subjects: Crime; Literary; Thrillers
Markets: Adult

Closed to approaches.

Closed to submissions until February 2019. Check website for current status. Publishes literary fiction and upmarket genre fiction only. No nonfiction, screenplays, children's books, or young adult. Send one-page synopsis and full ms (or three-chapter sample) by email.

P0602 Orion Children's Books
Publishing Imprint

Book Publisher: Hachette Children's Group (**P0350**)

P0603 Our Sunday Visitor
Book Publisher
200 Noll Plaza, Huntington, IN 46750
United States
Tel: +1 (260) 356-8400

https://www.osv.com

Nonfiction > *Nonfiction Books:* Catholicism

Non-profit Catholic publisher particularly interested in Apologetics and Catechetics, reference and prayer, heritage and saints, the family, and the parish.

P0604 Oxbow Books
Book Publisher
The Old Music Hall, 106-108 Cowley Road, OX4 1JE
United Kingdom
Tel: +44 (0) 1865 241249
Fax: +44 (0) 1865 794449

orders@oxbowbooks.com

https://www.oxbowbooks.com
https://www.facebook.com/oxbowbooks
https://www.twitter.com/oxbowbooks
https://www.linkedin.com/company/oxbow-books

ACADEMIC > **Nonfiction** > *Nonfiction Books:* Archaeology

Publisher of academic books on archaeology.

Editor: Richard Purslow

Publishing Imprint: Aris & Phillips

P0605 Oxford University Press
Book Publisher
Great Clarendon Street, Oxford, OX2 6DP
United Kingdom
Tel: +44 (0) 1865 556767
Fax: +44 (0) 1865 556646

onlinequeries.uk@oup.com

https://global.oup.com

Types: Fiction; Nonfiction
Formats: Reference
Subjects: Current Affairs; Drama; Finance; History; Legal; Literature; Medicine; Music;

Philosophy; Politics; Religion; Science;
Sociology
Markets: Academic; Adult; Children's;
Professional

Publishes academic works including journals,
schoolbooks, dictionaries, reference works,
classics, and children's fiction, and nonfiction.

Book Publisher: Nelson Thornes Limited

P0606 P8tech
Book Publisher
6 Woodside, Churnet View Road, Oakamoor,
Staffordshire, ST10 3AE
United Kingdom

info@P8tech.com

https://www.p8tech.com

Types: Nonfiction
Subjects: Technology
Markets: Professional

Publishes IT books and ebooks for technology
professionals. Current emphasis on Java and
Oracle technologies. Books are heavy on the
practical and full of code and screenshots.

P0607 Pace Press
Book Publisher
2006 S Mary St, Fresno, CA 93721
United States
Tel: +1 (800) 345-4447

kent@lindenpub.com

https://quilldriverbooks.com/pace-press/

Types: Fiction
Subjects: Fantasy; History; Horror; Mystery;
Romance; Science Fiction; Thrillers; Westerns
Markets: Adult

Closed to approaches.

**Closed to submissions as at January 2020.
Check website for current status.** Send query
by post or email with synopsis, author bio, and
first three or four chapters / 50 pages of your
manuscript. See website for full guidelines.

P0608 Pact Press
Book Publisher
Raleigh, NC
United States

info@regalhousepublishing.com

http://pactpress.com

Types: Fiction; Nonfiction; Poetry
Formats: Short Fiction
Subjects: Literary
Markets: Adult

Publishes short stories, poetry, nonfiction, and
literary fiction on themes such as social justice,
racism, discrimination, gender equality,
LGBTQ concerns, immigration, poverty and
homelessness. Submit via online submission
system. $5 submission fee.

P0609 Pale Fire Press
Book Publisher
United States
Tel: +1 (520) 282-1442

http://palefirepress.com

Fiction > *Novels:* Literary

Closed to approaches.

Closed to submissions as at January 2020.
Check website for current status.

P0610 Palgrave Macmillan
Book Publisher
United Kingdom

https://www.palgrave.com

Book Publisher: Springer Nature (**P0785**)

ACADEMIC > **Nonfiction**
  Nonfiction Books: Business; Culture;
  Economics; Environment; Films; Geography;
  Health; History; International; Journalism;
  Language; Literature; Media; Neuroscience;
  Philosophy; Politics; Psychology; Sociology;
  TV; Theatre
  Reference: Business; Philosophy
PROFESSIONAL > **Nonfiction** > *Nonfiction
Books*
  Business; Management

Send: Query; Submission Form; Author bio;
Writing sample

Download proposal form from website and
submit by email to relevant editorial contact.

Book Publisher: BFI Publishing

P0611 Pan Macmillan Australia
Book Publisher
Australia

pan.reception@macmillan.com.au

https://www.panmacmillan.com.au

Book Publisher: Pan Macmillan

ADULT
  Fiction > *Novels*
    Contemporary; Crime; Drama; Historical
    Fiction; Literary; Psychological Suspense;
    Saga; Thrillers

  Nonfiction > *Nonfiction Books*
    Contemporary; Crime; Health; History;
    Lifestyle; Memoir; Mind, Body, Spirit;
    Narrative Nonfiction
CHILDREN'S > **Fiction** > *Middle Grade*
YOUNG ADULT > **Fiction** > *Novels*

Send: Query; Author bio; Market info;
Synopsis; Proposal; Writing sample
How to send: Online submission system

Accepts submissions via online submission
system.

P0612 Pantheon
Publishing Imprint
United States

Book Publisher: Knopf Doubleday Publishing
Group (**P0475**)

P0613 Paradise Cay Publications
Book Publisher
120 Monda Way, Blue Lake, CA 95525
United States
Tel: +1 (707) 822-9063
Fax: +1 (707) 822-9163

info@paracay.com

http://www.paracay.com

ADULT > **Nonfiction**
  Gift Books: General, and in
  particular: Bigfoot
  Nonfiction Books: Outdoor Activities; Pacific
  Northwest; Sailing; Travel
CHILDREN'S
  Fiction > *Picture Books*
  Nonfiction > *Picture Books*

Publishes specialty book titles as well as an
ever expanding selection of field guides, travel
maps, and children's books.

Editors: Jim Morehouse; Matt Morehouse

Publishing Imprint: Pardey Books

P0614 Parthian Books
Book Publisher
The Old Surgery, Napier Street, Cardigan,
SA43 1ED
United Kingdom
Tel: +44 (0) 7890 968246

info@parthianbooks.com

https://www.parthianbooks.com

Fiction
  Novels: Literary
  Short Fiction: Literary
Nonfiction > *Nonfiction Books*
Poetry > *Poetry Collections*

Closed to approaches.

Publisher of poetry, fiction, and creative
nonfiction, of Welsh origin, in the English
language. Also publishes English language
translations of Welsh language work. Send
query with SAE, and (for fiction) a one-page
synopsis and first 30 pages, or (for poetry) a
sample of 15-20 poems. No email submissions,
genre fiction of any kind, or children's /
teenage fiction. See website for full submission
guidelines.

Author: Richard Owain Roberts

P0615 Partisan Press
Book Publisher
PO 11417, Norfolk, VA 23517
United States

red-ink@earthlink.net

https://www.partisanpress.org
https://www.angelfire.com/va/bcr/ptsn.html

Poetry > *Poetry Collections*: Working Class

Not for profit publisher of working class
poetry. Aims to create an awareness of and
involvement in working class culture as well as
to promote a progressive vision that will move
our class and our society forward toward a
more just and peaceful future.

Magazine: Blue Collar Review (**M0081**)

P0616 PassKey Publications
Book Publisher
5348 Vegas Drive PMB 1670, Las Vegas, NV
89108
United States

support@passkeyonline.com

https://www.passkeypublications.com

Types: Nonfiction
Subjects: Business; Finance
Markets: Adult

Publishes taxation and accountancy textbooks.

P0617 Pat-a-Cake
Publishing Imprint

Book Publisher: Hachette Children's Group
(**P0350**)

P0618 Patrician Press
Book Publisher
United Kingdom
Tel: +44 (0) 7968 288651

patricia@patricianpress.com

https://patricianpress.com

Types: Fiction; Nonfiction; Poetry
Formats: Short Fiction
Markets: Adult; Children's

Closed to approaches.

Small and independent non-profit press, with
the aim of encouraging and promoting writers
of high quality fiction and poetry. Imprint
publishes books for children. Contact by email
only.

Publishing Imprint: Pudding Press (*P0670*)

P0619 Paula Wiseman Books
Publishing Imprint

Book Publisher: Simon & Schuster Children's
Publishing (**P0768**)

P0620 Pavilion Books Group Limited
Book Publisher
43 Great Ormond Street, London, WC1N 3HZ
United Kingdom
Tel: +44 (0) 20 7462 1500

info@pavilionbooks.com

https://www.pavilionbooks.com

Types: Fiction; Nonfiction
Subjects: Arts; Beauty; Comedy / Humour;
Cookery; Crafts; Culture; Design; Fashion;
Gardening; History; Lifestyle
Markets: Adult; Children's

Send: Query
Don't send: Full text

Publishes nonfiction for adults and fiction and
nonfiction for children (including picture
books and colouring books). Send query with
SAE, outline, and sample chapter, by post. Due
to high volume of submissions, no
acknowledgement of receipt is provided.

Publishing Imprints: Batsford (*P0086*); Collins
& Brown; National Trust (*P0567*); Pavilion;
Pavilion Children's (*P0621*); Portico (*P0663*)

P0621 Pavilion Children's
Publishing Imprint

Book Publisher: Pavilion Books Group
Limited (**P0620**)

P0622 Pavilion Publishing
Book Publisher
Blue Sky Offices Shoreham, 25 Cecil Pashley
Way, Shoreham-by-Sea, West Sussex, BN43
5FF
United Kingdom
Tel: +44 (0) 1273 434943

info@pavpub.com

http://www.pavpub.com

Types: Nonfiction
Formats: Reference
Subjects: Health; Sociology
Markets: Professional

Publishes books and resources for public,
private and voluntary workers in the health,
social care, education and community safety
sectors. Welcomes submissions from both new
and established authors, and organisations that
are developing training materials.

P0623 Peepal Tree Press
Book Publisher
17 King's Avenue, Leeds, LS6 1QS
United Kingdom
Tel: +44 (0) 113 245 1703

contact@peepaltreepress.com

https://www.peepaltreepress.com

Fiction > *Short Fiction Collections*

Black People; Caribbean Diaspora;
Caribbean

Nonfiction > *Nonfiction Books*
Arts; Black People; Caribbean Diaspora;
Caribbean; Cultural Criticism; Literary
Criticism; Memoir

Poetry > *Poetry Collections*
Black People; Caribbean Diaspora;
Caribbean

Closed to approaches.

Publishes international Caribbean, Black
British, and south Asian writing. Submit
through online submission system.

P0624 Pelican Publishing Company
Book Publisher
990 N. Corporate Drive, Suite 100, New
Orleans, LA 70123
United States

editorial@pelicanpub.com

https://www.pelicanpub.com

Book Publisher: Arcadia Publishing

ADULT > **Nonfiction** > *Nonfiction Books*
Comedy / Humour; Music; Sport

CHILDREN'S
Fiction
Middle Grade: Adventure
Picture Books: Adventure; Holidays
Nonfiction
Middle Grade: Biography; Cookery;
Regional History
Picture Books: Biography; Holidays;
Regional History
YOUNG ADULT
Fiction > *Novels*: Adventure

Nonfiction > *Nonfiction Books*
Biography; Regional History

Send: Query; Author bio; Synopsis; Table of
Contents; Writing sample
How to send: Email

Publishes nonfiction for all ages and fiction for
children and young adults only. No adult
fiction. Send query by email. See website for
full guidelines.

Editor: Nina Kooij

P0625 Pen & Sword Aviation
Publishing Imprint

Book Publisher: Pen & Sword Books Ltd
(**P0626**)

P0626 Pen & Sword Books Ltd
Book Publisher
47 Church Street, Barnsley, South Yorkshire,
S70 2AS
United Kingdom
Tel: +44 (0) 1226 734222
Fax: +44 (0) 1226 734438

editorialoffice@pen-and-sword.co.uk

https://www.pen-and-sword.co.uk

Types: Nonfiction
Subjects: Antiques; Archaeology; Arts;
Autobiography; Crafts; Crime; Gardening;
Health; History; Lifestyle; Nature;
Photography; Science; Sociology; Sport;
Travel; Warfare
Markets: Adult

Send: Query
Don't send: Full text

Publishes across a number of areas including
military history, naval and maritime history,
aviation, local history, family history,
transport, discovery and exploration,
collectables and antiques, nostalgia and true
crime. In 2017, launched a new lifestyle
imprint which publishes books on areas such as
health and diet, hobbies and sport, gardening
and wildlife and space. Submit proposal using
form on website.

Editor: Lisa Hooson

Publishing Imprints: Frontline Books (**P0309**);
Leo Cooper (*P0485*); Pen & Sword Aviation
(*P0625*); Pen & Sword Maritime (*P0627*);
Remember When (**P0701**); Wharncliffe Books
(**P0923**); White Owl (*P0925*)

P0627 Pen & Sword Maritime
Publishing Imprint

Book Publisher: Pen & Sword Books Ltd
(**P0626**)

P0628 Penguin Books
Publishing Imprint
United States

Book Publisher: Penguin Publishing Group
(**P0633**)

P0629 Penguin Classics
Publishing Imprint
United States

Book Publisher: Penguin Publishing Group
(**P0633**)

P0630 Penguin General
Book Publisher

Book Publisher: Penguin Random House UK
(**P0635**)

P0631 Penguin Press
Book Publisher

Book Publisher: Penguin Random House UK
(**P0635**)

P0632 The Penguin Press
Publishing Imprint
United States

Book Publisher: Penguin Publishing Group
(**P0633**)

P0633 Penguin Publishing Group
Book Publisher
United States

Book Publisher: Penguin Group (USA)

Publishing Imprints: Avery (*P0067*); Berkley
(*P0094*); Blue Rider Press (*P0115*); DAW
(*P0217*); Dutton (*P0243*); Family Tree Books
(*P0281*); G.P. Putnam's Sons (*P0312*); Impact
(**P0434**); Interweave (**P0442**); Krause
Publications (**P0478**); North Light Books
(*P0579*); Penguin Books (*P0628*); Penguin
Classics (*P0629*); The Penguin Press (*P0632*);
Plume (*P0658*); Popular Woodworking Books
(**P0661**); Portfolio Penguin (*P0662*);
Riverhead Books (**P0707**); Sentinel (*P0754*);
TarcherPerigee (*P0811*); Viking (*P0886*);
Writer's Digest Books (*P0941*)

P0634 Penguin Random House Children's
Book Publisher

Book Publisher: Penguin Random House UK
(**P0635**)

Book Publisher: Puffin (UK) (**P0672**)

P0635 Penguin Random House UK
Book Publisher
One Embassy Gardens, 8 Viaduct Gardens,
London, SW11 7BW, 20 Vauxhall Bridge
Road, London, SW1V 2SA
United Kingdom
Tel: +44 (0) 20 7010 3000

https://www.penguin.co.uk
https://www.facebook.com/penguinbooks
https://www.instagram.com/penguinukbooks/
https://twitter.com/PenguinUKBooks
https://www.youtube.com/user/penguinbooks

Book Publisher: Penguin Random House

ADULT
  Fiction > *Novels*
  Nonfiction > *Nonfiction Books*

CHILDREN'S
  Fiction
    Chapter Books; *Early Readers*; *Middle
    Grade*; *Novels*; *Picture Books*
  Nonfiction > *Nonfiction Books*

How to send: Through a literary agent

Publishes a wide range of fiction, nonfiction,
poetry, and reference, for children and adults.
No queries or unsolicited MSS, other than
through a literary agent.

Audio Book Publisher: Penguin Random
House UK Audio

Book Publishers: Cornerstone (*P0191*); Ebury
(**P0247**); Michael Joseph (**P0544**); Penguin
General (*P0630*); Penguin Press (*P0631*);
Penguin Random House Children's (**P0634**);
Transworld Publishers (**P0835**); Vintage
(**P0891**)

P0636 Penguin Workshop
Publishing Imprint
United States

Book Publisher: Penguin Young Readers
Group (**P0638**)

P0637 Penguin Young Readers
Publishing Imprint
United States

Book Publisher: Penguin Young Readers
Group (**P0638**)

P0638 Penguin Young Readers Group
Book Publisher
United States

https://www.penguin.com/publishers/penguin-
young-readers-group/

Book Publisher: Penguin Group (USA)

Publishing Imprints: Dial Books for Young
Readers (**P0229**); Dutton Children's Books
(*P0244*); F. Warne & Co. (*P0275*); Firebird
(*P0291*); G.P. Putnam's Sons Books for Young
Readers (**P0313**); Kathy Dawson Books
(**P0464**); Kokila (*P0476*); Nancy Paulsen
Books (*P0565*); Penguin Workshop (*P0636*);
Penguin Young Readers (*P0637*); Penguin
Young Readers Licenses (*P0639*); Philomel
(*P0646*); Puffin (*P0671*); Razorbill (**P0695**);
Speak (*P0781*); Viking Children's Books
(*P0887*)

P0639 Penguin Young Readers Licenses
Publishing Imprint
United States

Book Publisher: Penguin Young Readers
Group (**P0638**)

P0640 Peony Press
Publishing Imprint

Book Publisher: Anness Publishing Ltd
(**P0039**)

P0641 Perseus Books
Book Publisher
United States

https://www.perseusbooks.com
https://www.facebook.com/pages/Perseus-
Books-Group/108204045874204
https://twitter.com/PerseusBooks
https://www.instagram.com/perseus_books/

Book Publisher: Hachette Book Group (**P0348**)

Nonfiction > *Nonfiction Books*

How to send: Through a literary agent

Independent publishing division acquired in 2016.

Publishing Imprints: Avalon Travel (*P0066*); Basic Books; Black Dog & Leventhal (*P0104*); Counterpoint Press; Da Capo Press; Hachette Books (*P0349*); Hachette Go! (*P0352*); PublicAffairs (*P0669*); Running Press (*P0717*); Westview Press

P0642 Peter Lang Oxford
Book Publisher
United Kingdom

editorial@peterlang.com

https://www.peterlang.com
https://www.facebook.com/pages/Peter-Lang-Oxford/260315267419469
https://twitter.com/peterlangoxford
http://peterlangoxford.wordpress.com/

ACADEMIC > **Nonfiction** > *Nonfiction Books*
Art History; Culture; Films; History; Ireland; Language; Literature; Media; Religion; Scotland; Sociology; South-East Asia; Sport; United Kingdom

Send: Query
How to send: Email

Select appropriate editor from website and query by email.

Editor: Na Li

Publishing Director: Lucy Melville

Senior Editors: Tony Mason; Dr Laurel Plapp

P0643 Peter Owen Publishers
Book Publisher
Conway Hall, 25 Red Lion Square, London, WC1R 4RL
United Kingdom

info@peterowen.com

https://www.peterowen.com
https://twitter.com/PeterOwenPubs
https://www.facebook.com/peter.owen.publishers
https://www.instagram.com/peterowenpublishing

Fiction > *Novels*
International; Literary

Nonfiction > *Nonfiction Books*

Does not want:

Nonfiction > *Nonfiction Books*
Memoir; Self Help; Spirituality; Sport

Closed to approaches.

Publishes general nonfiction and international literary fiction. No first novels, short stories, poetry, plays, sport, spirituality, self-help, or children's or genre fiction. Accepts query by email only, including cover letter, synopsis, and one or two sample chapters. No submissions by post. Prefers fiction to come from an agent or translator as appropriate.

Editorial Director: Antonia Owen

P0644 Phaidon Press
Book Publisher
United Kingdom

submissions@phaidon.com

https://www.phaidon.com
https://www.instagram.com/phaidonsnaps/
https://twitter.com/Phaidon
https://www.facebook.com/phaidoncom/
https://youtube.com/phaidonpress
https://linkedin.com/company/phaidon-press

ADULT > **Nonfiction** > *Nonfiction Books*
Architecture; Arts; Contemporary; Cookery; Cultural History; Culture; Design; Fashion; Films; Food; Interior Design; Music; Performing Arts; Photography; Travel

CHILDREN'S > **Nonfiction** > *Nonfiction Books*

Send: Outline; Author bio
How to send: Email

Publishes books in the areas of art, architecture, design, photography, film, fashion, contemporary culture, decorative arts, interior design, music, performing arts, cultural history, food, and cookery, travel, and books for children. No fiction or approaches by post. Send query by email only, with CV and short description of the project. Response only if interested.

Publishing Imprint: The Monacelli Press (**P0551**)

P0645 Phillimore
Publishing Imprint
United Kingdom

https://www.thehistorypress.co.uk

Book Publisher: The History Press (**P0406**)

Types: Nonfiction
Subjects: History
Markets: Adult

P0646 Philomel
Publishing Imprint
United States

Book Publisher: Penguin Young Readers Group (**P0638**)

P0647 Piatkus Books
Publishing Imprint
50 Victoria Embankment, London, EC4Y 0DZ

United Kingdom
Tel: +44 (0) 20 3122 7000

enquiries@hachette.co.uk

https://www.littlebrown.co.uk/imprint/piatkus/page/lbbg-imprint-piatkus/
https://business.facebook.com/piatkusfiction/?business_id=873802706096561
https://twitter.com/PiatkusBooks

Publishing Imprint: Little, Brown Book Group (**P0502**)

Fiction > *Novels*
Fantasy; Historical Fiction; Popular; Romance; Supernatural / Paranormal; Suspense

Nonfiction > *Nonfiction Books*
Business; Health; Mind, Body, Spirit; Parenting; Personal Development; Popular Psychology; Self Help

How to send: Through a literary agent

No longer accepts unsolicited submissions. Accepts material through a literary agent only.

Fiction Editor: Emma Beswetherick

Nonfiction Editor: Gill Bailey

P0648 Piatkus Constable & Robinson
Publishing Imprint

Publishing Imprint: Little, Brown Book Group (**P0502**)

P0649 Piccadilly Press
Book Publisher
80-81 Wimpole Street, London, W1G 9RE
United Kingdom
Tel: +44 (0) 20 7490 3875

hello@bonnierbooks.co.uk

http://www.piccadillypress.co.uk

Types: Fiction; Nonfiction
Subjects: Comedy / Humour; Contemporary
Markets: Children's; Young Adult

How to send: Through a literary agent

No longer accepts unsolicited submissions. Approach through a literary agent.

P0650 Pimpernel Press
Book Publisher
22 Marylands Road, London, W9 2DY
United Kingdom
Tel: +44 (0) 7976 047767

info@pimpernelpress.com

http://www.pimpernelpress.com
https://www.facebook.com/pimpernelpress/
https://twitter.com/pimpernelpress
https://www.pinterest.co.uk/pimpernelpress/

Nonfiction > *Nonfiction Books*
Arts; Design; Gardening; Houses

Publishes books on art, design, houses, and gardens.

P0651 Pimsleur
Publishing Imprint

Audio Book Publisher: Simon & Schuster Audio Publishing

P0652 Pineapple Press
Publishing Imprint
246 Goose Lane, 2nd Floor, Guilford, CT 06437
United States

http://pineapplepress.com
https://www.facebook.com/PineapplePress/

Book Publisher: The Globe Pequot Press (**P0329**)

ADULT

Fiction > *Novels*
Florida; Folklore, Myths, and Legends

Nonfiction
Nonfiction Books: Animals; Arts; Florida; Gardening; History; Nature; Travel
Reference: Florida

CHILDREN'S

Fiction > *Novels*: Florida

Nonfiction > *Nonfiction Books*: Florida

Send: Query; Outline; Table of Contents; Writing sample; Author bio; Market info
How to send: Email; Post

Publishes quality books that educate and entertain while making the real Florida accessible to readers nationwide. Topics include gardening, nature, art, folklore, history, travel, and children's books and fiction that feature the sunshine state.

Editor: June Cussen

P0653 Pinnacle
Publishing Imprint

Book Publisher: Kensington Publishing Corp. (**P0469**)

P0654 Pioneer Plus
Publishing Imprint

Book Publisher: Cedar Fort (**P0156**)

P0655 Plain Sight Publishing
Publishing Imprint

Book Publisher: Cedar Fort (**P0156**)

P0656 Platypus Media
Book Publisher
725 8th Street, SE, Washington DC 20003
United States
Tel: +1 (202) 546-1674

info@platypusmedia.com
submissions@platypusmedia.com

https://www.platypusmedia.com
https://www.facebook.com/PlatypusMedia/
https://twitter.com/PlatypusMedia

ADULT > **Nonfiction** > *Nonfiction Books*
Family; Parenting

CHILDREN'S > **Nonfiction** > *Nonfiction Books*
Animals; Family

PROFESSIONAL > **Nonfiction** > *Nonfiction Books*
Education; Family

Send: Query; Author bio; Writing sample; Full text; Market info; Self-Addressed Stamped Envelope (SASE)
How to send: Post
How not to send: Email

Publishes books focusing on the family and child development, including fiction and nonfiction for children, and parenting guides for adults. Send material with SASE for response.

P0657 Plexus Publishing Limited
Book Publisher
26 Dafforne Road, London, SW17 8TZ
United Kingdom

plexus@plexusuk.demon.co.uk

http://www.plexusbooks.com

Types: Nonfiction
Formats: Film Scripts
Subjects: Biography; Culture; Music
Markets: Adult

Publishes illustrated nonfiction books specialising in biography, popular culture, movies and music.

P0658 Plume
Publishing Imprint
United States

Book Publisher: Penguin Publishing Group (**P0633**)

P0659 Policy Press
Publishing Imprint

Book Publisher: Bristol University Press (**P0132**)

P0660 Pop Press
Publishing Imprint
United Kingdom

Book Publisher: Ebury (**P0247**)

P0661 Popular Woodworking Books
Publishing Imprint
United States

Book Publisher: Penguin Publishing Group (**P0633**)

Types: Nonfiction
Subjects: Crafts; Hobbies
Markets: Adult

Publishes books for woodwork enthusiasts.

P0662 Portfolio Penguin
Publishing Imprint
United States

Book Publisher: Penguin Publishing Group (**P0633**)

P0663 Portico
Publishing Imprint

Book Publisher: Pavilion Books Group Limited (**P0620**)

P0664 Praeger
Publishing Imprint
United States

Book Publisher: ABC-CLIO (**P0015**)

P0665 Press 53
Book Publisher
560 N. Trade Street, Suite 103, Winston-Salem, NC 27101
United States
Tel: +1 (336) 770-5353

editor@press53.com

http://www.press53.com

Types: Fiction; Poetry
Formats: Short Fiction
Subjects: Literary
Markets: Adult

Publishes collections of poetry and short stories. No novels or book length fiction. Finds authors through its competitions, and through writers being active in the literary community and literary magazines.

Editor: Kevin Morgan Watson

P0666 Profile Books
Publishing Imprint
29 Cloth Fair, London, EC1A 7JQ
United Kingdom
Tel: +44 (0) 20 7841 6300
Fax: +44 (0) 20 7833 3969

info@profilebooks.com

https://profilebooks.com

Publishing Imprint: Profile Books (**P0666**)

Types: Nonfiction
Subjects: Biography; Business; Comedy / Humour; Culture; Current Affairs; Finance; History; Politics; Psychology; Science
Markets: Adult

Closed to approaches.

Award-winning small publisher noted for author-friendly relations. Published the number-one Christmas bestseller in 2003.

Accepts direct queries by email (up to 250 words) with first 10 pages, with QUERY and the title of your work in the subject line. No attachments. See website for full guidelines.

Authors: Alan Bennett; Francis Fukuyama; Peter Nichols; Sue Unerman

Publishing Imprints: Economist Books. (*P0251*); Profile Books (**P0666**); Serpent's Tail

P0667 Prometheus
Publishing Imprint
United States

Book Publisher: The Globe Pequot Press (**P0329**)

P0668 Psyche
Publishing Imprint

Publishing Imprint: O-Books

P0669 PublicAffairs
Publishing Imprint
United States

Book Publisher: Perseus Books (**P0641**)

P0670 Pudding Press
Publishing Imprint

Book Publisher: Patrician Press (**P0618**)

P0671 Puffin
Publishing Imprint
United States

Book Publisher: Penguin Young Readers Group (**P0638**)

P0672 Puffin (UK)
Book Publisher
United Kingdom

https://www.penguin.co.uk/brands/puffin.html

Book Publisher: Penguin Random House Children's (**P0634**)

CHILDREN'S
 Fiction
  Chapter Books; *Middle Grade*; *Novels*; *Picture Books*
 Nonfiction > *Nonfiction Books*

Publishing Imprint: Tamarind Books (**P0809**)

P0673 Pulp! The Classics
Publishing Imprint
United Kingdom

Book Publisher: Oldcastle Books Group (**P0592**)

P0674 Purdue University Press
Book Publisher
504 West State Street, West Lafayette, IN

47907-2058
United States

pupress@purdue.edu

http://www.thepress.purdue.edu

ACADEMIC > **Nonfiction** > *Nonfiction Books*
 Agriculture; Anthropology; Business; Education; Engineering; Health; History; Indiana; Judaism; Language; Leadership; Literature; Philosophy; Politics; Science; Technology

PROFESSIONAL > **Nonfiction** > *Nonfiction Books*
 Agriculture; Business; Education; Engineering; Health; Leadership; Science; Technology

Send: Query; Author bio; Table of Contents; Proposal; Writing sample

Publishes scholarly and professional information. Welcomes proposals in its core subjects, which should be emailed to the Director.

Editorial Director: Justine Race

Managing Editor: Margaret Hunt

Publishing Imprint: PuP

P0675 PUSH
Publishing Imprint

Book Publisher: Scholastic (**P0740**)

P0676 QED Publishing
Publishing Imprint
The Old Brewery, 6 Blundell Street, London, N7 9BH
United Kingdom
Tel: +44 (0) 20 7812 8633

QuartoHomesSubmissions@Quarto.com

https://www.quartoknows.com/QED-Publishing

Book Publisher: The Quarto Group, Inc. (**P0679**)

CHILDREN'S
 Fiction > *Picture Books*
 Nonfiction > *Illustrated Books*

Send: Query; Proposal
How to send: Email

Publishes fresh, informative, high-quality books that will appeal to children, parents and teachers alike, from entertaining, innovative facts for the classroom to beautifully illustrated fiction that kids will want to take home. Always on the lookout for authors and artists with creative ideas that enhance and broaden their publishing list of children's books.

Publisher: Steve Evans

P0677 Quarry
Publishing Imprint

Book Publisher: The Quarto Group, Inc. (**P0679**)

P0678 Quarto Children's Books
Publishing Imprint

Book Publisher: The Quarto Group, Inc. (**P0679**)

P0679 The Quarto Group, Inc.
Book Publisher
The Old Brewery, 6 Blundell Street, London, N7 9BH
United Kingdom
Tel: +44 (0) 20 7700 6700
Fax: +44 (0) 20 7700 8066

http://www.quarto.com

ADULT > **Nonfiction** > *Nonfiction Books*

CHILDREN'S > **Nonfiction** > *Nonfiction Books*

Publisher of illustrated nonfiction books for adults and children.

Publishing Imprints: Apple Press; Aurum Press; Book Sales (*P0124*); Bright Press (*P0131*); Burgess Lea Press (*P0138*); Cool Springs Press (*P0189*); Epic Ink (*P0269*); Fair Winds Press (*P0278*); Frances Lincoln; Frances Lincoln Children's Books (**P0304**); Harvard Common Press (**P0391**); Iqon Editions (*P0444*); Ivy Kids (*P0446*); Ivy Press (*P0447*); Jacqui Small; Leaping Hare Press (*P0484*); Lincoln First Editions (*P0496*); Motorbooks (*P0556*); QED Publishing (**P0676**); Quarry (*P0677*); Quarto Children's Books (*P0678*); Quarto Publishing (*P0680*); Race Point Publishing (*P0687*); Rock Point Gift & Stationery (*P0708*); Rockport Publishing (*P0710*); SmartLab Toys (*P0773*); Union Books; Voyageur Press (**P0898**); Walter Foster Jr. (*P0903*); Walter Foster Publishing (**P0904**); Wellfleet Press (*P0917*); White Lion Publishing (*P0924*); Wide-Eyed Editions (**P0927**); Words & Pictures (**P0939**); becker&mayer! books (**P0091**); becker&mayer! kids (*P0092*); small world creations (*P0772*)

P0680 Quarto Publishing
Publishing Imprint

Book Publisher: The Quarto Group, Inc. (**P0679**)

P0681 Quattro Books
Book Publisher
12 Concord Ave, 2nd Floor, Toronto, Ontario, M6H 2P1
Canada
Tel: +1 (416) 893-7979

info@quattrobooks.ca

http://quattrobooks.ca

Types: Fiction; Poetry
Subjects: Literary
Markets: Adult

Publishes novellas of literary fiction, and poetry. Accepts work from Canadian citizens residing in Canada only. Novellas should be between 20,000 and 40,000 words. No genre fiction. Not accepting poetry manuscripts as at June 2019. No electronic submissions.

P0682 **Quercus Books**
Book Publisher
Carmelite House, 50 Victoria Embankment, London, EC4Y 0DZ
United Kingdom
Tel: +44 (0) 20 3122 6000

enquiries@quercusbooks.co.uk

https://www.quercusbooks.co.uk

Book Publisher: Hachette Livre (**P0353**)

Types: Fiction; Nonfiction
Subjects: Crime; Fantasy; Science Fiction
Markets: Adult; Children's

How to send: Through a literary agent

Publishes fiction and nonfiction. Accepts submissions only via a literary agent.

Publishing Imprint: Jo Fletcher Books (**P0453**)

P0683 **Quercus Children's Books**
Publishing Imprint

Book Publisher: Hachette Children's Group (**P0350**)

P0684 **Quill Driver Books**
Publishing Imprint
2006 South Mary Street, Fresno, CA 93721
United States
Tel: +1 (800) 345-4447
Fax: +1 (559) 233-6933

kent@lindenpub.com

https://quilldriverbooks.com

Book Publisher: Linden Publishing

Types: Nonfiction
Subjects: Architecture; Arts; Biography; Business; Comedy / Humour; Crime; Health; Hobbies; Lifestyle; Self Help; Spirituality; Technology; Travel
Markets: Adult

Send: Query
Don't send: Full text

Publishes nonfiction only. Send a book proposal including synopsis; commercial info; author platform; and sample chapters or supporting materials. See website for full guidelines.

Editor: Kent Sorsky

P0685 **Quiller Publishing Ltd**
Book Publisher
The Hill, Merrywalks, Stroud, GL5 4EP
United Kingdom
Tel: +44 (0) 1939 261616

info@quillerbooks.com

https://www.quillerpublishing.com
https://www.facebook.com/QuillerPublishing
https://twitter.com/QuillerBooks
https://www.pinterest.co.uk/QuillerPublishing/
https://instagram.com/quillerpublishing/

Nonfiction > *Nonfiction Books*
Archery; Arts; Biography; Canoeing; Climbing; Country Lifestyle; Crafts; Deer; Dogs; Environment; Equestrian; Falconry; Farming; Fishing; Food and Drink; History; Shooting

Send: Proposal; Synopsis; Writing sample; Table of Contents; Market info; Author bio; Self-Addressed Stamped Envelope (SASE)
How to send: Email; Post

Publishes books for all lovers of fishing, shooting, equestrian and country pursuits. Accepts unsolicited MSS from authors. Send submissions as hard copy only, with email address for reply or SAE if return of ms is required. Proposals may be sent by email.

Editor: Andrew Johnston

Publishing Imprints: The Sportsman's Press; Kenilworth Press (**P0466**); Quiller Press; Swan Hill Press

P0686 **Quintet Publishing**
Book Publisher
Ovest House, 58 West Street, Brighton, BN1 2RA
United Kingdom
Tel: +44 (0) 1273 716 000

mark.searle@quarto.com

https://www.quartoknows.com/Quintet-Publishing

Types: Nonfiction
Subjects: Cookery; Crafts; Culture; Lifestyle; Photography
Markets: Adult

Publishes illustrated nonfiction on a co-edition basis with partners around the world.

P0687 **Race Point Publishing**
Publishing Imprint

Book Publisher: The Quarto Group, Inc. (**P0679**)

P0688 **Radioactive Cloud**
Book Publisher
United States

https://radioactivecloud.weebly.com

Types: Poetry
Subjects: Literary
Markets: Adult

Send: Full text

Publishes poetry chapbooks between 15 and 30 pages in length. Submit via online submission system during submission window (December 1 – January 15).

P0689 **Rand McNally**
Book Publisher
United States
Tel: +1 (877) 446-4863

tndsupport@randmcnally.com

https://www.randmcnally.com
https://www.randmcnally.com/publishing

ADULT > **Nonfiction**
Activity Books: Travel
Reference: Road Atlases; Travel
CHILDREN'S > **Nonfiction** > *Activity Books*: Travel

Publishes road atlases and activity books for adults and children, focusing on travel.

P0690 **Random House**
Book Publisher
United States

http://www.randomhousebooks.com

Book Publisher: Penguin Random House

Fiction > *Novels*

Nonfiction > *Nonfiction Books*

How to send: Through a literary agent

Accepts queries through agents only – does not deal direct with aspiring writers.

Book Publishers: Bantam Doubleday Dell Books for Young Readers; Knopf Publishing Group

Publishing Imprints: 4 Color Books (**P0001**); Alibi; Ballantine (*P0077*); Bantam (**P0079**); Broadway Books; Clarkson Potter (**P0178**); Convergent Books (*P0188*); Crown; Crown Archetype (*P0202*); Crown Forum (*P0203*); Currency; Del Rey (*P0223*); Del Rey/LucasBooks (*P0224*); Delacorte Press; The Dial Press (*P0230*); Harmony Books (*P0362*); Hogarth (*P0411*); Image Books (*P0430*); Lorena Jones Books (*P0506*); Loveswept; Modern Library (*P0550*); One World (*P0597*); Random House (Imprint) (*P0691*); Rodale Books (*P0711*); Ten Speed Press (*P0817*); Three Rivers Press; Tim Duggan Books; WaterBrook Multnomah (*P0906*); Watson-Guptill (*P0909*)

P0691 **Random House (Imprint)**
Publishing Imprint

Book Publisher: Random House (**P0690**)

P0692 Ransom Note Press
Book Publisher
United States

editorial@ransomnotepress.com

http://www.ransomnotepress.com

Fiction > *Novels*
Mystery; Suspense

Send: Query; Synopsis; Author bio; Writing sample
Don't send: Full text
How to send: In the body of an email
How not to send: Email attachment; Post

Publishes mystery and suspense novels only. Accepts approaches via email only. See website for full submission guidelines.

P0693 Ransom Publishing Ltd
Book Publisher
Unit 7, Brocklands Farm, West Meon, Hampshire, GU32 1JN
United Kingdom
Tel: +44 (0) 1730 829091

steve@ransom.co.uk

http://www.ransom.co.uk

Types: Fiction; Nonfiction
Markets: Adult; Children's; Professional; Young Adult

Closed to approaches.

An independent specialist publisher of high quality, inspirational books that encourage and help children, young adults, and adults to develop their reading skills. Books are intended to have content which is age appropriate and engaging, but reading levels that would normally be appropriate for younger readers. Also publishes resources for both the library and classroom. No picture books or early years books. Will consider unsolicited mss. Email with synopsis and sample (up to three chapters) in first instance, or full ms if under thousand words.

Editor: Steve Rickard

P0694 Ravenstone
Publishing Imprint
Canada

info@turnstonepress.com

https://www.turnstonepress.com/books/ravenstone.html
https://www.facebook.com/turnstone.press.3
https://twitter.com/turnstonepress
http://www.pinterest.com/turnstonepress/
https://www.instagram.com/turnstone_press/
https://www.youtube.com/user/TurnstonePress
http://www.goodreads.com/user/show/16275125-turnstone-press

Book Publisher: Turnstone Press (**P0841**)

Fiction > *Novels*

Literary Mystery; Noir; Speculative; Thrillers; Urban Fantasy

Send: Full text
How to send: Online submission system

Publishes literary mysteries, thrillers, noir, speculative fiction, and urban fantasy.

P0695 Razorbill
Publishing Imprint
345 Hudson Street, New York, NY 10014
United States

http://www.razorbillbooks.com

Book Publisher: Penguin Young Readers Group (**P0638**)

Types: Fiction; Nonfiction
Subjects: Adventure; Comedy / Humour; Contemporary; Culture; Fantasy; Literary; Romance; Science Fiction; Suspense
Markets: Children's; Young Adult

Send: Query
Don't send: Full text

Publishes mainly fiction for middle grade and young adult. Send query with SASE, outline, target group, publishing credits (if any), and up to 30 pages. No picture books. Response only if interested.

P0696 REaDLips Press
Book Publisher
United States

readlipspress@gmail.com

https://readlipspress.com

Types: Fiction
Subjects: Literary
Markets: Adult

Send: Query
Don't send: Full text

Publishes literary fiction novellas between 20,000 and 60,000 words. Send blurb, bio, and summary by email. See website for full guidelines.

P0697 Rebel Base Books
Publishing Imprint

Book Publisher: Kensington Publishing Corp. (**P0469**)

P0698 Red Rattle Books
Book Publisher
United Kingdom

editor@redrattlebooks.co.uk

http://www.redrattlebooks.co.uk

Types: Fiction; Nonfiction
Subjects: Crime; Horror
Markets: Adult

Closed to approaches.

Not accepting submissions as at January 2019. Check website for current status. Independent, family run company, publishing new crime, horror and nonfiction books. Submit via website using online submission form.

P0699 Red Squirrel Publishing
Book Publisher
Suite 235, 15 Ingestre Place, London, W1F 0DU
United Kingdom

https://www.redsquirrelbooks.com

Nonfiction > *Nonfiction Books*
Culture; Society; United Kingdom

Publishes books aimed at helping people pass the British Citizenship test. No fiction, poetry, or children's.

Managing Director: Henry Dillon

P0700 Regency House Publishing Limited
Book Publisher
The Manor House, High Street, Buntingford, Hertfordshire, SG9 9AB
United Kingdom

https://beta.companieshouse.gov.uk/company/02673368

Nonfiction > *Nonfiction Books*

Publishes and packages mass-market nonfiction. Does not accept fiction or unsolicited MSS.

Chair: Brian Trodd

Managing Director: Nicolette Trodd

P0701 Remember When
Publishing Imprint
47 Church Street, Barnsley, South Yorkshire, S70 2AS
United Kingdom
Tel: +44 (0) 1226 734222
Fax: +44 (0) 1226 734438

editorialoffice@pen-and-sword.co.uk
enquiries@pen-and-sword.co.uk

https://www.pen-and-sword.co.uk
https://www.pen-and-sword.co.uk/Remember-When/i/6

Book Publisher: Pen & Sword Books Ltd (**P0626**)

Nonfiction > *Nonfiction Books*
Antiques; History; Nostalgia

Send: Synopsis; Market info; Author bio
How to send: Online submission system

Publishes books on nostalgia and antique collecting. Submit proposals via online submission system. See website.

Editor: Fiona Shoop

P0702 **Repeater Books**
Book Publisher
United Kingdom

https://repeaterbooks.com

Types: Fiction; Nonfiction; Poetry
Subjects: Arts; Culture; Current Affairs;
Literature; Music; Philosophy; Politics
Markets: Adult

Send: Full text

Aims to publish in every sphere and genre,
"combining vigorous dissent and a pragmatic
willingness to succeed". Submit complete ms
via online submission system.

P0703 **Richard Hollis**
Publishing Imprint

Book Publisher: Five Leaves Publications
(**P0295**)

P0704 **Richards Publishing**
Publishing Imprint
United Kingdom

Book Publisher: Brewin Books Ltd (**P0129**)

P0705 **Rider Books**
Publishing Imprint
United Kingdom

Book Publisher: Ebury (**P0247**)

P0706 **Rising Stars**
Book Publisher
Carmelite House, 50 Victoria Embankment,
London, EC4Y 0DZ
United Kingdom
Tel: +44 (0) 20 3122 6000

primary@hachette.co.uk

https://www.risingstars-uk.com
https://www.youtube.com/channel/
UCTO7hZc1TrfzBKFEo4i8qkQ
https://twitter.com/risingstarsedu
https://www.facebook.com/Rising-Stars-
547479242046479/timeline/
https://www.instagram.com/risingstarsedu

Book Publisher: Hodder Education (**P0410**)

ACADEMIC > **Nonfiction** > *Nonfiction*
Books: Education

Send: Query
How to send: Online submission system

Publisher of educational books and software
for children aged 3-18. Always looking for
people bursting with ideas and imagination and
a view of primary education. Complete survey
online in first instance.

Publishing Director: Ben Barton

P0707 **Riverhead Books**
Publishing Imprint
United States

Book Publisher: Penguin Publishing Group
(**P0633**)

Types: Fiction; Nonfiction
Subjects: Commercial; Contemporary; Literary
Markets: Adult

Publisher of bestselling literary fiction and
quality nonfiction.

Editor: Megan Lynch

P0708 **Rock Point Gift &
Stationery**
Publishing Imprint

Book Publisher: The Quarto Group, Inc.
(**P0679**)

P0709 **Rocket Science Press**
Publishing Imprint

Book Publisher: Shipwreckt Books Publishing
Company (**P0762**)

P0710 **Rockport Publishing**
Publishing Imprint

Book Publisher: The Quarto Group, Inc.
(**P0679**)

P0711 **Rodale Books**
Publishing Imprint

Book Publisher: Random House (**P0690**)

P0712 **Romance Publications**
Book Publisher
United States

romancepublications@gmail.com

https://www.facebook.com/romance.
publications/

Fiction
  Novelette: Romance
  Novellas: Romance
  Novels: Romance
  Short Fiction: Romance

How to send: Email

Publishes romantic stories that include a
central love story and emotionally satisfying
and optimistic ending. In addition to novels,
we publish novellas, novelettes, and short
stories. We are currently accepting short stores
(450-550) words to be published in our
monthly newsletters and anthologies of short
stories. Anthologies will be sold for a profit,
and the authors will receive a portion of the
royalties that is typically given to a single
author, which is 25%.

P0713 **Round Hall**
Publishing Imprint; Magazine Publisher
12/13 Exchange Place, International Financial
Services Centre, Dublin 1
Ireland

https://www.sweetandmaxwell.co.uk/
roundhall/

Book Publisher: Thomson Reuters

PROFESSIONAL > **Nonfiction**
  Articles: Legal
  Nonfiction Books: Legal

Send: Query
How to send: Email

Publishes information on Irish law in the form
of books, journals, periodicals, looseleaf
services, CD-ROMs and online services.
Contact by email.

Company Director: Martin McCann

Editor: Pamela Moran

P0714 **Route Publishing**
Book Publisher
PO Box 167, Pontefract, WF8 4WW
United Kingdom
Tel: +44 (0) 1977 793442

info@route-online.com

http://www.route-online.com

Types: Fiction; Nonfiction
Formats: Film Scripts
Subjects: Autobiography; Contemporary;
Culture; Music
Markets: Adult

Publisher of nonfiction (particularly music
books) and occasional fiction. Only accept a
handful of titles a year. Response no
guaranteed. If submitting by post, include SAE
if return of work required.

Editors: Ian Daley; Isabel Galan

P0715 **Routledge**
Book Publisher
United Kingdom

https://www.routledge.com

Book Publisher: Taylor & Francis Books

Types: Nonfiction
Subjects: Anthropology; Archaeology;
Architecture; Business; Crime; Finance;
Health; Legal; Nature; Politics; Psychology;
Science; Technology
Markets: Academic; Adult; Professional

Send: Query
Don't send: Full text

International academic imprint. Send proposal
with sample chapters and author CV (see
website for detailed guidelines). No fiction,
poetry, travel, or astrology.

Book Publisher: David Fulton (Publishers) Ltd

P0716 **Ruby Fiction**
Publishing Imprint
Penrose House, Crawley Drive, Camberley,
Surrey, GU15 2AB

United Kingdom
Tel: +44 (0)1276 586367

info@rubyfiction.com
submissions@rubyfiction.com

https://www.rubyfiction.com
https://twitter.com/rubyfiction
https://www.facebook.com/pages/RubyFiction

Book Publisher: Choc Lit (**P0169**)

Fiction > *Novels*
  Romance; Thrillers; Women's Fiction

Send: Author bio; Synopsis
How to send: Online submission system

Publishes thrillers, women's fiction and romances without the hero's point of view, between 60,000 and 100,000 words, suitable for a female adult audience.

P0717 Running Press
Publishing Imprint
United States

Book Publisher: Perseus Books (**P0641**)

P0718 Rutgers University Press
Book Publisher
106 Somerset St., 3rd Floor, New Brunswick, NJ 08901
United States

https://www.rutgersuniversitypress.org
https://www.pinterest.com/rutgersuniv0180/
http://www.facebook.com/pages/Rutgers-University-Press/212072346925
https://www.instagram.com/RutgersUPress/
https://twitter.com/RutgersUPress
https://www.youtube.com/user/RutgersUPress

ACADEMIC > **Nonfiction**
  Nonfiction Books: General, and in particular: 18th Century; African American; Anthropology; Architecture; Arts; Asia; Asian American; Biography; Business; Caribbean; Comic Books; Crime; Culture; Environment; Ethnic Groups; Films; Food; Gardening; Gender; Health; History; Judaism; LGBTQIA; Leadership; Legal; Leisure; Literature; Management; Media; Medicine; Memoir; Middle East; Military History; Music; Nature; New Jersey; New York City; New York State; Philosophy; Politics; Regional; Religion; Science; Social Issues; Sociology; South America; Sport; Travel; United States; Urban; Women's Studies
  Reference: General

Send: Outline; Table of Contents; Writing sample; Market info; Author bio
How to send: Post; Email

Publishes scholarly books, regional, social sciences and humanities. No original fiction or poetry. See website for full submission guidelines and individual editor contacts.

P0719 RYA (Royal Yachting Association)
Book Publisher
RYA House, Ensign Way, Hamble, Southampton, Hampshire, SO31 4YA
United Kingdom
Tel: +44 (0) 23 8060 4100

reception@rya.org.uk

https://www.rya.org.uk/

Nonfiction > *Nonfiction Books*
  Boats; Sailing; Yachts

Publisher of books on boating and sailing.

Editor: Phil Williams-Ellis

P0720 Ryland Peters & Small and CICO Books
Book Publisher
United Kingdom

enquiries@rps.co.uk

https://rylandpeters.com
https://www.facebook.com/RylandPetersandSmall
https://twitter.com/rylandpeters
https://www.pinterest.co.uk/rpscicobooks/
https://www.instagram.com/rylandpetersandsmall/
https://www.youtube.com/channel/UC-zcYDB1m8QxPJhWhRmytjA

ADULT > **Nonfiction** > *Illustrated Books*
  Comedy / Humour; Crafts; Food and Drink; Health; Interior Design; Mind, Body, Spirit; Popular Culture

CHILDREN'S > **Nonfiction** > *Illustrated Books*
  Crafts; Gardening; Science

Send: Query; Synopsis; Table of Contents; Author bio; Writing sample
How to send: Email

Independent, illustrated publisher creating books in the areas of interior design, food and drink, craft, mindfulness and spirituality, health, humour and pop culture. Also produces gifts and stationery, as well as books for kids.

Book Publisher: Cico Books

Managing Director: David Peters

Publishing Director: Alison Starling

P0721 Saddle Road Press
Book Publisher
1483 Wailuku Drive, Hilo, HI 96720
United States

info@saddleroadpress.com

http://saddleroadpress.com

Types: Fiction; Poetry
Formats: Short Fiction
Subjects: Autobiography; Literary
Markets: Adult

Closed to approaches.

Closed to submissions as at September 2019. Check website for current status. Small literary press publishing full-length poetry collections, poetry chapbooks, literary fiction, essays, memoir, and hybrid forms, in both print and eBook editions. Currently looking for collections of poetry and hybrid poetry/prose, and collections of short fiction and lyric essays. Submit through online submission system. $20 submission fee.

P0722 Safari Press
Book Publisher
15621 Chemical Lane, Huntington Beach, CA 92649
United States
Tel: +1 (714) 894-9080

info@safaripress.com

https://www.safaripress.com
https://www.facebook.com/SafariPress

Nonfiction > *Nonfiction Books*
  Firearms; Hunting

Publisher of big-game hunting, wingshooting, and sporting-firearms books.

Editor: Jacqueline Neufeld

P0723 Saffron Books
Book Publisher
EAPGROUP, PO Box 13666, London, SW14 8WF
United Kingdom
Tel: +44 (0) 20 8392 1122
Fax: +44 (0) 20 8392 1122

info@eapgroup.com

http://www.saffronbooks.com

Types: Fiction; Nonfiction
Subjects: Archaeology; Arts; Business; Culture; Current Affairs; Finance; History; Sociology
Markets: Adult

Send: Query
Don't send: Full text

Publishes books on art, archaeology and architecture, art history, current affairs and linguistics, with a particular emphasis on Asia, Africa, and the Middle East. Also publishes fiction. Welcomes proposals for books and monographs from new or established authors. Send query by email, post, or fax (not preferred for long documents). See website for full guidelines.

P0724 Saga Press
Publishing Imprint

Book Publisher: Simon & Schuster Children's Publishing (**P0768**)

P0725 Sage Publications
Book Publisher; Magazine Publisher
1 Oliver's Yard, 55 City Road, London, EC1Y
1SP
United Kingdom
Tel: +44 (0) 20 7324 8500
Fax: +44 (0) 20 7324 8600

info@sagepub.co.uk

https://uk.sagepub.com

Types: Nonfiction
Subjects: Anthropology; Archaeology; Arts;
Business; Crime; Finance; Health; History;
Media; Medicine; Politics; Psychology;
Religion; Science; Sociology; Technology
Markets: Academic; Professional

Publishes academic books and journals. See
website for guides for authors and making
submissions, etc.

Book Publisher: CQ Press

Magazine: Feminist Review (**M0203**)

P0726 Saint Andrew Press
Publishing Imprint
Norwich Books and Music, 13a Hellesdon
Park Road, Norwich, NR6 5DR
United Kingdom
Tel: +44 (0) 1603 785925
Fax: +44 (0) 1603 785915

admin@norwichbooksandmusic.co.uk

https://standrewpress.hymnsam.co.uk

Book Publisher: Hymns Ancient & Modern
Ltd (**P0424**)

Types: Nonfiction
Formats: Reference
Subjects: Religion
Markets: Adult; Children's

Send: Query
Don't send: Full text

Publisher of religious books for the UK and
international Christian retail and trade markets,
including general reference and children's
books. See website for full submission
guidelines.

P0727 Saint Julian Press
Book Publisher
2053 Cortlandt, Suite 200, Houston, TX 77008
United States
Tel: +1 (281) 734-8721

ronstarbuck@saintjulianpress.com

http://www.saintjulianpress.com

Types: Poetry
Subjects: Literary
Markets: Adult

Closed to approaches.

Literary poetry publisher. Charges reading fees
of between $50 and $80 depending on
manuscript length. Closed to submissions until

late 2019 / early 2020. Check website for
current status.

Editor: Ron Starbuck

P0728 Salaam Reads
Publishing Imprint

Book Publisher: Simon & Schuster Children's
Publishing (**P0768**)

P0729 The Salariya Book
Company
Book Publisher
25 Marlborough Place, Brighton, East Sussex,
BN1 1UB
United Kingdom
Tel: +44 (0) 1273 603306
Fax: +44 (0) 1273 621619

salariya@salariya.com

http://www.salariya.com

Types: Fiction; Nonfiction
Subjects: Adventure; Fantasy; History; Nature;
Science
Markets: Children's

Closed to approaches.

**Not accepting submissions as at February
2019. Check website for current
status.** Publishes books of fiction and
nonfiction for children.

Publishing Imprints: Book House (*P0123*);
Scribblers (*P0749*); Scribo (*P0750*)

P0730 Salo Press
Book Publisher
United Kingdom

editorsalopress@gmail.com

https://salopress.weebly.com

Types: Poetry
Subjects: Experimental; Literary
Markets: Adult

An independent micro publisher focusing on
poetry of an experimental / weird / surreal /
cerebral nature. See website for current
submission opportunities.

Editor: Sophie Essex

P0731 Salt Publishing Ltd
Book Publisher
12 Norwich Road, CROMER, Norfolk, NR27
0AX
United Kingdom
Tel: +44 (0) 1263 511011

submissions@saltpublishing.com

http://www.saltpublishing.com

Types: Fiction; Nonfiction; Poetry
Formats: Short Fiction
Subjects: Biography; Crime; Gothic; Literary
Criticism; Mystery; Thrillers
Markets: Adult; Children's

Currently accepting submissions of
contemporary adult poetry and nonfiction by
British residents. See website for full
submission guidelines.

P0732 Salvo Press
Publishing Imprint
221 River St, 9th Floor, Hoboken, NJ 07030
United States
Tel: +1 (212) 431-5455

info@salvopress.com

http://salvopress.com

Book Publisher: Start Publishing (**P0796**)

Types: Fiction
Subjects: Literary; Mystery; Thrillers
Markets: Adult

Publishes quality mysteries, thrillers, and
literary books in eBook and audiobook
formats.

P0733 Samosir Books
Book Publisher
United Kingdom

https://samosirbooksltd.blogspot.com

Types: Nonfiction
Subjects: Adventure; Comedy / Humour;
Culture; Travel
Markets: Adult

Dedicated to publishing and distributing travel
related literature worldwide.

Authors: Chris Raven; Simon Raven

P0734 Sandstone Press Ltd
Book Publisher
Suite 1, Willow House, Stoneyfield Business
Park, Inverness, IV2 7PA
United Kingdom
Tel: +44 (0) 1349 865484

submissions@sandstonepress.com
info@sandstonepress.com

https://sandstonepress.com
https://www.youtube.com/channel/
UC_36jtKtY2dy8roy5jQMQHg
https://www.facebook.com/SandstonePress
https://twitter.com/sandstonepress

Fiction > *Novels*

Nonfiction > *Nonfiction Books*

Send: Query; Submission Form; Synopsis;
Writing sample
How to send: Word file email attachment;
Through a literary agent

Accepts submissions of nonfiction from agents
and authors all year. Accepts submissions of
fiction from agents all year, but accepts
submissions of fiction from authors during
specific windows only. Check website for
status regarding fiction submissions from
authors. Accepts approaches via email only.
See website for full guidelines.

P0735 Saqi Books
Book Publisher
26 Westbourne Grove, London, W2 5RH
United Kingdom
Tel: +44 (0) 20 7221 9347
Fax: +44 (0) 20 7229 7492

elizabeth@saqibooks.com

http://www.saqibooks.com

Types: Fiction; Nonfiction
Subjects: Architecture; Arts; Cookery; History;
Literary; Politics
Markets: Academic; Adult

Send: Query
Don't send: Full text

Publisher of books related to the Arab world
and the Middle East (initially), but now also
covering South and Central Asia. Also
publishes European fiction. Not accepting
fiction submissions as at September 2019. See
website for full submission guidelines.

Publishing Imprint: Telegram Books (**P0814**)

P0736 Sarabande Books, Inc.
Book Publisher
822 E. Market St., Louisville, KY 40206
United States
Tel: +1 (502) 458-4028

info@sarabandebooks.org

http://www.sarabandebooks.org

Types: Fiction; Nonfiction; Poetry
Subjects: Literary
Markets: Adult

Send: Full text

Nonprofit literary press championing poetry,
fiction, and essays. Accepts submissions
through its annual competitions, for which an
entry fee must be paid.

P0737 Sasquatch Books
Book Publisher
1904 Third Avenue, Suite 710, Seattle,
Washington 98101
United States

custserve@sasquatchbooks.com

https://sasquatchbooks.com
https://www.facebook.com/
SasquatchBooksSeattle/
https://twitter.com/sasquatchbooks
https://www.instagram.com/sasquatchbooks/

Nonfiction > *Nonfiction Books*
Arts; Business; Family; Food; Gardening;
Literature; Nature; Politics; Wine

Send: Query; Proposal
How to send: Post

Publishes books by the most gifted writers,
artists, chefs, naturalists, and thought leaders in
the Pacific Northwest and on the West Coast,
and brings their talents to a national audience.

Publishing Imprints: Little Bigfoot (**P0498**);
Spruce Books (*P0786*)

P0738 Sawday's
Book Publisher
Merchants House, Wapping Road, Bristol, BS1
4RW
United Kingdom
Tel: +44 (0) 1172 047810

hello@sawdays.co.uk

https://www.sawdays.co.uk

Types: Nonfiction
Subjects: Nature; Travel
Markets: Adult

Publishes guidebooks and books on
environmental topics.

P0739 Schocken Books
Publishing Imprint
United States

Book Publisher: Knopf Doubleday Publishing
Group (**P0475**)

P0740 Scholastic
Book Publisher
557 Broadway, New York, NY 10012
United States

TeachingResources@Scholastic.com

https://www.scholastic.com
https://scholastic.force.com/scholasticfaqs/s/
article/How-do-I-submit-a-manuscript-for-
teaching-ideas

CHILDREN'S
 Fiction
   Chapter Books; *Early Readers*; *Middle
   Grade*; *Novels*; *Picture Books*
 Nonfiction
   Chapter Books; *Early Readers*; *Illustrated
   Books*; *Middle Grade*
PROFESSIONAL > **Nonfiction** > *Nonfiction
Books*: Education

Send: Query; Table of Contents; Writing
sample

The world's largest publisher and distributor of
children's books. Provides professional
services, classroom magazines, and produces
educational and popular children's media.

Book Publishers: Arthur A. Levine Books;
Chicken House Publishing; Scholastic UK
(**P0747**)

Publishing Imprints: AFK (*P0024*); Cartwheel
Books (*P0152*); Graphix (*P0341*); Klutz
(*P0473*); Orchard Books (*P0600*); PUSH
(*P0675*); Scholastic Audio (*P0741*); Scholastic
Focus (*P0743*); Scholastic Inc. (*P0744*);
Scholastic Press (*P0745*); Scholastic Reference
(*P0746*)

P0741 Scholastic Audio
Publishing Imprint

Book Publisher: Scholastic (**P0740**)

P0742 Scholastic Children's Books
Book Publisher

Book Publisher: Scholastic UK (**P0747**)

P0743 Scholastic Focus
Publishing Imprint

Book Publisher: Scholastic (**P0740**)

P0744 Scholastic Inc.
Publishing Imprint

Book Publisher: Scholastic (**P0740**)

P0745 Scholastic Press
Publishing Imprint

Book Publisher: Scholastic (**P0740**)

P0746 Scholastic Reference
Publishing Imprint

Book Publisher: Scholastic (**P0740**)

P0747 Scholastic UK
Book Publisher
Euston House, 24 Eversholt Street, London,
NW1 1DB, WITNEY:, Windrush Park, Range
Road, Witney, OXON, OX25 0YD,
SOUTHAM:, Westfield Road, Southam,
Warwickshire, CV47 0RA
United Kingdom
Tel: +44 (0) 1926 887799
Fax: +44 (0) 1926 883331

enquiries@scholastic.co.uk

https://www.scholastic.co.uk

Book Publisher: Scholastic (**P0740**)

Types: Fiction; Nonfiction
Markets: Children's

Publisher of fiction and nonfiction for children,
as well as educational material for primary
schools.

Book Publisher: Scholastic Children's Books
(*P0742*)

P0748 Scout Press
Publishing Imprint

Book Publisher: Simon & Schuster Adult
Publishing (**P0766**)

P0749 Scribblers
Publishing Imprint

Book Publisher: The Salariya Book Company
(**P0729**)

P0750 Scribo
Publishing Imprint

Book Publisher: The Salariya Book Company (**P0729**)

P0751 Seal Press

Publishing Imprint
1290 Avenue of the Americas, New York, NY 10104
United States

Seal.Press@hbgusa.com

https://www.sealpress.com
https://www.facebook.com/sealpress
https://twitter.com/sealpress
https://www.instagram.com/sealpress/

Publishing Imprint: Da Capo Press

Nonfiction > *Nonfiction Books*: Feminism

Founded in 1976 and stands as one of the most enduring feminist publishing houses to emerge from the women's press movement of the 1970s. Publishes radical and groundbreaking books that inspire and challenge readers, that humanize urgent issues, that build much-needed bridges in divisive times, and help us see the world in a new light.

P0752 Seaworthy Publications

Book Publisher
6300 N Wickham Road, Unit #130-416, Melbourne, FL 32940
United States
Tel: +1 (321) 610-3634

queries@seaworthy.com

http://www.seaworthy.com

Nonfiction > *Articles*
  Boats; Sailing

Send: Full text

Nautical book publisher specialising in recreational boating. Send query by email outlining your work and attaching sample table of contents and two or three sample chapters. See website for full submission guidelines.

P0753 SelfMadeHero

Book Publisher
139 Pancras Road, London, NW1 1UN
United Kingdom

submissions@selfmadehero.com

https://selfmadehero.com

Types: Fiction; Nonfiction
Subjects: Biography; Crime; Horror; Science Fiction
Markets: Adult

Publishes fiction and nonfiction graphic novels. Send query by email or by post with one-page synopsis and at least eight pages of sequential art (up to 5MB if sending by email). See website for full guidelines.

P0754 Sentinel

Publishing Imprint
United States

Book Publisher: Penguin Publishing Group (**P0633**)

P0755 September Publishing

Book Publisher
United Kingdom
Tel: +44 (0) 20 3637 0116

info@septemberpublishing.org

https://www.septemberpublishing.org

Types: Nonfiction
Subjects: Arts; Autobiography; Comedy / Humour; Politics; Travel
Markets: Adult

Publishes extraordinary lives and expert insight. Welcomes submissions from both authors and agents via form on website.

P0756 Seren Books

Book Publisher
Suite 6, 4 Derwen Road, Bridgend, CF31 1LH
United Kingdom
Tel: +44 (0) 1656 663018

Seren@SerenBooks.com

https://www.serenbooks.com
https://www.facebook.com/SerenBooks
http://www.twitter.com/SerenBooks
http://www.pinterest.com/SerenBooks

Fiction
  Novels: Literary
  Short Fiction: Literary

Nonfiction > *Nonfiction Books*
  Arts; Biography; Current Affairs; Drama; History; Literary Criticism; Memoir; Music; Photography; Sport; Travel

Poetry > *Poetry Collections*

Send: Full text

Publishes fiction, nonfiction, and poetry. Specialises in English-language writing from Wales and aims to bring Welsh culture, art, literature, and politics to a wider audience. Accepts nonfiction submissions by post or by email. Accepts poetry submissions by post only. Accepts fiction only from authors with whom there is an existing publishing relationship.

Poetry Editor: Amy Wack

Publisher: Mick Felton

P0757 Severn House Publishers

Book Publisher
Eardley House, 4 Uxbridge Street, London, W8 7SY
United Kingdom
Tel: +44 (0) 20 3011 0525

sales@severnhouse.com

http://severnhouse.com

Types: Fiction
Subjects: Crime; History; Horror; Mystery; Romance; Science Fiction; Thrillers
Markets: Adult

How to send: Through a literary agent

Accepts submissions via literary agents only. Targets the UK and US fiction library markets, and considers only authors with a significant background in these markets.

P0758 Shambhala Publications

Book Publisher
2129 13th Street, Boulder, CO 80302
United States

submissions@shambhala.com

https://www.shambhala.com
http://www.facebook.com/ShambhalaPublications
http://www.instagram.com/shambhala_publications/

Fiction > *Novels*: Adventure

Nonfiction > *Nonfiction Books*
  Activities; Arts; Buddhism; Christianity; Crafts; Creativity; Hinduism; Judaism; Martial Arts; Meditation; Memoir; Parenting; Philosophy; Psychology; Religion; Sufism; Taoism; Theravada Buddhism; Yoga; Zen

Poetry > *Poetry Collections*
  Classics / Ancient World; Contemporary; Inspirational; Spirituality

Send: Proposal
How to send: Email
How not to send: Post

Specialises in books that present creative and conscious ways of transforming individuals, society, and the planet. Focuses mainly on religion and philosophy, but covers a wide range of subjects including sciences, arts, Buddhism, Christianity, literature, poetry, psychology, etc. See website for full range of books published.

P0759 Shearsman Books

Book Publisher
PO Box 4239, Swindon, SN3 9FN
United Kingdom
Tel: +44 (0) 1179 572957

editor@shearsman.com

https://www.shearsman.com

Types: Nonfiction; Poetry; Translations
Subjects: Autobiography; Literary Criticism
Markets: Adult

Send: Query
Don't send: Full text

Publishes poetry books of at least 60 A5 pages. Publishes mainly poetry by British, Irish,

North American and Australian/New Zealand poets, plus poetry in translation from any language—although particular interest in German, Spanish and Latin American poetry. Submit only if MS is of appropriate length and most of it has already appeared in UK or US magazines of some repute. Send selection of 6-10 pages by post with SASE or by email with material embedded in the text or as PDF attachment. No other kind of attachments accepted. Also sometimes publishes literary criticism on poetry, and essays or memoirs by poets.

Editor: Tony Frazer

P0760 Shelf Stuff
Publishing Imprint

Book Publisher: HarperCollins

P0761 Shepheard-Walwyn (Publishers) Ltd
Book Publisher
107 Parkway House, Sheen Lane, London, SW14 8LS
United Kingdom
Tel: +44 (0) 20 8241 5927

books@shepheard-walwyn.co.uk

https://shepheard-walwyn.co.uk

Types: Nonfiction; Poetry
Subjects: Biography; Finance; History; Philosophy; Politics
Markets: Adult

Publishes mainly nonfiction, particularly the areas listed above and also books of Scottish interest, and gift books in calligraphy and / or illustrated. Also some poetry.

P0762 Shipwreckt Books Publishing Company
Book Publisher
Ruchford, MN
United States

contact@shipwrecktbooks.com

http://www.shipwrecktbooks.com

Types: Fiction; Nonfiction; Poetry
Subjects: Autobiography; Comedy / Humour; Culture; Current Affairs; Fantasy; Gardening; Health; History; Legal; Leisure; Lifestyle; Literary; Medicine; Mystery; Nature; Politics; Science Fiction; Spirituality; Sport; Suspense; Warfare; Women's Interests
Markets: Adult; Children's; Young Adult

Closed to approaches.

Not accepting submissions as at May 2020. Publishes books and literary magazine. Submit brief bio, synopsis, and first ten pages (or a couple of poems) using form on website.

Publishing Imprints: Lost Lake Folk Art (*P0508*); Rocket Science Press (*P0709*); Up On Big Rock Poetry (*P0880*)

P0763 Silvertail Books
Book Publisher
United Kingdom

editor@silvertailbooks.com

http://www.silvertailbooks.com

Types: Fiction; Nonfiction
Subjects: Commercial
Markets: Adult

Welcomes submissions for commercial fiction and nonfiction, either through an agent or direct from authors. Submit by email only. No postal submissions. Response not guaranteed.

Author / Literary Agent / Publisher: Humfrey Hunter (**L0490**)

P0764 Simon & Schuster
Book Publisher
United States

https://www.simonandschuster.com
https://www.facebook.com/simonandschuster
https://twitter.com/SimonSchuster
https://www.youtube.com/user/SimonSchusterVideos
https://instagram.com/simonandschuster

Fiction > *Novels*

Nonfiction > *Nonfiction Books*

How to send: Through a literary agent

Large publishing house covering a wide range of fiction and nonfiction.

Audio Book Publisher: Simon & Schuster Audio Publishing

Book Publishers: Simon & Schuster Adult Publishing (**P0766**); Simon & Schuster Children's Publishing (**P0768**)

Publishing Imprint: The Free Press

P0765 Simon & Schuster (Imprint)
Publishing Imprint

Book Publisher: Simon & Schuster Adult Publishing (**P0766**)

P0766 Simon & Schuster Adult Publishing
Book Publisher
United States

Book Publisher: Simon & Schuster (**P0764**)

How to send: Through a literary agent

Publishing Imprints: Adams Media (*P0021*); Atria (*P0061*); Avid Reader Press (*P0068*); Emily Bestler Books (*P0263*) Enliven (*P0266*); Folger Shakespeare Library (*P0300*); Free Press (*P0306*); Gallery (*P0315*); Howard (*P0419*); Jeter Publishing (*P0451*); One Signal (*P0596*); Scout Press (*P0748*); Scribner; Simon & Schuster (Imprint) (*P0765*); Threshold

(*P0822*); Tiller Press (*P0824*); Touchstone (*P0832*)

P0767 Simon & Schuster Audio
Publishing Imprint

Audio Book Publisher: Simon & Schuster Audio Publishing

P0768 Simon & Schuster Children's Publishing
Book Publisher
United States

https://www.simonandschuster.com/kids
https://www.facebook.com/simonandschuster
https://twitter.com/SimonSchuster
https://www.youtube.com/user/SimonSchusterVideos
https://instagram.com/simonandschuster

Book Publisher: Simon & Schuster (**P0764**)

CHILDREN'S
  Fiction
    Board Books; *Chapter Books*; *Early Readers*; *Middle Grade*; *Picture Books*
  Nonfiction
    Board Books; *Middle Grade*; *Picture Books*
YOUNG ADULT > **Fiction** > *Novels*

Closed to approaches.

Does not review, retain or return unsolicited materials or artwork.

Publishing Imprints: Aladdin (*P0026*); Atheneum (*P0056*); Beach Lane Books (*P0090*); Denene Millner Books (**P0225**); Little Simon; Margaret K. McElderry (*P0531*); Paula Wiseman Books (*P0619*); Saga Press (*P0724*); Salaam Reads (*P0728*); Simon & Schuster Books for Young Readers; Simon Pulse; Simon Spotlight

P0769 Simon & Schuster UK Limited
Book Publisher
1st Floor, 222 Gray's Inn Road, London, WC1X 8HB
United Kingdom
Tel: +44 (0) 20 7316 1900
Fax: +44 (0) 20 7316 0332

enquiries@simonandschuster.co.uk

https://www.simonandschuster.co.uk

Types: Fiction; Nonfiction
Subjects: Autobiography; Business; Comedy / Humour; Commercial; Cookery; Health; History; Literary; Politics; Science; Spirituality; Sport; Travel
Markets: Adult; Children's; Young Adult

How to send: Through a literary agent

Publisher of commercial and literary fiction and nonfiction for adults and children, including children's fiction and picture books. No unsolicited MSS.

Book Publisher: Martin Books (*P0535*)

Publishing Imprints: The Free Press; Pocket Books

P0770 Skip Jack Press
Publishing Imprint
United States

Book Publisher: The Globe Pequot Press (**P0329**)

P0771 Skyhorse Publishing, Inc.
Book Publisher

Book Publisher: Allworth Press (**P0030**)

Publishing Imprints: Arcade Publishing; Sky Pony Press

P0772 small world creations
Publishing Imprint

Book Publisher: The Quarto Group, Inc. (**P0679**)

P0773 SmartLab Toys
Publishing Imprint

Book Publisher: The Quarto Group, Inc. (**P0679**)

P0774 Smith/Doorstop Books
Book Publisher
The Poetry Business, Campo House, 54 Campo Lane, Sheffield, S1 2EG
United Kingdom
Tel: +44 (0) 1484 434840
Fax: +44 (0) 1484 426566

office@poetrybusiness.co.uk

https://poetrybusiness.co.uk

Types: Nonfiction; Poetry
Subjects: Arts; Autobiography; Crime; Culture; Literary; Literary Criticism
Markets: Adult; Children's

Resolves to discover new and exciting poetry to showcase and publish. Accepts unsolicited mss only during open calls for submissions to guest-edited anthologies. See website for upcoming anthology publication opportunities. Also publishes winners of annual competitions.

P0775 Smithsonian Institution
Magazine Publisher; Book Publisher
PO Box 37012, MRC 513, Washington, DC 20013-7012
United States

info@si.edu

https://www.si.edu
https://www.facebook.com/Smithsonian
https://instagram.com/smithsonian
https://www.pinterest.com/smithsonian/

https://smithsonian.tumblr.com/
https://twitter.com/smithsonian
https://www.youtube.com/c/smithsonian

Magazines: Air & Space Magazine (**M0018**); Smithsonian Magazine (**M0475**)

P0776 Snowbooks
Book Publisher
55 North Street, Thame, OXON, OX9 3BH
United Kingdom

submissions@snowbooks.com

http://www.snowbooks.com

Types: Fiction; Nonfiction
Subjects: Crafts; Crime; Fantasy; History; Horror; Leisure; Science Fiction; Sport; Thrillers
Markets: Adult

Send: Full text

Open to submissions of horror, science fiction, and fantasy novels over 70,000 words. Named joint Small Publisher of the Year at the 2006 British book Trade Awards. Friendly attitude towards authors and unsolicited approaches. See website for guidelines. Approach via email only – postal submissions will neither be read nor returned, even if sent through an agent.

Managing Director: Emma Barnes

P0777 Soho Press
Book Publisher
United States
Tel: +1 (212) 260-1900

soho@sohopress.com

https://sohopress.com

Types: Fiction
Subjects: Crime; Literary
Markets: Adult; Young Adult

Publishes bold literary voices, award-winning international crime fiction, and groundbreaking young adult fiction.

P0778 Somerville Press
Book Publisher
Dromore, Bantry, Co. Cork
Ireland
Tel: 353 (0) 28 32873

somervillepress@eircom.net

http://www.somervillepress.com

Types: Fiction; Nonfiction
Markets: Adult

Publishes fiction and nonfiction, mainly of Irish interest.

P0779 Sourcebooks
Book Publisher
1935 Brookdale Rd, Suite 139, Naperville, IL 60563
United States

Tel: +1 (630) 961-3900
Fax: +1 (630) 961-2168

info@sourcebooks.com
editorialsubmissions@sourcebooks.com

https://www.sourcebooks.com
https://linkedin.com/company/50434/
https://twitter.com/sourcebooks
https://facebook.com/sourcebooks
https://www.pinterest.com/sbjabberwockykids/
https://www.instagram.com/sourcebooks/
https://www.sourcebooks.com/contact-us.html

ADULT
Fiction > *Novels*
General, and in particular: Mystery; Romance

Nonfiction
Gift Books: General
Nonfiction Books: General, and in particular: Beauty; Biography; Business; Education; Entertainment; Health; History; Memoir; Parenting; Psychology; Relationships; Self Help; Women's Issues
Reference: General, and in particular: Education
CHILDREN'S > **Nonfiction** > *Nonfiction Books*

YOUNG ADULT > **Fiction** > *Novels*

Send: Query; Synopsis; Author bio; Table of Contents; Writing sample; Market info
Don't send: Full text
How to send: Email
How not to send: Post

We are interested in books that will establish a unique standard in their subject area. We look for books with a well-defined, strong target market. Our list includes most nonfiction categories, including memoir, history, college reference and study aids, entertainment, general self-help/psychology, business, parenting and special needs parenting, health and beauty, reference, education, biography, love and relationships, gift books and women's issues.

Publishing Imprints: Dawn Publications (**P0218**); Sourcebooks Casablanca; Sourcebooks Hysteria; Sourcebooks Landmark; Sourcebooks MediaFusion; Sphinx Publishing

P0780 Southwater.
Publishing Imprint

Book Publisher: Anness Publishing Ltd (**P0039**)

P0781 Speak
Publishing Imprint
United States

Book Publisher: Penguin Young Readers Group (**P0638**)

P0782 Special Interest Model Books Ltd

Book Publisher
50a Willis Way, Poole, Dorset, BH15 3SY
United Kingdom
Tel: +44 (0) 1202 649930
Fax: +44 (0) 1202 649950

orders@specialinterestmodelbooks.co.uk

https://www.specialinterestmodelbooks.co.uk

Nonfiction > *Nonfiction Books*
Amateur Radio; Amateur Winemaking;
Hobbies; Model Aircraft; Model Making;
Model Ships and Boats; Radio Control

Publishes practical manuals for hobbyists in
the fields of model engineering, scale
modelling, radio-controlled models and home
winemaking and brewing.

Editor: Chris Lloyd

P0783 Sphere

Publishing Imprint

Publishing Imprint: Little, Brown Book Group
(P0502)

P0784 SportsBooks Limited

Book Publisher
9 St Aubyns Place, York, YO24 1EQ
United Kingdom
Tel: +44 (0) 1904 613475

info@sportsbooks.ltd.uk

http://www.sportsbooks.ltd.uk

Types: Nonfiction
Subjects: Biography; Sport
Markets: Adult

Publishes sports nonfiction.

Publishing Imprint: BMM **(P0118)**

P0785 Springer Nature

Book Publisher

Book Publishers: Macmillan Education
(P0523); Palgrave Macmillan **(P0610)**;
Springer-Verlag London Ltd

P0786 Spruce Books

Publishing Imprint
United States

Book Publisher: Sasquatch Books **(P0737)**

P0787 Square Peg

Publishing Imprint
United Kingdom

Book Publisher: Vintage **(P0891)**

P0788 St Martin's Paperbacks

Publishing Imprint

Publishing Imprint: St Martin's Press **(P0789)**

P0789 St Martin's Press

Publishing Imprint
United States

publicity@stmartins.com

https://us.macmillan.com/smp

Book Publishers: Macmillan Publishers
(P0524); Macmillan

Types: Fiction; Nonfiction
Formats: Reference
Subjects: Biography; Crime; History; Mystery;
Politics; Self Help; Travel
Markets: Academic; Adult

How to send: Through a literary agent

Approach via literary agent only. Began by
importing UK authors to the States and
continues to buy heavily in the United
Kingdom. No unsolicited MSS or unagented
queries.

Publishing Imprints: Castle Point Books
(P0153); Griffin *(P0344)*; Minotaur *(P0547)*;
St Martin's Paperbacks *(P0788)*; Thomas
Dunne Books; Wednesday Books *(P0915)*

P0790 St Pauls

Book Publisher
2187 Victory Boulevard, Staten Island, NY
10314
United States
Tel: +1 (800) 343-2522
Fax: +1 (718) 698-8390

sales@stpauls.us

http://www.stpaulsusa.com

Types: Nonfiction
Subjects: Biography; Religion; Self Help
Markets: Adult

Send: Full text

Publishes books for a Roman Catholic
readership.

P0791 Stacey International

Book Publisher
14 Great College Street, London, SW1P 3RX
United Kingdom
Tel: +44 (0) 20 7221 7166

editorial@stacey-international.co.uk
info@stacey-international.co.uk

http://www.stacey-international.co.uk

Fiction > *Novels*

Nonfiction > *Nonfiction Books*
Archaeology; Biography; Cookery; Geology;
History; Language; Middle East; Nature;
Photography; Travel

Poetry > *Poetry Collections*

Send: Full text; Proposal; Self-Addressed
Stamped Envelope (SASE)
How to send: Email; Post

Publishes nonfiction, fiction, and poetry.
Submit manuscripts and proposals by email or
by post with SASE. See website for more
information.

P0792 Stackpole Books

Publishing Imprint
United States

http://www.stackpolebooks.com

Book Publisher: The Globe Pequot Press
(P0329)

Nonfiction
Nonfiction Books: American Civil War;
Crafts; Fly Fishing; Hobbies; Military
History; Nature; Outdoor Activities; World
War II
Reference: Military

Publishes titles in the categories of Outdoors,
Crafts and Military History. Strong in Fly
Fishing, Nature Guides, Civil War and World
War II History, Military Reference and
Specialty Crafts and Hobbies.

Editors: Candi Derr; Jay Nichols; Dave Reisch

Publisher: Judith Schnell

P0793 Stanford University Press

Book Publisher
485 Broadway, First Floor, Redwood City CA
94063-8460
United States
Tel: +1 (650) 723-9434
Fax: +1 (650) 725-3457

https://www.sup.org
http://www.facebook.com/
stanforduniversitypress
http://www.twitter.com/stanfordpress
https://www.youtube.com/channel/
UCmd8xj7yu0WGeLRqL39UjLA
http://instagram.com/stanfordupress

ACADEMIC > **Nonfiction** > *Nonfiction
Books*
Anthropology; Asia; Business; Economics;
Finance; History; Judaism; Legal; Literature;
Middle East; Philosophy; Politics; Religion;
Sociology; South America

Send: Query; Proposal; Author bio; Table of
Contents
How to send: Email; Post

Submit proposals by post, or see website for
list of editors and submit proposal to the
appropriate editor by email.

P0794 Stanley Gibbons

Book Publisher; Magazine Publisher
United Kingdom

support@stanleygibbons.com

https://www.stanleygibbons.com
https://www.stanleygibbons.com/publishing/
publishing-house

https://www.facebook.com/
stanleygibbonsgroup
https://twitter.com/StanleyGibbons
https://www.instagram.com/stanleygibbons/

Nonfiction > *Reference*: Stamp Collecting

Publishes handbooks and reference guides on stamps and stamp collecting.

P0795 Star Bright Books

Book Publisher
13 Landsdowne Street, Cambridge, MA 02139
United States
Tel: +1 (617) 354-1300
Fax: +1 (617) 354-1399

info@starbrightbooks.com

https://starbrightbooks.org

CHILDREN'S
  Fiction
    Chapter Books; *Picture Books*
  Nonfiction
    Chapter Books: General
    Picture Books: General, and in
    particular: Biography; Diversity

How to send: Post
How not to send: Email

Publishes books that are entertaining, meaningful and sensitive to the needs of all children. Welcomes submissions for picture books and longer works, both fiction and nonfiction. See website for full submission guidelines.

P0796 Start Publishing

Book Publisher

Publishing Imprint: Salvo Press (**P0732**)

P0797 Stash Books

Publishing Imprint
United States

Book Publisher: C&T Publishing (**P0140**)

P0798 The Stinging Fly Press

Book Publisher; Magazine Publisher
Ireland

submissions.stingingfly@gmail.com
editor@stingingfly.org
info@stingingfly.org

https://stingingfly.org
https://www.facebook.com/StingingFly
http://twitter.com/stingingfly

Fiction > *Short Fiction Collections*

Closed to approaches.

Publishes single-author short-story collections and multiple-author anthologies.

Publisher: Declan Meade

P0799 Stone Bridge Press

Book Publisher
1393 Solano Avenue, Suite C, Albany, CA
94706
United States
Tel: +1 (510) 524-8732

sbpedit@stonebridge.com

https://www.stonebridge.com

Types: Fiction; Nonfiction; Poetry;
Translations
Formats: Film Scripts; Reference
Subjects: Arts; Business; Crafts; Culture;
Design; Lifestyle; Literature; Spirituality;
Travel
Markets: Adult; Children's

Send: Query
Don't send: Full text

Publishes books about Asia and in particular Japan and China. Send brief query by email in the first instance.

P0800 Stonewood Press

Book Publisher
Submissions, Stonewood Press, Diversity
House, 72 Nottingham Road, Arnold,
Nottingham, NG5 6LF
United Kingdom

stonewoodpress@gmail.com

http://www.stonewoodpress.co.uk

Types: Fiction; Poetry
Formats: Short Fiction
Subjects: Contemporary
Markets: Adult

Note: Current submission status is unclear. The publisher's website states it is closed to new submissions, but that submissions re-open from the start of 2017. Independent publisher dedicated to promoting new writing, with an emphasis on contemporary short stories and poetry. Send query with biography, publishing history, and either one story and a brief outline of the others in the collection, or up to 10 poems and details of how many other poems are in the collection. Submit by post only. No children's books, creative nonfiction, novels, or drama.

Editor: Martin Parker

P0801 Strata Publishing, Inc.

Book Publisher
PO 1303, State College, PA 16804-1303
United States
Tel: +1 (814) 234-8545

stratapub@stratapub.com

http://www.stratapub.com

ACADEMIC > **Nonfiction** > *Nonfiction
Books*
  Communication; Journalism

PROFESSIONAL > **Nonfiction** > *Nonfiction
Books*
  Communication; Journalism

Send: Query; Outline; Market info; Table of
Contents; Author bio
How to send: Post
How not to send: Email attachment

An independent publishing house producing books for college students, scholars, and professionals in communication and journalism. Send query letter giving the working title, the course(s) for which the book is intended, brief description of your general approach, major competitors, and how your book is different from them.

Editor: Kathleen Domenig

P0802 Sublunary Editions

Book Publisher; Magazine Publisher
Seattle
United States

support@sublunaryeditions.com

https://sublunaryeditions.com
https://oleada.io/publication/sublunary-editions
https://twitter.com/sublunaryeds
https://instagram.com/sublunaryeditions

Fiction
  Novellas: Experimental; Literary
  Short Fiction: Experimental; Literary
Nonfiction > *Essays*
  Experimental; Literary
Poetry
  Any Poetic Form; *Experimental Poetry*

Started as a small-scale, DIY project in early 2019. For the first several months, the press's sole output as a regular envelope of new writing mailed (the old fashioned way) to subscribers. Since then, the press has expanded to publish 8-10 brief books every year, and, as of early 2021, a quarterly magazine

Magazine: Firmament (**M0210**)

P0803 Sunstone Press

Book Publisher
Box 2321, Santa Fe, NM 87504-2321
United States
Tel: +1 (505) 988-4418
Fax: +1 (505) 988-1025

http://www.sunstonepress.com

Types: Fiction; Nonfiction; Poetry
Formats: Reference; Short Fiction; Theatre
Scripts
Subjects: Adventure; Archaeology;
Architecture; Arts; Autobiography; Business;
Comedy / Humour; Cookery; Crafts; Crime;
Fantasy; Gardening; Health; History; How To;
Legal; Music; Mystery; Nature; Photography;
Politics; Religion; Romance; Science Fiction;
Sport; Travel; Warfare; Westerns; Women's
Interests
Markets: Adult; Children's

Send: Query
Don't send: Full text

Began in the 1970s with a focus on nonfiction about the American Southwest, but has since expanded its focus to include mainstream themes and categories in both fiction and nonfiction. Send query by post only with short summary, author bio, one sample chapter, table of contents, marketing plan, and statement on why this is the right publisher for your book.

P0804 Superbia Books
Publishing Imprint
United Kingdom

Book Publisher: DogHorn Publishing (**P0238**)

P0805 Swallow Press
Publishing Imprint

Book Publisher: Ohio University Press (**P0589**)

P0806 Sweet Cherry Publishing
Book Publisher
Unit 36, Vulcan House, Vulcan Road, Leicester, LE5 3EF
United Kingdom

submissions@sweetcherrypublishing.com

https://www.sweetcherrypublishing.com

CHILDREN'S > **Fiction**
  Middle Grade; Picture Books

Send: Query; Writing sample; Synopsis; Author bio
How to send: Email
How not to send: Post

Publishes books for children of all ages. Specialises in sets and series, so unlikely to take on a stand-alone title. Send submissions by email only. No postal submissions. See website for full submission guidelines.

Editor: Abdul Thadha

P0807 Sweetwater Books
Publishing Imprint

Book Publisher: Cedar Fort (**P0156**)

P0808 Tailwinds Press
Book Publisher
PO Box 2283, Radio City Station, New York, NY 10101-2283
United States

submissions@tailwindspress.com

http://www.tailwindspress.com

Types: Fiction; Nonfiction
Subjects: Literary
Markets: Adult

Send: Full text

New York City-based independent press specialising in high-quality literary fiction and nonfiction. Send submissions by post or email. See website for full guidelines.

P0809 Tamarind Books
Publishing Imprint
United Kingdom

puffin@penguinrandomhouse.co.uk

https://www.penguin.co.uk/puffin/tamarind.html

Book Publisher: Puffin (UK) (**P0672**)

CHILDREN'S
  Fiction
    Chapter Books: Diversity
    Middle Grade: Diversity
    Novels: Diversity

  Nonfiction > *Nonfiction Books:* Diversity

Publishes children's books and picture books with black, Asian, or mixed race children as the main protagonists.

Editor: Verna Wilkins

P0810 TANSTAAFL Press
Book Publisher
United States

submissions@tanstaaflpress.com

https://tanstaaflpress.com

Types: Fiction
Formats: Short Fiction
Subjects: Fantasy; Science Fiction
Markets: Adult

Send: Query
Don't send: Full text

Publishes science fiction, cyberpunk, alternative histories, post apocalyptic and fantasy of novel length. Will consider exceptional works in other genres of fiction, or short story compilations of the above topics. Send query by email with 300-500 word summary and first 1,000 words as a text attachment. See website for full guidelines.

P0811 TarcherPerigee
Publishing Imprint
United States

Book Publisher: Penguin Publishing Group (**P0633**)

P0812 Tate Publishing
Book Publisher
Millbank, London, SW1P 4RG
United Kingdom

submissions@tate.org.uk

https://www.tate.org.uk/publishing

Types: Nonfiction
Subjects: Arts; History
Markets: Adult; Children's

Send: Query
Don't send: Full text

Publishes exhibition-related and art-history titles, as well as books for children. Accepts proposals by post or by email. See website for guidelines.

P0813 TCK Publishing
Book Publisher; Ebook Publisher; Audio Book Publisher
16641 Brick Road, Granger, IN 46530
United States

info@tckpublishing.com
submissions@tckpublishing.com

https://www.tckpublishing.com

ADULT
  Fiction > *Novels*
    General, and in particular: Adventure; Fantasy; Historical Fiction; Mystery; Romance; Science Fiction; Suspense; Thrillers

  Nonfiction > *Nonfiction Books*
    General, and in particular: Business; Cookery; Gardening; Health; How To; Personal Development; Personal Finance; Relationships; Religion; Self Help; Spirituality; Wellbeing

CHILDREN'S > **Fiction** > *Middle Grade*

NEW ADULT > **Fiction** > *Novels*

YOUNG ADULT > **Fiction** > *Novels*

Send: Full text
How to send: Online submission system

A traditional book publisher that pays 50% gross royalties. We love to publish meaningful and inspirational fiction and nonfiction books that inspire and educate readers.

P0814 Telegram Books
Publishing Imprint
26 Westbourne Grove, London, W2 5RH
United Kingdom
Tel: +44 (0) 20 7221 9347
Fax: +44 (0) 20 7229 7492

elizabeth@saqibooks.com

https://saqibooks.com/imprint/telegram/

Book Publisher: Saqi Books (**P0735**)

Fiction > *Novels*

Closed to approaches.

Publishes fiction from around the world. Not accepting submissions as at November 2020.

P0815 Templar Books
Publishing Imprint
United Kingdom
Tel: +44 (0) 20 3770 8888

hello@templarco.co.uk

https://www.bonnierbooks.co.uk/childrens-imprints/templar-books/

Book Publisher: Bonnier Books (UK) **(P0122)**

CHILDREN'S
Fiction > *Picture Books*

Nonfiction
Board Books; *Gift Books*; *Illustrated Books*

How to send: Through a literary agent

Publishes children's fiction and picture and
novelty books. Encourage anybody who
wishes to have their work considered by one of
their imprints to seek representation by an
agent. No unsolicited mss or proposals.

P0816 **Temple Lodge Publishing**
Book Publisher
Hillside House, The Square, Forest Row,
RH18 5ES
United Kingdom

office@templelodge.com

https://www.templelodge.com

Types: Nonfiction
Subjects: Science; Spirituality
Markets: Adult

Send: Query
Don't send: Full text

Originally founded to develop the work of
Rudolf Steiner. Publishes nonfiction from a a
spiritual-scientific perspective. Send a
summary with list of chapters and sample
chapters by email or by post with SAE.

P0817 **Ten Speed Press**
Publishing Imprint

Book Publisher: Random House **(P0690)**

P0818 **Thames & Hudson Inc.**
Book Publisher
500 Fifth Avenue, New York, NY 10110
United States
Tel: +1 (212) 354-3763
Fax: +1 (212) 398-1252

bookinfo@thames.wwnorton.com

https://www.thamesandhudsonusa.com
https://www.instagram.com/
thamesandhudsonusa
https://twitter.com/ThamesHudsonUSA
https://www.facebook.com/
ThamesandHudsonUSA

Book Publisher: Thames and Hudson Ltd
(P0819)

ADULT
Fiction > *Novels*

Nonfiction
Nonfiction Books: Animals; Anthropology;
Antiques; Archaeology; Architecture; Arts;
Biography; Business; Classics / Ancient
World; Comedy / Humour; Comic Books;
Crafts; Design; Evolution; Fashion; Films;
Fitness; Folklore, Myths, and Legends;

Food; Games; Gardening; Health; History;
Houses; Interior Design; Literary
Criticism; Medicine; Military History;
Music; Nature; Philosophy; Photography;
Religion; Science; Spirituality; Sport; TV;
Theatre; Travel
Reference: General

Poetry > *Poetry Collections*

CHILDREN'S
Fiction
Chapter Books; *Early Readers*; *Picture
Books*
Nonfiction
Activity Books; *Nonfiction Books*; *Picture
Books*

Send: Query
Don't send: Full text
How to send: In the body of an email
How not to send: Email attachment

Send proposals up to six pages by email. No
attachments or unsolicited mss.

P0819 **Thames and Hudson Ltd**
Book Publisher
181A High Holborn, London, WC1V 7QX
United Kingdom
Tel: +44 (0) 20 7845 5000

submissions@thameshudson.co.uk

http://www.thamesandhudson.com

Types: Nonfiction
Formats: Reference
Subjects: Archaeology; Architecture; Arts;
Beauty; Biography; Crafts; Culture; Design;
Fashion; Gardening; History; Lifestyle;
Literature; Nature; Philosophy; Photography;
Religion; Science; Travel
Markets: Adult; Children's

Send: Query
Don't send: Full text

Publishes illustrated nonfiction only. No
fiction. Prefers to receive submissions by
email, but will accept submissions by post. See
website for full details.

Book Publisher: Thames & Hudson Inc.
(P0818)

P0820 **Thomas Nelson**
Publishing Imprint

Book Publisher: HarperCollins

P0821 **Three Hares Publishing**
Book Publisher
United Kingdom

submissions@threeharespublishing.com

https://threeharespublishing.com

Types: Fiction; Nonfiction
Subjects: Crime; Psychology; Thrillers
Markets: Adult; Children's

Closed to approaches.

**Closed to submissions as at July 2019.
Check website for current status.** Will
consider all kinds of fiction and nonfiction,
except picture books. Particularly interested in
crime/psychological thrillers and Middle Grade
fiction. Send query by email with one-page
synopsis and first three chapters. See website
for full guidelines.

P0822 **Threshold**
Publishing Imprint

Book Publisher: Simon & Schuster Adult
Publishing **(P0766)**

P0823 **Tiger of the Stripe**
Book Publisher
50 Albert Road, Richmond, Surrey, TW10
6DP
United Kingdom
Tel: +44 (0) 20 8940 8087

https://tigerofthestripe.co.uk

Fiction > *Novels*

Nonfiction > *Nonfiction Books*
Architecture; Books; Food; History;
Language; Medieval; Music

Eclectic but with an emphasis on well-
researched academic or semi-academic works.
Also interested in biographies, history,
language textbooks, cookbooks, typography.
Not currently accepting new fiction.

Authors: Gerrish Gray; Jay Landesman; Julia
Scott

Editor: Peter Danckwerts

P0824 **Tiller Press**
Publishing Imprint

Book Publisher: Simon & Schuster Adult
Publishing **(P0766)**

P0825 **Times Books**
Publishing Imprint
United Kingdom

Book Publisher: HarperCollins UK **(P0382)**

P0826 **Tiny Owl**
Book Publisher
6 Hatfield Road, Chiswick, London, W4 1AF
United Kingdom

info@tinyowl.co.uk

https://tinyowl.co.uk
https://www.facebook.com/tinyowlpublishing/
https://twitter.com/tinyowl_books
https://www.youtube.com/channel/
UCJkMec_cxEVzTf2iUGvk2Pg
https://www.instagram.com/
tiny_owl_publishing/

CHILDREN'S > **Fiction** > *Picture Books*

Closed to approaches.

Publisher of picture books for children.

P0827 Titan Books
Book Publisher
Titan House, 144 Southwark Street, London,
SE1 0UP
United Kingdom

https://www.titanbooks.com

Types: Fiction; Nonfiction
Formats: Film Scripts; Short Fiction; TV
Scripts
Subjects: Comedy / Humour; Entertainment;
Science Fiction
Markets: Adult; Young Adult

Send: Query
Don't send: Full text

Publisher of graphic novels, particularly with
film or television tie-ins, and books related to
film and TV. No unsolicited fiction or books
for children, but will consider ideas for
licensed projects they have already contracted.
Send query with synopsis by post only. No
email submissions.

P0828 Toad Hall Editions
Book Publisher; Self Publishing Service
United States

hello@toadhalleditions.ink

https://www.toadhalleditions.ink
https://www.instagram.com/toadhalleditions/

Fiction
Novels; *Short Fiction Collections*
Nonfiction > *Nonfiction Books*
Creative Nonfiction; Memoir; Personal
Essays

Poetry > *Poetry Collections*

Does not want:

> **Fiction** > *Novels*
> Fantasy; Historical Fiction; Horror;
> Mystery; Romance; Science Fiction;
> Thrillers
>
> **Nonfiction** > *Nonfiction Books*
> Finance; Motivational Self-Help

Send: Query; Synopsis; Author bio; Pitch
How to send: Email
How not to send: Email attachment

Costs: Offers services that writers have to pay
for.

Small press publisher that also provides self-
publishing services.

Magazines: Buttered Toast (**M0093**); Kerning
(**M0300**)

P0829 Tommy Nelson
Publishing Imprint

Book Publisher: HarperCollins

P0830 Top Publications, Ltd
Book Publisher
3100 Independence Parkway, Suite 311-359,
Plano, TX 75075
United States
Tel: +1 (972) 490-9686
Fax: +1 (972) 233-0713

submissions@toppub.com

http://www.toppub.com

Types: Fiction
Formats: Short Fiction
Subjects: Adventure; Commercial;
Contemporary; History; Horror; Mystery;
Romance; Science Fiction; Suspense; Warfare
Markets: Adult; Young Adult

Send: Query
Don't send: Full text

Small press publisher of mainstream fiction.
Authors should be willing to invest large
amounts of time promoting their book and
attending book-signings, etc. Send query letter
by email only, giving information about
yourself, your book, and your marketing ideas
for it. No queries or submissions by post.
Email approaches only. Any queries or
submissions sent through the post will not be
responded to.

Editor: Victoria Lam

P0831 Torrey House Press, LLC
Book Publisher
150 S. State St. Suite 100, Salt Lake City, UT
84111
United States
Tel: +1 (801) 209-1657

mail@torreyhouse.com

http://torreyhouse.com

Types: Fiction; Nonfiction
Subjects: Culture; History; Literary; Nature
Markets: Adult

Send: Query
Don't send: Full text

Publishes narrative nonfiction and literary
fiction with a natural history, environmental, or
a natural landscape theme, or about the politics
and practice of sustainable living. Submit using
online submission manager on website.

Editors: Kirsten Johanna Allen; Mark Bailey

P0832 Touchstone
Publishing Imprint

Book Publisher: Simon & Schuster Adult
Publishing (**P0766**)

P0833 TouchWood Editions
Book Publisher
Canada

submissions@touchwoodeditions.com

https://www.touchwoodeditions.com

Fiction
Novels: Contemporary; Historical Fiction;
Mystery; Supernatural / Paranormal
Short Fiction Collections: General

Nonfiction
Essays: General
Nonfiction Books: Alberta; Arctic; Arts;
Beer; Biography; British Columbia;
Contemporary; Cookery; Food; Gardening;
History; Memoir; Nature; Painting; Pets;
Photography; Travel; Vancouver Island;
Wine; Women

Send: Query; Outline; Proposal; Synopsis;
Marketing Plan; Author bio; Writing sample
How to send: PDF file email attachment

Accepts submissions by email only. Response
only if interested. Publishes Canadian authors
only. See website for full guidelines.

P0834 Transworld Ireland
Publishing Imprint

Book Publisher: Transworld Publishers
(**P0835**)

P0835 Transworld Publishers
Book Publisher
61-63 Uxbridge Road, Ealing, London, W5
5SA
United Kingdom
Tel: +44 (0) 20 8579 2652

info@transworld-publishers.co.uk

https://www.penguin.co.uk/company/
publishers/transworld.html

Book Publisher: Penguin Random House UK
(**P0635**)

Types: Fiction; Nonfiction
Subjects: Biography; Comedy / Humour;
Cookery; Crime; Fantasy; Health; History;
Literary; Literature; Music; Romance; Science;
Science Fiction; Spirituality; Sport; Thrillers;
Travel
Markets: Adult; Children's

How to send: Through a literary agent

Large publisher publishing a wide range of
fiction and nonfiction for children and adults.
No unsolicited MSS. Approach via a literary
agent only.

Publishing Imprints: Bantam Books (*P0080*);
Bantam Press (*P0081*); Black Swan (*P0107*);
Corgi (*P0190*); Transworld Ireland (*P0834*)

P0836 Travelers' Tales / Solas House
Book Publisher
2320 Bowdoin Street, Palo Alto CA 94306
United States
Tel: +1 (650) 462-2110
Fax: +1 (650) 462-6305

ttales@travelerstales.com

https://travelerstales.com
https://www.facebook.com/Travelers-Tales-197098590465058/
https://twitter.com/travelerstales

Nonfiction
Nonfiction Books: Travel
Short Nonfiction: Travel

How to send: Online submission system
How not to send: Post; Email

Publishes books and anthologies of true travel tales, whether funny, adventurous, frightening, or grim. No fiction. Submit through online submission system only. No submissions by post or email. Response only if interested.

P0837 Trentham Books
Publishing Imprint
United Kingdom

p.gordon-smith@ucl.ac.uk

https://www.ucl.ac.uk/ucl-press

Book Publisher: UCL Press (**P0848**)

Types: Nonfiction
Subjects: Design; Science; Sociology; Technology; Women's Interests
Markets: Academic

Send: Query
Don't send: Full text

Open access publisher of edited volumes, scholarly editions, textbooks and journals. Welcomes proposals.

Editor: Pat Gordon-Smith

P0838 Trotman Publishing
Book Publisher
21d Charles Street, Bath, BA1 1HX
United Kingdom
Tel: +44 (0) 3330 501023

info@trotman.co.uk

https://trotman.co.uk
https://twitter.com/TrotmanEd

ADULT > **Nonfiction** > *Nonfiction Books*
Career Development; Education; Walking Guides

PROFESSIONAL > **Nonfiction** > *Nonfiction Books*
Career Development; Education

Publishes books that help students get the career they want, and aid careers education professionals giving careers guidance. Also publishes walking guides.

Editor: David Lester

Publishing Imprint: White Ladder Press

P0839 TTA Press
Magazine Publisher; Book Publisher
United Kingdom

http://www.ttapress.com

Magazines: Black Static (**M0079**); Crimewave (**M0143**); Interzone (**M0282**)

P0840 Turner Publishing
Book Publisher

Publishing Imprint: Jewish Lights Publishing (**P0452**)

P0841 Turnstone Press
Book Publisher
Artspace Building, 206-100 Arthur Street, Winnipeg, Manitoba, Canada R3B 1H3
Canada
Tel: +1 (204) 947-1555
Fax: +1 (204) 947-1556

editor@turnstonepress.com

http://www.turnstonepress.com

Types: Fiction; Nonfiction; Poetry
Formats: Short Fiction
Subjects: Fantasy; Literary; Literary Criticism; Mystery; Thrillers
Markets: Adult

Literary publisher publishing the work of Canadian authors or landed immigrants only. Publishes literary fiction, literary non-fiction – including literary criticism – and poetry. Publishes literary mysteries, thrillers, noir, speculative fiction, and fantasy under imprint. No contact by email. All submissions must be by post with SASE. Mss without SASE will be recycled without response, as will submissions requesting response by email. See website for full guidelines.

Publishing Imprint: Ravenstone (**P0694**)

P0842 Turtle Books
Book Publisher
866 United Nations Plaza, Suite #525, New York, NY 10017
United States
Tel: +1 (212) 644-2020
Fax: +1 (212) 223-4387

http://www.turtlebooks.com

Types: Fiction; Nonfiction; Poetry
Subjects: Adventure; Culture; Fantasy; History; Literature; Nature; Sociology; Sport; Westerns
Markets: Children's

Send: Full text

Publishes children's illustrated books, often in both English and Spanish. Submit complete MS rather than sending a query.

Editor: John Whitman

P0843 Twelve
Publishing Imprint

Book Publisher: Grand Central Publishing (**P0337**)

P0844 Twenty-First Century Books
Publishing Imprint

Book Publisher: Lerner Publishing Group (**P0487**)

P0845 Two Rivers Press
Book Publisher
7 Denmark Road, Reading, RG1 5PA
United Kingdom

anne@tworiverspress.com

https://tworiverspress.com

Types: Nonfiction; Poetry
Subjects: Arts; Culture; Literary
Markets: Adult

Publishes poetry, art, culture, and local interest books, focusing on Reading and the surrounding area.

P0846 TwoDot
Publishing Imprint
United States

Book Publisher: The Globe Pequot Press (**P0329**)

P0847 Tyndale House Publishers, Inc.
Book Publisher
351 Executive Drive, Carol Stream, IL 60188
United States
Tel: +1 (855) 277-9400
Fax: +1 (866) 622-9474

https://www.tyndale.com
https://facebook.com/TyndaleHouse
https://twitter.com/TyndaleHouse
https://pinterest.com/TyndaleHouse/
https://instagram.com/tyndalehouse/
https://youtube.com/user/TyndaleHP/

ADULT
Fiction > *Novels*
Allegory; Christianity; Contemporary Romance; Contemporary; Historical Fiction; Mystery; Romantic Suspense; Suspense; Thrillers; Westerns

Nonfiction
Nonfiction Books: Archaeology; Arts; Autobiography; Biography; Business; Christian Living; Christianity; Comedy / Humour; Culture; Current Affairs; Education; Finance; Health; History; Judaism; Leadership; Leisure; Memoir; Mental Health; Personal Development; Politics; Psychology; Sport; Travel
Reference: Christianity

CHILDREN'S
Fiction
Chapbook: Christianity
Picture Books: Christianity

Nonfiction > *Nonfiction Books*
Christian Living; Christianity

TEEN
Fiction > *Novels*: Christianity

Nonfiction > *Nonfiction Books*
Christian Living; Christianity;
Relationships; Sex

How to send: Through a literary agent

Christian publisher, publishing bibles,
nonfiction, fiction, and books for kids and
teens.

P0848 UCL Press
Book Publisher
United Kingdom

c.penfold@ucl.ac.uk

https://www.ucl.ac.uk/ucl-press

Types: Nonfiction
Markets: Academic

Send: Query
Don't send: Full text

Open access publisher of scholarly
monographs, edited volumes, scholarly
editions, textbooks and journals in all subject
areas. Welcomes proposals.

Publishing Imprint: Trentham Books (**P0837**)

P0849 Ugly Duckling Presse
Book Publisher
The Old American Can Factory, 232 Third
Street, #E303 (corner Third Avenue),
Brooklyn, NY 11215
United States
Tel: +1 (347) 948-5170

office@uglyducklingpresse.org

https://uglyducklingpresse.org

Nonfiction > *Nonfiction Books*: Experimental
Poetry in Translation > *Poetry Collections*
Poetry > *Poetry Collections*
Closed to approaches.

Nonprofit publisher of poetry, translation,
experimental nonfiction, performance texts,
and books by artists. Check website for
specific calls for submissions.

P0850 UKA Press
Book Publisher
United Kingdom

andrea@ukapress.com

http://www.ukapress.com

Fiction > *Novels*
Nonfiction > *Nonfiction Books*
Poetry > *Poetry Collections*

Send: Query
How to send: Through a literary agent

This publisher was created to publish fresh,
exciting work by talented writers from around
the world.

We're looking for originality, sparkle and the
promise of something unexpected. Genre and
style aren't important; quality is.

Accepts submissions through literary agents
only.

P0851 Ulverscroft Ltd
Book Publisher
The Green, Bradgate Road, Anstey, Leicester,
LE7 7FU
United Kingdom
Tel: +44 (0) 1162 364325

m.merrill@ulverscroft.co.uk

https://www.ulverscroft.com

Types: Fiction; Nonfiction
Markets: Adult

Publishes a wide variety of large print titles in
hard and soft cover formats, as well as
abridged and unabridged audio books. Many
titles are written by the world's favourite
authors.

Book Publisher: F.A. Thorpe (Publishing)

Editor: Mark Merrill

P0852 Unbound Press
Book Publisher
20 St Thomas Street, London, SE1 9RS
United Kingdom
Tel: +44 (0) 20 3997 6790

support@unbound.com

https://unbound.com
https://facebook.com/unbound
https://twitter.com/unbounders
https://instagram.com/unbounders

Fiction > *Novels*
Nonfiction > *Nonfiction Books*

Send: Full text

Crowdfunding publisher. Submit manuscripts
via form on website.

P0853 Unicorn
Publishing Imprint

Book Publisher: Unicorn Publishing Group
(**P0854**)

P0854 Unicorn Publishing Group
Book Publisher
Charleston Studio, Meadow Business Centre,
Ringmer, Lewes, East Sussex, BN8 5RW
United Kingdom
Tel: +44 (0) 1273 812066

ian@unicornpublishing.org

http://www.unicornpublishing.org

Types: Fiction; Nonfiction
Formats: Reference
Subjects: Arts; Biography; Culture; History;
Warfare
Markets: Adult

Publishes books on the visual arts and cultural
history, military history, and historical fiction.
Approach by email or by post.

Editor: Lucy Duckworth

Publishing Imprints: Unicorn (*P0853*);
Uniform (*P0855*); Universe (*P0858*)

P0855 Uniform
Publishing Imprint

Book Publisher: Unicorn Publishing Group
(**P0854**)

P0856 Union Park Press
Publishing Imprint
United States

Book Publisher: The Globe Pequot Press
(**P0329**)

P0857 Unity
Book Publisher
Integrated Marketing Department, Attention:
Product Manager, 1901 NW Blue Parkway,
Unity Village, Missouri 64065-0001
United States
Tel: +1 (816) 524-3550

acquisitions@unityonline.org

https://www.unity.org

Types: Nonfiction
Subjects: Philosophy; Self Help; Spirituality
Markets: Adult

Send: Full text

Publisher of books on Spirituality, New
Thought, personal growth, spiritual leadership,
mind-body-spirit, and spiritual self-help. Send
query by email as PDF attachment. See
website for full guidelines.

P0858 Universe
Publishing Imprint

Book Publisher: Unicorn Publishing Group
(**P0854**)

P0859 The University of Akron Press
Book Publisher
120 E. Mill Street, Suite 415, Akron, OH
44308
United States

uapress@uakron.edu

https://www.uakron.edu/uapress/

Types: Nonfiction; Poetry
Subjects: Cookery; Culture; History; Sport
Markets: Adult

Send: Query
Don't send: Full text

For nonfiction, complete and submit form on website. Also publishes books of poetry, mainly through its annual competition.

P0860 University of Alaska Press
Book Publisher
Editorial Department, University of Alaska Press, PO Box 756240, 104 Eielson Building, Fairbanks, AK 99775-6240
United States
Tel: +1 (907) 474-5831
Fax: +1 (907) 474-5502

UA-acquisitions@alaska.edu

http://www.alaska.edu/uapress/

Types: Fiction; Nonfiction; Poetry; Translations
Subjects: Autobiography; Culture; History; Nature; Politics; Science; Sport
Markets: Academic; Adult

Closed to approaches.

Publisher based in Alaska, publishing academic and general trade books on an expanding range of subject areas, including politics and history, Native languages and cultures, science and natural history, biography and memoir, poetry, fiction and anthologies, and original translations. Send proposals by post. No unsolicited mss.

P0861 University of Arkansas Press
Book Publisher
McIlroy House, 105 N. McIlroy Avenue, Fayetteville, AR 72701
United States
Tel: +1 (479) 575-7544

mbieker@uark.edu

https://www.uapress.com

Types: Nonfiction; Poetry
Markets: Academic; Adult

Accepts unsolicited proposals for scholarly books in the social sciences and humanities as well as nonfiction works of local or regional interest. Also publishes poetry books through its poetry competitions, for which there is a standard entry fee. Submit via online submission system.

Editors: Mike Bieker; David Scott Cunningham

P0862 University of California Press
Book Publisher
United States

krobinson@ucpress.edu

https://www.ucpress.edu
https://twitter.com/ucpress
https://www.facebook.com/ucpress
https://www.instagram.com/uc_press/
https://www.youtube.com/channel/
UCX5V8BHO32jgshduh7nbR8Q
https://www.linkedin.com/company/university-of-california-press

ACADEMIC > **Nonfiction** > *Nonfiction Books*
    Africa; Anthropology; Arts; Asia; Classics / Ancient World; Crime; Economics; Environment; Films; Food; Gender; Health; History; Language; Legal; Literature; Media; Middle East; Music; Philosophy; Politics; Psychology; Religion; Science; Sexuality; Sociology; South America; Technology; United States; Wine

Scholarly publisher based in California.

Acquisitions Editor: Maura Roessner

Editorial Director: Kim Robinson

P0863 University of Exeter Press
Book Publisher
Reed Hall, Streatham Drive, Exeter, EX4 4QR
United Kingdom
Tel: +44 (0) 1392 263066
Fax: +44 (0) 1392 263064

n.massen@exeterpress.co.uk

http://www.exeterpress.co.uk

Types: Nonfiction
Formats: Film Scripts; Reference
Subjects: Archaeology; Culture; History; Literature; Philosophy; Religion; Sociology
Markets: Academic

Send: Query
Don't send: Full text

Publisher of academic books. See website for guidelines on submitting a proposal.

Editors: Anna Henderson; Hetty Marx; Nigel Massen

P0864 University of Hertfordshire Press
Book Publisher
College Lane, Hatfield, Hertfordshire, AL10 9AB
United Kingdom
Tel: +44 (0) 1707 284681

uhpress@herts.ac.uk

http://www.herts.ac.uk/UHPress

ACADEMIC > **Nonfiction** > *Nonfiction Books*
    History; Literature; Local History; Mathematics; Psychology; Theatre

Send: Query; Submission Form
How to send: Email

Publisher of academic books on local history, including imprints for Essex, West Midlands, and Hertfordshire.

Editor: Jane Housham

Publishing Imprints: Essex Publications (**P0270**); Hertfordshire Publications (**P0404**); West Midlands Publications (**P0920**)

P0865 University of Iowa Press
Book Publisher
119 West Park Road, 100 Kuhl House, Iowa City IA 52242-1000
United States
Tel: +1 (319) 335-2000
Fax: +1 (319) 335-2055

uipress@uiowa.edu

http://www.uiowapress.org

Types: Fiction; Nonfiction; Poetry
Formats: Short Fiction; Theatre Scripts
Subjects: Anthropology; Archaeology; Arts; Biography; Culture; History; Literary; Literature; Nature; Warfare
Markets: Academic; Adult

Send proposals for nonfiction by email. Accepts fiction and poetry through annual competitions only.

P0866 University of Maine Press
Book Publisher
5729 Fogler Library, Orono, ME 04469-5729
United States
Tel: +1 (207) 581-1652

alpert@maine.edu

https://umaine.edu/umpress/

ACADEMIC > **Nonfiction** > *Nonfiction Books*
    Arts; Maine; Science

ADULT > **Fiction** > *Novels*: Maine

Send: Query; Synopsis; Writing sample; Self-Addressed Stamped Envelope (SASE)
Don't send: Full text
How to send: Post; Email

Publishes scholarly books and original writing in science, the arts and the humanities, focusing on the intellectual concerns of the Maine region. Occasionally publishes regional fiction. Send query by email or by post with SASE between September 1 and October 31.

P0867 University of Massachusetts Press
Book Publisher
New Africa House, 180 Infirmary Way, 4th Floor, Amherst, MA 01003-9289
United States
Fax: +1 (413) 545-1226

cdougan@umpress.umass.edu

http://www.umass.edu/umpress

Types: Fiction; Nonfiction; Poetry
Subjects: Culture; History; Nature; Politics
Markets: Academic; Adult

Focuses primarily on books in the field of American studies, including books that explore the history, politics, literature, culture, and environment of the United States – as well as works with a transnational perspective. In addition to publishing works of scholarship, the Press produces books of more general interest for a wider readership. Also publishes poetry and fiction via its annual competitions only.

Editor-in-Chief: Matt Becker

P0868 University of Missouri Press

Book Publisher
113 Heinkel Building, 201 S 7th Street, Columbia, MO 65211
United States
Tel: +1 (573) 882-7641
Fax: +1 (573) 884-4498

upress@missouri.edu

https://upress.missouri.edu

Types: Nonfiction
Subjects: History; Literary Criticism; Politics; Warfare
Markets: Academic

Send: Query
Don't send: Full text

Scholarly publisher of a range of subject lists, with a focus on American History (esp. US Military, African American, Political), Journalism, Political Science, Missouri History and Regional Studies, and Literary Criticism (gen. American and British). Also happy to consider enquiries regarding work in any area of the humanities or natural history. No fiction or poetry. See website for full guidelines.

Editor-in-Chief: Andrew J. Davidson

P0869 University of Nevada Press

Book Publisher
University of Nevada Press, Morrill Hall Mail Stop 0166, Reno NV 89557-0166
United States
Tel: +1 (775) 784-6573

jbanducci@unpress.nevada.edu

https://www.unpress.nevada.edu

Types: Fiction; Nonfiction
Subjects: Anthropology; Arts; Culture; Current Affairs; Finance; History; Literature; Nature; Politics; Science; Sociology
Markets: Academic; Adult

Send: Query
Don't send: Full text

Publishes scholarly books in the humanities and social sciences in the fields of environmental studies, public health, mining studies, Native American studies, urban studies, Basque studies, gambling and commercial gaming, and select fiction. Will also publish books on any topic which contribute to our understanding of Nevada, the Great Basin, and American West. See website for full submission guidelines and submit proposals by email.

Editor: JoAnne Banducci

P0870 University of North Texas Press

Book Publisher
1155 Union Circle #311336, Denton, TX 76203-5017
United States
Tel: +1 (940) 565-2142
Fax: +1 (940) 369-8760

Ronald.Chrisman@unt.edu

https://untpress.unt.edu

Types: Fiction; Nonfiction; Poetry
Formats: Theatre Scripts
Subjects: Antiques; Architecture; Arts; Biography; Business; Comedy / Humour; Cookery; Crime; Finance; History; Legal; Literary Criticism; Medicine; Nature; Photography; Politics; Religion; Science; Sociology; Sport; Technology; Travel; Warfare; Women's Interests
Markets: Academic

Publishes titles on Texas, its history, military history, and social issues. Also covers women's interests and multicultural issues. Also publishes fiction and poetry through its annual competitions. See website for more details.

P0871 University of Oklahoma Press

Book Publisher
2800 Venture Drive, Norman, OK 73069-8216
United States

https://www.oupress.com

ACADEMIC > **Nonfiction** > *Nonfiction Books*
Arts; Autobiography; Biography; Business; Comedy / Humour; Cookery; Crafts; Drama; Economics; Education; Engineering; Family; Fitness; Health; History; Hobbies; Language; Legal; Literature; Music; Nature; Performing Arts; Pets; Philosophy; Photography; Politics; Psychology; Relationships; Religion; Science; Self Help; Sociology; Sport; Technology; Transport; Travel

How to send: Online submission system

Publishes scholarly books of significance to the state, region, nation, and world, both to convey the results of current research to other scholars and to offer broader presentations for the general public.

P0872 University of Pennsylvania Press

Book Publisher
3905 Spruce Street, Philadelphia, PA 19104-4112
United States
Tel: +1 (215) 898-6261
Fax: +1 (215) 898-0404

custserv@pobox.upenn.edu

https://www.upenn.edu/pennpress

ACADEMIC > **Nonfiction** > *Nonfiction Books*
African Diaspora; Atlantic; Culture; History; Intellectual History; Judaism; Literary Criticism; Medieval; North America; Political History; Renaissance; South America

Send: Query
How to send: Email

Send query by email to appropriate editor.

Associate Editor: Jenny Tan

Company Director: Eric Halpern

Editor-in-Chief: Walter Biggins

Senior Editors: Robert Lockhart; Jerome Singerman

P0873 University of Pittsburgh Press

Book Publisher
7500 Thomas Boulevard, Pittsburgh, PA 15260
United States

https://upittpress.org

ACADEMIC > **Nonfiction** > *Nonfiction Books*
Architecture; Arts; Asia; Biography; Eastern Europe; Environment; History; Literature; Medicine; Pennsylvania; Photography; Pittsburgh; Russia; Science; South America; Technology; Travel; Urban

ADULT > **Poetry** > *Any Poetic Form*

Send: Query
Don't send: Full text

Publishes books on Latin American studies, Russian and East European studies, Central Asian studies, composition and literacy studies, environmental studies, urban studies, the history of architecture and the built environment, and the history and philosophy of science, technology, and medicine. Describes its poetry series as representing many of the finest poets active today.

Acquisitions Editor: Joshua Shanholtzer

Editorial Directors: Abby Collier; Sandy Crooms

P0874 University of Tennessee Press

Book Publisher
110 Conference Center, Knoxville, TN 37996-4108
United States
Tel: +1 (865) 974-3321
Fax: +1 (865) 974-3724

utpress@utk.edu

https://utpress.org
https://www.facebook.com/utennpress/
https://twitter.com/utennpress

ACADEMIC > **Nonfiction** > *Nonfiction Books*
American Civil War; American History; Anthropology; Folklore, Myths, and Legends; Literature; Music; Popular Culture; Religion; Sport

Send: Query; Table of Contents; Writing sample; Author bio

The press is committed to preserving knowledge about Tennessee and the region and, by expanding its unique publishing program, it promotes a broad base of cultural understanding and, ultimately, improves life in the state.

Acquisitions Editor: Scot Danforth

P0875 University of Texas Press

Book Publisher
3001 Lake Austin Blvd, 2.200, Stop E4800, Austin, TX 78703-4206
United States

https://utpress.utexas.edu

ACADEMIC > **Nonfiction** > *Nonfiction Books*
Anthropology; Archaeology; Architecture; Arts; Biography; Classics / Ancient World; Cookery; Environment; Films; Food; History; Judaism; Media; Middle East; Music; Nature; Photography; Sexuality; South America; Southwestern United States; Texas; United States

ADULT > **Nonfiction** > *Nonfiction Books*
Art History; Arts; Culture; Current Affairs; Food; History; Music; Nature; Texas

Send: Query; Proposal; Table of Contents; Writing sample; Author bio; Submission Form
How to send: Email

Send query with proposal, table of contents, sample chapter, and CV. Publishes scholarly books and some general readership nonfiction. See website for full details.

P0876 University of Virginia Press

Book Publisher
University of Virginia Press, P.O. Box 400318 (Postal), 210 Sprigg Lane (Courier),

Charlottesville, VA 22904-4318
United States
Tel: +1 (434) 924-3468
Fax: +1 (434) 982-2655

vapress@virginia.edu

https://www.upress.virginia.edu/

Types: Nonfiction
Subjects: Architecture; History; Literary Criticism; Sociology
Markets: Academic

Considers academic books in areas including humanities, social sciences, American history, African-American studies, architecture, Victorian literature, Caribbean literature and ecocriticism.

P0877 The University of Wisconsin Press

Book Publisher
728 State Street, Suite 443, Madison, WI 53706
United States
Tel: +1 (608) 263-1101
Fax: +1 (608) 263-1173

uwiscpress@uwpress.wisc.edu

http://www.wisc.edu/wisconsinpress

Types: Fiction; Nonfiction; Poetry
Formats: Film Scripts; Short Fiction
Subjects: Anthropology; Autobiography; Culture; History; Media; Nature; Politics; Travel
Markets: Academic

Send: Query
Don't send: Full text

Publishes scholarly, general interest nonfiction books and books featuring the American midwest, along with a limited number of novels and short story collections. Publishes poetry via its annual competition only, for which there is an entry fee.

P0878 University Press of Mississippi

Book Publisher
United States

https://www.upress.state.ms.us

ACADEMIC > **Nonfiction** > *Nonfiction Books*
African American; Caribbean; Comic Books; Culture; Films; Folklore, Myths, and Legends; History; Literature; Media; Music; Popular Culture; US Southern States

How to send: Email

Publishes books that interpret the South and its culture to the nation and the world, scholarly books of the highest distinction, and books vital to readers in African American studies, Caribbean studies, comics studies, film and media studies, folklore, history, literary studies, music, and popular culture.

P0879 Unthank Books

Book Publisher
United Kingdom

information@unthankbooks.com

https://www.unthankbooks.com
https://www.facebook.com/UnthankBooks/
https://twitter.com/@unthankbooks

Fiction
Novels: Literary
Short Fiction Collections: Literary

An independent publisher nurturing distinct and vibrant literature, both in the novel and short form.

Editorial Director: Ashley Stokes

Publisher: Robin Jones

P0880 Up On Big Rock Poetry

Publishing Imprint

Book Publisher: Shipwreckt Books Publishing Company (**P0762**)

P0881 Usborne Publishing

Book Publisher
83-85 Saffron Hill, London, EC1N 8RT
United Kingdom
Tel: +44 (0) 20 7430 2800
Fax: +44 (0) 20 7430 1562

https://usborne.com

Types: Fiction; Nonfiction
Formats: Reference
Markets: Children's

How to send: Through a literary agent

Publisher of children's reference now expanding into children's fiction. All nonfiction written in-house and fiction submissions accepted via literary agents only.

P0882 Vallentine Mitchell

Publishing Imprint
Catalyst House, 720 Centennial Court, Centennial Park, Elstree, Herts, WD6 3SY
United Kingdom
Tel: +44 (0) 20 8292 5637

editor@vmbooks.com

https://www.vmbooksuk.com

Types: Nonfiction
Subjects: Culture; History; Philosophy; Religion
Markets: Academic; Adult

Send: Query
Don't send: Full text

Publishes books on Jewish history, culture and heritage, Jewish thought, Middle Eastern history, politics and culture and the Holocaust, for both academic and general readerships. Offices in Hertfordshire and Chicago, Illinois. Send proposals by email.

P0883 VanderWyk & Burnham
Book Publisher
1610 Long Leaf Circle, St. Louis, MO 63146
United States
Tel: +1 (314) 432-3435
Fax: +1 (314) 993-4485

quickpublishing@sbcglobal.net

http://www.vandb.com

Types: Nonfiction
Subjects: Lifestyle; Psychology; Self Help
Markets: Adult

Closed to approaches.

Not accepting unsolicited proposals or submissions as at May 2020.

P0884 Vegetarian Alcoholic Press
Book Publisher
United States

vegalpress@gmail.com

http://www.vegetarianalcoholicpress.com

Types: Fiction; Poetry
Formats: Short Fiction
Subjects: Literary
Markets: Adult

Send: Full text

Publishes poetry and short story collections. Send submissions by email.

P0885 Vermilion
Publishing Imprint
United Kingdom

Book Publisher: Ebury (**P0247**)

P0886 Viking
Publishing Imprint
United States

Book Publisher: Penguin Publishing Group (**P0633**)

P0887 Viking Children's Books
Publishing Imprint
United States

Book Publisher: Penguin Young Readers Group (**P0638**)

P0888 Viking Dog
Book Publisher
United States

contact@viking-dog.com

https://www.viking-dog.com
https://www.instagram.com/vikingdogent/
https://www.facebook.com/vikingdogent/
http://twitter.com/vikingdogent
https://www.youtube.com/channel/
UCmZtTxwsFYEKNa-eBrtHxhg?view_as=
subscriber
https://vimeo.com/user70568100

Fiction > *Novels*
  Adventure; Fantasy; Science Fiction; Thrillers; Westerns
Scripts
  Film Scripts: Adventure; Fantasy; Science Fiction; Thrillers; Westerns
  TV Scripts: Adventure; Fantasy; Science Fiction; Thrillers; Westerns

Send: Query
How to send: Email

A content company based in Los Angeles that creates, publishes and distributes film and book projects.

P0889 Vine Leaves Press
Book Publisher
Australia

submissions@vineleavespress.com

https://www.vineleavespress.com

Types: Fiction; Nonfiction
Formats: Reference; Short Fiction
Subjects: Autobiography; Literary
Markets: Adult

Send: Query
Don't send: Full text

Publishes novels (all genres accepted, but with a literary bent), memoirs / biographies / autobiographies, creative nonfiction, and writing / publishing reference books, and short story collections. Send query by email with first ten pages and author bio.

P0890 Vinspire Publishing
Book Publisher
PO Box 1165, Ladson, SC 29456-1165
United States
Tel: +1 (843) 695-7530

vinspirepublishingeic@gmail.com

https://www.vinspirepublishing.com

Types: Fiction
Subjects: Comedy / Humour; History; Mystery; Romance; Thrillers; Westerns
Markets: Adult; Young Adult

Closed to approaches.

Accepts agented approaches only, except during open submission calls, which are announced on the website and via social media.

P0891 Vintage
Book Publisher
United Kingdom

Book Publisher: Penguin Random House UK (**P0635**)

Publishing Imprints: The Bodley Head (*P0120*); Chatto & Windus (*P0166*); Harvill Secker (*P0393*); Hogarth Press (*P0412*); Jonathan Cape (**P0457**); Square Peg (*P0787*);

Vintage Classics (*P0893*); Vintage Paperbacks (*P0894*); Yellow Jersey (*P0945*)

P0892 Vintage Books
Publishing Imprint
United States

Book Publisher: Knopf Doubleday Publishing Group (**P0475**)

P0893 Vintage Classics
Publishing Imprint
United Kingdom

Book Publisher: Vintage (**P0891**)

P0894 Vintage Paperbacks
Publishing Imprint
United Kingdom

Book Publisher: Vintage (**P0891**)

P0895 Virago
Publishing Imprint

Publishing Imprint: Little, Brown Book Group (**P0502**)

P0896 Virgin Books
Publishing Imprint
United Kingdom

Book Publisher: Ebury (**P0247**)

P0897 Vision Paperbacks
Book Publisher
United Kingdom

https://www.visionpaperbacks.co.uk

Nonfiction > *Nonfiction Books*
  General, and in particular: Alternative Lifestyles; Autobiography; Biography; Current Affairs; Environment; Investigative Journalism; Media; Science; Sexuality; Society

Send: Synopsis; Full text; Writing sample; Market info
How to send: Online contact form

Accepts approaches from published and first-time authors for books that fit with their list. Submit material through online submission form.

Editor: Charlotte Cole

Publishing Imprint: Fusion Press

P0898 Voyageur Press
Publishing Imprint
Book Proposals, Voyageur Press, Quayside Publishing Group, 400 First Avenue North, Suite 300, Minneapolis, MN 55401
United States
Tel: +1 (800) 458-0454
Fax: +1 (612) 344-8691

customerservice@quaysidepub.com

http://www.voyageurpress.com

Book Publisher: The Quarto Group, Inc. (**P0679**)

Types: Nonfiction
Subjects: Culture; History; Lifestyle; Music; Nature; Photography; Travel
Markets: Adult

Send: Query
Don't send: Full text

Publishes books on nature and the

environment; country living and farming heritage; regional and cultural history; music;

travel and photography. See website for full submission guidelines.

P0899 W Publishing Group
Publishing Imprint

Book Publisher: HarperCollins

P0900 W.W. Norton & Company Ltd
Book Publisher
15 Carlisle Street, London, W1D 3BS
United Kingdom
Tel: +44 (0) 20 7323 1579

crussell1@wwnorton.com

https://wwnorton.co.uk
https://twitter.com/wwnortonUK
https://www.instagram.com/wwnortonuk/
https://medium.com/@W.W.NortonUK
https://www.pinterest.com/wwnortonuk/

ACADEMIC > **Nonfiction** > *Nonfiction Books*
African American; Anthropology; Astronomy; Biology; Chemistry; Classics / Ancient World; Computer Science; Films; Geology; History; Literature; Music; Oceanography; Philosophy; Physics; Politics; Popular Science; Psychology; Religion; Sociology; Statistics

ADULT
Fiction
Graphic Novels; *Novels*
Nonfiction
Essays: General
Nonfiction Books: Adventure; African American; Archaeology; Architecture; Arts; Astronomy; Biography; Business; Classics / Ancient World; Comedy / Humour; Crafts; Crime; Culture; Current Affairs; Design; Drama; Economics; Education; Environment; Films; Folklore, Myths, and Legends; Food and Drink; Games; Gardening; Health; History; Hobbies; Houses; LGBTQIA; Legal; Literature; Medicine; Memoir; Music; Nature; Parenting; Pets; Philosophy; Photography; Politics; Popular Science; Psychology; Psychotherapy; Religion; Self Help; Sociology; Sport; Statistics;

Technology; Transport; Travel; Women's Studies; Writing
Poetry > *Poetry Collections*

CHILDREN'S
Fiction
Chapter Books; *Early Readers*; *Picture Books*
Nonfiction > *Nonfiction Books*

PROFESSIONAL > **Nonfiction** > *Nonfiction Books*
Addiction; Anxiety Disorders; Architecture; Autism; Child Psychotherapy; Coaching; Couple Therapy; Depression; Design; Eating Disorders; Education; Family Therapy; Genetics; Geriatrics; Health; Hypnosis; Juvenile Psychotherapy; Medicine; Neurobiology; Neuropsychology; Neuroscience; Post Traumatic Stress Disorder; Psychiatry; Psychoanalysis; Psychological Trauma; Psychotherapy; Self Help; Sexuality

UK branch of a US publisher. No editorial office in the UK – contact the main office in New York (see separate listing).

P0901 Walden Pond Press
Publishing Imprint

Book Publisher: HarperCollins

P0902 Walker Books Ltd
Book Publisher
87 Vauxhall Walk, London, SE11 5HJ
United Kingdom
Tel: +44 (0) 20 7793 0909

editorial@walker.co.uk

http://www.walkerbooks.co.uk

Types: Fiction; Nonfiction
Markets: Children's

Publishes fiction and nonfiction for children, including illustrated books. Not accepting unsolicited fiction or picture books as at September 2019.

P0903 Walter Foster Jr.
Publishing Imprint

Book Publisher: The Quarto Group, Inc. (**P0679**)

P0904 Walter Foster Publishing
Publishing Imprint
Suite A, Irvine, CA 92618
United States
Tel: +1 (800) 426-0099
Fax: +1 (949) 380-7575

info@walterfoster.com

http://www.walterfoster.com

Book Publisher: The Quarto Group, Inc. (**P0679**)

Types: Nonfiction
Subjects: Crafts; How To
Markets: Adult; Children's; Young Adult

Publishes how-to craft books and kits for children and adults.

P0905 Washington State University Press
Book Publisher
Cooper Publications Building, PO Box 645910, Pullman, WA 99164-5910
United States
Tel: +1 (509) 335-8821
Fax: +1 (509) 335-8568

wsupress@wsu.edu

https://wsupress.wsu.edu

Types: Nonfiction
Subjects: Biography; Cookery; Culture; History; Nature; Politics; Westerns
Markets: Academic; Adult

Send: Query
Don't send: Full text

Send query by post or by email (preferred) with author CV, summary of proposed work, sample bio, and one or two sample chapters. Specialises in the American West, particularly the prehistory, history, environment, politics, and culture of the greater Northwest region. No fiction, poetry, or literary criticism. See website for full guidelines.

Editor-in-Chief: Linda Bathgate

P0906 WaterBrook Multnomah
Publishing Imprint

Book Publisher: Random House (**P0690**)

P0907 Watkins Media
Book Publisher

Book Publishers: Angry Robot (**P0038**); Watkins Publishing (**P0908**)

P0908 Watkins Publishing
Book Publisher
Unit 11, Shepperton House, 89 Shepperton Road, London, N1 3DF
United Kingdom
Tel: +44 (0) 20 3813 6940

enquiries@watkinspublishing.com

https://www.watkinspublishing.com

Book Publisher: Watkins Media (**P0907**)

Types: Nonfiction
Subjects: History; Lifestyle; Religion; Self Help
Markets: Adult

Publishes books in the field of Mind, Body and Spirit. Not accepting submissions as at April 2019. Check website for current status.

P0909 **Watson-Guptill**
Publishing Imprint

Book Publisher: Random House (**P0690**)

P0910 **Watson-Guptill Publications**
Publishing Imprint
United States

http://crownpublishing.com/archives/imprint/watson-guptill

Book Publisher: The Crown Publishing Group

Types: Nonfiction
Formats: Reference; Theatre Scripts
Subjects: Architecture; Arts; Crafts; Culture; Design; How To; Lifestyle; Music; Photography
Markets: Adult; Children's

Send: Query
Don't send: Full text

Publishes art and art instruction books.

P0911 **Wave Books**
Book Publisher
1938 Fairview Avenue East, Suite 201, Seattle, WA 98102
United States
Tel: +1 (206) 676-5337

info@wavepoetry.com

https://www.wavepoetry.com
http://twitter.com/WavePoetry
http://www.facebook.com/pages/Wave-Books/325354873993
http://wavepoetry.tumblr.com/

Poetry > *Poetry Collections*: Contemporary

Closed to approaches.

Independent poetry press based in Seattle. Accepts submissions only in response to specific calls for submissions posted on the website (see the submissions page).

Publisher: Charlie Wright

P0912 **Wayland Books**
Publishing Imprint

Book Publisher: Hachette Children's Group (**P0350**)

P0913 **Wayne State University Press**
Book Publisher
4809 Woodward Avenue, Detroit, Michigan 48201-1309
United States

annie.martin@wayne.edu

https://www.wsupress.wayne.edu

Types: Nonfiction
Subjects: Culture; Media; Religion
Markets: Academic

Send: Query
Don't send: Full text

Actively acquiring books in African American studies, media studies, fairy-tale studies, Jewish studies, citizenship studies, and regional studies: books about the state of Michigan, the city of Detroit, and the Great Lakes region. Send query by post or by email to appropriate acquisitions editor (see website for details and individual contact details).

P0914 **Weasel Press**
Book Publisher
United States

thedude@weaselpress.com

https://www.weaselpress.com

Types: Fiction; Nonfiction; Poetry
Formats: Short Fiction
Subjects: Experimental; Literary
Markets: Adult

From autumn 2020 will only accept work from authors of colour, or who identify as LGBTQ+, or who are disabled. Submit through online submission system.

P0915 **Wednesday Books**
Publishing Imprint

Publishing Imprint: St Martin's Press (**P0789**)

P0916 **Welbeck Publishing Group**
Book Publisher
20 Mortimer Street, London, W1T 3JW
United Kingdom
Tel: +44 (0) 20 7612 0400
Fax: +44 (0) 20 7612 0401

submissions@welbeckpublishing.com

https://www.welbeckpublishing.com
https://www.facebook.com/welbeckpublish/
https://www.instagram.com/welbeckpublish/
https://twitter.com/welbeckpublish
https://www.youtube.com/welbeckpublishinggroup
https://www.linkedin.com/company/welbeckpublishinggroup/

ADULT
  Fiction > *Novels*
    Commercial; Popular

  Nonfiction
    Illustrated Books: Comedy / Humour; Entertainment; Fashion; History; Lifestyle; Sport
    Nonfiction Books: Biography; Business; Crime; History; Memoir; Military; Narrative Nonfiction; Popular Culture; Popular Science; Psychology; Self Help; Sport
    Puzzle Books: General

CHILDREN'S
  Fiction > *Middle Grade*

  Nonfiction
    Illustrated Books: Environment; History; Hobbies; Mental Health; Nature
    Nonfiction Books: General
    Picture Books: General

Send: Query
Don't send: Full text

Publishes illustrated reference, sport, entertainment, commercial fiction and children's nonfiction. Synopses and ideas for suitable books are welcomed, but no unsolicited MSS, academic, or poetry. Send query by email only with short synopsis, author bio, market info, and up to two chapters up to a maximum of 20 pages. See website for full guidelines.

P0917 **Wellfleet Press**
Publishing Imprint

Book Publisher: The Quarto Group, Inc. (**P0679**)

P0918 **Wells College Press**
Book Publisher
170 Main St, Aurora, NY 13026
United States
Tel: +1 (315) 364-3420

bookartscenter@wells.edu

https://wellsbookartscenter.org/wells-college-press/

Types: Nonfiction; Poetry
Subjects: Arts; Design
Markets: Adult

Publishes poetry chapbooks and books on art, design, and typography.

P0919 **Wesleyan University Press**
Book Publisher
215 Long Lane, Middletown, CT 06459
United States
Tel: +1 (860) 685-7730
Fax: +1 (860) 685-7712

stamminen@wesleyan.edu

http://www.wesleyan.edu/wespress

Types: Nonfiction
Subjects: Music
Markets: Academic

Send: Query
Don't send: Full text

Accepting proposals in the areas of dance and music. See website for submission guidelines.

P0920 **West Midlands Publications**
Publishing Imprint
United Kingdom

http://www.uhpress.co.uk/subject-areas/west-midlands-publications

Book Publisher: University of Hertfordshire Press (**P0864**)

ACADEMIC > **Nonfiction** > *Nonfiction Books*: Local History

This series aims to publish scholarly, attractive, well-illustrated and accessible studies on the history of the English West Midlands, a region which broadly encompasses the historic counties of Derbyshire, Herefordshire, Shropshire, Staffordshire, Warwickshire and Worcestershire.

P0921 WestBow Press
Publishing Imprint

Book Publisher: HarperCollins

P0922 WH Allen
Publishing Imprint
United Kingdom

Book Publisher: Ebury (**P0247**)

P0923 Wharncliffe Books
Publishing Imprint
United Kingdom

https://www.pen-and-sword.co.uk/Wharncliffe-Books/i/8

Book Publisher: Pen & Sword Books Ltd (**P0626**)

Nonfiction > *Nonfiction Books*
History; Regional

Send: Query; Synopsis
How to send: Online submission system

Publishes local history books covering areas across the UK.

Editor: Rupert Harding

P0924 White Lion Publishing
Publishing Imprint

Book Publisher: The Quarto Group, Inc. (**P0679**)

P0925 White Owl
Publishing Imprint

Book Publisher: Pen & Sword Books Ltd (**P0626**)

P0926 Whitecap Books Ltd
Book Publisher
Suite 209, 314 West Cordova Street, Vancouver, BC, V6B 1E8
Canada

bookinfo@whitecap.ca

https://www.whitecap.ca

Types: Nonfiction
Subjects: Cookery; History; Nature
Markets: Adult

Closed to approaches.

Publishes visually appealing books on food, wine, health and well-being, regional history, and regional guidebooks.

P0927 Wide-Eyed Editions
Publishing Imprint
The Old Brewery, 6 Blundell Street, London, N7 9BH
United Kingdom
Tel: +44 (0) 20 7700 6700
Fax: +44 (0) 20 7700 8066

QuartoExploresSubmissions@Quartous.com

https://www.quartoknows.com/Wide-Eyed-Editions

Book Publisher: The Quarto Group, Inc. (**P0679**)

Types: Nonfiction
Subjects: Arts; Nature; Travel
Markets: Children's

Send: Query
Don't send: Full text

Publishes books on the arts, natural history and armchair travel. Send query with proposal by email. See website for full guidelines.

P0928 Wild Goose Publications
Book Publisher
The Iona Community, Suite 9, Fairfield, 1048 Govan Road, Glasgow, G51 4XS
United Kingdom
Tel: +44 (0) 1414 297281

admin@ionabooks.com

https://www.ionabooks.com

Nonfiction > *Nonfiction Books*: Christianity

Publisher of an ecumenical community of people from different walks of life and different traditions in the Christian church.

P0929 Wilderness Press
Book Publisher
c/o Keen Communications, 2204 First Avenue South, Suite 102, Birmingham, AL 35233
United States
Tel: +1 (800) 443-7227
Fax: +1 (205) 326-1012

https://www.wildernesspress.com/

Types: Nonfiction
Subjects: How To; Leisure; Nature; Travel
Markets: Adult

Publisher of books on the outdoors, travel, and outdoor activities.

P0930 Wiley-Blackwell
Publishing Imprint
9600 Garsington Road, Oxford, OX4 2DQ
United Kingdom
Tel: +44 (0) 1865 776868
Fax: +44 (0) 1865 714591

https://www.wiley.com/WileyCDA/Brand/id-35.html

Book Publisher: John Wiley & Sons, Inc.

PROFESSIONAL > **Nonfiction**
Nonfiction Books; *Reference*

A global provider of content-enabled solutions to improve outcomes in research, education and professional practice with online tools, journals, books, databases, reference works and laboratory protocols. Has strengths in every major academic, scientific and professional field. Partners with over 800 prestigious societies representing two million members.

P0931 William Collins
Publishing Imprint
United Kingdom

Book Publisher: HarperCollins UK (**P0382**)

P0932 William Morrow
Publishing Imprint

Book Publisher: HarperCollins

P0933 Windhorse Publications Ltd
Book Publisher
38 Newmarket Road, Cambridge, CB5 8DT
United Kingdom

info@windhorsepublications.com
dhammamegha@windhorsepublications.com

https://www.windhorsepublications.com
https://www.facebook.com/windhorse.publications/
https://twitter.com/WindhorsePubs
https://www.instagram.com/windhorsepubs/
https://issuu.com/windhorsepublications
https://vimeo.com/windhorsepublications
https://soundcloud.com/windhorsepublications
https://thebuddhistcentre.com/windhorsepublications?display=latest

Nonfiction > *Nonfiction Books*: Buddhism

Send: Query
Don't send: Proposal; Full text
How to send: Email

Publishes books exploring Buddhist ideas and practices, mainly by authors connected to the Triratna Buddhist Order and Community, but also relevant and accessible works by other authors. Send initial query by email before sending proposals or manuscripts.

P0934 Wise Music Group
Book Publisher

Book Publisher: Omnibus Press (**P0594**)

P0935 Witness
Publishing Imprint

Book Publisher: HarperCollins

P0936 **Wolfpack Publishing**
Book Publisher
5130 S. Fort Apache Rd. 215-380, Las Vegas,
NV 89148
United States
Tel: +1 (702) 689-3912

https://wolfpackpublishing.com
https://www.goodreads.com/group/show/
138635-wolfpack-publishing
https://www.facebook.com/WolfpackPub/
https://twitter.com/wolfpackpub

Fiction > *Novels*
Adventure; Crime; Historical Fiction;
Mystery; Suspense; Thrillers; Westerns

Send: Synopsis; Full text; Market info
How to send: Online submission system

An award winning indie publisher that began
life as a small Western Fiction publishing
company, but which now publishes across a
variety of genres. Continues to specialise in
Westerns, but not accepting submissions for
Westerns as at July 2021.

P0937 **Wolters Kluwer**
Book Publisher
PO Box 1030, 2400 BA, Alphen aan den Rijn
Netherlands

Book Publishers: Kluwer Law International
(**P0474**); Wolters Kluwer (UK) Ltd

P0938 **WordFarm**
Book Publisher
140 Lakeside Ave, Suite A-303, Seattle, WA
98122-6538
United States
Tel: +1 (312) 281-8806

info@wordfarm.net

http://www.wordfarm.net

Fiction > *Novels*: Literary

Nonfiction > *Nonfiction Books*: Literary

Poetry > *Any Poetic Form*

Closed to approaches.

Publishes collections of poetry, short fiction,
essays, and single works of fiction or literary
nonfiction.

Authors: Stacy Barton; Ruth Goring; Erin
Keane; Jack Leax; Lynda Rutledge; Luci
Shaw; Paul Willis

Editor: Andrew Craft

P0939 **Words & Pictures**
Publishing Imprint
The Old Brewery, 6 Blundell Street, London,
N7 9BH
United Kingdom
Tel: +44 (0) 20 770 6700

QuartoHomesSubmissions@Quarto.com

https://www.quartoknows.com/words-pictures

Book Publisher: The Quarto Group, Inc.
(**P0679**)

CHILDREN'S > **Fiction** > *Picture Books*

How to send: Email

Always on the lookout for authors and artists
with creative ideas to enhance and broaden
their list of children's books. See website for
submission guidelines.

Editor: Maxime Boucknooghe

Publisher: Rhiannon Findlay

P0940 **Wren & Rook**
Publishing Imprint

Book Publisher: Hachette Children's Group
(**P0350**)

P0941 **Writer's Digest Books**
Publishing Imprint
United States

Book Publisher: Penguin Publishing Group
(**P0633**)

P0942 **Wyldblood Press**
*Book Publisher; Magazine Publisher; Online
Publisher*
Thicket View, Bakers Row, Bakers Lane,
Maidenhead, SL6 6PX
United Kingdom
Tel: +44 (0) 7961 323023

admin@wyldblood.com

https://wyldblood.com
https://www.facebook.com/Wyldblood-Press-
115385210261475/

ADULT > **Fiction**
Novels: Fantasy; Science Fiction
Short Fiction: Fantasy; Science Fiction
YOUNG ADULT > **Fiction**
Novels: Fantasy; Science Fiction
Short Fiction: Fantasy; Science Fiction

Send: Query; Synopsis; Full text
How to send: Email attachment
How not to send: PDF file email attachment

We're a publisher of speculative and literary
fiction. We're based in England but sell all
over the world both online and in print. We
believe there's always room for high quality
writing and never enough spaces to find it, so
we're working hard to create a new home for
inspiring new work. By speculative we mean
science fiction and fantasy but that reflects our
tastes and not our limits. Good writing breaks
through boundaries and knows no genre limits.

We will be publishing novels, anthology
collections, a bimonthly magazine (from Jan
2021) (ebook and print) and flash fiction
(online only).

P0943 **Yale University Press
(London)**
Book Publisher
47 Bedford Square, London, WC1B 3DP
United Kingdom
Tel: +44 (0) 20 7079 4900

trade@yaleup.co.uk

https://www.yalebooks.co.uk

ADULT > **Nonfiction**
Nonfiction Books: Architecture; Arts;
Biography; Business; Computers; Current
Affairs; Economics; Fashion; Health;
History; Language; Legal; Literature;
Mathematics; Medicine; Memoir; Music;
Philosophy; Politics; Religion; Science;
Society; Sociology; Technology; Wellbeing
Reference: General

CHILDREN'S > **Nonfiction** > *Nonfiction
Books*: Education

Send: Query; Author bio; Market info; Table
of Contents; Writing sample
How to send: Post; Phone; Email

Publishes world class scholarship for a broad
readership.

Editor: Sophie Neve

Editorial Directors: Mark Eastment; Julian
Loose

Managing Director / Publisher: Heather
McCallum

Senior Editor: Joanna Godfrey

P0944 **Yellow Flag Press**
Book Publisher
United States

https://www.yellowflagpress.com

Types: Poetry
Subjects: Literary
Markets: Adult

Publishes trade paperback books as well as
handmade chapbooks and broadsides in limited
edition printings. Free open reading period in
April, but submissions can be made at other
times of the year with a $5 discounted sample
chapbook purchase.

Editor: J. Bruce Fuller

P0945 **Yellow Jersey**
Publishing Imprint
United Kingdom

Book Publisher: Vintage (**P0891**)

P0946 **Yes Poetry Chapbooks**
Book Publisher
United States

editor@yespoetry.com

https://www.yespoetry.com

Online Magazine: Yes Poetry Magazine (**M0570**)

Poetry > *Chapbook*

Closed to approaches.

Has published a poetry magazine since 2010, and since 2016 has also published poetry chapbooks. Closed to chapbook submissions as at October 2019. Check website for current status.

P0947 **YesYes Books**
Book Publisher
1614 NE Alberta Street, Portland, OR 97211
United States

info@yesyesbooks.com

https://www.yesyesbooks.com

Types: Fiction; Poetry
Subjects: Literary
Markets: Adult

Accepts submissions of fiction and poetry between April 1 and May 15, and via its two contests in autumn.

P0948 **Zebra Shout**
Publishing Imprint

Book Publisher: Kensington Publishing Corp. (**P0469**)

P0949 **ZED Press**
Book Publisher
Canada

zedpresschapbook@gmail.com

https://zedpresswindsor.wordpress.com

Types: Poetry
Subjects: Experimental; Literary
Markets: Adult

Send: Full text

Publishes poetry chapbooks. Looks for experimental work and seeks to highlight voices that are underrepresented in literature. Accepts manuscripts up to 32 pages in length, by email. See website for full guidelines.

P0950 **Zero Books**
Publishing Imprint
Portland, OR
United States

https://www.johnhuntpublishing.com/zer0-books/

Book Publisher: John Hunt Publishing Ltd

Types: Nonfiction
Subjects: Culture; Philosophy; Politics
Markets: Adult

Send: Full text

The modern world is at an impasse. Disasters scroll across our smartphone screens and we're invited to like, follow or upvote, but critical thinking is harder and harder to find. Rather than connecting us in common struggle and debate, the internet has sped up and deepened a long-standing process of alienation and atomization. We want to work against this trend.

Authors: Ben Burgis; Mark Fisher; Graham Harman; Owen Hatherley; Angela Nagle; Laurie Penny; Nina Power; Eugene Thacker

P0951 **Zest Books**
Publishing Imprint

Book Publisher: Lerner Publishing Group (**P0487**)

P0952 **Zonderkidz**
Publishing Imprint

Book Publisher: HarperCollins

P0953 **Zondervan**
Publishing Imprint

Book Publisher: HarperCollins

P0954 **Zondervan Academic**
Publishing Imprint

Book Publisher: HarperCollins

Index

Claim your free access to **www.firstwriter.com**: *See p.409*

Arts

See more specifically: Art History; Church Art; Painting; Performing Arts; Photography; Practical Art

336 Index | Book Club Women's Fiction

Sheil Land Associates Ltd L0906
Silberman, Jeff L0914
Stanton, Mark "Stan" L0934
Steed, Hayley L0935
Stringer, Marlene L0950
Yearwood, Susan L1059

Book Club Women's Fiction
See more broadly: Book Club Fiction; Women's Fiction
Beck, Rachel L0078
Eberly, Chelsea L0288

Book Extracts
Booklaunch M0083

Book Publishing
See more broadly: Publishing
NB Magazine M0362

Books
See more broadly: Media
Black Moon Magazine M0078
Cahoodaloodaling M0098
Event M0193
Foundation: The International Review of Science Fiction M0219
Fugue M0222
Future Fire, The M0225
Literary Mama M0312
Mid-American Review M0339
Mythaxis Review M0357
Poetry Wales M0408
Supplement, The M0501
Takahe M0507
Tiger of the Stripe P0823
Vagabond City M0541
Western Humanities Review M0556

Boy Books
Kimber, Natalie L0569

British Columbia
See more broadly: Canada
See more specifically: Vancouver Island
Arsenal Pulp Press P0053
Caitlin Press Inc. P0141
Heritage House P0402
TouchWood Editions P0833

Buddhism
See more broadly: Religion
See more specifically: Mahayana Buddhism; Theravada Buddhism
Mud Pie Books P0557
Shambhala Publications P0758
Urthona M0539
Windhorse Publications Ltd P0933

Building / Construction
See more broadly: Business
Rural Builder M0446

Buildings
See more specifically: Houses

Business
See more specifically: Building / Construction; Entrepreneurship; Film Industry; Management; Procurement; Publishing; Trade; Women in Business
ABC-CLIO / Greenwood P0016
Accountancy Age M0011
Aevitas L0016
Allen O'Shea Literary Agency L0027
Allworth Press P0030
AMACOM Books P0032
Arabelle Publishing P0046
Atlantic, The M0047
Authority Guides, The P0064
Baumer, Jan L0074
BCS (British Computer Society) P0088
Bell Lomax Moreton Agency L0081
Berrett-Koehler Publishers P0095
Birlinn Ltd P0098
Bradford Literary Agency L0117
Bristol University Press P0132
Business London M0092
Campbell, Charlie L0152
Changemakers P0161
Cheney Agency, The L0190
Clare Hulton Literary Agency L0200
Colourpoint Educational P0183
Columbia University Press P0184
Cowles Agency, The L0222
Creative Authors Ltd L0226
Croner-i Limited P0199
Dame M0154
Diversion Books P0233
DK (Dorling Kindersley Ltd) P0234
Dollarbooks PTY LTD P0239
Drummond Agency, The L0278
Economica M0178
Economist, The M0179
Elliott & Thompson P0259
Entrepreneur M0190
Entrepreneur Press P0268
Fakis, Delia Berrigan L0318
Felicia Eth Literary Representation L0324
Fernwood Publishing P0288
Fox & Howard Literary Agency L0351
Funny Times M0223
Gale P0314
Gerecke, Jeff L0390
Getzler, Josh L0391
Girard, Brenna L0395
Globe Pequot Press, The P0329
Graham Maw Christie Literary Agency L0408
Gregory, Evan L0423
Harmsworth, Esmond L0444
Harper Business P0366
Hart, Jim L0449
Harvard Business Publishing P0390
Harvey Klinger, Inc L0452
Hay House Publishers P0396
Hoffman, Scott L0476
InkWell Management L0499
Insomniac Press P0439
Insurance Age M0279
Investors Chronicle M0283
Joelle Delbourgo Associates, Inc. L0527
Jonathan Pegg Literary Agency L0530
Karinch, Maryann L0550
Kathi J. Paton Literary Agency L0556
Kensington Publishing Corp. P0469
Kneerim & Williams L0575
Knight Features L0577
Kruger Cowne L0583
LA Literary Agency, The L0586
Lakosil, Natalie L0588
Langtons International L0595
Limelight Management L0616
Lincolnshire Life M0309
Linda Konner Literary Agency L0617
Literary Management Group, Inc. L0623
Liza Dawson Associates L0625
Lowenstein Associates, Inc. L0635
MacGregor & Luedeke L0655
Management Today M0326
Mango Publishing Group P0527
Manor House Publishing P0529
Marcil O'Farrell Literary, LLC and Denise Marcil Literary Agency, LLC L0668
Mayfair Times M0332
Mehren, Jane von L0695
Mentor Books P0539
Michael Snell Literary Agency L0703
Oak Tree Press P0584
Ohio State University Press, The P0588
Palgrave Macmillan P0610
PassKey Publications P0616
Perry Literary, Inc. L0789
Piatkus Books P0647
Profile Books P0666
Purdue University Press P0674
Queen Literary Agency, Inc. L0817
Quill Driver Books P0684
Rees Literary Agency L0824
Regina Ryan Publishing Enterprises L0827
Rick Broadhead & Associates Literary Agency L0835
Rising Innovator M0443
Robert Dudley Agency L0843
Rothstein, Eliza L0865
Routledge P0715
Rutgers University Press P0718
Saffron Books P0723
Sage Publications P0725
Sasquatch Books P0737
Schneider, Kathy L0891
Sheree Bykofsky Associates, Inc. L0908
Shreve, Jeff L0909
Shuster, Todd L0911
Simon & Schuster UK Limited P0769
Smart Retailer M0474
Solow Literary Enterprises, Inc. L0925
Sourcebooks P0779
Speciality Food M0485
Specialty Fabrics Review M0486
Stanford University Press P0793
Stephanides, Myrsini L0937
Stone Bridge Press P0799
Successful Meetings M0499
Sunstone Press P0803
Targett, Simon L0968
TCK Publishing P0813
TD Magazine M0512
Thames & Hudson Inc. P0818
Tran, Jennifer Chen L0986
Tyndale House Publishers, Inc. P0847
Union Literary L0991
United Talent Agency (UTA) L0993
University of North Texas Press P0870
University of Oklahoma Press P0871
W.W. Norton & Company Ltd. P0900
Watson, Mackenzie Brady L1016
Weimann, Frank L1022
Welbeck Publishing Group P0916
Welsh Country M0554
Whimsy Literary Agency, LLC L1030
White, Melissa L1031
Writers' Representatives, LLC L1056
Yale University Press (London) P0943
Yearwood, Susan L1059

CIA
See more broadly: Secret Intelligence
Weimann, Frank L1022

California
See more broadly: United States
Naturegraph & Keven Brown Publications P0569

Canada
See more broadly: North America
See more specifically: Alberta; British Columbia; Yukon

Canoeing
See more broadly: Sport
Quiller Publishing Ltd P0685

Career Development
See more broadly: Personal Development
Beck, Rachel L0078
Berrett-Koehler Publishers P0095
Betsy Amster Literary Enterprises L0094
DK (Dorling Kindersley Ltd) P0234
Karinch, Maryann L0550
marie claire M0328
Pride M0418

Commercial Fantasy

Commercial Women's Fiction

Communication

Computer Programming

Computer Science

Computers

Contemporary

Cosmopolitan....................................M0134
Cowboys & Indians.........................M0138
Dollarbooks PTY LTD P0239
Elle..M0186
Enchanted Living.............................M0189
Fashion x Film.................................M0199
FHM...M0206
Grand Central Publishing P0337
Grazia..M0241
Hello!...M0254
InStyle...M0278
Irene Goodman Literary Agency
    (IGLA) L0501
Jacaranda Books Art Music Ltd.............P0449
Kruger Cowne..................................L0583
Laurence King Publishing Ltd P0482
marie claire M0328
Maxim..M0331
Mayfair Times M0332
My Weekly M0355
Pavilion Books Group Limited................P0620
Phaidon Press..................................P0644
Pride...M0418
Red Magazine M0438
Rosica Colin Ltd..............................L0860
Scottish Field...................................M0457
Stylist...M0497
Surface...M0502
Take a Break....................................M0508
Thames & Hudson Inc.....................P0818
Thames and Hudson Ltd..................P0819
Thompson Literary Agency.............L0975
Tran, Jennifer Chen L0986
Ulster Tatler.....................................M0531
Welbeck Publishing Group P0916
Woman & Home................................M0561
Woman's Weekly..............................M0562
Yale University Press (London)............P0943
Yours..M0574

Feminism
See more broadly: Gender
See more specifically: Intersectional Feminism
Andrew, Nelle...................................L0036
Atyeo, Charlotte L0050
Ballard, Sarah..................................L0060
Baxter, Veronique.............................L0075
Beaumont, Diana L0077
Beck, Rachel.....................................L0078
Cleis Press..P0179
Conscience.......................................M0131
Eberly, Chelsea.................................L0288
Feminist Press, The..........................P0287
Feminist Review................................M0203
Feminist Studies M0204
Finegan, Stevie.................................L0334
Forrester, Jemima.............................L0347
Future Fire, The................................M0225
Hakim, Serene..................................L0436
Hardman, Caroline L0442
Iris Blasi..L0506
Lakosil, Natalie................................L0588
Latshaw, Katherine...........................L0597
MacLeod, Lauren..............................L0660
Mango Publishing Group P0527
Mills, Rachel....................................L0717
Ostby, Kristin L0773
Perez, Kristina L0787
Richesin, Nicki L0832
Seal Press..P0751
Tibbets, Anne L0981
Understorey Magazine......................M0534
Feminist Romance
See more broadly: Romance
Cooper, Maggie................................L0220
Fiction
3 Seas Literary Agency L0001

30 North M0003
34th Parallel M0005
365 Tomorrows M0006
4RV Biblical Based P0003
4RV Children's Corner P0004
4RV Fiction......................................P0005
4RV Publishing................................P0007
4RV Tweens & Teens........................P0008
4RV Young Adult..............................P0009
4th Estate...P0010
a...p press..P0013
A.M. Heath & Company Limited,
    Author's Agents L0003
aaduna...M0007
Abdo Publishing Co.........................P0017
Abner Stein L0005
About Place Journal M0009
Abuzz Press.....................................P0019
Account, The....................................M0010
Acheampong, Kwaku........................ L0009
Adams Literary L0010
Adams, Seren................................... L0012
Aevitas L0016
Agency (London) Ltd, The L0018
Agony Opera.................................... M0016
Agora Books......................................P0025
Ahearn Agency, Inc, The L0020
Ahmed, Jamilah L0021
Albert Whitman & Company.............P0027
Alice Williams Literary L0025
Allison & Busby Ltd.........................P0029
Alma Books Ltd................................P0031
Ambassador Speakers Bureau &
    Literary Agency L0030
Ambit M0021
Amethyst Review.............................. M0026
Ampersand Agency Ltd, The.............. L0031
Anaverde Magazine M0027
And Magazine M0028
Andersen Press Ltd..........................P0037
Anderson, Darley............................. L0033
Andrew Nurnberg Associates, Ltd L0035
Andrew, Nelle.................................. L0036
Andy Ross Agency L0037
Angry Robot.....................................P0038
Anne Clark Literary Agency L0038
Anne Edelstein Literary Agency L0039
Annette Green Authors' Agency L0040
Antigonish Review, The M0029
Antioch Review, The M0030
Antony Harwood Limited................. L0042
Anvil Press Publishers P0041
Apex Publishing Ltd.........................P0042
Apostolides, Zoe L0043
Apple Tree Literary Ltd.................... L0044
April Gloaming M0045
Aquila M0031
Arcadia Books..................................P0049
Arena Fantasy M0033
Areopagus Magazine M0034
Arkansas Review............................... M0035
Arms, Victoria Wells L0046
Arsenal Pulp Press...........................P0053
Art Times Journal M0039
ARTmosterrific................................. M0042
Arts & Letters M0043
ASH Literary.................................... L0048
Asimov's Science Fiction M0044
Atlantean Publishing.........................P0057
Atlantic Books P0058
Atlantic, The M0047
Atyeo, Charlotte............................... L0050
Aurelia Leo P0062
Aurora Metro Press...........................P0063
Avon Books P0070
Award Publications Limited..................P0071

Awen M0050
Azantian Literary Agency....................L0054
Azantian, Jennifer L0055
Bacopa Literary Review....................M0052
Bad Nudes M0053
Bad Press Ink...................................P0074
Badger Learning...............................P0075
Baffler, The M0054
Baker Publishing Group...................P0076
Ballard, Sarah..................................L0060
Banipal M0055
Bantam P0079
Baobab Press....................................P0082
Barbara Levy Literary Agency L0061
Bare Fiction Magazine......................M0057
Barone Literary Agency....................L0066
Baror International, Inc.....................L0068
Barren Magazine M0058
Barrington Stoke P0084
BatCat Press P0085
Bath Literary Agency L0072
Bauman, Erica L0073
Baumer, Jan L0074
Baxter, Veronique L0075
Be About It Press P0089
Beal, Maile L0076
Beano, The M0063
Beaumont, Diana L0077
Beck, Rachel.....................................L0078
Beek, Emily Van L0079
Belford, Matt L0080
Bell Lomax Moreton Agency L0081
Bell, Madison Smartt L0085
Bellingham Review............................M0067
Belmont Story Review M0068
Beloit Fiction Journal.......................M0069
Bent Agency (UK), The L0089
Bent Agency, The..............................L0090
Berlyne, John L0093
Bess Press P0096
Betsy Amster Literary Enterprises..........L0094
Better Than Starbucks......................M0071
Beverley Slopen Literary Agency...........L0095
Bewley, Elizabeth L0096
Big Fiction.......................................M0072
Big Ugly Review, The M0073
BIGnews...M0074
Birlinn Ltd.......................................P0098
Bitter Lemon Press...........................P0099
Black & White Publishing Ltd...........P0101
Black Coffey Publishing P0103
Black Heron Press P0105
Black Moon Magazine M0078
Black Static M0079
Black Velvet Seductions P0108
Blackstaff Press P0110
Blair Partnership, The L0100
Blake Friedmann Literary Agency Ltd L0101
Bloomsbury Publishing Plc...............P0112
Blue Collar Review M0081
Blue Earth Review M0082
Bluemoose Books Ltd P0117
Blunt, Felicity..................................L0105
BOA Editions, Ltd P0119
Bolton, Camilla L0106
Bonnier Books (UK) P0122
Bonomi, Luigi L0107
Book Bureau Literary Agency, The........L0108
Book Group, The...............................L0109
Booklaunch M0083
Bookouture.......................................P0125
Bookseeker Agency L0110
BookStop Literary Agency, LLC L0111
Borstel, Stefanie Sanchez Von............L0112
Bowlin, Sarah L0114
Boyle, Katherine L0116

Literary Criticism

See more broadly: Literature

BCS (British Computer Society).............P0088
Bloomsbury Publishing Plc...................P0112
British Medical Journal (BMJ)...............M0086
Business London M0092
Childswork / ChildsPLAY, LLC............P0168
Croner-i Limited....................................P0199
dbS Productions....................................P0219
Deracine..M0163
Dollarbooks PTY LTD.........................P0239
Drummond Agency, The.......................L0278
Eastland Press......................................P0246
Elsevier Ltd P0261
Entrepreneur Press...............................P0268
Facet Publishing...................................P0276
Farm & Ranch Living..........................M0197
Farming Magazine................................M0198
Fiscal Publications...............................P0293
Frances Kelly Agency L0357
Gale...P0314
Government Publications P0335
Gryphon House, Inc.............................P0347
Harper Business...................................P0366
HarperCollins Leadership.....................P0381
Harvard Business Publishing................P0390
Human Kinetics....................................P0422
Idyll Arbor..P0428
InfoWorld..M0275
Insurance Age......................................M0279
International Piano................................M0280
Investors Chronicle..............................M0283
IOP Publishing....................................P0443
Jolly Learning.....................................P0456
Kluwer Law International P0474
Linguist, The.......................................M0310
Management Today M0326
Nursery World M0373
Oak Tree Press.....................................P0584
Open University Press..........................P0599
Our Dogs M0382
Oxford University Press.......................P0605
P8tech...P0606
Palgrave Macmillan..............................P0610
Pavilion Publishing..............................P0622
Photographer, The M0399
Pilot..M0401
Platypus Media P0656
Practising Midwife, The M0415
Practitioner, The M0416
Purdue University Press.......................P0674
Ransom Publishing Ltd P0693
Rising Innovator M0443
Round Hall...P0713
Routledge...P0715
Rural Builder M0446
Sage Publications.................................P0725
Scholastic...P0740
Scottish Farmer, The M0456
Screen International..............................M0461
Sea Breezes M0465
Seen and Heard M0466
Ships Monthly Magazine......................M0468
Smart Retailer......................................M0474
Speciality Food....................................M0485
Specialty Fabrics Review M0486
Strata Publishing, Inc..........................P0801
Strategic Finance M0496
Successful Meetings.............................M0499
Sunshine Artist M0500
TD Magazine M0512
Trotman Publishing P0838
W.W. Norton & Company Ltd...............P0900
Wiley-Blackwell...................................P0930

Project Management
See more broadly: Management
BCS (British Computer Society).............P0088

Prose Poetry
Better Than Starbucks..........................M0071
Ink Sweat and Tears.............................M0276
Tears in the Fence M0513

Psychiatry
See more broadly: Medicine
W.W. Norton & Company Ltd...............P0900

Psychoanalysis
See more broadly: Psychology
W.W. Norton & Company Ltd...............P0900

Psychological Horror
See more broadly: Horror
Azantian, Jennifer L0055
Lightner, Kayla L0615
Soloway, Jennifer March L0927
Tibbets, Anne.......................................L0981

Psychological Suspense
See more broadly: Suspense
See more specifically: Psychological Suspense Thrillers
Blunt, Felicity L0105
Chanchani, Sonali L0182
Cho, Catherine......................................L0194
Combemale, Chris L0212
Forrester, Jemima.................................L0347
Hordern, Kate.......................................L0481
Hornsley, Sarah....................................L0482
Pan Macmillan Australia P0611
Posner, Marcy......................................L0809
Power, Anna...L0811
Preston, Amanda..................................L0815
Ritchie, Rebecca L0838
Savvides, Marilia L0884
Soloway, Jennifer March L0927
Tannenbaum, Amy L0967
Terlip, Paige..L0972

Psychological Suspense Thrillers
See more broadly: Psychological Suspense; Psychological Thrillers

Psychological Thrillers
See more broadly: Thrillers
See more specifically: Psychological Suspense Thrillers
Azantian, Jennifer L0055
Bookouture...P0125
Chambers-Black, Jemiscoe....................L0180
Coombes, Clare.....................................L0216
Fabien, Samantha L0316
Fergusson, Julie L0329
Guillory, Robbie L0428
Kate Barker Literary, TV, & Film
Agency L0553
Langtry, Elena......................................L0596
Moylett, Lisa..L0730
Ogden, Hellie L0767
Williams, Laura L1039

Psychological Trauma
See more broadly: Psychology
See more specifically: Post Traumatic Stress Disorder
W.W. Norton & Company Ltd...............P0900

Psychology
See more specifically: Anxiety Disorders; Depression; Eating Disorders; Hypnosis; Neuropsychology; Popular Psychology; Psychoanalysis; Psychological Trauma; Psychotherapy
ABC-CLIO / Greenwood........................P0016
Aevitas L0016
Anne Edelstein Literary Agency L0039
Bal, Emma L0058
Betsy Amster Literary Enterprises L0094
Blake Friedmann Literary Agency Ltd....L0101
C+W (Conville & Walsh)......................L0147
Cambridge University Press P0143
Caroline Davidson Literary Agency........L0162

Chang, Nicola.......................................L0185
Changemakers P0161
Childswork / ChildsPLAY, LLC P0168
Cho, Catherine......................................L0194
Columbia University Press.....................P0184
Dollarbooks PTY LTD...........................P0239
Drummond Agency, The.........................L0278
Ekstrom, Rachel L0298
Esersky, Gareth L0306
Ethan Ellenberg Literary Agency L0308
Felicia Eth Literary Representation L0324
Fox & Howard Literary Agency..............L0351
Free Association Books Ltd....................P0305
Garbuz, Sulamita L0381
Geiger, Ellen L0384
Hardman, Caroline................................L0442
Harmsworth, Esmond.............................L0444
Harvey Klinger, Inc...............................L0452
Hay House Publishers P0396
Hoffman, Scott L0476
Icon Books Ltd P0427
Idyll Arbor...P0428
Ink and Colors Ltd L0498
InkWell Management..............................L0499
Jean V. Naggar Literary Agency, The L0519
Joelle Delbourgo Associates, Inc............L0527
Karen Gantz Literary Management L0549
Kirby, Robert..L0572
Kneerim & Williams L0575
Kruger Cowne L0583
LA Literary Agency, The.......................L0586
Lakosil, Natalie L0588
Linda Konner Literary Agency L0617
Liza Dawson Associates L0625
Lowenstein Associates, Inc....................L0635
Marion Boyars Publishers P0533
Massie & McQuilkin..............................L0680
Michael Snell Literary Agency L0703
Mills, Rachel L0717
Open University Press...........................P0599
Palgrave Macmillan P0610
Perry Literary, Inc.................................L0789
Profile Books..P0666
Queen Literary Agency, Inc...................L0817
Rees Literary Agency.............................L0824
Regina Ryan Publishing Enterprises........L0827
Rosenberg Group, The L0858
Rosica Colin Ltd L0860
Rothstein, Eliza L0865
Routledge...P0715
Sage Publications P0725
Shambhala Publications P0758
Sheil Land Associates Ltd.....................L0906
Sheree Bykofsky Associates, Inc............L0908
Solow Literary Enterprises, Inc. L0925
Sourcebooks...P0779
Susan Schulman Literary Agency...........L0955
Sutherland, Kari L0957
Three Hares Publishing P0821
Tran, Jennifer Chen L0986
Tyndale House Publishers, Inc. P0847
University of California Press.................P0862
University of Hertfordshire Press P0864
University of Oklahoma Press P0871
VanderWyk & Burnham P0883
W.W. Norton & Company Ltd P0900
Welbeck Publishing Group.....................P0916
Whimsy Literary Agency, LLC L1030
Wyckoff, Joanne L1057

Psychotherapy
See more broadly: Psychology
See more specifically: Juvenile Psychotherapy
W.W. Norton & Company Ltd P0900

Publishing
See more broadly: Business

Shipwreckt Books Publishing
  Company P0762
Simon & Schuster UK Limited P0769
Spirituality & Health M0487
Stone Bridge Press P0799
TCK Publishing P0813
Temple Lodge Publishing P0816
Thames & Hudson Inc. P0818
Thompson Literary Agency L0975
Transworld Publishers P0835
Unity P0857
Wyckoff, Joanne L1057

Sport
See more specifically: Archery; Baseball;
  Canoeing; Climbing; Cycling; Darts;
  Equestrian; Falcony; Football / Soccer;
  Golf; Horse Racing; Hunting; Martial Arts;
  Motorsports; Rugby; Shooting; Skiing;
  Snowboarding
Abdo Publishing Co P0017
Allen O'Shea Literary Agency L0027
Anness Publishing Ltd. P0039
Annette Green Authors' Agency L0040
Antigonish Review, The M0029
Apex Publishing Ltd. P0042
Ashley Drake Publishing Ltd P0054
Atyeo, Charlotte L0050
Bell Lomax Moreton Agency L0081
Birlinn Ltd P0098
Black & White Publishing Ltd P0101
Blackstaff Press P0110
Brattle Agency LLC, The L0121
Brewin Books Ltd. P0129
Brick M0085
Brouckaert, Justin L0133
Bucci, Chris L0139
C+W (Conville & Walsh) L0147
Caitlin Press Inc. P0141
Campbell, Charlie L0152
Chambliss, Jamie L0181
Charles River Press P0163
Charlie Campbell Literary Agents L0188
Cheney Agency, The L0190
Corridor of Uncertainty, The M0133
Country Life M0135
Crowood Press, The P0204
Cull & Co. Ltd L0230
Darton, Longman & Todd Ltd P0216
David Luxton Associates L0246
Diver Magazine M0166
Diversion Books P0233
DK (Dorling Kindersley Ltd) P0234
Dollarbooks PTY LTD P0239
Duduit, Del L0282
E. J. McCarthy Agency L0286
Edwards, Max L0291
Elks Magazine, The M0185
Elliott & Thompson P0259
Felicia Eth Literary Representation L0324
Fernwood Publishing P0288
FHM M0206
Flaneur M0213
Fort Publishing P0302
Frances Goldin Literary Agency, Inc. L0356
Garden & Gun M0226
Gerecke, Jeff L0390
Gill Books P0326
Gregory, Evan L0423
HarperCollins UK P0382
Harriot, Michael L0446
Harvey Klinger, Inc L0452
Haynes Publishing P0397
Heritage House P0402
hhb agency ltd L0468
Human Kinetics P0422
Icon Books Ltd P0427

Insomniac Press P0439
James Fitzgerald Agency, The L0512
Jane Judd Literary Agency L0515
Jean V. Naggar Literary Agency, The L0519
Jenny Brown Associates L0521
Jewish Chronicle M0293
Kahn, Jody L0544
Karinch, Maryann L0550
Kates Hill Press, The P0462
Kathi J. Paton Literary Agency L0556
Kelpies P0465
Kneerim & Williams L0575
Krause Publications P0478
Kruger Cowne L0583
LA Literary Agency, The L0586
Lightner, Kayla L0615
Limelight Management L0616
Loaded M0315
Lutterworth Press, The P0513
Luxton, David L0648
MacGregor & Luedeke L0655
Mad M0323
Marcil O'Farrell Literary, LLC and
  Denise Marcil Literary Agency,
  LLC L0668
Marr, Jill L0674
Massie & McQuilkin L0680
Maxim M0331
McGowan, Matt L0693
Mentor Books P0539
Merlin Unwin Books P0541
Methuen Publishing Ltd P0543
Michael Greer Literary Agency, The L0702
Mundy, Toby L0731
Munson, Oli L0733
New Holland Publishers Australia P0576
Ohio University Press P0589
Outside M0383
Pelican Publishing Company P0624
Pen & Sword Books Ltd P0626
Perry Literary, Inc. L0789
Peter Lang Oxford P0642
Philips, Ariana L0796
Queen Literary Agency, Inc. L0817
Regina Ryan Publishing Enterprises L0827
Robert Dudley Agency L0843
Robertson Murray Literary Agency L0845
Rosica Colin Ltd L0860
Rutgers University Press P0718
SAIL Magazine M0451
Seren Books P0756
Shipwreckt Books Publishing
  Company P0762
Signorelli, Michael L0913
Silberman, Jeff L0914
Simon & Schuster UK Limited P0769
Skier & Snowboarder Magazine M0472
Snowbooks P0776
SnoWest M0477
Sports Afield M0488
SportsBooks Limited P0784
Stanton, Mark "Stan" L0934
Sunstone Press P0803
Targett, Simon L0968
Thames & Hudson Inc. P0818
Thayer, Henry L0973
Thompson Literary Agency L0975
Transworld Publishers P0835
Turtle Books P0842
Tyndale House Publishers, Inc. P0847
University of Akron Press, The P0859
University of Alaska Press P0860
University of North Texas Press P0870
University of Oklahoma Press P0871
University of Tennessee Press P0874
W.W. Norton & Company Ltd P0900

Walters, Nick L1014
Weimann, Frank L1022
Welbeck Publishing Group P0916
Willms, Kathryn L1043
Wilson, Ed L1046
Wyckoff, Joanne L1057
Yachting World M0565
Sports Cars
See more broadly: Cars
Classic & Sports Car M0117
Sports Celebrity
See more broadly: Celebrity
FRA (Futerman, Rose, & Associates) L0354
Richter, Rick L0834
Spy Thrillers
See more broadly: Thrillers
Good Literary Agency, The L0405
Stamp Collecting
See more broadly: Hobbies
Stanley Gibbons P0794
Statistics
See more broadly: Mathematics
Addison Wesley P0022
Cambridge University Press P0143
W.W. Norton & Company Ltd P0900
Steam Engines
See more broadly: Steam Power; Vehicles
Old Glory M0378
Steam Power
See more broadly: Technology
See more specifically: Steam Engines
Old Glory M0378
Sub-Culture
See more broadly: Culture
Eisenmann, Caroline L0297
McGowan, Matt L0693
Sufism
See more broadly: Islam
Shambhala Publications P0758
Superhero Fantasy
See more broadly: Fantasy
Unreal Magazine M0537
Supernatural / Paranormal
See more specifically: Ghost Stories; Mysticism;
  Supernatural / Paranormal Romance;
  Vampires; Witches
Beek, Emily Van L0079
Black Velvet Seductions P0108
Burning Chair P0139
Chambers-Black, Jemiscoe L0180
Fate M0200
Oghma Creative Media P0586
Piatkus Books P0647
TouchWood Editions P0833
Supernatural / Paranormal Romance
See more broadly: Romance; Supernatural /
  Paranormal
Avon Books P0070
Bradford Literary Agency L0117
Carina Press P0150
Perez, Kristina L0787
Surreal
Agony Opera M0016
ASH Literary L0048
Asimov's Science Fiction M0044
Neon M0363
Suspense
See more specifically: Domestic Suspense;
  Psychological Suspense; Romantic Suspense
Agora Books P0025
Ahearn Agency, Inc, The L0020
Andrew, Nelle L0036
Black Coffey Publishing P0103
Blake Friedmann Literary Agency Ltd L0101
Bolton, Camilla L0106
Brower, Michelle L0134

Youth Culture
See more broadly: Culture

Yukon
See more broadly: Canada

Zen
See more broadly: Mahayana Buddhism

Zombies
See more broadly: Horror

Get Free Access to the firstwriter.com Website

To claim your free access to the firstwriter.com website simply go to the website at https://www.firstwriter.com/subscribe and begin the subscription process as normal. On the second page, enter the required details (such as your name and address, etc.) then for "Voucher / coupon number" enter the following promotional code:

- **A45Q-UTC2**

This will reduce the cost of creating a subscription by up to $15 / £10 / €15, making it free to create a monthly, quarterly, or combination subscription. Alternatively, you can use the discount to take out an annual or life subscription at a reduced rate.

Continue the process until your account is created. Please note that you will need to provide your payment details, even if there is no up-front payment. This is in case you choose to leave your subscription running after the free initial period, but there is no obligation for you to do so.

When you use this code to take out a free subscription you are under no obligation to make any payments whatsoever and you are free to cancel your account before you make any payments if you wish.

If you need any assistance, please email support@firstwriter.com.

If you have found this book useful, please consider leaving a review on the website where you bought it.

What you get

Once you have set up access to the site you will be able to benefit from all the following features:

Databases

All our databases are updated almost every day, and include powerful search facilities to help you find exactly what you need. Searches that used to take you hours or even days in print books or on search engines can now be done in seconds, and produce more accurate and up-to-date information. Our agents database also includes independent reports from at least three separate sources, showing you which are the top agencies and helping you avoid the scams that are all over the internet. You can try out any of our databases before you subscribe:

- Search dozens of **current competitions**.
- Search **over 2,300 literary agents and agencies.**
- Search **over 2,300 magazines**.
- Search **over 2,800 book publishers** that **don't** charge fees.

Plus advanced features to help you with your search:

- Save searches and save time – set multiple search parameters specific to your work, save them, and then access the search results with a single click whenever you log in. You can even save multiple different searches if you have different types of work you are looking to place.
- Add personal notes to listings, visible only to you and fully searchable – helping you to organise your actions.
- Set reminders on listings to notify you when to submit your work, when to follow up, when to expect a reply, or any other custom action.
- Track which listings you've viewed and when, to help you organise your search – any listings which have changed since you last viewed them will be highlighted for your attention!

Daily email updates

As a subscriber you will be able to take advantage of our email alert service, meaning you can specify your particular interests and we'll send you automatic email updates when we change or add a listing that matches them. So if you're interested in agents dealing in romantic fiction in the United States you can have us send you emails with the latest updates about them – keeping you up to date without even having to log in.

User feedback

Our agent, publisher, and magazine databases all include a user feedback feature that allows our subscribers to leave feedback on each listing – giving you not only the chance to have your say about the markets you contact, but giving a unique authors' perspective on the listings.

Save on copyright protection fees

If you're sending your work away to publishers, competitions, or literary agents, it's vital that you first protect your copyright. As a subscriber to firstwriter.com you can do this through our site and save 10% on the copyright registration fees normally payable for protecting your work internationally through the Intellectual Property Rights Office.

Monthly newsletter

When you subscribe to firstwriter.com you also receive our monthly email newsletter – described by one publishing company as "the best in the business" – including articles, news, and interviews for writers. And the best part is that you can continue to receive the newsletter even after you stop your paid subscription – at no cost!

Terms and conditions

The promotional code contained in this publication may be used by the owner of the book only to create one subscription to firstwriter.com at a reduced cost, or for free. It may not be used by or disseminated to third parties. Should the code be misused then the owner of the book will be liable for any costs incurred, including but not limited to payment in full at the standard rate for the subscription in question. The code may be used at any time until the end of the calendar year named in the title of the publication, after which time it will become invalid. The code may be redeemed against the creation of a new account only – it cannot be redeemed against the ongoing costs of keeping a subscription open. In order to create a subscription a method of payment must be provided, but there is no obligation to make any payment. Subscriptions may be cancelled at any time, and if an account is cancelled before any payment becomes due then no payment will be made. Once a subscription has been created, the normal schedule of payments will begin on a monthly, quarterly, or annual basis, unless a life Subscription is selected, or the subscription is cancelled prior to the first payment becoming due. Subscriptions may be cancelled at any time, but if they are left open beyond the date at which the first payment becomes due and is processed then payments will not be refundable.

Made in the USA
Columbia, SC
18 April 2022

59123257R00230